Case Studies in Critical Controversy

Edgar Allan Poe
Selected Poetry, Tales, and Essays

D0217432

Case Studies in Critical Controversy

SERIES EDITORS: Gerald Graff, *The University of Illinois at Chicago*

James Phelan, *The Ohio State University*

Edgar Allan Poe
Selected Poetry, Tales, and Essays

Authoritative Texts with Essays on Three Critical Controversies

EDITED BY

Jared Gardner
The Ohio State University

Elizabeth Hewitt
The Ohio State University

Bedford/St. Martin's
A Macmillan Education Imprint

Boston • New York

For Bedford/St. Martin's

Vice President, Editorial, Macmillan Higher Education Humanities:
  Edwin Hill
Editorial Director, English and Music: Karen S. Henry
Senior Executive Editor: Stephen A. Scipione
Publishing Services Manager: Andrea Cava
Production Supervisor: Carolyn Quimby
Marketing Manager: Joy Fisher Williams
Project Management: DeMasi Design and Publishing Services
Director of Rights and Permissions: Hilary Newman
Senior Art Director: Anna Palchik
Cover Design: William Boardman
Cover Art: In the Year Before II, Portrait of Edgar Allan Poe (1809–49) 1982
  (w/c on paper), Janssen, Horst (1929–95) / Private Collection / Bridgeman
  Images © 2015 Artists Rights Society (ARS), New York / VG Bild-Kunst,
  Bonn
Composition: Achorn International, Inc.
Printing and Binding: RR Donnelley and Sons

Manufactured in the United States of America.

0   9   8   7   6   5
f   e   d   c   b   a

For information, write: Bedford/St. Martin's, 75 Arlington Street,
Boston, MA 02116   (617-399-4000)

ISBN 978-1-4576-2932-7

Acknowledgments

Text acknowledgments and copyrights appear at the back of the book on page 567, which constitutes an extension of the copyright page. It is a violation of the law to reproduce these selections by any means whatsoever without the written permission of the copyright holder.

Distributed outside North America by PALGRAVE MACMILLAN
Houndmills, Basingstoke, Hampshire RG21 6XS

About the Series

Each volume in the Case Studies in Critical Controversy series reprints an authoritative text of a classic literary work—or, as in this case, a selection of shorter texts by a major author—along with documents and critical essays that have been chosen to introduce the chief critical debates and cultural conflicts concerning the work or the author.

Like the first two volumes in the series, one devoted to Mark Twain's *Adventures of Huckleberry Finn* and the other to William Shakespeare's *The Tempest*, this book emphasizes debate and controversy because we believe that reading with absorption and enjoyment and talking, even arguing, with others about what we read are deeply interdependent activities. All of us most fruitfully read a book (or watch a film, or look at a painting, or, indeed, experience almost any event) when our attention is directed and intensified by our awareness of others' responses, an awareness that can also inspire us to make our own contributions to the ongoing discussion. Thus, this case study emphasizes controversy, which, increasingly, is the form contemporary discourse about books and culture takes.

This approach to the Case Studies in Critical Controversy series grows out of our own undergraduate experiences, coming to college from families where book-talk and intellectual conversation were not everyday events. Like so many students today, we wondered why the academy put so much emphasis on reading literature for its "hidden meanings" when, from our perspectives, literature was something primarily to be enjoyed, not elaborately analyzed. This attitude left us at a loss, however, when we were assigned to write an English essay and had to find something to *say* about a literary work. For as our correspondent James Berger has pointed out, "You don't learn to write an English paper by reading a novel."

We eventually discovered that the best way to learn to write an English paper about a literary work was by listening and responding to something said about the work in a class discussion or by reading the debates of stimulating critics about it. We each eventually found that exposure to pertinent critical controversies in the classroom helped greatly to dispel our initial fear and confusion, and to show us why the meanings of texts, and the debates about those meanings, can indeed matter.[1]

We know from our experience in teaching today's students that many of them face the same problems we did as we tried to become socialized into the conversations of literary study. When students are shy and silent in class discussions and find critical essays difficult to write, the reason often lies in the mysterious and intimidating nature of literary critical discourse.

To be sure, an instructor can alleviate the problem by telling such students to forget intellectual academic talk and just respond in their own voices. "Never mind what the critics say about Poe; tell us how you feel when you read 'The Raven.'" Though such a tactic is understandable—perhaps even essential—at the beginning stages of literary study, it is not a long-term solution. It widens rather than bridges the already large gulf between the discourse of the teacher and that of the student. More important, it widens the gulf between those students who "talk the talk" of the academy—the ones who get the As and who are destined for professional career tracks—and those who settle for lesser awards and ambitions.

Bridging the gulf between literary critical discourse and student discourse is important if higher education in the humanities is to be effective. And the best way to bridge the gulf is to think of reading, discussing, and writing about literature as a process of entering into a conversation about it.

---

[1] See Gerald Graff's *Beyond the Culture Wars* (New York: Norton, 1992, pp. 67–68) for an account of how his awareness of controversies about *Huckleberry Finn* helped him begin to like books.

Learning by controversy offers a practical sol
polarized debates of our time. Indeed, this strategy
how the quality of cultural debate in our societ
improved. It is a common prediction that the cultu
century will continue to put a premium on people'
ductively with conflict and cultural difference. Lean
is sound training for citizenship in that future.

The University

The (

About This Volume

Edgar Allan Poe is the odd man out in American literary history. Although one of the most widely read nineteenth-century American authors today, his writing stubbornly resists the larger stories we tell about American literature. Although born in Boston, Poe was not a New Englander and thus he cannot be merged into a literary history that emphasizes American puritanism and transcendentalism. And although he lived most of his life below the Mason-Dixon line and served as editor for the *Virginia Literary Messenger*, his work tenaciously continues to resist easy identification as a southern and regionalist. Unlike his contemporaries, the Fireside Poets (Henry Wadsworth Longfellow, John Greenleaf Whittier, and James Russell Lowell), Poe was not especially popular. But unlike the other two canonical American poets of the nineteenth century, Walt Whitman and Emily Dickinson, Poe deliberately and flamboyantly courted the popular literary market. No matter how we try to fit him into our American literature courses, there is Poe thumbing his nose at our attempts to make him play a tidy role in the stories we would tell. Of course, it is just this feature of Poe that most attracts us to him.

As one of the most gifted critics and cultural observers of his age, Poe knew well its predominant tastes and tendencies. He knew them, and he rejected them. At a time when authors were scrambling after the success of James Fenimore Cooper in forging a uniquely "American" national literature, Poe deliberately set the vast majority of his fictions in foreign landscapes. And when most successful fiction writers were publishing novels, Poe wrote almost exclusively in the short story form. In a period that seemingly rewarded authenticity and genuine senti- ment as the index of literary and moral value, Poe cultivated deception, hoaxes, and satire. So what makes Poe doubly fascinating is that even as he refused the conventions of his time, he very much *craved* the approval of his time—both popular and critical. Nonetheless, as we will see in the pages to follow, he frequently attacked the very critics or liter- ary luminaries most inclined to grant him the laurels he coveted, instead putting his trust in Rufus Griswold, one of American literary history's most unreliable guardians. Everywhere we turn when it comes to Poe one finds contradiction, perversity, and, of course, controversy.

Not only Poe's work but also his life has occasioned critical contro- versy, and thus Part One begins with a biographical essay that sketches Poe's short tragic life, focusing particularly on his publishing career. Part One then offers a selection of Poe's poems, tales, and essays. Many of the included texts are among the best known in Poe's corpus: even a casual student of American literature has probably read (or at least seen an episode of *The Simpsons* that references) "The Raven," "Annabel Lee," "The Tell-Tale Heart," or "The Cask of Amontillado." We selected other works because of their central role in the controversies on which the book focuses. For example, "The Fall of the House of Usher" has served as a central text in all three of the controversies we address, while "Hop-Frog" has been of special interest in recent years to critics debating Poe's attitudes toward race, and Poe's infamous statement about the "death of a beautiful woman" in "Philosophy of Composition" has been a lightning rod for critical conversations about gender. We also wanted our selections to include important examples of Poe's foundational work in the development of new genres such as detective fiction, whose growing popularity would put increasing pres- sure on the emerging distinction between the "popular" and the "liter- ary"; we include here two examples of Poe's detective fiction: "The Purloined Letter" and "The Murders in the Rue Morgue."

Part Two comprises three different sections, each focused on a dis- tinct critical controversy. The first concerns the status of Poe's writing itself and assembles texts from more than 150 years of debate as to the literary value, or lack thereof, of Poe's writing. The second section focuses on an issue that has emerged more recently as crucial to Poe criticism: the representation of slavery, racism, and race in Poe's work. And finally, the third section concentrates on the animated critical debate about Poe's representation of women, a debate that has offered a fierce contestation about Poe's sexual politics.

As we hope readers will discover, to study the controversies surrounding Edgar Allan Poe is to plug into some of the most highly charged questions facing literary studies. What is "literature"? Who determines its value? What role does an author's life play in the meanings we bring to a literary text? What responsibility do authors have to respond to the pressing political and ethical issues of their day? How do we locate those judgments, and how do we, in our own time, respond to them? Not only does a study of Poe's controversies allow us access to these wide-ranging issues of literary and cultural criticism, but it also brings us into intimate contact with the unique power of this essentially controversial writer. More than almost any figure in American literary history, Poe is deeply polarizing—both in his own lifetime and our present moment. Few readers are neutral on Poe: he tends to inspire worship or loathing, declarations of genius or of hucksterism. In the pages that follow, it will sometimes seem that Poe perversely tried to cultivate these radically different responses. Indeed, it is this obstinate refusal of moderation and temperate conciliation in both his work and his life that makes Edgar Allan Poe such a compelling author and perhaps (though he would have hated the label) an essentially *American* one. Writing contemporaneously with Poe, the French theorist of American democracy Alexander de Tocqueville described what he saw as the unique aesthetic possibility of American literature:

> Style will frequently be fantastic, incorrect, overburdened and loose—almost vehement and bold. Authors will aim at rapidity of execution, more than at perfection of detail. Small productions will be more common than bulky books; there will be more wit than erudition, more imagination than profundity; and literary performances will bear marks of an untutored and rude vigor of thought.

Tocqueville is not writing about Poe, but his celebration of American vehemence, imagination, and vigor seem to imagine Poe with remarkable precision. And indeed subsequent generations of French readers and critics were to be some of Poe's most impassioned admirers, praising him as the American artist who cried out in the face of his nation's bland conformity.

An author who generated controversy from his entrance on the literary scene, Poe remains one of the few American writers almost everyone has read and arrived at some opinion about. Somewhere out there, beyond the veil, we sense Poe laughing. Certainly no one would enjoy this volume more than he.

A NOTE ON POE'S TEXTS

Readers may notice that Poe is often inconsistent in his spelling, sometimes using what we would term British spellings and sometimes American spellings, even within the same story. We have retained these inconsistencies for several reasons. First, spelling in the first half of the nineteenth century was often inconsistent and nonstandardized. The notion of proper spelling in English is a relatively modern invention: the publication of Samuel Johnson's *Dictionary of the English Language* only a century before Poe was one of the first attempts to codify standardized spelling. And the idea of an "American" spelling didn't emerge until after the first Webster dictionary in 1828, and did not fully solidify until the 1840s, with the second edition. Not surprisingly then, during the period Poe wrote and published, very few editors were overly punctilious about these spelling differences. Further complicating our natural desire to regularize spellings is the fact that many of Poe's tales (and poems) are voiced by unreliable narrators, and thus the irregular spellings can sometimes tell us something about their state of mind. One extreme example found in the pages to follow is "How to Write a Blackwood Article," where the narrator's word choice and poor spelling is an object of satire. To regularize Zenobia's spelling would be to lose all the fun of the story.

Further complicating matters, there are in many cases multiple versions of individual stories and poems, both in manuscript and in print, often with different spellings and other changes. For these and related reasons, the practice in Poe textual scholarship has been to rely primarily on what have been determined to be the authoritative versions of the individual texts, as established by generations of Poe scholars, especially James A. Harrison and Thomas Ollive Mabbott. In most cases we have followed the text choices established by these scholars and agreed upon by the field of Poe studies, with the occasional silent change made in the interest of readability.

All citations to Poe's writings not included in this volume will reference the two-volume edition of Poe's work from the Library of America. Parenthetical references to *ER* direct the reader to the *Essays and Reviews* volume edited by G. R. Thompson, and references to *PT* refer to the *Poetry and Tales* volume edited by Patrick Quinn, both published in 1984. Citations from Poe's letters will reference *The Collected Letters of Edgar Allan Poe*, edited by John Ward Ostrom, Burton R. Pollin, and Jeffrey A. Savoye, published by Gordian Press in 2008, using the abbreviation *L* in parenthetical citations.

ACKNOWLEDGMENTS

Our indebtedness to the many people who helped bring this project into existence is perhaps the only thing that is genuinely uncontroversial in this volume. First we must thank James Phelan and Gerald Graff who first encouraged us to translate our own complicated relationship with teaching Edgar Allan Poe into a volume in their Case Studies in Critical Controversy series. This book would not have happened without their invaluable advice, editorship, and assistance. We are also grateful to Alexander L. Hammond, Kent P. Ljungquist, Leland S. Person, Scott Peeples, John Carlos Rowe, and the anonymous readers who reviewed the initial prospectus and offered invaluable suggestions and advice that significantly improved this volume. We also want to thank Joan E. Feinberg, the former president of Bedford/St. Martin's, who gave the project the green light, and the vice president of Editorial, Humanities, Edwin Hill; editorial director and literature publisher Karen S. Henry; editorial assistant Eliza Kritz; text permissions manager Kalina Ingham and permissions editor Barbara Hernandez; William Boardman, cover designer; Andrea Cava, manager of publishing services, and Linda DeMasi of DeMasi Design and Publishing Services; and executive marketing manager Joy Fisher Williams. Thanks to Elijah Gardner and Ben Novotny Owen who spent many long hours helping us prepare the manuscript. And finally we are extremely fortunate to have been able to work with Steve Scipione, our editor at Bedford/St. Martin's, who has masterfully shepherded the project from the very beginning. His editorial acuity, wisdom, and generosity were vital to the project—we couldn't be more grateful.

Jared Gardner
Elizabeth Hewitt

Contents

PART ONE
Edgar Allan Poe: Life and Work

PART TWO
A Case Study in Critical Controversy

Why Study Critical Controversies about the Work of Edgar Allan Poe?   237

The Controversy over Aesthetics and the Literary Marketplace; or, Is Poe a Literary Genius or a Pop-Culture Hack?   248

The Controversy over Race; or, What Did Poe Have to Say about African Americans and Slavery? 339

The Controversy over Gender and Sexuality; or, Why Is Poe So Obsessed with Dead Women? 473

How to Write about Critical Controversy over the Work of Edgar Allan Poe 557

About the Editors 565

Case Studies in Critical Controversy

Edgar Allan Poe
Selected Poetry, Tales, and Essays

PART ONE

Edgar Allan Poe:
Life and Work

The Life of Edgar Allan Poe

Edgar Poe was born in Boston on January 19, 1809, to David and Elizabeth Poe, both actors working at the time with Powell's Company. Living the itinerant life of actors, the parents left their newborn with his paternal grandparents in Baltimore while they finished their tour. Thus from the first weeks of his life, Poe found himself at once a Northerner and a Southerner, a division that would shape his life and career in fundamental ways.

Though Poe's parents were both actors, by all accounts Elizabeth was the more talented, receiving several positive reviews while David was often overlooked or even disdained. By the fall of 1809, David Poe's career on stage was over, and less than two years later he deserted his wife and three children. Despite the support of friends and family, Elizabeth Poe deteriorated rapidly both physically and emotionally after her husband left. On December 8, 1811, she passed away, and the Poe siblings were dispersed to the households of different friends and relatives.

Edgar passed into the care of John and Frances Allan of Richmond, Virginia. John Allan was a successful merchant, and in 1815 he brought his wife and Edgar to England, a business trip deferred by the outbreak of the War of 1812. After visiting with relatives in Scotland, the Allans settled in London. Edgar attended boarding school in Chelsea and by all accounts thrived.

By spring of 1819, however, Allan's firm suffered financial difficulties when credit dried up after the Panic of 1819 as the nation's first major depression took hold. In June of 1820, the Allans and Edgar returned to Richmond after almost five years away. Back in Virginia, relations between Allan and Poe began to strain—familiar adolescent tensions between father and son were no doubt exacerbated by disruptions brought on by the move and financial tensions at home. Despite the clear causes of the familial friction, Allan and Poe, both extremely strong-willed, took the cooling of relations very much to heart. The fact that Allan's business partnership dissolved just as Poe was beginning to imagine for himself a career as a poet no doubt added tension to an already fraught relationship.

In early 1826, Poe began his studies at the University of Virginia, which had opened its doors only one year earlier. Unfortunately, Poe's time at the university would be cut short, despite his successes in the classroom. Money became an increasing source of tension between Allan and Poe, exacerbated by Poe's newly discovered interest in gambling and disinterest in following his foster father into business. Unable to convince Allan to cover his considerable gambling debts, Poe withdrew from the university at the end of his first year. As Poe's fortunes began what would be a fairly steady decline, his foster father began to see his own situation improve. In addition to being named a director of the Bank of Virginia, Allan came into a considerable inheritance. Poe, meanwhile, made his way to Boston, the city of his birth, on a coal vessel.

Poe had left Boston as a baby, too early to form any personal attachment to the city; nonetheless, the city carried a lot of meaning for the young man. In addition to being the hometown of his deceased parents, Boston had emerged as the center of the literary culture to which Poe increasingly aspired. Poe's older brother Henry had begun publishing poems early in 1827, and in the summer of that year Edgar's own first volume, *Tamerlane and Other Poems*, was published in a small run of only fifty copies, attributed anonymously to "A Bostonian." The edition quickly vanished into obscurity.

By the time *Tamerlane* came out, Poe had enlisted in the U.S. Army under the pseudonym Edgar A. Perry, and by fall his unit was ordered to South Carolina, sending the would-be Bostonian back south of the Mason-Dixon line. After a year in the army, Poe wrote his foster father, seeking Allan's influence in securing a reference to West Point. "I . . . am no longer a boy tossing about on the world without aim or consistency," he assured Allan. Allan did help secure Poe's discharge and references for admission to the military academy, and following the death of Poe's foster mother, Frances Allen, Allan and Poe seemed to be moving toward reconciliation, drawn together by shared grief. It wasn't long, however, before familiar issues of money and Allan's disappointment over Poe's increasing determination to pursue a literary career once again strained their relationship.

While waiting for his appointment to West Point, at the end of 1829, Poe published a second volume of poems, *Al Aaraaf, Tamerlane, and Minor Poems.* This time, the edition of 250 copies received some small notice in the literary press. In 1830, Poe was accepted into West Point, arriving in June. Four months later John Allan married Louisa Patterson, a woman who appears to have taken an active dislike to Poe well before she even met him at her husband's deathbed in 1834.

Poe found life at West Point uncongenial, and he blamed Allan for not providing for him properly, forcing him to live "like a beggar" at the school. Almost immediately he made up his mind to resign. Having committed for five years of service, the only way out was to neglect his studies and duties and face expulsion. Sure enough, by the end of January 1831, Poe was court-martialed and expelled from the academy. From West Point he made his way to Baltimore, where he joined his aunt Maria Clemm, along with Clemm's daughter, Virginia, Clemm's mother, and Poe's older brother, Henry. Here Poe would fall in love with his young cousin Virginia, who later became his wife. More immediately, however, Poe found in the Clemm household a community supportive of his literary ambitions and confident in his success— precisely the environment he most needed at the outset of his career as a professional writer.

From the start of Poe's new life, however, his literary achievements would be accompanied, almost relentlessly, by tragedy and hardship. In August 1833, just as Poe was beginning to place stories in periodicals, his brother died of tuberculosis following a long decline, exacerbated by alcoholism. In October, the *Saturday Visiter* published "MS. Found in a Bottle" which had won the magazine's fifty-dollar contest. Riding a wave of publicity from the contest, Poe announced that a collection of his stories, *Tales of the Folio Club,* would be published by subscription. Before the volume was published, however, a son was born to John and Louisa Allan, forever ending Poe's hopes for a reconciliation that might restore his place as Allan's heir. Poe now knew he would need to depend on his writing for his survival and the care of Maria and Virginia Clemm.

In 1834, a new journal dedicated to promoting Southern literature was founded by Thomas W. White, and in 1835, failing to secure meaningful employment in the Baltimore area, Poe moved to Richmond to take on the responsibilities of managing editor at the *Southern Literary Messenger*. It is here that Poe found his voice as an insightful and often acerbic critic, and he began to earn more attention for his critical writing than he had received for his poetry or tales. But as would prove so often the case in the years to follow, success did not sit easily with Poe. After just a few months Poe abruptly left his position, only to beg White to be reinstated a short time later. White knew Poe's strengths as an editor and writer, but he was also keenly aware of his weaknesses, and so he took Poe back only on the condition that it was "expressly understood by us that all engagements on my part would be dissolved, the moment you get drunk."

Reinstalled as editor, Poe brought his aunt and cousin to live with him in Richmond, marrying Virginia in May of 1836. Even as the reputation of *The Messenger* grew under Poe's management, the Poes found themselves continuing to live in severely straitened conditions. Eager to expand the subscription rolls of the magazine, Poe's criticism becomes increasingly ferocious, leading him to develop a reputation as a literary "savage." At the cost of making many enemies along the way, by the end of 1836, Poe's name was a familiar one in literary circles.

Unfortunately, White had finally run out of patience with his editor, and Poe began 1837 without a job once again. However, while White was unwilling to trust his magazine to Poe's management, he was more than eager to pay for his contributions. In February, encouraged by the publisher Harper and Brothers that a novel would prove more profitable than a collection of stories, Poe began serializing *Arthur Gordon Pym* in the pages of the *Messenger*. Early in 1838, Poe moved his family to Philadelphia in hopes of securing a new magazine position, and in July of that year Harper and Brothers published *Pym* in New York. The novel, while favorably reviewed in several periodicals, failed to sell as Poe hoped it would.

Even as he began publishing what would be some of his most celebrated tales, Poe remained in poverty. In 1839, he was hired as an assistant editor for *Burton's Gentleman's Magazine* at a salary of ten dollars a week. In addition to the meager salary, Poe had other reasons to be dissatisfied with the post, as Burton treated Poe as a drudge, granting him none of the editorial authority he had exercised at the *Messenger*. Nonetheless, the tenure at *Burton's* provided a forum for the publication of "The Fall of the House of Usher," and one month later of "William Wilson." These two stories served as highlights in Poe's *Tales of the Grotesque and Arabesque*, issued by Lea & Blanchard in December 1839. Although this collection includes some of Poe's most famous stories, the volume once again did not sell well.

Early in 1840, Burton put his magazine up for sale, and Poe determined that the time was finally right to start his own journal, which he planned to call *The Penn Magazine*. Despite encouragement from press and public, Poe was unable to secure the funds necessary to start his magazine. His frantic efforts on behalf of the would-be magazine left Poe exhausted and seriously ill. Just when things seemed most dire for the Poe household, however, the newly launched *Graham's Magazine* offered Poe the position of book review editor and an opportunity to publish his fiction and essays.

His new relationship with *Graham's* made 1841 a good year for Poe. The magazine published stories such as Poe's "The Murders in the Rue Morgue" and his review of Charles Dickens's novel *Barnaby Rudge*. And it was in 1841 that Poe first met Rufus Griswold, a young poet and editor who would play such a key role in Poe's legacy, as we will see in the first controversy collected in this volume (p. 252). In almost every respect things were looking up for Poe: he had a productive working relationship with *Graham's* and a rapidly growing national reputation.

But 1842 began with a dark cloud that would haunt Poe for the remainder of his days. On January 20, while singing at home with her family, Virginia Poe experienced a pulmonary hemorrhage. The meaning was immediately obvious to all assembled: Virginia had tuberculosis, an incurable disease throughout the nineteenth century. Virginia survived five painful years before finally succumbing to the disease in January 1847. As he watched his beloved wife's health slowly degenerate, Poe increasingly turned to alcohol to dull his own pain, which in turn contributed to his own declining health and fortunes until his death in 1849.

With his wife's illness, Poe realized he needed more financial security than his post at *Graham's* could provide. He resigned his position to attempt once more to start his own periodical or secure a political appointment—anything to provide more money for his struggling family. After a grueling and ultimately fruitless attempt to secure a political appointment in the Custom House, Poe put all of his energies into his frequently deferred magazine, now retitled *The Stylus*. Poe continued to work on behalf of the magazine until the end of his life, but was never able to raise the funds necessary to get his project off the ground.

In the final years of his career, Poe's fame and struggles continued to grow in equal measure. In 1843, for example, he won a hundred-dollar prize for his story "The Gold-Bug," but the funds proved inadequate to meet the growing financial challenges facing his struggling household. Late in 1843, Poe began a new career as a lecturer to supplement his income, a vocation that brought him new attention but also new enemies, as he frequently voiced his negative impressions of prominent literary figures.

A year later, in October 1844, Poe began working as an assistant to the poet Nathaniel P. Willis, editor of the new *Evening Mirror*. It is in the *Evening Mirror* that Poe published "The Raven" in 1845, the high point of his literary fame during his lifetime. Encouraged by his celebrity, Poe resigned his position with Willis and signed on as a founding partner of the weekly *Broadway Journal*. For the first time Poe found himself moving in some of the highest literary and social circles, and it is during this period that Poe delivered a disastrous speech at the Boston Lyceum that will be discussed in more detail in the introduction to the "Aesthetics" controversy (p. 248). By year's end the *Broadway Journal* ceased publication, and by spring of 1846, after becoming caught up in society gossip, Poe's social invitations dried up as well.

With Virginia's illness heading into its final chapter, Poe moved his family to a small cottage where they lived in isolation and mounting poverty until her death in January 1847 at the age of twenty-four. From that point on, Poe's biography is the story of a man bouncing from one city to the next, seeking out lectureships, sponsors for his phantom *Stylus*, and, too often, the solace of the bottle. But it is also during this time that Poe met some of the women whose friendships sustained him intellectually and emotionally during his final years, especially the poet Sarah Helen Whitman with whom Poe became involved romantically. Ultimately, their brief engagement was called off at the end of 1848 when Poe once again proved himself unable to abstain from alcohol, despite solemn promises.[1]

His final months were devoted to one last stab at happiness, as he courted a widow he had romanced many years earlier when both were young. Mrs. Elmira Royster Shelton finally accepted his proposal, perhaps encouraged by Poe having joined the Richmond chapter of the Sons of Temperance. On September 27, 1849, Poe departed from

---

[1] In the nineteenth century, alcoholism was almost as much of a death sentence as was tuberculosis, as Alcoholics Anonymous and other programs and treatments for alcohol dependency did not yet exist.

Richmond for New York City, planning to bring his mother-in-law, Mrs. Clemm, back with him to his new life with Mrs. Shelton. Along the way, however, Poe stopped in Baltimore where he disappeared for five days, and was ultimately found in a comatose state. On October 7, 1849, at the age of forty, Edgar Allan Poe died at the Washington College Hospital.

Within days of Poe's untimely demise, the struggle over his literary legacy began—a debate that continues to the present day, as we will see in Part Two.

Selected Poetry, Tales, and Essays

Tamerlane°

Kind solace in a dying hour!
    Such, father, is not (now) my theme—
I will not madly deem that power
      Of Earth may shrive me of the sin
5   Unearthly pride hath revell'd in—
I have no time to dote or dream:
You call it hope—that fire of fire!
It is but agony of desire:
If I *can* hope—Oh God! I can—
10   Its fount is holier—more divine—
I would not call thee fool, old man,
    But such is not a gift of thine.

Know thou the secret of a spirit
    Bow'd from its wild pride into shame.
15 O yearning heart! I did inherit
    Thy withering portion with the fame,

Tamerlane: European name of the Central Asian king Timur (1336–1405) who conquered much of Asia and founded the Timurid dynasty.

The searing glory which hath shone
Amid the Jewels of my throne,
Halo of Hell! and with a pain
20   Not Hell shall make me fear again—
O craving heart, for the lost flowers
And sunshine of my summer hours!
The undying voice of that dead time,
With its interminable chime,
25   Rings, in the spirit of a spell,
Upon thy emptiness—a knell.

I have not always been as now:
The fever'd diadem on my brow
      I claim'd and won usurpingly——
30   Hath not the same fierce heirdom given
         Rome to the Caesar—this to me?
            The heritage of a kingly mind,
And a proud spirit which hath striven
Triumphantly with human kind.

35   On mountain soil I first drew life:
         The mists of the Taglay have shed
         Nightly their dews upon my head,
And, I believe, the winged strife
And tumult of the headlong air
40   Have nestled in my very hair.

So late from Heaven—that dew—it fell
      ('Mid dreams of an unholy night)
Upon me with the touch of Hell,
      While the red flashing of the light
45   From clouds that hung, like banners, o'er,
         Appeared to my half-closing eye
         The pageantry of monarchy,
And the deep trumpet-thunder's roar
         Came hurriedly upon me, telling
50   Of human battle, where my voice,
My own voice, silly child!—was swelling
         (O! how my spirit would rejoice,
And leap within me at the cry)
The battle-cry of Victory!

55   The rain came down upon my head
         Unshelter'd—and the heavy wind
         Rendered me mad and deaf and blind.

It was but man, I thought, who shed
   Laurels upon me: and the rush—
60 The torrent of the chilly air
Gurgled within my ear the crush
   Of empires—with the captive's prayer—
The hum of suitors—and the tone
Of flattery 'round a sovereign's throne.

65 My passions, from that hapless hour,
   Usurp'd a tyranny which men
Have deem'd, since I have reach'd to power,
   My innate nature—be it so:
But, father, there liv'd one who, then,
70 Then—in my boyhood—when their fire
   Burn'd with a still intenser glow
(For passion must, with youth, expire)
   E'en *then* who knew this iron heart
In woman's weakness had a part.

75 I have no words—alas!—to tell
The loveliness of loving well!
Nor would I now attempt to trace
The more than beauty of a face
Whose lineaments, upon my mind,
80 Are——shadows on th' unstable wind:
Thus I remember having dwelt
   Some page of early lore upon,
With loitering eye, till I have felt
The letters—with their meaning—melt
85   To fantasies—with none.

O, she was worthy of all love!
   Love—as in infancy was mine—
'Twas such as angel minds above
   Might envy; her young heart the shrine
90 On which my every hope and thought
   Were incense—then a goodly gift,
      For they were childish and upright—
Pure——as her young example taught:
   Why did I leave it, and, adrift,
95   Trust to the fire within, for light?

We grew in age—and love—together—
   Roaming the forest, and the wild;

My breast her shield in wintry weather—
   And, when the friendly sunshine smil'd,
100 And she would mark the opening skies,
   I saw no Heaven—but in her eyes.

Young Love's first lesson is——the heart:
   For 'mid that sunshine, and those smiles,
When, from our little cares apart,
105   And laughing at her girlish wiles,
I'd throw me on her throbbing breast,
   And pour my spirit out in tears—
There was no need to speak the rest—
   No need to quiet any fears
110 Of her—who ask'd no reason why,
But turn'd on me her quiet eye!

Yet *more* than worthy of the love
My spirit struggled with, and strove,
When, on the mountain peak, alone,
115 Ambition lent it a new tone—
I had no being—but in thee:
   The world, and all it did contain
In the earth—the air—the sea—
   Its joy—its little lot of pain
120 That was new pleasure——the ideal,
   Dim, vanities of dreams by night—
And dimmer nothings which were real—
   (Shadows—and a more shadowy light!)
Parted upon their misty wings,
125   And, so, confusedly, became
   Thine image, and—a name—a name!
Two separate—yet most intimate things.

I was ambitious—have you known
   The passion, father? You have not:
130 A cottager, I mark'd a throne
Of half the world as all my own,
   And murmur'd at such lowly lot—
But, just like any other dream,
   Upon the vapor of the dew
135 My own had past, did not the beam
   Of beauty which did while it thro'
The minute—the hour—the day—oppress
My mind with double loveliness.

We walk'd together on the crown
140 Of a high mountain which look'd down
Afar from its proud natural towers
    Of rock and forest, on the hills—
The dwindled hills! begirt with bowers
    And shouting with a thousand rills.

145 I spoke to her of power and pride,
    But mystically—in such guise
That she might deem it nought beside
    The moment's converse; in her eyes
I read, perhaps too carelessly—
150   A mingled feeling with my own—
The flush on her bright cheek, to me
    Seem'd to become a queenly throne
Too well that I should let it be
    Light in the wilderness alone.

155 I wrapp'd myself in grandeur then
    And donn'd a visionary crown——
        Yet it was not that Fantasy
        Had thrown her mantle over me—
But that, among the rabble—men,
160   Lion ambition is chain'd down—
And crouches to a keeper's hand—
Not so in deserts where the grand—
The wild—the terrible conspire
With their own breath to fan his fire.

165 Look 'round thee now on Samarcand!°—
    Is she not queen of Earth? her pride
Above all cities? in her hand
    Their destinies? in all beside
Of glory which the world hath known
170 Stands she not nobly and alone?
Falling—her veriest stepping-stone
Shall form the pedestal of a throne—
And who her sovereign? Timour—he
    Whom the astonished people saw
175 Striding o'er empires haughtily
    A diadem'd outlaw!

Samarcand: Capital of the Timurid empire (in what is now Uzbekistan) during the
fourteenth and fifteenth centuries.

O, human love! thou spirit given,
On Earth, of all we hope in Heaven!
Which fall'st into the soul like rain
180 Upon the Siroc-wither'd° plain,
And, failing in thy power to bless,
But leav'st the heart a wilderness!
Idea! which bindest life around
With music of so strange a sound
185 And beauty of so wild a birth—
Farewell! for I have won the Earth.

When Hope, the eagle that tower'd, could see
　　No cliff beyond him in the sky,
His pinions were bent droopingly—
190 　　And homeward turn'd his soften'd eye.
'Twas sunset: when the sun will part
There comes a sullenness of heart
To him who still would look upon
The glory of the summer sun.
195 That soul will hate the ev'ning mist
So often lovely, and will list
To the sound of the coming darkness (known
To those whose spirits harken) as one
Who, in a dream of night, *would* fly
200 But *cannot* from a danger nigh.

What tho' the moon—the white moon
Shed all the splendor of her noon,
Her smile is chilly—and *her* beam,
In that time of dreariness, will seem
205 (So like you gather in your breath)
A portrait taken after death.
And boyhood is a summer sun
Whose waning is the dreariest one—
For all we live to know is known
210 And all we seek to keep hath flown—
Let life, then, as the day-flower, fall
With the noon-day beauty—which is all.

I reach'd my home—my home no more—
　　For all had flown who made it so.
215 I pass'd from out its mossy door,
　　And, tho' my tread was soft and low,

Siroc: A hot desert wind.

A voice came from the threshold stone
Of one whom I had earlier known—
　　O, I defy thee, Hell, to show
220　On beds of fire that burn below,
　　An humbler heart—a deeper wo.

Father, I firmly do believe—
　　I *know*—for Death who comes for me
　　　From regions of the blest afar,
225　Where there is nothing to deceive,
　　　Hath left his iron gate ajar,
　　And rays of truth you cannot see
　　Are flashing thro' Eternity—
I do believe that Eblis° hath
230　A snare in every human path—
　　Else how, when in the holy grove
　　I wandered of the idol, Love,
　　Who daily scents his snowy wings
　　With incense of burnt offerings
235　From the most unpolluted things,
　　Whose pleasant bowers are yet so riven
　　Above with trellic'd rays from Heaven
　　No mote may shun—no tiniest fly—
　　The light'ning of his eagle eye—
240　How was it that Ambition crept,
　　　Unseen, amid the revels there,
　　Till growing bold, he laughed and leapt
　　　In the tangles of Love's very hair?

The Sleeper

At midnight, in the month of June,
I stand beneath the mystic moon.
An opiate vapour, dewy, dim,
Exhales from out her golden rim,
5　And, softly dripping, drop by drop,
Upon the quiet mountain top,
Steals drowsily and musically
Into the universal valley.
The rosemary nods upon the grave;
10　The lily lolls upon the wave;
Wrapping the fog about its breast,
The ruin moulders into rest;

Eblis: A Koranic term for the principal evil spirit or the devil.

Looking like Lethë,° see! the lake
A conscious slumber seems to take,
15 And would not, for the world, awake.
All Beauty sleeps!—and lo! where lies
Irenë, with her Destinies!

Oh, lady bright! can it be right—
This window open to the night?
20 The wanton airs, from the tree-top,
Laughingly through the lattice drop—
The bodiless airs, a wizard rout,
Flit through thy chamber in and out,
And wave the curtain canopy
25 So fitfully—so fearfully—
Above the closed and fringéd lid
'Neath which thy slumb'ring soul lies hid,
That o'er the floor and down the wall,
Like ghosts the shadows rise and fall!
30 Oh, lady dear, hast thou no fear?
Why and what art thou dreaming here?
Sure thou art come o'er far-off seas,
A wonder to these garden trees!
Strange is thy pallor! strange thy dress!
35 Strange, above all, thy length of tress,
And this all solemn silentness!

The lady sleeps! Oh, may her sleep,
Which is enduring, so be deep!
Heaven have her in its sacred keep!
40 This chamber changed for one more holy,
This bed for one more melancholy,
I pray to God that she may lie
Forever with unopened eye,
While the pale sheeted ghosts go by!

45 My love, she sleeps! Oh, may her sleep,
As it is lasting, so be deep!
Soft may the worms about her creep!
Far in the forest, dim and old,
For her may some tall vault unfold—
50 Some vault that oft hath flung its black

Lethë: One of the five rivers of Hades in Greek mythology. Those who drink the waters of Lethë forget everything.

And wingéd pannels° fluttering back,
Triumphant, o'er the crested palls,
Of her grand family funerals—
Some sepulchre, remote, alone,
55 Against whose portal she hath thrown,
In childhood, many an idle stone—
Some tomb from out whose sounding door
She ne'er shall force an echo more,
Thrilling to think, poor child of sin!
60 It was the dead who groaned within.

The City in the Sea

Lo! Death has reared himself a throne
In a strange city lying alone
Far down within the dim West,
Where the good and the bad and the worst
    and the best
5 Have gone to their eternal rest.
There shrines and palaces and towers
(Time-eaten towers that tremble not!)
Resemble nothing that is ours.
Around, by lifting winds forgot,
10 Resignedly beneath the sky
The melancholy waters lie.

No rays from the holy heaven come down
On the long night-time of that town;
But light from out the lurid sea
15 Streams up the turrets silently—
Gleams up the pinnacles far and free—
Up domes—up spires—up kingly halls—
Up fanes—up Babylon-like walls—
Up shadowy long-forgotten bowers
20 Of sculptured ivy and stone flowers—
Up many and many a marvellous shrine
Whose wreathéd friezes intertwine
The viol, the violet, and the vine.

Resignedly beneath the sky
25 The melancholy waters lie.
So blend the turrets and shadows there
That all seem pendulous in air,

pannels: Heavy doors. Used frequently by Poe.

While from a proud tower in the town
Death looks gigantically down.

30 There open fanes and gaping graves
Yawn level with the luminous waves;
But not the riches there that lie
In each idol's diamond eye —
Not the gaily-jewelled dead
35 Tempt the waters from their bed;
For no ripples curl, alas!
Along that wilderness of glass —
No swellings tell that winds may be
Upon some far-off happier sea —
40 No heavings hint that winds have been
On seas less hideously serene.

But lo, a stir is in the air!
The wave — there is a movement there!
As if the towers had thrust aside,
45 In slightly sinking, the dull tide —
As if their tops had feebly given
A void within the filmy Heaven.
The waves have now a redder glow —
The hours are breathing faint and low —
50 And when, amid no earthly moans,
Down, down that town shall settle hence.
Hell, rising from a thousand thrones,
Shall do it reverence.

To Helen

Helen, thy beauty is to me
    Like those Nicéan barks° of yore,
That gently, o'er a perfum'd sea,
    The weary, way-worn wanderer bore
5   To his own native shore.

On desperate seas long wont to roam,
    Thy hyacinth hair, thy classic face,
Thy Naiad airs have brought me home
    To the glory that was Greece,
10   And the grandeur that was Rome.

Nicéan barks: Although there is no consensus to this allusion, it likely refers to ships
from the Greek city Nicaea.

Lo! in yon brilliant window-niche
 How statue-like I see thee stand,
The agate lamp within thy hand!
 Ah, Psyche, from the regions which
15 Are Holy-Land!

Lenore

Ah, broken is the golden bowl!—the spirit
 flown forever!
Let the bell toll!—a saintly soul floats on the
 Stygian river:—
And, Guy De Vere, hast *thou* no tear?—weep
 now or never more!
See! on yon drear and rigid bier low lies thy
 love, Lenore!
5 Come, let the burial rite be read—the funeral
 song be sung!—
An anthem for the queenliest dead that ever
 died so young—
A dirge for her the doubly dead in that she
 died so young.

"Wretches! ye loved her for her wealth and ye
 hated her for her pride;
And, when she fell in feeble health, ye blessed
 her—that she died:—
10 How *shall* the ritual then be read—the
 requiem how be sung
By you—by yours, the evil eye—by yours the
 slanderous tongue
That did to death the innocence that died and
 died so young?"

Peccavimus:°—yet rave not thus! but let a
 Sabbath song
Go up to God so solemnly the dead may feel
 no wrong!
15 The sweet Lenore hath gone before, with
 Hope that flew beside,
Leaving thee wild for the dear child that
 should have been thy bride—

Peccavimus: We have sinned.

For her, the fair and debonair, that now so
   lowly lies,
The life upon her yellow hair, but not within
   her eyes—
The life still there upon her hair, the death
   upon her eyes.

20 "Avaunt!—avaunt! to friends from fiends the
   indignant ghost is riven—
From Hell unto a high estate within the
   utmost Heaven—
From moan and groan to a golden throne
   beside the King of Heaven:—
Let *no* bell toll, then, lest her soul, amid its
   hallowed mirth
Should catch the note as it doth float up from
   the damnéd Earth!
25 And I—tonight my heart is light:—no dirge
   will I upraise,
But waft the angel on her flight with a Paean
   of old days!"

Israfel°

In Heaven a spirit doth dwell
   "Whose heart-strings are a lute;"
None sing so wildly well
As the angel Israfel,
5 And the giddy stars (so legends tell)
Ceasing their hymns, attend the spell
   Of his voice, all mute.

Tottering above
   In her highest noon,
10   The enamoured moon
Blushes with love,
   While, to listen, the red levin°
   (With the rapid Pleiads, even,
   Which were seven,)
15   Pauses in Heaven.

Israfel: "And the angel Israfel, whose heart-strings are a lute, and who has the sweetest
voice of all God's creatures.—KORAN." [Poe's note.]   **levin:** Thunderbolt.

And they say (the starry choir
    And the other listening things)
That Israfeli's fire
Is owing to that lyre
20   By which he sits and sings—
The trembling living wire
Of those unusual strings.

But the skies that angel trod,
    Where deep thoughts are a duty—
25 Where Love's a grown up God—
    Where the Houri glances are
Imbued with all the beauty
    Which we worship in a star.

Therefore, thou art not wrong,
30   Israfeli, who despises
An unimpassioned song;
To thee the laurels belong,
    Best bard, because the wisest!
Merrily live, and long!

35 The ecstacies above
    With thy burning measures suit—
Thy grief, thy joy, thy hate, thy love,
With the fervour of thy lute—
    Well may the stars be mute!

40 Yes, Heaven is thine; but this
    Is a world of sweets and sours;
    Our flowers are merely—flowers,
And the shadow of thy perfect bliss
    Is the sunshine of ours.

45 If I could dwell
Where Israfel
    Hath dwelt, and he where I,
He might not sing so wildly well
    A mortal melody,
50 While a bolder note than this might swell
    From my lyre within the sky.

The Raven

Once upon a midnight dreary, while I
  pondered, weak and weary,
Over many a quaint and curious volume of
  forgotten lore—
While I nodded, nearly napping, suddenly
  there came a tapping,
As of some one gently rapping, rapping at my
  chamber door.
5 " 'Tis some visiter," I muttered, "tapping at
  my chamber door—
    Only this and nothing more."

Ah, distinctly I remember it was in the bleak
  December;
And each separate dying ember wrought its
  ghost upon the floor.
Eagerly I wished the morrow;—vainly I had
  sought to borrow
10 From my books surcease of sorrow—sorrow
  for the lost Lenore—
For the rare and radiant maiden whom the
  angels name Lenore—
    Nameless *here* for evermore.

And the silken, sad, uncertain rustling of each
  purple curtain
Thrilled me—filled me with fantastic terrors
  never felt before;
15 So that now, to still the beating of my heart, I
  stood repeating
" 'Tis some visiter entreating entrance at my
  chamber door—
Some late visiter entreating entrance at my
  chamber door;—
    This it is and nothing more."

Presently my soul grew stronger; hesitating
  then no longer,
20 "Sir," said I, "or Madam, truly your
  forgiveness I implore;
But the fact is I was napping, and so gently
  you came rapping,

And so faintly you came tapping, tapping at
   my chamber door,
That I scarce was sure I heard you"—here I
   opened wide the door;——
     Darkness there and nothing more.

25 Deep into that darkness peering, long I stood
   there wondering, fearing,
Doubting, dreaming dreams no mortal ever
   dared to dream before;
But the silence was unbroken, and the stillness
   gave no token,
And the only word there spoken was the
   whispered word, "Lenore?"
This I whispered, and an echo murmured back
   the word, "Lenore!"
30   Merely this and nothing more.

Back into the chamber turning, all my soul
   within me burning,
Soon again I heard a tapping somewhat louder
   than before.
"Surely," said I, "surely that is something at
   my window lattice;
Let me see, then, what thereat is, and this
   mystery explore—
35 Let my heart be still a moment and this
   mystery explore;—
     'Tis the wind and nothing more!"

Open here I flung the shutter, when, with
   many a flirt and flutter,
In there stepped a stately Raven of the saintly
   days of yore;
Not the least obeisance made he; not a minute
   stopped or stayed he;
40 But, with mien of lord or lady, perched above
   my chamber door—
Perched upon a bust of Pallas° just above my
   chamber door—
     Perched, and sat, and nothing more.

Pallas: Another name for Athena, the goddess of wisdom.

Then this ebony bird beguiling my sad fancy
   into smiling,
By the grave and stern decorum of the
   countenance it wore,
45 "Though thy crest be shorn and shaven,
   thou," I said, "art sure no craven,
Ghastly grim and ancient Raven wandering
   from the Nightly shore—
Tell me what thy lordly name is on the Night's
   Plutonian shore!"
     Quoth the Raven "Nevermore."

Much I marvelled this ungainly fowl to hear
   discourse so plainly,
50 Though its answer little meaning—little
   relevancy bore;
For we cannot help agreeing that no living
   human being
Ever yet was blessed with seeing bird above his
   chamber door—
Bird or beast upon the sculptured bust above
   his chamber door,
     With such name as "Nevermore."

55 But the Raven, sitting lonely on the placid
   bust, spoke only
That one word, as if his soul in that one word
   he did outpour.
Nothing farther then he uttered—not a
   feather then he fluttered—
Till I scarcely more than muttered "Other
   friends have flown before—
On the morrow *he* will leave me, as my Hopes
   have flown before."
60   Then the bird said "Nevermore."

Startled at the stillness broken by reply so aptly
   spoken,
"Doubtless," said I, "what it utters is its only
   stock and store
Caught from some unhappy master whom
   unmerciful Disaster
Followed fast and followed faster till his songs
   one burden bore—

65 Till the dirges of his Hope that melancholy
       burden bore
           Of 'Never—nevermore.' "

But the Raven still beguiling my sad fancy into
       smiling,
Straight I wheeled a cushioned seat in front of
       bird, and bust and door;
Then, upon the velvet sinking, I betook myself
       to linking
70 Fancy unto fancy, thinking what this ominous
       bird of yore—
What this grim, ungainly, ghastly, gaunt, and
       ominous bird of yore
           Meant in croaking "Nevermore."

This I sat engaged in guessing, but no syllable
       expressing
To the fowl whose fiery eyes now burned into
       my bosom's core;
75 This and more I sat divining, with my head at
       ease reclining
On the cushion's velvet lining that the
       lamp-light gloated o'er,
But whose velvet-violet lining with the
       lamp-light gloating o'er,
           She shall press, ah, nevermore!

Then, methought, the air grew denser,
       perfumed from an unseen censer°
80 Swung by seraphim° whose foot-falls tinkled
       on the tufted floor.
"Wretch," I cried, "thy God hath lent thee—
       by these angels he hath sent thee
Respite—respite and nepenthe,° from thy
       memories of Lenore;
Quaff, oh quaff this kind nepenthe and forget
       this lost Lenore!"
           Quoth the Raven "Nevermore."

---

censer: Vessel for burning incense.   **seraphim:** Plural of *seraph*, the highest order of
angels in Christianity.   **nepenthe:** In ancient Greek literature, a drug used to remove
sorrow.

85 "Prophet!" said I, "thing of evil!—prophet
    still, if bird or devil!—
  Whether Tempter sent, or whether tempest
    tossed thee here ashore,
  Desolate yet all undaunted, on this desert land
    enchanted—
  On this home by Horror haunted—tell me
    truly, I implore—
  Is there—*is* there balm in Gilead?—tell me—
    tell me, I implore!"
90   Quoth the Raven "Nevermore."

  "Prophet!" said I, "thing of evil!—prophet
    still, if bird or devil!
  By that Heaven that bends above us—by that
    God we both adore—
  Tell this soul with sorrow laden if, within the
    distant Aidenn,°
  It shall clasp a sainted maiden whom the
    angels name Lenore—
95 Clasp a rare and radiant maiden whom the
    angels name Lenore."
      Quoth the Raven "Nevermore."

  "Be that word our sign of parting, bird or
    fiend!" I shrieked, upstarting—
  "Get thee back into the tempest and the
    Night's Plutonian shore!
  Leave no black plume as a token of that lie thy
    soul hath spoken!
100 Leave my loneliness unbroken!—quit the bust
    above my door!
  Take thy beak from out my heart, and take thy
    form from off my door!"
      Quoth the Raven "Nevermore."

  And the Raven, never flitting, still is sitting,
    still is sitting
  On the pallid bust of Pallas just above my
    chamber door;
105 And his eyes have all the seeming of a demon's
    that is dreaming,

Aidenn: The Garden of Eden.

And the lamp-light o'er him streaming throws
   his shadow on the floor;
And my soul from out that shadow that lies
   floating on the floor
     Shall be lifted—nevermore!

To Marie Louise

Not long ago, the writer of these lines,
In the mad pride of intellectuality,
Maintained "the power of words"—denied that ever
A thought arose within the human brain
5 Beyond the utterance of the human tongue;
And now, as if in mockery of that boast,
Two words—two foreign soft dissyllables—
Italian tones made only to be murmured
By angels dreaming in the moonlit "dew
10 That hangs like chains of pearl on Hermon hill"—
Have stirred from out the abysses of his heart,
Unthought-like thoughts that are the souls of thought,
Richer, far wilder, far diviner visions
Than even the seraph harper, Israfel,
15 Who has "the sweetest voice of all God's creatures,"
Could hope to utter. And I! my spells are broken.
The pen falls powerless from my shivering hand.
With thy dear name as text, though bidden by thee,
I cannot write—I cannot speak or think,
20 Alas! I cannot feel; for 'tis not feeling,
This standing motionless upon the golden
Threshold of the wide-open gate of dreams,
Gazing, entranced, adown the gorgeous vista,
And thrilling as I see upon the right,
25 Upon the left, and all the way along
Amid empurpled vapors, far away
To where the prospect terminates—*thee only.*

Annabel Lee

It was many and many a year ago,
   In a kingdom by the sea,
That a maiden lived whom you may know
   By the name of Annabel Lee;—

5 And this maiden she lived with no other thought
     Than to love and be loved by me.

  She was a child and *I* was a child,
     In this kingdom by the sea,
  But we loved with a love that was more than love—
10   I and my Annabel Lee—
  With a love that the wingéd seraphs of Heaven
     Coveted her and me.

  And this was the reason that, long ago,
     In this kingdom by the sea,
15 A wind blew out of a cloud by night
     Chilling my Annabel Lee;
  So that her high-born kinsmen came
     And bore her away from me,
  To shut her up in a sepulchre
20   In this kingdom by the sea.

  The angels, not half so happy in Heaven,
     Went envying her and me;
  Yes! that was the reason (as all men know,
     In this kingdom by the sea)
25 That the wind came out of the cloud, chilling
     And killing my Annabel Lee.

  But our love it was stronger by far than the love
     Of those who were older than we—
     Of many far wiser than we—
30 And neither the angels in Heaven above
     Nor the demons down under the sea
  Can ever dissever my soul from the soul
     Of the beautiful Annabel Lee:—

  For the moon never beams without bringing me dreams
     Of the beautiful Annabel Lee;
  And the stars never rise but I see the bright eyes
35   Of the beautiful Annabel Lee;
  And so, all the night-tide, I lie down by the side
  Of my darling, my darling, my life and my bride
40   In her sepulchre there by the sea—
     In her tomb by the side of the sea.

For Annie

Thank Heaven! the crisis—
    The danger is past,
And the lingering illness
    Is over at last—
5 And the fever called "Living"
    Is conquered at last.

Sadly, I know
    I am shorn of my strength,
And no muscle I move
10   As I lie at full length—
But no matter!—I feel
    I am better at length.

And I rest so composedly,
    Now, in my bed,
15 That any beholder
    Might fancy me dead—
Might start at beholding me,
    Thinking me dead.

The moaning and groaning,
20   The sighing and sobbing,
Are quieted now,
    With that horrible throbbing
At heart:—ah, that horrible,
    Horrible throbbing!

25 The sickness—the nausea—
    The pitiless pain—
Have ceased, with the fever
    That maddened my brain—
With the fever called "Living"
30   That burned in my brain.

And oh! of all tortures
    That torture the worst
Has abated—the terrible
    Torture of thirst

35 For the napthaline° river
  Of Passion accurst:—
I have drank of a water
  That quenches all thirst:—

Of a water that flows,
40   With a lullaby sound,
From a spring but a very few
  Feet under ground—
From a cavern not very far
  Down under ground.

45 And ah! let it never
  Be foolishly said
That my room it is gloomy
  And narrow my bed;
For man never slept
50   In a different bed—
And, to *sleep*, you must slumber
  In just such a bed.

My tantalized spirit
  Here blandly reposes,
55 Forgetting, or never
  Regretting its roses—
Its old agitations
  Of myrtles and roses:

For now, while so quietly
60   Lying, it fancies
A holier odor
  About it, of pansies—
A rosemary odor,
  Commingled with pansies—
65 With rue and the beautiful
  Puritan pansies.

And so it lies happily,
  Bathing in many

napthaline: A material made from coal tar that could be used for light; usually spelled "naphthalene."

A dream of the truth
70   And the beauty of Annie—
Drowned in a bath
    Of the tresses of Annie.

She tenderly kissed me,
    She fondly caressed,
75 And then I fell gently
    To sleep on her breast—
Deeply to sleep
    From the heaven of her breast.

When the light was extinguished,
80   She covered me warm,
And she prayed to the angels
    To keep me from harm—
To the queen of the angels
    To shield me from harm.

85 And I lie so composedly,
    Now, in my bed,
(Knowing her love)
    That you fancy me dead—
And I rest so contentedly,
90   Now in my bed,
(With her love at my breast)
    That you fancy me dead—
That you shudder to look at me,
    Thinking me dead:—

95 But my heart it is brighter
    Than all of the many
Stars in the sky,
    For it sparkles with Annie—
It glows with the light
100   Of the love of my Annie—
With the thought of the light
    Of the eyes of my Annie.

TALES

Metzengerstein

Pestis eram vivus—moriens tua mors ero.°

–MARTIN LUTHER

Horror and fatality have been stalking abroad in all ages. Why then give a date to this story I have to tell? Let it suffice to say, that at the period of which I speak, there existed, in the interior of Hungary, a settled although hidden belief in the doctrines of the Metempsychosis.° Of the doctrines themselves—that is, of their falsity, or of their proba-bility—I say nothing. I assert, however, that much of our incredulity (as La Bruyere says of all our unhappiness) *"vient de ne pouvoir être seuls."* °

But there were some points in the Hungarian superstition which were fast verging to absurdity. They—the Hungarians—differed very essentially from their Eastern authorities. For example. *"The soul,"* said the former—I give the words of an acute and intelligent Parisian— *"ne demeure qu'un seul fois dans un corps sensible: au reste—un cheval, un chien, un homme meme, n'est que la ressemblance peu tangible de ces animaux."* °

The families of Berlifitzing and Metzengerstein had been at vari-ance for centuries. Never before were two houses so illustrious, mutu-ally embittered by hostility so deadly. The origin of this enmity seems to be found in the words of an ancient prophecy—"A lofty name shall have a fearful fall when, as the rider over his horse, the mortality of Metzengerstein shall triumph over the immortality of Berlifitzing."

To be sure the words themselves had little or no meaning. But more trivial causes have given rise—and that no long while ago—to conse-quences equally eventful. Besides, the estates, which were contiguous, had long exercised a rival influence in the affairs of a busy government. Moreover, near neighbors are seldom friends; and the inhabitants of the Castle Berlifitzing might look, from their lofty buttresses, into the very

---

Pestis eram ... mors ero: Living, I was your plague—dying I shall be your death. *Metempsychosis:* The transmigration of the soul after death into another body. *vient...* *seuls:* The French passage is adapted from Jean de La Bruyère (1645–1696), a French philosopher and writer, who writes about the unhappiness that comes from not being able "to be alone." *ne demeure ... animaux:* The French passage is not entirely translatable, but suggests that souls are located in the very different physical bodies of all animals: horses, dogs, and even humans.

windows of the Palace Metzengerstein. Least of all had the more than feudal magnificence thus discovered, a tendency to allay the irritable feelings of the less ancient and less wealthy Berlifitzings. What wonder, then, that the words, however silly, of that prediction, should have succeeded in setting and keeping at variance two families already predisposed to quarrel by every instigation of hereditary jealousy? The prophecy seemed to imply—if it implied anything—a final triumph on the part of the already more powerful house; and was of course remembered with the more bitter animosity by the weaker and less influential.

Wilhelm, Count Berlifitzing, although loftily descended, was, at the epoch of this narrative, an infirm and doting old man, remarkable for nothing but an inordinate and inveterate personal antipathy to the family of his rival, and so passionate a love of horses, and of hunting, that neither bodily infirmity, great age, nor mental incapacity, prevented his daily participation in the dangers of the chase.

Frederick, Baron Metzengerstein, was, on the other hand, not yet of age. His father, the Minister G——, died young. His mother, the Lady Mary, followed him quickly. Frederick was, at that time, in his eighteenth year. In a city, eighteen years are no long period: but in a wilderness—in so magnificent a wilderness as that old principality, the pendulum vibrates with a deeper meaning.

From some peculiar circumstances attending the administration of his father, the young Baron, at the decease of the former, entered immediately upon his vast possessions. Such estates were seldom held before by a nobleman of Hungary. His castles were without number. The chief in point of splendor and extent was the "Palace Metzengerstein." The boundary line of his dominions was never clearly defined; but his principal park embraced a circuit of fifty miles.

Upon the succession of a proprietor so young, with a character so well known, to a fortune so unparalleled, little speculation was afloat in regard to his probable course of conduct. And, indeed, for the space of three days, the behavior of the heir out-heroded Herod, and fairly surpassed the expectations of his most enthusiastic admirers. Shameful debaucheries—flagrant treacheries—unheard-of atrocities—gave his trembling vassals quickly to understand that no servile submission on their part—no punctilios of conscience on his own—were thenceforward to prove any security against the remorseless fangs of a petty Caligula. On the night of the fourth day, the stables of the Castle Berlifitzing were discovered to be on fire; and the unanimous opinion of the neighborhood added the crime of the incendiary to the already hideous list of the Baron's misdemeanors and enormities.

But during the tumult occasioned by this occurrence, the young nobleman himself, sat apparently buried in meditation, in a vast and desolate upper apartment of the family palace of Metzengerstein. The rich although faded tapestry hangings which swung gloomily upon the walls, represented the shadowy and majestic forms of a thousand illustrious ancestors. *Here*, rich-ermined priests, and pontifical dignitaries, familiarly seated with the autocrat and the sovereign, put a veto on the wishes of a temporal king, or restrained with the fiat of papal supremacy the rebellious sceptre of the Arch-enemy. *There*, the dark, tall statures of the Princes Metzengerstein—their muscular war-coursers plunging over the carcasses of fallen foes—startled the steadiest nerves with their vigorous expression: and *here*, again, the voluptuous and swan-like figures of the dames of days gone by, floated away in the mazes of an unreal dance to the strains of imaginary melody.

But as the Baron listened, or affected to listen, to the gradually increasing uproar in the stables of Berlifitzing—or perhaps pondered upon some more novel, some more decided act of audacity—his eyes were turned unwittingly to the figure of an enormous, and unnaturally colored horse, represented in the tapestry as belonging to a Saracen° ancestor of the family of his rival. The horse itself, in the fore-ground of the design, stood motionless and statue-like—while, farther back, its discomfited rider perished by the dagger of a Metzengerstein.

On Frederick's lip arose a fiendish expression, as he became aware of the direction which his glance had, without his consciousness, assumed. Yet he did not remove it. On the contrary, he could by no means account for the overwhelming anxiety which appeared falling like a pall upon his senses. It was with difficulty that he reconciled his dreamy and incoherent feelings with the certainty of being awake. The longer he gazed, the more absorbing became the spell—the more impossible did it appear that he could ever withdraw his glance from the fascination of that tapestry. But the tumult without becoming suddenly more violent, with a compulsory exertion he diverted his attention to the glare of ruddy light thrown full by the flaming stables upon the windows of the apartment.

The action, however, was but momentary; his gaze returned mechanically to the wall. To his extreme horror and astonishment, the head of the gigantic steed had, in the meantime, altered its position. The neck of the animal, before arched, as if in compassion, over the prostrate body of its lord, was now extended, at full length, in the direction of the

Saracen: Medieval European term for a Muslim.

Baron. The eyes, before invisible, now wore an energetic and human expression, while they gleamed with a fiery and unusual red; and the distended lips of the apparently enraged horse left in full view his sepulchral and disgusting teeth.

Stupified with terror, the young nobleman tottered to the door. As he threw it open, a flash of red light, streaming far into the chamber, flung his shadow with a clear outline against the quivering tapestry; and he shuddered to perceive that shadow—as he staggered awhile upon the threshold—assuming the exact position, and precisely filling up the contour, of the relentless and triumphant murderer of the Saracen Berlifitzing.

To lighten the depression of his spirits, the Baron hurried into the open air. At the principal gate of the palace he encountered three equerries.° With much difficulty, and at the imminent peril of their lives, they were restraining the convulsive plunges of a gigantic and fiery-colored horse.

"Whose horse? Where did you get him?" demanded the youth, in a querulous and husky tone, as he became instantly aware that the mysterious steed in the tapestried chamber was the very counterpart of the furious animal before his eyes.

"He is your own property, sire," replied one of the equerries, "at least he is claimed by no other owner. We caught him flying, all smoking and foaming with rage, from the burning stables of the Castle Berlifitzing. Supposing him to have belonged to the old Count's stud of foreign horses, we led him back as an estray. But the grooms there disclaim any title to the creature; which is strange, since he bears evident marks of having made a narrow escape from the flames."

"The letters W. V. B. are also branded very distinctly on his forehead," interrupted a second equerry, "I supposed them, of course, to be the initials of Wilhelm Von Berlifitzing—but all at the castle are positive in denying any knowledge of the horse."

"Extremely singular!" said the young Baron, with a musing air, and apparently unconscious of the meaning of his words. "He is, as you say, a remarkable horse—a prodigious horse! although, as you very justly observe, of a suspicious and untractable character; let him be mine, however," he added, after a pause, "perhaps a rider like Frederick of Metzengerstein, may tame even the devil from the stables of Berlifitzing."

"You are mistaken, my lord; the horse, as I think we mentioned, is *not* from the stables of the Count. If such had been the case, we know

---

equerries: Senior attendants who oversee the stables for a noble family.

our duty better than to bring him into the presence of a noble of your family."

"True!" observed the Baron, drily; and at that instant a page of the bed-chamber came from the palace with a heightened color, and a precipitate step. He whispered into his master's ear an account of the sudden disappearance of a small portion of the tapestry, in an apartment which he designated; entering, at the same time, into particulars of a minute and circumstantial character; but from the low tone of voice in which these latter were communicated, nothing escaped to gratify the excited curiosity of the equerries.

The young Frederick, during the conference, seemed agitated by a variety of emotions. He soon, however, recovered his composure, and an expression of determined malignancy settled upon his countenance, as he gave peremptory orders that the apartment in question should be immediately locked up, and the key placed in his own possession.

"Have you heard of the unhappy death of the old hunter Berlifitzing?" said one of his vassals to the Baron, as, after the departure of the page, the huge steed which that nobleman had adopted as his own, plunged and curveted, with redoubled fury, down the long avenue which extended from the palace to the stables of Metzengerstein.

"No!" said the Baron, turning abruptly towards the speaker, "dead! say you?"

"It is indeed true, my lord; and, to the noble of your name, will be, I imagine, no unwelcome intelligence."

A rapid smile shot over the countenance of the listener. "How died he?"

"In his rash exertions to rescue a favorite portion of his hunting stud, he has himself perished miserably in the flames."

"I—n—d—e—e—d—!" ejaculated the Baron, as if slowly and deliberately impressed with the truth of some exciting idea.

"Indeed;" repeated the vassal.

"Shocking!" said the youth, calmly, and turned quietly into the palace.

From this date a marked alteration took place in the outward demeanor of the dissolute young Baron Frederick Von Metzengerstein. Indeed, his behaviour disappointed every expectation, and proved little in accordance with the views of many a manoeuvring mamma; while his habits and manner, still less than formerly, offered anything congenial with those of the neighboring aristocracy. He was never to be seen beyond the limits of his own domain, and, in this wide and social world, was utterly companionless—unless, indeed, that unnatural, impetuous, and fiery-colored horse, which he henceforward continually bestrode, had any mysterious right to the title of his friend.

Numerous invitations on the part of the neighborhood for a long time, however, periodically came in. "Will the Baron honor our festivals with his presence?" "Will the Baron join us in a hunting of the boar?" — "Metzengerstein does not hunt;" "Metzengerstein will not attend," were the haughty and laconic answers.

These repeated insults were not to be endured by an imperious nobility. Such invitations became less cordial — less frequent — in time they ceased altogether. The widow of the unfortunate Count Berlifitzing was even heard to express a hope "that the Baron might be at home when he did not wish to be at home, since he disdained the company of his equals; and ride when he did not wish to ride, since he preferred the society of a horse." This to be sure was a very silly explosion of hereditary pique; and merely proved how singularly unmeaning our sayings are apt to become, when we desire to be unusually energetic.

The charitable, nevertheless, attributed the alteration in the conduct of the young nobleman to the natural sorrow of a son for the untimely loss of his parents; — forgetting, however, his atrocious and reckless behavior during the short period immediately succeeding that bereavement. Some there were, indeed, who suggested a too haughty idea of self-consequence and dignity. Others again (among them may be mentioned the family physician) did not hesitate in speaking of morbid melancholy, and hereditary ill-health; while dark hints, of a more equivocal nature, were current among the multitude.

Indeed, the Baron's perverse attachment to his lately-acquired charger — an attachment which seemed to attain new strength from every fresh example of the animal's ferocious and demon-like propensities — at length became, in the eyes of all reasonable men, a hideous and unnatural fervor. In the glare of noon — at the dead hour of night — in sickness or in health — in calm or in tempest — the young Metzengerstein seemed riveted to the saddle of that colossal horse, whose intractable audacities so well accorded with his own spirit.

There were circumstances, moreover, which, coupled with late events, gave an unearthly and portentous character to the mania of the rider, and to the capabilities of the steed. The space passed over in a single leap had been accurately measured, and was found to exceed by an astounding difference, the wildest expectations of the most imaginative. The Baron, besides, had no particular *name* for the animal, although all the rest in his collection were distinguished by characteristic appellations. His stable, too, was appointed at a distance from the rest; and with regard to grooming and other necessary offices, none but the owner in person had ventured to officiate, or even to enter the enclosure of that horse's particular stall. It was also to be observed, that although the three grooms, who had caught the steed as he fled from the conflagration at Berlifitzing, had succeeded in arresting his course, by means of a chain-bridle and noose—yet no one of the three could with any certainty affirm that he had, during that dangerous struggle, or at any period thereafter, actually placed his hand upon the body of the beast. Instances of peculiar intelligence in the demeanor of a noble and high-spirited horse are not to be supposed capable of exciting unreasonable attention, but there were certain circumstances which intruded themselves per force upon the most skeptical and phlegmatic; and it is said there were times when the animal caused the gaping crowd who stood around to recoil in horror from the deep and impressive meaning of his terrible stamp—times when the young Metzengerstein turned pale and shrunk away from the rapid and searching expression of his earnest and human-looking eye.

Among all the retinue of the Baron, however, none were found to doubt the ardor of that extraordinary affection which existed on the part of the young nobleman for the fiery qualities of his horse; at least, none but an insignificant and misshapen little page, whose deformities were in every body's way, and whose opinions were of the least possible importance. He (if his ideas are worth mentioning at all,) had the effrontery to assert that his master never vaulted into the saddle, without an unaccountable and almost imperceptible shudder; and that, upon his return from every long-continued and habitual ride, an expression of triumphant malignity distorted every muscle in his countenance.

One tempestuous night, Metzengerstein, awaking from heavy slumber, descended like a maniac from his chamber, and, mounting in hot haste, bounded away into the mazes of the forest. An occurrence so common attracted no particular attention, but his return was looked for with intense anxiety on the part of his domestics, when, after some hours' absence, the stupendous and magnificent battlements of the Palace Metzengerstein, were discovered crackling and rocking to their very foundation, under the influence of a dense and livid mass of ungovernable fire.

As the flames, when first seen, had already made so terrible a progress that all efforts to save any portion of the building were evidently futile, the astonished neighborhood stood idly around in silent, if not apathetic wonder. But a new and fearful object soon riveted the attention of the multitude, and proved how much more intense is the excitement wrought in the feelings of a crowd by the contemplation of human agony, than that brought about by the most appalling spectacles of inanimate matter.

Up the long avenue of aged oaks which led from the forest to the main entrance of the Palace Metzengerstein, a steed, bearing an unbonneted and disordered rider, was seen leaping with an impetuosity which outstripped the very Demon of the Tempest.

The career of the horseman was indisputably, on his own part, uncontrollable. The agony of his countenance, the convulsive struggle of his frame, gave evidence of superhuman exertion: but no sound, save a solitary shriek, escaped from his lacerated lips, which were bitten through and through in the intensity of terror. One instant, and the clattering of hoofs resounded sharply and shrilly above the roaring of the flames and the shrieking of the winds—another, and, clearing at a single plunge the gate-way and the moat, the steed bounded far up the tottering staircases of the palace, and, with its rider, disappeared amid the whirlwind of chaotic fire.

The fury of the tempest immediately died away, and a dead calm sullenly succeeded. A white flame still enveloped the building like a shroud, and, streaming far away into the quiet atmosphere, shot forth a glare of preternatural light; while a cloud of smoke settled heavily over the battlements in the distinct colossal figure of—*a horse*.

Berenice

Dicebant mihi sodales, si sepulchrum amicae, visitarem, curas meas aliquantulum fore levatas.

–EBN ZAIAT°

Misery is manifold. The wretchedness of earth is multiform. Over-reaching the wide horizon as the rainbow, its hues are as various as the hues of that arch,—as distinct too, yet as intimately blended. Over-reaching the wide horizon as the rainbow! How is it that from beauty I have derived a type of unloveliness?—from the covenant of peace a simile of sorrow? But as, in ethics, evil is a consequence of good, so, in fact, out of joy is sorrow born. Either the memory of past bliss is the anguish of to-day, or the agonies which *are* have their origin in the ecstasies which *might have been*.

Dicebant . . . fore levatas: My companions told me that I might find some little alleviation of my misery, in visiting the grave of my beloved. Ebn Zaiat was a Bagdad poet of the third century.

My baptismal name is Egaeus; that of my family I will not mention. Yet there are no towers in the land more time-honored than my gloomy, gray, hereditary halls. Our line has been called a race of visionaries; and in many striking particulars—in the character of the family mansion— in the frescos of the chief saloon—in the tapestries of the dormitories—in the chiselling of some buttresses in the armory—but more especially in the gallery of antique paintings—in the fashion of the library chamber—and, lastly, in the very peculiar nature of the library's contents, there is more than sufficient evidence to warrant the belief.

The recollections of my earliest years are connected with that chamber, and with its volumes—of which latter I will say no more. Here died my mother. Herein was I born. But it is mere idleness to say that I had not lived before—that the soul has no previous existence. You deny it?—let us not argue the matter. Convinced myself, I seek not to convince. There is, however, a remembrance of aërial forms—of spiritual and meaning eyes—of sounds, musical yet sad—a remembrance which will not be excluded; a memory like a shadow, vague, variable, indefinite, unsteady; and like a shadow, too, in the impossibility of my getting rid of it while the sunlight of my reason shall exist.

In that chamber was I born. Thus awaking from the long night of what seemed, but was not, nonentity, at once into the very regions of fairy-land—into a palace of imagination—into the wild dominions of monastic thought and erudition—it is not singular that I gazed around me with a startled and ardent eye—that I loitered away my boyhood in books, and dissipated my youth in reverie; but it *is* singular that as years rolled away, and the noon of manhood found me still in the mansion of my fathers—it *is* wonderful what stagnation there fell upon the springs of my life—wonderful how total an inversion took place in the character of my commonest thought. The realities of the world affected me as visions, and as visions only, while the wild ideas of the land of dreams became, in turn,—not the material of my everyday existence—but in very deed that existence utterly and solely in itself.

* * *

Berenice and I were cousins, and we grew up together in my paternal halls. Yet differently we grew—I ill of health and buried in gloom— she, agile, graceful, and overflowing with energy—hers the ramble on the hill-side—mine the studies of the cloister—I living within my own heart, and addicted body and soul to the most intense and painful meditation—she roaming carelessly through life with no thought of the shadows in her path, or the silent flight of the raven-winged hours. Berenice!—I call upon her name—Berenice!—and from the gray ruins of memory a thousand tumultuous recollections are startled at the sound! Ah! vividly is her image before me now, as in the early days of her light-heartedness and joy! Oh! gorgeous yet fantastic beauty! Oh! sylph amid the shrubberies of Arnheim!°—Oh! Naiad among its fountains!—and then—then all is mystery and terror, and a tale which should not be told. Disease—a fatal disease—fell like the simoon° upon her frame, and, even while I gazed upon her, the spirit of change swept over her, pervading her mind, her habits, and her character, and, in a manner the most subtle and terrible, disturbing even the identity of her person! Alas! the destroyer came and went,—and the victim—where was she? I knew her not—or knew her no longer as Berenice.

Among the numerous train of maladies superinduced by that fatal and primary one which effected a revolution of so horrible a kind in the moral and physical being of my cousin, may be mentioned as the most distressing and obstinate in its nature, a species of epilepsy not unfrequently terminating in *trance* itself—trance very nearly resembling positive dissolution, and from which her manner of recovery was, in most instances, startlingly abrupt. In the mean time my own disease—for I have been told that I should call it by no other appelation—my own disease, then, grew rapidly upon me, and assumed finally a monomaniac character of a novel and extraordinary form—hourly and momently gaining vigor—and at length obtaining over me the most incomprehensible ascendancy. This monomania, if I must so term it, consisted in a morbid irritability of those properties of the mind in metaphysical science termed the *attentive*. It is more than probable that I am not understood; but I fear, indeed, that it is in no manner possible to convey to the mind of the merely general reader, an adequate idea of that nervous *intensity of interest* with which, in my case, the powers of meditation (not to speak technically) busied and buried themselves, in the contemplation of even the most ordinary objects of the universe.

To muse for long unwearied hours, with my attention riveted to some frivolous device on the margin, or in the typography of a book; to become absorbed for the better part of a summer's day in a quaint shadow falling aslant upon the tapestry, or upon the floor; to lose myself for an entire night in watching the steady flame of a lamp, or the embers of a fire; to dream away whole days over the perfume of a flower; to

---

Arnheim: A small city in the east of the Netherlands.   **simoon:** A strong, dry wind that blows in the Arabian Peninsula.

repeat monotonously some common word, until the sound, by dint of frequent repetition, ceased to convey any idea whatever to the mind; to lose all sense of motion or physical existence, by means of absolute bodily quiescence long and obstinately persevered in:—such were a few of the most common and least pernicious vagaries induced by a condition of the mental faculties, not, indeed, altogether unparalleled, but certainly bidding defiance to anything like analysis or explanation.

Yet let me not be misapprehended.—The undue, earnest, and morbid attention thus excited by objects in their own nature frivolous, must not be confounded in character with that ruminating propensity common to all mankind, and more especially indulged in by persons of ardent imagination. It was not even, as might be at first supposed, an extreme condition, or exaggeration of such propensity, but primarily and essentially distinct and different. In the one instance, the dreamer, or enthusiast, being interested by an object usually *not* frivolous, imperceptibly loses sight of this object in a wilderness of deductions and suggestions issuing therefrom, until, at the conclusion of a day dream *often replete with luxury*, he finds the *incitamentum* or first cause of his musings entirely vanished and forgotten. In my case the primary object was *invariably frivolous*, although assuming, through the medium of my distempered vision, a refracted and unreal importance. Few deductions, if any, were made; and those few pertinaciously returning in upon the original object as a centre. The meditations were *never* pleasurable; and, at the termination of the reverie, the first cause, so far from being out of sight, had attained that supernaturally exaggerated interest which was the prevailing feature of the disease. In a word, the powers of mind more particularly exercised were, with me, as I have said before, the *attentive*, and are, with the day-dreamer, the *speculative*.

My books, at this epoch, if they did not actually serve to irritate the disorder, partook, it will be perceived, largely, in their imaginative and inconsequential nature, of the characteristic qualities of the disorder itself. I well remember, among others, the treatise of the noble Italian Coelius Secundus Curio, "*de Amplitudine Beati Regni Dei;*" St. Austin's great work, the "City of God;" and Tertullian's "*de Carne Christi,*" in which the paradoxical sentence "*Mortuus est Dei filius; credible est quia ineptum est; et sepultus resurrexit; certum est quia impossibile est*"° occupied my undivided time, for many weeks of laborious and fruitless investigation.

Mortuus . . . impossibile est: Dead is the son of God; absurd, and hence believable; and he rose from the dead; certainly, because impossible.

Thus it will appear that, shaken from its balance only by trivial things, my reason bore resemblance to that ocean-crag spoken of by Ptolemy Hephestion, which steadily resisting the attacks of human violence, and the fiercer fury of the waters and the winds, trembled only to the touch of the flower called Asphodel. And although, to a careless thinker, it might appear a matter beyond doubt, that the alteration produced by her unhappy malady, in the *moral* condition of Berenice, would afford me many objects for the exercise of that intense and abnormal meditation whose nature I have been at some trouble in explaining, yet such was not in any degree the case. In the lucid intervals of my infirmity, her calamity, indeed, gave me pain, and, taking deeply to heart that total wreck of her fair and gentle life, I did not fail to ponder, frequently and bitterly, upon the wonder-working means by which so strange a revolution had been so suddenly brought to pass. But these reflections partook not of the idiosyncrasy of my disease, and were such as would have occurred, under similar circumstances, to the ordinary mass of mankind. True to its own character, my disorder revelled in the less important but more startling changes wrought in the *physical* frame of Berenice—in the singular and most appalling distortion of her personal identity.

During the brightest days of her unparalleled beauty, most surely I had never loved her. In the strange anomaly of my existence, feelings with me, *had never been* of the heart, and my passions *always were* of the mind. Through the gray of the early morning—among the trellissed shadows of the forest at noon-day—and in the silence of my library at night, she had flitted by my eyes, and I had seen her—not as the living and breathing Berenice, but as the Berenice of a dream—not as a being of the earth, earthy, but as the abstraction of such a being—not as a thing to admire, but to analyze—not as an object of love, but as the theme of the most abstruse although desultory speculation. And *now*— now I shuddered in her presence, and grew pale at her approach; yet, bitterly lamenting her fallen and desolate condition, I called to mind that she had loved me long, and, in an evil moment, I spoke to her of marriage.

And at length the period of our nuptials was approaching, when, upon an afternoon in the winter of the year,—one of those unseasonably warm, calm, and misty days which are the nurse of the beautiful Halcyon,°—I sat, (and sat, as I thought, alone,) in the inner apartment of the library. But uplifting my eyes I saw that Berenice stood before me.

Halcyon: "For as Jove, during the winter season, gives twice seven days of warmth, men have called this clement and temperate time the nurse of the beautiful Halcyon.— *Simonides.*" [Poe's note.]

Was it my own excited imagination—or the misty influence of the atmosphere—or the uncertain twilight of the chamber—or the gray draperies which fell around her figure—that caused in it so vacillating and indistinct an outline? I could not tell. She spoke no word, and I—not for worlds could I have uttered a syllable. An icy chill ran through my frame; a sense of insufferable anxiety oppressed me; a consuming curiosity pervaded my soul; and sinking back upon the chair, I remained for some time breathless and motionless, with my eyes riveted upon her person. Alas! its emaciation was excessive, and not one vestige of the former being, lurked in any single line of the contour. My burning glances at length fell upon the face.

The forehead was high, and very pale, and singularly placid; and the once jetty hair fell partially over it, and overshadowed the hollow temples with innumerable ringlets now of a vivid yellow, and jarring discordantly, in their fantastic character, with the reigning melancholy of the countenance. The eyes were lifeless, and lustreless, and seemingly pupilless, and I shrank involuntarily from their glassy stare to the contemplation of the thin and shrunken lips. They parted; and in a smile of peculiar meaning, *the teeth* of the changed Berenice disclosed themselves slowly to my view. Would to God that I had never beheld them, or that, having done so, I had died!

* * *

The shutting of a door disturbed me, and, looking up, I found that my cousin had departed from the chamber. But from the disordered chamber of my brain, had not, alas! departed, and would not be driven away, the white and ghastly *spectrum* of the teeth. Not a speck on their surface—not a shade on their enamel—not an indenture in their edges—but what that brief period of her smile had sufficed to brand in upon my memory. I saw them *now* even more unequivocally than I beheld them *then*. The teeth!—the teeth!—they were here, and there, and everywhere, and visibly and palpably before me; long, narrow, and excessively white, with the pale lips writhing about them, as in the very moment of their first terrible development. Then came the full fury of my *monomania*, and I struggled in vain against its strange and irresistible influence. In the multiplied objects of the external world I had no thoughts but for the teeth. For these I longed with a phrenzied desire. All other matters and all different interests became absorbed in their single contemplation. They—they alone were present to the mental eye, and they, in their sole individuality, became the essence of my

mental life. I held them in every light. I turned them in every attitude.
I surveyed their characteristics. I dwelt upon their peculiarities. I pondered upon their conformation. I mused upon the alteration in their
nature. I shuddered as I assigned to them in imagination a sensitive and
sentient power, and even when unassisted by the lips, a capability of
moral expression. Of Mad'selle Sallé° it has been well said, "*que tous ses
pas etaient des sentiments,*"° and of Berenice I more seriously believed
que tous ses dents etaient des idées. Des idées!°—ah here was the idiotic
thought that destroyed me! *Des idées!*—ah *therefore* it was that I coveted them so madly! I felt that their possession could alone ever restore
me to peace, in giving me back to reason.

And the evening closed in upon me thus—and then the darkness
came, and tarried, and went—and the day again dawned—and the
mists of a second night were now gathering around—and still I sat
motionless in that solitary room, and still I sat buried in meditation,
and still the *phantasma* of the teeth maintained its terrible ascendancy
as, with the most vivid and hideous distinctness, it floated about amid
the changing lights and shadows of the chamber. At length there broke
in upon my dreams a cry as of horror and dismay; and thereunto, after
a pause, succeeded the sound of troubled voices, intermingled with
many low moanings of sorrow, or of pain. I arose from my seat, and,
throwing open one of the doors of the library, saw standing out in the
antechamber a servant maiden, all in tears, who told me that Berenice
was—no more. She had been seized with epilepsy in the early morning,
and now, at the closing in of the night, the grave was ready for its tenant, and all the preparations for the burial were completed.

*   *   *

I found myself sitting in the library, and again sitting there alone. It
seemed that I had newly awakened from a confused and exciting dream.
I knew that it was now midnight, and I was well aware that since the
setting of the sun Berenice had been interred. But of that dreary period
which intervened I had no positive—at least no definite comprehension. Yet its memory was replete with horror—horror more horrible
from being vague, and terror more terrible from ambiguity. It was a
fearful page in the record of my existence, written all over with dim,

---

Mad'selle Sallé: Marie Sallé (1707–1756), innovative French dancer and choreographer.
que tous se pas . . . sentiments: That all her steps were feelings.   *que tous se dents . . .
idées!:* That all her teeth were ideas. Ideas!

and hideous, and unintelligible recollections. I strived to decypher them, but in vain; while ever and anon, like the spirit of a departed sound, the shrill and piercing shriek of a female voice seemed to be ringing in my ears. I had done a deed—what was it? I asked myself the question aloud, and the whispering echoes of the chamber answered me, "*what was it?*"

On the table beside me burned a lamp, and near it lay a little box. It was of no remarkable character, and I had seen it frequently before, for it was the property of the family physician; but how came it *there*, upon my table, and why did I shudder in regarding it? These things were in no manner to be accounted for, and my eyes at length dropped to the open pages of a book, and to a sentence underscored therein. The words were the singular but simple ones of the poet Ebn Zaiat. *"Dicebant mihi sodales, si sepulchrum amicae, visitarem, curas meas aliquantulum fore levatas."* Why then, as I perused them, did the hairs of my head erect themselves on end, and the blood of my body become congealed within my veins?

There came a light tap at the library door, and pale as the tenant of a tomb, a menial entered upon tiptoe. His looks were wild with terror, and he spoke to me in a voice tremulous, husky, and very low. What said he?—some broken sentences I heard. He told of a wild cry disturbing the silence of the night—of the gathering together of the household—of a search in the direction of the sound;—and then his tones grew thrillingly distinct as he whispered me of a violated grave—of a disfigured body enshrouded, yet still breathing, still palpitating, *still alive!*

He pointed to my garments;—they were muddy and clotted with gore. I spoke not, and he took me gently by the hand;—it was indented with the impress of human nails. He directed my attention to some object against the wall;—I looked at it for some minutes;—it was a spade. With a shriek I bounded to the table, and grasped the box that lay upon it. But I could not force it open; and in my tremor it slipped from my hands, and fell heavily, and burst into pieces; and from it, with a rattling sound, there rolled out some instruments of dental surgery, intermingled with thirty-two small, white and ivory-looking substances that were scattered to and fro about the floor.

Ligeia

And the will therein lieth, which dieth not. Who knoweth the mysteries of the will, with its vigor? For God is but a great will pervading all things by nature of its intentness. Man doth not

yield himself to the angels, nor unto death utterly, save only
through the weakness of his feeble will.

–JOSEPH GLANVILL

I cannot, for my soul, remember how, when, or even precisely
where, I first became acquainted with the lady Ligeia. Long years have
since elapsed, and my memory is feeble through much suffering. Or,
perhaps, I cannot *now* bring these points to mind, because, in truth, the
character of my beloved, her rare learning, her singular yet placid cast
of beauty, and the thrilling and enthralling eloquence of her low musical language, made their way into my heart by paces so steadily and
stealthily progressive that they have been unnoticed and unknown. Yet
I believe that I met her first and most frequently in some large, old,
decaying city near the Rhine. Of her family—I have surely heard her
speak. That it is of a remotely ancient date cannot be doubted. Ligeia!
Ligeia! Buried in studies of a nature more than all else adapted to
deaden impressions of the outward world, it is by that sweet word
alone—by Ligeia—that I bring before mine eyes in fancy the image of
her who is no more. And now, while I write, a recollection flashes upon
me that I have *never known* the paternal name of her who was my friend
and my betrothed, and who became the partner of my studies, and
finally the wife of my bosom. Was it a playful charge on the part of my
Ligeia? or was it a test of my strength of affection, that I should institute no inquiries upon this point? or was it rather a caprice of my own—a
wildly romantic offering on the shrine of the most passionate devotion? I but indistinctly recall the fact itself—what wonder that I have
utterly forgotten the circumstances which originated or attended it?
And, indeed, if ever that spirit which is entitled *Romance*—if ever she,
the wan and the misty-winged *Ashtophet°* of idolatrous Egypt, presided,
as they tell, over marriages ill-omened, then most surely she presided
over mine.

There is one dear topic, however, on which my memory fails me
not. It is the *person* of Ligeia. In stature she was tall, somewhat slender,
and, in her latter days, even emaciated. I would in vain attempt to portray the majesty, the quiet ease, of her demeanor, or the incomprehensible lightness and elasticity of her footfall. She came and departed as a
shadow. I was never made aware of her entrance into my closed study
save by the dear music of her low sweet voice, as she placed her marble
hand upon my shoulder. In beauty of face no maiden ever equalled her.

Ashtophet: Imagined Egyptian fertility or marriage goddess.

It was the radiance of an opium dream—an airy and spirit-lifting vision more wildly divine than the phantasies which hovered about the slumbering souls of the daughters of Delos. Yet her features were not of that regular mould which we have been falsely taught to worship in the classical labors of the heathen. "There is no exquisite beauty," says Bacon, Lord Verulam, speaking truly of all the forms and *genera* of beauty, "without some *strangeness* in the proportion." Yet, although I saw that the features of Ligeia were not of a classic regularity—although I perceived that her loveliness was indeed "exquisite," and felt that there was much of "strangeness" pervading it, yet I have tried in vain to detect the irregularity and to trace home my own perception of "the strange." I examined the contour of the lofty and pale forehead—it was faultless—how cold indeed that word when applied to a majesty so divine!—the skin rivalling the purest ivory, the commanding extent and repose, the gentle prominence of the regions above the temples; and then the raven-black, the glossy, the luxuriant and naturally-curling tresses, setting forth the full force of the Homeric epithet, "hyacinthine!" I looked at the delicate outlines of the nose—and nowhere but in the graceful medallions of the Hebrews had I beheld a similar perfection. There were the same luxurious smoothness of surface, the same scarcely perceptible tendency to the aquiline, the same harmoniously curved nostrils speaking the free spirit. I regarded the sweet mouth. Here was indeed the triumph of all things heavenly—the magnificent turn of the short upper lip—the soft, voluptuous slumber of the under—the dimples which sported, and the color which spoke—the teeth glancing back, with a brilliancy almost startling, every ray of the holy light which fell upon them in her serene and placid, yet most exultingly radiant of all smiles. I scrutinized the formation of the chin—and here, too, I found the gentleness of breadth, the softness and the majesty, the fullness and the spirituality, of the Greek—the contour which the God Apollo revealed but in a dream, to Cleomenes, the son of the Athenian. And then I peered into the large eyes of Ligeia.

For eyes we have no models in the remotely antique. It might have been, too, that in these eyes of my beloved lay the secret to which Lord Verulam alludes. They were, I must believe, far larger than the ordinary eyes of our own race. They were even fuller than the fullest of the gazelle eyes of the tribe of the valley of Nourjahad. Yet it was only at intervals—in moments of intense excitement—that this peculiarity became more than slightly noticeable in Ligeia. And at such moments was her beauty—in my heated fancy thus it appeared perhaps—the beauty of beings either above or apart from the earth—the beauty of

the fabulous Houri of the Turk. The hue of the orbs was the most brilliant of black, and, far over them, hung jetty lashes of great length. The
brows, slightly irregular in outline, had the same tint. The "strangeness," however, which I found in the eyes, was of a nature distinct from
the formation, or the color, or the brilliancy of the features, and must,
after all, be referred to the *expression*. Ah, word of no meaning! behind
whose vast latitude of mere sound we intrench our ignorance of so
much of the spiritual. The expression of the eyes of Ligeia! How for
long hours have I pondered upon it! How have I, through the whole of
a midsummer night, struggled to fathom it! What was it—that something more profound than the well of Democritus°—which lay far
within the pupils of my beloved? What *was* it? I was possessed with a
passion to discover. Those eyes! those large, those shining, those divine
orbs! they became to me twin stars of Leda, and I to them devoutest of
astrologers.

There is no point, among the many incomprehensible anomalies of
the science of mind, more thrillingly exciting than the fact—never, I
believe, noticed in the schools—that, in our endeavors to recall to
memory something long forgotten, we often find ourselves *upon the
very verge* of remembrance, without being able, in the end, to remember. And thus how frequently, in my intense scrutiny of Ligeia's eyes,
have I felt approaching the full knowledge of their expression—felt it
approaching—yet not quite be mine—and so at length entirely depart!
And (strange, oh strangest mystery of all!) I found, in the commonest
objects of the universe, a circle of analogies to that expression. I mean
to say that, subsequently to the period when Ligeia's beauty passed into
my spirit, there dwelling as in a shrine, I derived, from many existences
in the material world, a sentiment such as I felt always aroused within me
by her large and luminous orbs. Yet not the more could I define that
sentiment, or analyze, or even steadily view it. I recognized it, let me
repeat, sometimes in the survey of a rapidly-growing vine—in the contemplation of a moth, a butterfly, a chrysalis, a stream of running water.
I have felt it in the ocean; in the falling of a meteor. I have felt it in the
glances of unusually aged people. And there are one or two stars in
heaven—(one especially, a star of the sixth magnitude, double and
changeable, to be found near the large star in Lyra) in a telescopic scrutiny of which I have been made aware of the feeling. I have been filled
with it by certain sounds from stringed instruments, and not unfre-

---

Democritus: A reference to a statement by the Greek philosopher Democritus, "Of a truth
we know nothing, for truth is an abyss."

quently by passages from books. Among innumerable other instances, I well remember something in a volume of Joseph Glanvill, which (perhaps merely from its quaintness—who shall say?) never failed to inspire me with the sentiment;—"And the will therein lieth, which dieth not. Who knoweth the mysteries of the will, with its vigor? For God is but a great will pervading all things by nature of its intentness. Man doth not yield him to the angels, nor unto death utterly, save only through the weakness of his feeble will."

Length of years, and subsequent reflection, have enabled me to trace, indeed, some remote connection between this passage in the English moralist and a portion of the character of Ligeia. An *intensity* in thought, action, or speech, was possibly, in her, a result, or at least an index, of that gigantic volition which, during our long intercourse, failed to give other and more immediate evidence of its existence. Of all the women whom I have ever known, she, the outwardly calm, the ever-placid Ligeia, was the most violently a prey to the tumultuous vultures of stern passion. And of such passion I could form no estimate, save by the miraculous expansion of those eyes which at once so delighted and appalled me—by the almost magical melody, modulation, distinctness and placidity of her very low voice—and by the fierce energy (rendered doubly effective by contrast with her manner of utterance) of the wild words which she habitually uttered.

I have spoken of the learning of Ligeia: it was immense—such as I have never known in woman. In the classical tongues was she deeply proficient, and as far as my own acquaintance extended in regard to the modern dialects of Europe, I have never known her at fault. Indeed upon any theme of the most admired, because simply the most abstruse of the boasted erudition of the academy, have I *ever* found Ligeia at fault? How singularly—how thrillingly, this one point in the nature of my wife has forced itself, at this late period only, upon my attention! I said her knowledge was such as I have never known in woman—but where breathes the man who has traversed, and successfully, *all* the wide areas of moral, physical, and mathematical science? I saw not then what I now clearly perceive, that the acquisitions of Ligeia were gigantic, were astounding; yet I was sufficiently aware of her infinite supremacy to resign myself, with a child-like confidence, to her guidance through the chaotic world of metaphysical investigation at which I was most busily occupied during the earlier years of our marriage. With how vast a triumph—with how vivid a delight—with how much of all that is ethereal in hope—did I *feel*, as she bent over me in studies but little sought—but less known—that delicious vista by slow degrees expanding before me, down whose long, gorgeous, and all untrodden path, I might at length pass onward to the goal of a wisdom too divinely precious not to be forbidden!

How poignant, then, must have been the grief with which, after some years, I beheld my well-grounded expectations take wings to themselves and fly away! Without Ligeia I was but as a child groping benighted. Her presence, her readings alone, rendered vividly luminous the many mysteries of the transcendentalism in which we were immersed. Wanting the radiant lustre of her eyes, letters, lambent and golden, grew duller than Saturnian lead. And now those eyes shone less and less frequently upon the pages over which I pored. Ligeia grew ill. The wild eyes blazed with a too—too glorious effulgence; the pale fingers became of the transparent waxen hue of the grave, and the blue veins upon the lofty forehead swelled and sank impetuously with the tides of the most gentle emotion. I saw that she must die—and I struggled desperately in spirit with the grim Azrael.° And the struggles of the passionate wife were, to my astonishment, even more energetic than my own. There had been much in her stern nature to impress me with the belief that, to her, death would have come without its terrors;—but not so. Words are impotent to convey any just idea of the fierceness of resistance with which she wrestled with the Shadow. I groaned in anguish at the pitiable spectacle. I would have soothed—I would have reasoned; but, in the intensity of her wild desire for life,—for life—*but* for life—solace and reason were alike the uttermost of folly. Yet not until the last instance, amid the most convulsive writhings of her fierce spirit, was shaken the external placidity of her demeanor. Her voice grew more gentle—grew more low—yet I would not wish to dwell upon the wild meaning of the quietly uttered words. My brain reeled as I hearkened, entranced, to a melody more than mortal—to assumptions and aspirations which mortality had never before known.

That she loved me I should not have doubted; and I might have been easily aware that, in a bosom such as hers, love would have reigned no ordinary passion. But in death only, was I fully impressed with the strength of her affection. For long hours, detaining my hand, would she pour out before me the overflowing of a heart whose more than passionate devotion amounted to idolatry. How had I deserved to be so blessed by such confessions?—how had I deserved to be so cursed with the removal of my beloved in the hour of her making them? But upon this subject I cannot bear to dilate. Let me say only, that in Ligeia's

Azrael: The angel of death.

more than womanly abandonment to a love, alas! all unmerited, all unworthily bestowed, I at length recognized the principle of her longing with so wildly earnest a desire for the life which was now fleeing so rapidly away. It is this wild longing — it is this eager vehemence of desire for life — *but* for life — that I have no power to portray — no utterance capable of expressing.

At high noon of the night in which she departed, beckoning me, peremptorily, to her side, she bade me repeat certain verses composed by herself not many days before. I obeyed her. — They were these:

Lo! 'tis a gala night
   Within the lonesome latter years!
An angel throng, bewinged, bedight°
   In veils, and drowned in tears,
Sit in a theatre, to see
   A play of hopes and fears,
While the orchestra breathes fitfully
   The music of the spheres.

Mimes, in the form of God on high,
   Mutter and mumble low,
And hither and thither fly —
   Mere puppets they, who come and go
At bidding of vast formless things
   That shift the scenery to and fro,
Flapping from out their Condor wings
   Invisible Wo!

That motley drama! — oh, be sure
   It shall not be forgot!
With its Phantom chased forevermore,
   By a crowd that seize it not,
Through a circle that ever returneth in
   To the self-same spot,
And much of Madness and more of Sin,
   And Horror the soul of the plot.

But see, amid the mimic rout,
   A crawling shape intrude!
A blood-red thing that writhes from out
   The scenic solitude!

bedight: Adorned.

It writhes!—it writhes!—with mortal pangs
　　The mimes become its food,
And the seraphs sob at vermin fangs
　　In human gore imbued.

Out—out are the lights—out all!
　　And over each quivering form,
The curtain, a funeral pall,
　　Comes down with the rush of a storm,
And the angels, all pallid and wan,
　　Uprising, unveiling, affirm
That the play is the tragedy, "Man,"
　　And its hero the Conqueror Worm.

"O God!" half shrieked Ligeia, leaping to her feet and extending her arms aloft with a spasmodic movement, as I made an end of these lines—"O God! O Divine Father!—shall these things be undeviatingly so?—shall this Conqueror be not once conquered? Are we not part and parcel in Thee? Who—who knoweth the mysteries of the will with its vigor? Man doth not yield him to the angels, *nor unto death utterly*, save only through the weakness of his feeble will."

And now, as if exhausted with emotion, she suffered her white arms to fall, and returned solemnly to her bed of Death. And as she breathed her last sighs, there came mingled with them a low murmur from her lips. I bent to them my ear and distinguished, again, the concluding words of the passage in Glanvill—*"Man doth not yield him to the angels, nor unto death utterly, save only through the weakness of his feeble will."*

She died;—and I, crushed into the very dust with sorrow, could no longer endure the lonely desolation of my dwelling in the dim and decaying city by the Rhine. I had no lack of what the world calls wealth. Ligeia had brought me far more, very far more than ordinarily falls to the lot of mortals. After a few months, therefore, of weary and aimless wandering, I purchased, and put in some repair, an abbey, which I shall not name, in one of the wildest and least frequented portions of fair England. The gloomy and dreary grandeur of the building, the almost savage aspect of the domain, the many melancholy and time-honored memories connected with both, had much in unison with the feelings of utter abandonment which had driven me into that remote and unsocial region of the country. Yet although the external abbey, with its verdant decay hanging about it, suffered but little alteration, I gave way, with a child-like perversity, and perchance with a faint hope of alleviating my sorrows, to a display of more than regal magnificence within. For such follies, even in childhood, I had imbibed a taste and now they came back to me as if in the dotage of grief. Alas, I feel how much even of incipient madness might have been discovered in the gorgeous and fantastic draperies, in the solemn carvings of Egypt, in the wild cornices and furniture, in the Bedlam patterns of the carpets of tufted gold! I had become a bounden slave in the trammels of opium, and my labors and my orders had taken a coloring from my dreams. But these absurdities I must not pause to detail. Let me speak only of that one chamber, ever accursed, whither in a moment of mental alienation, I led from the altar as my bride—as the successor of the unforgotten Ligeia—the fair-haired and blue-eyed Lady Rowena Trevanion, of Tremaine.

There is no individual portion of the architecture and decoration of that bridal chamber which is not now visibly before me. Where were the souls of the haughty family of the bride, when, through thirst of gold, they permitted to pass the threshold of an apartment *so* bedecked, a maiden and a daughter so beloved? I have said that I minutely remember the details of the chamber—yet I am sadly forgetful on topics of deep moment—and here there was no system, no keeping, in the fantastic display, to take hold upon the memory. The room lay in a high turret of the castellated abbey, was pentagonal in shape, and of capacious size. Occupying the whole southern face of the pentagon was the sole window—an immense sheet of unbroken glass from Venice—a single pane, and tinted of a leaden hue, so that the rays of either the sun or moon, passing through it, fell with a ghastly lustre on the objects within. Over the upper portion of this huge window, extended the trellice-work of an aged vine, which clambered up the massy walls of the turret. The ceiling, of gloomy-looking oak, was excessively lofty, vaulted, and elaborately fretted with the wildest and most grotesque specimens of a semi-Gothic, semi-Druidical device. From out the most central recess of this melancholy vaulting, depended, by a single chain of gold with long links, a huge censer of the same metal, Saracenic in pattern, and with many perforations so contrived that there writhed in and out of them, as if endued with a serpent vitality, a continual succession of parti-colored fires.

Some few ottomans and golden candelabra, of Eastern figure, were in various stations about—and there was the couch, too—the bridal couch—of an Indian model, and low, and sculptured of solid ebony, with a pall-like canopy above. In each of the angles of the chamber stood on end a gigantic sarcophagus of black granite, from the tombs of the kings over against Luxor, with their aged lids full of immemorial sculpture. But in the draping of the apartment lay, alas! the chief phantasy of all. The lofty walls, gigantic in height—even unproportionably so—were hung from summit to foot, in vast folds, with a heavy and massive-looking tapestry—tapestry of a material which was found alike as a carpet on the floor, as a covering for the ottomans and the ebony bed, as a canopy for the bed, and as the gorgeous volutes of the curtains which partially shaded the window. The material was the richest cloth of gold. It was spotted all over, at irregular intervals, with arabesque figures, about a foot in diameter, and wrought upon the cloth in patterns of the most jetty black. But these figures partook of the true character of the arabesque only when regarded from a single point of view. By a contrivance now common, and indeed traceable to a very remote period of antiquity, they were made changeable in aspect. To one entering the room, they bore the appearance of simple monstrosities; but upon a farther advance, this appearance gradually departed; and step by step, as the visiter moved his station in the chamber, he saw himself surrounded by an endless succession of the ghastly forms which belong to the superstition of the Norman, or arise in the guilty slumbers of the monk. The phantasmagoric effect was vastly heightened by the artificial introduction of a strong continual current of wind behind the draperies—giving a hideous and uneasy animation to the whole.

In halls such as these—in a bridal chamber such as this—I passed, with the Lady of Tremaine, the unhallowed hours of the first month of our marriage—passed them with but little disquietude. That my wife dreaded the fierce moodiness of my temper—that she shunned me and loved me but little—I could not help perceiving; but it gave me rather pleasure than otherwise. I loathed her with a hatred belonging more to demon than to man. My memory flew back, (oh, with what intensity of regret!) to Ligeia, the beloved, the august, the beautiful, the entombed. I revelled in recollections of her purity, of her wisdom, of her lofty, her ethereal nature, of her passionate, her idolatrous love. Now, then, did my spirit fully and freely burn with more than all the fires of her own. In the excitement of my opium dreams (for I was habitually fettered in the shackles of the drug) I would call aloud upon her name, during the silence of the night, or among the sheltered recesses of the glens by day, as if, through the wild eagerness, the solemn passion, the consuming ardor of my longing for the departed, I could restore her to the pathway she had abandoned—ah, *could* it be forever?—upon the earth.

About the commencement of the second month of the marriage, the Lady Rowena was attacked with sudden illness, from which her recovery was slow. The fever which consumed her rendered her nights uneasy; and in her perturbed state of half-slumber, she spoke of sounds, and of motions, in and about the chamber of the turret, which I concluded had no origin save in the distemper of her fancy, or perhaps in the phantasmagoric influences of the chamber itself. She became at length convalescent—finally well. Yet but a brief period elapsed, ere a second more violent disorder again threw her upon a bed of suffering; and from this attack her frame, at all times feeble, never altogether recovered. Her illnesses were, after this epoch, of alarming character, and of more alarming recurrence, defying alike the knowledge and the great exertions of her physicians. With the increase of the chronic disease which had thus, apparently, taken too sure hold upon her constitution to be eradicated by human means, I could not fail to observe a similar increase in the nervous irritation of her temperament, and in her excitability by trivial causes of fear. She spoke again, and now more frequently and pertinaciously, of the sounds—of the slight sounds—and of the unusual motions among the tapestries, to which she had formerly alluded.

One night, near the closing in of September, she pressed this distressing subject with more than usual emphasis upon my attention. She had just awakened from an unquiet slumber, and I had been watching, with feelings half of anxiety, half of vague terror, the workings of her emaciated countenance. I sat by the side of her ebony bed, upon one of the ottomans of India. She partly arose, and spoke, in an earnest low whisper, of sounds which she *then* heard, but which I could not hear—of motions which she *then* saw, but which I could not perceive. The wind was rushing hurriedly behind the tapestries, and I wished to show her (what, let me confess it, I could not *all* believe) that those almost inarticulate breathings, and those very gentle variations of the figures upon the wall, were but the natural effects of that customary rushing of the wind. But a deadly pallor, over-spreading her face, had proved to me that my exertions to reassure her would be fruitless. She appeared to be fainting, and no attendants were within call. I remembered where was deposited a decanter of light wine which had been ordered by her physicians, and hastened across the chamber to procure it. But, as I stepped beneath the light of the censer, two circumstances of a startling nature attracted my attention. I had felt that some palpable although invisible object had passed lightly by my person; and I saw that there lay upon the golden carpet, in the very middle of the rich lustre thrown from the censer, a shadow—a faint, indefinite shadow of angelic aspect—such as might be fancied for the shadow of a shade.

But I was wild with the excitement of an immoderate dose of opium, and heeded these things but little, nor spoke of them to Rowena. Having found the wine, I recrossed the chamber, and poured out a gobletful, which I held to the lips of the fainting lady. She had now partially recovered, however, and took the vessel herself, while I sank upon an ottoman near me, with my eyes fastened upon her person. It was then that I became distinctly aware of a gentle foot-fall upon the carpet, and near the couch; and in a second thereafter, as Rowena was in the act of raising the wine to her lips, I saw, or may have dreamed that I saw, fall within the goblet, as if from some invisible spring in the atmosphere of the room, three or four large drops of a brilliant and ruby colored fluid. If this I saw—not so Rowena. She swallowed the wine unhesitatingly, and I forbore to speak to her of a circumstance which must, after all, I considered, have been but the suggestion of a vivid imagination, rendered morbidly active by the terror of the lady, by the opium, and by the hour.

Yet I cannot conceal it from my own perception that, immediately subsequent to the fall of the ruby-drops, a rapid change for the worse took place in the disorder of my wife; so that, on the third subsequent night, the hands of her menials prepared her for the tomb, and on the fourth, I sat alone, with her shrouded body, in that fantastic chamber which had received her as my bride. Wild visions, opium-engendered, flitted, shadow-like, before me. I gazed with unquiet eye upon the sarcophagi in the angles of the room, upon the varying figures of the drapery, and upon the writhing of the parti-colored fires in the censer overhead. My eyes then fell, as I called to mind the circumstances of a former night, to the spot beneath the glare of the censer where I had seen the faint traces of the shadow. It was there, however, no longer; and breathing with greater freedom, I turned my glances to the pallid and rigid figure upon the bed. Then rushed upon me a thousand memories of Ligeia—and then came back upon my heart, with the turbulent violence of a flood, the whole of that unutterable wo with which I had regarded *her* thus enshrouded. The night waned; and still, with a bosom full of bitter thoughts of the one only and supremely beloved, I remained gazing upon the body of Rowena.

It might have been midnight, or perhaps earlier, or later, for I had taken no note of time, when a sob, low, gentle, but very distinct, startled me from my revery.—I *felt* that it came from the bed of ebony—the bed of death. I listened in an agony of superstitious terror—but there was no repetition of the sound. I strained my vision to detect any motion in the corpse—but there was not the slightest perceptible. Yet I could not have been deceived. I *had* heard the noise, however faint, and my soul was awakened within me. I resolutely and perseveringly kept my attention riveted upon the body. Many minutes elapsed before any circumstance occurred tending to throw light upon the mystery. At length it became evident that a slight, a very feeble, and barely noticeable tinge of color had flushed up within the cheeks, and along the sunken small veins of the eyelids. Through a species of unutterable horror and awe, for which the language of mortality has no sufficiently energetic expression, I felt my heart cease to beat, my limbs grow rigid where I sat. Yet a sense of duty finally operated to restore my self-possession. I could no longer doubt that we had been precipitate in our preparations—that Rowena still lived. It was necessary that some immediate exertion be made; yet the turret was altogether apart from the portion of the abbey tenanted by the servants—there were none within call—I had no means of summoning them to my aid without leaving the room for many minutes—and this I could not venture to do. I therefore struggled alone in my endeavors to call back the spirit still hovering. In a short period it was certain, however, that a relapse had taken place; the color disappeared from both eyelid and cheek, leaving a wanness even more than that of marble; the lips became doubly shrivelled and pinched up in the ghastly expression of death; a repulsive clamminess and coldness overspread rapidly the surface of the body; and all the usual rigorous stiffness immediately supervened. I fell back with a shudder upon the couch from which I had been so startlingly aroused, and again gave myself up to passionate waking visions of Ligeia.

An hour thus elapsed when (could it be possible?) I was a second time aware of some vague sound issuing from the region of the bed. I listened—in extremity of horror. The sound came again—it was a sigh. Rushing to the corpse, I saw—distinctly saw—a tremor upon the lips. In a minute afterward they relaxed, disclosing a bright line of the pearly teeth. Amazement now struggled in my bosom with the profound awe which had hitherto reigned there alone. I felt that my vision grew dim, that my reason wandered; and it was only by a violent effort that I at length succeeded in nerving myself to the task which duty thus once more had pointed out. There was now a partial glow upon the forehead and upon the cheek and throat; a perceptible warmth pervaded the whole frame; there was even a slight pulsation at the heart. The lady *lived*; and with redoubled ardor I betook myself to the task of restoration. I chafed and bathed the temples and the hands, and used every exertion which experience, and no little medical reading, could suggest.

But in vain. Suddenly, the color fled, the pulsation ceased, the lips resumed the expression of the dead, and, in an instant afterward, the whole body took upon itself the icy chilliness, the livid hue, the intense rigidity, the sunken outline, and all the loathsome peculiarities of that which has been, for many days, a tenant of the tomb.

And again I sunk into visions of Ligeia—and again, (what marvel that I shudder while I write?) *again* there reached my ears a low sob from the region of the ebony bed. But why shall I minutely detail the unspeakable horrors of that night? Why shall I pause to relate how, time after time, until near the period of the gray dawn, this hideous drama of revivification was repeated; how each terrific relapse was only into a sterner and apparently more irredeemable death; how each agony wore the aspect of a struggle with some invisible foe; and how each struggle was succeeded by I know not what of wild change in the personal appearance of the corpse? Let me hurry to a conclusion.

The greater part of the fearful night had worn away, and she who had been dead, once again stirred—and now more vigorously than hitherto, although arousing from a dissolution more appalling in its utter hopelessness than any. I had long ceased to struggle or to move, and remained sitting rigidly upon the ottoman, a helpless prey to a whirl of violent emotions, of which extreme awe was perhaps the least terrible, the least consuming. The corpse, I repeat, stirred, and now more vigorously than before. The hues of life flushed up with unwonted energy into the countenance—the limbs relaxed—and, save that the eyelids were yet pressed heavily together, and that the bandages and draperies of the grave still imparted their charnel character to the figure, I might have dreamed that Rowena had indeed shaken off, utterly, the fetters of Death. But if this idea was not, even then, altogether adopted, I could at least doubt no longer, when, arising from the bed, tottering, with feeble steps, with closed eyes, and with the manner of one bewildered in a dream, the thing that was enshrouded advanced bodily and palpably into the middle of the apartment.

I trembled not—I stirred not—for a crowd of unutterable fancies connected with the air, the stature, the demeanor of the figure, rushing hurriedly through my brain, had paralyzed—had chilled me into stone. I stirred not—but gazed upon the apparition. There was a mad disorder in my thoughts—a tumult unappeasable. Could it, indeed, be the *living* Rowena who confronted me? Could it indeed be Rowena *at all*—the fair-haired, the blue-eyed Lady Rowena Trevanion of Tremaine? Why, *why* should I doubt it? The bandage lay heavily about the mouth—but then might it not be the mouth of the breathing Lady of

Tremaine? And the cheeks—there were the roses as in her noon of life—yes, these might indeed be the fair cheeks of the living Lady of Tremaine. And the chin, with its dimples, as in health, might it not be hers?—but *had she then grown taller since her malady?* What inexpressible madness seized me with that thought? One bound, and I had reached her feet! Shrinking from my touch, she let fall from her head the ghastly cerements° which had confined it, and there streamed forth, into the rushing atmosphere of the chamber, huge masses of long and dishevelled hair; *it was blacker than the wings of the midnight!* And now slowly opened *the eyes* of the figure which stood before me. "Here then, at least," I shrieked aloud, "can I never—can I never be mistaken—these are the full, and the black, and the wild eyes—of my lost love—of the lady—of the LADY LIGEIA!"

How to Write a Blackwood° Article

"In the name of the Prophet—figs!!"
–CRY OF THE TURKISH FIG-PEDDLER

I presume every body has heard of me. My name is the Signora Psyche Zenobia. This I know to be a fact. No body but my enemies ever calls me Suky Snobbs. I have been assured that Suky is but a vulgar corruption of Psyche, which is good Greek, and means "the soul" (that's me, I'm *all* soul) and sometimes "a butterfly," which latter meaning undoubtedly alludes to my appearance in my new crimson satin dress, with the sky-blue Arabian *mantelet,*° and the trimmings of green *agraffas,*° and the seven flounces of orange-colored *auriculas,*° As for Snobbs—any person who should look at me would be instantly aware that my name wasn't Snobbs. Miss Tabitha Turnip propagated that report through sheer envy. Tabitha Turnip indeed! Oh the little wretch! But what can we expect from a turnip? Wonder if she remembers the old adage about "blood out of a turnip, &c." [Mem: put her in mind of it the first opportunity.] [Mem: again—pull her nose.] Where was I? Ah! I have been assured that Snobbs is a mere corruption of Zenobia, and that Zenobia was a queen—(So am I. Dr. Moneypenny, always calls me the Queen of Hearts)—and that Zenobia, as well as Psyche, is good Greek, and that my father was "a Greek," and

---

cerements: Waxed cloth used to wrap corpses.   ***Blackwood:*** *Blackwood's Edinburgh Magazine*, published in Britain from 1817 to 1980.   ***mantelet:*** A sleeveless cloak or shawl.   ***agraffas:*** Ornamental clasps.   ***auriculas:*** An alpine flower.

that consequently I have a right to our patronymic, which is Zenobia, and not by any means Snobbs. Nobody but Tabitha Turnip calls me Suky Snobbs. I am the Signora Psyche Zenobia.

As I said before, every body has heard of me. I am that very Signora Psyche Zenobia, so justly celebrated as corresponding secretary to the "*Philadelphia, Regular, Exchange, Tea, Total, Young, Belles, Lettres, Universal, Experimental, Bibliographical, Association, To, Civilize, Humanity.*" Dr. Moneypenny made the title for us, and says he chose it because it sounded big like an empty rum-puncheon.° (A vulgar man that sometimes — but he's deep.) We all sign the initials of the society after our names, in the fashion of the R. S. A., Royal Society of Arts — the S. D. U. K., Society for the Diffusion of Useful Knowledge, &c, &c. Dr. Moneypenny says that S stands for *stale*, and that D. U. K. spells duck, (but it don't,) and that S. D. U. K. stands for Stale Duck, and not for Lord Brougham's society° — but then Dr. Moneypenny is such a queer man that I am never sure when he is telling me the truth. At any rate we always add to our names the initials P. R. E. T. T. Y. B. L. U. E. B. A. T. C. H. — that is to say, Philadelphia, Regular, Exchange, Tea, Total, Young, Belles, Lettres, Universal, Experimental, Bibliographical, Association, To, Civilize, Humanity — one letter for each word, which is a decided improvement upon Lord Brougham. Dr. Moneypenny will have it that our initials give our true character — but for my life I can't see what he means.

Notwithstanding the good offices of the Doctor, and the strenuous exertions of the association to get itself into notice, it met with no very great success until I joined it. The truth is, members indulged in too flippant a tone of discussion. The papers read every Saturday evening were characterized less by depth than buffoonery. They were all whipped syllabub.° There was no investigation of first causes, first principles. There was no investigation of anything at all. There was no attention paid to that great point, the "fitness of things." In short there was no fine writing like this. It was all low — very! No profundity, no reading, no metaphysics — nothing which the learned call spirituality, and which the unlearned choose to stigmatize as cant. [Dr. M. says I ought to spell "cant" with a capital K — but I know better.]

When I joined the society it was my endeavor to introduce a better style of thinking and writing, and all the world knows how well I have succeeded. We get up as good papers now in the P. R. E. T. T. Y.

---

rum-puncheon: A large cask for holding liquids.   *Lord Brougham's society:* The Society for the Diffusion of Useful Knowledge, founded by Henry Peter Brougham in 1825.   *syllabub:* A whipped cream dessert usually flavored with wine or sherry.

B. L. U. E. B. A. T. C. H. as any to be found even in Blackwood. I say, Blackwood, because I have been assured that the finest writing, upon every subject, is to be discovered in the pages of that justly celebrated Magazine. We now take it for our model upon all themes, and are getting into rapid notice accordingly. And, after all, it's not so very difficult a matter to compose an article of the genuine Blackwood stamp, if one only goes properly about it. Of course I don't speak of the political articles. Everybody knows how *they* are managed, since Dr. Moneypenny explained it. Mr. Blackwood has a pair of tailor's-shears, and three apprentices who stand by him for orders. One hands him the "Times," another the "Examiner," and a third a "Gulley's New Compendium of Slang-Whang." Mr. B. merely cuts out and intersperses. It is soon done—nothing but Examiner, Slang-Whang, and Times—then Times, Slang-Whang, and Examiner—and then Times, Examiner, and Slang-Whang.

But the chief merit of the Magazine lies in its miscellaneous articles; and the best of these come under the head of what Dr. Moneypenny calls the *bizarreries* (whatever that may mean) and what everybody else calls the *intensities*. This is a species of writing which I have long known how to appreciate, although it is only since my late visit to Mr. Blackwood (deputed by the society) that I have been made aware of the exact method of composition. This method is very simple, but not so much so as the politics. Upon my calling at Mr. B.'s, and making known to him the wishes of the society, he received me with great civility, took me into his study, and gave me a clear explanation of the whole process.

"My dear madam," said he, evidently struck with my majestic appearance, for I had on the crimson satin, with the green *agraffas*, and orange-coloured *auriculas*. "My *dear* madam," said he, "sit down. The matter stands thus: In the first place, your writer of intensities must have very black ink, and a very big pen, with a very blunt nib. And, mark me, Miss Psyche Zenobia!" he continued, after a pause, with the most impressive energy and solemnity of manner, "mark me!—*that pen—must—never be mended!* Herein, madam, lies the secret, the soul, of intensity. I assume it upon myself to say, that no individual, of however great genius, ever wrote with a good pen,—understand me,—a good article. You may take it for granted, that when manuscript can be read it is never worth reading. This is a leading principle in our faith, to which if you cannot readily assent, our conference is at an end."

He paused. But, of course, as I had no wish to put an end to the conference, I assented to a proposition so very obvious, and one, too, of whose truth I had all along been sufficiently aware. He seemed pleased, and went on with his instructions.

"It may appear invidious in me, Miss Psyche Zenobia, to refer you to an article, or set of articles, in the way of model or study; yet perhaps I may as well call your attention to a few cases. Let me see. There was '*The Dead Alive*,' a capital thing!—the record of a gentleman's sensations, when entombed before the breath was out of his body—full of taste, terror, sentiment, metaphysics, and erudition. You would have sworn that the writer had been born and brought up in a coffin. Then we had the '*Confessions of an Opium-eater*'—fine, very fine!—glorious imagination—deep philosophy—acute speculation—plenty of fire and fury, and a good spicing of the decidedly unintelligible. That was a nice bit of flummery, and went down the throats of the people delightfully. They would have it that Coleridge wrote the paper—but not so. It was composed by my pet baboon, Juniper, over a rummer of Hollands and water, 'hot, without sugar.'" [This I could scarcely have believed had it been any body but Mr. Blackwood, who assured me of it.] "Then there was '*The Involuntary Experimentalist*,' all about a gentleman who got baked in an oven, and came out alive and well, although certainly done to a turn. And then there was '*The Diary of a Late Physician*,' where the merit lay in good rant, and indifferent Greek—both of them taking things, with the public. And then there was '*The Man in the Bell*,' a paper by-the-bye, Miss Zenobia, which I cannot sufficiently recommend to your attention. It is the history of a young person who goes to sleep under the clapper of a church bell, and is awakened by its tolling for a funeral. The sound drives him mad, and, accordingly, pulling out his tablets, he gives a record of his sensations. Sensations are the great things after all. Should you ever be drowned or hung, be sure and make a note of your sensations—they will be worth to you ten guineas a sheet. If you wish to write forcibly, Miss Zenobia, pay minute attention to the sensations."

"That I certainly will, Mr. Blackwood," said I.

"Good!" he replied. "I see you are a pupil after my own heart. But I must put you *au fait* to the details necessary in composing what may be denominated a genuine Blackwood article of the sensation stamp—the kind which you will understand me to say I consider the best for all purposes.

"The first thing requisite is to get yourself into such a scrape as no one ever got into before. The oven, for instance,—that was a good hit. But if you have no oven, or big bell, at hand, and if you cannot conveniently tumble out of a balloon, or be swallowed up in an earthquake, or get stuck fast in a chimney, you will have to be contented with simply imagining some similar misadventure. I should prefer, however, that you have the actual fact to bear you out. Nothing so well assists the fancy, as an experimental knowledge of the matter in hand. 'Truth is strange,' you know, 'stranger than fiction'—besides being more to the purpose."

Here I assured him I had an excellent pair of garters, and would go and hang myself forthwith.

"Good!" he replied, "do so;—although hanging is somewhat hack-neyed. Perhaps you might do better. Take a dose of Brandreth's pills,° and then give us your sensations. However, my instructions will apply equally well to any variety of misadventure, and in your way home you may easily get knocked in the head, or run over by an omnibus, or bit-ten by a mad dog, or drowned in a gutter. But to proceed.

"Having determined upon your subject, you must next consider the tone, or manner, of your narration. There is the tone didactic, the tone enthusiastic, the tone natural—all common-place enough. But then there is the tone laconic, or curt, which has lately come much into use. It consists in short sentences. Somehow thus. Can't be too brief. Can't be too snappish. Always a full stop. And never a paragraph.

"Then there is the tone elevated, diffusive, and interjectional. Some of our best novelists patronize this tone. The words must be all in a whirl, like a humming-top, and make a noise very similar, which answers remarkably well instead of meaning. This is the best of all possible styles where the writer is in too great a hurry to think.

"The tone metaphysical is also a good one. If you know any big words this is your chance for them. Talk of the Ionic and Eleatic schools—of Archytas, Gorgias, and Alcmoeon. Say something about objectivity and subjectivity. Be sure and abuse a man named Locke. Turn up your nose at things in general, and when you let slip anything a little *too* absurd, you need not be at the trouble of scratching it out, but just add a foot-note, and say that you are indebted for the above profound observation to the '*Kritik der reinen Vernunft*,' or to the '*Metaphysische Anfangsgrunde der Naturwissenchaft.*'° This would look erudite and—and—and frank.

Brandeth's pills: A brand of purgative medicine widely known due to the advertising skill of Benjamin Brandreth (1809–1880). *Kritik...der Naturwissenchaft:* Both texts are by the German philosopher Immanuel Kant (1724–1804). In English, their titles are *The Critique of Pure Reason* and *Metaphysicial Foundations of Natural Science.*

"There are various other tones of equal celebrity, but I shall mention only two more—the tone transcendental and the tone heterogeneous. In the former the merit consists in seeing into the nature of affairs a very great deal farther than any body else. This second sight is very efficient when properly managed. A little reading of the 'Dial'° will carry you a great way. Eschew, in this case, big words; get them as small as possible, and write them upside down. Look over Channing's° poems and quote what he says about a 'fat little man with a delusive show of Can.' Put in something about the Supernal Oneness. Don't say a syllable about the Infernal Twoness. Above all, study innuendo. Hint every thing—assert nothing. If you feel inclined to say 'bread and butter,' do not by any means say it outright. You may say anything and every thing *approaching* to 'bread and butter.' You may hint at buckwheat cake, or you may even go so far as to insinuate oat-meal porridge, but if bread and butter be your real meaning, be cautious, my *dear* Miss Psyche, not on any account to say 'bread and butter!' "

I assured him that I should never say it again as long as I lived. He kissed me and continued:

"As for the tone heterogeneous, it is merely a judicious mixture, in equal proportions, of all the other tones in the world, and is consequently made up of everything deep, great, odd, piquant, pertinent, and pretty.

"Let us suppose now you have determined upon your incidents and tone. The most important portion,—in fact the soul of the whole business, is yet to be attended to—I allude to *the filling up*. It is not to be supposed that a lady or gentleman either has been leading the life of a book-worm. And yet above all things it is necessary that your article have an air of erudition, or at least afford evidence of extensive general reading. Now I'll put you in the way of accomplishing this point. See here!" (pulling down some three or four ordinary looking volumes, and opening them at random.) "By casting your eye down almost any page of any book in the world, you will be able to perceive at once a host of little scraps of either learning or *bel-esprit-ism*, which are the very thing for the spicing of a Blackwood article. You might as well note down a few while I read them to you. I shall make two divisions: first, *Piquant Facts for the Manufacture of Similes*; and, second, *Piquant Expressions to be introduced as occasion may require*. Write now!—" and I wrote as he dictated.

Dial: Boston magazine, which between 1840 and 1844 served as a main publication of American transcendentalism.   *Channing:* William Ellery Channing (1818–1901), American transcendentalist poet.

"PIQUANT FACTS FOR SIMILES. 'There were originally but three Muses—Melete, Mneme, and Aoede—meditation, memory, and singing.' You may make a good deal of that little fact if properly worked. You see it is not generally known, and looks *recherché*. You must be careful and give the thing with a downright improviso air.

"Again. 'The river Alpheus passed beneath the sea, and emerged without injury to the purity of its waters.' Rather stale that, to be sure, but, if properly dressed and dished up, will look quite as fresh as ever.

"Here is something better. 'The Persian Iris appears to some persons to possess a sweet and very powerful perfume, while to others it is perfectly scentless.' Fine that, and very delicate! Turn it about a little, and it will do wonders. We'll have something else in the botanical line. There's nothing goes down so well, especially with the help of a little Latin. Write!

"'*The Epidendrum Flos Aeris*, of Java, bears a very beautiful flower, and will live when pulled up by the roots. The natives suspend it by a cord from the ceiling, and enjoy its fragrance for years.' That's capital! That will do for the similes. Now for the Piquant Expressions.

"PIQUANT EXPRESSIONS. '*The venerable Chinese novel Ju-Kiao-Li.*' Good! By introducing these few words with dexterity you will evince your intimate acquaintance with the language and literature of the Chinese. With the aid of this you may either get along without either Arabic, or Sanscrit, or Chickasaw. There is no passing muster, however, without Spanish, Italian, German, Latin, and Greek. I must look you out a little specimen of each. Any scrap will answer, because you must depend upon your own ingenuity to make it fit into your article. Now write!

"'*Aussi tendre que Zaïre*'—as tender as Zaire—French. Alludes to the frequent repetition of the phrase, *la tendre Zaïre*, in the French tragedy of that name. Properly introduced, will show not only your knowledge of the language, but your general reading and wit. You can say, for instance, that the chicken you were eating (write an article about being choked to death by a chicken-bone) was not altogether *aussi tendre que Zaïre*. Write!

'*Van muerte tan escondida,*
 Que no te sienta venir,
Porque el plazer del morir,
 No me torne a dar la vida.'

That's Spanish—from Miguel de Cervantes. 'Come quickly O death! but be sure and don't let me see you coming, lest the pleasure I shall feel at your appearance should unfortunately bring me back again to life.' This you may slip in quite *à propos* when you are struggling in the last agonies with the chicken-bone. Write!

> '*Il pover 'huomo che non se'n era accorto,*
> *Andava combattendo, e era morto.*'

That's Italian, you perceive,—from Ariosto. It means that a great hero, in the heat of combat, not perceiving that he had been fairly killed, continued to fight valiantly, dead as he was. The application of this to your own case is obvious—for I trust, Miss Psyche, that you will not neglect to kick for at least an hour and a half after you have been choked to death by that chicken-bone. Please to write!

> '*Und sterb'ich doch, no sterb'ich denn*
> *Durch sie—durch sie!*'

That's German—from Schiller. 'And if I die, at least I die—for thee— for thee!' Here it is clear that you are apostrophizing the *cause* of your disaster, the chicken. Indeed what gentleman (or lady either) of sense, *would'nt* die, I should like to know, for a well fattened capon of the right Molucca breed, stuffed with capers and mushrooms, and served up in a salad-bowl, with orange-jellies *en mosäiques.* Write! (You can get them that way at Tortoni's,)—Write, if you please!

"Here is a nice little Latin phrase, and rare too, (one can't be too *recherché* or brief in one's Latin, it's getting so common,)—*ignoratio elenchi.°* He has committed an *ignoratio elenchi*—that is to say, he has understood the words of your proposition, but not the ideas. The man was a *fool,* you see. Some poor fellow whom you address while choking with that chicken-bone, and who therefore didn't precisely understand what you were talking about. Throw the *ignoratio elenchi* in his teeth, and, at once, you have him annihilated. If he dares to reply, you can tell him from Lucan (here it is) that speeches are mere *anemonae verborum*, anemone words. The anemone, with great brilliancy, has no smell. Or, if he begins to bluster, you may be down upon him with *insomnia Jovis*, reveries of Jupiter—a phrase which Silius Italicus (see here!) applies to thoughts pompous and inflated. This will be sure and cut him to the heart. He can do nothing but roll over and die. Will you be kind enough to write?

---

ignoratio elenchi: An error in reasoning.

"In Greek we must have something pretty—from Demosthenes, for example. Ανερ ο φευγων χαι παλιν μαχεσεται. [Aner o pheogon kai palin makesetai]. There is a tolerably good translation of it in Hudibras—

For he that flies may fight again,
Which he can never do that's slain.

In a Blackwood article nothing makes so fine a show as your Greek. The very letters have an air of profundity about them. Only observe, madam, the astute look of that Epsilon! That Phi ought certainly to be a bishop! Was ever there a smarter fellow than that Omicron? Just twig that Tau! In short, there is nothing like Greek for a genuine sensation-paper. In the present case your application is the most obvious thing in the world. Rap out the sentence, with a huge oath, and by way of *ultimatum* at the good-for-nothing dunder-headed villain who couldn't understand your plain English in relation to the chicken-bone. He'll take the hint and be off, you may depend upon it."

These were all the instructions Mr. B. could afford me upon the topic in question, but I felt they would be entirely sufficient. I was, at length, able to write a genuine Blackwood article, and determined to do it forthwith. In taking leave of me, Mr. B. made a proposition for the purchase of the paper when written; but as he could offer me only fifty guineas a sheet, I thought it better to let our society have it, than sacrifice it for so paltry a sum. Notwithstanding this niggardly spirit, however, the gentleman showed his consideration for me in all other respects, and indeed treated me with the greatest civility. His parting words made a deep impression upon my heart, and I hope I shall always remember them with gratitude.

"My dear Miss Zenobia," he said, while the tears stood in his eyes, "is there *any*thing else I can do to promote the success of your laudable undertaking? Let me reflect! It is just possible that you may not be able, so soon as convenient, to—to—get yourself drowned, or—choked with a chicken-bone, or—or hung,—or—bitten by a—but stay! Now I think me of it, there are a couple of very excellent bull-dogs in the yard—fine fellows, I assure you—savage, and all that—indeed just the thing for your money—they'll have you eaten up, *auriculas* and all, in less than five minutes (here's my watch!)—and then only think of the sensations! Here! I say— Tom!—Peter!—Dick, you villain!—let out those"—but as I was really in a great hurry, and had not another moment to spare, I was reluctantly forced to expedite my departure, and accordingly took leave *at once*—somewhat more abruptly, I admit, than strict courtesy would have otherwise, allowed.

It was my primary object, upon quitting Mr. Blackwood, to get into some immediate difficulty, pursuant to his advice, and with this view I spent the greater part of the day in wandering about Edinburgh, seeking for desperate adventures—adventures adequate to the intensity of my feelings, and adapted to the vast character of the article I intended to write. In this excursion I was attended by one negro-servant Pompey, and my little lap-dog Diana, whom I had brought with me from Philadelphia. It was not, however, until late in the afternoon that I fully succeeded in my arduous undertaking. An important event then happened of which the following Blackwood article, in the tone heterogeneous, is the substance and result.

A Predicament

What chance, good lady, hath bereft you thus?

–COMUS

It was a quiet and still afternoon when I strolled forth in the goodly city of Edina. The confusion and bustle in the streets were terrible. Men were talking. Women were screaming. Children were choking. Pigs were whistling. Carts they rattled. Bulls they bellowed. Cows they lowed. Horses they neighed. Cats they caterwauled. Dogs they danced. *Danced!* Could it then be possible? *Danced!* Alas, thought I, *my* dancing days are over! Thus it is ever. What a host of gloomy recollections will ever and anon be awakened in the mind of genius and imaginative contemplation, especially of a genius doomed to the everlasting, and eternal, and continual, and, as one might say, the—*continued*—yes, the *continued and continuous*, bitter, harassing, disturbing, and, if I may be allowed the expression, the *very* disturbing influence of the serene, and godlike, and heavenly, and exalting, and elevated, and, purifying effect of what may be rightly termed the most enviable, the most *truly* enviable—nay! the most benignly beautiful, the most deliciously ethereal, and, as it were, the most *pretty* (if I may use so bold an expression) *thing* (pardon me, gentle reader!) in the world—but I am always led away by my feelings. In *such* a mind, I repeat, what a host of recollections are stirred up by a trifle! The dogs danced! *I*—I *could* not! They frisked—I wept. They capered—I sobbed aloud. Touching circumstances! which cannot fail to bring to the recollection of the classical reader that exquisite passage in relation to the fitness of things, which is to be found in the commencement of the third volume of that admirable and venerable Chinese novel, the *Jo-Go-Slow*.

In my solitary walk through the city I had two humble but faithful companions. Diana, my poodle! sweetest of creatures! She had a quantity of hair over her one eye, and a blue riband tied fashionably around her neck. Diana was not more than five inches in height, but her head was somewhat bigger than her body, and her tail, being cut off exceedingly close, gave an air of injured innocence to the interesting animal which rendered her a favorite with all.

And Pompey, my negro!—sweet Pompey! how shall I ever forget thee? I had taken Pompey's arm. He was three feet in height (I like to be particular) and about seventy, or perhaps eighty, years of age. He had bow-legs and was corpulent. His mouth should not be called small, nor his ears short. His teeth, however, were like pearl, and his large full eyes were deliciously white. Nature had endowed him with no neck, and had placed his ankles (as usual with that race) in the middle of the upper portion of the feet. He was clad with a striking simplicity. His sole garments were a stock of nine inches in height, and a nearly-new drab overcoat which had formerly been in the service of the tall, stately, and illustrious Dr. Moneypenny. It was a good overcoat. It was well cut. It was well made. The coat was nearly new. Pompey held it up out of the dirt with both hands.

There were three persons in our party, and two of them have already been the subject of remark. There was a third—that person was myself. I am the Signora Psyche Zenobia. I am *not* Suky Snobbs. My appearance is commanding. On the memorable occasion of which I speak I was habited in a crimson satin dress, with a sky-blue Arabian mantelet. And the dress had trimmings of green agraffas, and seven graceful flounces of the orange colored auricula. I thus formed the third of the party. There was the poodle. There was Pompey. There was myself. We were *three*. Thus it is said there were originally but three Furies—Melty, Nimmy and Hetty—Meditation, Memory, and Fiddling.

Leaning upon the arm of the gallant Pompey, and attended at a respectable distance by Diana, I proceeded down one of the populous and very pleasant streets of the now deserted Edina. On a sudden, there presented itself to view a church—a Gothic cathedral—vast, venerable, and with a tall steeple, which towered into the sky. What madness now possessed me? Why did I rush upon my fate? I was seized with an uncontrollable desire to ascend the giddy pinnacle, and thence survey the immense extent of the city. The door of the cathedral stood invitingly open. My destiny prevailed. I entered the ominous archway.

Where then was my guardian angel?—if indeed such angels there be. *If!* Distressing monosyllable! what world of mystery, and meaning, and doubt, and uncertainty is there involved in thy two letters! I entered the ominous archway! I entered; and, without injury to my orange-colored auriculas, I passed beneath the portal, and emerged within the vestibule! Thus it is said the immense river Alfred passed, unscathed, and unwetted, beneath the sea.

I thought the staircase would never have an end. *Round!* Yes, they went round and up, and round and up and round and up, until I could not help surmising, with the sagacious Pompey, upon whose supporting arm I leaned in all the confidence of early affection—I *could* not help surmising that the upper end of the continuous spiral ladder had been accidentally, or perhaps designedly, removed. I paused for breath; and, in the meantime, an accident occurred of too momentous a nature in a moral, and also in a metaphysical point of view, to be passed over without notice. It appeared to me—indeed I was quite confident of the fact—I could not be mistaken—no! I had, for some moments, carefully and anxiously observed the motions of my Diana— I say that *I could not be* mistaken—Diana *smelt a rat!* At once I called Pompey's attention to the subject, and he—he agreed with me. There was then no longer any reasonable room for doubt. The rat had been smelled—and by Diana. Heavens! shall I ever forget the intense excitement of the moment? Alas! what is the boasted intellect of man? The rat!—it was there—that is to say, it was somewhere. Diana smelled the rat. I—*I could* not! Thus it is said the Prussian Isis has, for some persons, a sweet and very powerful perfume, while to others it is perfectly scentless.

The staircase had been surmounted, and there were now only three or four more upward steps intervening between us and the summit. We still ascended, and now only one step remained. One step! One little, little step! Upon one such little step in the great staircase of human life how vast a sum of human happiness or misery often depends! I thought of myself, then of Pompey, and then of the mysterious and inexplicable destiny which surrounded us. I thought of Pompey!—alas, I thought of love! I thought of my many false *steps* which have been taken, and may be taken again. I resolved to be more cautious, more reserved. I abandoned the arm of Pompey, and, without his assistance, surmounted the one remaining step, and gained the chamber of the belfry. I was followed immediately afterwards by my poodle. Pompey alone remained behind. I stood at the head of the staircase, and encouraged him to ascend. He stretched forth to me his hand, and unfortunately in so doing was forced to abandon his firm hold upon the overcoat. Will the gods never cease their persecution? The overcoat it dropped, and, with one of his feet, Pompey stepped upon the long and trailing skirt of the overcoat. He stumbled and fell—this consequence was inevitable. He fell forwards, and, with his accursed head, striking me full in the—in the breast, precipitated me headlong, together with himself, upon the hard, filthy and detestable floor of the belfry. But my revenge was sure, sudden and complete. Seizing him furiously by the wool with both hands, I tore out a vast quantity of black, and crisp, and curling material, and tossed it from me with every manifestation of disdain. It fell among the ropes of the belfry and remained. Pompey arose, and said no word. But he regarded me piteously with his large eyes and—sighed. Ye Gods—that sigh! It sunk into my heart. And the hair—the wool! Could I have reached that wool I would have bathed it with my tears, in testimony of regret. But alas! it was now far beyond my grasp. As it dangled among the cordage of the bell, I fancied it still alive. I fancied that it stood on end with indignation. Thus the *happy dandy Flos Aeris* of Java bears, it is said, a beautiful flower, which will live when pulled up by the roots. The natives suspend it by a cord from the ceiling and enjoy its fragrance for years.

Our quarrel was now made up, and we looked about the room for an aperture through which to survey the city of Edina. Windows there were none. The sole light admitted into the gloomy chamber proceeded from a square opening, about a foot in diameter, at a height of about seven feet from the floor. Yet what will the energy of true genius not effect? I resolved to clamber up to this hole. A vast quantity of wheels, pinions, and other cabalistic-looking machinery stood opposite the hole, close to it; and through the hole there passed an iron rod from the machinery. Between the wheels and the wall where the hole lay, there was barely room for my body—yet I was desperate, and determined to persevere. I called Pompey to my side.

"You perceive that aperture, Pompey. I wish to look through it. You will stand here just beneath the hole—so. Now, hold out one of your hands, Pompey, and let me step upon it—thus. Now, the other hand, Pompey, and with its aid I will get upon your shoulders."

He did everything I wished, and I found, upon getting up, that I could easily pass my head and neck through the aperture. The prospect was sublime. Nothing could be more magnificent. I merely paused a moment to bid Diana behave herself, and assure Pompey that I would be considerate and bear as lightly as possible upon his shoulders. I told him I would be tender of his feelings—*ossi tender que beefsteak*. Having done this justice to my faithful friend, I gave myself up with great zest and enthusiasm to the enjoyment of the scene which so obligingly spread itself out before my eyes.

Upon this subject, however, I shall forbear to dilate. I will not describe the city of Edinburgh. Every one has been to Edinburgh—the classic Edina. I will confine myself to the momentous details of my own lamentable adventure. Having, in some measure, satisfied my curiosity in regard to the extent, situation, and general appearance of the city, I had leisure to survey the church in which I was, and the delicate architecture of the steeple. I observed that the aperture through which I had thrust my head was an opening in the dial-plate of a gigantic clock, and must have appeared, from the street, as a large key-hole, such as we see in the face of the French watches. No doubt the true object was to admit the arm of an attendant, to adjust, when necessary, the hands of the clock from within. I observed also, with surprise, the immense size of these hands, the longest of which could not have been less than ten feet in length, and, where broadest, eight or nine inches in breadth. They were of solid steel apparently, and their edges appeared to be sharp. Having noticed these particulars, and some others, I again turned my eyes upon the glorious prospect below, and soon became absorbed in contemplation.

From this, after some minutes, I was aroused by the voice of Pompey, who declared that he could stand it no longer, and requested that I would be so kind as to come down. This was unreasonable, and I told him so in a speech of some length. He replied, but with an evident misunderstanding of my ideas upon the subject. I accordingly grew angry, and told him in plain words, that he was a fool, that he had committed an *ignoramus e-clench-eye*, that his notions were mere *insommary Bovis*, and his words little better than *an enemy-werrybor'em*. With this he appeared satisfied, and I resumed my contemplations.

It might have been half an hour after this altercation when, as I was deeply absorbed in the heavenly scenery beneath me, I was startled by something very cold which pressed with a gentle pressure on the back of my neck. It is needless to say that I felt inexpressibly alarmed. I knew that Pompey was beneath my feet, and that Diana was sitting, according to my explicit directions, upon her hind legs in the farthest corner of the room. What could it be? Alas! I but too soon discovered. Turning my head gently to one side, I perceived, to my extreme horror, that the huge, glittering, scimetar-like minute-hand of the clock, had, in the course of its hourly revolution, *descended upon my neck*. There was, I knew, not a second to be lost. I pulled back at once—but it was too late. There was no chance of forcing my head through the mouth of that terrible trap in which it was so fairly caught, and which grew narrower and narrower with a rapidity too horrible to be conceived. The agony of that moment is not to be imagined. I threw up my hands and endeavored, with all my strength, to force upward the ponderous iron bar. I might as well have tried to lift the cathedral itself. Down, down, down it came, closer and yet closer. I screamed to Pompey for aid: but he said that I had hurt his feelings by calling him "an ignorant old squint eye:" I yelled to Diana; but she only said "bow-wow-wow," and that "I had told her on no account to stir from the corner." Thus I had no relief to expect from my associates.

Meantime the ponderous and terrific *Scythe of Time* (for I now discovered the literal import of that classical phrase) had not stopped, nor was it likely to stop, in its career. Down and still down, it came. It had already buried its sharp edge a full inch in my flesh, and my sensations grew indistinct and confused. At one time I fancied myself in Philadelphia with the stately Dr. Moneypenny, at another in the back parlor of Mr. Blackwood receiving his invaluable instructions. And then again the sweet recollection of better and earlier times came over me, and I thought of that happy period when the world was not all a desert, and Pompey not altogether cruel.

The ticking of the machinery amused me. *Amused me*, I say, for my sensations now bordered upon perfect happiness, and the most trifling circumstances afforded me pleasure. The eternal *click-clack, click-clack, click-clack*, of the clock was the most melodious of music in my ears, and occasionally even put me in mind of the grateful sermonic harangues of Dr. Ollapod. Then there were the great figures upon the dial-plate— how intelligent, how intellectual, they all looked! And presently they took to dancing the Mazurka, and I think it was the figure V who performed the most to my satisfaction. She was evidently a lady of breeding. None of your swaggerers, and nothing at all indelicate in her motions. She did the pirouette to admiration—whirling round upon her apex. I made an endeavor to hand her a chair, for I saw that she appeared fatigued with her exertions—and it was not until then that I fully perceived my lamentable situation. Lamentable indeed! The bar had buried itself two inches in my neck. I was aroused to a sense of exquisite pain. I prayed for death, and, in the agony of the moment, could not help repeating those exquisite verses of the poet Miguel De Cervantes:

Vanny Buren, tan escondida
Query no te senty venny
Pork and pleasure, delly morry
Nommy, torny, darry, widdy!

But now a new horror presented itself, and one indeed sufficient to startle the strongest nerves. My eyes, from the cruel pressure of the machine, were absolutely starting from their sockets. While I was thinking how I should possibly manage without them, one actually tumbled out of my head, and, rolling down the steep side of the steeple, lodged in the rain gutter which ran along the eaves of the main building. The loss of the eye was not so much as the insolent air of independence and contempt with which it regarded me after it was out. There it lay in the gutter just under my nose, and the airs it gave itself would have been ridiculous had they not been disgusting. Such a winking and blinking were never before seen. This behavior on the part of my eye in the gutter was not only irritating on account of its manifest insolence and shameful ingratitude, but was also exceedingly inconvenient on account of the sympathy which always exists between two eyes of the same head, however far apart. I was forced, in a manner, to wink and to blink, whether I would or not, in exact concert with the scoundrelly thing that lay just under my nose. I was presently relieved, however, by the dropping out of the other eye. In falling it took the same direction (possibly a concerted plot) as its fellow. Both rolled out of the gutter together, and in truth I was very glad to get rid of them.

The bar was now four inches and a half deep in my neck, and there was only a little bit of skin to cut through. My sensations were those of entire happiness, for I felt that in a few minutes, at farthest, I should be relieved from my disagreeable situation. And in this expectation I was not at all deceived. At twenty-five minutes past five in the afternoon precisely, the huge minute-hand had proceeded sufficiently far on its terrible revolution to sever the small remainder of my neck. I was not sorry to see the head which had occasioned me so much embarrassment at length make a final separation from my body. It first rolled down the side of the steeple, then lodged, for a few seconds, in the gutter, and then made its way, with a plunge, into the middle of the street.

I will candidly confess that my feelings were now of the most singular — nay of the most mysterious, the most perplexing and incomprehensible character. My senses were here and there at one and the same moment. With my head I imagined, at one time, that I the head, was the real Signora Psyche Zenobia—at another I felt convinced that myself, the body, was the proper identity. To clear my ideas on this topic I felt in my pocket for my snuff-box, but, upon getting it, and endeavoring to apply a pinch of its grateful contents in the ordinary manner, I became immediately aware of my peculiar deficiency, and threw the box at once down to my head. It took a pinch with great satisfaction, and smiled me an acknowledgement in return. Shortly afterwards it made me a speech, which I could hear but indistinctly without ears. I gathered enough, however, to know that it was astonished at my wishing to remain alive under such circumstances. In the concluding sentences it quoted the noble words of Ariosto—

> *Il pover hommy che non sera corty*
> *And have a combat tenty erry morty;*

thus comparing me to the hero who, in the heat of the combat, not perceiving that he was dead, continued to contest the battle with inextinguishable valor. There was nothing now to prevent my getting down from my elevation, and I did so. What it was that Pompey saw so *very* peculiar in my appearance I have never yet been able to find out. The fellow opened his mouth from ear to ear, and shut his two eyes as if he were endeavoring to crack nuts between the lids. Finally, throwing off his overcoat, he made one spring for the staircase and disappeared. I hurled after the scoundrel these vehement words of Demosthenes—

> *Andrew O'Phlegethon, you really make haste to fly,*

and then turned to the darling of my heart, to the one-eyed! the shaggy-haired Diana. Alas! what a horrible vision affronted my eyes? *Was* that a rat I saw skulking into his hole? *Are* these the picked bones of the little angel who has been cruelly devoured by the monster? Ye Gods! and what *do* I behold—*is* that the departed spirit, the shade, the ghost of my beloved puppy, which I perceive sitting with a grace so melancholy, in the corner? Harken! for she speaks, and, heavens! it is in the German of Schiller—

> "Unt stubby duk, so stubby dun
> Duk she! duk she!"

Alas! and are not her words too true?

> And if I died at least I died
> For thee—for thee.

Sweet creature! she *too* has sacrificed herself in my behalf. Dogless, niggerless, headless, what *now* remains for the unhappy Signora Psyche Zenobia? Alas—*nothing*! I have done.

The Man That Was Used Up

A Tale of the Late Bugaboo and Kickapoo Campaign

Pleurez, pleurez, mes yeux, et fondez vous en eau!
La moitie de ma vie a mis l'autre au tombeau.

–CORNEILLE°

I cannot just now remember when or where I first made the acquaintance of that truly fine-looking fellow, Brevet Brigadier General John A. B. C. Smith. Some one *did* introduce me to the gentleman, I am sure—at some public meeting, I know very well—held about something of great importance, no doubt—at some place or other, I feel convinced,—whose name I have unaccountably forgotten. The truth is—that the introduction was attended, upon my part, with a degree of anxious embarrassment which operated to prevent any definite impressions of either time or place. I am constitutionally nervous—this, with me, is a family failing, and I can't help it. In especial, the slightest appearance of mystery—of any point I cannot exactly comprehend—puts me at once into a pitiable state of agitation.

There was something, as it were, remarkable—yes, *remarkable*, although this is but a feeble term to express my full meaning—about the entire individuality of the personage in question. He was, perhaps, six feet in height, and of a presence singularly commanding. There was an *air distingué* pervading the whole man, which spoke of high breeding, and hinted at high birth. Upon this topic—the topic of Smith's personal appearance—I have a kind of melancholy satisfaction in being minute. His head of hair would have done honor to a Brutus;—nothing could be more richly flowing, or possess a brighter gloss. It was of a jetty black;—which was also the color, or more properly the no color of his unimaginable whiskers. You perceive I cannot speak of these latter without enthusiasm; it is not too much to say that they were the

---

Pleurez . . . Corneille: Poe translates this epigraph, "Weep, weep, my eyes! It is no time to laugh / For half myself has buried the other half." The passage is from the tragedy *Le Cid* by Pierre Corneille (1606–1684).

handsomest pair of whiskers under the sun. At all events, they encircled, and at times partially overshadowed, a mouth utterly unequalled. Here were the most entirely even, and the most brilliantly white of all conceivable teeth. From between them, upon every proper occasion, issued a voice of surpassing clearness, melody, and strength. In the matter of eyes, also, my acquaintance was pre-eminently endowed. Either one of such a pair was worth a couple of the ordinary ocular organs. They were of a deep hazel, exceedingly large and lustrous; and there was perceptible about them, ever and anon, just that amount of interesting obliquity which gives pregnancy to expression.

The bust of the General was unquestionably the finest bust I ever saw. For your life you could not have found a fault with its wonderful proportion. This rare peculiarity set off to great advantage a pair of shoulders which would have called up a blush of conscious inferiority into the countenance of the marble Apollo. I have a passion for fine shoulders, and may say that I never beheld them in perfection before. The arms altogether were admirably modelled. Nor were the lower limbs less superb. These were, indeed, the *ne plus ultra* of good legs. Every connoisseur in such matters admitted the legs to be good. There was neither too much flesh, nor too little,—neither rudeness nor fragility. I could not imagine a more graceful curve than that of the *os femoris*, and there was just that due gentle prominence in the rear of the *fibula* which goes to the conformation of a properly proportioned calf. I wish to God my young and talented friend Chiponchipino, the sculptor, had but seen the legs of Brevet Brigadier General John A. B. C. Smith.

But although men so absolutely fine-looking are neither as plenty as reasons or blackberries, still I could not bring myself to believe that *the remarkable* something to which I alluded just now,—that the odd air of *je ne sais quoi* which hung about my new acquaintance,—lay altogether, or indeed at all, in the supreme excellence of his bodily endowments. Perhaps it might be traced to the *manner*;—yet here again I could not pretend to be positive. There *was* a primness, not to say stiffness, in his carriage—a degree of measured, and, if I may so express it, of rectangular precision, attending his every movement, which, observed in a more diminutive figure, would have had the least little savor in the world, of affectation, pomposity or constraint, but which noticed in a gentleman of his undoubted dimensions, was readily placed to the account of reserve, *hauteur*—of a commendable sense, in short, of what is due to the dignity of colossal proportion.

The kind friend who presented me to General Smith whispered in my ear some few words of comment upon the man. He was a *remarkable* man—a *very* remarkable man—indeed one of the *most* remarkable men of the age. He was an especial favorite, too, with the ladies—chiefly on account of his high reputation for courage.

"In *that* point he is unrivalled—indeed he is a perfect desperado—a down-right fire-eater, and no mistake," said my friend, here dropping his voice excessively low, and thrilling me with the mystery of his tone.

"A downright fire-eater, and *no* mistake. Showed *that*, I should say, to some purpose, in the late tremendous swamp-fight away down South, with the Bugaboo and Kickapoo Indians." [Here my friend opened his eyes to some extent.] "Bless my soul!—blood and thunder, and all that!—*prodigies* of valor!—heard of him of course?—you know he's the man"——

"Man alive, how *do* you do? why, how *are* ye? very glad to see ye, indeed!" here interrupted the General himself, seizing my companion by the hand as he drew near, and bowing stiffly, but profoundly, as I was presented. I then thought, (and I think so still,) that I never heard a clearer nor a stronger voice, nor beheld a finer set of teeth: but I *must* say that I was sorry for the interruption just at that moment, as, owing to the whispers and insinuations aforesaid, my interest had been greatly excited in the hero of the Bugaboo and Kickapoo campaign.

However, the delightfully luminous conversation of Brevet Brigadier General John A. B. C. Smith soon completely dissipated this chagrin. My friend leaving us immediately, we had quite a long *tête-à-tête*, and I was not only pleased but *really*—instructed. I never heard a more fluent talker, or a man of greater general information. With becoming modesty, he forebore, nevertheless, to touch upon the theme I had just then most at heart—I mean the mysterious circumstances attending the Bugaboo war—and, on my own part, what I conceive to be a proper sense of delicacy forbade me to broach the subject; although, in truth, I was exceedingly tempted to do so. I perceived, too, that the gallant soldier preferred topics of philosophical interest, and that he delighted, especially, in commenting upon the rapid march of mechanical invention. Indeed, lead him where I would, this was a point to which he invariably came back.

"There is nothing at all like it," he would say; "we are a wonderful people, and live in a wonderful age. Parachutes and rail-roads—man-traps and spring-guns! Our steam-boats are upon every sea, and the Nassau balloon packet is about to run regular trips (fare either way only twenty pounds sterling) between London and Timbuctoo. And who shall calculate the immense influence upon social life—upon arts—upon commerce—upon literature—which will be the immediate result of the great principles of electro magnetics! Nor, is this all, let me assure you! There is really no end to the march of invention. The most wonderful—the most ingenious—and let me add, Mr.—Mr.—Thompson, I believe, is your name—let me add, I say, the most *useful*—the most truly *useful* mechanical contrivances, are daily springing up like mushrooms, if I may so express myself, or, more figuratively, like—ah—grasshoppers—like grasshoppers, Mr. Thompson—about us and ah—ah—ah—around us!"

Thompson, to be sure, is not my name; but it is needless to say that I left General Smith with a heightened interest in the man, with an exalted opinion of his conversational powers, and a deep sense of the valuable privileges we enjoy in living in this age of mechanical invention. My curiosity, however, had not been altogether satisfied, and I resolved to prosecute immediate inquiry among my acquaintances touching the Brevet Brigadier General himself, and particularly respecting the tremendous events *quorum pars magna fuit*,° during the Bugaboo and Kickapoo campaign.

The first opportunity which presented itself, and which (*horresco referens*°) I did not in the least scruple to seize, occurred at the Church of the Reverend Doctor Drummummupp, where I found myself established, one Sunday, just at sermon time, not only in the pew, but by the side, of that worthy and communicative little friend of mine, Miss Tabitha T. Thus seated, I congratulated myself, and with much reason, upon the very flattering state of affairs. If any person knew anything about Brevet Brigadier General John A. B. C. Smith, that person, it was clear to me, was Miss Tabitha T. We telegraphed a few signals, and then commenced, *soto voce*, a brisk *tête-à-tête*.

"Smith!" said she, in reply to my very earnest inquiry; "Smith!—why, not General John A. B. C.? Bless me, I thought you *knew* all about *him!* This is a wonderfully inventive age! Horrid affair that!—a bloody set of wretches, those Kickapoos!—fought like a hero—prodigies of valor—immortal renown. Smith!—Brevet Brigadier General John A. B. C.! why, you know he's the man"——

"Man," here broke in Doctor Drummummupp, at the top of his voice, and with a thump that came near knocking the pulpit about our ears; "man that is born of a woman hath but a short time to live; he cometh up and is cut down like a flower!" I started to the extremity of the pew, and perceived by the animated looks of the divine, that the

---

quorum pars magna fuit: Of which things he was an important part.   *horresco referens:* Shudder to recall. This phrase and the preceding are from the *Aeneid*, Book II.

wrath which had nearly proved fatal to the pulpit had been excited by the whispers of the lady and myself. There was no help for it; so I submitted with a good grace, and listened, in all the martyrdom of dignified silence, to the balance of that very capital discourse.

Next evening found me a somewhat late visitor at the Rantipole theatre, where I felt sure of satisfying my curiosity at once, by merely stepping into the box of those exquisite specimens of affability and omniscience, the Misses Arabella and Miranda Cognoscenti. That fine tragedian, Climax, was doing Iago to a very crowded house, and I experienced some little difficulty in making my wishes understood; especially, as our box was next the slips, and completely overlooked the stage.

"Smith?" said Miss Arabella, as she at length comprehended the purport of my query; "Smith?—why, not General John A. B. C.?"

"Smith?" inquired Miranda, musingly. "God bless me, did you ever behold a finer figure?"

"Never, madam, but *do* tell me"———

"Or so inimitable grace?"

"Never, upon my word!—But pray inform me"———

"Or so just an appreciation of stage effect?"

"Madam!"

"Or a more delicate sense of the true beauties of Shakespeare? Be so good as to look at that leg!"

"The devil!" and I turned again to her sister.

"Smith?" said she, "why, not General John A. B. C.? Horrid affair that, wasn't it?—great wretches, those Bugaboos—savage and so on—but we live in a wonderfully inventive age!—Smith!—O yes! great man!—perfect desperado—immortal renown—prodigies of valor! *Never heard!*" [This was given in a scream.] "Bless my soul! why, he's the man"———

"———mandragora
Nor all the drowsy syrups of the world
Shall ever medicine thee to that sweet sleep
Which thou owd'st yesterday!"°

here roared our Climax just in my ear, and shaking his fist in my face all the time, in a way that I *couldn't* stand, and I *wouldn't*. I left the Misses Cognoscenti immediately, went behind the scenes forthwith, and gave the beggarly scoundrel such a thrashing as I trust he will remember to the day of his death.

---

mandragora / . . . owd'st yesterday: From *Othello,* act 3, scene 3, 330–33.

At the *soirée* of the lovely widow, Mrs. Kathleen O'Trump, I was confident that I should meet with no similar disappointment. Accordingly, I was no sooner seated at the card-table, with my pretty hostess for a *vis-à-vis*, than I propounded those questions the solution of which had become a matter so essential to my peace.

"Smith?" said my partner, "why, not General John A. B. C.? Horrid affair that, wasn't it?—diamonds, did you say?—terrible wretches those Kickapoos!—we are playing *whist*, if you please, Mr. Tattle—however, this is the age of invention, most certainly *the* age, one may say—*the* age *par excellence*—speak French?—oh, quite a hero—perfect desperado!—*no hearts*, Mr. Tattle? I don't believe it!—immortal renown and all that!—prodigies of valor! *Never heard!!*—why, bless me, he's the man"———

"Mann?—*Captain* Mann?" here screamed some little feminine interloper from the farthest corner of the room. "Are you talking about Captain Mann and the duel?—oh, I *must* hear—do tell—go on, Mrs. O'Trump!—do now go on!" And go on Mrs. O'Trump did—all about a certain Captain Mann, who was either shot or hung, or should have been both shot and hung. Yes! Mrs. O'Trump, she went on, and I—I went off. There was no chance of hearing anything farther that evening in regard to Brevet Brigadier General John A. B. C. Smith.

Still I consoled myself with the reflection that the tide of ill luck would not run against me forever, and so determined to make a bold push for information at the rout of that bewitching little angel, the graceful Mrs. Pirouette.

"Smith?" said Mrs. P., as we twirled about together in a *pas de zephyr*,° "Smith?—why, not General John A. B. C.? Dreadful business that of the Bugaboos, wasn't it?—dreadful creatures, those Indians!—*do* turn out your toes! I really am ashamed of you—man of great courage, poor fellow!—but this is a wonderful age for invention—O dear me, I'm out of breath—quite a desperado—prodigies of valor—*never heard!!*—can't believe it—I shall have to sit down and enlighten you—Smith! why, he's the man"———

"Man-*Fred*, I tell you!" here bawled out Miss Bas-Bleu, as I led Mrs. Pirouette to a seat. "Did ever anybody hear the like? It's Man-*Fred*, I say, and not at all by any means Man-*Friday*." Here Miss Bas-Bleu beckoned to me in a very peremptory manner; and I was obliged, will I nill I, to leave Mrs. P. for the purpose of deciding a dispute touching the title of a certain poetical drama of Lord Byron's. Although I

---

pas de zephyr: A term used to describe a stretched foot in dance.

pronounced, with great promptness, that the true title was Man-*Friday*, and not by any means Man-*Fred*, yet when I returned to seek Mrs. Pirouette she was not to be discovered, and I made my retreat from the house in a very bitter spirit of animosity against the whole race of the Bas-Bleus.

Matters had now assumed a really serious aspect, and I resolved to call at once upon my particular friend, Mr. Theodore Sinivate; for I knew that here at least I should get something like definite information.

"Smith?" said he, in his well-known peculiar way of drawling out his syllables; "Smith?—why, not General John A. B. C.? Savage affair that with the Kickapo-o-o-os, wasn't it? Say! don't you think so?—perfect despera-a-ado—great pity, 'pon my honor!—wonderfully inventive age!—pro-o-odigies of valor! By the by, did you ever hear about Captain Ma-a-a-a-n?"

"Captain Mann be d——d!" said I; "please to go on with your story."

"Hem!—oh well!—quite *la même cho-o-ose*, as we say in France. Smith, eh? Brigadier General John A. B. C.? I say"—[here Mr. S. thought proper to put his finger to the side of his nose]—"I say, you don't mean to insinuate now, really and truly, and conscientiously, that you don't know all about that affair of Smith's, as well as I do, eh? Smith? John A—B—C.? Why, bless me, he's the ma-a-an"——

"*Mr.* Sinivate," said I, imploringly, "*is* he the man in the mask?"

"No-o-o!" said he, looking wise, "nor the man in the mo-o-o-o-on."

This reply I considered a pointed and positive insult, and so left the house at once in high dudgeon, with a firm resolve to call my friend, Mr. Sinivate, to a speedy account for his ungentlemanly conduct and ill-breeding.

In the meantime, however, I had no notion of being thwarted touching the information I desired. There was one resource left me yet. I would go to the fountain head. I would call forthwith upon the General himself, and demand, in explicit terms, a solution of this abominable piece of mystery. Here, at least, there should be no chance for equivocation. I would be plain, positive, peremptory—as short as piecrust—as concise as Tacitus or Montesquieu.

It was early when I called, and the General was dressing; but I pleaded urgent business, and was shown at once into his bed-room by an old negro valet, who remained in attendance during my visit. As I entered the chamber, I looked about, of course, for the occupant, but did not immediately perceive him. There was a large and exceedingly odd-looking bundle of something which lay close by my feet on the floor, and, as I was not in the best humor in the world, I gave it a kick out of the way.

"Hem! ahem! rather civil that, I should say!" said the bundle, in one of the smallest, and altogether the funniest little voices, between a squeak and a whistle, that I ever heard in all the days of my existence.

"Ahem! rather civil that, I should observe."

I fairly shouted with terror, and made off, at a tangent, into the farthest extremity of the room.

"God bless me! my dear fellow," here again whistled the bundle, "what—what—what—why, what *is* the matter? I really believe you don't know me at all."

What *could* I say to all this—what *could* I? I staggered into an arm-chair, and, with staring eyes and open mouth, awaited the solution of the wonder.

"Strange you shouldn't know me though, isn't it?" presently re-squeaked the nondescript, which I now perceived was performing, upon the floor, some inexplicable evolution, very analogous to the drawing on of a stocking. There was only a single leg, however, apparent.

"Strange you shouldn't know me, though, isn't it? Pompey, bring me that leg!" Here Pompey handed the bundle, a very capital cork leg, already dressed, which it screwed on in a trice; and then it stood up upright before my eyes.

"And a bloody action it *was*," continued the thing, as if in a soliloquy; "but then one mustn't fight with the Bugaboos and Kickapoos, and think of coming off with a mere scratch. Pompey, I'll thank you now for that arm. Thomas" [turning to me] "is decidedly the best hand at a cork leg; but if you should ever want an arm, my dear fellow, you must really let me recommend you to Bishop." Here Pompey screwed on an arm.

"We had rather hot work of it, that you may say. Now, you dog, slip on my shoulders and bosom! Pettitt makes the best shoulders, but for a bosom you will have to go to Ducrow."

"Bosom!" said I.

"Pompey, will you *never* be ready with that wig? Scalping is a rough process after all; but then you can procure such a capital scratch at De L'Orme's."

"Scratch!"

"Now, you nigger, my teeth! For a *good* set of these you had better go to Parmly's at once; high prices, but excellent work. I swallowed some very capital articles, though, when the big Bugaboo rammed me down with the butt end of his rifle."

"Butt end! ram down!! my eye!!"

"O yes, by-the-by, my eye—here, Pompey, you scamp, screw it in! Those Kickapoos are not so very slow at a gouge; but he's a belied man, that Dr. Williams, after all; you can't imagine how well I see with the eyes of his make."

I now began very clearly to perceive that the object before me was nothing more nor less than my new acquaintance, Brevet Brigadier General John A. B. C. Smith. The manipulations of Pompey had made, I must confess, a very striking difference in the appearance of the personal man. The voice, however, still puzzled me no little; but even this apparent mystery was speedily cleared up.

"Pompey, you black rascal," squeaked the General, "I really do believe you would let me go out without my palate."

Hereupon, the negro, grumbling out an apology, went up to his master, opened his mouth with the knowing air of a horse-jockey, and adjusted therein a somewhat singular-looking machine, in a very dexterous manner, that I could not altogether comprehend. The alteration, however, in the entire expression of the General's countenance was instantaneous and surprising. When he again spoke, his voice had resumed all that rich melody and strength which I had noticed upon our original introduction.

"D——n the vagabonds!" said he, in so clear a tone that I positively started at the change, "D——n the vagabonds! they not only knocked in the roof of my mouth, but took the trouble to cut off at least seven-eighths of my tongue. There isn't Bonfanti's equal, however, in America, for really good articles of this description. I can recommend you to him with confidence," [here the General bowed,] "and assure you that I have the greatest pleasure in so doing."

I acknowledged his kindness in my best manner, and took leave of him at once, with a perfect understanding of the true state of affairs—with a full comprehension of the mystery which had troubled me so long. It was evident. It was a clear case. Brevet Brigadier General John A. B. C. Smith was the man——— was *the man that was used up*.

The Fall of the House of Usher

Son coeur est un luth suspendu; Sitôt qu'on le touche il résonne.
–DE BÉRANGER°

During the whole of a dull, dark, and soundless day in the autumn of the year, when the clouds hung oppressively low in the heavens, I had been passing alone, on horseback, through a singularly dreary tract

---

Son coeur . . . De Béranger: The epigraph is from the French poet Pierre Jean de Béranger (1780–1857); it translates: "His heart is a lute; touch it, and at once it sounds."

of country; and at length found myself, as the shades of the evening drew on, within view of the melancholy House of Usher. I know not how it was—but, with the first glimpse of the building, a sense of insufferable gloom pervaded my spirit. I say insufferable; for the feeling was unrelieved by any of that half-pleasurable, because poetic, sentiment, with which the mind usually receives even the sternest natural images of the desolate or terrible. I looked upon the scene before me—upon the mere house, and the simple landscape features of the domain—upon the bleak walls—upon the vacant eye-like windows—upon a few rank sedges—and upon a few white trunks of decayed trees—with an utter depression of soul which I can compare to no earthly sensation more properly than to the after-dream of the reveller upon opium—the bitter lapse into everyday life—the hideous dropping off of the veil. There was an iciness, a sinking, a sickening of the heart—an unredeemed dreariness of thought which no goading of the imagination could torture into aught of the sublime. What was it—I paused to think—what was it that so unnerved me in the contemplation of the House of Usher? It was a mystery all insoluble; nor could I grapple with the shadowy fancies that crowded upon me as I pondered. I was forced to fall back upon the unsatisfactory conclusion, that while, beyond doubt, there *are* combinations of very simple natural objects which have the power of thus affecting us, still the analysis of this power lies among considerations beyond our depth. It was possible, I reflected, that a mere different arrangement of the particulars of the scene, of the details of the picture, would be sufficient to modify, or perhaps to annihilate its capacity for sorrowful impression; and, acting upon this idea, I reined my horse to the precipitous brink of a black and lurid tarn° that lay in unruffled lustre by the dwelling, and gazed down—but with a shudder even more thrilling than before—upon the remodelled and inverted images of the gray sedge, and the ghastly tree-stems, and the vacant and eye-like windows.

Nevertheless, in this mansion of gloom I now proposed to myself a sojourn of some weeks. Its proprietor, Roderick Usher, had been one of my boon companions in boyhood; but many years had elapsed since our last meeting. A letter, however, had lately reached me in a distant part of the country—a letter from him—which, in its wildly importunate nature, had admitted of no other than a personal reply. The MS. gave evidence of nervous agitation. The writer spoke of acute bodily illness—of a mental disorder which oppressed him—and of an earnest desire to see me, as his best, and indeed his only personal friend, with a

tarn: Small mountain lake.

view of attempting, by the cheerfulness of my society, some alleviation of his malady. It was the manner in which all this, and much more, was said—it was the apparent *heart* that went with his request—which allowed me no room for hesitation; and I accordingly obeyed forthwith what I still considered a very singular summons.

Although, as boys, we had been even intimate associates, yet I really knew little of my friend. His reserve had been always excessive and habitual. I was aware, however, that his very ancient family had been noted, time out of mind, for a peculiar sensibility of temperament, displaying itself, through long ages, in many works of exalted art, and manifested, of late, in repeated deeds of munificent yet unobtrusive charity, as well as in a passionate devotion to the intricacies, perhaps even more than to the orthodox and easily recognisable beauties, of musical science. I had learned, too, the very remarkable fact, that the stem of the Usher race, all time-honored as it was, had put forth, at no period, any enduring branch; in other words, that the entire family lay in the direct line of descent, and had always, with very trifling and very temporary variation, so lain. It was this deficiency, I considered, while running over in thought the perfect keeping of the character of the premises with the accredited character of the people, and while speculating upon the possible influence which the one, in the long lapse of centuries, might have exercised upon the other—it was this deficiency, perhaps, of collateral issue, and the consequent undeviating transmission, from sire to son, of the patrimony with the name, which had, at length, so identified the two as to merge the original title of the estate in the quaint and equivocal appellation of the "House of Usher"—an appellation which seemed to include, in the minds of the peasantry who used it, both the family and the family mansion.

I have said that the sole effect of my somewhat childish experiment—that of looking down within the tarn—had been to deepen the first singular impression. There can be no doubt that the consciousness of the rapid increase of my superstition—for why should I not so term it?—served mainly to accelerate the increase itself. Such, I have long known, is the paradoxical law of all sentiments having terror as a basis. And it might have been for this reason only, that, when I again uplifted my eyes to the house itself, from its image in the pool, there grew in my mind a strange fancy—a fancy so ridiculous, indeed, that I but mention it to show the vivid force of the sensations which oppressed me. I had so worked upon my imagination as really to believe that about the whole mansion and domain there hung an atmosphere peculiar to themselves and their immediate vicinity—an atmosphere which had no affinity with the air of heaven, but which had reeked up from the decayed trees, and the gray wall, and the silent tarn—a pestilent and mystic vapor, dull, sluggish, faintly discernible, and leaden-hued.

Shaking off from my spirit what *must* have been a dream, I scanned more narrowly the real aspect of the building. Its principal feature seemed to be that of an excessive antiquity. The discoloration of ages had been great. Minute fungi overspread the whole exterior, hanging in a fine tangled web-work from the eaves. Yet all this was apart from any extraordinary dilapidation. No portion of the masonry had fallen; and there appeared to be a wild inconsistency between its still perfect adaptation of parts, and the crumbling condition of the individual stones. In this there was much that reminded me of the specious totality of old wood-work which has rotted for long years in some neglected vault, with no disturbance from the breath of the external air. Beyond this indication of extensive decay, however, the fabric gave little token of instability. Perhaps the eye of a scrutinizing observer might have discovered a barely perceptible fissure, which, extending from the roof of the building in front, made its way down the wall in a zigzag direction, until it became lost in the sullen waters of the tarn.

Noticing these things, I rode over a short causeway to the house. A servant in waiting took my horse, and I entered the Gothic archway of the hall. A valet, of stealthy step, thence conducted me, in silence, through many dark and intricate passages in my progress to the *studio* of his master. Much that I encountered on the way contributed, I know not how, to heighten the vague sentiments of which I have already spoken. While the objects around me—while the carvings of the ceilings, the sombre tapestries of the walls, the ebon blackness of the floors, and the phantasmagoric armorial trophies which rattled as I strode, were but matters to which, or to such as which, I had been accustomed from my infancy—while I hesitated not to acknowledge how familiar was all this—I still wondered to find how unfamiliar were the fancies which ordinary images were stirring up. On one of the staircases, I met the physician of the family. His countenance, I thought, wore a mingled expression of low cunning and perplexity. He accosted me with trepidation and passed on. The valet now threw open a door and ushered me into the presence of his master.

The room in which I found myself was very large and lofty. The windows were long, narrow, and pointed, and at so vast a distance from the black oaken floor as to be altogether inaccessible from within. Feeble gleams of encrimsoned light made their way through the trellissed panes, and served to render sufficiently distinct the more prominent objects around; the eye, however, struggled in vain to reach the remoter angles of the chamber, or the recesses of the vaulted and fretted ceiling. Dark draperies hung upon the walls. The general furniture was profuse, comfortless, antique, and tattered. Many books and musical instruments lay scattered about, but failed to give any vitality to the scene. I felt that I breathed an atmosphere of sorrow. An air of stern, deep, and irredeemable gloom hung over and pervaded all.

Upon my entrance, Usher arose from a sofa on which he had been lying at full length, and greeted me with a vivacious warmth which had much in it, I at first thought, of an overdone cordiality—of the constrained effort of the *ennuyé* man of the world. A glance, however, at his countenance, convinced me of his perfect sincerity. We sat down; and for some moments, while he spoke not, I gazed upon him with a feeling half of pity, half of awe. Surely, man had never before so terribly altered, in so brief a period, as had Roderick Usher! It was with difficulty that I could bring myself to admit the identity of the wan being before me with the companion of my early boyhood. Yet the character of his face had been at all times remarkable. A cadaverousness of complexion; an eye large, liquid, and luminous beyond comparison; lips somewhat thin and very pallid, but of a surpassingly beautiful curve; a nose of a delicate Hebrew model, but with a breadth of nostril unusual in similar formations; a finely moulded chin, speaking, in its want of prominence, of a want of moral energy; hair of a more than web-like softness and tenuity; these features, with an inordinate expansion above the regions of the temple, made up altogether a countenance not easily to be forgotten. And now in the mere exaggeration of the prevailing character of these features, and of the expression they were wont to convey, lay so much of change that I doubted to whom I spoke. The now ghastly pallor of the skin, and the now miraculous lustre of the eye, above all things startled and even awed me. The silken hair, too, had been suffered to grow all unheeded, and as, in its wild gossamer texture, it floated rather than fell about the face, I could not, even with effort, connect its Arabesque expression with any idea of simple humanity.

In the manner of my friend I was at once struck with an incoherence—an inconsistency; and I soon found this to arise from a series of feeble and futile struggles to overcome an habitual trepidancy—an excessive nervous agitation. For something of this nature I had indeed been prepared, no less by his letter, than by reminiscences of certain boyish traits, and by conclusions deduced from his peculiar physical conformation and temperament. His action was alternately vivacious and sullen. His voice varied rapidly from a tremulous indecision (when the animal

spirits seemed utterly in abeyance) to that species of energetic concision—that abrupt, weighty, unhurried, and hollow-sounding enunciation—that leaden, self-balanced and perfectly modulated guttural utterance, which may be observed in the lost drunkard, or the irreclaimable
eater of opium, during the periods of his most intense excitement.

It was thus that he spoke of the object of my visit, of his earnest
desire to see me, and of the solace he expected me to afford him. He
entered, at some length, into what he conceived to be the nature of his
malady. It was, he said, a constitutional and a family evil, and one for
which he despaired to find a remedy—a mere nervous affection, he
immediately added, which would undoubtedly soon pass off. It displayed itself in a host of unnatural sensations. Some of these, as he
detailed them, interested and bewildered me; although, perhaps, the
terms, and the general manner of the narration had their weight. He
suffered much from a morbid acuteness of the senses; the most insipid
food was alone endurable; he could wear only garments of certain texture; the odors of all flowers were oppressive; his eyes were tortured by
even a faint light; and there were but peculiar sounds, and these from
stringed instruments, which did not inspire him with horror.

To an anomalous species of terror I found him a bounden slave. "I
shall perish," said he, "I *must* perish in this deplorable folly. Thus, thus,
and not otherwise, shall I be lost. I dread the events of the future, not in
themselves, but in their results. I shudder at the thought of any, even the
most trivial, incident, which may operate upon this intolerable agitation
of soul. I have, indeed, no abhorrence of danger, except in its absolute
effect—in terror. In this unnerved—in this pitiable condition—I feel
that the period will sooner or later arrive when I must abandon life and
reason together, in some struggle with the grim phantasm, FEAR."

I learned, moreover, at intervals, and through broken and equivocal hints, another singular feature of his mental condition. He was
enchained by certain superstitious impressions in regard to the dwelling
which he tenanted, and whence, for many years, he had never ventured
forth—in regard to an influence whose supposititious force was conveyed in terms too shadowy here to be re-stated—an influence which
some peculiarities in the mere form and substance of his family mansion, had, by dint of long sufferance, he said, obtained over his
spirit—an effect which the *physique* of the gray walls and turrets, and of
the dim tarn into which they all looked down, had, at length, brought
about upon the *morale* of his existence.

He admitted, however, although with hesitation, that much of the
peculiar gloom which thus afflicted him could be traced to a more

natural and far more palpable origin—to the severe and long-continued illness—indeed to the evidently approaching dissolution—of a tenderly beloved sister—his sole companion for long years—his last and only relative on earth. "Her decease," he said, with a bitterness which I can never forget, "would leave him (him the hopeless and the frail) the last of the ancient race of the Ushers." While he spoke, the lady Madeline (for so was she called) passed slowly through a remote portion of the apartment, and, without having noticed my presence, disappeared. I regarded her with an utter astonishment not unmingled with dread— and yet I found it impossible to account for such feelings. A sensation of stupor oppressed me, as my eyes followed her retreating steps. When a door, at length, closed upon her, my glance sought instinctively and eagerly the countenance of the brother—but he had buried his face in his hands, and I could only perceive that a far more than ordinary wanness had overspread the emaciated fingers through which trickled many passionate tears.

The disease of the lady Madeline had long baffled the skill of her physicians. A settled apathy, a gradual wasting away of the person, and frequent although transient affections of a partially cataleptical character, were the unusual diagnosis. Hitherto she had steadily borne up against the pressure of her malady, and had not betaken herself finally to bed; but, on the closing in of the evening of my arrival at the house, she succumbed (as her brother told me at night with inexpressible agitation) to the prostrating power of the destroyer; and I learned that the glimpse I had obtained of her person would thus probably be the last I should obtain—that the lady, at least while living, would be seen by me no more.

For several days ensuing, her name was unmentioned by either Usher or myself: and during this period I was busied in earnest endeavors to alleviate the melancholy of my friend. We painted and read together; or I listened, as if in a dream, to the wild improvisations of his speaking guitar. And thus, as a closer and still closer intimacy admitted me more unreservedly into the recesses of his spirit, the more bitterly did I perceive the futility of all attempt at cheering a mind from which darkness, as if an inherent positive quality, poured forth upon all objects of the moral and physical universe, in one unceasing radiation of gloom.

I shall ever bear about me a memory of the many solemn hours I thus spent alone with the master of the House of Usher. Yet I should fail in any attempt to convey an idea of the exact character of the studies, or of the occupations, in which he involved me, or led me the way. An excited and highly distempered ideality threw a sulphureous lustre over all. His long improvised dirges will ring forever in my ears. Among other things, I hold painfully in mind a certain singular perversion and amplification of the wild air of the last waltz of Von Weber.° From the paintings over which his elaborate fancy brooded, and which grew, touch by touch, into vaguenesses at which I shuddered the more thrillingly, because I shuddered knowing not why;—from these paintings (vivid as their images now are before me) I would in vain endeavor to educe more than a small portion which should lie within the compass of merely written words. By the utter simplicity, by the nakedness of his designs, he arrested and overawed attention. If ever mortal painted an idea, that mortal was Roderick Usher. For me at least—in the circumstances then surrounding me—there arose out of the pure abstractions which the hypochondriac contrived to throw upon his canvass, an intensity of intolerable awe, no shadow of which felt I ever yet in the contemplation of the certainly glowing yet too concrete reveries of Fuseli.°

One of the phantasmagoric conceptions of my friend, partaking not so rigidly of the spirit of abstraction, may be shadowed forth, although feebly, in words. A small picture presented the interior of an immensely long and rectangular vault or tunnel, with low walls, smooth, white, and without interruption or device. Certain accessory points of the design served well to convey the idea that this excavation lay at an exceeding depth below the surface of the earth. No outlet was observed in any portion of its vast extent, and no torch, or other artificial source of light was discernible; yet a flood of intense rays rolled throughout, and bathed the whole in a ghastly and inappropriate splendor.

I have just spoken of that morbid condition of the auditory nerve which rendered all music intolerable to the sufferer, with the exception of certain effects of stringed instruments. It was, perhaps, the narrow limits to which he thus confined himself upon the guitar, which gave birth, in great measure, to the fantastic character of his performances. But the fervid *facility* of his *impromptus* could not be so accounted for. They must have been, and were, in the notes, as well as in the words of his wild fantasias (for he not unfrequently accompanied himself with rhymed verbal improvisations), the result of that intense mental collectedness and concentration to which I have previously alluded as observable only in particular moments of the highest artificial excitement. The words of one of these rhapsodies I easily remembered. I was, perhaps, the more forcibly impressed with it, as he gave it,

---

Von Weber: Carl Maria von Weber (1786–1826), a German Romantic composer and musician.   ***Fuseli:*** Swiss painter Henry Fuseli (1741–1825).

because, in the under or mystic current of its meaning, I fancied that I perceived, and for the first time, a full consciousness on the part of Usher, of the tottering of his lofty reason upon her throne. The verses, which were entitled "The Haunted Palace," ran very nearly, if not accurately, thus:

I

In the greenest of our valleys,
   By good angels tenanted,
Once a fair and stately palace —
   Radiant palace — reared its head.
In the monarch Thought's dominion —
   It stood there!
Never seraph spread a pinion
   Over fabric half so fair.

II

Banners yellow, glorious, golden,
   On its roof did float and flow;
(This — all this — was in the olden
   Time long ago)
And every gentle air that dallied,
   In that sweet day,
Along the ramparts plumed and pallid,
   A winged odor went away.

III

Wanderers in that happy valley
   Through two luminous windows saw
Spirits moving musically
   To a lute's well-tunéd law,
Round about a throne, where sitting
   (Porphyrogene!°)
In state his glory well befitting,
   The ruler of the realm was seen.

IV

And all with pearl and ruby glowing
   Was the fair palace door,

Porphyrogene: A neologism created by Poe.

Through which came flowing, flowing, flowing,
    And sparkling evermore,
A troop of Echoes whose sweet duty
    Was but to sing,
In voices of surpassing beauty,
    The wit and wisdom of their king.

V

But evil things, in robes of sorrow,
    Assailed the monarch's high estate;
(Ah, let us mourn, for never morrow
    Shall dawn upon him, desolate!)
And, round about his home, the glory
    That blushed and bloomed
Is but a dim-remembered story
    Of the old time entombed.

VI

And travellers now within that valley,
    Through the red-litten windows, see
Vast forms that move fantastically
    To a discordant melody;
While, like a rapid ghastly river,
    Through the pale door,
A hideous throng rush out forever,
    And laugh—but smile no more.

I well remember that suggestions arising from this ballad, led us into a train of thought wherein there became manifest an opinion of Usher's which I mention not so much on account of its novelty, (for other men° have thought thus,) as on account of the pertinacity with which he maintained it. This opinion, in its general form, was that of the sentience of all vegetable things. But, in his disordered fancy, the idea had assumed a more daring character, and trespassed, under certain conditions, upon the kingdom of inorganization. I lack words to express the full extent, or the earnest *abandon* of his persuasion. The belief, however, was connected (as I have previously hinted) with the gray stones of the home of his forefathers. The conditions of the sentience had been here, he imagined, fulfilled in the method of collocation of these stones—in the

for other men: Watson, Dr. Percival, Spallanzani, and especially the Bishop of Landaff.—
See "Chemical Essays," vol v. [Poe's note.]

order of their arrangement, as well as in that of the many *fungi* which overspread them, and of the decayed trees which stood around—above all, in the long undisturbed endurance of this arrangement, and in its reduplication in the still waters of the tarn. Its evidence—the evidence of the sentience—was to be seen, he said, (and I here started as he spoke,) in the gradual yet certain condensation of an atmosphere of their own about the waters and the walls. The result was discoverable, he added, in that silent, yet importunate and terrible influence which for centuries had moulded the destinies of his family, and which made *him* what I now saw him—what he was. Such opinions need no comment, and I will make none.

Our books—the books which, for years, had formed no small portion of the mental existence of the invalid—were, as might be supposed, in strict keeping with this character of phantasm. We pored together over such works as the Ververt et Chartreuse of Gresset; the Belphegor of Machiavelli; the Heaven and Hell of Swedenborg; the Subterranean Voyage of Nicholas Klimm by Holberg; the Chiromancy of Robert Flud, of Jean D'Indaginé, and of De la Chambre; the Journey into the Blue Distance of Tieck; and the City of the Sun of Campanella. One favorite volume was a small octavo edition of the *Directorium Inquisitorium*, by the Dominican Eymeric de Gironne; and there were passages in Pomponius Mela, about the old African Satyrs and OEgipans, over which Usher would sit dreaming for hours. His chief delight, however, was found in the perusal of an exceedingly rare and curious book in quarto Gothic—the manual of a forgotten church—the *Vigiliae Mortuorum secundum Chorum Ecclesiae Maguntinae.*°

I could not help thinking of the wild ritual of this work, and of its probable influence upon the hypochondriac, when, one evening, having informed me abruptly that the lady Madeline was no more, he stated his intention of preserving her corpse for a fortnight, (previously to its final interment,) in one of the numerous vaults within the main walls of the building. The worldly reason, however, assigned for this singular proceeding, was one which I did not feel at liberty to dispute. The brother had been led to his resolution (so he told me) by consideration of the unusual character of the malady of the deceased, of certain obtrusive and eager inquiries on the part of her medical men, and of the remote and exposed situation of the burial-ground of the family. I will not deny that when I called to mind the sinister countenance of

---

Vigiliae . . . Maguntinae: Vigils for the Dead according to the Church of Mainz.

the person whom I met upon the staircase, on the day of my arrival at the house, I had no desire to oppose what I regarded as at best but a harmless, and by no means an unnatural, precaution.

At the request of Usher, I personally aided him in the arrangements for the temporary entombment. The body having been encoffined, we two alone bore it to its rest. The vault in which we placed it (and which had been so long unopened that our torches, half smothered in its oppressive atmosphere, gave us little opportunity for investigation) was small, damp, and entirely without means of admission for light; lying, at great depth, immediately beneath that portion of the building in which was my own sleeping apartment. It had been used, apparently, in remote feudal times, for the worst purposes of a donjon°-keep, and, in later days, as a place of deposit for powder, or some other highly combustible substance, as a portion of its floor, and the whole interior of a long archway through which we reached it, were carefully sheathed with copper. The door, of massive iron, had been, also, similarly protected. Its immense weight caused an unusually sharp grating sound, as it moved upon its hinges.

Having deposited our mournful burden upon tressels within this region of horror, we partially turned aside the yet unscrewed lid of the coffin, and looked upon the face of the tenant. A striking similitude between the brother and sister now first arrested my attention; and Usher, divining, perhaps, my thoughts, murmured out some few words from which I learned that the deceased and himself had been twins, and that sympathies of a scarcely intelligible nature had always existed between them. Our glances, however, rested not long upon the dead—for we could not regard her unawed. The disease which had thus entombed the lady in the maturity of youth, had left, as usual in all maladies of a strictly cataleptical character, the mockery of a faint blush upon the bosom and the face, and that suspiciously lingering smile upon the lip which is so terrible in death. We replaced and screwed down the lid, and, having secured the door of iron, made our way, with toil, into the scarcely less gloomy apartments of the upper portion of the house.

And now, some days of bitter grief having elapsed, an observable change came over the features of the mental disorder of my friend. His ordinary manner had vanished. His ordinary occupations were neglected or forgotten. He roamed from chamber to chamber with hurried, unequal, and objectless step. The pallor of his countenance had assumed, if possible, a more ghastly hue—but the luminousness of his eye had

donjon: Archaic spelling of dungeon.

utterly gone out. The once occasional huskiness of his tone was heard no more; and a tremulous quaver, as if of extreme terror, habitually characterized his utterance. There were times, indeed, when I thought his unceasingly agitated mind was laboring with some oppressive secret, to divulge which he struggled for the necessary courage. At times, again, I was obliged to resolve all into the mere inexplicable vagaries of madness, for I beheld him gazing upon vacancy for long hours, in an attitude of the profoundest attention, as if listening to some imaginary sound. It was no wonder that his condition terrified—that it infected me. I felt creeping upon me, by slow yet certain degrees, the wild influences of his own fantastic yet impressive superstitions.

It was, especially, upon retiring to bed late in the night of the seventh or eighth day after the placing of the lady Madeline within the donjon, that I experienced the full power of such feelings. Sleep came not near my couch—while the hours waned and waned away. I struggled to reason off the nervousness which had dominion over me. I endeavored to believe that much, if not all of what I felt, was due to the bewildering influence of the gloomy furniture of the room—of the dark and tattered draperies, which, tortured into motion by the breath of a rising tempest, swayed fitfully to and fro upon the walls, and rustled uneasily about the decorations of the bed. But my efforts were fruitless. An irrepressible tremor gradually pervaded my frame; and, at length, there sat upon my very heart an incubus of utterly causeless alarm. Shaking this off with a gasp and a struggle, I uplifted myself upon the pillows, and, peering earnestly within the intense darkness of the chamber, harkened—I know not why, except that an instinctive spirit prompted me—to certain low and indefinite sounds which came, through the pauses of the storm, at long intervals, I knew not whence. Overpowered by an intense sentiment of horror, unaccountable yet unendurable, I threw on my clothes with haste (for I felt that I should sleep no more during the night), and endeavored to arouse myself from the pitiable condition into which I had fallen, by pacing rapidly to and fro through the apartment.

I had taken but few turns in this manner, when a light step on an adjoining staircase arrested my attention. I presently recognised it as that of Usher. In an instant afterward he rapped, with a gentle touch, at my door, and entered, bearing a lamp. His countenance was, as usual, cadaverously wan—but, moreover, there was a species of mad hilarity in his eyes—an evidently restrained *hysteria* in his whole demeanor. His air appalled me—but anything was preferable to the solitude which I had so long endured, and I even welcomed his presence as a relief.

"And you have not seen it?" he said abruptly, after having stared about him for some moments in silence—"you have not then seen it?—but, stay! you shall." Thus speaking, and having carefully shaded his lamp, he hurried to one of the casements, and threw it freely open to the storm.

The impetuous fury of the entering gust nearly lifted us from our feet. It was, indeed, a tempestuous yet sternly beautiful night, and one wildly singular in its terror and its beauty. A whirlwind had apparently collected its force in our vicinity; for there were frequent and violent alterations in the direction of the wind; and the exceeding density of the clouds (which hung so low as to press upon the turrets of the house) did not prevent our perceiving the life-like velocity with which they flew careering from all points against each other, without passing away into the distance. I say that even their exceeding density did not prevent our perceiving this—yet we had no glimpse of the moon or stars—nor was there any flashing forth of the lightning. But the under surfaces of the huge masses of agitated vapor, as well as all terrestrial objects immediately around us, were glowing in the unnatural light of a faintly luminous and distinctly visible gaseous exhalation which hung about and enshrouded the mansion.

"You must not—you shall not behold this!" said I, shudderingly, to Usher, as I led him, with a gentle violence, from the window to a seat. "These appearances, which bewilder you, are merely electrical phenomena not uncommon—or it may be that they have their ghastly origin in the rank miasma of the tarn. Let us close this casement;—the air is chilling and dangerous to your frame. Here is one of your favorite romances. I will read, and you shall listen;—and so we will pass away this terrible night together."

The antique volume which I had taken up was the "Mad Trist" of Sir Launcelot Canning; but I had called it a favorite of Usher's more in sad jest than in earnest; for, in truth, there is little in its uncouth and unimaginative prolixity which could have had interest for the lofty and spiritual ideality of my friend. It was, however, the only book immediately at hand; and I indulged a vague hope that the excitement which now agitated the hypochondriac, might find relief (for the history of mental disorder is full of similar anomalies) even in the extremeness of the folly which I should read. Could I have judged, indeed, by the wild overstrained air of vivacity with which he harkened, or apparently harkened, to the words of the tale, I might well have congratulated myself upon the success of my design.

I had arrived at that well-known portion of the story where Ethel-red, the hero of the Trist, having sought in vain for peaceable admission into the dwelling of the hermit, proceeds to make good an entrance by force. Here, it will be remembered, the words of the narrative run thus:

"And Ethelred, who was by nature of a doughty heart, and who was now mighty withal, on account of the powerfulness of the wine which he had drunken, waited no longer to hold parley with the hermit, who, in sooth, was of an obstinate and maliceful turn, but, feeling the rain upon his shoulders, and fearing the rising of the tempest, uplifted his mace outright, and, with blows, made quickly room in the plankings of the door for his gauntleted hand; and now pulling therewith sturdily, he so cracked, and ripped, and tore all asunder, that the noise of the dry and hollow-sounding wood alarummed and reverberated throughout the forest."

At the termination of this sentence I started, and for a moment, paused; for it appeared to me (although I at once concluded that my excited fancy had deceived me)—it appeared to me that, from some very remote portion of the mansion, there came, indistinctly, to my ears, what might have been, in its exact similarity of character, the echo (but a stifled and dull one certainly) of the very cracking and ripping sound which Sir Launcelot had so particularly described. It was, beyond doubt, the coincidence alone which had arrested my attention; for, amid the rattling of the sashes of the casements, and the ordinary commingled noises of the still increasing storm, the sound, in itself, had nothing, surely, which should have interested or disturbed me. I continued the story:

"But the good champion Ethelred, now entering within the door, was sore enraged and amazed to perceive no signal of the maliceful hermit; but, in the stead thereof, a dragon of a scaly and prodigious demeanor, and of a fiery tongue, which sate in guard before a palace of gold, with a floor of silver; and upon the wall there hung a shield of shining brass with this legend enwritten—

Who entereth herein, a conqueror hath bin;
Who slayeth the dragon, the shield he shall win;

And Ethelred uplifted his mace, and struck upon the head of the dragon, which fell before him, and gave up his pesty breath, with a shriek so horrid and harsh, and withal so piercing, that Ethelred had fain to close his ears with his hands against the dreadful noise of it, the like whereof was never before heard."

Here again I paused abruptly, and now with a feeling of wild amazement—for there could be no doubt whatever that, in this instance, I
did actually hear (although from what direction it proceeded I found it
impossible to say) a low and apparently distant, but harsh, protracted,
and most unusual screaming or grating sound—the exact counterpart
of what my fancy had already conjured up for the dragon's unnatural
shriek as described by the romancer.

Oppressed, as I certainly was, upon the occurrence of this second
and most extraordinary coincidence, by a thousand conflicting sensations, in which wonder and extreme terror were predominant, I still
retained sufficient presence of mind to avoid exciting, by any observation, the sensitive nervousness of my companion. I was by no means
certain that he had noticed the sounds in question; although, assuredly,
a strange alteration had, during the last few minutes, taken place in his
demeanor. From a position fronting my own, he had gradually brought
round his chair, so as to sit with his face to the door of the chamber; and
thus I could but partially perceive his features, although I saw that his
lips trembled as if he were murmuring inaudibly. His head had dropped
upon his breast—yet I knew that he was not asleep, from the wide and
rigid opening of the eye as I caught a glance of it in profile. The motion
of his body, too, was at variance with this idea—for he rocked from side
to side with a gentle yet constant and uniform sway. Having rapidly
taken notice of all this, I resumed the narrative of Sir Launcelot, which
thus proceeded:

"And now, the champion, having escaped from the terrible fury of
the dragon, bethinking himself of the brazen shield, and of the breaking
up of the enchantment which was upon it, removed the carcass from out
of the way before him, and approached valorously over the silver pavement of the castle to where the shield was upon the wall; which in sooth
tarried not for his full coming, but fell down at his feet upon the silver
floor, with a mighty great and terrible ringing sound."

No sooner had these syllables passed my lips, than—as if a shield of
brass had indeed, at the moment, fallen heavily upon a floor of silver—I became aware of a distinct, hollow, metallic, and clangorous, yet
apparently muffled reverberation. Completely unnerved, I leaped to my
feet; but the measured rocking movement of Usher was undisturbed. I
rushed to the chair in which he sat. His eyes were bent fixedly before
him, and throughout his whole countenance there reigned a stony
rigidity. But, as I placed my hand upon his shoulder, there came a
strong shudder over his whole person; a sickly smile quivered about his
lips; and I saw that he spoke in a low, hurried, and gibbering murmur,

as if unconscious of my presence. Bending closely over him, I at length drank in the hideous import of his words.

"Not hear it?—yes, I hear it, and *have* heard it. Long—long—long—many minutes, many hours, many days, have I heard it—yet I dared not—oh, pity me, miserable wretch that I am!—I dared not—I *dared* not speak! *We have put her living in the tomb!* Said I not that my senses were acute? I *now* tell you that I heard her first feeble movements in the hollow coffin. I heard them—many, many days ago—yet I dared not—*I dared not speak!* And now—to-night—Ethelred—ha! ha!—the breaking of the hermit's door, and the death-cry of the dragon, and the clangor of the shield!—say, rather, the rending of her coffin, and the grating of the iron hinges of her prison, and her struggles within the coppered archway of the vault! Oh whither shall I fly? Will she not be here anon? Is she not hurrying to upbraid me for my haste? Have I not heard her footstep on the stair? Do I not distinguish that heavy and horrible beating of her heart? Madman!"—here he sprang furiously to his feet, and shrieked out his syllables, as if in the effort he were giving up his soul—"*Madman! I tell you that she now stands without the door!*"

As if in the superhuman energy of his utterance there had been found the potency of a spell—the huge antique pannels to which the speaker pointed, threw slowly back, upon the instant, their ponderous and ebony jaws. It was the work of the rushing gust—but then without those doors there *did* stand the lofty and enshrouded figure of the lady Madeline of Usher. There was blood upon her white robes, and the evidence of some bitter struggle upon every portion of her emaciated frame. For a moment she remained trembling and reeling to and fro upon the threshold—then, with a low moaning cry, fell heavily inward upon the person of her brother, and in her violent and now final death-agonies, bore him to the floor a corpse, and a victim to the terrors he had anticipated.

From that chamber, and from that mansion, I fled aghast. The storm was still abroad in all its wrath as I found myself crossing the old causeway. Suddenly there shot along the path a wild light, and I turned to see whence a gleam so unusual could have issued; for the vast house and its shadows were alone behind me. The radiance was that of the full, setting, and blood-red moon, which now shone vividly through that once barely-discernible fissure, of which I have before spoken as extending from the roof of the building, in a zigzag direction, to the base. While I gazed, this fissure rapidly widened—there came a fierce breath of the whirlwind—the entire orb of the satellite burst at once upon my sight—my brain reeled as I saw the mighty walls rushing asunder—there was a long tumultuous shouting sound like the voice of a thousand waters—and the deep and dank tarn at my feet closed sullenly and silently over the fragments of the "House of Usher."

William Wilson

> What say of it? what say CONSCIENCE grim,
> That spectre in my path?
>
> —CHAMBERLAIN'S *PHARRONIDA*°

Let me call myself, for the present, William Wilson. The fair page now lying before me need not be sullied with my real appellation. This has been already too much an object for the scorn—for the horror—for the detestation of my race. To the uttermost regions of the globe have not the indignant winds bruited its unparalleled infamy? Oh, outcast of all outcasts most abandoned!—to the earth art thou not forever dead? to its honors, to its flowers, to its golden aspirations?—and a cloud, dense, dismal, and limitless, does it not hang eternally between thy hopes and heaven?

I would not, if I could, here or to-day, embody a record of my later years of unspeakable misery, and unpardonable crime. This epoch—these later years—took unto themselves a sudden elevation in turpitude, whose origin alone it is my present purpose to assign. Men usually grow base by degrees. From me, in an instant, all virtue dropped bodily as a mantle. From comparatively trivial wickedness I passed, with the stride of a giant, into more than the enormities of an Elah-Gabalus.° What chance—what one event brought this evil thing to pass, bear with me while I relate. Death approaches; and the shadow which foreruns him has thrown a softening influence over my spirit. I long, in passing through the dim valley, for the sympathy—I had nearly said for the pity—of my fellow men. I would fain have them believe that I have been, in some measure, the slave of circumstances beyond human control. I would wish them to seek out for me, in the details I am about to give, some little oasis of *fatality* amid a wilderness of error. I would have them allow—what they cannot refrain from allowing—that, although temptation may have erewhile existed as great, man was never

---

Pharronida: Poe references William Chamberlayne's poem *Pharonnida* (1659), although the passage is not located in the work.   *Elah-Gabalus:* Roman emperor Elagabalus who ruled from 218 to 222.

thus, at least, tempted before — certainly, never *thus* fell. And is it therefore that he has never thus suffered? Have I not indeed been living in a
dream? And am I not now dying a victim to the horror and the mystery
of the wildest of all sublunary visions?

I am the descendant of a race whose imaginative and easily excitable
temperament has at all times rendered them remarkable; and, in my
earliest infancy, I gave evidence of having fully inherited the family character. As I advanced in years it was more strongly developed; becoming,
for many reasons, a cause of serious disquietude to my friends, and of
positive injury to myself. I grew self-willed, addicted to the wildest ca-
prices, and a prey to the most ungovernable passions. Weak-minded,
and beset with constitutional infirmities akin to my own, my parents
could do but little to check the evil propensities which distinguished me.
Some feeble and ill-directed efforts resulted in complete failure on their
part, and, of course, in total triumph on mine. Thenceforward my voice
was a household law; and at an age when few children have abandoned
their leading-strings, I was left to the guidance of my own will, and became, in all but name, the master of my own actions.

My earliest recollections of a school-life, are connected with a large,
rambling, Elizabethan house, in a misty-looking village of England,
where were a vast number of gigantic and gnarled trees, and where all
the houses were excessively ancient. In truth, it was a dream-like and
spirit-soothing place, that venerable old town. At this moment, in fancy,
I feel the refreshing chilliness of its deeply-shadowed avenues, inhale
the fragrance of its thousand shrubberies, and thrill anew with undefin-
able delight, at the deep hollow note of the church-bell, breaking, each
hour, with sullen and sudden roar, upon the stillness of the dusky atmosphere in which the fretted Gothic steeple lay imbedded and asleep.

It gives me, perhaps, as much of pleasure as I can now in any manner experience, to dwell upon minute recollections of the school and its
concerns. Steeped in misery as I am — misery, alas! only too real — I
shall be pardoned for seeking relief, however slight and temporary, in
the weakness of a few rambling details. These, moreover, utterly trivial,
and even ridiculous in themselves, assume, to my fancy, adventitious
importance, as connected with a period and a locality when and where
I recognise the first ambiguous monitions of the destiny which afterwards so fully overshadowed me. Let me then remember.

The house, I have said, was old and irregular. The grounds were
extensive, and a high and solid brick wall, topped with a bed of mortar
and broken glass, encompassed the whole. This prison-like rampart
formed the limit of our domain; beyond it we saw but thrice a week—

once every Saturday afternoon, when, attended by two ushers, we were permitted to take brief walks in a body through some of the neighbouring fields—and twice during Sunday, when we were paraded in the same formal manner to the morning and evening service in the one church of the village. Of this church the principal of our school was pastor. With how deep a spirit of wonder and perplexity was I wont to regard him from our remote pew in the gallery, as, with step solemn and slow, he ascended the pulpit! This reverend man, with countenance so demurely benign, with robes so glossy and so clerically flowing, with wig so minutely powdered, so rigid and so vast,—could this be he who, of late, with sour visage, and in snuffy habiliments, administered, ferule in hand, the Draconian laws of the academy? Oh, gigantic paradox, too utterly monstrous for solution!

At an angle of the ponderous wall frowned a more ponderous gate. It was riveted and studded with iron bolts, and surmounted with jagged iron spikes. What impressions of deep awe did it inspire! It was never opened save for the three periodical egressions and ingressions already mentioned; then, in every creak of its mighty hinges, we found a plenitude of mystery—a world of matter for solemn remark, or for more solemn meditation.

The extensive enclosure was irregular in form, having many capacious recesses. Of these, three or four of the largest constituted the play-ground. It was level, and covered with fine hard gravel. I well remember it had no trees, nor benches, nor anything similar within it. Of course it was in the rear of the house. In front lay a small parterre, planted with box and other shrubs; but through this sacred division we passed only upon rare occasions indeed—such as a first advent to school or final departure thence, or perhaps, when a parent or friend having called for us, we joyfully took our way home for the Christmas or Midsummer holy-days.

But the house!—how quaint an old building was this!—to me how veritably a palace of enchantment! There was really no end to its windings—to its incomprehensible subdivisions. It was difficult, at any given time, to say with certainty upon which of its two stories one happened to be. From each room to every other there were sure to be found three or four steps either in ascent or descent. Then the lateral branches were innumerable—inconceivable—and so returning in upon themselves, that our most exact ideas in regard to the whole mansion were not very far different from those with which we pondered upon infinity. During the five years of my residence here, I was never able to ascertain with precision, in what remote locality lay the little sleeping apartment assigned to myself and some eighteen or twenty other scholars.

The school-room was the largest in the house—I could not help thinking, in the world. It was very long, narrow, and dismally low, with pointed Gothic windows and a ceiling of oak. In a remote and terror-inspiring angle was a square enclosure of eight or ten feet, comprising the *sanctum*, "during hours," of our principal, the Reverend Dr. Bransby. It was a solid structure, with massy door, sooner than open which in the absence of the "Dominie," we would all have willingly perished by the *peine forte et dure.*° In other angles were two other similar boxes, far less reverenced, indeed, but still greatly matters of awe. One of these was the pulpit of the "classical" usher, one of the "English and mathematical." Interspersed about the room, crossing and re-crossing in endless irregularity, were innumerable benches and desks, black, ancient, and time-worn, piled desperately with much-bethumbed books, and so beseamed with initial letters, names at full length, grotesque figures, and other multiplied efforts of the knife, as to have entirely lost what little of original form might have been their portion in days long departed. A huge bucket with water stood at one extremity of the room, and a clock of stupendous dimensions at the other.

Encompassed by the massy walls of this venerable academy, I passed, yet not in tedium or disgust, the years of the third lustrum° of my life. The teeming brain of childhood requires no external world of incident to occupy or amuse it; and the apparently dismal monotony of a school was replete with more intense excitement than my riper youth has derived from luxury, or my full manhood from crime. Yet I must believe that my first mental development had in it much of the uncommon—even much of the *outré*. Upon mankind at large the events of very early existence rarely leave in mature age any definite impression. All is gray shadow—a weak and irregular remembrance—an indistinct regathering of feeble pleasures and phantasmagoric pains. With me this is not so. In childhood I must have felt with the energy of a man what I now find stamped upon memory in lines as vivid, as deep, and as durable as the *exergues* of the Carthaginian medals.

Yet in fact—in the fact of the world's view—how little was there to remember! The morning's awakening, the nightly summons to bed; the connings, the recitations; the periodical half-holidays, and peram-

---

peine forte et dure: Hard and forceful punishment. The term refers to physical torture in which the subject is slowly crushed to death.   *lustrum:* A period of five years.

bulations; the play-ground, with its broils, its pastimes, its intrigues;—
these, by a mental sorcery long forgotten, were made to involve a wilderness of sensation, a world of rich incident, an universe of varied
emotion, of excitement the most passionate and spirit-stirring. *"Oh, le
bon temps, que ce siecle de fer!"*°

In truth, the ardor, the enthusiasm, and the imperiousness of my
disposition, soon rendered me a marked character among my schoolmates, and by slow, but natural gradations, gave me an ascendancy over
all not greatly older than myself;—over all with a single exception. This
exception was found in the person of a scholar, who, although no relation, bore the same Christian and surname as myself;—a circumstance,
in fact, little remarkable; for, notwithstanding a noble descent, mine
was one of those every-day appellations which seem, by prescriptive
right, to have been, time out of mind, the common property of the
mob. In this narrative I have therefore designated myself as William Wilson,—a fictitious title not very dissimilar to the real. My namesake alone,
of those who in school-phraseology constituted "our set," presumed to
compete with me in the studies of the class—in the sports and broils of
the play-ground—to refuse implicit belief in my assertions, and submission to my will—indeed, to interfere with my arbitrary dictation in any
respect whatsoever. If there is on earth a supreme and unqualified despotism, it is the despotism of a master mind in boyhood over the less energetic spirits of its companions.

Wilson's rebellion was to me a source of the greatest embarrassment;—the more so as, in spite of the bravado with which in public I
made a point of treating him and his pretensions, I secretly felt that I
feared him, and could not help thinking the equality which he maintained so easily with myself, a proof of his true superiority; since not to
be overcome cost me a perpetual struggle. Yet this superiority—even
this equality—was in truth acknowledged by no one but myself; our
associates, by some unaccountable blindness, seemed not even to suspect it. Indeed, his competition, his resistance, and especially his impertinent and dogged interference with my purposes, were not more
pointed than private. He appeared to be destitute alike of the ambition
which urged, and of the passionate energy of mind which enabled me
to excel. In his rivalry he might have been supposed actuated solely
by a whimsical desire to thwart, astonish, or mortify myself; although
there were times when I could not help observing, with a feeling made

Oh, le bon . . . de fer!: Oh those good times, it was the age of iron!

up of wonder, abasement, and pique, that he mingled with his injuries, his insults, or his contradictions, a certain most inappropriate, and assuredly most unwelcome *affectionateness* of manner. I could only conceive this singular behavior to arise from a consummate self-conceit assuming the vulgar airs of patronage and protection.

Perhaps it was this latter trait in Wilson's conduct, conjoined with our identity of name, and the mere accident of our having entered the school upon the same day, which set afloat the notion that we were brothers, among the senior classes in the academy. These do not usually inquire with much strictness into the affairs of their juniors. I have before said, or should have said, that Wilson was not, in the most remote degree, connected with my family. But assuredly if we *had* been brothers we must have been twins; for, after leaving Dr. Bransby's, I casually learned that my namesake was born on the nineteenth of January, 1813—and this is a somewhat remarkable coincidence; for the day is precisely that of my own nativity.

It may seem strange that in spite of the continual anxiety occasioned me by the rivalry of Wilson, and his intolerable spirit of contradiction, I could not bring myself to hate him altogether. We had, to be sure, nearly every day a quarrel in which, yielding me publicly the palm of victory, he, in some manner, contrived to make me feel that it was he who had deserved it; yet a sense of pride on my part, and a veritable dignity on his own, kept us always upon what are called "speaking terms," while there were many points of strong congeniality in our tempers, operating to awake in me a sentiment which our position alone, perhaps, prevented from ripening into friendship. It is difficult, indeed, to define, or even to describe, my real feelings towards him. They formed a motley and heterogeneous admixture;—some petulant animosity, which was not yet hatred, some esteem, more respect, much fear, with a world of uneasy curiosity. To the moralist it will be unnecessary to say, in addition, that Wilson and myself were the most inseparable of companions.

It was no doubt the anomalous state of affairs existing between us, which turned all my attacks upon him, (and they were many, either open or covert) into the channel of banter or practical joke (giving pain while assuming the aspect of mere fun) rather than into a more serious and determined hostility. But my endeavours on this head were by no means uniformly successful, even when my plans were the most wittily concocted; for my namesake had much about him, in character, of that unassuming and quiet austerity which, while enjoying the poignancy of its own jokes, has no heel of Achilles in itself, and absolutely refuses to be laughed at. I could find, indeed, but one vulnerable point, and that, lying in a personal peculiarity, arising, perhaps, from constitutional disease, would have been spared by any antagonist less at his wit's end than myself;—my rival had a weakness in the faucial or guttural organs, which precluded him from raising his voice at anytime *above a very low whisper.* Of this defect I did not fail to take what poor advantage lay in my power.

Wilson's retaliations in kind were many; and there was one form of his practical wit that disturbed me beyond measure. How his sagacity first discovered at all that so petty a thing would vex me, is a question I never could solve; but, having discovered, he habitually practised the annoyance. I had always felt aversion to my uncourtly patronymic, and its very common, if not plebeian praenomen.° The words were venom in my ears; and when, upon the day of my arrival, a second William Wilson came also to the academy, I felt angry with him for bearing the name, and doubly disgusted with the name because a stranger bore it, who would be the cause of its twofold repetition, who would be constantly in my presence, and whose concerns, in the ordinary routine of the school business, must inevitably, on account of the detestable coincidence, be often confounded with my own.

The feeling of vexation thus engendered grew stronger with every circumstance tending to show resemblance, moral or physical, between my rival and myself. I had not then discovered the remarkable fact that we were of the same age; but I saw that we were of the same height, and I perceived that we were even singularly alike in general contour of person and outline of feature. I was galled, too, by the rumor touching a relationship, which had grown current in the upper forms. In a word, nothing could more seriously disturb me, (although I scrupulously concealed such disturbance,) than any allusion to a similarity of mind, person, or condition existing between us. But, in truth, I had no reason to believe that (with the exception of the matter of relationship, and in the case of Wilson himself,) this similarity had ever been made a subject of comment, or even observed at all by our schoolfellows. That *he* observed it in all its bearings, and as fixedly as I, was apparent; but that he could discover in such circumstances so fruitful a field of annoyance, can only be attributed, as I said before, to his more than ordinary penetration.

His cue, which was to perfect an imitation of myself, lay both in words and in actions; and most admirably did he play his part. My dress it was an easy matter to copy; my gait and general manner were, without difficulty, appropriated; in spite of his constitutional defect, even my

praenomen: First name.

voice did not escape him. My louder tones were, of course, unattempted, but then the key, it was identical; *and his singular whisper, it grew the very echo of my own.*

How greatly this most exquisite portraiture harassed me, (for it could not justly be termed a caricature,) I will not now venture to describe. I had but one consolation—in the fact that the imitation, apparently, was noticed by myself alone, and that I had to endure only the knowing and strangely sarcastic smiles of my namesake himself. Satisfied with having produced in my bosom the intended effect, he seemed to chuckle in secret over the sting he had inflicted, and was characteristically disregardful of the public applause which the success of his witty endeavours might have so easily elicited. That the school, indeed, did not feel his design, perceive its accomplishment, and participate in his sneer, was, for many anxious months, a riddle I could not resolve. Perhaps the *gradation* of his copy rendered it not so readily perceptible; or, more possibly, I owed my security to the masterly air of the copyist, who, disdaining the letter, (which in a painting is all the obtuse can see,) gave but the full spirit of his original for my individual contemplation and chagrin.

I have already more than once spoken of the disgusting air of patronage which he assumed toward me, and of his frequent officious interference with my will. This interference often took the ungracious character of advice; advice not openly given, but hinted or insinuated. I received it with a repugnance which gained strength as I grew in years. Yet, at this distant day, let me do him the simple justice to acknowledge that I can recall no occasion when the suggestions of my rival were on the side of those errors or follies so usual to his immature age and seeming inexperience; that his moral sense, at least, if not his general talents and worldly wisdom, was far keener than my own; and that I might, to-day, have been a better, and thus a happier man, had I less frequently rejected the counsels embodied in those meaning whispers which I then but too cordially hated and too bitterly despised.

As it was, I at length grew restive in the extreme under his distasteful supervision, and daily resented more and more openly what I considered his intolerable arrogance. I have said that, in the first years of our connexion as schoolmates, my feelings in regard to him might have been easily ripened into friendship: but, in the latter months of my residence at the academy, although the intrusion of his ordinary manner had, beyond doubt, in some measure, abated, my sentiments, in nearly similar proportion, partook very much of positive hatred. Upon one occasion he saw this, I think, and afterwards avoided, or made a show of avoiding me.

It was about the same period, if I remember aright, that, in an altercation of violence with him, in which he was more than usually thrown off his guard, and spoke and acted with an openness of demeanor rather foreign to his nature, I discovered, or fancied I discovered, in his accent, his air, and general appearance, a something which first startled, and then deeply interested me, by bringing to mind dim visions of my earliest infancy—wild, confused and thronging memories of a time when memory herself was yet unborn. I cannot better describe the sensation which oppressed me than by saying that I could with difficulty shake off the belief of my having been acquainted with the being who stood before me, at some epoch very long ago—some point of the past even infinitely remote. The delusion, however, faded rapidly as it came; and I mention it at all but to define the day of the last conversation I there held with my singular namesake.

The huge old house, with its countless subdivisions, had several large chambers communicating with each other, where slept the greater number of the students. There were, however, (as must necessarily happen in a building so awkwardly planned,) many little nooks or recesses, the odds and ends of the structure; and these the economic ingenuity of Dr. Bransby had also fitted up as dormitories; although, being the merest closets, they were capable of accommodating but a single individual. One of these small apartments was occupied by Wilson.

One night, about the close of my fifth year at the school, and immediately after the altercation just mentioned, finding every one wrapped in sleep, I arose from bed, and, lamp in hand, stole through a wilderness of narrow passages from my own bedroom to that of my rival. I had long been plotting one of those ill-natured pieces of practical wit at his expense in which I had hitherto been so uniformly unsuccessful. It was my intention, now, to put my scheme in operation, and I resolved to make him feel the whole extent of the malice with which I was imbued. Having reached his closet, I noiselessly entered, leaving the lamp, with a shade over it, on the outside. I advanced a step, and listened to the sound of his tranquil breathing. Assured of his being asleep, I returned, took the light, and with it again approached the bed. Close curtains were around it, which, in the prosecution of my plan, I slowly and quietly withdrew, when the bright rays fell vividly upon the sleeper, and my eyes, at the same moment, upon his countenance. I looked;—and a numbness, an iciness of feeling instantly pervaded my frame. My breast heaved, my knees tottered, my whole spirit became possessed with an objectless yet intolerable horror. Gasping for breath, I lowered the lamp in still nearer proximity to the face. Were these—*these* the lineaments of William Wilson? I saw, indeed, that they were his, but I shook as if with a fit of the ague in fancying they were not. What *was* there about them to confound me in this manner? I gazed;—while my brain reeled with a multitude of incoherent thoughts. Not thus he appeared—assuredly not *thus*—in the vivacity of his waking hours. The same name! the same contour of person! the same day of arrival at the academy! And then his dogged and meaningless imitation of my gait, my voice, my habits, and my manner! Was it, in truth, within the bounds of human possibility, that *what I now saw* was the result, merely, of the habitual practice of this sarcastic imitation? Awe-stricken, and with a creeping shudder, I extinguished the lamp, passed silently from the chamber, and left, at once, the halls of that old academy, never to enter them again.

After a lapse of some months, spent at home in mere idleness, I found myself a student at Eton. The brief interval had been sufficient to enfeeble my remembrance of the events at Dr. Bransby's, or at least to effect a material change in the nature of the feelings with which I remembered them. The truth—the tragedy—of the drama was no more. I could now find room to doubt the evidence of my senses; and seldom called up the subject at all but with wonder at the extent of human credulity, and a smile at the vivid force of the imagination which I hereditarily possessed. Neither was this species of skepticism likely to be diminished by the character of the life I led at Eton. The vortex of thoughtless folly into which I there so immediately and so recklessly plunged, washed away all but the froth of my past hours, engulfed at once every solid or serious impression, and left to memory only the veriest levities of a former existence.

I do not wish, however, to trace the course of my miserable profligacy here—a profligacy which set at defiance the laws, while it eluded the vigilance of the institution. Three years of folly, passed without profit, had but given me rooted habits of vice, and added, in a somewhat unusual degree, to my bodily stature, when, after a week of soulless dissipation, I invited a small party of the most dissolute students to a secret carousal in my chambers. We met at a late hour of the night; for our debaucheries were to be faithfully protracted until morning. The wine flowed freely, and there were not wanting other and perhaps more dangerous seductions; so that the grey dawn had already faintly appeared in the east, while our delirious extravagance was at its height.

Madly flushed with cards and intoxication, I was in the act of insisting upon a toast of more than wonted profanity, when my attention was suddenly diverted by the violent, although partial unclosing of the door of the apartment, and by the eager voice of a servant from without. He said that some person, apparently in great haste, demanded to speak with me in the hall.

Wildly excited with wine, the unexpected interruption rather delighted than surprised me. I staggered forward at once, and a few steps brought me to the vestibule of the building. In this low and small room there hung no lamp; and now no light at all was admitted, save that of the exceedingly feeble dawn which made its way through the semicircular window. As I put my foot over the threshold, I became aware of the figure of a youth about my own height, and habited in a white kerseymere° morning frock, cut in the novel fashion of the one I myself wore at the moment. This the faint light enabled me to perceive; but the features of his face I could not distinguish. Upon my entering, he strode hurriedly up to me, and, seizing me by the arm with a gesture of petulant impatience, whispered the words "William Wilson!" in my ear.

I grew perfectly sober in an instant.

There was that in the manner of the stranger, and in the tremulous shake of his uplifted finger, as he held it between my eyes and the light, which filled me with unqualified amazement; but it was not this which had so violently moved me. It was the pregnancy of solemn admonition in the singular, low, hissing utterance; and, above all, it was the character, the tone, *the key*, of those few, simple, and familiar, yet *whispered* syllables, which came with a thousand thronging memories of by-gone days, and struck upon my soul with the shock of a galvanic battery. Ere I could recover the use of my senses he was gone.

Although this event failed not of a vivid effect upon my disordered imagination, yet was it evanescent as vivid. For some weeks, indeed, I busied myself in earnest inquiry, or was wrapped in a cloud of morbid speculation. I did not pretend to disguise from my perception the identity of the singular individual who thus perseveringly interfered with my affairs, and harassed me with his insinuated counsel. But who and what was this Wilson?—and whence came he?—and what were his purposes? Upon neither of these points could I be satisfied; merely ascertaining, in regard to him, that a sudden accident in his family had caused his removal from Dr. Bransby's academy on the afternoon of the day in which I myself had eloped. But in a brief period I ceased to think upon

---

kerseymere: A fine woolen cloth.

the subject; my attention being all absorbed in a contemplated departure for Oxford. Thither I soon went; the uncalculating vanity of my parents furnishing me with an outfit and annual establishment, which would enable me to indulge at will in the luxury already so dear to my heart,—to vie in profuseness of expenditure with the haughtiest heirs of the wealthiest earldoms in Great Britain.

Excited by such appliances to vice, my constitutional temperament broke forth with redoubled ardor, and I spurned even the common restraints of decency in the mad infatuation of my revels. But it were absurd to pause in the detail of my extravagance. Let it suffice, that among spendthrifts I out-Heroded Herod, and that, giving name to a multitude of novel follies, I added no brief appendix to the long catalogue of vices then usual in the most dissolute university of Europe.

It could hardly be credited, however, that I had, even here, so utterly fallen from the gentlemanly estate, as to seek acquaintance with the vilest arts of the gambler by profession, and, having become an adept in his despicable science, to practise it habitually as a means of increasing my already enormous income at the expense of the weak-minded among my fellow collegians. Such, nevertheless, was the fact. And the very enormity of this offence against all manly and honourable sentiment proved, beyond doubt, the main if not the sole reason of the impunity with which it was committed. Who, indeed, among my most abandoned associates, would not rather have disputed the clearest evidence of his senses, than have suspected of such courses, the gay, the frank, the generous William Wilson—the noblest and most liberal commoner at Oxford—him whose follies (said his parasites) were but the follies of youth and unbridled fancy—whose errors but inimitable whim—whose darkest vice but a careless and dashing extravagance?

I had been now two years successfully busied in this way, when there came to the university a young *parvenu* nobleman, Glendinning—rich, said report, as Herodes Atticus°—his riches, too, as easily acquired. I soon found him of weak intellect, and, of course, marked him as a fitting subject for my skill. I frequently engaged him in play, and contrived, with the gambler's usual art, to let him win considerable sums, the more effectually to entangle him in my snares. At length, my schemes being ripe, I met him (with the full intention that this meeting should be final and decisive) at the chambers of a fellow-commoner, (Mr. Preston,) equally intimate with both, but who, to do him justice, entertained not even a remote suspicion of my design. To give to this a

Herodes Atticus (101–177) was a Roman senator and wealthy patron to the arts.

better coloring, I had contrived to have assembled a party of some eight or ten, and was solicitously careful that the introduction of cards should appear accidental, and originate in the proposal of my contemplated dupe himself. To be brief upon a vile topic, none of the low finesse was omitted, so customary upon similar occasions that it is a just matter for wonder how any are still found so besotted as to fall its victim.

We had protracted our sitting far into the night, and I had at length effected the manoeuvre of getting Glendinning as my sole antagonist. The game, too, was my favorite *écarté*. The rest of the company, interested in the extent of our play, had abandoned their own cards, and were standing around us as spectators. The *parvenu*, who had been induced by my artifices in the early part of the evening, to drink deeply, now shuffled, dealt, or played, with a wild nervousness of manner for which his intoxication, I thought, might partially, but could not altogether account. In a very short period he had become my debtor to a large amount, when, having taken a long draught of port, he did precisely what I had been coolly anticipating—he proposed to double our already extravagant stakes. With a well-feigned show of reluctance, and not until after my repeated refusal had seduced him into some angry words which gave a color of *pique* to my compliance, did I finally comply. The result, of course, did but prove how entirely the prey was in my toils; in less than an hour he had quadrupled his debt. For some time his countenance had been losing the florid tinge lent it by the wine; but now, to my astonishment, I perceived that it had grown to a pallor truly fearful. I say to my astonishment. Glendinning had been represented to my eager inquiries as immeasurably wealthy; and the sums which he had as yet lost, although in themselves vast, could not, I supposed, very seriously annoy, much less so violently affect him. That he was overcome by the wine just swallowed, was the idea which most readily presented itself; and, rather with a view to the preservation of my own character in the eyes of my associates, than from any less interested motive, I was about to insist, peremptorily, upon a discontinuance of the play, when some expressions at my elbow from among the company, and an ejaculation evincing utter despair on the part of Glendinning, gave me to understand that I had effected his total ruin under circumstances which, rendering him an object for the pity of all, should have protected him from the ill offices even of a fiend.

What now might have been my conduct it is difficult to say. The pitiable condition of my dupe had thrown an air of embarrassed gloom over all; and, for some moments, a profound silence was maintained, during which I could not help feeling my cheeks tingle with the many

burning glances of scorn or reproach cast upon me by the less abandoned of the party. I will even own that an intolerable weight of anxiety
was for a brief instant lifted from my bosom by the sudden and extraordinary interruption which ensued. The wide, heavy folding doors of
the apartment were all at once thrown open, to their full extent, with a
vigorous and rushing impetuosity that extinguished, as if by magic,
every candle in the room. Their light, in dying, enabled us just to perceive that a stranger had entered, about my own height, and closely
muffled in a cloak. The darkness, however, was now total; and we could
only *feel* that he was standing in our midst. Before any one of us could
recover from the extreme astonishment into which this rudeness had
thrown all, we heard the voice of the intruder.

"Gentlemen," he said, in a low, distinct, and never-to-be-forgotten
whisper which thrilled to the very marrow of my bones, "Gentlemen, I
make no apology for this behaviour, because in thus behaving, I am but
fulfilling a duty. You are, beyond doubt, uninformed of the true character of the person who has to-night won at *écarté* a large sum of money
from Lord Glendinning. I will therefore put you upon an expeditious
and decisive plan of obtaining this very necessary information. Please to
examine, at your leisure, the inner linings of the cuff of his left sleeve,
and the several little packages which may be found in the somewhat
capacious pockets of his embroidered morning wrapper."

While he spoke, so profound was the stillness that one might have
heard a pin drop upon the floor. In ceasing, he departed at once, and as
abruptly as he had entered. Can I—shall I describe my sensations?—
must I say that I felt all the horrors of the damned? Most assuredly I
had little time given for reflection. Many hands roughly seized me upon
the spot, and lights were immediately reprocured. A search ensued. In
the lining of my sleeve were found all the court cards essential in *écarté*,
and, in the pockets of my wrapper, a number of packs, fac-similes of
those used at our sittings, with the single exception that mine were of
the species called, technically, *arrondées*; the honors being slightly convex at the ends, the lower cards slightly convex at the sides. In this
disposition, the dupe who cuts, as customary, at the length of the pack,
will invariably find that he cuts his antagonist an honor; while the gambler, cutting at the breadth, will, as certainly, cut nothing for his victim
which may count in the records of the game.

Any burst of indignation upon this discovery would have affected
me less than the silent contempt, or the sarcastic composure, with which
it was received.

"Mr. Wilson," said our host, stooping to remove from beneath his feet an exceedingly luxurious cloak of rare furs, "Mr. Wilson, this is your property." (The weather was cold; and, upon quitting my own room, I had thrown a cloak over my dressing wrapper, putting it off upon reaching the scene of play.) "I presume it is supererogatory to seek here (eyeing the folds of the garment with a bitter smile) for any farther evidence of your skill. Indeed, we have had enough. You will see the necessity, I hope, of quitting Oxford—at all events, of quitting instantly my chambers."

Abased, humbled to the dust as I then was, it is probable that I should have resented this galling language by immediate personal violence, had not my whole attention been at the moment arrested by a fact of the most startling character. The cloak which I had worn was of a rare description of fur; how rare, how extravagantly costly, I shall not venture to say. Its fashion, too, was of my own fantastic invention; for I was fastidious to an absurd degree of coxcombry,° in matters of this frivolous nature. When, therefore, Mr. Preston reached me that which he had picked up upon the floor, and near the folding doors of the apartment, it was with an astonishment nearly bordering upon terror, that I perceived my own already hanging on my arm, (where I had no doubt unwittingly placed it,) and that the one presented me was but its exact counterpart in every, in even the minutest possible particular. The singular being who had so disastrously exposed me, had been muffled, I remembered, in a cloak; and none had been worn at all by any of the members of our party with the exception of myself. Retaining some presence of mind, I took the one offered me by Preston; placed it, unnoticed, over my own; left the apartment with a resolute scowl of defiance; and, next morning ere dawn of day, commenced a hurried journey from Oxford to the continent, in a perfect agony of horror and of shame.

I fled in vain. My evil destiny pursued me as if in exultation, and proved, indeed, that the exercise of its mysterious dominion had as yet only begun. Scarcely had I set foot in Paris ere I had fresh evidence of the detestable interest taken by this Wilson in my concerns. Years flew, while I experienced no relief. Villain!—at Rome, with how untimely, yet with how spectral an officiousness, stepped he in between me and my ambition! At Vienna, too—at Berlin—and at Moscow! Where, in truth, had I *not* bitter cause to curse him within my heart? From his

coxcombry: Foppery.

inscrutable tyranny did I at length flee, panic-stricken, as from a pestilence; and to the very ends of the earth *I fled in vain.*

And again, and again, in secret communion with my own spirit,
would I demand the questions "Who is he?—whence came he?—and
what are his objects?" But no answer was there found. And now I scrutinized, with a minute scrutiny, the forms, and the methods, and the
leading traits of his impertinent supervision. But even here there was
very little upon which to base a conjecture. It was noticeable, indeed,
that, in no one of the multiplied instances in which he had of late
crossed my path, had he so crossed it except to frustrate those schemes,
or to disturb those actions, which, if fully carried out, might have
resulted in bitter mischief. Poor justification this, in truth, for an authority so imperiously assumed! Poor indemnity for natural rights of self-
agency so pertinaciously, so insultingly denied!

I had also been forced to notice that my tormentor, for a very long
period of time, (while scrupulously and with miraculous dexterity maintaining his whim of an identity of apparel with myself,) had so contrived
it, in the execution of his varied interference with my will, that I saw
not, at any moment, the features of his face. Be Wilson what he might,
this, at least, was but the veriest of affectation, or of folly. Could he,
for an instant, have supposed that, in my admonisher at Eton—in the
destroyer of my honor at Oxford,—in him who thwarted my ambition
at Rome, my revenge at Paris, my passionate love at Naples, or what
he falsely termed my avarice in Egypt,—that in this, my arch-enemy
and evil genius, could fail to recognise the William Wilson of my school
boy days,—the namesake, the companion, the rival,—the hated and
dreaded rival at Dr. Bransby's? Impossible!—But let me hasten to the
last eventful scene of the drama.

Thus far I had succumbed supinely to this imperious domination.
The sentiment of deep awe with which I habitually regarded the elevated character, the majestic wisdom, the apparent omnipresence and
omnipotence of Wilson, added to a feeling of even terror, with which
certain other traits in his nature and assumptions inspired me, had operated, hitherto, to impress me with an idea of my own utter weakness
and helplessness, and to suggest an implicit, although bitterly reluctant
submission to his arbitrary will. But, of late days, I had given myself up
entirely to wine; and its maddening influence upon my hereditary temper rendered me more and more impatient of control. I began to murmur,—to hesitate,—to resist. And was it only fancy which induced me
to believe that, with the increase of my own firmness, that of my tormentor underwent a proportional diminution? Be this as it may, I now

began to feel the inspiration of a burning hope, and at length nurtured in my secret thoughts a stern and desperate resolution that I would submit no longer to be enslaved.

It was at Rome, during the Carnival of 18—, that I attended a masquerade in the palazzo of the Neapolitan Duke Di Broglio. I had indulged more freely than usual in the excesses of the wine-table; and now the suffocating atmosphere of the crowded rooms irritated me beyond endurance. The difficulty, too, of forcing my way through the mazes of the company contributed not a little to the ruffling of my temper; for I was anxiously seeking, (let me not say with what unworthy motive) the young, the gay, the beautiful wife of the aged and doting Di Broglio. With a too unscrupulous confidence she had previously communicated to me the secret of the costume in which she would be habited, and now, having caught a glimpse of her person, I was hurrying to make my way into her presence.—At this moment I felt a light hand placed upon my shoulder, and that ever-remembered, low, damnable *whisper* within my ear.

In an absolute frenzy of wrath, I turned at once upon him who had thus interrupted me, and seized him violently by the collar. He was attired, as I had expected, in a costume altogether similar to my own; wearing a Spanish cloak of blue velvet, begirt about the waist with a crimson belt sustaining a rapier. A mask of black silk entirely covered his face.

"Scoundrel!" I said, in a voice husky with rage, while every syllable I uttered seemed as new fuel to my fury, "scoundrel! impostor! accursed villain! you shall not—you *shall not* dog me unto death! Follow me, or I stab you where you stand!"—and I broke my way from the ball-room into a small ante-chamber adjoining—dragging him unresistingly with me as I went.

Upon entering, I thrust him furiously from me. He staggered against the wall, while I closed the door with an oath, and commanded him to draw. He hesitated but for an instant; then, with a slight sigh, drew in silence, and put himself upon his defence.

The contest was brief indeed. I was frantic with every species of wild excitement, and felt within my single arm the energy and power of a multitude. In a few seconds I forced him by sheer strength against the wainscoting, and thus, getting him at mercy, plunged my sword, with brute ferocity, repeatedly through and through his bosom.

At that instant some person tried the latch of the door. I hastened to prevent an intrusion, and then immediately returned to my dying antagonist. But what human language can adequately portray *that* astonishment, *that* horror which possessed me at the spectacle then presented to view? The brief moment in which I averted my eyes had been sufficient to produce, apparently, a material change in the arrangements at the upper or farther end of the room. A large mirror,—so at first it seemed to me in my confusion—now stood where none had been perceptible before; and, as I stepped up to it in extremity of terror, mine own image, but with features all pale and dabbled in blood, advanced to meet me with a feeble and tottering gait.

Thus it appeared I say, but was not. It was my antagonist—it was Wilson, who then stood before me in the agonies of his dissolution. His mask and cloak lay, where he had thrown them, upon the floor. Not a thread in all his raiment—not a line in all the marked and singular lineaments of his face which was not, even in the most absolute identity, *mine own!*

It was Wilson; but he spoke no longer in a whisper, and I could have fancied that I myself was speaking while he said:

"*You have conquered, and I yield. Yet, henceforward art thou also dead—dead to the World, to Heaven and to Hope! In me didst thou exist—and, in my death, see by this image, which is thine own, how utterly thou hast murdered thyself.*"

The Man of the Crowd

Ce grand malheur, de ne pouvoir être seul.

—LA BRUYÈRE°

It was well said of a certain German book that "*er lasst sich nicht lesen*"—it does not permit itself to be read. There are some secrets which do not permit themselves to be told. Men die nightly in their beds, wringing the hands of ghostly confessors, and looking them piteously in the eyes—die with despair of heart and convulsion of throat, on account of the hideousness of mysteries which will not *suffer themselves* to be revealed. Now and then, alas, the conscience of man takes up a burthen so heavy in horror that it can be thrown down only into the grave. And thus the essence of all crime is undivulged.

Ce grand . . . La Bruyère: The misfortune of not being alone. From French philosopher Jean de La Bruyère (1645–1696).

Not long ago, about the closing in of an evening in autumn, I sat at the large bow window of the D—— Coffee-House in London. For some months I had been ill in health, but was now convalescent, and, with returning strength, found myself in one of those happy moods which are so precisely the converse of *ennui*—moods of the keenest appetency, when the film from the mental vision departs—the αχλυς ος πριν επηεν°—and the intellect, electrified, surpasses as greatly its every-day condition, as does the vivid yet candid reason of Leibnitz,° the mad and flimsy rhetoric of Gorgias.° Merely to breathe was enjoyment; and I derived positive pleasure even from many of the legitimate sources of pain. I felt a calm but inquisitive interest in every thing. With a cigar in my mouth and a newspaper in my lap, I had been amusing myself for the greater part of the afternoon, now in poring over advertisements, now in observing the promiscuous company in the room, and now in peering through the smoky panes into the street.

This latter is one of the principal thoroughfares of the city, and had been very much crowded during the whole day. But, as the darkness came on, the throng momently increased; and, by the time the lamps were well lighted, two dense and continuous tides of population were rushing past the door. At this particular period of the evening I had never before been in a similar situation, and the tumultuous sea of human heads filled me, therefore, with a delicious novelty of emotion. I gave up, at length, all care of things within the hotel, and became absorbed in contemplation of the scene without.

At first my observations took an abstract and generalizing turn. I looked at the passengers in masses, and thought of them in their aggregate relations. Soon, however, I descended to details, and regarded with minute interest the innumerable varieties of figure, dress, air, gait, visage, and expression of countenance.

By far the greater number of those who went by had a satisfied business-like demeanor, and seemed to be thinking only of making their way through the press. Their brows were knit, and their eyes rolled quickly; when pushed against by fellow-wayfarers they evinced no symptom of impatience, but adjusted their clothes and hurried on. Others, still a numerous class, were restless in their movements, had flushed faces, and talked and gesticulated to themselves, as if feeling in solitude on account of the very denseness of the company around. When impeded in

αχλυς ος πριν επηεν: Poe's Greek is loosely taken from the *Iliad* 5.127 and translates: "Darkness which before was upon [them]." **Leibnitz:** Gottfried Wilhelm Leibniz (1646–1716), German mathematician and philosopher. **Gorgias:** Pre-Socratic philosopher and rhetorician (485–380 BCE).

their progress, these people suddenly ceased muttering, but re-doubled their gesticulations, and awaited, with an absent and overdone smile upon the lips, the course of the persons impeding them. If jostled, they bowed profusely to the jostlers, and appeared overwhelmed with confusion.—There was nothing very distinctive about these two large classes beyond what I have noted. Their habiliments belonged to that order which is pointedly termed the decent. They were undoubtedly noblemen, merchants, attorneys, tradesmen, stock-jobbers—the Eupatrids° and the common-places of society—men of leisure and men actively engaged in affairs of their own—conducting business upon their own responsibility. They did not greatly excite my attention.

The tribe of clerks was an obvious one and here I discerned two remarkable divisions. There were the junior clerks of flash houses°— young gentlemen with tight coats, bright boots, well-oiled hair, and supercilious lips. Setting aside a certain dapperness of carriage, which may be termed *deskism* for want of a better word, the manner of these persons seemed to me an exact facsimile of what had been the perfection of *bon ton* about twelve or eighteen months before. They wore the cast-off graces of the gentry;—and this, I believe, involves the best definition of the class.

The division of the upper clerks of staunch firms, or of the "steady old fellows," it was not possible to mistake. These were known by their coats and pantaloons of black or brown, made to sit comfortably, with white cravats and waistcoats, broad solid-looking shoes, and thick hose or gaiters.—They had all slightly bald heads, from which the right ears, long used to pen-holding, had an odd habit of standing off on end. I observed that they always removed or settled their hats with both hands, and wore watches, with short gold chains of a substantial and ancient pattern. Theirs was the affectation of respectability;—if indeed there be an affectation so honorable.

There were many individuals of dashing appearance, whom I easily understood as belonging to the race of swell pick-pockets, with which all great cities are infested. I watched these gentry with much inquisitiveness, and found it difficult to imagine how they should ever be mistaken for gentlemen by gentlemen themselves. Their voluminousness of wristband, with an air of excessive frankness, should betray them at once.

Eupatrids: Nobility of ancient Athens.   *flash houses:* Pubs and saloons frequented by criminals.

The gamblers, of whom I descried not a few, were still more easily recognisable. They wore every variety of dress, from that of the desperate thimble-rig bully, with velvet waistcoat, fancy neckerchief, gilt chains, and filagreed buttons, to that of the scrupulously inornate clergyman, than which nothing could be less liable to suspicion. Still all were distinguished by a certain sodden swarthiness of complexion, a filmy dimness of eye, and pallor and compression of lip. There were two other traits, moreover, by which I could always detect them;—a guarded lowness of tone in conversation, and a more than ordinary extension of the thumb in a direction at right angles with the fingers.—Very often, in company with these sharpers, I observed an order of men somewhat different in habits, but still birds of a kindred feather. They may be defined as the gentlemen who live by their wits. They seem to prey upon the public in two battalions—that of the dandies and that of the military men. Of the first grade the leading features are long locks and smiles; of the second frogged coats and frowns.

Descending in the scale of what is termed gentility, I found darker and deeper themes for speculation. I saw Jew pedlars, with hawk eyes flashing from countenances whose every other feature wore only an expression of abject humility; sturdy professional street beggars scowling upon mendicants of a better stamp, whom despair alone had driven forth into the night for charity; feeble and ghastly invalids, upon whom death had placed a sure hand, and who sidled and tottered through the mob, looking every one beseechingly in the face, as if in search of some chance consolation, some lost hope; modest young girls returning from long and late labor to a cheerless home, and shrinking more tearfully than indignantly from the glances of ruffians, whose direct contact, even, could not be avoided; women of the town of all kinds and of all ages—the unequivocal beauty in the prime of her womanhood, putting one in mind of the statue in Lucian, with the surface of Parian marble, and the interior filled with filth—the loathsome and utterly lost leper in rags—the wrinkled, bejewelled and paint-begrimed beldame, making a last effort at youth—the mere child of immature form, yet, from long association, an adept in the dreadful coquetries of her trade, and burning with a rabid ambition to be ranked the equal of her elders in vice; drunkards innumerable and indescribable—some in shreds and patches, reeling, inarticulate, with bruised visage and lacklustre eyes—some in whole although filthy garments, with a slightly unsteady swagger, thick sensual lips, and hearty-looking rubicund faces—others clothed in materials which had once been good, and which even now were scrupulously well brushed—men who walked

with a more than naturally firm and springy step, but whose countenances were fearfully pale, whose eyes hideously wild and red, and who
clutched with quivering fingers, as they strode through the crowd, at
every object which came within their reach; beside these, pie-men, por-
ters, coal-heavers, sweeps; organ-grinders, monkey-exhibiters and ballad mongers, those who vended with those who sang; ragged artizans
and exhausted laborers of every description, and all full of a noisy and
inordinate vivacity which jarred discordantly upon the ear, and gave an
aching sensation to the eye.

As the night deepened, so deepened to me the interest of the scene;
for not only did the general character of the crowd materially alter (its
gentler features retiring in the gradual withdrawal of the more orderly
portion of the people, and its harsher ones coming out into bolder
relief, as the late hour brought forth every species of infamy from its
den,) but the rays of the gas-lamps, feeble at first in their struggle with
the dying day, had now at length gained ascendancy, and threw over
every thing a fitful and garish lustre. All was dark yet splendid — as that
ebony to which has been likened the style of Tertullian.°

The wild effects of the light enchained me to an examination of
individual faces; and although the rapidity with which the world of light
flitted before the window, prevented me from casting more than a
glance upon each visage, still it seemed that, in my then peculiar mental
state, I could frequently read, even in that brief interval of a glance, the
history of long years.

With my brow to the glass, I was thus occupied in scrutinizing the
mob, when suddenly there came into view a countenance (that of a
decrepit old man, some sixty-five or seventy years of age,) — a countenance which at once arrested and absorbed my whole attention, on
account of the absolute idiosyncracy of its expression. Any thing even
remotely resembling that expression I had never seen before. I well
remember that my first thought, upon beholding it, was that Retzch,°
had he viewed it, would have greatly preferred it to his own pictural
incarnations of the fiend. As I endeavored, during the brief minute of
my original survey, to form some analysis of the meaning conveyed,
there arose confusedly and paradoxically within my mind, the ideas of
vast mental power, of caution, of penuriousness, of avarice, of coolness,
of malice, of blood-thirstiness, of triumph, of merriment, of excessive
terror, of intense — of supreme despair. I felt singularly aroused, star-

---

Tertullian: Quintus Septimius Florens Tertullianus (160–225), early Christian author
from Carthage.   **Retzch:** Friedrich August Moritz Retzsch (1799–1857), German
painter and engraver.

tled, fascinated. "How wild a history," I said to myself, "is written within that bosom!" Then came a craving desire to keep the man in view — to know more of him. Hurriedly putting on an overcoat, and seizing my hat and cane, I made my way into the street, and pushed through the crowd in the direction which I had seen him take; for he had already disappeared. With some little difficulty I at length came within sight of him, approached, and followed him closely, yet cautiously, so as not to attract his attention.

I had now a good opportunity of examining his person. He was short in stature, very thin, and apparently very feeble. His clothes, generally, were filthy and ragged; but as he came, now and then, within the strong glare of a lamp, I perceived that his linen, although dirty, was of beautiful texture; and my vision deceived me, or, through a rent in a closely-buttoned and evidently second-handed *roquelaire*° which enveloped him, I caught a glimpse both of a diamond and of a dagger. These observations heightened my curiosity, and I resolved to follow the stranger whithersoever he should go.

It was now fully night-fall, and a thick humid fog hung over the city, soon ending in a settled and heavy rain. This change of weather had an odd effect upon the crowd, the whole of which was at once put into new commotion, and overshadowed by a world of umbrellas. The waver, the jostle, and the hum increased in a tenfold degree. For my own part I did not much regard the rain — the lurking of an old fever in my system rendering the moisture somewhat too dangerously pleasant. Tying a handkerchief about my mouth, I kept on. For half an hour the old man held his way with difficulty along the great thoroughfare; and I here walked close at his elbow through fear of losing sight of him. Never once turning his head to look back, he did not observe me. By and bye he passed into a cross street, which, although densely filled with people, was not quite so much thronged as the main one he had quitted. Here a change in his demeanor became evident. He walked more slowly and with less object than before — more hesitatingly. He crossed and re-crossed the way repeatedly without apparent aim; and the press was still so thick that, at every such movement, I was obliged to follow him closely. The street was a narrow and long one, and his course lay within it for nearly an hour, during which the passengers had gradually diminished to about that number which is ordinarily seen at noon in Broadway near the Park — so vast a difference is there between a London populace and that of the most frequented American city. A

roquelaire: Knee-length coat trimmed with fur.

second turn brought us into a square, brilliantly lighted, and overflowing with life. The old manner of the stranger re-appeared. His chin fell upon his breast, while his eyes rolled wildly from under his knit brows, in every direction, upon those who hemmed him in. He urged his way steadily and perseveringly. I was surprised, however, to find, upon his having made the circuit of the square, that he turned and retraced his steps. Still more was I astonished to see him repeat the same walk several times — once nearly detecting me as he came round with a sudden movement.

In this exercise he spent another hour, at the end of which we met with far less interruption from passengers than at first. The rain fell fast; the air grew cool; and the people were retiring to their homes. With a gesture of impatience, the wanderer passed into a bye-street comparatively deserted. Down this, some quarter of a mile long, he rushed with an activity I could not have dreamed of seeing in one so aged, and which put me to much trouble in pursuit. A few minutes brought us to a large and busy bazaar, with the localities of which the stranger appeared well acquainted, and where his original demeanor again became apparent, as he forced his way to and fro, without aim, among the host of buyers and sellers.

During the hour and a half, or thereabouts, which we passed in this place, it required much caution on my part to keep him within reach without attracting his observation. Luckily I wore a pair of caoutchouc° over-shoes, and could move about in perfect silence. At no moment did he see that I watched him. He entered shop after shop, priced nothing, spoke no word, and looked at all objects with a wild and vacant stare. I was now utterly amazed at his behaviour, and firmly resolved that we should not part until I had satisfied myself in some measure respecting him.

A loud-toned clock struck eleven, and the company were fast deserting the bazaar. A shop-keeper, in putting up a shutter, jostled the old man, and at the instant I saw a strong shudder come over his frame. He hurried into the street, looked anxiously around him for an instant, and then ran with incredible swiftness through many crooked and people-less lanes, until we emerged once more upon the great thoroughfare whence we had started — the street of the D—— Hotel. It no longer wore, however, the same aspect. It was still brilliant with gas; but the rain fell fiercely, and there were few persons to be seen. The stranger grew pale. He walked moodily some paces up the once populous ave-

caoutchouc: Rubber.

nue, then, with a heavy sigh, turned in the direction of the river, and, plunging through a great variety of devious ways, came out, at length, in view of one of the principal theatres. It was about being closed, and the audience were thronging from the doors. I saw the old man gasp as if for breath while he threw himself amid the crowd; but I thought that the intense agony of his countenance had, in some measure, abated. His head again fell upon his breast; he appeared as I had seen him at first. I observed that he now took the course in which had gone the greater number of the audience — but, upon the whole, I was at a loss to comprehend the waywardness of his actions.

As he proceeded, the company grew more scattered, and his old uneasiness and vacillation were resumed. For some time he followed closely a party of some ten or twelve roisterers; but from this number one by one dropped off, until three only remained together, in a narrow and gloomy lane little frequented. The stranger paused, and, for a moment, seemed lost in thought; then, with every mark of agitation, pursued rapidly a route which brought us to the verge of the city, amid regions very different from those we had hitherto traversed. It was the most noisome quarter of London, where every thing wore the worst impress of the most deplorable poverty, and of the most desperate crime. By the dim light of an accidental lamp, tall, antique, worm-eaten, wooden tenements were seen tottering to their fall, in directions so many and capricious that scarce the semblance of a passage was discernible between them. The paving-stones lay at random, displaced from their beds by the rankly-growing grass. Horrible filth festered in the dammed-up gutters. The whole atmosphere teemed with desolation. Yet, as we proceeded, the sounds of human life revived by sure degrees, and at length large bands of the most abandoned of a London populace were seen reeling to and fro. The spirits of the old man again flickered up, as a lamp which is near its death-hour. Once more he strode onward with elastic tread. Suddenly a corner was turned, a blaze of light burst upon our sight, and we stood before one of the huge suburban temples of Intemperance — one of the palaces of the fiend, Gin.

It was now nearly day-break; but a number of wretched inebriates still pressed in and out of the flaunting entrance. With a half shriek of joy the old man forced a passage within, resumed at once his original bearing, and stalked backward and forward, without apparent object, among the throng. He had not been thus long occupied, however, before a rush to the doors gave token that the host was closing them for the night. It was something even more intense than despair that I then observed upon the countenance of the singular being whom I had watched so pertinaciously. Yet he did not hesitate in his career, but, with a mad energy, retraced his steps at once, to the heart of the mighty London. Long and swiftly he fled, while I followed him in the wildest amazement, resolute not to abandon a scrutiny in which I now felt an interest all-absorbing. The sun arose while we proceeded, and, when we had once again reached that most thronged mart of the populous town, the street of the D—— Hotel, it presented an appearance of human bustle and activity scarcely inferior to what I had seen on the evening before. And here, long, amid the momently increasing confusion, did I persist in my pursuit of the stranger. But, as usual, he walked to and fro, and during the day did not pass from out the turmoil of that street. And, as the shades of the second evening came on, I grew wearied unto death, and, stopping fully in front of the wanderer, gazed at him steadfastly in the face. He noticed me not, but resumed his solemn walk, while I, ceasing to follow, remained absorbed in contemplation. "This old man," I said at length, "is the type and the genius of deep crime. He refuses to be alone. *He is the man of the crowd.* It will be in vain to follow; for I shall learn no more of him, nor of his deeds. The worst heart of the world is a grosser book than the 'Hortulus Animae,'° and perhaps it is but one of the great mercies of God that '*er lasst sich nicht lesen.*' "

The Murders in the Rue Morgue

What song the Syrens sang, or what name Achilles assumed when he hid himself among women, although puzzling questions, are not beyond *all* conjecture.

–SIR THOMAS BROWNE

The mental features discoursed of as the analytical, are, in themselves, but little susceptible of analysis. We appreciate them only in their effects. We know of them, among other things, that they are always to their possessor, when inordinately possessed, a source of the liveliest enjoyment. As the strong man exults in his physical ability, delighting in such exercises as call his muscles into action, so glories the analyst in that moral activity which *disentangles.* He derives pleasure from even the most trivial occupations bringing his talent into play. He is fond of enigmas, of conundrums, of hieroglyphics; exhibiting in his solutions

Hortulus Animae: "The *Hortulus Animæ cum Oratiunculis Aliquibus Superadditis* of Grünninger." [Poe's note.]

of each a degree of *acumen* which appears to the ordinary apprehension praeternatural. His results, brought about by the very soul and essence of method, have, in truth, the whole air of intuition.

The faculty of re-solution is possibly much invigorated by mathematical study, and especially by that highest branch of it which, unjustly, and merely on account of its retrograde operations, has been called, as if *par excellence*, analysis. Yet to calculate is not in itself to analyse. A chess-player, for example, does the one without effort at the other. It follows that the game of chess, in its effects upon mental character, is greatly misunderstood. I am not now writing a treatise, but simply prefacing a somewhat peculiar narrative by observations very much at random; I will, therefore, take occasion to assert that the higher powers of the reflective intellect are more decidedly and more usefully tasked by the unostentatious game of draughts° than by all the elaborate frivolity of chess. In this latter, where the pieces have different and *bizarre* motions, with various and variable values, what is only complex is mistaken (a not unusual error) for what is profound. The *attention* is here called powerfully into play. If it flag for an instant, an oversight is committed, resulting in injury or defeat. The possible moves being not only manifold but involute, the chances of such oversights are multiplied; and in nine cases out of ten it is the more concentrative rather than the more acute player who conquers. In draughts, on the contrary, where the moves are *unique* and have but little variation, the probabilities of inadvertence are diminished, and the mere attention being left comparatively unemployed, what advantages are obtained by either party are obtained by superior *acumen*. To be less abstract—Let us suppose a game of draughts where the pieces are reduced to four kings, and where, of course, no oversight is to be expected. It is obvious that here the victory can be decided (the players being at all equal) only by some *recherché* movement, the result of some strong exertion of the intellect. Deprived of ordinary resources, the analyst throws himself into the spirit of his opponent, identifies himself therewith, and not unfrequently sees thus, at a glance, the sole methods (sometimes indeed absurdly simple ones) by which he may seduce into error or hurry into miscalculation.

Whist has long been noted for its influence upon what is termed the calculating power; and men of the highest order of intellect have been known to take an apparently unaccountable delight in it, while eschewing chess as frivolous. Beyond doubt there is nothing of a similar nature

draughts: The game of checkers.

so greatly tasking the faculty of analysis. The best chess-player in Chris-
tendom *may* be little more than the best player of chess; but proficiency
in whist implies capacity for success in all those more important under-
takings where mind struggles with mind. When I say proficiency, I mean
that perfection in the game which includes a comprehension of *all* the
sources whence legitimate advantage may be derived. These are not only
manifold but multiform, and lie frequently among recesses of thought
altogether inaccessible to the ordinary understanding. To observe attentively is to remember distinctly; and, so far, the concentrative chess-
player will do very well at whist; while the rules of Hoyle (themselves
based upon the mere mechanism of the game) are sufficiently and generally comprehensible. Thus to have a retentive memory, and to proceed by "the book," are points commonly regarded as the sum total of
good playing. But it is in matters beyond the limits of mere rule that the
skill of the analyst is evinced. He makes, in silence, a host of observations and inferences. So, perhaps, do his companions; and the difference in the extent of the information obtained, lies not so much in the
validity of the inference as in the quality of the observation. The necessary knowledge is that of *what* to observe. Our player confines himself
not at all; nor, because the game is the object, does he reject deductions
from things external to the game. He examines the countenance of his
partner, comparing it carefully with that of each of his opponents. He
considers the mode of assorting the cards in each hand; often counting
trump by trump, and honor by honor, through the glances bestowed
by their holders upon each. He notes every variation of face as the play
progresses, gathering a fund of thought from the differences in the
expression of certainty, of surprise, of triumph, or of chagrin. From the
manner of gathering up a trick he judges whether the person taking it
can make another in the suit. He recognises what is played through
feint, by the air with which it is thrown upon the table. A casual or
inadvertent word; the accidental dropping or turning of a card, with
the accompanying anxiety or carelessness in regard to its concealment;
the counting of the tricks, with the order of their arrangement; embarrassment, hesitation, eagerness or trepidation — all afford, to his apparently intuitive perception, indications of the true state of affairs. The
first two or three rounds having been played, he is in full possession of
the contents of each hand, and thenceforward puts down his cards with
as absolute a precision of purpose as if the rest of the party had turned
outward the faces of their own.

The analytical power should not be confounded with simple ingenuity; for while the analyst is necessarily ingenious, the ingenious man

is often remarkably incapable of analysis. The constructive or combining power, by which ingenuity is usually manifested, and to which the phrenologists (I believe erroneously) have assigned a separate organ, supposing it a primitive faculty, has been so frequently seen in those whose intellect bordered otherwise upon idiocy, as to have attracted general observation among writers on morals. Between ingenuity and the analytic ability there exists a difference far greater, indeed, than that between the fancy and the imagination, but of a character very strictly analogous. It will be found, in fact, that the ingenious are always fanciful, and the *truly* imaginative never otherwise than analytic.

The narrative which follows will appear to the reader somewhat in the light of a commentary upon the propositions just advanced.

Residing in Paris during the spring and part of the summer of 18—, I there became acquainted with a Monsieur C. Auguste Dupin. This young gentleman was of an excellent—indeed of an illustrious family, but, by a variety of untoward events, had been reduced to such poverty that the energy of his character succumbed beneath it, and he ceased to bestir himself in the world, or to care for the retrieval of his fortunes. By courtesy of his creditors, there still remained in his possession a small remnant of his patrimony; and, upon the income arising from this, he managed, by means of a rigorous economy, to procure the necessaries of life, without troubling himself about its superfluities. Books, indeed, were his sole luxuries, and in Paris these are easily obtained.

Our first meeting was at an obscure library in the Rue Montmartre, where the accident of our both being in search of the same very rare and very remarkable volume, brought us into closer communion. We saw each other again and again. I was deeply interested in the little family history which he detailed to me with all that candor which a Frenchman indulges whenever mere self is his theme. I was astonished, too, at the vast extent of his reading; and, above all, I felt my soul enkindled within me by the wild fervor, and the vivid freshness of his imagination. Seeking in Paris the objects I then sought, I felt that the society of such a man would be to me a treasure beyond price; and this feeling I frankly confided to him. It was at length arranged that we should live together during my stay in the city; and as my worldly circumstances were somewhat less embarrassed than his own, I was permitted to be at the expense of renting, and furnishing in a style which suited the rather fantastic gloom of our common temper, a time-eaten and grotesque mansion, long deserted through superstitions into which we did not inquire, and tottering to its fall in a retired and desolate portion of the Faubourg St. Germain.

Had the routine of our life at this place been known to the world, we should have been regarded as madmen—although, perhaps, as madmen of a harmless nature. Our seclusion was perfect. We admitted no visitors. Indeed the locality of our retirement had been carefully kept a secret from my own former associates; and it had been many years since Dupin had ceased to know or be known in Paris. We existed within ourselves alone.

It was a freak of fancy in my friend (for what else shall I call it?) to be enamored of the Night for her own sake; and into this *bizarrerie*, as into all his others, I quietly fell; giving myself up to his wild whims with a perfect *abandon*. The sable divinity would not herself dwell with us always; but we could counterfeit her presence. At the first dawn of the morning we closed all the messy shutters of our old building; lighting a couple of tapers which, strongly perfumed, threw out only the ghastliest and feeblest of rays. By the aid of these we then busied our souls in dreams—reading, writing, or conversing, until warned by the clock of the advent of the true Darkness. Then we sallied forth into the streets, arm in arm, continuing the topics of the day, or roaming far and wide until a late hour, seeking, amid the wild lights and shadows of the populous city, that infinity of mental excitement which quiet observation can afford.

At such times I could not help remarking and admiring (although from his rich ideality I had been prepared to expect it) a peculiar analytic ability in Dupin. He seemed, too, to take an eager delight in its exercise—if not exactly in its display—and did not hesitate to confess the pleasure thus derived. He boasted to me, with a low chuckling laugh, that most men, in respect to himself, wore windows in their bosoms, and was wont to follow up such assertions by direct and very startling proofs of his intimate knowledge of my own. His manner at these moments was frigid and abstract; his eyes were vacant in expression; while his voice, usually a rich tenor, rose into a treble which would have sounded petulantly but for the deliberateness and entire distinctness of the enunciation. Observing him in these moods, I often dwelt meditatively upon the old philosophy of the Bi-Part Soul, and amused myself with the fancy of a double Dupin—the creative and the resolvent.

Let it not be supposed, from what I have just said, that I am detailing any mystery, or penning any romance. What I have described in the Frenchman, was merely the result of an excited, or perhaps of a diseased intelligence. But of the character of his remarks at the periods in question an example will best convey the idea.

We were strolling one night down a long dirty street, in the vicinity of the Palais Royal. Being both, apparently, occupied with thought, neither of us had spoken a syllable for fifteen minutes at least. All at once Dupin broke forth with these words:

"He is a very little fellow, that's true, and would do better for the *Théâtre des Variétés*."°

"There can be no doubt of that," I replied unwittingly, and not at first observing (so much had I been absorbed in reflection) the extraordinary manner in which the speaker had chimed in with my meditations. In an instant afterward I recollected myself, and my astonishment was profound.

"Dupin," said I, gravely, "this is beyond my comprehension. I do not hesitate to say that I am amazed, and can scarcely credit my senses. How was it possible you should know I was thinking of———?" Here I paused, to ascertain beyond a doubt whether he really knew of whom I thought.

———"of Chantilly," said he, "why do you pause? You were remarking to yourself that his diminutive figure unfitted him for tragedy."

This was precisely what had formed the subject of my reflections. Chantilly was a *quondam* cobbler of the Rue St. Denis, who, becoming stage-mad, had attempted the role of Xerxes, in Crébillon's tragedy so called, and been notoriously Pasquinaded° for his pains.

"Tell me, for Heaven's sake," I exclaimed, "the method—if method there is—by which you have been enabled to fathom my soul in this matter." In fact I was even more startled than I would have been willing to express.

"It was the fruiterer," replied my friend, "who brought you to the conclusion that the mender of soles was not of sufficient height for Xerxes *et id genus omne*."°

"The fruiterer!—you astonish me—I know no fruiterer whomsoever."

"The man who ran up against you as we entered the street—it may have been fifteen minutes ago."

I now remembered that, in fact, a fruiterer, carrying upon his head a large basket of apples, had nearly thrown me down, by accident, as we passed from the Rue C——— into the thoroughfare where we

---

Théâtre des Variétés: Parisian theater that opened in 1807.   ***Pasquinaded:*** Satirized.
et id genus omne: And all of that kind.

stood; but what this had to do with Chantilly I could not possibly understand.

There was not a particle of *charlâtanerie* about Dupin. "I will explain," he said, "and that you may comprehend all clearly, we will first retrace the course of your meditations, from the moment in which I spoke to you until that of the *rencontre* with the fruiterer in question. The larger links of the chain run thus—Chantilly, Orion, Dr. Nichols, Epicurus, Stereotomy, the street stones, the fruiterer."

There are few persons who have not, at some period of their lives, amused themselves in retracing the steps by which particular conclusions of their own minds have been attained. The occupation is often full of interest; and he who attempts it for the first time is astonished by the apparently illimitable distance and incoherence between the starting-point and the goal. What, then, must have been my amazement when I heard the Frenchman speak what he had just spoken, and when I could not help acknowledging that he had spoken the truth. He continued:

"We had been talking of horses, if I remember aright, just before leaving the Rue C———. This was the last subject we discussed. As we crossed into this street, a fruiterer, with a large basket upon his head, brushing quickly past us, thrust you upon a pile of paving-stones collected at a spot where the causeway is undergoing repair. You stepped upon one of the loose fragments, slipped, slightly strained your ankle, appeared vexed or sulky, muttered a few words, turned to look at the pile, and then proceeded in silence. I was not particularly attentive to what you did; but observation has become with me, of late, a species of necessity.

"You kept your eyes upon the ground—glancing, with a petulant expression, at the holes and ruts in the pavement, (so that I saw you were still thinking of the stones,) until we reached the little alley called Lamartine, which has been paved, by way of experiment, with the overlapping and riveted blocks. Here your countenance brightened up, and, perceiving your lips move, I could not doubt that you murmured the word 'stereotomy,' a term very affectedly applied to this species of pavement. I knew that you could not say to yourself 'stereotomy' without being brought to think of atomies, and thus of the theories of Epicurus; and since, when we discussed this subject not very long ago, I mentioned to you how singularly, yet with how little notice, the vague guesses of that noble Greek had met with confirmation in the late nebular cosmogony, I felt that you could not avoid casting your eyes upward to the great *nebula* in Orion, and I certainly expected that you would do so. You did look up; and I was now assured that I had correctly followed your steps. But in that bitter *tirade* upon Chantilly, which appeared in yesterday's '*Musée*,' the satirist, making some disgraceful allusions to the cobbler's change of name upon assuming the buskin, quoted a Latin line about which we have often conversed. I mean the line

Perdidit antiquum litera prima sonum°

I had told you that this was in reference to Orion, formerly written Urion; and, from certain pungencies connected with this explanation, I was aware that you could not have forgotten it. It was clear, therefore, that you would not fail to combine the two ideas of Orion and Chantilly. That you did combine them I saw by the character of the smile which passed over your lips. You thought of the poor cobbler's immolation. So far, you had been stooping in your gait; but now I saw you draw yourself up to your full height. I was then sure that you reflected upon the diminutive figure of Chantilly. At this point I interrupted your meditations to remark that as, in fact, he *was* a very little fellow—that Chantilly—he would do better at the *Théâtre des Variétés.*"

Not long after this, we were looking over an evening edition of the "Gazette des Tribunaux," when the following paragraphs arrested our attention.

"EXTRAORDINARY MURDERS.—This morning, about three o'clock, the inhabitants of the Quartier St. Roch were aroused from sleep by a succession of terrific shrieks, issuing, apparently, from the fourth story of a house in the Rue Morgue, known to be in the sole occupancy of one Madame L'Espanaye, and her daughter, Mademoiselle Camille L'Espanaye. After some delay, occasioned by a fruitless attempt to procure admission in the usual manner, the gateway was broken in with a crowbar, and eight or ten of the neighbors entered, accompanied by two *gendarmes*. By this time the cries had ceased; but, as the party rushed up the first flight of stairs, two or more rough voices, in angry contention, were distinguished, and seemed to proceed from the upper part of the house. As the second landing was reached, these sounds, also, had ceased, and everything remained perfectly quiet. The party spread themselves, and hurried from room to room. Upon arriving at a large back chamber in the fourth story, (the door of which, being found locked, with the key inside, was forced open,) a spectacle presented itself which struck every one present not less with horror than with astonishment.

Perdidit . . . sonum: The first letter has lost its original sound.

"The apartment was in the wildest disorder—the furniture broken and thrown about in all directions. There was only one bedstead; and from this the bed had been removed, and thrown into the middle of the floor. On a chair lay a razor, besmeared with blood. On the hearth were two or three long and thick tresses of grey human hair, also dabbled in blood, and seeming to have been pulled out by the roots. Upon the floor were found four Napoleons, an ear-ring of topaz, three large silver spoons, three smaller of *métal d'Alger*, and two bags, containing nearly four thousand francs in gold. The drawers of a *bureau*, which stood in one corner, were open, and had been, apparently, rifled, although many articles still remained in them. A small iron safe was discovered under the *bed* (not under the bedstead). It was open, with the key still in the door. It had no contents beyond a few old letters, and other papers of little consequence.

"Of Madame L'Espanaye no traces were here seen; but an unusual quantity of soot being observed in the fire-place, a search was made in the chimney, and (horrible to relate!) the corpse of the daughter, head downward, was dragged therefrom; it having been thus forced up the narrow aperture for a considerable distance. The body was quite warm. Upon examining it, many excoriations were perceived, no doubt occasioned by the violence with which it had been thrust up and disengaged. Upon the face were many severe scratches, and, upon the throat, dark bruises, and deep indentations of finger nails, as if the deceased had been throttled to death.

"After a thorough investigation of every portion of the house, without farther discovery, the party made its way into a small paved yard in the rear of the building, where lay the corpse of the old lady, with her throat so entirely cut that, upon an attempt to raise her, the head fell off. The body, as well as the head, was fearfully mutilated—the former so much so as scarcely to retain any semblance of humanity.

"To this horrible mystery there is not as yet, we believe, the slightest clew."

The next day's paper had these additional particulars.

"*The Tragedy in the Rue Morgue*. Many individuals have been examined in relation to this most extraordinary and frightful affair." [The word '*affaire*' has not yet, in France, that levity of import which it conveys with us,] "but nothing whatever has transpired to throw light upon it. We give below all the material testimony elicited.

"*Pauline Dubourg*, laundress, deposes that she has known both the deceased for three years, having washed for them during that period.

The old lady and her daughter seemed on good terms—very affectionate towards each other. They were excellent pay. Could not speak in regard to their mode or means of living. Believed that Madame L. told fortunes for a living. Was reputed to have money put by. Never met any persons in the house when she called for the clothes or took them home. Was sure that they had no servant in employ. There appeared to be no furniture in any part of the building except in the fourth story.

"*Pierre Moreau*, tobacconist, deposes that he has been in the habit of selling small quantities of tobacco and snuff to Madame L'Espanaye for nearly four years. Was born in the neighborhood, and has always resided there. The deceased and her daughter had occupied the house in which the corpses were found, for more than six years. It was formerly occupied by a jeweller, who under-let the upper rooms to various persons. The house was the property of Madame L. She became dissatisfied with the abuse of the premises by her tenant, and moved into them herself, refusing to let any portion. The old lady was childish. Witness had seen the daughter some five or six times during the six years. The two lived an exceedingly retired life—were reputed to have money. Had heard it said among the neighbors that Madame L. told fortunes—did not believe it. Had never seen any person enter the door except the old lady and her daughter, a porter once or twice, and a physician some eight or ten times.

"Many other persons, neighbors, gave evidence to the same effect. No one was spoken of as frequenting the house. It was not known whether there were any living connexions of Madame L. and her daughter. The shutters of the front windows were seldom opened. Those in the rear were always closed, with the exception of the large back room, fourth story. The house was a good house—not very old.

"*Isidore Musèt, gendarme*, deposes that he was called to the house about three o'clock in the morning, and found some twenty or thirty persons at the gateway, endeavoring to gain admittance. Forced it open, at length, with a bayonet—not with a crowbar. Had but little difficulty in getting it open, on account of its being a double or folding gate, and bolted neither at bottom nor top. The shrieks were continued until the gate was forced—and then suddenly ceased. They seemed to be screams of some person (or persons) in great agony—were loud and drawn out, not short and quick. Witness led the way up stairs. Upon reaching the first landing, heard two voices in loud and angry contention—the one a gruff voice, the other much shriller—a very strange voice. Could distinguish some words of the former, which was that of a Frenchman.

Was positive that it was not a woman's voice. Could distinguish the words '*sacré*' and '*diable.*' The shrill voice was that of a foreigner. Could not be sure whether it was the voice of a man or of a woman. Could not make out what was said, but believed the language to be Spanish. The state of the room and of the bodies was described by this witness as we described them yesterday.

"*Henri Duval*, a neighbor, and by trade a silver-smith, deposes that he was one of the party who first entered the house. Corroborates the testimony of Musèt in general. As soon as they forced an entrance, they reclosed the door, to keep out the crowd, which collected very fast, notwithstanding the lateness of the hour. The shrill voice, this witness thinks, was that of an Italian. Was certain it was not French. Could not be sure that it was a man's voice. It might have been a woman's. Was not acquainted with the Italian language. Could not distinguish the words, but was convinced by the intonation that the speaker was an Italian. Knew Madame L. and her daughter. Had conversed with both frequently. Was sure that the shrill voice was not that of either of the deceased.

"—— *Odenheimer, restaurateur.* This witness volunteered his testimony. Not speaking French, was examined through an interpreter. Is a native of Amsterdam. Was passing the house at the time of the shrieks. They lasted for several minutes—probably ten. They were long and loud—very awful and distressing. Was one of those who entered the building. Corroborated the previous evidence in every respect but one. Was sure that the shrill voice was that of a man—of a Frenchman. Could not distinguish the words uttered. They were loud and quick—unequal—spoken apparently in fear as well as in anger. The voice was harsh—not so much shrill as harsh. Could not call it a shrill voice. The gruff voice said repeatedly '*sacré*,' '*diable*,' and once '*mon Dieu.*'

"*Jules Mignaud*, banker, of the firm of Mignaud et Fils, Rue Deloraine. Is the elder Mignaud. Madame L'Espanaye had some property. Had opened an account with his banking house in the spring of the year——(eight years previously). Made frequent deposits in small sums. Had checked for nothing until the third day before her death, when she took out in person the sum of 4000 francs. This sum was paid in gold, and a clerk went home with the money.

"*Adolphe Le Bon*, clerk to Mignaud et Fils, deposes that on the day in question, about noon, he accompanied Madame L'Espanaye to her residence with the 4000 francs, put up in two bags. Upon the door being opened, Mademoiselle L. appeared and took from his hands one of the bags, while the old lady relieved him of the other. He then bowed and departed. Did not see any person in the street at the time. It is a bye-street — very lonely.

"*William Bird*, tailor deposes that he was one of the party who entered the house. Is an Englishman. Has lived in Paris two years. Was one of the first to ascend the stairs. Heard the voices in contention. The gruff voice was that of a Frenchman. Could make out several words, but cannot now remember all. Heard distinctly '*sacré*' and '*mon Dieu.*' There was a sound at the moment as if of several persons struggling — a scraping and scuffling sound. The shrill voice was very loud — louder than the gruff one. Is sure that it was not the voice of an Englishman. Appeared to be that of a German. Might have been a woman's voice. Does not understand German.

"Four of the above-named witnesses, being recalled, deposed that the door of the chamber in which was found the body of Mademoiselle L. was locked on the inside when the party reached it. Every thing was perfectly silent — no groans or noises of any kind. Upon forcing the door no person was seen. The windows, both of the back and front room, were down and firmly fastened from within. A door between the two rooms was closed, but not locked. The door leading from the front room into the passage was locked, with the key on the inside. A small room in the front of the house, on the fourth story, at the head of the passage, was open, the door being ajar. This room was crowded with old beds, boxes, and so forth. These were carefully removed and searched. There was not an inch of any portion of the house which was not carefully searched. Sweeps were sent up and down the chimneys. The house was a four story one, with garrets (*mansardes.*) A trap-door on the roof was nailed down very securely — did not appear to have been opened for years. The time elapsing between the hearing of the voices in contention and the breaking open of the room door, was variously stated by the witnesses. Some made it as short as three minutes — some as long as five. The door was opened with difficulty.

"*Alfonzo Garcio*, undertaker, deposes that he resides in the Rue Morgue. Is a native of Spain. Was one of the party who entered the house. Did not proceed up stairs. Is nervous, and was apprehensive of the consequences of agitation. Heard the voices in contention. The gruff voice was that of a Frenchman. Could not distinguish what was said. The shrill voice was that of an Englishman — is sure of this. Does not understand the English language, but judges by the intonation.

"*Alberto Montani*, confectioner, deposes that he was among the first to ascend the stairs. Heard the voices in question. The gruff voice was that of a Frenchman. Distinguished several words. The speaker appeared to be expostulating. Could not make out the words of the shrill voice. Spoke quick and unevenly. Thinks it the voice of a Russian. Corroborates the general testimony. Is an Italian. Never conversed with a native of Russia.

"Several witnesses, recalled, here testified that the chimneys of all the rooms on the fourth story were too narrow to admit the passage of a human being. By 'sweeps' were meant cylindrical sweeping-brushes, such as are employed by those who clean chimneys. These brushes were passed up and down every flue in the house. There is no back passage by which any one could have descended while the party proceeded up stairs. The body of Mademoiselle L'Espanaye was so firmly wedged in the chimney that it could not be got down until four or five of the party united their strength.

"*Paul Dumas,* physician, deposes that he was called to view the bodies about day-break. They were both then lying on the sacking of the bedstead in the chamber where Mademoiselle L. was found. The corpse of the young lady was much bruised and excoriated. The fact that it had been thrust up the chimney would sufficiently account for these appearances. The throat was greatly chafed. There were several deep scratches just below the chin, together with a series of livid spots which were evidently the impression of fingers. The face was fearfully discolored, and the eye-balls protruded. The tongue had been partially bitten through. A large bruise was discovered upon the pit of the stomach, produced, apparently, by the pressure of a knee. In the opinion of M. Dumas, Mademoiselle L'Espanaye had been throttled to death by some person or persons unknown. The corpse of the mother was horribly mutilated. All the bones of the right leg and arm were more or less shattered. The left *tibia* much splintered, as well as all the ribs of the left side. Whole body dreadfully bruised and discolored. It was not possible to say how the injuries had been inflicted. A heavy club of wood, or a broad bar of iron—a chair—any large, heavy, and obtuse weapon would have produced such results, if wielded by the hands of a very powerful man. No woman could have inflicted the blows with any weapon. The head of the deceased, when seen by witness, was entirely separated from the body, and was also greatly shattered. The throat had evidently been cut with some very sharp instrument—probably with a razor.

"*Alexandre Etienne,* surgeon, was called with M. Dumas to view the bodies. Corroborated the testimony, and the opinions of M. Dumas.

"Nothing farther of importance was elicited, although several other persons were examined. A murder so mysterious, and so perplexing in all its particulars, was never before committed in Paris—if indeed a murder has been committed at all. The police are entirely at fault—an unusual occurrence in affairs of this nature. There is not, however, the shadow of a clew apparent."

The evening edition of the paper stated that the greatest excitement still continued in the Quartier St. Roch—that the premises in question had been carefully re-searched, and fresh examinations of witnesses instituted, but all to no purpose. A postscript, however, mentioned that Adolphe Le Bon had been arrested and imprisoned—although nothing appeared to criminate him, beyond the facts already detailed.

Dupin seemed singularly interested in the progress of this affair—at least so I judged from his manner, for he made no comments. It was only after the announcement that Le Bon had been imprisoned, that he asked me my opinion respecting the murders.

I could merely agree with all Paris in considering them an insoluble mystery. I saw no means by which it would be possible to trace the murderer.

"We must not judge of the means," said Dupin, "by this shell of an examination. The Parisian police, so much extolled for *acumen*, are cunning, but no more. There is no method in their proceedings, beyond the method of the moment. They make a vast parade of measures; but, not unfrequently, these are so ill adapted to the objects proposed, as to put us in mind of Monsieur Jourdain's calling for his *robe-de-chambre—pour mieux entendre la musique.*° The results attained by them are not unfrequently surprising, but, for the most part, are brought about by simple diligence and activity. When these qualities are unavailing, their schemes fail. Vidocq,° for example, was a good guesser, and a persevering man. But, without educated thought, he erred continually by the very intensity of his investigations. He impaired his vision by holding the object too close. He might see, perhaps, one or two points with unusual clearness, but in so doing he, necessarily, lost sight of the matter as a whole. Thus there is such a thing as being too profound. Truth is not always in a well. In fact, as regards the more important knowledge, I do believe that she is invariably superficial. The depth lies in the valleys where we seek her, and not upon the mountain-tops where she is found. The modes and sources of this kind of error are well typified in the contemplation of the heavenly bodies. To look at a star by

robe-de-chambre . . . la musique: Dressing gown—to better hear the music.   **Vidocq:** Francois Eugène Vidocq (1775–1857), French criminal and criminalist who is said to have founded the French police and modern criminology.

glances—to view it in a side-long way, by turning toward it the exterior portions of the *retina* (more susceptible of feeble impressions of light than the interior), is to behold the star distinctly—is to have the best appreciation of its lustre—a lustre which grows dim just in proportion as we turn our vision *fully* upon it. A greater number of rays actually fall upon the eye in the latter case, but, in the former, there is the more refined capacity for comprehension. By undue profundity we perplex and enfeeble thought; and it is possible to make even Venus herself vanish from the firmament by a scrutiny too sustained, too concentrated, or too direct.

"As for these murders, let us enter into some examinations for ourselves, before we make up an opinion respecting them. An inquiry will afford us amusement," [I thought this an odd term, so applied, but said nothing] "and, besides, Le Bon once rendered me a service for which I am not ungrateful. We will go and see the premises with our own eyes. I know G———, the Prefect of Police, and shall have no difficulty in obtaining the necessary permission."

The permission was obtained, and we proceeded at once to the Rue Morgue. This is one of those miserable thoroughfares which intervene between the Rue Richelieu and the Rue St. Roch. It was late in the afternoon when we reached it; as this quarter is at a great distance from that in which we resided. The house was readily found; for there were still many persons gazing up at the closed shutters, with an objectless curiosity, from the opposite side of the way. It was an ordinary Parisian house, with a gateway, on one side of which was a glazed watch-box, with a sliding panel in the window, indicating a *loge de concierge*. Before going in we walked up the street, turned down an alley, and then, again turning, passed in the rear of the building—Dupin, meanwhile, examining the whole neighborhood, as well as the house, with a minuteness of attention for which I could see no possible object.

Retracing our steps, we came again to the front of the dwelling, rang, and, having shown our credentials, were admitted by the agents in charge. We went up stairs—into the chamber where the body of Mademoiselle L'Espanaye had been found, and where both the deceased still lay. The disorders of the room had, as usual, been suffered to exist. I saw nothing beyond what had been stated in the "Gazette des Tribunaux." Dupin scrutinized every thing—not excepting the bodies of the victims. We then went into the other rooms, and into the yard; a *gendarme* accompanying us throughout. The examination occupied us until dark, when we took our departure. On our way home my companion stepped in for a moment at the office of one of the daily papers.

I have said that the whims of my friend were manifold, and that *Je les ménagais*°:—for this phrase there is no English equivalent. It was his humor, now, to decline all conversation on the subject of the murder, until about noon the next day. He then asked me, suddenly, if I had observed any thing *peculiar* at the scene of the atrocity.

There was something in his manner of emphasizing the word "peculiar," which caused me to shudder, without knowing why.

"No, nothing *peculiar*," I said; "nothing more, at least, than we both saw stated in the paper."

"The 'Gazette,'" he replied, "has not entered, I fear, into the unusual horror of the thing. But dismiss the idle opinions of this print. It appears to me that this mystery is considered insoluble, for the very reason which should cause it to be regarded as easy of solution—I mean for the *outré* character of its features. The police are confounded by the seeming absence of motive—not for the murder itself—but for the atrocity of the murder. They are puzzled, too, by the seeming impossibility of reconciling the voices heard in contention, with the facts that no one was discovered up stairs but the assassinated Mademoiselle L'Espanaye, and that there were no means of egress without the notice of the party ascending. The wild disorder of the room; the corpse thrust, with the head downward, up the chimney; the frightful mutilation of the body of the old lady; these considerations, with those just mentioned, and others which I need not mention, have sufficed to paralyze the powers, by putting completely at fault the boasted *acumen*, of the government agents. They have fallen into the gross but common error of confounding the unusual with the abstruse. But it is by these deviations from the plane of the ordinary, that reason feels its way, if at all, in its search for the true. In investigations such as we are now pursuing, it should not be so much asked 'what has occurred,' as 'what has occurred that has never occurred before.' In fact, the facility with which I shall arrive, or have arrived, at the solution of this mystery, is in the direct ratio of its apparent insolubility in the eyes of the police."

I stared at the speaker in mute astonishment.

"I am now awaiting," continued he, looking toward the door of our apartment—"I am now awaiting a person who, although perhaps not the perpetrator of these butcheries, must have been in some measure implicated in their perpetration. Of the worst portion of the crimes committed, it is probable that he is innocent. I hope that I am right in this supposition; for upon it I build my expectation of reading the

Je les ménagais: I treated them carefully.

entire riddle. I look for the man here—in this room—every moment. It is true that he may not arrive; but the probability is that he will. Should he come, it will be necessary to detain him. Here are pistols; and we both know how to use them when occasion demands their use."

I took the pistols, scarcely knowing what I did, or believing what I heard, while Dupin went on, very much as if in a soliloquy. I have already spoken of his abstract manner at such times. His discourse was addressed to myself; but his voice, although by no means loud, had that intonation which is commonly employed in speaking to some one at a great distance. His eyes, vacant in expression, regarded only the wall.

"That the voices heard in contention," he said, "by the party upon the stairs, were not the voices of the women themselves, was fully proved by the evidence. This relieves us of all doubt upon the question whether the old lady could have first destroyed the daughter, and afterward have committed suicide. I speak of this point chiefly for the sake of method; for the strength of Madame L'Espanaye would have been utterly unequal to the task of thrusting her daughter's corpse up the chimney as it was found; and the nature of the wounds upon her own person entirely pre-clude the idea of self-destruction. Murder, then, has been committed by some third party; and the voices of this third party were those heard in contention. Let me now advert—not to the whole testimony respecting these voices—but to what was *peculiar* in that testimony. Did you observe any thing peculiar about it?"

I remarked that, while all the witnesses agreed in supposing the gruff voice to be that of a Frenchman, there was much disagreement in regard to the shrill, or, as one individual termed it, the harsh voice.

"That was the evidence itself," said Dupin, "but it was not the pecu-liarity of the evidence. You have observed nothing distinctive. Yet there *was* something to be observed. The witnesses, as you remark, agreed about the gruff voice; they were here unanimous. But in regard to the shrill voice, the peculiarity is—not that they disagreed—but that, while an Italian, an Englishman, a Spaniard, a Hollander, and a Frenchman attempted to describe it, each one spoke of it as that *of a foreigner.* Each is sure that it was not the voice of one of his own countrymen. Each lik-ens it—not to the voice of an individual of any nation with whose lan-guage he is conversant—but the converse. The Frenchman supposes it the voice of a Spaniard, and 'might have distinguished some words *had he been acquainted with the Spanish.*' The Dutchman maintains it to have been that of a Frenchman; but we find it stated that '*not understanding French this witness was examined through an interpreter.*' The Englishman thinks it the voice of a German, and '*does not understand German.*' The Spaniard 'is sure' that it was that of an Englishman, but 'judges by the intonation' altogether, '*as he has no knowledge of the English.*' The Italian believes it the voice of a Russian, but '*has never conversed with a native of Russia.*' A second Frenchman differs, moreover, with the first, and is positive that the voice was that of an Italian; but, *not being cognizant of that tongue,* is, like the Spaniard, 'convinced by the intonation.' Now, how strangely unusual must that voice have really been, about which such testimony as this *could* have been elicited!—in whose *tones,* even, denizens of the five great divisions of Europe could recognise nothing familiar! You will say that it might have been the voice of an Asiatic—of an African. Neither Asiatics nor Africans abound in Paris; but, without denying the inference, I will now merely call your attention to three points. The voice is termed by one witness 'harsh rather than shrill.' It is represented by two others to have been 'quick and *unequal.*' No words—no sounds resembling words—were by any witness mentioned as distinguishable.

"I know not," continued Dupin, "what impression I may have made, so far, upon your own understanding; but I do not hesitate to say that legitimate deductions even from this portion of the testimony—the portion respecting the gruff and shrill voices—are in themselves sufficient to engender a suspicion which should give direction to all farther progress in the investigation of the mystery. I said 'legitimate deductions;' but my meaning is not thus fully expressed. I designed to imply that the deductions are the *sole* proper ones, and that the suspicion arises *inevitably* from them as the single result. What the suspicion is, however, I will not say just yet. I merely wish you to bear in mind that, with myself, it was sufficiently forcible to give a definite form—a certain tendency—to my inquiries in the chamber.

"Let us now transport ourselves, in fancy, to this chamber. What shall we first seek here? The means of egress employed by the murderers. It is not too much to say that neither of us believe in praeternatural events. Madame and Mademoiselle L'Espanaye were not destroyed by spirits. The doers of the deed were material, and escaped materially. Then how? Fortunately, there is but one mode of reasoning upon the point, and that mode *must* lead us to a definite decision.—Let us examine, each by each, the possible means of egress. It is clear that the assassins were in the room where Mademoiselle L'Espanaye was found, or at least in the room adjoining, when the party ascended the stairs. It is then only from these two apartments that we have to seek issues. The police have laid bare the floors, the ceilings, and the masonry of the walls, in every direction. No *secret* issues could have escaped their vigilance. But, not trusting to *their* eyes, I examined with my own. There were, then, *no* secret issues. Both doors leading from the rooms into the passage were securely locked, with the keys inside. Let us turn to the chimneys. These, although of ordinary width for some eight or ten feet above the hearths, will not admit, throughout their extent, the body of a large cat. The impossibility of egress, by means already stated, being thus absolute, we are reduced to the windows. Through those of the front room no one could have escaped without notice from the crowd in the street. The murderers *must* have passed, then, through those of the back room. Now, brought to this conclusion in so unequivocal a manner as we are, it is not our part, as reasoners, to reject it on account of apparent impossibilities. It is only left for us to prove that these apparent 'impossibilities' are, in reality, not such.

"There are two windows in the chamber. One of them is unobstructed by furniture, and is wholly visible. The lower portion of the other is hidden from view by the head of the unwieldy bedstead which is thrust close up against it. The former was found securely fastened from within. It resisted the utmost force of those who endeavored to raise it. A large gimlet-hole had been pierced in its frame to the left, and a very stout nail was found fitted therein, nearly to the head. Upon examining the other window, a similar nail was seen similarly fitted in it; and a vigorous attempt to raise this sash, failed also. The police were now entirely satisfied that egress had not been in these directions. And, *therefore*, it was thought a matter of supererogation to withdraw the nails and open the windows.

"My own examination was somewhat more particular, and was so for the reason I have just given — because here it was, I knew, that all apparent impossibilities *must* be proved to be not such in reality.

"I proceeded to think thus — *à posteriori*. The murderers *did* escape from one of these windows. This being so, they could not have re-fastened the sashes from the inside, as they were found fastened; — the consideration which put a stop, through its obviousness, to the scrutiny of the police in this quarter. Yet the sashes *were* fastened. They *must*, then, have the power of fastening themselves. There was no escape from this conclusion. I stepped to the unobstructed casement, withdrew the nail with some difficulty, and attempted to raise the sash. It resisted all my efforts, as I had anticipated. A concealed spring must, I now knew, exist; and this corroboration of my idea convinced me that my premises, at least, were correct, however mysterious still appeared the circumstances attending the nails. A careful search soon brought to light the hidden spring. I pressed it, and, satisfied with the discovery, forbore to upraise the sash.

"I now replaced the nail and regarded it attentively. A person passing out through this window might have reclosed it, and the spring would have caught—but the nail could not have been replaced. The conclusion was plain, and again narrowed in the field of my investigations. The assassins *must* have escaped through the other window. Supposing, then, the springs upon each sash to be the same, as was probable, there *must* be found a difference between the nails, or at least between the modes of their fixture. Getting upon the sacking of the bedstead, I looked over the head-board minutely at the second casement. Passing my hand down behind the board, I readily discovered and pressed the spring, which was, as I had supposed, identical in character with its neighbor. I now looked at the nail. It was as stout as the other, and apparently fitted in the same manner—driven in nearly up to the head.

"You will say that I was puzzled; but, if you think so, you must have misunderstood the nature of the inductions. To use a sporting phrase, I had not been once 'at fault.' The scent had never for an instant been lost. There was no flaw in any link of the chain. I had traced the secret to its ultimate result,—and that result was *the nail*. It had, I say, in every respect, the appearance of its fellow in the other window; but this fact was an absolute nullity (conclusive as it might seem to be) when compared with the consideration that here, at this point, terminated the clew. 'There *must* be something wrong,' I said, 'about the nail.' I touched it; and the head, with about a quarter of an inch of the shank, came off in my fingers. The rest of the shank was in the gimlet-hole, where it had been broken off. The fracture was an old one (for its edges were incrusted with rust), and had apparently been accomplished by the blow of a hammer, which had partially imbedded, in the top of the bottom sash, the head portion of the nail. I now carefully replaced this head portion in the indentation whence I had taken it, and the resemblance to a perfect nail was complete—the fissure was invisible. Pressing the spring, I gently raised the sash for a few inches; the head went up with it, remaining firm in its bed. I closed the window, and the semblance of the whole nail was again perfect.

"The riddle, so far, was now unriddled. The assassin had escaped through the window which looked upon the bed. Dropping of its own accord upon his exit (or perhaps purposely closed), it had become fastened by the spring; and it was the retention of this spring which had been mistaken by the police for that of the nail,—farther inquiry being thus considered unnecessary.

"The next question is that of the mode of descent. Upon this point I had been satisfied in my walk with you around the building. About five feet and a half from the casement in question there runs a lightning-rod. From this rod it would have been impossible for any one to reach the window itself, to say nothing of entering it. I observed, however, that the shutters of the fourth story were of the peculiar kind called by Parisian carpenters *ferrades*—a kind rarely employed at the present day, but frequently seen upon very old mansions at Lyons and Bourdeaux. They are in the form of an ordinary door, (a single, not a folding door) except that the lower half is latticed or worked in open trellis—thus affording an excellent hold for the hands. In the present instance these shutters are fully three feet and a half broad. When we saw them from the rear of the house, they were both about half open—that is to say, they stood off at right angles from the wall. It is probable that the police, as well as myself, examined the back of the tenement; but, if so, in looking at these *ferrades* in the line of their breadth (as they must have done), they did not perceive this great breadth itself, or, at all events, failed to take it into due consideration. In fact, having once satisfied themselves that no egress could have been made in this quarter, they would naturally bestow here a very cursory examination. It was clear to me, however, that the shutter belonging to the window at the head of the bed, would, if swung fully back to the wall, reach to within two feet of the lightning-rod. It was also evident that, by exertion of a very unusual degree of activity and courage, an entrance into the window, from the rod, might have been thus effected. — By reaching to the distance of two feet and a half (we now suppose the shutter open to its whole extent) a robber might have taken a firm grasp upon the trellis-work. Letting go, then, his hold upon the rod, placing his feet securely against the wall, and springing boldly from it, he might have swung the shutter so as to close it, and, if we imagine the window open at the time, might even have swung himself into the room.

"I wish you to bear especially in mind that I have spoken of a *very* unusual degree of activity as requisite to success in so hazardous and so difficult a feat. It is my design to show you, first, that the thing might possibly have been accomplished:—but, secondly and *chiefly*, I wish to impress upon your understanding the *very extraordinary*— the almost praeternatural character of that agility which could have accomplished it.

"You will say, no doubt, using the language of the law, that 'to make out my case,' I should rather undervalue, than insist upon a full estimation of the activity required in this matter. This may be the practice in law, but it is not the usage of reason. My ultimate object is only the truth. My immediate purpose is to lead you to place in juxtaposition, that *very unusual* activity of which I have just spoken, with that *very peculiar* shrill (or harsh) and *unequal* voice, about whose nationality no two persons could be found to agree, and in whose utterance no syllabification could be detected."

At these words a vague and half-formed conception of the meaning of Dupin flitted over my mind. I seemed to be upon the verge of comprehension, without power to comprehend—as men, at times, find themselves upon the brink of remembrance, without being able, in the end, to remember. My friend went on with his discourse.

"You will see," he said, "that I have shifted the question from the mode of egress to that of ingress. It was my design to suggest the idea that both were effected in the same manner, at the same point. Let us now revert to the interior of the room. Let us survey the appearances here. The drawers of the bureau, it is said, had been rifled, although many articles of apparel still remained within them. The conclusion here is absurd. It is a mere guess—a very silly one—and no more. How are we to know that the articles found in the drawers were not all these drawers had originally contained? Madame L'Espanaye and her daughter lived an exceedingly retired life—saw no company—seldom went out—had little use for numerous changes of habiliment. Those found were at least of as good quality as any likely to be possessed by these ladies. If a thief had taken any, why did he not take the best—why did he not take all? In a word, why did he abandon four thousand francs in gold to encumber himself with a bundle of linen? The gold *was* abandoned. Nearly the whole sum mentioned by Monsieur Mignaud, the banker, was discovered, in bags, upon the floor. I wish you, therefore, to discard from your thoughts the blundering idea of *motive*, engendered in the brains of the police by that portion of the evidence which speaks of money delivered at the door of the house. Coincidences ten times as remarkable as this (the delivery of the money, and murder committed within three days upon the party receiving it), happen to all of us every hour of our lives, without attracting even momentary notice. Coincidences, in general, are great stumbling-blocks in the way of that class of thinkers who have been educated to know nothing of the theory of probabilities—that theory to which the most glorious objects of human research are indebted for the most glorious of illustration. In the present instance, had the gold been gone, the fact of its delivery three days before would have formed something more than a coincidence. It would have been corroborative of this idea of motive. But, under the real circumstances of the case, if we are to suppose gold the motive of this outrage, we must also imagine the perpetrator so vacillating an idiot as to have abandoned his gold and his motive together.

"Keeping now steadily in mind the points to which I have drawn your attention—that peculiar voice, that unusual agility, and that startling absence of motive in a murder so singularly atrocious as this—let us glance at the butchery itself. Here is a woman strangled to death by manual strength, and thrust up a chimney, head downward. Ordinary assassins employ no such modes of murder as this. Least of all, do they thus dispose of the murdered. In the manner of thrusting the corpse up the chimney, you will admit that there was something *excessively outré*—something altogether irreconcilable with our common notions of human action, even when we suppose the actors the most depraved of men. Think, too, how great must have been that strength which could have thrust the body *up* such an aperture so forcibly that the united vigor of several persons was found barely sufficient to drag it *down!*

"Turn, now, to other indications of the employment of a vigor most marvellous. On the hearth were thick tresses—very thick tresses—of grey human hair. These had been torn out by the roots. You are aware of the great force necessary in tearing thus from the head even twenty or thirty hairs together. You saw the locks in question as well as myself. Their roots (a hideous sight!) were clotted with fragments of the flesh of the scalp—sure token of the prodigious power which had been exerted in uprooting perhaps half a million of hairs at a time. The throat of the old lady was not merely cut, but the head absolutely severed from the body: the instrument was a mere razor. I wish you also to look at the *brutal* ferocity of these deeds. Of the bruises upon the body of Madame L'Espanaye I do not speak. Monsieur Dumas, and his worthy coadjutor Monsieur Etienne, have pronounced that they were inflicted by some obtuse instrument; and so far these gentlemen are very correct. The obtuse instrument was clearly the stone pavement in the yard, upon which the victim had fallen from the window which looked in upon the bed. This idea, however simple it may now seem, escaped the police for the same reason that the breadth of the shutters escaped them—because, by the affair of the nails, their perceptions had been hermetically sealed against the possibility of the windows having ever been opened at all.

"If now, in addition to all these things, you have properly reflected upon the odd disorder of the chamber, we have gone so far as to combine the ideas of an agility astounding, a strength superhuman, a ferocity brutal, a butchery without motive, a *grotesquerie* in horror absolutely alien from humanity, and a voice foreign in tone to the ears of men of many nations, and devoid of all distinct or intelligible syllabification. What result, then, has ensued? What impression have I made upon your fancy?"

I felt a creeping of the flesh as Dupin asked me the question. "A madman," I said, "has done this deed — some raving maniac, escaped from a neighboring *Maison de Santé.*"

"In some respects," he replied, "your idea is not irrelevant. But the voices of madmen, even in their wildest paroxysms, are never found to tally with that peculiar voice heard upon the stairs. Madmen are of some nation, and their language, however incoherent in its words, has always the coherence of syllabification. Besides, the hair of a madman is not such as I now hold in my hand. I disentangled this little tuft from the rigidly clutched fingers of Madame L'Espanaye. Tell me what you can make of it."

"Dupin!" I said, completely unnerved; "this hair is most unusual — this is no *human* hair."

"I have not asserted that it is," said he; "but, before we decide this point, I wish you to glance at the little sketch I have here traced upon this paper. It is a *fac-simile* drawing of what has been described in one portion of the testimony as 'dark bruises, and deep indentations of finger nails,' upon the throat of Mademoiselle L'Espanaye, and in another, (by Messrs. Dumas and Etienne,) as a 'series of livid spots, evidently the impression of fingers.'

"You will perceive," continued my friend, spreading out the paper upon the table before us, "that this drawing gives the idea of a firm and fixed hold. There is no *slipping* apparent. Each finger has retained — possibly until the death of the victim — the fearful grasp by which it originally imbedded itself. Attempt, now, to place all your fingers, at the same time, in the respective impressions as you see them."

I made the attempt in vain.

"We are possibly not giving this matter a fair trial," he said. "The paper is spread out upon a plane surface; but the human throat is cylindrical. Here is a billet of wood, the circumference of which is about that of the throat. Wrap the drawing around it, and try the experiment again."

I did so; but the difficulty was even more obvious than before. "This," I said, "is the mark of no human hand."

"Read now," replied Dupin, "this passage from Cuvier."°

It was a minute anatomical and generally descriptive account of the large fulvous Ourang-Outang of the East Indian Islands. The gigantic stature, the prodigious strength and activity, the wild ferocity, and the imitative propensities of these mammalia are sufficiently well known to all. I understood the full horrors of the murder at once.

"The description of the digits," said I, as I made an end of reading, "is in exact accordance with this drawing. I see that no animal but an Ourang-Outang, of the species here mentioned, could have impressed the indentations as you have traced them. This tuft of tawny hair, too, is identical in character with that of the beast of Cuvier. But I cannot possibly comprehend the particulars of this frightful mystery. Besides, there were *two* voices heard in contention, and one of them was unquestionably the voice of a Frenchman."

"True; and you will remember an expression attributed almost unanimously, by the evidence, to this voice,—the expression, '*mon Dieu!*' This, under the circumstances, has been justly characterized by one of the witnesses (Montani, the confectioner,) as an expression of remonstrance or expostulation. Upon these two words, therefore, I have mainly built my hopes of a full solution of the riddle. A Frenchman was cognizant of the murder. It is possible—indeed it is far more than probable—that he was innocent of all participation in the bloody transactions which took place. The Ourang-Outang may have escaped from him. He may have traced it to the chamber; but, under the agitating circumstances which ensued, he could never have re-captured it. It is still at large. I will not pursue these guesses—for I have no right to call them more—since the shades of reflection upon which they are based are scarcely of sufficient depth to be appreciable by my own intellect, and since I could not pretend to make them intelligible to the understanding of another. We will call them guesses then, and speak of them as such. If the Frenchman in question is indeed, as I suppose, innocent of this atrocity, this advertisement, which I left last night, upon our return home, at the office of 'Le Monde,' (a paper devoted to the shipping interest, and much sought by sailors,) will bring him to our residence."

He handed me a paper, and I read thus:

CAUGHT— *In the Bois de Boulogne, early in the morning of the* —— *inst.,* (the morning of the murder,) *a very large, tawny*

Cuvier: Georges Cuvier (1769–1832), French naturalist and zoologist.

*Ourang-Outang of the Bornese species. The owner, (who is ascer-
tained to be a sailor, belonging to a Maltese vessel,) may have the
animal again, upon identifying it satisfactorily, and paying a few
charges arising from its capture and keeping. Call at No. ——,
Rue ——, Faubourg St. Germain—au troisième.*

"How was it possible," I asked, "that you should know the man to
be a sailor, and belonging to a Maltese vessel?"

"I do *not* know it," said Dupin. "I am not *sure* of it. Here, however,
is a small piece of ribbon, which from its form, and from its greasy
appearance, has evidently been used in tying the hair in one of those
long *queues* of which sailors are so fond. Moreover, this knot is one
which few besides sailors can tie, and is peculiar to the Maltese. I picked
the ribbon up at the foot of the lightning-rod. It could not have
belonged to either of the deceased. Now if, after all, I am wrong in my
induction from this ribbon, that the Frenchman was a sailor belonging
to a Maltese vessel, still I can have done no harm in saying what I did
in the advertisement. If I am in error, he will merely suppose that I
have been misled by some circumstance into which he will not take the
trouble to inquire. But if I am right, a great point is gained. Cognizant
although innocent of the murder, the Frenchman will naturally hesitate
about replying to the advertisement—about demanding the Ourang-
Outang. He will reason thus:—'I am innocent; I am poor; my Ourang-
Outang is of great value—to one in my circumstances a fortune of
itself—why should I lose it through idle apprehensions of danger? Here
it is, within my grasp. It was found in the Bois de Boulogne—at a vast
distance from the scene of that butchery. How can it ever be suspected
that a brute beast should have done the deed? The police are at
fault—they have failed to procure the slightest clew. Should they even
trace the animal, it would be impossible to prove me cognizant of the
murder, or to implicate me in guilt on account of that cognizance.
Above all, *I am known*. The advertiser designates me as the possessor
of the beast. I am not sure to what limit his knowledge may extend.
Should I avoid claiming a property of so great value, which it is known
that I possess, I will render the animal at least, liable to suspicion. It is
not my policy to attract attention either to myself or to the beast. I will
answer the advertisement, get the Ourang-Outang, and keep it close
until this matter has blown over.'"

At this moment we heard a step upon the stairs.

"Be ready," said Dupin, "with your pistols, but neither use them
nor show them until at a signal from myself."

The front door of the house had been left open, and the visiter had entered, without ringing, and advanced several steps upon the staircase. Now, however, he seemed to hesitate. Presently we heard him descending. Dupin was moving quickly to the door, when we again heard him coming up. He did not turn back a second time, but stepped up with decision, and rapped at the door of our chamber.

"Come in," said Dupin, in a cheerful and hearty tone.

A man entered. He was a sailor, evidently,—a tall, stout, and muscular-looking person, with a certain dare-devil expression of countenance, not altogether unprepossessing. His face, greatly sunburnt, was more than half hidden by whisker and *mustachio*. He had with him a huge oaken cudgel, but appeared to be otherwise unarmed. He bowed awkwardly, and bade us "good evening," in French accents, which, although somewhat Neufchatelish, were still sufficiently indicative of a Parisian origin.

"Sit down, my friend," said Dupin. "I suppose you have called about the Ourang-Outang. Upon my word, I almost envy you the possession of him; a remarkably fine, and no doubt a very valuable animal. How old do you suppose him to be?"

The sailor drew a long breath, with the air of a man relieved of some intolerable burden, and then replied, in an assured tone:

"I have no way of telling—but he can't be more than four or five years old. Have you got him here?"

"Oh no; we had no conveniences for keeping him here. He is at a livery stable in the Rue Dubourg, just by. You can get him in the morning. Of course you are prepared to identify the property?"

"To be sure I am, sir."

"I shall be sorry to part with him," said Dupin.

"I don't mean that you should be at all this trouble for nothing, sir," said the man. "Couldn't expect it. Am very willing to pay a reward for the finding of the animal—that is to say, any thing in reason."

"Well," replied my friend, "that is all very fair, to be sure. Let me think!—what should I have? Oh! I will tell you. My reward shall be this. You shall give me all the information in your power about these murders in the Rue Morgue."

Dupin said the last words in a very low tone, and very quietly. Just as quietly, too, he walked toward the door, locked it, and put the key in his pocket. He then drew a pistol from his bosom and placed it, without the least flurry, upon the table.

The sailor's face flushed up as if he were struggling with suffocation. He started to his feet and grasped his cudgel; but the next moment he fell back into his seat, trembling violently, and with the countenance of death itself. He spoke not a word. I pitied him from the bottom of my heart.

"My friend," said Dupin, in a kind tone, "you are alarming yourself unnecessarily—you are indeed. We mean you no harm whatever. I pledge you the honor of a gentleman, and of a Frenchman, that we intend you no injury. I perfectly well know that you are innocent of the atrocities in the Rue Morgue. It will not do, however, to deny that you are in some measure implicated in them. From what I have already said, you must know that I have had means of information about this matter—means of which you could never have dreamed. Now the thing stands thus. You have done nothing which you could have avoided—nothing, certainly, which renders you culpable. You were not even guilty of robbery, when you might have robbed with impunity. You have nothing to conceal. You have no reason for concealment. On the other hand, you are bound by every principle of honor to confess all you know. An innocent man is now imprisoned, charged with that crime of which you can point out the perpetrator."

The sailor had recovered his presence of mind, in a great measure, while Dupin uttered these words; but his original boldness of bearing was all gone.

"So help me God," said he, after a brief pause, "I *will* tell you all I know about this affair;—but I do not expect you to believe one half I say—I would be a fool indeed if I did. Still, I *am* innocent, and I will make a clean breast if I die for it."

What he stated was, in substance, this. He had lately made a voyage to the Indian Archipelago. A party, of which he formed one, landed at Borneo, and passed into the interior on an excursion of pleasure. Himself and a companion had captured the Ourang-Outang. This companion dying, the animal fell into his own exclusive possession. After great trouble, occasioned by the intractable ferocity of his captive during the home voyage, he at length succeeded in lodging it safely at his own residence in Paris, where, not to attract toward himself the unpleasant curiosity of his neighbors, he kept it carefully secluded, until such time as it should recover from a wound in the foot, received from a splinter on board ship. His ultimate design was to sell it.

Returning home from some sailors' frolic on the night, or rather in the morning of the murder, he found the beast occupying his own bedroom, into which it had broken from a closet adjoining, where it had been, as was thought, securely confined. Razor in hand, and fully lathered, it was sitting before a looking-glass, attempting the operation of shaving, in which it had no doubt previously watched its master through the key-hole of the closet. Terrified at the sight of so dangerous a weapon in the possession of an animal so ferocious, and so well able to use it, the man, for some moments, was at a loss what to do. He had been accustomed, however, to quiet the creature, even in its fiercest moods, by the use of a whip, and to this he now resorted. Upon sight of it, the Ourang-Outang sprang at once through the door of the chamber, down the stairs, and thence, through a window, unfortunately open, into the street.

The Frenchman followed in despair; the ape, razor still in hand, occasionally stopping to look back and gesticulate at its pursuer, until the latter had nearly come up with it. It then again made off. In this manner the chase continued for a long time. The streets were profoundly quiet, as it was nearly three o'clock in the morning. In passing down an alley in the rear of the Rue Morgue, the fugitive's attention was arrested by a light gleaming from the open window of Madame L'Espanaye's chamber, in the fourth story of her house. Rushing to the building, it perceived the lightning-rod, clambered up with inconceivable agility, grasped the shutter, which was thrown fully back against the wall, and, by its means, swung itself directly upon the headboard of the bed. The whole feat did not occupy a minute. The shutter was kicked open again by the Ourang-Outang as it entered the room.

The sailor, in the meantime, was both rejoiced and perplexed. He had strong hopes of now recapturing the brute, as it could scarcely escape from the trap into which it had ventured, except by the rod, where it might be intercepted as it came down. On the other hand, there was much cause for anxiety as to what it might do in the house. This latter reflection urged the man still to follow the fugitive. A lightning-rod is ascended without difficulty, especially by a sailor; but, when he had arrived as high as the window, which lay far to his left, his career was stopped; the most that he could accomplish was to reach over so as to obtain a glimpse of the interior of the room. At this glimpse he nearly fell from his hold through excess of horror. Now it was that those hideous shrieks arose upon the night, which had startled from slumber the inmates of the Rue Morgue. Madame L'Espanaye and her daughter, habited in their night clothes, had apparently been occupied in arranging some papers in the iron chest already mentioned, which had been wheeled into the middle of the room. It was open, and its contents lay beside it on the floor. The victims must have been sitting with their backs toward the window; and, from the time elapsing between the ingress of the beast and the screams, it seems probable that it was not immediately perceived. The flapping-to of the shutter would naturally have been attributed to the wind.

As the sailor looked in, the gigantic animal had seized Madame L'Espanaye by the hair, (which was loose, as she had been combing it,) and was flourishing the razor about her face, in imitation of the motions of a barber. The daughter lay prostrate and motionless; she had swooned. The screams and struggles of the old lady (during which the hair was torn from her head) had the effect of changing the probably pacific purposes of the Ourang-Outang into those of wrath. With one determined sweep of its muscular arm it nearly severed her head from her body. The sight of blood inflamed its anger into phrenzy. Gnashing its teeth, and flashing fire from its eyes, it flew upon the body of the girl, and imbedded its fearful talons in her throat, retaining its grasp until she expired. Its wandering and wild glances fell at this moment upon the head of the bed, over which the face of its master, rigid with horror, was just discernible. The fury of the beast, who no doubt bore still in mind the dreaded whip, was instantly converted into fear. Conscious of having deserved punishment, it seemed desirous of concealing its bloody deeds, and skipped about the chamber in an agony of nervous agitation; throwing down and breaking the furniture as it moved, and dragging the bed from the bedstead. In conclusion, it seized first the corpse of the daughter, and thrust it up the chimney, as it was found; then that of the old lady, which it immediately hurled through the window headlong.

As the ape approached the casement with its mutilated burden, the sailor shrank aghast to the rod, and, rather gliding than clambering down it, hurried at once home—dreading the consequences of the butchery, and gladly abandoning, in his terror, all solicitude about the fate of the Ourang-Outang. The words heard by the party upon the staircase were the Frenchman's exclamations of horror and affright, commingled with the fiendish jabberings of the brute.

I have scarcely anything to add. The Ourang-Outang must have escaped from the chamber, by the rod, just before the breaking of the door. It must have closed the window as it passed through it. It was subsequently caught by the owner himself, who obtained for it a very large sum at the *Jardin des Plantes.*° Le Bon was instantly released, upon our narration of the circumstances (with some comments from Dupin) at the *bureau* of the Prefect of Police. This functionary, however well

Jardin des Plantes: The Ménagerie du Jardin des Plantes was a zoo located in a large botanical garden in central Paris, founded in 1793.

disposed to my friend, could not altogether conceal his chagrin at the turn which affairs had taken, and was fain to indulge in a sarcasm or two, about the propriety of every person minding his own business.

"Let him talk," said Dupin, who had not thought it necessary to reply. "Let him discourse; it will ease his conscience. I am satisfied with having defeated him in his own castle. Nevertheless, that he failed in the solution of this mystery, is by no means that matter for wonder which he supposes it; for, in truth, our friend the Prefect is somewhat too cunning to be profound. In his wisdom is no stamen. It is all head and no body, like the pictures of the Goddess Laverna,—or, at best, all head and shoulders, like a codfish. But he is a good creature after all. I like him especially for one master stroke of cant, by which he has attained his reputation for ingenuity. I mean the way he has '*de nier ce qui est, et d'expliquer ce qui n'est pas°.*'"

The Oval Portrait

The chateau into which my valet had ventured to make forcible entrance, rather than permit me, in my desperately wounded condition, to pass a night in the open air, was one of those piles of commingled gloom and grandeur which have so long frowned among the Appenines,° not less in fact than in the fancy of Mrs. Radcliffe.° To all appearance it had been temporarily and very lately abandoned. We established ourselves in one of the smallest and least sumptuously furnished apartments. It lay in a remote turret of the building. Its decorations were rich, yet tattered and antique. Its walls were hung with tapestry and bedecked with manifold and multiform armorial trophies, together with an unusually great number of very spirited modern paintings in frames of rich golden arabesque. In these paintings, which depended from the walls not only in their main surfaces, but in very many nooks which the bizarre architecture of the chateau rendered necessary—in these paintings my incipient delirium, perhaps, had caused me to take deep interest; so that I bade Pedro to close the heavy shutters of the room—since it was already night—to light the tongues of a tall candelabrum which stood by the head of my bed—and to throw open far and wide the fringed curtains of black velvet which enveloped the bed itself. I wished all this done that I might resign myself, if not to sleep, at least alternately to the contemplation of these pictures, and the perusal of

---

de nier . . . n'est pas: Rousseau—Nouvella Heloise. [Poe's note.] The passage translates, "To deny what is, and explain what is not." **Appenines:** The Apennine Mountains of Italy. **Mrs. Radcliffe:** Ann Radcliffe (1764–1823), British gothic novelist.

a small volume which had been found upon the pillow, and which purported to criticise and describe them.

Long—long I read—and devoutly, devotedly I gazed. Rapidly and
gloriously the hours flew by, and the deep midnight came. The position
of the candelabrum displeased me, and outreaching my hand with difficulty, rather than disturb my slumbering valet, I placed it so as to
throw its rays more fully upon the book.

But the action produced an effect altogether unanticipated. The
rays of the numerous candles (for there were many) now fell within a
niche of the room which had hitherto been thrown into deep shade by
one of the bed-posts. I thus saw in vivid light a picture all unnoticed
before. It was the portrait of a young girl just ripening into womanhood. I glanced at the painting hurriedly, and then closed my eyes. Why
I did this was not at first apparent even to my own perception. But
while my lids remained thus shut, I ran over in my mind my reason for
so shutting them. It was an impulsive movement to gain time for
thought—to make sure that my vision had not deceived me—to calm
and subdue my fancy for a more sober and more certain gaze. In a very
few moments I again looked fixedly at the painting.

That I now saw aright I could not and would not doubt; for the first
flashing of the candles upon that canvas had seemed to dissipate the
dreamy stupor which was stealing over my senses, and to startle me at
once into waking life.

The portrait, I have already said, was that of a young girl. It was a
mere head and shoulders, done in what is technically termed a *vignette*
manner; much in the style of the favorite heads of Sully.° The arms, the
bosom and even the ends of the radiant hair, melted imperceptibly into
the vague yet deep shadow which formed the back-ground of the whole.
The frame was oval, richly gilded and filagreed in *Moresque*. As a thing of
art nothing could be more admirable than the painting itself. But it could
have been neither the execution of the work, nor the immortal beauty of
the countenance, which had so suddenly and so vehemently moved me.
Least of all, could it have been that my fancy, shaken from its half slumber, had mistaken the head for that of a living person. I saw at once that
the peculiarities of the design, of the *vignetting*, and of the frame, must
have instantly dispelled such idea—must have prevented even its momentary entertainment. Thinking earnestly upon these points, I remained,
for an hour perhaps, half sitting, half reclining, with my vision riveted
upon the portrait. At length, satisfied with the true secret of its effect, I

Sully: Thomas Sully (1783–1872), British-born American portrait painter.

fell back within the bed. I had found the spell of the picture in an absolute *life-likeliness* of expression, which, at first startling, finally confounded, subdued and appalled me. With deep and reverent awe I
replaced the candelabrum in its former position. The cause of my deep
agitation being thus shut from view, I sought eagerly the volume which
discussed the paintings and their histories. Turning to the number which
designated the oval portrait, I there read the vague and quaint words
which follow:

"She was a maiden of rarest beauty, and not more lovely than full of
glee. And evil was the hour when she saw, and loved, and wedded the
painter. He, passionate, studious, austere, and having already a bride in
his Art: she a maiden of rarest beauty, and not more lovely than full of
glee: all light and smiles, and frolicksome as the young fawn: loving and
cherishing all things: hating only the Art which was her rival: dreading
only the pallet and brushes and other untoward instruments which
deprived her of the countenance of her lover. It was thus a terrible thing
for this lady to hear the painter speak of his desire to pourtray even his
young bride. But she was humble and obedient, and sat meekly for
many weeks in the dark high turret-chamber where the light dripped
upon the pale canvas only from overhead. But he, the painter, took
glory in his work, which went on from hour to hour and from day to
day. And he was a passionate, and wild and moody man, who became
lost in reveries; so that he *would* not see that the light which fell so
ghastlily in that lone turret withered the health and the spirits of his
bride, who pined visibly to all but him. Yet she smiled on and still
on, uncomplainingly, because she saw that the painter, (who had high
renown,) took a fervid and burning pleasure in his task, and wrought
day and night to depict her who so loved him, yet who grew daily more
dispirited and weak. And in sooth some who beheld the portrait spoke
of its resemblance in low words, as of a mighty marvel, and a proof not
less of the power of the painter than of his deep love for her whom he
depicted so surpassingly well. But at length, as the labor drew nearer to
its conclusion, there were admitted none into the turret; for the painter
had grown wild with the ardor of his work, and turned his eyes from the
canvas rarely, even to regard the countenance of his wife. And he *would*
not see that the tints which he spread upon the canvas were drawn from
the cheeks of her who sat beside him. And when many weeks had
passed, and but little remained to do, save one brush upon the mouth
and one tint upon the eye, the spirit of the lady again flickered up as
the flame within the socket of the lamp. And then the brush was given,
and then the tint was placed; and, for one moment, the painter stood

entranced before the work which he had wrought; but in the next, while he yet gazed, he grew tremulous and very pallid, and aghast, and crying with a loud voice 'This is indeed *Life* itself!' turned suddenly to regard his beloved: — *She was dead.*"

The Pit and the Pendulum

Impia tortorum longas hic turba furores
Sanguinis innocui, non satiata, aluit.
Sospite nunc patria, fracto nunc funeris antro,
Mors ubi dira fuit vita salusque patent.°
  —[QUATRAIN COMPOSED FOR THE GATES OF A MARKET TO BE ERECTED
      UPON THE SITE OF THE JACOBIN CLUB° HOUSE AT PARIS.]

I was sick — sick unto death with that long agony; and when they at length unbound me, and I was permitted to sit, I felt that my senses were leaving me. The sentence — the dread sentence of death — was the last of distinct accentuation which reached my ears. After that, the sound of the inquisitorial voices seemed merged in one dreamy indeterminate hum. It conveyed to my soul the idea of *revolution* — perhaps from its association in fancy with the burr of a mill-wheel. This only for a brief period; for presently I heard no more. Yet, for a while, I saw; but with how terrible an exaggeration! I saw the lips of the black-robed judges. They appeared to me white — whiter than the sheet upon which I trace these words — and thin even to grotesqueness; thin with the intensity of their expression of firmness — of immoveable resolution — of stern contempt of human torture. I saw that the decrees of what to me was Fate, were still issuing from those lips. I saw them writhe with a deadly locution. I saw them fashion the syllables of my name; and I shuddered because no sound succeeded. I saw, too, for a few moments of delirious horror, the soft and nearly imperceptible waving of the sable draperies which enwrapped the walls of the apartment. And then my vision fell upon the seven tall candles upon the table. At first they wore the aspect of charity, and seemed white and slender angels who would save me; but then, all at once, there came a most deadly nausea over my spirit, and I felt every fibre in my frame thrill as if I had touched

---

Impia tortorum . . . salusque patent: Here the wicked mob, unappeased / Long cherished a hatred of innocent blood. / Now that the fatherland has been saved, and the cave of death demolished, / Where grim death has been, life and health appear. **Jacobin Club:** The Jacobin Club was the most important political group of the French Revolution.

the wire of a galvanic battery, while the angel forms became meaning-less spectres, with heads of flame, and I saw that from them there would be no help. And then there stole into my fancy, like a rich musical note, the thought of what sweet rest there must be in the grave. The thought came gently and stealthily, and it seemed long before it attained full appreciation; but just as my spirit came at length properly to feel and entertain it, the figures of the judges vanished, as if magically, from before me; the tall candles sank into nothingness; their flames went out utterly; the blackness of darkness supervened; all sensations appeared swallowed up in a mad rushing descent as of the soul into Hades. Then silence, and stillness, and night were the universe.

I had swooned; but still will not say that all of consciousness was lost. What of it there remained I will not attempt to define, or even to describe; yet all was not lost. In the deepest slumber—no! In delir-ium—no! In a swoon—no! In death—no! even in the grave all *is not* lost. Else there is no immortality for man. Arousing from the most pro-found of slumbers, we break the gossamer web of *some* dream. Yet in a second afterward, (so frail may that web have been) we remember not that we have dreamed. In the return to life from the swoon there are two stages; first, that of the sense of mental or spiritual; secondly, that of the sense of physical, existence. It seems probable that if, upon reach-ing the second stage, we could recall the impressions of the first, we should find these impressions eloquent in memories of the gulf beyond. And that gulf is—what? How at least shall we distinguish its shadows from those of the tomb? But if the impressions of what I have termed the first stage, are not, at will, recalled, yet, after long interval, do they not come unbidden, while we marvel whence they come? He who has never swooned, is not he who finds strange palaces and wildly familiar faces in coals that glow; is not he who beholds floating in mid-air the sad visions that the many may not view; is not he who ponders over the perfume of some novel flower—is not he whose brain grows bewildered with the meaning of some musical cadence which has never before arrested his attention.

Amid frequent and thoughtful endeavors to remember; amid ear-nest struggles to regather some token of the state of seeming nothing-ness into which my soul had lapsed, there have been moments when I have dreamed of success; there have been brief, very brief periods when I have conjured up remembrances which the lucid reason of a later epoch assures me could have had reference only to that condition of seeming unconsciousness. These shadows of memory tell, indistinctly, of tall figures that lifted and bore me in silence down—down—still down—till a hideous dizziness oppressed me at the mere idea of the interminableness of the descent. They tell also of a vague horror at my heart, on account of that heart's unnatural stillness. Then comes a sense of sudden motionlessness throughout all things; as if those who bore me (a ghastly train!) had outrun, in their descent, the limits of the limitless, and paused from the wearisomeness of their toil. After this I call to mind flatness and dampness; and then all is *madness*—the madness of a memory which busies itself among forbidden things.

Very suddenly there came back to my soul motion and sound—the tumultuous motion of the heart, and, in my ears, the sound of its beating. Then a pause in which all is blank. Then again sound, and motion, and touch—a tingling sensation pervading my frame. Then the mere consciousness of existence, without thought—a condition which lasted long. Then, very suddenly, *thought*, and shuddering terror, and earnest endeavor to comprehend my true state. Then a strong desire to lapse into insensibility. Then a rushing revival of soul and a successful effort to move. And now a full memory of the trial, of the judges, of the sable draperies, of the sentence, of the sickness, of the swoon. Then entire forgetfulness of all that followed; of all that a later day and much earnestness of endeavor have enabled me vaguely to recall.

So far, I had not opened my eyes. I felt that I lay upon my back, unbound. I reached out my hand, and it fell heavily upon something damp and hard. There I suffered it to remain for many minutes, while I strove to imagine where and *what* I could be. I longed, yet dared not to employ my vision. I dreaded the first glance at objects around me. It was not that I feared to look upon things horrible, but that I grew aghast lest there should be *nothing* to see. At length, with a wild desperation at heart, I quickly unclosed my eyes. My worst thoughts, then, were confirmed. The blackness of eternal night encompassed me. I struggled for breath. The intensity of the darkness seemed to oppress and stifle me. The atmosphere was intolerably close. I still lay quietly, and made effort to exercise my reason. I brought to mind the inquisitorial proceedings, and attempted from that point to deduce my real condition. The sentence had passed; and it appeared to me that a very long interval of time had since elapsed. Yet not for a moment did I suppose myself actually dead. Such a supposition, notwithstanding what we read in fiction, is altogether inconsistent with real existence;—but where and in what state was I? The condemned to death, I knew, perished usually at the *auto-da-fes*,° and one of these had been held on the very

---

auto-da-fes: The burning of a heretic by the Spanish Inquisition.

night of the day of my trial. Had I been remanded to my dungeon, to await the next sacrifice, which would not take place for many months? This I at once saw could not be. Victims had been in immediate demand. Moreover, my dungeon, as well as all the condemned cells at Toledo, had stone floors, and light was not altogether excluded.

A fearful idea now suddenly drove the blood in torrents upon my heart, and for a brief period, I once more relapsed into insensibility. Upon recovering, I at once started to my feet, trembling convulsively in every fibre. I thrust my arms wildly above and around me in all directions. I felt nothing; yet dreaded to move a step, lest I should be impeded by the walls of a *tomb*. Perspiration burst from every pore, and stood in cold big beads upon my forehead. The agony of suspense, grew at length intolerable, and I cautiously moved forward, with my arms extended, and my eyes straining from their sockets, in the hope of catching some faint ray of light. I proceeded for many paces; but still all was blackness and vacancy. I breathed more freely. It seemed evident that mine was not, at least, the most hideous of fates.

And now, as I still continued to step cautiously onward, there came thronging upon my recollection a thousand vague rumors of the horrors of Toledo. Of the dungeons there had been strange things narrated—fables I had always deemed them—but yet strange, and too ghastly to repeat, save in a whisper. Was I left to perish of starvation in this subterranean world of darkness; or what fate, perhaps even more fearful, awaited me? That the result would be death, and a death of more than customary bitterness, I knew too well the character of my judges to doubt. The mode and the hour were all that occupied or distracted me.

My outstretched hands at length encountered some solid obstruction. It was a wall, seemingly of stone masonry—very smooth, slimy, and cold. I followed it up; stepping with all the careful distrust with which certain antique narratives had inspired me. This process, however, afforded me no means of ascertaining the dimensions of my dungeon; as I might make its circuit, and return to the point whence I set out, without being aware of the fact; so perfectly uniform seemed the wall. I therefore sought the knife which had been in my pocket, when led into the inquisitorial chamber; but it was gone; my clothes had been exchanged for a wrapper of coarse serge. I had thought of forcing the blade in some minute crevice of the masonry, so as to identify my point of departure. The difficulty, nevertheless, was but trivial; although, in the disorder of my fancy, it seemed at first insuperable. I tore a part of the hem from the robe and placed the fragment at full length, and at right angles to the wall. In groping my way around the prison, I could not fail to encounter this rag upon completing the circuit. So, at least I thought: but I had not counted upon the extent of the dungeon, or upon my own weakness. The ground was moist and slippery. I staggered onward for some time, when I stumbled and fell. My excessive fatigue induced me to remain prostrate; and sleep soon overtook me as I lay.

Upon awaking, and stretching forth an arm, I found beside me a loaf and a pitcher with water. I was too much exhausted to reflect upon this circumstance, but ate and drank with avidity. Shortly afterward, I resumed my tour around the prison, and with much toil, came at last upon the fragment of the serge. Up to the period when I fell, I had counted fifty-two paces, and, upon resuming my walk, I had counted forty-eight more — when I arrived at the rag. There were in all, then, a hundred paces; and, admitting two paces to the yard, I presumed the dungeon to be fifty yards in circuit. I had met, however, with many angles in the wall, and thus I could form no guess at the shape of the vault; for vault I could not help supposing it to be.

I had little object — certainly no hope — in these researches; but a vague curiosity prompted me to continue them. Quitting the wall, I resolved to cross the area of the enclosure. At first, I proceeded with extreme caution, for the floor, although seemingly of solid material, was treacherous with slime. At length, however, I took courage, and did not hesitate to step firmly — endeavoring to cross in as direct a line as possible. I had advanced some ten or twelve paces in this manner, when the remnant of the torn hem of my robe became entangled between my legs. I stepped on it, and fell violently on my face.

In the confusion attending my fall, I did not immediately apprehend a somewhat startling circumstance, which yet, in a few seconds afterward, and while I still lay prostrate, arrested my attention. It was this: my chin rested upon the floor of the prison, but my lips, and the upper portion of my head, although seemingly at a less elevation than the chin, touched nothing. At the same time, my forehead seemed bathed in a clammy vapor, and the peculiar smell of decayed fungus arose to my nostrils. I put forward my arm, and shuddered to find that I had fallen at the very brink of a circular pit, whose extent, of course, I had no means of ascertaining at the moment. Groping about the masonry just below the margin, I succeeded in dislodging a small fragment, and let it fall into the abyss. For many seconds I hearkened to its reverberations as it dashed against the sides of the chasm in its descent: at length, there was a sullen plunge into water, succeeded by loud echoes. At the same moment, there came a sound resembling the quick opening, and as rapid closing of a door overhead, while a faint gleam of light flashed suddenly through the gloom, and as suddenly faded away.

I saw clearly the doom which had been prepared for me, and congratulated myself upon the timely accident by which I had escaped. Another step before my fall, and the world had seen me no more. And the death just avoided, was of that very character which I had regarded as fabulous and frivolous in the tales respecting the Inquisition. To the victims of its tyranny, there was the choice of death with its direst physical agonies, or death with its most hideous moral horrors. I had been reserved for the latter. By long suffering my nerves had been unstrung, until I trembled at the sound of my own voice, and had become in every respect a fitting subject for the species of torture which awaited me.

Shaking in every limb, I groped my way back to the wall—resolving there to perish rather than risk the terrors of the wells, of which my imagination now pictured many in various positions about the dungeon. In other conditions of mind, I might have had courage to end my misery at once, by a plunge into one of these abysses; but now I was the veriest of cowards. Neither could I forget what I had read of these pits—that the *sudden* extinction of life formed no part of their most horrible plan.

Agitation of spirit kept me awake for many long hours; but at length I again slumbered. Upon arousing, I found by my side, as before, a loaf and a pitcher of water. A burning thirst consumed me, and I emptied the vessel at a draught. It must have been drugged—for scarcely had I drunk, before I became irresistibly drowsy. A deep sleep fell upon me— a sleep like that of death. How long it lasted, of course, I know not; but when, once again, I unclosed my eyes, the objects around me were visible. By a wild, sulphurous lustre, the origin of which I could not at first determine, I was enabled to see the extent and aspect of the prison.

In its size I had been greatly mistaken. The whole circuit of its walls did not exceed twenty-five yards. For some minutes this fact occasioned me a world of vain trouble; vain indeed—for what could be of less importance, under the terrible circumstances which environed me, then the mere dimensions of my dungeon? But my soul took a wild interest in trifles, and I busied myself in endeavors to account for the error I had committed in my measurement. The truth at length flashed upon me. In my first attempt at exploration, I had counted fifty-two paces, up to the period when I fell: I must then have been within a pace or two of the fragment of serge; in fact, I had nearly performed the circuit of the vault. I then slept—and, upon awaking, I must have returned upon my steps—thus supposing the circuit nearly double what it actually was. My confusion of mind prevented me from observing that I began my tour with the wall to the left, and ended it with the wall to the right.

I had been deceived, too, in respect to the shape of the enclosure. In feeling my way, I had found many angles, and thus deduced an idea of great irregularity; so potent is the effect of total darkness upon one arousing from lethargy or sleep! The angles were simply those of a few slight depressions, or niches, at odd intervals. The general shape of the prison was square. What I had taken for masonry seemed now to be iron, or some other metal, in huge plates, whose sutures or joints occasioned the depression. The entire surface of this metallic enclosure was rudely daubed in all the hideous and repulsive devices to which the charnel superstition of the monks has given rise. The figures of fiends in aspects of menace, with skeleton forms, and other more really fearful images, overspread and disfigured the walls. I observed that the outlines of these monstrosities were sufficiently distinct, but that the colors seemed faded and blurred, as if from the effects of a damp atmosphere. I now noticed the floor, too, which was of stone. In the centre yawned the circular pit from whose jaws I had escaped; but it was the only one in the dungeon.

All this I saw indistinctly and by much effort—for my personal condition had been greatly changed during slumber. I now lay upon my back, and at full length, on a species of low framework of wood. To this I was securely bound by a long strap resembling a surcingle.° It passed in many convolutions about my limbs and body, leaving at liberty only my head, and my left arm to such extent, that I could, by dint of much exertion, supply myself with food from an earthen dish which lay by my side on the floor. I saw, to my horror, that the pitcher had been removed. I say, to my horror—for I was consumed with intolerable thirst. This thirst it appeared to be the design of my persecutors to stimulate—for the food in the dish was meat pungently seasoned.

Looking upward, I surveyed the ceiling of my prison. It was some thirty or forty feet overhead, and constructed much as the side walls. In one of its panels a very singular figure riveted my whole attention. It was the painted figure of Time as he is commonly represented, save that, in lieu of a scythe, he held what, at a casual glance, I supposed to be the pictured image of a huge pendulum, such as we see on antique clocks. There was something, however, in the appearance of this

surcingle: A belt used to attach equipment to a horse.

machine which caused me to regard it more attentively. While I gazed directly upward at it, (for its position was immediately over my own,) I fancied that I saw it in motion. In an instant afterward the fancy was confirmed. Its sweep was brief, and of course slow. I watched it for some minutes, somewhat in fear, but more in wonder. Wearied at length with observing its dull movement, I turned my eyes upon the other objects in the cell.

A slight noise attracted my notice, and, looking to the floor, I saw several enormous rats traversing it. They had issued from the well, which lay just within view to my right. Even then, while I gazed, they came up in troops, hurriedly, with ravenous eyes, allured by the scent of the meat. From this it required much effort and attention to scare them away.

It might have been half an hour, perhaps even an hour, (for I could take but imperfect note of time,) before I again cast my eyes upward. What I then saw, confounded and amazed me. The sweep of the pendulum had increased in extent by nearly a yard. As a natural consequence, its velocity was also much greater. But what mainly disturbed me, was the idea that it had perceptibly *descended*. I now observed — with what horror it is needless to say — that its nether extremity was formed of a crescent of glittering steel, about a foot in length from horn to horn; the horns upward, and the under edge evidently as keen as that of a razor. Like a razor also, it seemed massy and heavy, tapering from the edge into a solid and broad structure above. It was appended to a weighty rod of brass, and the whole *hissed* as it swung through the air.

I could no longer doubt the doom prepared for me by monkish ingenuity in torture. My cognizance of the pit had become known to the inquisitorial agents — *the pit*, whose horrors had been destined for so bold a recusant as myself — *the pit*, typical of hell, and regarded by rumor as the Ultima Thule° of all their punishments. The plunge into this pit I had avoided by the merest of accidents, and I knew that surprise, or entrapment into torment, formed an important portion of all the grotesquerie of these dungeon deaths. Having failed to fall, it was no part of the demon plan to hurl me into the abyss; and thus (there being no alternative) a different and a milder destruction awaited me. Milder! I half smiled in my agony as I thought of such application of such a term.

What boots it to tell of the long, long hours of horror more than mortal, during which I counted the rushing oscillations of the steel! Inch by inch — line by line — with a descent only appreciable at inter-

Ultima Thule: A remote goal or ideal.

vals that seemed ages—down and still down it came! Days passed—it might have been that many days passed—ere it swept so closely over me as to fan me with its acrid breath. The odor of the sharp steel forced itself into my nostrils. I prayed—I wearied heaven with my prayer for its more speedy descent. I grew frantically mad, and struggled to force myself upward against the sweep of the fearful scimitar. And then I fell suddenly calm, and lay smiling at the glittering death, as a child at some rare bauble.

There was another interval of utter insensibility; it was brief; for, upon again lapsing into life, there had been no perceptible descent in the pendulum. But it might have been long—for I knew there were demons who took note of my swoon, and who could have arrested the vibration at pleasure. Upon my recovery, too, I felt very—oh, inexpressibly—sick and weak, as if through long inanition. Even amid the agonies of that period, the human nature craved food. With painful effort I outstretched my left arm as far as my bonds permitted, and took possession of the small remnant which had been spared me by the rats. As I put a portion of it within my lips, there rushed to my mind a half-formed thought of joy—of hope. Yet what business had *I* with hope? It was, as I say, a half-formed thought—man has many such, which are never completed. I felt that it was of joy—of hope; but I felt also that it had perished in its formation. In vain I struggled to perfect—to regain it. Long suffering had nearly annihilated all my ordinary powers of mind. I was an imbecile—an idiot.

The vibration of the pendulum was at right angles to my length. I saw that the crescent was designed to cross the region of the heart. It would fray the serge of my robe—it would return and repeat its operations—again—and again. Notwithstanding its terrifically wide sweep, (some thirty feet or more,) and the hissing vigor of its descent, sufficient to sunder these very walls of iron, still the fraying of my robe would be all that, for several minutes, it would accomplish. And at this thought I paused. I dared not go farther than this reflection. I dwelt upon it with a pertinacity of attention—as if, in so dwelling, I could arrest *here* the descent of the steel. I forced myself to ponder upon the sound of the crescent as it should pass across the garment—upon the peculiar thrilling sensation which the friction of cloth produces on the nerves. I pondered upon all this frivolity until my teeth were on edge.

Down—steadily down it crept. I took a frenzied pleasure in contrasting its downward with its lateral velocity. To the right—to the left—far and wide—with the shriek of a damned spirit! to my heart,

with the stealthy pace of the tiger! I alternately laughed and howled, as
the one or the other idea grew predominant.

Down—certainly, relentlessly down! It vibrated within three inches
of my bosom! I struggled violently—furiously—to free my left arm.
This was free only from the elbow to the hand. I could reach the latter,
from the platter beside me, to my mouth, with great effort, but no farther. Could I have broken the fastenings above the elbow, I would have
seized and attempted to arrest the pendulum. I might as well have
attempted to arrest an avalanche!

Down—still unceasingly—still inevitably down! I gasped and
struggled at each vibration. I shrunk convulsively at its every sweep. My
eyes followed its outward or upward whirls with the eagerness of the
most unmeaning despair; they closed themselves spasmodically at the
descent, although death would have been a relief, oh, how unspeakable! Still I quivered in every nerve to think how slight a sinking of the
machinery would precipitate that keen, glistening axe upon my bosom.
It was *hope* that prompted the nerve to quiver—the frame to shrink. It
was *hope*—the hope that triumphs on the rack—that whispers to the
death-condemned even in the dungeons of the Inquisition.

I saw that some ten or twelve vibrations would bring the steel in
actual contact with my robe—and with this observation there suddenly
came over my spirit all the keen, collected calmness of despair. For the
first time during many hours—or perhaps days—I *thought*. It now
occurred to me, that the bandage, or surcingle, which enveloped me,
was *unique*. I was tied by no separate cord. The first stroke of the razor-
like crescent athwart any portion of the band, would so detach it that it
might be unwound from my person by means of my left hand. But how
fearful, in that case, the proximity of the steel! The result of the slightest struggle, how deadly! Was it likely, moreover, that the minions of
the torturer had not foreseen and provided for this possibility? Was it
probable that the bandage crossed my bosom in the track of the pendulum? Dreading to find my faint, and, as it seemed, my last hope frustrated, I so far elevated my head as to obtain a distinct view of my
breast. The surcingle enveloped my limbs and body close in all directions—*save in the path of the destroying crescent.*

Scarcely had I dropped my head back into its original position,
when there flashed upon my mind what I cannot better describe than
as the unformed half of that idea of deliverance to which I have previously alluded, and of which a moiety only floated indeterminately
through my brain when I raised food to my burning lips. The whole
thought was now present—feeble, scarcely sane, scarcely definite—but

still entire. I proceeded at once, with the nervous energy of despair, to attempt its execution.

For many hours the immediate vicinity of the low framework upon which I lay, had been literally swarming with rats. They were wild, bold, ravenous—their red eyes glaring upon me as if they waited but for motionlessness on my part to make me their prey. "To what food," I thought, "have they been accustomed in the well?"

They had devoured, in spite of all my efforts to prevent them, all but a small remnant of the contents of the dish. I had fallen into an habitual see-saw, or wave of the hand about the platter; and, at length, the unconscious uniformity of the movement deprived it of effect. In their voracity, the vermin frequently fastened their sharp fangs in my fingers. With the particles of the oily and spicy viand which now remained, I thoroughly rubbed the bandage wherever I could reach it; then, raising my hand from the floor, I lay breathlessly still.

At first, the ravenous animals were startled and terrified at the change—at the cessation of movement. They shrank alarmedly back; many sought the well. But this was only for a moment. I had not counted in vain upon their voracity. Observing that I remained without motion, one or two of the boldest leaped upon the frame-work, and smelt at the surcingle. This seemed the signal for a general rush. Forth from the well they hurried in fresh troops. They clung to the wood—they overran it, and leaped in hundreds upon my person. The measured movement of the pendulum disturbed them not at all. Avoiding its strokes, they busied themselves with the anointed bandage. They pressed—they swarmed upon me in ever accumulating heaps. They writhed upon my throat; their cold lips sought my own; I was half stifled by their thronging pressure; disgust, for which the world has no name, swelled my bosom, and chilled, with a heavy clamminess, my heart. Yet one minute, and I felt that the struggle would be over. Plainly I perceived the loosening of the bandage. I knew that in more than one place it must be already severed. With a more than human resolution I lay *still*.

Nor had I erred in my calculations—nor had I endured in vain. I at length felt that I was *free*. The surcingle hung in ribands from my body. But the stroke of the pendulum already pressed upon my bosom. It had divided the serge of the robe. It had cut through the linen beneath. Twice again it swung, and a sharp sense of pain shot through every nerve. But the moment of escape had arrived. At a wave of my hand my deliverers hurried tumultuously away. With a steady movement—cautious, sidelong, shrinking, and slow—I slid from the embrace of the bandage and beyond the reach of the scimitar. For the moment, at least, *I was free.*

Free!—and in the grasp of the Inquisition! I had scarcely stepped from my wooden bed of horror upon the stone floor of the prison, when the motion of the hellish machine ceased, and I beheld it drawn up, by some invisible force, through the ceiling. This was a lesson which I took desperately to heart. My every motion was undoubtedly watched. Free!—I had but escaped death in one form of agony, to be delivered unto worse than death in some other. With that thought I rolled my eyes nervously around on the barriers of iron that hemmed me in. Something unusual—some change which, at first, I could not appreciate distinctly—it was obvious, had taken place in the apartment. For many minutes of a dreamy and trembling abstraction, I busied myself in vain, unconnected conjecture. During this period, I became aware, for the first time, of the origin of the sulphurous light which illumined the cell. It proceeded from a fissure, about half an inch in width, extending entirely around the prison at the base of the walls, which thus appeared, and were completely separated from the floor. I endeavored, but of course in vain, to look through the aperture.

As I arose from the attempt, the mystery of the alteration in the chamber broke at once upon my understanding. I have observed that, although the outlines of the figures upon the walls were sufficiently distinct, yet the colors seemed blurred and indefinite. These colors had now assumed, and were momentarily assuming, a startling and most intense brilliancy, that gave to the spectral and fiendish portraitures an aspect that might have thrilled even firmer nerves than my own. Demon eyes, of a wild and ghastly vivacity, glared upon me in a thousand directions, where none had been visible before, and gleamed with the lurid lustre of a fire that I could not force my imagination to regard as unreal.

Unreal!—Even while I breathed there came to my nostrils the breath of the vapor of heated iron! A suffocating odor pervaded the prison! A deeper glow settled each moment in the eyes that glared at my agonies! A richer tint of crimson diffused itself over the pictured horrors of blood. I panted! I gasped for breath! There could be no doubt of the design of my tormentors—oh! most unrelenting! oh! most demoniac of men! I shrank from the glowing metal to the centre of the cell. Amid the thought of the fiery destruction that impended, the idea of the coolness of the well came over my soul like balm. I rushed to its deadly brink. I threw my straining vision below. The glare from the enkindled roof illumined its inmost recesses. Yet, for a wild moment, did my spirit refuse to comprehend the meaning of what I saw. At length it forced—it wrestled its way into my soul—it burned itself in upon my shuddering reason. Oh! for a voice to speak!—oh! horror!—oh! any horror but this! With a shriek, I rushed from the margin, and buried my face in my hands—weeping bitterly.

The heat rapidly increased, and once again I looked up, shuddering as with a fit of the ague. There had been a second change in the cell—and now the change was obviously in the *form*. As before, it was in vain that I at first endeavored to appreciate or understand what was taking place. But not long was I left in doubt. The Inquisitorial vengeance had been hurried by my two-fold escape, and there was to be no more dallying with the King of Terrors. The room had been square. I saw that two of its iron angles were now acute—two, consequently, obtuse. The fearful difference quickly increased with a low rumbling or moaning sound. In an instant the apartment had shifted its form into that of a lozenge. But the alteration stopped not here—I neither hoped nor desired it to stop. I could have clasped the red walls to my bosom as a garment of eternal peace. "Death," I said, "any death but that of the pit!" Fool! might I have not known that *into the pit* it was the object of the burning iron to urge me? Could I resist its glow? or if even that, could I withstand its pressure? And now, flatter and flatter grew the lozenge, with a rapidity that left me no time for contemplation. Its centre, and of course, its greatest width, came just over the yawning gulf. I shrank back—but the closing walls pressed me resistlessly onward. At length for my seared and writhing body there was no longer an inch of foothold on the firm floor of the prison. I struggled no more, but the agony of my soul found vent in one loud, long, and final scream of despair. I felt that I tottered upon the brink—I averted my eyes—

There was a discordant hum of human voices! There was a loud blast as of many trumpets! There was a harsh grating as of a thousand thunders! The fiery walls rushed back! An outstretched arm caught my own as I fell, fainting, into the abyss. It was that of General Lasalle.° The French army had entered Toledo. The Inquisition was in the hands of its enemies.

The Tell-Tale Heart

True!—nervous—very, very dreadfully nervous I had been and am; but why *will* you say that I am mad? The disease had sharpened my

---

General Lasalle: Antoine Charles Louis de Lasalle (1775–1809), French general during the French Revolution and Napoleonic Wars. He fought in Spain during the Peninsular War in 1808.

senses—not destroyed—not dulled them. Above all was the sense of hearing acute. I heard all things in the heaven and in the earth. I heard many things in hell. How, then, am I mad? Hearken! and observe how healthily—how calmly I can tell you the whole story.

It is impossible to say how first the idea entered my brain; but once conceived, it haunted me day and night. Object there was none. Passion there was none. I loved the old man. He had never wronged me. He had never given me insult. For his gold I had no desire. I think it was his eye! yes, it was this! One of his eyes resembled that of a vulture—a pale blue eye, with a film over it. Whenever it fell upon me, my blood ran cold; and so by degrees—very gradually—I made up my mind to take the life of the old man, and thus rid myself of the eye forever.

Now this is the point. You fancy me mad. Madmen know nothing. But you should have seen *me*. You should have seen how wisely I proceeded—with what caution—with what foresight—with what dissimulation I went to work! I was never kinder to the old man than during the whole week before I killed him. And every night, about midnight, I turned the latch of his door and opened it—oh, so gently! And then, when I had made an opening sufficient for my head, I put in a dark lantern, all closed, closed, so that no light shone out, and then I thrust in my head. Oh, you would have laughed to see how cunningly I thrust it in! I moved it slowly—very, very slowly, so that I might not disturb the old man's sleep. It took me an hour to place my whole head within the opening so far that I could see him as he lay upon his bed. Ha!—would a madman have been so wise as this? And then, when my head was well in the room, I undid the lantern cautiously—oh, so cautiously—cautiously (for the hinges creaked)—I undid it just so much that a single thin ray fell upon the vulture eye. And this I did for seven long nights—every night just at midnight—but I found the eye always closed; and so it was impossible to do the work; for it was not the old man who vexed me, but his Evil Eye. And every morning, when the day broke, I went boldly into the chamber, and spoke courageously to him, calling him by name in a hearty tone, and inquiring how he had passed the night. So you see he would have been a very profound old man, indeed, to suspect that every night, just at twelve, I looked in upon him while he slept.

Upon the eighth night I was more than usually cautious in opening the door. A watch's minute hand moves more quickly than did mine. Never before that night had I *felt* the extent of my own powers—of my sagacity. I could scarcely contain my feelings of triumph. To think that there I was, opening the door, little by little, and he not even to dream of my secret deeds or thoughts. I fairly chuckled at the idea; and perhaps he heard me; for he moved on the bed suddenly, as if startled. Now you may think that I drew back—but no. His room was as black as pitch with the thick darkness, (for the shutters were close fastened, through fear of robbers,) and so I knew that he could not see the opening of the door, and I kept pushing it on steadily, steadily.

I had my head in, and was about to open the lantern, when my thumb slipped upon the tin fastening, and the old man sprang up in the bed, crying out—"Who's there?"

I kept quite still and said nothing. For a whole hour I did not move a muscle, and in the meantime I did not hear him lie down. He was still sitting up in the bed listening;—just as I have done, night after night, hearkening to the death watches in the wall.

Presently I heard a slight groan, and I knew it was the groan of mortal terror. It was not a groan of pain or of grief—oh, no!—it was the low stifled sound that arises from the bottom of the soul when overcharged with awe. I knew the sound well. Many a night, just at midnight, when all the world slept, it has welled up from my own bosom, deepening, with its dreadful echo, the terrors that distracted me. I say I knew it well. I knew what the old man felt, and pitied him, although I chuckled at heart. I knew that he had been lying awake ever since the first slight noise, when he had turned in the bed. His fears had been ever since growing upon him. He had been trying to fancy them causeless, but could not. He had been saying to himself—"It is nothing but the wind in the chimney—it is only a mouse crossing the floor," or "it is merely a cricket which has made a single chirp." Yes, he has been trying to comfort himself with these suppositions: but he had found all in vain. *All in vain*; because Death, in approaching him had stalked with his black shadow before him, and enveloped the victim. And it was the mournful influence of the unperceived shadow that caused him to feel—although he neither saw nor heard—to *feel* the presence of my head within the room.

When I had waited a long time, very patiently, without hearing him lie down, I resolved to open a little—a very, very little crevice in the lantern. So I opened it—you cannot imagine how stealthily, stealthily—until, at length a single dim ray, like the thread of the spider, shot from out the crevice and fell upon the vulture eye.

It was open—wide, wide open—and I grew furious as I gazed upon it. I saw it with perfect distinctness—all a dull blue, with a hideous veil over it that chilled the very marrow in my bones; but I could see nothing else of the old man's face or person: for I had directed the ray as if by instinct, precisely upon the damned spot.

And now have I not told you that what you mistake for madness is but over acuteness of the senses? — now, I say, there came to my ears a low, dull, quick sound, such as a watch makes when enveloped in cotton. I knew *that* sound well, too. It was the beating of the old man's heart. It increased my fury, as the beating of a drum stimulates the soldier into courage.

But even yet I refrained and kept still. I scarcely breathed. I held the lantern motionless. I tried how steadily I could maintain the ray upon the eye. Meantime the hellish tattoo of the heart increased. It grew quicker and quicker, and louder and louder every instant. The old man's terror *must* have been extreme! It grew louder, I say, louder every moment! — do you mark me well? I have told you that I am nervous: so I am. And now at the dead hour of the night, amid the dreadful silence of that old house, so strange a noise as this excited me to uncontrollable terror. Yet, for some minutes longer I refrained and stood still. But the beating grew louder, louder! I thought the heart must burst. And now a new anxiety seized me — the sound would be heard by a neighbor! The old man's hour had come! With a loud yell, I threw open the lantern and leaped into the room. He shrieked once — once only. In an instant I dragged him to the floor, and pulled the heavy bed over him. I then smiled gaily, to find the deed so far done. But, for many minutes, the heart beat on with a muffled sound. This, however, did not vex me; it would not be heard through the wall. At length it ceased. The old man was dead. I removed the bed and examined the corpse. Yes, he was stone, stone dead. I placed my hand upon the heart and held it there many minutes. There was no pulsation. He was stone dead. His eye would trouble me no more.

If still you think me mad, you will think so no longer when I describe the wise precautions I took for the concealment of the body. The night waned, and I worked hastily, but in silence. First of all I dismembered the corpse. I cut off the head and the arms and the legs.

I then took up three planks from the flooring of the chamber, and deposited all between the scantlings. I then replaced the boards so cleverly, so cunningly, that no human eye — not even *his* — could have detected any thing wrong. There was nothing to wash out — no stain of any kind — no blood-spot whatever. I had been too wary for that. A tub had caught all — ha! ha!

When I had made an end of these labors, it was four o'clock — still dark as midnight. As the bell sounded the hour, there came a knocking at the street door. I went down to open it with a light heart,—for what had I *now* to fear? There entered three men, who introduced themselves, with perfect suavity, as officers of the police. A shriek had been heard by a neighbor during the night; suspicion of foul play had been aroused; information had been lodged at the police office, and they (the officers) had been deputed to search the premises.

I smiled,—for *what* had I to fear? I bade the gentlemen welcome. The shriek, I said, was my own in a dream. The old man, I mentioned, was absent in the country. I took my visitors all over the house. I bade them search—search *well*. I led them, at length, to *his* chamber. I showed them his treasures, secure, undisturbed. In the enthusiasm of my confidence, I brought chairs into the room, and desired them *here* to rest from their fatigues, while I myself, in the wild audacity of my perfect triumph, placed my own seat upon the very spot beneath which reposed the corpse of the victim.

The officers were satisfied. My *manner* had convinced them. I was singularly at ease. They sat, and while I answered cheerily, they chatted of familiar things. But, ere long, I felt myself getting pale and wished them gone. My head ached, and I fancied a ringing in my ears: but still they sat and still chatted. The ringing became more distinct:—it continued and became more distinct: I talked more freely to get rid of the feeling: but it continued and gained definitiveness—until, at length, I found that the noise was *not* within my ears.

No doubt I now grew *very* pale;—but I talked more fluently, and with a heightened voice. Yet the sound increased—and what could I do? It was *a low, dull, quick sound—much such a sound as a watch makes when enveloped in cotton*. I gasped for breath—and yet the officers heard it not. I talked more quickly—more vehemently; but the noise steadily increased. I arose and argued about trifles, in a high key and with violent gesticulations; but the noise steadily increased. Why *would* they not be gone? I paced the floor to and fro with heavy strides, as if excited to fury by the observations of the men—but the noise steadily increased. Oh God! what *could* I do? I foamed—I raved—I swore! I swung the chair upon which I had been sitting, and grated it upon the boards, but the noise arose over all and continually increased. It grew louder—louder—*louder!* And still the men chatted pleasantly, and smiled. Was it possible they heard not? Almighty God!—no, no! They heard!—they suspected!—they *knew!*—they were making a mockery of my horror!—this I thought, and this I think. But anything was better than this agony! Anything was more tolerable than this derision! I could bear those hypocritical smiles no longer! I felt that I must scream or die!—and now—again!—hark! louder! louder! louder! *louder!*—

"Villains!" I shrieked, "dissemble no more! I admit the deed!—tear up the planks!—here, here!—it is the beating of his hideous heart!"

The Black Cat

For the most wild, yet most homely narrative which I am about to pen, I neither expect nor solicit belief. Mad indeed would I be to expect it, in a case where my very senses reject their own evidence. Yet, mad am I not—and very surely do I not dream. But to-morrow I die, and to-day I would unburthen my soul. My immediate purpose is to place before the world, plainly, succinctly, and without comment, a series of mere household events. In their consequences, these events have terrified—have tortured—have destroyed me. Yet I will not attempt to expound them. To me, they have presented little but Horror—to many they will seem less terrible than *barroques.*° Hereafter, perhaps, some intellect may be found which will reduce my phantasm to the common-place—some intellect more calm, more logical, and far less excitable than my own, which will perceive, in the circumstances I detail with awe, nothing more than an ordinary succession of very natural causes and effects.

From my infancy I was noted for the docility and humanity of my disposition. My tenderness of heart was even so conspicuous as to make me the jest of my companions. I was especially fond of animals, and was indulged by my parents with a great variety of pets. With these I spent most of my time, and never was so happy as when feeding and caressing them. This peculiarity of character grew with my growth, and, in my manhood, I derived from it one of my principal sources of pleasure. To those who have cherished an affection for a faithful and sagacious dog, I need hardly be at the trouble of explaining the nature or the intensity of the gratification thus derivable. There is something in the unselfish and self-sacrificing love of a brute, which goes directly to the heart of him who has had frequent occasion to test the paltry friendship and gossamer fidelity of mere *Man.*

I married early, and was happy to find in my wife a disposition not uncongenial with my own. Observing my partiality for domestic pets,

---

barroques: Properly, the term refers to something in the baroque style (ornate, complex, etc.), but Poe here uses the word to mean *bizarre.*

she lost no opportunity of procuring those of the most agreeable kind. We had birds, goldfish, a fine dog, rabbits, a small monkey, and *a cat*.

This latter was a remarkably large and beautiful animal, entirely black, and sagacious to an astonishing degree. In speaking of his intelligence, my wife, who at heart was not a little tinctured with superstition, made frequent allusion to the ancient popular notion, which regarded all black cats as witches in disguise. Not that she was ever *serious* upon this point—and I mention the matter at all for no better reason than that it happens, just now, to be remembered.

Pluto—this was the cat's name—was my favorite pet and playmate. I alone fed him, and he attended me wherever I went about the house. It was even with difficulty that I could prevent him from following me through the streets.

Our friendship lasted, in this manner, for several years, during which my general temperament and character—through the instrumentality of the Fiend Intemperance—had (I blush to confess it) experienced a radical alteration for the worse. I grew, day by day, more moody, more irritable, more regardless of the feelings of others. I suffered myself to use intemperate language to my wife. At length, I even offered her personal violence. My pets, of course, were made to feel the change in my disposition. I not only neglected, but ill-used them. For Pluto, however, I still retained sufficient regard to restrain me from maltreating him, as I made no scruple of maltreating the rabbits, the monkey, or even the dog, when by accident, or through affection, they came in my way. But my disease grew upon me—for what disease is like Alcohol!—and at length even Pluto, who was now becoming old, and consequently somewhat peevish—even Pluto began to experience the effects of my ill temper.

One night, returning home, much intoxicated, from one of my haunts about town, I fancied that the cat avoided my presence. I seized him; when, in his fright at my violence, he inflicted a slight wound upon my hand with his teeth. The fury of a demon instantly possessed me. I knew myself no longer. My original soul seemed, at once, to take its flight from my body; and a more than fiendish malevolence, gin-nurtured, thrilled every fibre of my frame. I took from my waistcoat-pocket a pen-knife, opened it, grasped the poor beast by the throat, and deliberately cut one of its eyes from the socket! I blush, I burn, I shudder, while I pen the damnable atrocity.

When reason returned with the morning—when I had slept off the fumes of the night's debauch—I experienced a sentiment half of horror, half of remorse, for the crime of which I had been guilty; but it was, at best, a feeble and equivocal feeling, and the soul remained untouched. I again plunged into excess, and soon drowned in wine all memory of the deed.

In the meantime the cat slowly recovered. The socket of the lost eye presented, it is true, a frightful appearance, but he no longer appeared to suffer any pain. He went about the house as usual, but, as might be expected, fled in extreme terror at my approach. I had so much of my old heart left, as to be at first grieved by this evident dislike on the part of a creature which had once so loved me. But this feeling soon gave place to irritation. And then came, as if to my final and irrevocable overthrow, the spirit of PERVERSENESS. Of this spirit philosophy takes no account. Yet I am not more sure that my soul lives, than I am that perverseness is one of the primitive impulses of the human heart—one of the indivisible primary faculties, or sentiments, which give direction to the character of Man. Who has not, a hundred times, found himself committing a vile or a silly action, for no other reason than because he knows he should *not*? Have we not a perpetual inclination, in the teeth of our best judgment, to violate that which is *Law*, merely because we understand it to be such? This spirit of perverseness, I say, came to my final overthrow. It was this unfathomable longing of the soul *to vex itself*—to offer violence to its own nature—to do wrong for the wrong's sake only—that urged me to continue and finally to consummate the injury I had inflicted upon the unoffending brute. One morning, in cool blood, I slipped a noose about its neck and hung it to the limb of a tree;—hung it with the tears streaming from my eyes, and with the bitterest remorse at my heart;—hung it *because* I knew that it had loved me, and *because* I felt it had given me no reason of offence;—hung it *because* I knew that in so doing I was committing a sin—a deadly sin that would so jeopardize my immortal soul as to place it—if such a thing were possible—even beyond the reach of the infinite mercy of the Most Merciful and Most Terrible God.

On the night of the day on which this cruel deed was done, I was aroused from sleep by the cry of fire. The curtains of my bed were in flames. The whole house was blazing. It was with great difficulty that my wife, a servant, and myself, made our escape from the conflagration. The destruction was complete. My entire worldly wealth was swallowed up, and I resigned myself thenceforward to despair.

I am above the weakness of seeking to establish a sequence of cause and effect, between the disaster and the atrocity. But I am detailing a chain of facts—and wish not to leave even a possible link imperfect.

On the day succeeding the fire, I visited the ruins. The walls, with one exception, had fallen in. This exception was found in a compartment wall, not very thick, which stood about the middle of the house, and against which had rested the head of my bed. The plastering had here, in great measure, resisted the action of the fire—a fact which I attributed to its having been recently spread. About this wall a dense crowd were collected, and many persons seemed to be examining a particular portion of it with very minute and eager attention. The words "strange!" "singular!" and other similar expressions, excited my curiosity. I approached and saw, as if graven in *bas relief* upon the white surface, the figure of a gigantic *cat*. The impression was given with an accuracy truly marvellous. There was a rope about the animal's neck.

When I first beheld this apparition—for I could scarcely regard it as less—my wonder and my terror were extreme. But at length reflection came to my aid. The cat, I remembered, had been hung in a garden adjacent to the house. Upon the alarm of fire, this garden had been immediately filled by the crowd—by some one of whom the animal must have been cut from the tree and thrown, through an open window, into my chamber. This had probably been done with the view of arousing me from sleep. The falling of other walls had compressed the victim of my cruelty into the substance of the freshly-spread plaster; the lime of which, with the flames, and the *ammonia* from the carcass, had then accomplished the portraiture as I saw it.

Although I thus readily accounted to my reason, if not altogether to my conscience, for the startling fact just detailed, it did not the less fail to make a deep impression upon my fancy. For months I could not rid myself of the phantasm of the cat; and, during this period, there came back into my spirit a half-sentiment that seemed, but was not, remorse. I went so far as to regret the loss of the animal, and to look about me, among the vile haunts which I now habitually frequented, for another pet of the same species, and of somewhat similar appearance, with which to supply its place.

One night as I sat, half stupified, in a den of more than infamy, my attention was suddenly drawn to some black object, reposing upon the head of one of the immense hogsheads of Gin, or of Rum, which constituted the chief furniture of the apartment. I had been looking steadily at the top of this hogshead for some minutes, and what now caused me surprise was the fact that I had not sooner perceived the object thereupon. I approached it, and touched it with my hand. It was a black cat—a very large one—fully as large as Pluto, and closely resembling him in every respect but one. Pluto had not a white hair upon any portion of his body; but this cat had a large, although indefinite splotch of white, covering nearly the whole region of the breast.

Upon my touching him, he immediately arose, purred loudly, rubbed against my hand, and appeared delighted with my notice. This, then, was the very creature of which I was in search. I at once offered to purchase it of the landlord; but this person made no claim to it—knew nothing of it—had never seen it before.

I continued my caresses, and, when I prepared to go home, the animal evinced a disposition to accompany me. I permitted it to do so; occasionally stooping and patting it as I proceeded. When it reached the house it domesticated itself at once, and became immediately a great favorite with my wife.

For my own part, I soon found a dislike to it arising within me. This was just the reverse of what I had anticipated; but—I know not how or why it was—its evident fondness for myself rather disgusted and annoyed. By slow degrees, these feelings of disgust and annoyance rose into the bitterness of hatred. I avoided the creature; a certain sense of shame, and the remembrance of my former deed of cruelty, preventing me from physically abusing it. I did not, for some weeks, strike, or otherwise violently ill use it; but gradually—very gradually—I came to look upon it with unutterable loathing, and to flee silently from its odious presence, as from the breath of a pestilence.

What added, no doubt, to my hatred of the beast, was the discovery, on the morning after I brought it home, that, like Pluto, it also had been deprived of one of its eyes. This circumstance, however, only endeared it to my wife, who, as I have already said, possessed, in a high degree, that humanity of feeling which had once been my distinguishing trait, and the source of many of my simplest and purest pleasures.

With my aversion to this cat, however, its partiality for myself seemed to increase. It followed my footsteps with a pertinacity which it would be difficult to make the reader comprehend. Whenever I sat, it would crouch beneath my chair, or spring upon my knees, covering me with its loathsome caresses. If I arose to walk it would get between my feet and thus nearly throw me down, or, fastening its long and sharp claws in my dress, clamber, in this manner, to my breast. At such times, although I longed to destroy it with a blow, I was yet withheld from so doing, partly by a memory of my former crime, but chiefly—let me confess it at once—by absolute *dread* of the beast.

This dread was not exactly a dread of physical evil—and yet I should be at a loss how otherwise to define it. I am almost ashamed to own—yes, even in this felon's cell, I am almost ashamed to own—that the terror and horror with which the animal inspired me, had been heightened by one of the merest chimaeras it would be possible to conceive. My wife had called my attention, more than once, to the character of the mark of white hair, of which I have spoken, and which constituted the sole visible difference between the strange beast and the one I had destroyed. The reader will remember that this mark, although large, had been originally very indefinite; but, by slow degrees—degrees nearly imperceptible, and which for a long time my Reason struggled to reject as fanciful—it had, at length, assumed a rigorous distinctness of outline. It was now the representation of an object that I shudder to name—and for this, above all, I loathed, and dreaded, and would have rid myself of the monster *had I dared*—it was now, I say, the image of a hideous—of a ghastly thing—of the GALLOWS!—oh, mournful and terrible engine of Horror and of Crime—of Agony and of Death!

And now was I indeed wretched beyond the wretchedness of mere Humanity. And *a brute beast*—whose fellow I had contemptuously destroyed—*a brute beast* to work out for *me*—for me a man, fashioned in the image of the High God—so much of insufferable wo! Alas! neither by day nor by night knew I the blessing of Rest any more! During the former the creature left me no moment alone; and, in the latter, I started, hourly, from dreams of unutterable fear, to find the hot breath of *the thing* upon my face, and its vast weight—an incarnate Night-Mare that I had no power to shake off—incumbent eternally upon my *heart!*

Beneath the pressure of torments such as these, the feeble remnant of the good within me succumbed. Evil thoughts became my sole intimates—the darkest and most evil of thoughts. The moodiness of my usual temper increased to hatred of all things and of all mankind; while, from the sudden, frequent, and ungovernable outbursts of a fury to which I now blindly abandoned myself, my uncomplaining wife, alas! was the most usual and the most patient of sufferers.

One day she accompanied me, upon some household errand, into the cellar of the old building which our poverty compelled us to inhabit. The cat followed me down the steep stairs, and, nearly throwing me headlong, exasperated me to madness. Uplifting an axe, and forgetting, in my wrath, the childish dread which had hitherto stayed my hand, I aimed a blow at the animal which, of course, would have proved instantly fatal had it descended as I wished. But this blow was arrested by the hand of my wife. Goaded, by the interference, into a rage more than demoniacal, I withdrew my arm from her grasp and buried the axe in her brain. She fell dead upon the spot, without a groan.

This hideous murder accomplished, I set myself forthwith, and with entire deliberation, to the task of concealing the body. I knew that I could not remove it from the house, either by day or by night, without the risk of being observed by the neighbors. Many projects entered my mind. At one period I thought of cutting the corpse into minute fragments, and destroying them by fire. At another, I resolved to dig a grave for it in the floor of the cellar. Again, I deliberated about casting it in the well in the yard—about packing it in a box, as if merchandize, with the usual arrangements, and so getting a porter to take it from the house. Finally I hit upon what I considered a far better expedient than either of these. I determined to wall it up in the cellar—as the monks of the middle ages are recorded to have walled up their victims.

For a purpose such as this the cellar was well adapted. Its walls were loosely constructed, and had lately been plastered throughout with a rough plaster, which the dampness of the atmosphere had prevented from hardening. Moreover, in one of the walls was a projection, caused by a false chimney, or fireplace, that had been filled up, and made to resemble the rest of the cellar. I made no doubt that I could readily displace the bricks at this point, insert the corpse, and wall the whole up as before, so that no eye could detect any thing suspicious.

And in this calculation I was not deceived. By means of a crow-bar I easily dislodged the bricks, and, having carefully deposited the body against the inner wall, I propped it in that position, while, with little trouble, I re-laid the whole structure as it originally stood. Having procured mortar, sand, and hair, with every possible precaution, I prepared a plaster which could not be distinguished from the old, and with this I very carefully went over the new brick-work. When I had finished, I felt satisfied that all was right. The wall did not present the slightest appearance of having been disturbed. The rubbish on the floor was picked up with the minutest care. I looked around triumphantly, and said to myself—"Here at least, then, my labor has not been in vain."

My next step was to look for the beast which had been the cause of so much wretchedness; for I had, at length, firmly resolved to put it to death. Had I been able to meet with it, at the moment, there could have been no doubt of its fate; but it appeared that the crafty animal had been alarmed at the violence of my previous anger, and forebore to present itself in my present mood. It is impossible to describe, or to imagine, the deep, the blissful sense of relief which the absence of the detested creature occasioned in my bosom. It did not make its appearance during the night—and thus for one night at least, since its introduction into the house, I soundly and tranquilly slept; aye, *slept* even with the burden of murder upon my soul!

The second and the third day passed, and still my tormentor came not. Once again I breathed as a freeman. The monster, in terror, had fled the premises forever! I should behold it no more! My happiness was supreme! The guilt of my dark deed disturbed me but little. Some few inquiries had been made, but these had been readily answered. Even a search had been instituted—but of course nothing was to be discovered. I looked upon my future felicity as secured.

Upon the fourth day of the assassination, a party of the police came, very unexpectedly, into the house, and proceeded again to make rigorous investigation of the premises. Secure, however, in the inscrutability of my place of concealment, I felt no embarrassment whatever. The officers bade me accompany them in their search. They left no nook or corner unexplored. At length, for the third or fourth time, they descended into the cellar. I quivered not in a muscle. My heart beat calmly as that of one who slumbers in innocence. I walked the cellar from end to end. I folded my arms upon my bosom, and roamed easily to and fro. The police were thoroughly satisfied and prepared to depart. The glee at my heart was too strong to be restrained. I burned to say if but one word, by way of triumph, and to render doubly sure their assurance of my guiltlessness.

"Gentlemen," I said at last, as the party ascended the steps, "I delight to have allayed your suspicions. I wish you all health, and a little more courtesy. By the bye, gentlemen, this—this is a very well constructed house." [In the rabid desire to say something easily, I scarcely knew what I uttered at all.]—"I may say an *excellently* well constructed house. These walls—are you going, gentlemen?—these walls are solidly put together;" and here, through the mere phrenzy of bravado, I rapped heavily, with a cane which I held in my hand, upon that very portion of the brick-work behind which stood the corpse of the wife of my bosom.

But may God shield and deliver me from the fangs of the Arch-Fiend! No sooner had the reverberation of my blows sunk into silence, than I was answered by a voice from within the tomb!—by a cry, at first muffled and broken, like the sobbing of a child, and then quickly swelling into one long, loud, and continuous scream, utterly anomalous and inhuman—a howl—a wailing shriek, half of horror and half of triumph, such as might have arisen only out of hell, conjointly from the throats of the dammed in their agony and of the demons that exult in the damnation.

Of my own thoughts it is folly to speak. Swooning, I staggered to the opposite wall. For one instant the party upon the stairs remained motionless, through extremity of terror and of awe. In the next, a dozen stout arms were toiling at the wall. It fell bodily. The corpse, already greatly decayed and clotted with gore, stood erect before the eyes of the spectators. Upon its head, with red extended mouth and solitary eye of fire, sat the hideous beast whose craft had seduced me into murder, and whose informing voice had consigned me to the hangman. I had walled the monster up within the tomb!

The Purloined Letter

Nil sapientiae odiosius acumine nimio.°

—SENECA

At Paris, just after dark one gusty evening in the autumn of 18—, I was enjoying the twofold luxury of meditation and a meerschaum,° in company with my friend C. Auguste Dupin, in his little back library, or book-closet, *au troisiême, No. 33, Rue Dunôt, Faubourg St. Germain.* For one hour at least we had maintained a profound silence; while each, to any casual observer, might have seemed intently and exclusively occupied with the curling eddies of smoke that oppressed the atmosphere of the chamber. For myself, however, I was mentally discussing certain topics which had formed matter for conversation between us at an earlier period of the evening; I mean the affair of the Rue Morgue, and the mystery attending the murder of Marie Rogêt. I looked upon it, therefore, as something of a coincidence, when the door of our apartment was thrown open and admitted our old acquaintance, Monsieur G——, the Prefect of the Parisian police.

We gave him a hearty welcome; for there was nearly half as much of the entertaining as of the contemptible about the man, and we had not seen him for several years. We had been sitting in the dark, and Dupin now arose for the purpose of lighting a lamp, but sat down again, without doing so, upon G.'s saying that he had called to consult us, or

---

Nil sapientiae . . . nimio: There is nothing wisdom hates more than cleverness.   ***meerschaum:*** A smoking pipe.

rather to ask the opinion of my friend, about some official business which had occasioned a great deal of trouble.

"If it is any point requiring reflection," observed Dupin, as he forebore to enkindle the wick, "we shall examine it to better purpose in the dark."

"That is another of your odd notions," said the Prefect, who had a fashion of calling every thing "odd" that was beyond his comprehension, and thus lived amid an absolute legion of "oddities."

"Very true," said Dupin, as he supplied his visiter with a pipe, and rolled towards him a comfortable chair.

"And what is the difficulty now?" I asked. "Nothing more in the assassination way, I hope?"

"Oh no; nothing of that nature. The fact is, the business is *very* simple indeed, and I make no doubt that we can manage it sufficiently well ourselves; but then I thought Dupin would like to hear the details of it, because it is so excessively *odd*."

"Simple and odd," said Dupin.

"Why, yes; and not exactly that, either. The fact is, we have all been a good deal puzzled because the affair *is* so simple, and yet baffles us altogether."

"Perhaps it is the very simplicity of the thing which puts you at fault," said my friend.

"What nonsense you *do* talk!" replied the Prefect, laughing heartily.

"Perhaps the mystery is a little *too* plain," said Dupin.

"Oh, good heavens! who ever heard of such an idea?"

"A little *too* self-evident."

"Ha! ha! ha!—ha! ha! ha!—ho! ho! ho!" roared our visiter, profoundly amused, "oh, Dupin, you will be the death of me yet!"

"And what, after all, *is* the matter on hand?" I asked.

"Why, I will tell you," replied the Prefect, as he gave a long, steady, and contemplative puff, and settled himself in his chair. "I will tell you in a few words; but, before I begin, let me caution you that this is an affair demanding the greatest secrecy, and that I should most probably lose the position I now hold, were it known that I confided it to any one."

"Proceed," said I.

"Or not," said Dupin.

"Well, then; I have received personal information, from a very high quarter, that a certain document of the last importance, has been purloined from the royal apartments. The individual who purloined it is known; this beyond a doubt; he was seen to take it. It is known, also, that it still remains in his possession."

"How is this known?" asked Dupin.

"It is clearly inferred," replied the Prefect, "from the nature of the document, and from the non-appearance of certain results which would at once arise from its passing *out* of the robber's possession;—that is to say, from his employing it as he must design in the end to employ it."

"Be a little more explicit," I said.

"Well, I may venture so far as to say that the paper gives its holder a certain power in a certain quarter where such power is immensely valuable." The Prefect was fond of the cant of diplomacy.

"Still I do not quite understand," said Dupin.

"No? Well; the disclosure of the document to a third person, who shall be nameless, would bring in question the honor of a personage of most exalted station; and this fact gives the holder of the document an ascendancy over the illustrious personage whose honor and peace are so jeopardized."

"But this ascendancy," I interposed, "would depend upon the robber's knowledge of the loser's knowledge of the robber. Who would dare—"

"The thief," said G., "is the Minister D——, who dares all things, those unbecoming as well as those becoming a man. The method of the theft was not less ingenious than bold. The document in question—a letter, to be frank—had been received by the personage robbed while alone in the royal *boudoir*. During its perusal she was suddenly interrupted by the entrance of the other exalted personage from whom especially it was her wish to conceal it. After a hurried and vain endeavor to thrust it in a drawer, she was forced to place it, open as it was, upon a table. The address, however, was uppermost, and, the contents thus unexposed, the letter escaped notice. At this juncture enters the Minister D——. His lynx eye immediately perceives the paper, recognises the handwriting of the address, observes the confusion of the personage addressed, and fathoms her secret. After some business transactions, hurried through in his ordinary manner, he produces a letter somewhat similar to the one in question, opens it, pretends to read it, and then places it in close juxtaposition to the other. Again he converses, for some fifteen minutes, upon the public affairs. At length, in taking leave, he takes also from the table the letter to which he had no claim. Its rightful owner saw, but, of course, dared not call attention to the act, in the presence of the third personage who stood at her elbow. The minister decamped; leaving his own letter—one of no importance—upon the table."

"Here, then," said Dupin to me, "you have precisely what you demand to make the ascendancy complete—the robber's knowledge of the loser's knowledge of the robber."

"Yes," replied the Prefect; "and the power thus attained has, for some months past, been wielded, for political purposes, to a very dangerous extent. The personage robbed is more thoroughly convinced, every day, of the necessity of reclaiming her letter. But this, of course, cannot be done openly. In fine, driven to despair, she has committed the matter to me."

"Than whom," said Dupin, amid a perfect whirlwind of smoke, "no more sagacious agent could, I suppose, be desired, or even imagined."

"You flatter me," replied the Prefect; "but it is possible that some such opinion may have been entertained."

"It is clear," said I, "as you observe, that the letter is still in possession of the minister; since it is this possession, and not any employment of the letter, which bestows the power. With the employment the power departs."

"True," said G.; "and upon this conviction I proceeded. My first care was to make thorough search of the minister's hotel; and here my chief embarrassment lay in the necessity of searching without his knowledge. Beyond all things, I have been warned of the danger which would result from giving him reason to suspect our design."

"But," said I, "you are quite *au fait*° in these investigations. The Parisian police have done this thing often before."

"O yes; and for this reason I did not despair. The habits of the minister gave me, too, a great advantage. He is frequently absent from home all night. His servants are by no means numerous. They sleep at a distance from their master's apartment, and, being chiefly Neapolitans, are readily made drunk. I have keys, as you know, with which I can open any chamber or cabinet in Paris. For three months a night has not passed, during the greater part of which I have not been engaged, personally, in ransacking the D—— Hotel. My honor is interested, and, to mention a great secret, the reward is enormous. So I did not abandon the search until I had become fully satisfied that the thief is a more astute man than myself. I fancy that I have investigated every nook and corner of the premises in which it is possible that the paper can be concealed."

au fait: Familiar; informed.

"But is it not possible," I suggested, "that although the letter may be in possession of the minister, as it unquestionably is, he may have concealed it elsewhere than upon his own premises?"

"This is barely possible," said Dupin. "The present peculiar condition of affairs at court, and especially of those intrigues in which D—— is known to be involved, would render the instant availability of the document—its susceptibility of being produced at a moment's notice—a point of nearly equal importance with its possession."

"Its susceptibility of being produced?" said I.

"That is to say, of being *destroyed*," said Dupin.

"True," I observed; "the paper is clearly then upon the premises. As for its being upon the person of the minister, we may consider that as out of the question."

"Entirely," said the Prefect. "He has been twice waylaid, as if by footpads, and his person rigorously searched under my own inspection."

"You might have spared yourself this trouble," said Dupin. "D——, I presume, is not altogether a fool, and, if not, must have anticipated these waylayings, as a matter of course."

"Not *altogether* a fool," said G., "but then he's a poet, which I take to be only one remove from a fool."

"True," said Dupin, after a long and thoughtful whiff from his meerschaum, "although I have been guilty of certain doggrel myself."

"Suppose you detail," said I, "the particulars of your search."

"Why the fact is, we took our time, and we searched *every where*. I have had long experience in these affairs. I took the entire building, room by room; devoting the nights of a whole week to each. We examined, first, the furniture of each apartment. We opened every possible drawer; and I presume you know that, to a properly trained police agent, such a thing as a *secret* drawer is impossible. Any man is a dolt who permits a 'secret' drawer to escape him in a search of this kind. The thing is *so* plain. There is a certain amount of bulk—of space—to be accounted for in every cabinet. Then we have accurate rules. The fiftieth part of a line could not escape us. After the cabinets we took the chairs. The cushions we probed with the fine long needles you have seen me employ. From the tables we removed the tops."

"Why so?"

"Sometimes the top of a table, or other similarly arranged piece of furniture, is removed by the person wishing to conceal an article; then the leg is excavated, the article deposited within the cavity, and the top replaced. The bottoms and tops of bedposts are employed in the same way."

"But could not the cavity be detected by sounding?" I asked.

"By no means, if, when the article is deposited, a sufficient wadding of cotton be placed around it. Besides, in our case, we were obliged to proceed without noise."

"But you could not have removed—you could not have taken to pieces *all* articles of furniture in which it would have been possible to make a deposit in the manner you mention. A letter may be compressed into a thin spiral roll, not differing much in shape or bulk from a large knitting-needle, and in this form it might be inserted into the rung of a chair, for example. You did not take to pieces all the chairs?"

"Certainly not; but we did better—we examined the rungs of every chair in the hotel, and, indeed the jointings of every description of furniture, by the aid of a most powerful microscope. Had there been any traces of recent disturbance we should not have failed to detect it instantly. A single grain of gimlet-dust, for example, would have been as obvious as an apple. Any disorder in the glueing—any unusual gaping in the joints—would have sufficed to insure detection."

"I presume you looked to the mirrors, between the boards and the plates, and you probed the beds and the bed-clothes, as well as the curtains and carpets."

"That of course; and when we had absolutely completed every particle of the furniture in this way, then we examined the house itself. We divided its entire surface into compartments, which we numbered, so that none might be missed; then we scrutinized each individual square inch throughout the premises, including the two houses immediately adjoining, with the microscope, as before."

"The two houses adjoining!" I exclaimed; "you must have had a great deal of trouble."

"We had; but the reward offered is prodigious."

"You include the *grounds* about the houses?"

"All the grounds are paved with brick. They gave us comparatively little trouble. We examined the moss between the bricks, and found it undisturbed."

"You looked among D——'s papers, of course, and into the books of the library?"

"Certainly; we opened every package and parcel; we not only opened every book, but we turned over every leaf in each volume, not contenting ourselves with a mere shake, according to the fashion of some of our police officers. We also measured the thickness of every book-*cover*, with the most accurate admeasurement, and applied to each the most jealous scrutiny of the microscope. Had any of the bindings been recently meddled with, it would have been utterly impossible that the fact should have escaped observation. Some five or six volumes, just from the hands of the binder, we carefully probed, longitudinally, with the needles."

"You explored the floors beneath the carpets?"

"Beyond doubt. We removed every carpet, and examined the boards with the microscope."

"And the paper on the walls?"

"Yes."

"You looked into the cellars?"

"We did."

"Then," I said, "you have been making a miscalculation, and the letter is *not* upon the premises, as you suppose."

"I fear you are right there," said the Prefect. "And now, Dupin, what would you advise me to do?"

"To make a thorough re-search of the premises."

"That is absolutely needless," replied G——. "I am not more sure that I breathe than I am that the letter is not at the Hotel."

"I have no better advice to give you," said Dupin. "You have, of course, an accurate description of the letter?"

"Oh yes!"—And here the Prefect, producing a memorandum-book proceeded to read aloud a minute account of the internal, and especially of the external appearance of the missing document. Soon after finishing the perusal of this description, he took his departure, more entirely depressed in spirits than I had ever known the good gentleman before.

In about a month afterwards he paid us another visit, and found us occupied very nearly as before. He took a pipe and a chair and entered into some ordinary conversation. At length I said,—

"Well, but G——, what of the purloined letter? I presume you have at last made up your mind that there is no such thing as overreaching the Minister?"

"Confound him, say I—yes; I made the re-examination, however, as Dupin suggested—but it was all labor lost, as I knew it would be."

"How much was the reward offered, did you say?" asked Dupin.

"Why, a very great deal—a *very* liberal reward—I don't like to say how much, precisely; but one thing I *will* say, that I wouldn't mind giving my individual check for fifty thousand francs to any one who could obtain me that letter. The fact is, it is becoming of more and more importance every day; and the reward has been lately doubled. If it were trebled, however, I could do no more than I have done."

"Why, yes," said Dupin, drawlingly, between the whiffs of his meer-schaum, "I really—think, G——, you have not exerted yourself—to the utmost in this matter. You might—do a little more, I think, eh?"

"How?—in what way?'

"Why—puff, puff—you might—puff, puff—employ counsel in the matter, eh?—puff, puff, puff. Do you remember the story they tell of Abernethy?"

"No; hang Abernethy!"

"To be sure! hang him and welcome. But, once upon a time, a certain rich miser conceived the design of spunging upon this Abernethy for a medical opinion. Getting up, for this purpose, an ordinary conversation in a private company, he insinuated his case to the physician, as that of an imaginary individual.

" 'We will suppose,' said the miser, 'that his symptoms are such and such; now, doctor, what would *you* have directed him to take?' "

" 'Take!' said Abernethy, 'why, take *advice*, to be sure.' "

"But," said the Prefect, a little discomposed, "I am *perfectly* willing to take advice, and to pay for it. I would *really* give fifty thousand francs to any one who would aid me in the matter."

"In that case," replied Dupin, opening a drawer, and producing a check-book, "you may as well fill me up a check for the amount mentioned. When you have signed it, I will hand you the letter."

I was astounded. The Prefect appeared absolutely thunder-stricken. For some minutes he remained speechless and motionless, looking incredulously at my friend with open mouth, and eyes that seemed starting from their sockets; then, apparently recovering himself in some measure, he seized a pen, and after several pauses and vacant stares, finally filled up and signed a check for fifty thousand francs, and handed it across the table to Dupin. The latter examined it carefully and deposited it in his pocket-book; then, unlocking an *escritoire*,° took thence a letter and gave it to the Prefect. This functionary grasped it in a perfect agony of joy, opened it with a trembling hand, cast a rapid glance at its contents, and then, scrambling and struggling to the door, rushed at length unceremoniously from the room and from the house, without having uttered a syllable since Dupin had requested him to fill up the check.

When he had gone, my friend entered into some explanations.

---

escritoire: Small, covered writing desk.

"The Parisian police," he said, "are exceedingly able in their way. They are persevering, ingenious, cunning, and thoroughly versed in the knowledge which their duties seem chiefly to demand. Thus, when G—— detailed to us his mode of searching the premises at the Hotel D——, I felt entire confidence in his having made a satisfactory investigation—so far as his labors extended."

"So far as his labors extended?" said I.

"Yes," said Dupin. "The measures adopted were not only the best of their kind, but carried out to absolute perfection. Had the letter been deposited within the range of their search, these fellows would, beyond a question, have found it."

I merely laughed—but he seemed quite serious in all that he said.

"The measures, then," he continued, "were good in their kind, and well executed; their defect lay in their being inapplicable to the case, and to the man. A certain set of highly ingenious resources are, with the Prefect, a sort of Procrustean bed,° to which he forcibly adapts his designs. But he perpetually errs by being too deep or too shallow, for the matter in hand; and many a schoolboy is a better reasoner than he. I knew one about eight years of age, whose success at guessing in the game of 'even and odd' attracted universal admiration. This game is simple, and is played with marbles. One player holds in his hand a number of these toys, and demands of another whether that number is even or odd. If the guess is right, the guesser wins one; if wrong, he loses one. The boy to whom I allude won all the marbles of the school. Of course he had some principle of guessing; and this lay in mere observation and admeasurement of the astuteness of his opponents. For example, an arrant simpleton is his opponent, and, holding up his closed hand, asks, 'are they even or odd?' Our schoolboy replies, 'odd,' and loses; but upon the second trial he wins, for he then says to himself, 'the simpleton had them even upon the first trial, and his amount of cunning is just sufficient to make him have them odd upon the second; I will therefore guess odd;'—he guesses odd, and wins. Now, with a simpleton a degree above the first, he would have reasoned thus: 'This fellow finds that in the first instance I guessed odd, and, in the second, he will propose to himself, upon the first impulse, a simple variation from even to odd, as did the first simpleton; but then a second thought will suggest that this is too simple a variation, and finally he will decide upon putting it even as before. I will therefore guess even;'—he guesses

Procrustean bed: An arbitrary standard to which all must conform.

even, and wins. Now this mode of reasoning in the schoolboy, whom his fellows termed 'lucky,'—what, in its last analysis, is it?"

"It is merely," I said, "an identification of the reasoner's intellect with that of his opponent."

"It is," said Dupin; "and, upon inquiring of the boy by what means he effected the *thorough* identification in which his success consisted, I received answer as follows: 'When I wish to find out how wise, or how stupid, or how good, or how wicked is any one, or what are his thoughts at the moment, I fashion the expression of my face, as accurately as possible, in accordance with the expression of his, and then wait to see what thoughts or sentiments arise in my mind or heart, as if to match or correspond with the expression.' This response of the schoolboy lies at the bottom of all the spurious profundity which has been attributed to Rochefoucault, to La Bougive, to Machiavelli, and to Campanella."

"And the identification," I said, "of the reasoner's intellect with that of his opponent, depends, if I understand you aright, upon the accuracy with which the opponent's intellect is admeasured."

"For its practical value it depends upon this," replied Dupin; "and the Prefect and his cohort fail so frequently, first, by default of this identification, and, secondly, by ill-admeasurement, or rather through non-admeasurement, of the intellect with which they are engaged. They consider only their *own* ideas of ingenuity; and, in searching for anything hidden, advert only to the modes in which *they* would have hidden it. They are right in this much—that their own ingenuity is a faithful representative of that of *the mass*; but when the cunning of the individual felon is diverse in character from their own, the felon foils them, of course. This always happens when it is above their own, and very usually when it is below. They have no variation of principle in their investigations; at best, when urged by some unusual emergency—by some extraordinary reward—they extend or exaggerate their old modes of *practice*, without touching their principles. What, for example, in this case of D——, has been done to vary the principle of action? What is all this boring, and probing, and sounding, and scrutinizing with the microscope, and dividing the surface of the building into registered square inches—what is it all but an exaggeration *of the application* of the one principle or set of principles of search, which are based upon the one set of notions regarding human ingenuity, to which the Prefect, in the long routine of his duty, has been accustomed? Do you not see he has taken it for granted that *all* men proceed to conceal a letter,— not exactly in a gimlet-hole bored in a chair-leg—but, at least, in *some* out-of-the-way hole or corner suggested by the same tenor of thought which would urge a man to secrete a letter in a gimlet-hole bored in a chair-leg? And do you not see also, that such *recherchés* nooks for concealment are adapted only for ordinary occasions, and would be adopted only by ordinary intellects; for, in all cases of concealment, a disposal of the article concealed—a disposal of it in this *recherché* manner,—is, in the very first instance, presumable and presumed; and thus its discovery depends, not at all upon the acumen, but altogether upon the mere care, patience, and determination of the seekers; and where the case is of importance—or, what amounts to the same thing in the policial eyes, when the reward is of magnitude,—the qualities in question have *never* been known to fail. You will now understand what I meant in suggesting that, had the purloined letter been hidden any where within the limits of the Prefect's examination—in other words, had the principle of its concealment been comprehended within the principles of the Prefect—its discovery would have been a matter altogether beyond question. This functionary, however, has been thoroughly mystified; and the remote source of his defeat lies in the supposition that the Minister is a fool, because he has acquired renown as a poet. All fools are poets; this the Prefect *feels*; and he is merely guilty of a *non distributio medii*° in thence inferring that all poets are fools."

"But is this really the poet?" I asked. "There are two brothers, I know; and both have attained reputation in letters. The Minister I believe has written learnedly on the Differential Calculus. He is a mathematician, and no poet."

"You are mistaken; I know him well; he is both. As poet *and* mathematician, he would reason well; as mere mathematician, he could not have reasoned at all, and thus would have been at the mercy of the Prefect."

"You surprise me," I said, "by these opinions, which have been contradicted by the voice of the world. You do not mean to set at naught the well-digested idea of centuries. The mathematical reason has long been regarded as *the* reason *par excellence*."

"'*Il y a à parier*,'" replied Dupin, quoting from Chamfort, "'*que toute idée publique, toute convention reçue est une sottise, car elle a convenue au plus grand nombre*.'° The mathematicians, I grant you, have done their best to promulgate the popular error to which you allude,

---

non distributio medii: Undistributed middle; a term used to describe a logical fallacy.
Il y a à parier . . . grand nombre: You can count on the fact that all popular notions and accepted conventions are stupid since the majority has found them acceptable.

and which is none the less an error for its promulgation as truth. With an art worthy a better cause, for example, they have insinuated the term 'analysis' into application to algebra. The French are the originators of this particular deception; but if a term is of any importance—if words derive any value from applicability—then 'analysis' conveys 'algebra' about as much as, in Latin, '*ambitus*' implies 'ambition,' '*religio*' 'religion,' or '*homines honesti*,' a set of *honorable* men."

"You have a quarrel on hand, I see," said I, "with some of the algebraists of Paris; but proceed."

"I dispute the availability, and thus the value, of that reason which is cultivated in any especial form other than the abstractly logical. I dispute, in particular, the reason educed by mathematical study. The mathematics are the science of form and quantity; mathematical reasoning is merely logic applied to observation upon form and quantity. The great error lies in supposing that even the truths of what is called *pure* algebra, are abstract or general truths. And this error is so egregious that I am confounded at the universality with which it has been received. Mathematical axioms are *not* axioms of general truth. What is true of *relation*—of form and quantity—is often grossly false in regard to morals, for example. In this latter science it is very usually *un*true that the aggregated parts are equal to the whole. In chemistry also the axiom fails. In the consideration of motive it fails; for two motives, each of a given value, have not, necessarily, a value when united, equal to the sum of their values apart. There are numerous other mathematical truths which are only truths within the limits of *relation*. But the mathematician argues, from his *finite truths*, through habit, as if they were of an absolutely general applicability—as the world indeed imagines them to be. Bryant, in his very learned 'Mythology,' mentions an analogous source of error, when he says that 'although the Pagan fables are not believed, yet we forget ourselves continually, and make inferences from them as existing realities.' With the algebraists, however, who are Pagans themselves, the 'Pagan fables' *are* believed, and the inferences are made, not so much through lapse of memory, as through an unaccountable addling of the brains. In short, I never yet encountered the mere mathematician who could be trusted out of equal roots, or one who did not clandestinely hold it as a point of his faith that $x^2 + px$ was absolutely and unconditionally equal to q. Say to one of these gentlemen, by way of experiment, if you please, that you believe occasions may occur where $x^2 + px$ is *not* altogether equal to q, and, having made him understand what you mean, get out of his reach as speedily as convenient, for, beyond doubt, he will endeavor to knock you down.

"I mean to say," continued Dupin, while I merely laughed at his last observations, "that if the Minister had been no more than a mathematician, the Prefect would have been under no necessity of giving me this check. I knew him, however, as both mathematician and poet, and my measures were adapted to his capacity, with reference to the circumstances by which he was surrounded. I knew him as a courtier, too, and as a bold *intriguant.* Such a man, I considered, could not fail to be aware of the ordinary policial modes of action. He could not have failed to anticipate—and events have proved that he did not fail to anticipate—the waylayings to which he was subjected. He must have foreseen, I reflected, the secret investigations of his premises. His frequent absences from home at night, which were hailed by the Prefect as certain aids to his success, I regarded only as *ruses*, to afford opportunity for thorough search to the police, and thus the sooner to impress them with the conviction to which G——, in fact, did finally arrive—the conviction that the letter was not upon the premises. I felt, also, that the whole train of thought, which I was at some pains in detailing to you just now, concerning the invariable principle of policial action in searches for articles concealed—I felt that this whole train of thought would necessarily pass through the mind of the Minister. It would imperatively lead him to despise all the ordinary *nooks* of concealment. *He* could not, I reflected, be so weak as not to see that the most intricate and remote recess of his hotel would be as open as his commonest closets to the eyes, to the probes, to the gimlets, and to the microscopes of the Prefect. I saw, in fine, that he would be driven, as a matter of course, to *simplicity*, if not deliberately induced to it as a matter of choice. You will remember, perhaps, how desperately the Prefect laughed when I suggested, upon our first interview, that it was just possible this mystery troubled him so much on account of its being so *very* self-evident."

"Yes," said I, "I remember his merriment well. I really thought he would have fallen into convulsions."

"The material world," continued Dupin, "abounds with very strict analogies to the immaterial; and thus some color of truth has been given to the rhetorical dogma, that metaphor, or simile, may be made to strengthen an argument, as well as to embellish a description. The principle of the *vis inertiae*,° for example, seems to be identical in physics and metaphysics. It is not more true in the former, that a large body is with more difficulty set in motion than a smaller one, and that its

vis inertiae: Force of inertia.

subsequent *momentum* is commensurate with this difficulty, than it is, in the latter, that intellects of the vaster capacity, while more forcible, more constant, and more eventful in their movements than those of inferior grade, are yet the less readily moved, and more embarrassed and full of hesitation in the first few steps of their progress. Again: have you ever noticed which of the street signs, over the shop-doors, are the most attractive of attention?"

"I have never given the matter a thought," I said.

"There is a game of puzzles," he resumed, "which is played upon a map. One party playing requires another to find a given word—the name of town, river, state or empire—any word, in short, upon the motley and perplexed surface of the chart. A novice in the game gener-ally seeks to embarrass his opponents by giving them the most minutely lettered names; but the adept selects such words as stretch, in large characters, from one end of the chart to the other. These, like the over-largely lettered signs and placards of the street, escape observation by dint of being excessively obvious; and here the physical oversight is precisely analogous with the moral inapprehension by which the intel-lect suffers to pass unnoticed those considerations which are too obtru-sively and too palpably self-evident. But this is a point, it appears, some-what above or beneath the understanding of the Prefect. He never once thought it probable, or possible, that the Minister had deposited the letter immediately beneath the nose of the whole world, by way of best preventing any portion of that world from perceiving it.

"But the more I reflected upon the daring, dashing, and discriminat-ing ingenuity of D——; upon the fact that the document must always have been *at hand*, if he intended to use it to good purpose; and upon the decisive evidence, obtained by the Prefect, that it was not hidden within the limits of that dignitary's ordinary search—the more satisfied I became that, to conceal this letter, the Minister had resorted to the com-prehensive and sagacious expedient of not attempting to conceal it at all.

"Full of these ideas, I prepared myself with a pair of green spec-tacles, and called one fine morning, quite by accident, at the Ministerial hotel. I found D—— at home, yawning, lounging, and dawdling, as usual, and pretending to be in the last extremity of *ennui*. He is, per-haps, the most really energetic human being now alive—but that is only when nobody sees him.

"To be even with him, I complained of my weak eyes, and lamented the necessity of the spectacles, under cover of which I cautiously and thoroughly surveyed the whole apartment, while seemingly intent only upon the conversation of my host.

"I paid especial attention to a large writing-table near which he sat, and upon which lay confusedly, some miscellaneous letters and other papers, with one or two musical instruments and a few books. Here, however, after a long and very deliberate scrutiny, I saw nothing to excite particular suspicion.

"At length my eyes, in going the circuit of the room, fell upon a trumpery fillagree card-rack of pasteboard, that hung dangling by a dirty blue ribbon, from a little brass knob just beneath the middle of the mantel-piece. In this rack, which had three or four compartments, were five or six visiting cards and a solitary letter. This last was much soiled and crumpled. It was torn nearly in two, across the middle—as if a design, in the first instance, to tear it entirely up as worthless, had been altered, or stayed, in the second. It had a large black seal, bearing the D—— cipher *very* conspicuously, and was addressed, in a diminutive female hand, to D——, the minister, himself. It was thrust carelessly, and even, as it seemed, contemptuously, into one of the uppermost divisions of the rack.

"No sooner had I glanced at this letter, than I concluded it to be that of which I was in search. To be sure, it was, to all appearance, radically different from the one of which the Prefect had read us so minute a description. Here the seal was large and black, with the D—— cipher; there it was small and red, with the ducal arms of the S—— family. Here, the address, to the Minister, was diminutive and feminine; there the superscription, to a certain royal personage, was markedly bold and decided; the size alone formed a point of correspondence. But, then, the *radicalness* of these differences, which was excessive; the dirt; the soiled and torn condition of the paper, so inconsistent with the *true* methodical habits of D——, and so suggestive of a design to delude the beholder into an idea of the worthlessness of the document; these things, together with the hyper-obtrusive situation of this document, full in the view of every visiter, and thus exactly in accordance with the conclusions to which I had previously arrived; these things, I say, were strongly corroborative of suspicion, in one who came with the intention to suspect.

"I protracted my visit as long as possible, and, while I maintained a most animated discussion with the Minister, upon a topic which I knew well had never failed to interest and excite him, I kept my attention really riveted upon the letter. In this examination, I committed to memory its external appearance and arrangement in the rack; and also fell, at length, upon a discovery which set at rest whatever trivial doubt I might have entertained. In scrutinizing the edges of the paper, I observed them to be more *chafed* than seemed necessary. They presented the *broken* appearance which is manifested when a stiff paper, having been once folded and pressed with a folder, is refolded in a reversed direction, in the same creases or edges which had formed the original fold. This discovery was sufficient. It was clear to me that the letter had been turned, as a glove, inside out, re-directed, and re-sealed. I bade the Minister good morning, and took my departure at once, leaving a gold snuff-box upon the table.

"The next morning I called for the snuff-box, when we resumed, quite eagerly, the conversation of the preceding day. While thus engaged, however, a loud report, as if of a pistol, was heard immediately beneath the windows of the hotel, and was succeeded by a series of fearful screams, and the shoutings of a terrified mob. D—— rushed to a casement, threw it open, and looked out. In the meantime, I stepped to the card-rack, took the letter, put it in my pocket, and replaced it by a *fac-simile*, (so far as regards externals,) which I had carefully prepared at my lodgings—imitating the D—— cipher, very readily, by means of a seal formed of bread.

"The disturbance in the street had been occasioned by the frantic behavior of a man with a musket. He had fired it among a crowd of women and children. It proved, however, to have been without ball, and the fellow was suffered to go his way as a lunatic or a drunkard. When he had gone, D—— came from the window, whither I had followed him immediately upon securing the object in view. Soon afterwards I bade him farewell. The pretended lunatic was a man in my own pay."

"But what purpose had you," I asked, "in replacing the letter by a *fac-simile*? Would it not have been better, at the first visit, to have seized it openly, and departed?"

"D——," replied Dupin, "is a desperate man, and a man of nerve. His hotel, too, is not without attendants devoted to his interests. Had I made the wild attempt you suggest, I might never have left the Ministerial presence alive. The good people of Paris might have heard of me no more. But I had an object apart from these considerations. You know my political prepossessions. In this matter, I act as a partisan of the lady concerned. For eighteen months the Minister has had her in his power. She has now him in hers—since, being unaware that the letter is not in his possession, he will proceed with his exactions as if it was. Thus will he inevitably commit himself, at once, to his political destruction. His downfall, too, will not be more precipitate than awkward. It is all very well to talk about the *facilis descensus Averni*;° but in all kinds

---

facilis descensus Averni: The descent to Avernus [evil] is easy.

of climbing, as Catalani said of singing, it is far more easy to get up than to come down. In the present instance I have no sympathy—at least no pity—for him who descends. He is that *monstrum horrendum*, an unprincipled man of genius. I confess, however, that I should like very well to know the precise character of his thoughts, when, being defied by her whom the Prefect terms 'a certain personage,' he is reduced to opening the letter which I left for him in the card-rack."

"How? did you put any thing particular in it?"

"Why—it did not seem altogether right to leave the interior blank—that would have been insulting. D——, at Vienna once, did me an evil turn, which I told him, quite good-humoredly, that I should remember. So, as I knew he would feel some curiosity in regard to the identity of the person who had outwitted him, I thought it a pity not to give him a clue. He is well acquainted with my MS., and I just copied into the middle of the blank sheet the words—

> " '——— Un dessein si funeste,
> S'il n'est digne d'Atrée, est digne de Thyeste.°
> They are to be found in Crébillon's 'Atrée.' "

The Imp of the Perverse

In the consideration of the faculties and impulses—of the *prima mobilia*° of the human soul, the phrenologists have failed to make room for a propensity which, although obviously existing as a radical, primitive, irreducible sentiment, has been equally overlooked by all the moralists who have preceded them. In the pure arrogance of the reason, we have all overlooked it. We have suffered its existence to escape our senses, solely through want of belief—of faith;—whether it be faith in Revelation, or faith in the Kabbala. The idea of it has never occurred to us, simply because of its supererogation. We saw no *need* of the impulse—for the propensity. We could not perceive its necessity. We could not understand, that is to say, we could not have understood, had the notion of this *primum mobile* ever obtruded itself;—we could not have understood in what manner it might be made to further the objects of humanity, either temporal or eternal. It cannot be denied that phrenology and, in great measure, all metaphysicianism, have been concocted *à priori*. The intellectual or logical man, rather than the understanding or observant man, set himself to imagine designs—to

---

Un dessein . . . de Thyeste: "A plan so terrible, if not worthy of Atrée, is worthy of Thyeste." The lines come from the French poet Prosper Jolyot de Crébillon's revenge tragedy, *Atrée et Thyeste.*   **prima mobilia:** Primary cause.

dictate purposes to God. Having thus fathomed, to his satisfaction, the intentions of Jehovah, out of these intentions he built his innumerable systems of mind. In the matter of phrenology, for example, we first determined, naturally enough, that it was the design of the Deity that man should eat. We then assigned to man an organ of alimentiveness, and this organ is the scourge with which the Deity compels man, will-I nill-I, into eating. Secondly, having settled it to be God's will that man should continue his species, we discovered an organ of amativeness, forthwith. And so with combativeness, with ideality, with causality, with constructiveness, — so, in short, with every organ, whether representing a propensity, a moral sentiment, or a faculty of the pure intellect. And in these arrangements of the *principia* of human action, the Spurzheimites,° whether right or wrong, in part, or upon the whole, have but followed, in principle, the footsteps of their predecessors; deducing and establishing every thing from the preconceived destiny of man, and upon the ground of the objects of his Creator.

It would have been wiser, it would have been safer to classify, (if classify we must,) upon the basis of what man usually or occasionally did, and was always occasionally doing, rather than upon the basis of what we took it for granted the Deity intended him to do. If we cannot comprehend God in his visible works, how then in his inconceivable thoughts, that call the works into being? If we cannot understand him in his objective creatures, how then in his substantive moods and phases of creation?

Induction, *à posteriori*, would have brought phrenology to admit, as an innate and primitive principle of human action, a paradoxical something, which we may call *perverseness*, for want of a more characteristic term. In the sense I intend, it is, in fact, a *mobile* without motive, a motive not *motivirt*.° Through its promptings we act without comprehensible object; or, if this shall be understood as a contradiction in terms, we may so far modify the proposition as to say, that through its promptings we act, for the reason that we should *not*. In theory, no reason can be more unreasonable; but, in fact, there is none more strong. With certain minds, under certain conditions, it becomes absolutely irresistible. I am not more certain that I breathe, than that the assurance of the wrong or error of any action is often the one unconquerable *force* which impels us, and alone impels us to its prosecution. Nor will this overwhelming tendency to do wrong for the wrong's sake, admit of analysis, or resolution into ulterior elements. It is a radical, a

Spurzheimites: Followers of Johann Spurzheim (1776–1832), German physician and phrenologist.   *mobile ... motivirt:* Movement without motive, a motive without motivation (here Poe misspells the German "motiviert").

primitive impulse—elementary. It will be said, I am aware, that when we persist in acts because we feel we should *not* persist in them, our conduct is but a modification of that which ordinarily springs from the combativeness of phrenology. But a glance will show the fallacy of this idea. The phrenological *combativeness* has for its essence, the necessity of self-defence. It is our safeguard against injury. Its principle regards our well-being; and thus the desire to be well, is excited simultaneously with its development. It follows, that the desire to be well must be excited simultaneously with any principle which shall be merely a modification of combativeness, but in the case of that something which I term *perverseness*, the desire to be well is not only not aroused, but a strongly antagonistical sentiment exists.

An appeal to one's own heart is, after all, the best reply to the sophistry just noticed. No one who trustingly consults and thoroughly questions his own soul, will be disposed to deny the entire radicalness of the propensity in question. It is not more incomprehensible than distinctive. There lives no man who at some period, has not been tormented, for example, by an earnest desire to tantalize a listener by circumlocution. The speaker is aware that he displeases; he has every intention to please; he is usually curt, precise, and clear; the most laconic and luminous language is struggling for utterance upon his tongue; it is only with difficulty that he restrains himself from giving it flow; he dreads and deprecates the anger of him whom he addresses; yet, the thought strikes him, that by certain involutions and parentheses, this anger may be engendered. That single thought is enough. The impulse increases to a wish, the wish to a desire, the desire to an uncontrollable longing, and the longing, (to the deep regret and mortification of the speaker, and in defiance of all consequences,) is indulged.

We have a task before us which must be speedily performed. We know that it will be ruinous to make delay. The most important crisis of our life calls, trumpet-tongued, for immediate energy and action. We glow, we are consumed with eagerness to commence the work, with the anticipation of whose glorious result our whole souls are on fire. It must, it shall be undertaken to-day, and yet we put it off until to-morrow, and why? There is no answer, except that we feel *perverse*, using the word with no comprehension of the principle. To-morrow arrives; and with it a more impatient anxiety to do our duty, but with this very increase of anxiety arrives, also, a nameless, a positively fearful, because unfathomable craving for delay. This craving gathers strength as the moments fly. The last hour for action is at hand. We tremble with the violence of the conflict within us,—of the definite with the indefinite—of the substance with the shadow. But, if the contest have proceeded thus far, it is the shadow which prevails,—we struggle in vain. The clock strikes, and is the knell of our welfare. At the same time, it is the chanticleer-note to the ghost that has so long overawed us. It flies—it disappears—we are free. The old energy returns. We will labor *now*. Alas, it is *too late!*

We stand upon the brink of a precipice. We peer into the abyss—we grow sick and dizzy. Our first impulse is to shrink from the danger. Unaccountably we remain. By slow degrees our sickness and dizziness, and horror become merged in a cloud of unnameable feeling. By grada-tions, still more imperceptible, this cloud assumes shape, as did the vapor from the bottle out of which arose the genius in the Arabian Nights. But out of this *our* cloud upon the precipice's edge, there grows into palpability, a shape, far more terrible than any genius, or any demon of a tale, and yet it is but a thought, although a fearful one, and one which chills the very marrow of our bones with the fierceness of the delight of its horror. It is merely the idea of what would be our sensa-tions during the sweeping precipitancy of a fall from such a height. And this fall—this rushing annihilation—for the very reason that it involves that one most ghastly and loathsome of all the most ghastly and loath-some images of death and suffering which have ever presented them-selves to our imagination—for this very cause do we now the most vividly desire it. And because our reason violently deters us from the brink, *therefore*, do we the most impetuously approach it. There is no passion in nature so demoniacally impatient, as that of him, who shud-dering upon the edge of a precipice, thus meditates a plunge. To indulge for a moment, in any attempt at *thought*, is to be inevitably lost; for reflection but urges us to forbear, and *therefore* it is, I say, that we *cannot*. If there be no friendly arm to check us, or if we fail in a sudden effort to prostrate ourselves backward from the abyss, we plunge, and are destroyed.

Examine these similar actions as we will, we shall find them result-ing solely from the spirit of the *Perverse*. We perpetrate them because we feel that we should *not*. Beyond or behind this, there is no intelli-gible principle: and we might, indeed, deem this perverseness a direct instigation of the arch-fiend, were it not occasionally known to operate in furtherance of good.

I have said thus much, that in some measure I may answer your question—that I may explain to you why I am here—that I may assign to you something that shall have at least the faint aspect of a cause for my wearing these fetters, and for my tenanting this cell of the condemned. Had I not been thus prolix, you might either have misunderstood me altogether, or, with the rabble, have fancied me mad. As it is, you will easily perceive that I am one of the many uncounted victims of the Imp of the Perverse.

It is impossible that any deed could have been wrought with a more thorough deliberation. For weeks, for months, I pondered upon the means of the murder. I rejected a thousand schemes, because their accomplishment involved a *chance* of detection. At length, in reading some French memoirs, I found an account of a nearly fatal illness that occurred to Madame Pilau, through the agency of a candle accidentally poisoned. The idea struck my fancy at once. I knew my victim's habit of reading in bed. I knew, too, that his apartment was narrow and ill-ventilated. But I need not vex you with impertinent details. I need not describe the easy artifices by which I substituted, in his bed-room candle-stand, a wax-light of my own making, for the one which I there found. The next morning he was discovered dead in his bed, and the Coroner's verdict was,— "Death by the visitation of God."

Having inherited his estate, all went well with me for years. The idea of detection never once entered my brain. Of the remains of the fatal taper, I had myself carefully disposed. I had left no shadow of a clue by which it would be possible to convict, or even to suspect me of the crime. It is inconceivable how rich a sentiment of satisfaction arose in my bosom as I reflected upon my absolute security. For a very long period of time, I was accustomed to revel in this sentiment. It afforded me more real delight than all the mere worldly advantages accruing from my sin. But there arrived at length an epoch, from which the pleasurable feeling grew, by scarcely perceptible gradations, into a haunting and harassing thought. It harassed because it haunted. I could scarcely get rid of it for an instant. It is quite a common thing to be thus annoyed with the ringing in our ears, or rather in our memories, of the burthen of some ordinary song, or some unimpressive snatches from an opera. Nor will we be the less tormented if the song in itself be good, or the opera air meritorious. In this manner, at last, I would perpetually catch myself pondering upon my security, and repeating, in a low, undertone, the phrase, "I am safe."

One day, whilst sauntering along the streets, I arrested myself in the act of murmuring, half aloud, these customary syllables. In a fit of petulance, I re-modelled them thus:— "I am safe—I am safe—yes—if I be not fool enough to make open confession!"

No sooner had I spoken these words, than I felt an icy chill creep to my heart. I had had some experience in these fits of perversity, (whose nature I have been at some trouble to explain,) and I remembered well, that in no instance, I had successfully resisted their attacks. And now my own casual self-suggestion, that I might possibly be fool enough to confess the murder of which I had been guilty, confronted me, as if the very ghost of him whom I had murdered—and beckoned me on to death.

At first, I made an effort to shake off this nightmare of the soul. I walked vigorously—faster—still faster—at length I ran. I felt a maddening desire to shriek aloud. Every succeeding wave of thought overwhelmed me with new terror, for, alas! I well, too well understood that, to *think*, in my situation, was to be lost. I still quickened my pace. I bounded like a madman through the crowded thoroughfares. At length, the populace took the alarm, and pursued me. I felt *then* the consummation of my fate. Could I have torn out my tongue, I would have done it—but a rough voice resounded in my ears—a rougher grasp seized me by the shoulder. I turned—I gasped for breath. For a moment I experienced all the pangs of suffocation; I became blind, and deaf, and giddy; and then some invisible fiend, I thought, struck me with his broad palm upon the back. The long-imprisoned secret burst forth from my soul.

They say that I spoke with a distinct enunciation, but with marked emphasis and passionate hurry, as if in dread of interruption before concluding the brief but pregnant sentences that consigned me to the hangman and to hell.

Having related all that was necessary for the fullest judicial conviction, I fell prostrate in a swoon.

But why shall I say more? To-day I wear these chains, and am *here!* To-morrow I shall be fetterless!—*but where?*

The Cask of Amontillado

The thousand injuries of Fortunato I had borne as I best could; but when he ventured upon insult, I vowed revenge. You, who so well know the nature of my soul, will not suppose, however, that I gave utterance to a threat. *At length* I would be avenged; this was a point definitively settled—but the very definitiveness with which it was resolved, precluded the idea of risk. I must not only punish, but punish with impunity. A wrong is unredressed when retribution overtakes its redresser. It is equally unredressed when the avenger fails to make himself felt as such to him who has done the wrong.

It must be understood, that neither by word nor deed had I given Fortunato cause to doubt my good will. I continued, as was my wont, to smile in his face, and he did not perceive that my smile *now* was at the thought of his immolation.

He had a weak point—this Fortunato—although in other regards he was a man to be respected and even feared. He prided himself on his connoisseurship in wine. Few Italians have the true virtuoso spirit. For the most part their enthusiasm is adopted to suit the time and opportunity—to practise imposture upon the British and Austrian *millionaires*. In painting and gemmary Fortunato, like his countrymen, was a quack—but in the matter of old wines he was sincere. In this respect I did not differ from him materially: I was skilful in the Italian vintages myself, and bought largely whenever I could.

It was about dusk, one evening during the supreme madness of the carnival season, that I encountered my friend. He accosted me with excessive warmth, for he had been drinking much. The man wore motley. He had on a tight-fitting parti-striped dress, and his head was surmounted by the conical cap and bells. I was so pleased to see him, that I thought I should never have done wringing his hand.

I said to him—"My dear Fortunato, you are luckily met. How remarkably well you are looking to-day! But I have received a pipe of what passes for Amontillado, and I have my doubts."

"How?" said he. "Amontillado? A pipe? Impossible! And in the middle of the carnival!"

"I have my doubts," I replied; "and I was silly enough to pay the full Amontillado price without consulting you in the matter. You were not to be found, and I was fearful of losing a bargain."

"Amontillado!"

"I have my doubts."

"Amontillado!"

"And I must satisfy them."

"Amontillado!"

"As you are engaged, I am on my way to Luchesi. If any one has a critical turn, it is he. He will tell me——"

"Luchesi cannot tell Amontillado from Sherry."

"And yet some fools will have it that his taste is a match for your own."

"Come, let us go."

"Whither?"

"To your vaults."

"My friend, no; I will not impose upon your good nature. I perceive you have an engagement. Luchesi——"

"I have no engagement;—come."

"My friend, no. It is not the engagement, but the severe cold with which I perceive you are afflicted. The vaults are insufferably damp. They are encrusted with nitre."

"Let us go, nevertheless. The cold is merely nothing. Amontillado! You have been imposed upon. And as for Luchesi, he cannot distinguish Sherry from Amontillado."

Thus speaking, Fortunato possessed himself of my arm. Putting on a mask of black silk, and drawing a *roquelaire*° closely about my person, I suffered him to hurry me to my palazzo.

There were no attendants at home; they had absconded to make merry in honor of the time. I had told them that I should not return until the morning, and had given them explicit orders not to stir from the house. These orders were sufficient, I well knew, to insure their immediate disappearance, one and all, as soon as my back was turned.

I took from their sconces two flambeaux, and giving one to Fortunato, bowed him through several suites of rooms to the archway that led into the vaults. I passed down a long and winding staircase, requesting him to be cautious as he followed. We came at length to the foot of the descent, and stood together on the damp ground of the catacombs of the Montresors.

The gait of my friend was unsteady, and the bells upon his cap jingled as he strode.

"The pipe," said he.

"It is farther on," said I; "but observe the white web-work which gleams from these cavern walls."

He turned towards me, and looked into my eyes with two filmy orbs that distilled the rheum of intoxication.

"Nitre?" he asked, at length.

"Nitre," I replied. "How long have you had that cough?"

"Ugh! ugh! ugh!—ugh! ugh! ugh!—ugh! ugh! ugh!—ugh! ugh! ugh!—ugh! ugh! ugh!"

My poor friend found it impossible to reply for many minutes.

"It is nothing," he said, at last.

"Come," I said, with decision, "we will go back; your health is precious. You are rich, respected, admired, beloved; you are happy, as once I was. You are a man to be missed. For me it is no matter. We will go back; you will be ill, and I cannot be responsible. Besides, there is Luchesi——"

"Enough," he said; "the cough is a mere nothing; it will not kill me. I shall not die of a cough."

"True—true," I replied; "and, indeed, I had no intention of alarming you unnecessarily—but you should use all proper caution. A draught of this Medoc will defend us from the damps."

---

roquelaire: A roquelaure, as more commonly spelled, is a knee-length cloak, often with bright lining and fur trim, fashionable in the eighteenth century.

Here I knocked off the neck of a bottle which I drew from a long row of its fellows that lay upon the mould.

"Drink," I said, presenting him the wine.

He raised it to his lips with a leer. He paused and nodded to me familiarly, while his bells jingled.

"I drink," he said, "to the buried that repose around us."

"And I to your long life."

He again took my arm, and we proceeded.

"These vaults," he said, "are extensive."

"The Montresors," I replied, "were a great and numerous family."

"I forget your arms."

"A huge human foot d'or, in a field azure; the foot crushes a serpent rampant whose fangs are imbedded in the heel."

"And the motto?"

"Nemo me impune lacessit."°

"Good!" he said.

The wine sparkled in his eyes and the bells jingled. My own fancy grew warm with the Medoc. We had passed through walls of piled bones, with casks and puncheons intermingling, into the inmost recesses of the catacombs. I paused again, and this time I made bold to seize Fortunato by an arm above the elbow.

"The nitre!" I said: "see, it increases. It hangs like moss upon the vaults. We are below the river's bed. The drops of moisture trickle among the bones. Come, we will go back ere it is too late. Your cough——"

"It is nothing," he said; "let us go on. But first, another draught of the Medoc."

I broke and reached him a flaçon of De Grâve. He emptied it at a breath. His eyes flashed with a fierce light. He laughed and threw the bottle upwards with a gesticulation I did not understand.

I looked at him in surprise. He repeated the movement—a grotesque one.

"You do not comprehend?" he said.

"Not I," I replied.

"Then you are not of the brotherhood."

"How?"

"You are not of the masons."

"Yes, yes," I said, "yes, yes."

"You? Impossible! A mason?"

"A mason," I replied.

Nemo me impune lacessit: No one can attack me and get away with it.

"A sign," he said.

"It is this," I answered, producing a trowel from beneath the folds of my *roquelaire.*

"You jest," he exclaimed, recoiling a few paces. "But let us proceed to the Amontillado."

"Be it so," I said, replacing the tool beneath the cloak, and again offering him my arm. He leaned upon it heavily. We continued our route in search of the Amontillado. We passed through a range of low arches, descended, passed on, and descending again, arrived at a deep crypt, in which the foulness of the air caused our flambeaux rather to glow than flame.

At the most remote end of the crypt there appeared another less spacious. Its walls had been lined with human remains, piled to the vault overhead, in the fashion of the great catacombs of Paris. Three sides of this interior crypt were still ornamented in this manner. From the fourth the bones had been thrown down, and lay promiscuously upon the earth, forming at one point a mound of some size. Within the wall thus exposed by the displacing of the bones, we perceived a still interior recess, in depth about four feet, in width three, in height six or seven. It seemed to have been constructed for no especial use in itself, but formed merely the interval between two of the colossal supports of the roof of the catacombs, and was backed by one of their circumscribing walls of solid granite.

It was in vain that Fortunato, uplifting his dull torch, endeavored to pry into the depths of the recess. Its termination the feeble light did not enable us to see.

"Proceed," I said; "herein is the Amontillado. As for Luchesi——"

"He is an ignoramus," interrupted my friend, as he stepped unsteadily forward, while I followed immediately at his heels. In an instant he had reached the extremity of the niche, and finding his progress arrested by the rock, stood stupidly bewildered. A moment more and I had fettered him to the granite. In its surface were two iron staples, distant from each other about two feet, horizontally. From one of these depended a short chain, from the other a padlock. Throwing the links about his waist, it was but the work of a few seconds to secure it. He was too much astounded to resist. Withdrawing the key I stepped back from the recess.

"Pass your hand," I said, "over the wall; you cannot help feeling the nitre. Indeed it is *very* damp. Once more let me *implore* you to return. No? Then I must positively leave you. But I must first render you all the little attentions in my power."

"The Amontillado!" ejaculated my friend, not yet recovered from his astonishment.

"True," I replied; "the Amontillado."

As I said these words I busied myself among the pile of bones of which I have before spoken. Throwing them aside, I soon uncovered a quantity of building stone and mortar. With these materials and with the aid of my trowel, I began vigorously to wall up the entrance of the niche.

I had scarcely laid the first tier of my masonry when I discovered that the intoxication of Fortunato had in a great measure worn off. The earliest indication I had of this was a low moaning cry from the depth of the recess. It was *not* the cry of a drunken man. There was then a long and obstinate silence. I laid the second tier, and the third, and the fourth; and then I heard the furious vibrations of the chain. The noise lasted for several minutes, during which, that I might hearken to it with the more satisfaction, I ceased my labors and sat down upon the bones. When at last the clanking subsided, I resumed the trowel, and finished without interruption the fifth, the sixth, and the seventh tier. The wall was now nearly upon a level with my breast. I again paused, and holding the flambeaux over the mason-work, threw a few feeble rays upon the figure within.

A succession of loud and shrill screams, bursting suddenly from the throat of the chained form, seemed to thrust me violently back. For a brief moment I hesitated—I trembled. Unsheathing my rapier, I began to grope with it about the recess: but the thought of an instant reassured me. I placed my hand upon the solid fabric of the catacombs, and felt satisfied. I reapproached the wall. I replied to the yells of him who clamored. I re-echoed—I aided—I surpassed them in volume and in strength. I did this, and the clamorer grew still.

It was now midnight, and my task was drawing to a close. I had completed the eighth, the ninth, and the tenth tier. I had finished a portion of the last and the eleventh; there remained but a single stone to be fitted and plastered in. I struggled with its weight; I placed it partially in its destined position. But now there came from out the niche a low laugh that erected the hairs upon my head. It was succeeded by a sad voice, which I had difficulty in recognising as that of the noble Fortunato. The voice said—

"Ha! ha! ha!—he! he!—a very good joke indeed—an excellent jest. We will have many a rich laugh about it at the palazzo—he! he! he!—over our wine—he! he! he!"

"The Amontillado!" I said.

"He! he! he!—he! he! he!—yes, the Amontillado. But is it not getting late? Will not they be awaiting us at the palazzo, the Lady Fortunato and the rest? Let us be gone."

"Yes," I said, "let us be gone."

"For the love of God, Montresor!"

"Yes," I said, "for the love of God!"

But to these words I hearkened in vain for a reply. I grew impatient. I called aloud—

"Fortunato!"

No answer. I called again—

"Fortunato!"

No answer still. I thrust a torch through the remaining aperture and let it fall within. There came forth in return only a jingling of the bells. My heart grew sick—on account of the dampness of the catacombs. I hastened to make an end of my labor. I forced the last stone into its position; I plastered it up. Against the new masonry I re-erected the old rampart of bones. For the half of a century no mortal has disturbed them. *In pace requiescat!*°

Hop-Frog

I never knew any one so keenly alive to a joke as the king was. He seemed to live only for joking. To tell a good story of the joke kind, and to tell it well, was the surest road to his favor. Thus it happened that his seven ministers were all noted for their accomplishments as jokers. They all took after the king, too, in being large, corpulent, oily men, as well as inimitable jokers. Whether people grow fat by joking, or whether there is something in fat itself which predisposes to a joke, I have never been quite able to determine; but certain it is that a lean joker is a *rara avis in terris.*°

About the refinements, or, as he called them, the "ghosts" of wit, the king troubled himself very little. He had an especial admiration for *breadth* in a jest, and would often put up with *length*, for the sake of it. Over-niceties wearied him. He would have preferred Rabelais's "Gargantua," to the "Zadig" of Voltaire: and, upon the whole, practical jokes suited his taste far better than verbal ones.

At the date of my narrative, professing jesters had not altogether gone out of fashion at court. Several of the great continental "powers" still retained their "fools," who wore motley, with caps and bells, and

In pace requiescat: Rest in peace.   *rara avis in terris:* A rare bird in the world. The passage is taken from Juvenal's Satires.

who were expected to be always ready with sharp witticisms, at a moment's notice, in consideration of the crumbs that fell from the royal table.

Our king, as a matter of course, retained his "fool." The fact is, he *required* something in the way of folly—if only to counterbalance the heavy wisdom of the seven wise men who were his ministers—not to mention himself.

His fool, or professional jester, was not *only* a fool, however. His value was trebled in the eyes of the king, by the fact of his being also a dwarf and a cripple. Dwarfs were as common at court, in those days, as fools; and many monarchs would have found it difficult to get through their days (days are rather longer at court than elsewhere) without both a jester to laugh *with*, and a dwarf to laugh *at*. But, as I have already observed, your jesters, in ninety-nine cases out of a hundred, are fat, round and unwieldy—so that it was no small source of self-gratulation with our king that, in Hop-Frog (this was the fool's name,) he possessed a triplicate treasure in one person.

I believe the name "Hop-Frog" was *not* that given to the dwarf by his sponsors at baptism, but it was conferred upon him, by general consent of the several ministers, on account of his inability to walk as other men do. In fact, Hop-Frog could only get along by a sort of interjectional gait—something between a leap and a wriggle—a movement that afforded illimitable amusement, and of course consolation, to the king, for (notwithstanding the protuberance of his stomach and a constitutional swelling of the head) the king, by his whole court, was accounted a capital figure.

But although Hop-Frog, through the distortion of his legs, could move only with great pain and difficulty along a road or floor, the prodigious muscular power which nature seemed to have bestowed upon his arms, by way of compensation for deficiency in the lower limbs, enabled him to perform many feats of wonderful dexterity, where trees or ropes were in question, or anything else to climb. At such exercises he certainly much more resembled a squirrel, or a small monkey, than a frog.

I am not able to say, with precision, from what country Hop-Frog originally came. It was from some barbarous region, however, that no person ever heard of—a vast distance from the court of our king. Hop-Frog, and a young girl very little less dwarfish than himself (although of exquisite proportions, and a marvellous dancer,) had been forcibly carried off from their respective homes in adjoining provinces, and sent as presents to the king, by one of his ever-victorious generals.

Under these circumstances, it is not to be wondered at that a close intimacy arose between the two little captives. Indeed, they soon became sworn friends. Hop-Frog, who, although he made a great deal of sport, was by no means popular, had it not in his power to render Trippetta many services; but *she*, on account of her grace and exquisite beauty (although a dwarf,) was universally admired and petted: so she possessed much influence; and never failed to use it, whenever she could, for the benefit of Hop-Frog.

On some grand state occasion—I forgot what—the king determined to have a masquerade, and whenever a masquerade or anything of that kind, occurred at our court, then the talents both of Hop-Frog and Trippetta were sure to be called in play. Hop-Frog, in especial, was so inventive in the way of getting up pageants, suggesting novel characters, and arranging costume, for masked balls, that nothing could be done, it seems, without his assistance.

The night appointed for the *fête* had arrived. A gorgeous hall had been fitted up, under Trippetta's eye, with every kind of device which could possibly give *éclât* to a masquerade. The whole court was in a fever of expectation. As for costumes and characters, it might well be supposed that everybody had come to a decision on such points. Many had made up their minds (as to what *rôles* they should assume) a week, or even a month, in advance; and, in fact, there was not a particle of indecision anywhere—except in the case of the king and his seven ministers. Why *they* hesitated I never could tell, unless they did it by way of a joke. More probably, they found it difficult, on account of being so fat, to make up their minds. At all events, time flew; and, as a last resource, they sent for Trippetta and Hop-Frog.

When the two little friends obeyed the summons of the king, they found him sitting at his wine with the seven members of his cabinet council; but the monarch appeared to be in a very ill humor. He knew that Hop-Frog was not fond of wine; for it excited the poor cripple almost to madness; and madness is no comfortable feeling. But the king loved his practical jokes, and took pleasure in forcing Hop-Frog to drink and (as the king called it) "to be merry."

"Come here, Hop-Frog," said he, as the jester and his friend entered the room: "swallow this bumper to the health of your absent friends [here Hop-Frog sighed,] and then let us have the benefit of your invention. We want characters—*characters*, man—something novel—out of the way. We are wearied with this everlasting sameness. Come, drink! the wine will brighten your wits."

Hop-Frog endeavored, as usual, to get up a jest in reply to these advances from the king; but the effort was too much. It happened to be the poor dwarf's birthday, and the command to drink to his "absent friends" forced the tears to his eyes. Many large, bitter drops fell into the goblet as he took it, humbly, from the hand of the tyrant.

"Ah! ha! ha! ha!" roared the latter, as the dwarf reluctantly drained the beaker. "See what a glass of good wine can do! Why, your eyes are shining already!"

Poor fellow! his large eyes *gleamed*, rather than shone; for the effect of wine on his excitable brain was not more powerful than instantaneous. He placed the goblet nervously on the table, and looked round upon the company with a half-insane stare. They all seemed highly amused at the success of the king's "*joke.*"

"And now to business," said the prime minister, a *very* fat man.

"Yes," said the king; "Come, Hop-Frog, lend us your assistance. Characters, my fine fellow; we stand in need of characters—all of us—ha! ha! ha!" and as this was seriously meant for a joke, his laugh was chorused by the seven.

Hop-Frog also laughed, although feebly and somewhat vacantly.

"Come, come," said the king, impatiently, "have you nothing to suggest?"

"I am endeavoring to think of something *novel*," replied the dwarf, abstractedly, for he was quite bewildered by the wine.

"Endeavoring!" cried the tyrant, fiercely; "what do you mean by *that*? Ah, I perceive. You are sulky, and want more wine. Here, drink this!" and he poured out another goblet full and offered it to the cripple, who merely gazed at it, gasping for breath.

"Drink, I say!" shouted the monster, "or by the fiends—"

The dwarf hesitated. The king grew purple with rage. The courtiers smirked. Trippetta, pale as a corpse, advanced to the monarch's seat, and, falling on her knees before him, implored him to spare her friend.

The tyrant regarded her, for some moments, in evident wonder at her audacity. He seemed quite at a loss what to do or say—how most becomingly to express his indignation. At last, without uttering a syllable, he pushed her violently from him, and threw the contents of the brimming goblet in her face.

The poor girl got up as best she could, and, not daring even to sigh, resumed her position at the foot of the table.

There was a dead silence for about half a minute, during which the falling of a leaf, or of a feather, might have been heard. It was interrupted by a low, but harsh and protracted *grating* sound which seemed to come at once from every corner of the room.

"What—what—*what* are you making that noise for?" demanded the king, turning furiously to the dwarf.

The latter seemed to have recovered, in great measure, from his intoxication, and looking fixedly but quietly into the tyrant's face, merely ejaculated:

"I—I? How could it have been me?"

"The sound appeared to come from without," observed one of the courtiers. "I fancy it was the parrot at the window, whetting his bill upon his cage-wires."

"True," replied the monarch, as if much relieved by the suggestion; "but, on the honor of a knight, I could have sworn that it was the gritting of this vagabond's teeth."

Hereupon the dwarf laughed (the king was too confirmed a joker to object to any one's laughing), and displayed a set of large, powerful, and very repulsive teeth. Moreover, he avowed his perfect willingness to swallow as much wine as desired. The monarch was pacified; and having drained another bumper with no very perceptible ill effect, Hop-Frog entered at once, and with spirit, into the plans for the masquerade.

"I cannot tell what was the association of idea," observed he, very tranquilly, and as if he had never tasted wine in his life, "but *just after* your majesty had struck the girl and thrown the wine in her face—*just after* your majesty had done this, and while the parrot was making that odd noise outside the window, there came into my mind a capital diversion—one of my own country frolics—often enacted among us, at our masquerades: but here it will be new altogether. Unfortunately, however, it requires a company of eight persons, and—"

"Here we *are!*" cried the king, laughing at his acute discovery of the coincidence; "eight to a fraction—I and my seven ministers. Come! what is the diversion?"

"We call it," replied the cripple, "the Eight Chained Ourang-Outangs, and it really is excellent sport if well enacted."

"*We* will enact it," remarked the king, drawing himself up, and lowering his eyelids.

"The beauty of the game," continued Hop-Frog, "lies in the fright it occasions among the women."

"Capital!" roared in chorus the monarch and his ministry.

"*I* will equip you as ourang-outangs," proceeded the dwarf; "leave all that to me. The resemblance shall be so striking, that the company of masqueraders will take you for real beasts—and of course, they will be as much terrified as astonished."

"O, this is exquisite!" exclaimed the king. "Hop-Frog! I will make a man of you."

"The chains are for the purpose of increasing the confusion by their jangling. You are supposed to have escaped, *en masse*, from your keepers. Your majesty cannot conceive the *effect* produced, at a masquerade, by eight chained ourang-outangs, imagined to be real ones by most of the company; and rushing in with savage cries, among the crowd of delicately and gorgeously habited men and women. The *contrast* is inimitable."

"It *must* be," said the king: and the council arose hurriedly (as it was growing late), to put in execution the scheme of Hop-Frog.

His mode of equipping the party as ourang-outangs was very simple, but effective enough for his purposes. The animals in question had, at the epoch of my story, very rarely been seen in any part of the civilized world; and as the imitations made by the dwarf were sufficiently beast-like and more than sufficiently hideous, their truthfulness to nature was thus thought to be secured.

The king and his ministers were first encased in tight-fitting stocki-net° shirts and drawers. They were then saturated with tar. At this stage of the process, some one of the party suggested feathers; but the suggestion was at once overruled by the dwarf, who soon convinced the eight, by ocular demonstration, that the hair of such a brute as the ourang-outang was much more efficiently represented by *flax*. A thick coating of the latter was accordingly plastered upon the coating of tar. A long chain was now procured. First, it was passed about the waist of the king, *and tied*; then about another of the party, and also tied; then about all successively, in the same manner. When this chaining arrangement was complete, and the party stood as far apart from each other as possible, they formed a circle; and to make all things appear natural, Hop-Frog passed the residue of the chain, in two diameters, at right angles, across the circle, after the fashion adopted, at the present day, by those who capture Chimpanzees, or other large apes, in Borneo.

The grand saloon in which the masquerade was to take place, was a circular room, very lofty, and receiving the light of the sun only through a single window at top. At night (the season for which the apartment was especially designed,) it was illuminated principally by a large chandelier, depending by a chain from the centre of the sky-light, and low-

---

stockinet: A knitted elastic fabric, primarily used for undergarments.

ered, or elevated, by means of a counter-balance as usual; but (in order
not to look unsightly) this latter passed outside the cupola and over the
roof.

The arrangements of the room had been left to Trippetta's superin-
tendence; but, in some particulars, it seems, she had been guided by the
calmer judgment of her friend the dwarf. At his suggestion it was that,
on this occasion, the chandelier was removed. Its waxen drippings
(which, in weather so warm, it was quite impossible to prevent,) would
have been seriously detrimental to the rich dresses of the guests, who,
on account of the crowded state of the saloon, could not *all* be expected
to keep from out its centre—that is to say, from under the chandelier.
Additional sconces were set in various parts of the hall, out of the way;
and a flambeau, emitting sweet odor, was placed in the right hand of
each of the Caryatides° that stood against the wall—some fifty or sixty
altogether.

The eight ourang-outangs, taking Hop-Frog's advice, waited patiently until midnight (when the room was thoroughly filled with masqueraders) before making their appearance. No sooner had the clock
ceased striking, however, than they rushed, or rather rolled in, all together—for the impediment of their chains caused most of the party to
fall, and all to stumble as they entered.

The excitement among the masqueraders was prodigious, and filled
the heart of the king with glee. As had been anticipated, there were not
a few of the guests who supposed the ferocious-looking creatures to be
beasts of *some* kind in reality, if not precisely ourang-outangs. Many of
the women swooned with affright; and had not the king taken the precaution to exclude all weapons from the saloon, his party might soon
have expiated their frolic in their blood. As it was, a general rush was
made for the doors; but the king had ordered them to be locked immediately upon his entrance; and, at the dwarf's suggestion, the keys had
been deposited with *him*.

While the tumult was at its height, and each masquerader attentive
only to his own safety—(for, in fact, there was much *real* danger from
the pressure of the excited crowd,)—the chain by which the chandelier
ordinarily hung, and which had been drawn up on its removal, might
have been seen very gradually to descend, until its hooked extremity
came within three feet of the floor.

Caryatides: Supporting architectural columns sculpted in the form of a draped female
figure.

Soon after this, the king and his seven friends, having reeled about the hall in all directions, found themselves, at length, in its centre, and, of course, in immediate contact with the chain. While they were thus situated, the dwarf, who had followed closely at their heels, inciting them to keep up the commotion, took hold of their own chain at the intersection of the two portions which crossed the circle diametrically and at right angles. Here, with the rapidity of thought, he inserted the hook from which the chandelier had been wont to depend; and, in an instant, by some unseen agency, the chandelier-chain was drawn so far upward as to take the hook out of reach, and, as an inevitable consequence, to drag the ourang-outangs together in close connection, and face to face.

The masqueraders, by this time, had recovered, in some measure, from their alarm; and, beginning to regard the whole matter as a well-contrived pleasantry, set up a loud shout of laughter at the predicament of the apes.

"Leave them to *me!*" now screamed Hop-Frog, his shrill voice making itself easily heard through all the din. "Leave them to *me*. I fancy *I* know them. If I can only get a good look at them, *I* can soon tell who they are."

Here, scrambling over the heads of the crowd, he managed to get to the wall; when, seizing a flambeau from one of the Caryatides, he returned, as he went, to the centre of the room—leaped, with the agility of a monkey, upon the king's head—and thence clambered a few feet up the chain—holding down the torch to examine the group of ourang-outangs, and still screaming, "*I* shall soon find out who they are!"

And now, while the whole assembly (the apes included) were convulsed with laughter, the jester suddenly uttered a shrill whistle; when the chain flew violently up for about thirty feet—dragging with it the dismayed and struggling ourang-outangs, and leaving them suspended in mid-air between the sky-light and the floor. Hop-Frog, clinging to the chain as it rose, still maintained his relative position in respect to the eight maskers, and still (as if nothing were the matter) continued to thrust his torch down towards them, as though endeavoring to discover who they were.

So thoroughly astonished were the whole company at this ascent, that a dead silence, of about a minute's duration, ensued. It was broken by just such a low, harsh, *grating* sound, as had before attracted the attention of the king and his councillors, when the former threw the wine in the face of Trippetta. But, on the present occasion, there could be no question as to *whence* the sound issued. It came from the fang-like teeth of the dwarf, who ground them and gnashed them as he foamed at the mouth, and glared, with an expression of maniacal rage, into the upturned countenances of the king and his seven companions.

"Ah, ha!" said at length the infuriated jester. "Ah, ha! I begin to see who these people *are*, now!" Here, pretending to scrutinize the king more closely, he held the flambeau to the flaxen coat which enveloped him, and which instantly burst into a sheet of vivid flame. In less than half a minute the whole eight ourang-outangs were blazing fiercely, amid the shrieks of the multitude who gazed at them from below, horror-stricken, and without the power to render them the slightest assistance.

At length the flames, suddenly increasing in virulence, forced the jester to climb higher up the chain, to be out of their reach; and, as he made this movement, the crowd again sank, for a brief instant, into silence. The dwarf seized his opportunity, and once more spoke:

"I now see *distinctly*," he said, "what manner of people these maskers are. They are a great king and his seven privy-councillors—a king who does not scruple to strike a defenceless girl, and his seven councillors who abet him in the outrage. As for myself, I am simply Hop-Frog, the jester—and *this is my last jest*."

Owing to the high combustibility of both the flax and the tar to which it adhered, the dwarf had scarcely made an end of his brief speech before the work of vengeance was complete. The eight corpses swung in their chains, a fetid, blackened, hideous, and indistinguishable mass. The cripple hurled his torch at them, clambered leisurely to the ceiling, and disappeared through the sky-light.

It is supposed that Trippetta, stationed on the roof of the saloon, had been the accomplice of her friend in his fiery revenge, and that, together, they effected their escape to their own country: for neither was seen again.

ESSAYS

Some Secrets of the Magazine Prison-House

The want of an International Copy-Right Law, by rendering it nearly impossible to obtain anything from the booksellers in the way of remuneration for literary labor, has had the effect of forcing many of our very best writers into the service of the Magazines and Reviews, which with a pertinacity that does them credit, keep up in a certain or uncertain degree the good old saying, that even in the thankless field of Letters the laborer is worthy of his hire. How — by dint of what dogged instinct of the honest and proper, these journals have contrived to persist in their paying practices, in the very teeth of the opposition got up by the Fosters and Leonard Scotts, who furnish for eight dollars any four of the British periodicals for a year, is a point we have had much difficulty in settling to our satisfaction, and we have been forced to settle it, at last, upon no more reasonable ground than that of a still lingering *esprit de patrie*.° That Magazines can live, and not only live but thrive, and not only thrive but afford to disburse money for original contributions, are facts which can only be solved, under the circumstances, by the really fanciful but still agreeable supposition, that there is somewhere still existing an ember not altogether quenched among the fires of good feeling for letters and literary men, that once animated the American bosom.

It would *not do* (perhaps this is the idea) to let our poor devil authors absolutely starve, while we grow fat, in a literary sense, on the good things of which we unblushingly pick the pocket of all Europe: it would not be exactly the thing *comme il faut*,° to permit a positive atrocity of this kind and hence we have Magazines, and hence we have a portion of the public who subscribe to these Magazines (through sheer pity), and hence we have Magazine publishers (who sometimes take upon themselves the duplicate title of "editor *and* proprietor,") — publishers, we say, who, under certain conditions of good conduct, occasional puffs, and decent subserviency at all times, make it a point of conscience to encourage the poor devil author with a dollar or two, more or less as he behaves himself properly and abstains from the indecent habit of turning up his nose.

We hope, however, that we are not so prejudiced or so vindictive as to insinuate that what certainly does look like illiberality on the part of

esprit de patrie: Patriotism.   *comme il faut:* Properly.

them (the Magazine publishers) is really an illiberality chargeable to *them*. In fact, it will be seen at once, that what we have said has a tendency directly the reverse of any such accusation. These publishers pay *something*—other publishers nothing at all. Here certainly is a difference—although a mathematician might contend that the difference might be infinitesimally small. Still, these Magazine editors and proprietors *pay* (that is the word), and with your true poor-devil author the smallest favors are sure to be thankfully received. No: the illiberality lies at the door of the demagogue-ridden public, who suffer their anointed delegates (or perhaps arointed—which is it?) to insult the common sense of them (the public) by making orations in our national halls on the beauty and conveniency of robbing the Literary Europe on the highway, and on the gross absurdity in especial of admitting so unprincipled a principle, that a man has any right and title either to his own brains or to the flimsy material that he chooses to spin out of them, like a confounded caterpillar as he is. If anything of this gossamer character stands in need of protection, why we have our hands full at once with the silk-worms and the *morus multicaulis*.°

But if we cannot, under the circumstances, complain of the absolute illiberality of the Magazine publishers (since pay they do), there is at least one particular in which we have against them good grounds of accusation. Why (since pay they must) do they not pay with a good grace, and *promptly*. Were we in an ill humor at this moment, we could a tale unfold which would erect the hair on the head of Shylock. A young author, struggling with Despair itself in the shape of a ghastly poverty, which has no alleviation—no sympathy from an every-day world, that cannot understand his necessities, and that would pretend not to understand them if it comprehended them ever so well—this young author is politely requested to compose an article, for which he will "be handsomely paid." Enraptured, he neglects perhaps for a month the sole employment which affords him the chance of a livelihood, and having starved through the month (he and his family) completes at length the month of starvation and the article, and despatches the latter (with a broad hint about the former) to the pursy "editor" and bottle-nosed "proprietor" who has condescended to honor him (the poor devil) with his patronage. A month (starving still), and no reply. Another month—still none. Two months more—still none. A second letter, modestly hinting that the article may not have reached its destination—still no reply. At the expiration of six additional months,

---

morus multicaulis: Mulberry plant, the leaves of which feed silkworms.

personal application is made at the "editor and proprietor's" office. Call again. The poor devil goes out, and does not fail to call again. Still call again;—and call again is the word for three or four months more. His patience exhausted, the article is demanded. No—he can't have it (the truth is, it was too good to be given up so easily)—"it is in print," and "contributions of this character are never paid for (it is a *rule* we have) under six months after publication. Call in six months after the issue of your affair, and your money is ready for you—for we are business men, ourselves—prompt." With this the poor devil is satisfied, and makes up his mind that the "editor and proprietor" is a gentleman, and that of course he (the poor devil) will wait as requested. And it is supposable that he would have waited if he could—but Death in the meantime would not. He dies, and by the good luck of his decease (which came by starvation) the fat "editor and proprietor" is fat henceforward and for ever to the amount of five and twenty dollars, very cleverly saved, to be spent generously in canvas-backs and champagne.

There are two things which we hope the reader will not do, as he runs over this article: first, we hope that he will not believe that we write from any personal experience of our own, for we have only the reports of actual sufferers to depend upon, and second, that he will not make any personal application of our remarks to any Magazine publisher now living, it being well known that they are all as remarkable for their generosity and urbanity, as for their intelligence, and appreciation of Genius.

The Philosophy of Composition

Charles Dickens, in a note now lying before me, alluding to an examination I once made of the mechanism of "Barnaby Rudge," says—"By the way, are you aware that Godwin wrote his 'Caleb Williams' backwards? He first involved his hero in a web of difficulties, forming the second volume, and then, for the first, cast about him for some mode of accounting for what had been done."

I cannot think this the *precise* mode of procedure on the part of Godwin—and indeed what he himself acknowledges, is not altogether in accordance with Mr. Dickens' idea—but the author of "Caleb Williams" was too good an artist not to perceive the advantage derivable from at least a somewhat similar process. Nothing is more clear than that every plot, worth the name, must be elaborated to its *dénouement* before any thing be attempted with the pen. It is only with the *dénouement* constantly in view that we can give a plot its indispensable air of consequence, or causation, by making the incidents, and especially the tone at all points, tend to the development of the intention.

There is a radical error, I think, in the usual mode of constructing a story. Either history affords a thesis—or one is suggested by an incident of the day—or, at best, the author sets himself to work in the combination of striking events to form merely the basis of his narrative—designing, generally, to fill in with description, dialogue, or autorial comment, whatever crevices of fact, or action, may, from page to page, render themselves apparent.

I prefer commencing with the consideration of an *effect*. Keeping originality *always* in view—for he is false to himself who ventures to dispense with so obvious and so easily attainable a source of interest—I say to myself, in the first place, "Of the innumerable effects, or impressions, of which the heart, the intellect, or (more generally) the soul is susceptible, what one shall I, on the present occasion, select?" Having chosen a novel, first, and secondly a vivid effect, I consider whether it can best be wrought by incident or tone—whether by ordinary incidents and peculiar tone, or the converse, or by peculiarity both of incident and tone—afterward looking about me (or rather within) for such combinations of event, or tone, as shall best aid me in the construction of the effect.

I have often thought how interesting a magazine paper might be written by any author who would—that is to say, who could—detail, step by step, the processes by which any one of his compositions attained its ultimate point of completion. Why such a paper has never been given to the world, I am much at a loss to say—but, perhaps, the autorial vanity has had more to do with the omission than any one other cause. Most writers—poets in especial—prefer having it understood that they compose by a species of fine frenzy—an ecstatic intuition—and would positively shudder at letting the public take a peep behind the scenes, at the elaborate and vacillating crudities of thought—at the true purposes seized only at the last moment—at the innumerable glimpses of idea that arrived not at the maturity of full view—at the fully matured fancies discarded in despair as unmanageable—at the cautious selections and rejections—at the painful erasures and interpolations—in a word, at the wheels and pinions—the tackle for scene-shifting—the step-ladders and demon-traps—the cock's feathers, the red paint and the black patches, which, in ninety-nine cases out of the hundred, constitute the properties of the literary *histrio*.

I am aware, on the other hand, that the case is by no means common, in which an author is at all in condition to retrace the steps by

which his conclusions have been attained. In general, suggestions, having arisen pell-mell, are pursued and forgotten in a similar manner.

For my own part, I have neither sympathy with the repugnance
alluded to, nor, at any time, the least difficulty in recalling to mind the
progressive steps of any of my compositions; and, since the interest of
an analysis, or reconstruction, such as I have considered a *desideratum*,
is quite independent of any real or fancied interest in the thing analyzed, it will not be regarded as a breach of decorum on my part to
show the *modus operandi* by which some one of my own works was put
together. I select "The Raven," as most generally known. It is my
design to render it manifest that no one point in its composition is
referrible either to accident or intuition—that the work proceeded,
step by step, to its completion with the precision and rigid consequence
of a mathematical problem.

Let us dismiss, as irrelevant to the poem *per se*, the circumstance—or
say the necessity—which, in the first place, gave rise to the intention of
composing *a* poem that should suit at once the popular and the critical
taste.

We commence, then, with this intention.

The initial consideration was that of extent. If any literary work is
too long to be read at one sitting, we must be content to dispense with
the immensely important effect derivable from unity of impression—
for, if two sittings be required, the affairs of the world interfere, and
every thing like totality is at once destroyed. But since, *ceteris paribus*,°
no poet can afford to dispense with *any thing* that may advance his
design, it but remains to be seen whether there is, in extent, any advantage to counterbalance the loss of unity which attends it. Here I say no,
at once. What we term a long poem is, in fact, merely a succession of
brief ones—that is to say, of brief poetical effects. It is needless to demonstrate that a poem is such, only inasmuch as it intensely excites, by
elevating, the soul; and all intense excitements are, through a psychal
necessity, brief. For this reason, at least one half of the "Paradise Lost"
is essentially prose—a succession of poetical excitements interspersed,
inevitably, with corresponding depressions—the whole being deprived,
through the extremeness of its length, of the vastly important artistic
element, totality, or unity, of effect.

It appears evident, then, that there is a distinct limit, as regards
length, to all works of literary art—the limit of a single sitting—and
that, although in certain classes of prose composition, such as "Rob-

ceteris paribus: All things being equal.

inson Crusoe," (demanding no unity,) this limit may be advantageously overpassed, it can never properly be overpassed in a poem. Within this limit, the extent of a poem may be made to bear mathematical relation to its merit—in other words, to the excitement or elevation—again in other words, to the degree of the true poetical effect which it is capable of inducing; for it is clear that the brevity must be in direct ratio of the intensity of the intended effect:—this, with one proviso—that a certain degree of duration is absolutely requisite for the production of any effect at all.

Holding in view these considerations, as well as that degree of excitement which I deemed not above the popular, while not below the critical, taste, I reached at once what I conceived the proper *length* for my intended poem—a length of about one hundred lines. It is, in fact, a hundred and eight.

My next thought concerned the choice of an impression, or effect, to be conveyed: and here I may as well observe that, throughout the construction, I kept steadily in view the design of rendering the work *universally* appreciable. I should be carried too far out of my immediate topic were I to demonstrate a point upon which I have repeatedly insisted, and which, with the poetical, stands not in the slightest need of demonstration—the point, I mean, that Beauty is the sole legitimate province of the poem. A few words, however, in elucidation of my real meaning, which some of my friends have evinced a disposition to misrepresent. That pleasure which is at once the most intense, the most elevating, and the most pure, is, I believe, found in the contemplation of the beautiful. When, indeed, men speak of Beauty, they mean, precisely, not a quality, as is supposed, but an effect—they refer, in short, just to that intense and pure elevation of *soul*—*not* of intellect, or of heart—upon which I have commented, and which is experienced in consequence of contemplating "the beautiful." Now I designate Beauty as the province of the poem, merely because it is an obvious rule of Art that effects should be made to spring from direct causes—that objects should be attained through means best adapted for their attainment—no one as yet having been weak enough to deny that the peculiar elevation alluded to, is *most readily* attained in the poem. Now the object, Truth, or the satisfaction of the intellect, and the object Passion, or the excitement of the heart, are, although attainable, to a certain extent, in poetry, far more readily attainable in prose. Truth, in fact, demands a precision, and Passion, a *homeliness* (the truly passionate will comprehend me) which are absolutely antagonistic to that Beauty which, I maintain, is the excitement, or pleasurable elevation, of the soul. It by no means follows from any thing here said, that passion, or even truth, may not be introduced, and even profitably introduced, into a poem—for they may serve in elucidation, or aid the general effect, as do discords in music, by contrast—but the true artist will always contrive, first, to tone them into proper subservience to the predominant aim, and, secondly, to enveil them, as far as possible, in that Beauty which is the atmosphere and the essence of the poem.

Regarding, then, Beauty as my province, my next question referred to the *tone* of its highest manifestation—and all experience has shown that this tone is one of *sadness.* Beauty of whatever kind, in its supreme development, invariably excites the sensitive soul to tears. Melancholy is thus the most legitimate of all the poetical tones.

The length, the province, and the tone, being thus determined, I betook myself to ordinary induction, with the view of obtaining some artistic piquancy which might serve me as a key-note in the construction of the poem—some pivot upon which the whole structure might turn. In carefully thinking over all the usual artistic effects—or more properly *points*, in the theatrical sense—I did not fail to perceive immediately that no one had been so universally employed as that of the *refrain*. The universality of its employment sufficed to assure me of its intrinsic value, and spared me the necessity of submitting it to analysis. I considered it, however, with regard to its susceptibility of improvement, and soon saw it to be in a primitive condition. As commonly used, the *refrain*, or burden, not only is limited to lyric verse, but depends for its impression upon the force of monotone—both in sound and thought. The pleasure is deduced solely from the sense of identity—of repetition. I resolved to diversify, and so vastly heighten, the effect, by adhering, in general, to the monotone of sound, while I continually varied that of thought: that is to say, I determined to produce continuously novel effects, by the variation *of the application* of the *refrain*—the *refrain* itself remaining, for the most part, unvaried.

These points being settled, I next bethought me of the *nature* of my *refrain*. Since its application was to be repeatedly varied, it was clear that the *refrain* itself must be brief, for there would have been an insurmountable difficulty in frequent variations of application in any sentence of length. In proportion to the brevity of the sentence, would, of course, be the facility of the variation. This led me at once to a single word as the best *refrain*.

The question now arose as to the *character* of the word. Having made up my mind to a *refrain*, the division of the poem into stanzas was, of course, a corollary: the *refrain* forming the close to each stanza.

That such a close, to have force, must be sonorous and susceptible of protracted emphasis, admitted no doubt: and these considerations inevitably led me to the long *o* as the most sonorous vowel, in connection with *r* as the most producible consonant.

The sound of the *refrain* being thus determined, it became necessary to select a word embodying this sound, and at the same time in the fullest possible keeping with that melancholy which I had predetermined as the tone of the poem. In such a search it would have been absolutely impossible to overlook the word "Nevermore." In fact, it was the very first which presented itself.

The next *desideratum* was a pretext for the continuous use of the one word "nevermore." In observing the difficulty which I at once found in inventing a sufficiently plausible reason for its continuous repetition, I did not fail to perceive that this difficulty arose solely from the pre-assumption that the word was to be so continuously or monotonously spoken by *a human* being—I did not fail to perceive, in short, that the difficulty lay in the reconciliation of this monotony with the exercise of reason on the part of the creature repeating the word. Here, then, immediately arose the idea of a *non*-reasoning creature capable of speech; and, very naturally, a parrot, in the first instance, suggested itself, but was superseded forthwith by a Raven, as equally capable of speech, and infinitely more in keeping with the intended *tone*.

I had now gone so far as the conception of a Raven—the bird of ill omen—monotonously repeating the one word, "Nevermore," at the conclusion of each stanza, in a poem of melancholy tone, and in length about one hundred lines. Now, never losing sight of the object *supremeness*, or perfection, at all points, I asked myself—"Of all melancholy topics, what, according to the *universal* understanding of mankind, is the *most* melancholy?" Death—was the obvious reply. "And when," I said, "is this most melancholy of topics most poetical?" From what I have already explained at some length, the answer, here also, is obvious—"When it most closely allies itself to *Beauty*: the death, then, of a beautiful woman is, unquestionably, the most poetical topic in the world—and equally is it beyond doubt that the lips best suited for such topic are those of a bereaved lover."

I had now to combine the two ideas, of a lover lamenting his deceased mistress and a Raven continuously repeating the word "Nevermore"—I had to combine these, bearing in mind my design of varying, at every turn, the *application* of the word repeated; but the only intelligible mode of such combination is that of imagining the Raven employing the word in answer to the queries of the lover. And here it was that I saw at once the opportunity afforded for the effect on which I had been depending—that is to say, the effect of the *variation of application*. I saw that I could make the first query propounded by the lover—the first query to which the Raven should reply "Nevermore"—that I could make this first query a commonplace one—the second less so—the third still less, and so on—until at length the lover, startled from his original *nonchalance* by the melancholy character of the word itself—by its frequent repetition—and by a consideration of the ominous reputation of the fowl that uttered it—is at length excited to superstition, and wildly propounds queries of a far different character—queries whose solution he has passionately at heart—propounds them half in superstition and half in that species of despair which delights in self-torture—propounds them not altogether because he believes in the prophetic or demoniac character of the bird (which, reason assures him, is merely repeating a lesson learned by rote) but because he experiences a phrenzied pleasure in so modeling his questions as to receive from the *expected* "Nevermore" the most delicious because the most intolerable of sorrow. Perceiving the opportunity thus afforded me—or, more strictly, thus forced upon me in the progress of the construction—I first established in mind the climax, or concluding query—that to which "Nevermore" should be in the last place an answer—that in reply to which this word "Nevermore" should involve the utmost conceivable amount of sorrow and despair.

Here then the poem may be said to have its beginning—at the end, where all works of art should begin—for it was here, at this point of my preconsiderations, that I first put pen to paper in the composition of the stanza:

> "Prophet," said I, "thing of evil!—prophet still if bird or devil!
> By that Heaven that bends above us—by that God we both adore—
> Tell this soul with sorrow laden, if within the distant Aidenn,
> It shall clasp a sainted maiden whom the angels name Lenore—
> Clasp a rare and radiant maiden whom the angels name Lenore."
> Quoth the Raven—"Nevermore."

I composed this stanza, at this point, first that, by establishing the climax, I might the better vary and graduate, as regards seriousness and importance, the preceding queries of the lover—and, secondly, that I might definitely settle the rhythm, the metre, and the length and general arrangement of the stanza—as well as graduate the stanzas which were to precede, so that none of them might surpass this in rhythmical effect. Had I been able, in the subsequent composition, to construct more vigorous stanzas, I should, without scruple, have purposely enfeebled them, so as not to interfere with the climacteric effect.

And here I may as well say a few words of the versification. My first object (as usual) was originality. The extent to which this has been neglected, in versification, is one of the most unaccountable things in the world. Admitting that there is little possibility of variety in mere *rhythm*, it is still clear that the possible varieties of metre and stanza are absolutely infinite—and yet, *for centuries, no man, in verse, has ever done, or ever seemed to think of doing, an original thing.* The fact is, originality (unless in minds of very unusual force) is by no means a matter, as some suppose, of impulse or intuition. In general, to be found, it must be elaborately sought, and although a positive merit of the highest class, demands in its attainment less of invention than negation.

Of course, I pretend to no originality in either the rhythm or metre of the "Raven." The former is trochaic—the latter is octameter acatalectic, alternating with heptameter catalectic repeated in the *refrain* of the fifth verse, and terminating with tetrameter catalectic. Less pedantically—the feet employed throughout (trochees) consist of a long syllable followed by a short: the first line of the stanza consists of eight of these feet—the second of seven and a half (in effect two-thirds)—the third of eight—the fourth of seven and a half—the fifth the same—the sixth three and a half. Now, each of these lines, taken individually, has been employed before, and what originality the "Raven" has, is in their *combination into stanza*; nothing even remotely approaching this combination has ever been attempted. The effect of this originality of combination is aided by other unusual, and some altogether novel effects, arising from an extension of the application of the principles of rhyme and alliteration.

The next point to be considered was the mode of bringing together the lover and the Raven—and the first branch of this consideration was the *locale*. For this the most natural suggestion might seem to be a forest, or the fields—but it has always appeared to me that a close *circumscription of space* is absolutely necessary to the effect of insulated incident:—it has the force of a frame to a picture. It has an indisputable moral power in keeping concentrated the attention, and, of course, must not be confounded with mere unity of place.

I determined, then, to place the lover in his chamber—in a chamber rendered sacred to him by memories of her who had frequented it. The room is represented as richly furnished—this in mere pursuance of the ideas I have already explained on the subject of Beauty, as the sole true poetical thesis.

The *locale* being thus determined, I had now to introduce the bird—and the thought of introducing him through the window, was inevitable. The idea of making the lover suppose, in the first instance, that the flapping of the wings of the bird against the shutter, is a "tapping" at the door, originated in a wish to increase, by prolonging, the reader's curiosity, and in a desire to admit the incidental effect arising from the lover's throwing open the door, finding all dark, and thence adopting the half-fancy that it was the spirit of his mistress that knocked.

I made the night tempestuous, first, to account for the Raven's seeking admission, and secondly, for the effect of contrast with the (physical) serenity within the chamber.

I made the bird alight on the bust of Pallas, also for the effect of contrast between the marble and the plumage—it being understood that the bust was absolutely *suggested* by the bird—the bust of *Pallas* being chosen, first, as most in keeping with the scholarship of the lover, and, secondly, for the sonorousness of the word, Pallas, itself.

About the middle of the poem, also, I have availed myself of the force of contrast, with a view of deepening the ultimate impression. For example, an air of the fantastic—approaching as nearly to the ludicrous as was admissible—is given to the Raven's entrance. He comes in "with many a flirt and flutter.

> Not the *least obeisance made he*; not a moment stopped or stayed
> he;
> But with *mien of lord or lady*, perched above my chamber door—

In the two stanzas which follow, the design is more obviously carried out:—

> Then this ebony bird beguiling my sad fancy into smiling,
> By the *grave and stern decorum of the countenance it wore*,
> "Though thy *crest be shorn and shaven* thou," I said, "art sure no
> craven,
> Ghastly grim and ancient Raven wandering from the Nightly shore—
> Tell me what thy lordly name is on the Night's Plutonian shore!"
> Quoth the Raven "Nevermore."

> ————

> Much I marvelled *this ungainly fowl* to hear discourse so plainly,
> Though its answer little meaning—little relevancy bore;
> For we cannot help agreeing that no living human being
> *Ever yet was blessed with seeing bird above his chamber door*—
> *Bird or beast upon the sculptured bust above his chamber door*,
> With such name as "Nevermore."

The effect of the *dénouement* being thus provided for, I immediately drop the fantastic for a tone of the most profound seriousness:—this tone commencing in the stanza directly following the one last quoted, with the line,

> But the Raven, sitting lonely on that placid bust, spoke only, etc.

From this epoch the lover no longer jests—no longer sees any thing even of the fantastic in the Raven's demeanor. He speaks of him as a "grim, ungainly, ghastly, gaunt, and ominous bird of yore," and feels the "fiery eyes" burning into his "bosom's core." This revolution of thought, or fancy, on the lover's part, is intended to induce a similar one on the part of the reader—to bring the mind into a proper frame for the *dénouement*—which is now brought about as rapidly and as *directly* as possible.

With the *dénouement* proper—with the Raven's reply, "Nevermore," to the lover's final demand if he shall meet his mistress in another world—the poem, in its obvious phase, that of a simple narrative, may be said to have its completion. So far, every thing is within the limits of the accountable—of the real. A raven, having learned by rote the single word "Nevermore," and having escaped from the custody of its owner, is driven, at midnight, through the violence of a storm, to seek admission at a window from which a light still gleams—the chamber-window of a student, occupied half in poring over a volume, half in dreaming of a beloved mistress deceased. The casement being thrown open at the fluttering of the bird's wings, the bird itself perches on the most convenient seat out of the immediate reach of the student, who, amused by the incident and the oddity of the visiter's demeanor, demands of it, in jest and without looking for a reply, its name. The raven addressed, answers with its customary word, "Nevermore"—a word which finds immediate echo in the melancholy heart of the student, who, giving utterance aloud to certain thoughts suggested by the occasion, is again startled by the fowl's repetition of "Nevermore." The student now guesses the state of the case, but is impelled, as I have before explained, by the human thirst for self-torture, and in part by superstition, to propound such queries to the bird as will bring him, the lover, the most of the luxury of sorrow, through the anticipated answer "Nevermore." With the indulgence, to the utmost extreme, of this self-torture, the narration, in what I have termed its first or obvious phase, has a natural termination, and so far there has been no overstepping of the limits of the real.

But in subjects so handled, however skillfully, or with however vivid an array of incident, there is always a certain hardness or nakedness, which repels the artistical eye. Two things are invariably required—first, some amount of complexity, or more properly, adaptation; and, secondly, some amount of suggestiveness—some under-current, however indefinite of meaning. It is this latter, in especial, which imparts to a work of art so much of that *richness* (to borrow from colloquy a forcible term) which we are too fond of confounding with *the ideal.* It is the *excess* of the suggested meaning—it is the rendering this the upper instead of the under-current of the theme—which turns into prose (and that of the very flattest kind) the so called poetry of the so called transcendentalists.

Holding these opinions, I added the two concluding stanzas of the poem—their suggestiveness being thus made to pervade all the narrative which has preceded them. The under-current of meaning is rendered first apparent in the lines—

"Take thy beak from out *my heart*, and take thy form from off my
    door!"
    Quoth the Raven "Nevermore!"

It will be observed that the words, "from out my heart," involve the first metaphorical expression in the poem. They, with the answer, "Nevermore," dispose the mind to seek a moral in all that has been previously narrated. The reader begins now to regard the Raven as emblematical—but it is not until the very last line of the very last stanza, that the intention of making him emblematical of *Mournful and Never-ending Remembrance* is permitted distinctly to be seen:

And the Raven, never flitting, still is sitting, *still* is sitting,
On the pallid bust of Pallas just above my chamber door;
And his eyes have all the seeming of a demon's that is dreaming,
And the lamp-light o'er him streaming throws his shadow on the
    floor;
And my soul *from out that shadow* that lies floating on the floor
    Shall be lifted—nevermore!

PART TWO

A Case Study in Critical Controversy

Why Study Critical Controversies about the Work of Edgar Allan Poe?

As college students, both of us had the experience of being initially baffled about literary works—and about the "litcritspeak" that our instructors employed to discuss it. To use an expression that we often hear from our students today, we found some of our reading—and almost all of the classroom discussion of it—"unrelatable." Over time, however, we picked up enough of the codes governing "litcritspeak" not only to find it comprehensible but also to see that its underlying logic actually made "lit" itself more relatable. In this essay we explain why studying critical controversies can save you much of the floundering that we experienced and how that pedagogy is especially relevant to the work of Edgar Allan Poe. We start with the mini-controversy about the term *relatable* (and its twin *relate to*).

The controversy arises because students find the term, which means "easy to connect with," quite useful, whereas instructors often find it objectionable. For example, students might contrast their different responses to William Shakespeare's *Hamlet* and his *Timon of Athens* by saying that they find Hamlet's story "relatable" and Timon's "unrelatable." Instructors object to this way of speaking because they hold that a major value of literature is its ability to take us outside of our personal comfort zones, exposing us to people and situations that are challenging precisely because we might initially find it difficult to relate to them.

In our view both sides have a point. Students can enrich their engagement with literature by seeking personal connections with it. But students should not reject out of hand story worlds and characters that are not immediately familiar to them. Instructors are right about the value of literature that takes readers outside their comfort zones. But instructors should not assume that students will be able to connect with all literature just because instructors believe that such connection is a good thing. We think that an excellent way to bridge this gap between students and teachers is by studying controversies about literary works, because such study can help students connect with literature that they initially have trouble relating to, and because such study can help students and teachers connect more fully with each other.

This edition of Edgar Allan Poe's work is designed to help you relate to his work more easily and more substantially by placing it in the context of debates about his theories, stories, and poems. We call the approach behind this edition "learning by controversy," and in this essay we explain the principles underlying the approach by responding to questions and objections that students and teachers sometimes pose to us about it.

THE HIDDEN MEANING PROBLEM

When students say they have trouble relating to the academic study of literature, they often are objecting to what they regard as their teachers' preoccupation with hidden meanings. Students often ask, Why can't we just enjoy literature? Why spoil that enjoyment by probing every sentence or every line for its complexities? These questions have special force for the work of Edgar Allan Poe, since stories such as "The Fall of the House of Usher" and "The Cask of Amontillado" offer the appeal of thrillers, and poems such as "Annabel Lee" combine the pleasures of musical verse with an emotional response to love and loss.

To some students, then, the debates between critics about such works come across as a double dose of the hidden meaning problem—with several opposing critical interpretations of those works to deal with instead of just one. Who cares about the squabbles between literary interpreters, especially since paying attention to them creates more distance between the works and our enjoyment of them?

Since so many students share such objections, we take them seriously and believe they need to be addressed head-on. We note, first, that both objections—to looking for hidden meanings in literature and to entering into debates about those meanings—are based on an underlying opposition between reading for pleasure and reading for analysis. Under careful scrutiny, however, this opposition is hard to sustain. If you reflect on your activities and conversations outside your formal classes, we believe you will find that you are frequently doing criticism and entering critical controversy by another name (on some occasions that name is "snark") and that you assume it is better to do it well than poorly.

In other words, you are already doing criticism the moment you begin to talk about a blog post, a TV show, a YouTube video, a sports event, or a friend's behavior, not to mention a book, a play, or a film. Furthermore, you become embroiled in controversy as soon as you discuss these things with a friend who has a different take on them. Even the most modest assertions about any of these things imply claims about its meaning, value, or consequences in the world, and the more interesting these claims are the more likely they are to be debatable. For example, if you say to a friend that a story is "a great read" (or "a snooze"), or that the person who interviewed you for a part-time job is "a jerk," you are engaging in a rudimentary act of criticism that can quickly get you into a disagreement. "A jerk? I thought he was a pretty cool guy!" If you go on to give a reason or two for your judgment—"Poe's Dupin is smarter and less neurotic than Sherlock Holmes"; "the interviewer was far more interested in himself than in my qualifications for the job"— you are moving toward a more sophisticated critical act that also invites further disagreement.

Furthermore, in making and debating such critical judgments, you are also implicitly beginning to practice what has come to be called "theory." When you argue that someone is "a jerk" or that a television show is "boring," you are operating with a set of principles (and thus an implicit theory) about what qualities in a person or a show are acceptable or unacceptable and why. In a similar way, when you say that you rate Dupin more highly than Sherlock Holmes, you are theorizing that the quality of a detective story can be judged in part by the intelligence and overall appeal of the detective. Of course, articulating the principles underlying your likes and dislikes risks adding another layer of abstrac tion to literary discussion and so may deepen the "hidden meaning" problem. But when you become theoretically explicit about your assumptions in this way, you make it easier to compare your reasons for your judgments with the reasons of others for theirs, and when those reasons clash, controversy emerges.

Of course we recognize that there is a difference between your straight up assessment of a book as boring and the complicated and all-too-often obscure cogitations and controversies of sophisticated literary critics and theorists. Because of this very difference, however, and the intimidation you may feel reading the published debates of literary critics, we want to emphasize that these debates have their roots in the same kind of arguments you have. Some of the issues in the debates among Poe critics arise out of their different answers to such basic questions as "Whom do I like in this short story?" "Is the character I like the one that Poe seems to want me to like?" and "How do I know?" In other words, you can think of academic critical and theoretical debate as formalized versions of the kinds of conversations you have all the time. Such debate is book-talk elevated to the level of rigorous argumentation.

We suspect that when students (and sometimes teachers) are turned off by literary critical debate and resist the idea of bringing it directly into class discussion, they are reacting—understandably enough—to encounters with abstruse, arid, or jargon-ridden examples of interpretive or theoretical analysis. Or they may be reacting to literary criticism in which nobody steps back to ask what's the point—that is, criticism that fails to make clear to the reader why the analysis is worthwhile, what's at stake in the analysis, and why it matters. As we believe the selections in this volume show, the most useful critics both spell out their main points and indicate why their readers should care about those points. But it is a good idea to ask the "so-what question" about these essays and, indeed, about any potential contribution to the debates about Poe, including your own.

Another reason that criticism and theory are inescapable is that they play a significant role in numerous practical decisions that students and teachers make. Students, for example, must decide such matters as which courses to take and which aspects of those courses to give their greatest attention, while teachers must decide which courses to offer and which books and writing assignments to put on their syllabi. All these decisions require us to make evaluative judgments that are themselves based on underlying principles (do you choose courses based on how they fit into your weekly schedule, or on their expected contribution to your course of study, or for some other reason?). Even some things that may initially appear to involve wholly subjective judgments are ultimately matters that depend on theoretical principles and reasons. For example, if you are asked to determine whether Poe is as good a writer as his contemporary Nathaniel Hawthorne, you may be tempted to shrug your shoulders and reply that the answer is a matter of opinion. While some readers are likely to enjoy Poe's work more than Hawthorne's, who is to say which writer is ultimately better? Why waste time debating these matters of subjective taste?

There is a long history of philosophic attempts, going back at least to Plato, to address this question of whether value judgments can ever be more than subjective, and we encourage you to at least sample these attempts. For now we offer a practical answer. We need to debate questions about value (and therefore examine the principles underlying our apparently subjective judgments) because so many of our individual and collective decisions about how to be and what to do involve value judgments that go beyond matters of subjective taste. For example, you are studying Poe and the other writers featured in your literature courses because the collective wisdom of scholars and teachers is that these authors are better than the thousands whose texts have either never been available in the Literary History Bookstore or been relegated to its discard bin. Although this collective wisdom is neither purely objective nor infallible, it is far from simply subjective: it is the result of countless value judgments—and debates about those judgments—that ultimately rest on reasoned arguments about the details of those writers' texts.

Another way to view our point is to consider any situation in which your community has to decide on a policy—over what texts to study in school, say, or if tax money should be invested in schools or a new sports arena. In this situation, you and your fellow citizens do not have the luxury of saying, "It's all a matter of opinion." Instead, your community has to make a value judgment that one choice is better than the other, and if you want your choice to carry the day, you and your allies need to be able to make persuasive arguments in favor of it. To opt out of the debate is to surrender one of the most important forms of action available to a citizen in a democracy. In sum, value judgments and debates about how to make them are inescapable, important, and more than matters of individual opinion.

AN OBJECTION FROM TEACHERS: CRITICS AND THEIR DEBATES DISTRACT STUDENTS FROM LITERATURE ITSELF

Some teachers who would concede that finding "hidden meaning" in literature is legitimate would nevertheless oppose asking students to read critical debates. In their view, reading critics only distracts students from the primary and immediate experience of reading the text itself, substituting the critics' responses for the students' own. These teachers might grant that reading critics and their debates is appropriate enough at the graduate level, where students are being trained as professionals in a discipline. But they would argue that criticism has no place in undergraduate courses, where the goal is to teach students to understand and appreciate literature itself. These teachers, then, implicitly distinguish between a student's "direct" and "unmediated" response to the text and the secondary book-talk engaged in by professional critics. For these teachers, such secondary book-talk at best diverts students' attention from their primary responses and at worst distorts the text as the critic pursues his own agenda.

We respectfully disagree with these teachers. First, we think that the distinction between a direct, or primary, and a mediated, or secondary, response to a text is at least as difficult to sustain as the distinction between reading for pleasure and reading for analysis. All responses are mediated to some degree. It is not possible, for example, to read Poe today without the mediating filter of his reputation as an important but eccentric American writer. It is not possible for any class approaching Poe's work to escape the mediation established by the context of the whole course—reading "Ligeia" in a course on literature and gender will be different from reading it in a course on the grotesque—and by the instructor's particular approach to the material. The choice is not between mediated and unmediated reading but between different kinds of mediation.

Second, as students you have an obvious stake in being exposed to the kind of discourse you are assigned to produce. In most undergraduate literature courses, you are asked to do literary criticism, in the written form of papers and in the oral discourse of class discussion. How can we teachers expect you to produce effective literary criticism unless we provide you with examples of it? Just as it would be strange to ask you to shoot free throws while telling you to never watch a basketball game, or to play a piano sonata without ever having seen a pianist play one, it seems strange to ask you to make the "moves" critics make without giving you the opportunity to watch and listen to some critics in action.

Third, as noted above, we believe that debates between critics can help to make literary works more intelligible and interesting by sharpening your sense of what to look for when you read them. Far from interfering with your spontaneous reactions to Poe's stories and poems, reading the critical debates about these works should help you engage more deeply with their language, techniques, structures, and themes.

The debates should help you connect these elements of the works with larger issues that can be raised about them and to see some of what is at stake in analyzing them. The moves made by literary critics become more meaningful and engaging when you watch them performing these moves on texts that you've had some response to, whether that response was one of delight, disappointment, or befuddlement. Indeed, as we discuss in our essay, "How to Write about Critical Controversy about Poe's Work" (p. 557), we believe that triangulating a text, your ideas about the text, and others' ideas about that text provides an excellent strategy for deepening your engagement with it.

To put these points another way, we believe that, as with basketball or piano playing, you learn by doing. You learn how to make the moves on the court or the keyboard when you cease being a spectator and start playing games and pieces yourself. Similarly you learn to make the moves in the game of Poe criticism by entering the critical fray and joining some of the debates that have gone on and continue to go on about his theories, stories, and poems.

CAN WE KNOW WHAT POE MEANT, AND, IF SO, HOW?

This question poses a challenge to the whole enterprise of learning by controversy. For if we can't know what Poe meant, aren't critics who debate about the meanings of Poe's works wasting their time? And how can we know what Poe meant, since he obviously is not around to tell us, having been dead for more than 150 years (his dates are 1809 to 1849)?

The kind and degree of access we readers and critics can legitimately claim to the intentions of authors has itself been a matter of intense debate among literary theorists. Virtually all theorists acknowledge that determining an author's intention is a difficult task, and some categorically deny that knowing an intention is possible. Others, however, and we count ourselves among their number, argue that although certain knowledge of another's intention is rare, we can and do make accurate inferences about each other's intentions all the time and could hardly communicate if we did not. We make these inferences with the aid of the feedback loop established among context, author, text, and audience. In effect, we ask and answer (often with well-justified confidence) the question, What does this use of this language by this person to this audience in this context most probably mean?

Consider, for example, the way we routinely identify verbal mistakes, something that would not be possible if we could not claim to discern a speaker's or writer's intention. When we decide a speaker must be making a mistake, saying one thing when he actually means another, we do so by differentiating between the speaker's actual words and the meaning he intends to convey. In one of the funniest scenes in Woody Allen's film *Take the Money and Run,* Allen in his role as a would-be bank robber pushes a note demanding money at a bank teller. With his less than perfect handwriting, however, Allen's character Virgil Starkwell has scrawled on the note what looks like "I've got a gub." The teller immediately gets into a discussion with Virgil, asking him, "What does this say? 'I've got a gub?'" The humor lies not just in Virgil's ineptness but also in the teller's absurd single-minded focus on the three-letter word even as he's being threatened with death. Allen relies on his audience to recognize that, in a real-life bank robbery, a teller (audience) would readily infer that a masked man (author) who handed him such a note (text) in such a context (the bank during business hours) must intend "gub" to mean "gun." While we are laughing at the scene, we may overlook the remarkable phenomenon that, although "gub" is not an English word, we have no trouble understanding what Virgil intends it to mean.

But even though knowing an author's intention is possible, it is not always easy, and thus we might pose the next question this way: Given that most literary works are more complex communications than "I have a gub," how can we maximize the probability that we are correctly inferring the intentions of those communications? We believe that one excellent way is to carefully examine and to participate in the debates about their meanings, because these debates collectively illuminate the various components of the feedback loop. Is Poe trying to create great art or is he a mere entertainer? Is he racist? Sexist? To answer, the critics in this collection examine, to one degree or another, Poe's life, his texts, his readers, and the multiple contexts in which he wrote. You can then examine these matters and come to your own conclusions.

For us, it follows that learning by controversy is not about proliferating debates that never reach resolution. Instead, it is a process that promotes the testing of multiple hypotheses about the meaning of a text against the details of that text and the multiple factors that influenced the shaping of those details. The goal of the testing is not to proliferate debate for its own sake but rather to find a persuasive answer to the question that generated the clashing hypotheses. But the process of testing also teaches us that we ought to view our answers not as permanent conclusions but as tentative resolutions subject to further debate and testing by others—and even by ourselves at a later date.

Reading for intention can be understood as "reading with the grain" of the text in an effort to see the text as the author designed it for an audience. Such readings are especially valuable when we find the author's designs to be admirable according to one or more measures (say, aesthetic or ethical or political). But reading with the grain is not the only valuable kind of engagement with a text, especially because (1) sometimes what happens to Allen's Virgil Starkwell happens to authors on a grander—and more serious—scale and because (2) we sometimes want to counter the results of reading with the grain. In these cases, we will want to read "against the grain" of the text and its intentions.

Our utterances can carry meanings that we are not personally conscious of, and may even deny when they are pointed out to us, but are recognizably present in our language. In other words, while intention can override meaning in a case like "I've got a gub," on other occasions meaning will override intention because our culture has assigned some inescapable meanings to our language whether or not we are aware of those meanings. For example, a man may be telling the truth when he says he never intended to offend anyone by using the word *chicks* to refer to women. But this man, as anyone living in our time should know, would be demeaning women without consciously intending to, because our culture has assigned a derogatory connotation to the word *chicks*. No matter how suspicious we may be of psychoanalyzing other people, virtually all of us have at times read "between the lines" of what they said and found meanings in them that the speakers did not intend but which betrayed questionable assumptions they absorbed from their culture or upbringing. Sometimes we will want to challenge rather than simply accept those assumptions. Critics, especially but not exclusively politically oriented critics, sometimes do this reading between the lines of an author's work in order to highlight significant meanings that escape readings with the grain.

Even when there is no gap between an author's apparent intention and her textual meanings, we may want to read her text against the grain in order to challenge its underlying beliefs and values. Many feminist critics have demonstrated the value of reading against the grain of texts that take the inferiority of women for granted. Paired with such readings, these texts are less able to get away with this ethically and politically deficient assumption than they may have been when they were originally published.

As we hope is clear, since both reading with and reading against the grain can provide valuable engagements with texts, there is no need to debate whether all readings should be intentional readings. At the same time, we would like to note that the concept of intention plays an important, if often silent, role in reading against the grain, precisely because the power of such reading depends in part on some under-standing of a reading with the grain. In other words, to appreciate the force of a reading against the grain we need to make decisions about what the grain itself is.

LEARNING BY CONTROVERSY AND OTHER APPROACHES TO TEACHING

Since we recognize that not all your courses will follow the learning by controversy approach, we would like to offer some reflections on how it relates to other pedagogies. You have probably already discov-ered that certain codes and buzzwords (e.g., "empowerment," "the decentered classroom," and "dialogue") often betray a given teacher's allegiance to one or another of the diverse theories of pedagogy—and that failing to decode their signals can cause you problems. For some professors, your role as a student is to master the knowledge they pre-sent and to reproduce that knowledge in examinations. For other pro-fessors, who reject this "banking" model of education (as they call it), with its assumption that knowledge is a substance to be deposited in and then withdrawn from the student's brain, your role is to be an active *constructor* of knowledge. In class, these teachers may try to get out of your way, intervening little in the discussion in order to "empower" you and your classmates to take control over your own learning. For still other professors, the best teacher is a passionate activist who tries to transform your presumably not-yet-enlightened consciousness, turning you against the dominant culture's patriarchal, racist, and homophobic attitudes that you presumably brought to the classroom, and converting you into an agent of social change. For yet another set of professors, this last group in turn may be viewed as an unprofessional and intolerant cadre of ideologues bent on coercing you into political correctness.

Learning by controversy assumes that just as a diversity of interpre-tations about Poe and his work is a good thing for education, so too is a diversity of pedagogical theories and teaching styles. In our view, there is no magic formula for teaching, no single right way for all teach-ers and all students to follow, and we know of good and bad teachers who represent each of the modes of pedagogy described above (though our commitment to learning by controversy means that we are skeptical about teachers, regardless of their pedagogical approaches, who are so sure about their own "truths" that they make no room in their class-rooms for opposing views). We also believe, however, that just as you should take part in the controversies over subject matters and inter-pretations, you should also be brought into the controversies about authority and pedagogy.

We recognize that conflict and controversy are not themselves neu-tral terms or activities. "Learning by controversy" may strike some of you—and some of your teachers—as a symptom of a masculinist pro-fessional and cultural ethic, one that rewards critical John Waynes who excel in shoot-outs with rival critics and critical schools. Others may be put off by what seems to them an aridly legalistic approach to literature that seems to treat authors almost as if they were accused parties on trial, with their fates in the hands of critical prosecuting attorneys and defense lawyers.

We want to be clear that for us the aim of literary education is not to determine who is the best critical prosecuting attorney or fastest critical gunslinger (or, for that matter, bullslinger). The reason for introducing you to critical conflicts is not to encourage you to unleash your aggres-sions, but to help you excel in the kind of analysis and reasoned argument that will make you an effective citizen as well as a good student. If clumsy uses of our approach run the risk of turning classroom discussions into the academic equivalent of Western shootouts or prosecutorial bullying of authors, effective uses have the potential for the significant pedagogi-cal gains we have been discussing. The first key is to distinguish between productive and unproductive critical controversies; the second is to engage with the more productive controversies in ways that open up insights into texts rather than merely lock us into rigid oppositions or that elevate winning over understanding.

You be the judge. "Why study critical controversies about the work of Edgar Allan Poe?" See how you might answer our initial question after you have worked through the texts in the rest of this book. And if you want to argue with us, we'd be glad to hear from you, since we seek to practice what we preach and that means regarding the answers we offer in this essay as hypotheses subject to further testing against the ideas of others, including you.

Gerald Graff
James Phelan

The Controversy over Aesthetics and the Literary Marketplace; or, Is Poe a Literary Genius or a Pop-Culture Hack?

Although his place in the American literary canon is firmly established, Poe has always been the odd man out among the American Romantics—the one canonical author from the period who is not included, for example, in F. O. Mathiessen's foundational *American Renaissance* (1941). As literary critic Shoshana Felman writes, "No poet has been so highly acclaimed and, at the same time, so violently disclaimed," and none "has engendered so much disagreement and so many critical contradictions" (27). This section attempts to give expression to some of the many voices that have both acclaimed and disclaimed Poe—occasionally both at the same time.

The contradictory assessment of Poe was one that Poe to some degree cultivated, as he loudly rejected both the provincialism of the nascent American literary establishment and the crassness of an emerging mass marketplace—while simultaneously courting the favor of both. Many of the documents in this section reveal the consequences of Poe's alternately obsequious and combative relationship to the newly emerging distinctions between "high" and "low" culture, between the "popular" and the "literary" that would shape his reception in the century following his death. This section also provides an opportunity to see how changing priorities in academic scholarship can dramatically reorient readings of canonical authors. In the case of Poe, for example, we see that questions of aesthetic judgment move increasingly into the background in the post–World War II period. As Harold Bloom put it, somewhat regretfully, in 2008, "The first principle in writing about Poe is never to discuss how badly he performed in both prose and verse" (vii). And yet, as we will see, many writers do pose such aesthetic challenges, even as others stage defenses of Poe's works in terms that his contemporaries might not have recognized.

*   *   *

James Russell Lowell was at the early stages of his own literary career when Poe solicited him to write an essay about him for the ongoing "Our Contributors" series in *Graham's Magazine*, where Poe had served as editor for a little more than a year. Ten years Lowell's senior, Poe had watched Lowell's rise, with interest and jealousy, from the publication of his earliest poems in 1840. It was hard for Poe not to attribute some of Lowell's growing fame to the advantages the young New Englander enjoyed, including Harvard degrees and the support of the Northern literary establishment.

Though it might have galled him, Poe was eager for entry to that establishment and saw Lowell as perhaps his best reference. Two years earlier Lowell had published Poe's story "The Tell-Tale Heart" in his own short-lived magazine *The Pioneer*; and as Poe hoped the 1845 portrait in *Graham's* would be reprinted numerous times, introducing Poe to the attention of and (at least briefly) embrace by the writers and critics behind the Young America literary movement, a group of writers devoted to establishing a nationalistic literary tradition independent of European influence. Poe himself was no literary nationalist and certainly no democrat, and thus he shared little in common with the movement aside from a contempt for current standards of American literary criticism.

Even as he was agreeing to Poe's request for the profile, which proved so instrumental to the consolidation of Poe's literary personality and popularity, Lowell was beginning to have doubts about Poe. In March 1844, Poe had written a decidedly mixed review of Lowell's *Poems*, describing them as "infected with the poetical conventionalities of the day," most particularly "the error of *didacticism*" which for Poe prevented Lowell's work from achieving "the sole legitimate object of the true poem": "the *creation of beauty*." That Lowell was aware of Poe's review is made clear in his profile in *Graham's*, where he questions—and indeed comes close to mocking—Poe's dictum. But Lowell generously attributed Poe's review to what he saw as certain "prejudices" that blinded his otherwise keen-eyed vision.

For numerous reasons, the literary alliance between Lowell and Poe was doomed even before it began. In Poe's 1849 review of Lowell's *Fable for Critics*, we perhaps get a clearer sense as to the nature of the prejudices that early on divided Poe and Lowell, albeit here Poe lays these entirely at Lowell's feet. "His prejudices on the topic of slavery break out every where in his present book," Poe declared in his review for the proslavery *Southern Literary Messenger*. Lowell believed deeply in the power of poetry to do political work, and as a committed abolitionist, the issue of slavery appears frequently in his early works. Whatever Poe's sentiments about the institution of slavery (see "The Controversy over Race"), Poe disdained didactic poetry in general and abolitionist poetry in particular. For example, of the great abolitionist poet John Greenleaf Whittier, Poe wrote dismissively in 1841, "his themes are *never* to our liking."

By the time Poe reviewed Lowell's *Fable for Critics*, their relationship had soured entirely, as evidenced by Lowell's very different assessment of Poe in the excerpt from *Fable* presented in this section. And whatever the differences between the two men on the topic of slavery, their falling out was already well in motion from other forces even as the profile in *Graham's* was in circulation.

Surely it was against his better judgment that Lowell arranged for Poe to speak at the Lyceum in Boston, despite Poe's continuing practice of lacing his reviews of Lowell's work with barbs, and, more urgently, Poe's new campaign against Lowell's friend Henry Wadsworth Longfellow, arguably the most respected American poet of the age. Having publicly associated himself with Poe's *Graham's*, Lowell felt the need to assure Longfellow that "I have had no communication with" him on these matters lest the poet think Lowell was somehow in sympathy with Poe's attacks. Lowell was certainly having misgivings about Poe's visit to Boston when he was informed later that spring that Poe had taken up drinking to excess again after a period of relative sobriety. Visiting Poe in New York Lowell found Poe "a little tipsy, as if he were recovering from a fit of drunkenness, & with that over-solemnity with which men in such cases try to convince you of their sobriety."

Things went from bad to worse when, in August, two months before his Boston appearance, Poe accused Lowell of "a palpable plagiarism" from Wordsworth. As Lowell wrote shortly after the accusation was published:

> Poe, I am afraid, is wholly lacking in that element of manhood which, for want of a better name, we call *character*. . . . As I prognosticated, I have made Poe my enemy by doing him a service. . . . He has accused me of plagiarism, and *misquoted* Wordsworth to sustain his charge. . . . Any one who had ever read the whole of Wordsworth's poem would see that there was no resemblance between the two passages. Poe wishes to kick down the ladder by which he rose. (p. 1: 142–43)

So even before the Lyceum appearance in October of 1845, the fragile friendship between the two writers had soured irrevocably. However, thanks to Lowell's portrait in *Graham's* and to the enormous popularity of "The Raven," Poe's newfound celebrity made him too attractive a guest for the Lyceum to disinvite, and the $50 offered for the reading of an original poem was too desperately needed by the perpetually bankrupt Poe for him to refuse. Unfortunately, neither the financial incentive nor the chance to hold court in the heart of the New England literary establishment were enough to summon the muse for the occasion, and Poe proved unable to produce the required original poem. Instead he read from "Al Aaraaf," a poem published when the poet was twenty (and written when he was still younger), presenting the work as if it were composed for the occasion.

It was Poe himself who exposed the true origin of the work over dinner following his performance. A series of accusations and charges followed, in which Longfellow's defenders pointed to the performance as evidence of Poe's untrustworthiness, while Poe attempted to pass it off as a hoax that exposed the hollowness of his hosts' critical faculties. When it was all said and done, however, the "Longfellow war" and the Lyceum affair had combined to effectively end any hopes Poe might have had of a working relationship with literary New England.

While this literary tempest is unlikely to engage the partisan spirits of readers today, we pause over these events from 1845 as a reminder of the degree to which Poe was involved in and even actively courted controversy in his own lifetime. Lowell, for example, would not have missed the barbed edge to Poe's long-winded "apology" before beginning his reading of "Al Aaraaf" for not being able to produce the kind of "didactic" poetry of which New Englanders were so very fond, a fairly direct slap against the man who had sponsored his invitation to the Lyceum in the first place. And the choice to read "Al Aaraaf" as if it were an original poem is all the more provocative in that Lowell had in fact singled that poem out in his original 1845 portrait for *Graham's* as an example of the quality of Poe's juvenilia: "the most remarkable boyish poems that we have ever read."

Despite the public feud, Poe and Lowell were in many ways kindred spirits—both writers struggled to found magazines and to establish themselves as fearless and insightful critics. It makes sense that Poe sought Lowell out, just as we can understand, even if the motives are perhaps somewhat obscure, why Poe would to some degree willfully sabotage the relationship. Far more obscure is Poe's relationship with editor and critic Rufus Griswold, and few incidents in Poe's life are as unaccountable as his decision to entrust his literary legacy to a man who made little secret of his contempt for Poe.

From their first meeting in 1841, Poe and Griswold seemed doomed to be sworn enemies. At the time, Griswold was reinventing himself from an unsuccessful Baptist minister into a literary editor, while Poe was managing his own attempted transformation from Southern editor to national writer. By 1842, their enmity seemed sealed when Griswold replaced Poe as editor at *Graham's* and Poe, paid by Griswold to write a favorable review of his *The Poets and Poetry of America*, offered instead what was at best a lukewarm assessment. By 1843, Poe was openly denouncing Griswold's volume and talents.

Still, the two could not be rid of each other. *The Poets and Poetry of America* had proved immensely successful, and when Griswold began work on a companion volume, *The Prose Writers of America*, Poe very much wished to be included. Poe's own rising literary stature made it impossible for Griswold to deny his rival inclusion in this volume. So began a brief but momentous period in 1845 of what Poe termed "hope of reconciliation." Poe even felt emboldened by this period of relative warmth to ask Griswold for a fifty-dollar loan. But even as their professional deportment toward each other improved for a time, the personal animosity increased on other fronts, largely due to their shared fascination with the poet and socialite Frances Sargent Osgood.

Given this history, Poe's choice of Griswold as literary executor is baffling, and his friends and allies (then and now) doubted the status of Griswold's claims to the title. Griswold also claimed that Poe had requested he write Poe's official biography after his death. Given that Poe had gone out of his way to ensure that Lowell, and *not* Griswold, write his portrait in *Graham's*, the claim seemed to stretch credulity, and Griswold's treatment of Poe following his death certainly endorsed the suspicions of Poe's friends—particularly the inclusion in his biography of seemingly forged documents. Yet the biography did much to establish the identity of Poe as literary outcast and source of postmortem controversy, and we see in the selections that follow how its influence would prove in many ways intractable.

So incensed by the treatment of their late friend were Poe's allies that many immediately came to his defense following Griswold's earliest salvos on the recently deceased writer's reputation, including authors George Lippard, Nathaniel Parker Willis, and Frances Osgood. The writer Lambert Wilmer was perhaps the most vociferous, denouncing the early biographical portrait Griswold published under the name "LUDWIG," as "a hypocritical canting document" published by a "slanderous and malicious miscreant." "Some circumstances mentioned by the slanderous hypocrite we *know* to be false, and we have no doubt in the world that nearly all of his statements intended to throw odium and discredit on the character of the deceased are scandalous inventions." (It says something perhaps of Poe's judgment that he believed Wilmer to be his enemy because Wilmer had at one time expressed anxieties that Poe's drinking would carry him "headlong to destruction, moral, physical and intellectual.")

The most extensive defense of Poe from his friends came from poet Sarah Helen Whitman in *Edgar Poe and His Critics*, which she began after Griswold's death in 1857. Poe and Whitman had been romantically involved toward the end of his life, and there is evidence that she refused his offer of marriage only because of deep concerns about his drinking. Like Osgood, Whitman remained fiercely loyal to Poe and offered her volume in opposition to Griswold's assertion that Poe "had few or no friends" (p. 268). Although Whitman championed Poe as a writer, her primary concern in her portrait was to rescue his memory from Griswold's character assassination attempts of the previous decade.

Even before Whitman's volume was published, however, another defense arrived from one who never knew Poe personally, beginning a very different chapter in the long story of the afterlife of Poe's reputation. Writing from France and introducing Poe to a new continental readership, Charles Baudelaire presented a very different Poe than that defined by either his friends or detractors in America up to that point. This was Poe the rebel, the romantic outcast, whose life and work, as Baudelaire put it, served as an "admirable protest" against everything that is wrong with the young nation — mercantilism, democracy, mediocrity. Baudelaire's Poe was born into an environment hostile to everything he valued — beauty, truth, art, and taste — values, not coincidentally, shared by the French poet himself.

Indeed, Baudelaire's celebration of Poe is in large measure an occasion to lay out his own theories of poetry and the role of the poet in a society increasingly dominated by profit and pragmatism. Baudelaire's Poe is Baudelaire himself, in many ways, or Baudelaire imagining himself born in a society even more antithetical to art and beauty than that which he found contemporary France to be. But his Poe—the romantic visionary protesting against modernity—would prove a powerful one for generations of readers on both sides of the Atlantic and would play a vital role in what we might understand as the cult of Poe that thrives to the present day.

A generation later, it was Baudelaire's enthusiasm for Poe that Henry James turned to as evidence of the French poet's aesthetic failings, or "primitive stage of reflection" (p. 291). Conversely, the playwright George Bernard Shaw pointed to America's failure to appreciate Poe as evidence of *its* state of cultural damnation. The striking difference of opinion between these contemporary great men of letters points to how deep were the divisions regarding the aesthetic value of Poe's work and the degree to which admiring or hating Poe's work had become a litmus test of sorts. For James, Poe represented everything he wanted to leave behind in America when he moved permanently to England. Shaw's appreciation of Poe, on the other hand, as the exception to the American rule, resembles the terms of Baudelaire's own positive assessment, albeit from a very different place. Where Baudelaire was a self-professed literary aristocrat who saw Poe as an antidemocratic kindred spirit, Shaw was a socialist who saw Poe as a fiercely independent author capable of rejecting the excesses of capitalism that blinded his countrymen to the true power of his work.

Baudelaire, James, and Shaw were of course writing of Poe and his legacy from across the ocean. In the 1920s and 30s, however, Americans began to take increased interest in their own literary history—an interest that would take on more urgency with the rise of the Cold War and the deeply felt need for an American culture to rally against the perceived dangers of Soviet communism. During this period, many writers of the nineteenth century who had been largely unknown or underappreciated during their own lifetime—writers such as Emily Dickinson or Herman Melville—were rediscovered, and other writers who occupied a relatively narrow literary sphere during their time—such as Ralph Waldo Emerson and Henry David Thoreau—began to occupy increasingly central roles in the emerging literary history being written. It was, in other words, a period of profound change and reevaluation—and for every writer rescued from obscurity, another writer long famed and held immortal began to slip steadily into historical obscurity.

(How many students of American literature today read, for example, formerly canonical authors such as John Greenleaf Whittier?)

In this climate, it was inevitable that Poe's value once more came under fierce scrutiny. The 1920s saw an explosion of interest in Poe. The Edgar Allen Poe Society was formed in 1923, and three biographies of Poe were published in 1926 alone. The revival of Poe's fortunes in the early twentieth century in his home country—fortunes Griswold had hoped to dispatch in his capacity as "executor"—finds its sources in a combination of forces, including growing American cultural nationalism after World War I; a desire on the part of the post-Reconstruction South for literary forefathers; the establishment of literary marketplaces for science fiction and detective fiction, both of which could claim Poe as a founding father; and the emergence of psychoanalytic criticism, to which Poe's works would prove especially amenable.

It was in this environment that American poet and critic Yvor Winters turned his attention to Poe in 1937 and, as he put it, started to "awaken to the fact" that to declare Poe "exceptionally bad" both as a theorist and a practitioner of literature was now considered an act of "heresy" (p. 294). For Winters the sudden canonization of Poe boded ill for the field of American literary scholarship only just emerging from the shadow of British domination. As a result, Winters's systematic dismantling of Poe's writings, and especially his criticism, was an attempt to distinguish the brand of literary criticism he and his associates among the New Critics were championing: an approach to literature that largely eschewed biographical and other contextual evidence in favor of a rigorous analysis of the text as a self-contained system. This is not to say that Winters did not genuinely believe Poe to be a vastly overrated writer: clearly he did. However, Winters was also motivated to take charge of debunking this reputation by the kind of criticism Poe was *inspiring* in the 1920s and 30s: psychological, biographical, and historical criticism that relied heavily on external context and methods imported from outside the text.

Writing from a position of self-imposed exile from his native America, like Henry James more than a half century earlier, the poet and critic T. S. Eliot, himself something of a spiritual godfather to the New Criticism with which Winters was associated, takes a somewhat more ambivalent approach to Poe. Like Winters, he finds "slipshod writing" and "puerile thinking unsupported by wide reading or profound scholarship" (p. 301). But he also suggests that Poe looks very different if we put aside the rigorous microscope of close reading and instead take what he calls here "a distant view." As Eliot suggests, Poe continues to haunt a century after his death, even to the point where Eliot—a poet who seems as unlike Poe as can be imagined—professes to be uncertain whether Poe has influenced even him. And it is undeniably the case, Eliot points out, that insofar as modernist poetry owes much to the influence of three French poets—Baudelaire, Mallarme, and Valéry—then Poe's influence on literary modernism is undeniable. Try as we might to outgrow Poe, Eliot suggests, he haunts us still as do few writers of the previous century. We might find his influence uncomfortable (science fiction writer Thomas Disch describes Poe as "our embarrassing ancestor" [32]), but Eliot suggests that to dismiss the traditions at whose headwaters he stands is to deny the wellsprings of much of our literary history.

Twenty years after Eliot, poet and critic Allen Tate, another associate of New Criticism, returned to Poe yet again. Clearly, something in Poe's work particularly fascinated and frustrated the New Critics. Writing toward the end of his career (and as New Criticism was being challenged for dominance in the American academy by other approaches, especially those who came to be associated with poststructuralism), Tate suggests that Poe might present an example of a writer whose work does not lend itself to formalist close reading, suggesting, prophetically as it turns out, that historical models of criticism might be more productive in this case. As we will see in the subsequent sections, Poe came under increasing critical attention in the 1970s and 80s with the rise of historical criticism. Much of this attention, however, is not of the kind that Tate (or Poe) would have likely appreciated.

Tate is in a nostalgic mode in the essay reprinted here, returning to Poe as he first encountered him as a child, before he was aware of the distinction between literature and popular writing that would mean so much in his adult life. Looking back, Tate notes that Poe alone remains with him of all his youthful reading, and it is Poe alone to whom he returns. In Tate's hands, Poe becomes the inventor of existentialism a good half century before that worldview became fashionable at the hands of European philosophers, a pragmatic writer who was as widely known as a critic as he was as a poet or fiction writer, and a poet of poems that are great despite the fact that they are at times "badly, even vulgarly written" (p. 315). Although he does not say so directly in his appraisal of Poe, it is also certainly the case that Poe's "southernness" was an important component of Tate's lifelong interest in the writer. Tate began his career as a self-identified Southern poet and he was a core member of the Southern Agrarians of the 1930s, a literary and political movement dedicated to a Southern literary renaissance and opposed to the forces of industrialization and urbanization.

It was in a very different context that the New Yorker E. L. Doctorow turned to Poe late in his own career. Although trained at Kenyon College by John Crowe Ransom, one of the leading figures of the New Criticism, Doctorow's approach to Poe is of a decidedly different stamp. Where Tate—even as he suggests that the New Criticism has not adequately accounted for Poe's powers—seeks to exile biographical facts and historical contexts from the consideration of the author ("Whether the poem was addressed to an older lady who was kind to Poe when he was a boy is irrelevant" [p. 312]), to Doctorow's eyes, they are the crux of the fascinating paradoxes that keep Poe so very much with us. For Doctorow, Poe's life and times and his odd, even perverse, response to both his biography and his time and place mark him as exceptional—a "genius hack" (p. 317)—and, simultaneously, "an allegory for all literary life" (p. 318).

As the selections in this section make clear, much of the work of debating Poe's aesthetics and his place in literary history has fallen to fellow writers, especially in the twentieth century when, for better or worse, literary critics often explicitly steer clear of such evaluative judgments. However, it is worth pausing here over a crucial moment in the afterlife of Poe's reputation that is not directly represented in the selections to follow. In the second half of the twentieth century, French scholars once again proved more sympathetic readers of Poe than many of his American critics. At almost the same moment that Tate was suggesting Poe's work is of interest only to cultural historians and not literary scholars, French psychoanalyst Jacques Lacan turned to Poe as a central subject in a yearlong seminar. Lacan focused on Poe's detective story, "The Purloined Letter," which he declares to be "essential for a psychoanalyst" (179). Although Lacan was not a literary critic, his analysis of Poe's story, first published in 1956, became a pivotal text for literary theorists when French theorist Jacques Derrida challenged Lacan's reading of Poe in his own essay, "Le facteur de la vérité" ("The Purveyor of Truth") in 1975. This critical dispute between Derrida and Lacan about language and truth, waged in a close analysis of Poe's tale of contestation between his detective Dupin and a state minister, itself became the catalyst for numerous essays in the 1970s and 80s. We do not include examples of this impassioned critical exchange in this volume, largely because these essays were collected in *The Purloined Poe: Lacan, Derrida, and Psychoanalytic Reading* in 1988, a volume that more than twenty-five years later remains in print, but also because they do require some background in the specialized language of psychoanalytic and poststructuralist theory. Commenting on the significance of this moment in literary critical history, Donald Pease noted that not only were the French once again responsible for rekindling Poe's "literary reputation," but their focused attention on Poe was largely responsible for popularizing the French critical field of deconstructionism among American literary critics.

This section concludes with assessments of this debate from literary scholars. Both J. Gerald Kennedy and Scott Peeples pose the question that is surely on the minds of all readers of this section by this point: If there is such debate about the quality of Poe's literary achievement, why is it Poe, of all the important American writers from the nineteenth century, who remains today the most recognizable and popular author, the one whose influence on popular culture can be felt from *The Simpsons* to the NFL?

Kennedy explains Poe's relevance for the twentieth and twenty-first centuries in terms of his being essentially a man ahead of his time: plugged into the heart of darkness—the "internal flaw of violence" (p. 323)—in American life, while also able to imagine aesthetic and philosophical strategies for navigating this world that would be articulated a century after his death with the rise of postmodernism. For Kennedy, more than any other writer of his time, Poe was a man of *our* time, speaking for *us* as much or more than for his own contemporaries.

Peeples offers a history of popular-culture engagements with Poe across a range of media, from popular theater to film to comic books. For Peeples, these adaptations, appropriations, and homages tell us as much as the scholarly engagements about how and why Poe continues to haunt our contemporary culture. The changing ways in which Poe's life and work get imagined across a range of media—from nineteenth-century theater to the new media mashups of the digital age—demonstrate our continued fascination with Poe, despite the range of challenges to his legacy as a writer that have been offered over the generations, including some by Poe himself.

WORKS CITED

Bloom, Harold. "Introduction." *Bloom's How to Write about Edgar Allan Poe.* By Susan Amper. New York: Infobase, 2007. Print.

Disch, Thomas M. *The Dreams Our Stuff Is Made Of: How Science Fiction Conquered the World.* New York: Simon, 2000. Print.

Felman, Shoshana. *Jacques Lacan and the Adventure of Insight: Psychoanalysis in Contemporary Culture.* Cambridge: Harvard UP, 1987. Print.

Lacan, Jacques. *The Ego in Freud's Theory and in the Technique of Psychoanalysis, 1954–55.* Vol. 2 of *The Seminar of Jacques Lacan.* Trans. Sylvana Tomaselli. Ed. Jacques-Alain Miller. New York: Norton, 1991.

Lowell, James Russell. *Letters.* Ed. Charles Eliot Norton. Boston: Houghton, Mifflin, 1904. Print.

Muller, John P., and William J. Richardson, eds. *The Purloined Poe: Lacan, Derrida, and Psychoanalytic Reading.* Baltimore: Johns Hopkins UP, 1988. Print.

Pease, Donald. "Marginal Politics and 'The Purloined Letter': A Review Essay," *Poe Studies* 15.1 (June 1982): 18–23. Print.

FURTHER READING
IN THE CONTROVERSY

Carlson, Eric W. *A Companion to Poe Studies.* Westport: Greenwood, 1996. Print.

Dauber, Kenneth. *The Idea of Authorship in America: Democratic Poetics from Franklin to Melville.* Madison: U of Wisconsin P, 1990. Print.

Dwight, Thomas, and David K. Jackson. *The Poe Log: A Documentary Life of Edgar Allan Poe, 1809–1849.* Boston: G. K. Hall, 1987. Print.

Hartmann, Jonathan. *The Marketing of Edgar Allan Poe.* New York: Routledge, 2011. Print.

Hayes, Kevin J. *Edgar Allan Poe in Context.* New York: Cambridge UP, 2013. Print.

Kennedy, J. Gerald, and Jerome McGann, eds. *Poe and the Remapping of Antebellum Print Culture.* Baton Rouge: Louisiana State UP, 2013. Print.

Neimeyer, Mark. "Poe and Popular Culture." *The Cambridge Companion to Edgar Allan Poe.* Ed. Kevin J. Hayes. New York: Cambridge UP. 205–24. Print.

Peeples, Scott. *The Afterlife of Edgar Allan Poe.* Rochester: Camden House, 2007. Print.

Scherman, Timothy H. "The Authority Effect: Poe and the Politics of Reputation in the Pre-Industry of American Publishing." *Arizona Quarterly* 49 (1993): 1–19. Print.

Walker, I. M. *Edgar Allan Poe: The Critical Heritage.* New York: Routledge, 1986. Print.

Whalen, Terence. *Edgar Allan Poe and the Masses: The Political Economy of Literature in Antebellum America.* Princeton: Princeton UP, 1999. Print.

Wreszin, Michael. "Edgar Allan Poe? I Dig Him." *Edgar Allan Poe Review* 3 (Spring 2002): 18–26. Print.

JAMES RUSSELL LOWELL

Edgar Allan Poe

James Russell Lowell (1819–1891) was a member of the Fireside Poets, a popular group of New England writers who helped bring international respectability to American letters in the mid-nineteenth century. Lowell was also an important critic and editor, coming into national prominence through the publication in 1848 of A Fable for Critics *and as the first editor of the* Atlantic Monthly. *In 1855, Lowell was named as Henry Wadsworth Longfellow's successor to the Professorship of Modern Languages and Belles-Lettres at Harvard University, a position Longfellow had held for twenty years. Following the Civil War, Lowell spent much of his remaining professional life as a diplomat, serving as U.S. minister first to Spain and then to England. During the course of his long career as a poet, critic, editor, and professor, Lowell emerged as arguably the most influential American writer of the nineteenth century.*

The two selections from Lowell offered here are written only a few short years apart — 1845 and 1848 — and yet the attitude toward Poe in the two could not be more different.

The situation of American literature is anomalous. It has no centre, or, if it have, it is like that of the sphere of Hermes. It is divided into many systems, each revolving round its several sun, and often presenting to the rest only the faint glimmer of a milk-and-watery way. Our capital city, unlike London or Paris, is not a great central heart, from which life and vigor radiate to the extremities, but resembles more an isolated umbilicus, stuck down as near as may be to the centre of the land, and seeming rather to tell a legend of former usefulness than to serve any present need. Boston, New York, Philadelphia, each has its literature almost more distinct than those of the different dialects of Germany; and the Young

Queen of the West[1] has also one of her own, of which some articulate rumor barely has reached us dwellers by the Atlantic. Meanwhile, a great babble is kept up concerning a national literature, and the country, having delivered itself of the ugly likeness of a paint-bedaubed, filthy savage, smilingly dandles the rag-baby upon her maternal knee, as if it were veritable flesh and blood, and would grow timely to bone and sinew.

But, before we have an American literature, we must have an American criticism. We have, it is true, some scores of "American Macaulays,"[2] the faint echoes of defunct originalities, who will discourse learnedly at an hour's notice upon matters, to be even a sciolist in which would ask the patient study and self-denial of years—but, with a few rare exceptions, America is still to seek a profound, original, and esthetic criticism. Our criticism, which from its nature might be expected to pass most erudite judgment upon the merit of thistles, undertakes to decide upon

"The plant and flower of light."[3]

There is little life in it, little conscientiousness, little reverence; nay, it has seldom the mere physical merit of fearlessness. It may be best likened to an intellectual gathering of chips to keep the critical pot of potatoes or reputations boiling. Too often, indeed, with the cast garments of some pigmy Gifford,[4] or other foreign notoriety, which he has picked up at the rag-fair of literature, our critic sallies forth, a self-dubbed Amadis,[5] armed with a pen, which, more wonderful even than the fairy-gifts in an old ballad, becomes at will either the lance couched terribly at defiant windmills, or the trumpet for a half-penny paean.

Perhaps there is no task more difficult than the just criticism of contemporary literature. It is even more grateful to give praise where it is needed than where it is deserved, and friendship so often seduces the iron stylus of justice into a vague flourish, that she writes what seems rather like an epitaph than a criticism. Yet if praise be given as an alms, we could not drop so poisonous a one into any man's hat. The critic's

---

[1]Cincinnati, Ohio.

[2]A reference to American imitators of Thomas Babington Macaulay (1800–1859), British historian and politician.

[3]From Ben Jonson (1572–1637), "A Part of an Ode to the Immortal Memory and Friendship of that noble pair, Sir Lucius Cary and Sir H. Morison."

[4]William Gifford (1756–1826), British literary critic and editor.

[5]Legendary knight of Spanish literature.

ink may suffer equally from too large an infusion of nutgalls[6] or of sugar. But it is easier to be generous than to be just, though there are some who find it equally hard to be either, and we might readily put faith in that fabulous direction to the hiding-place of truth, did we judge from the amount of water which we usually find mixed with it.

We were very naturally led into some remarks on American criticism by the subject of the present sketch. Mr. Poe is at once the most discriminating, philosophical, and fearless critic upon imaginative works who has written in America. It may be that we should qualify our remark a little and say that he *might be*, rather than that he always *is*, for he seems sometimes to mistake his phial of prussic-acid for his inkstand. If we do not always agree with him in his premises, we are, at least, satisfied that his deductions are logical, and that we are reading the thoughts of a man who thinks for himself, and says what he thinks, and knows well what he is talking about. His analytic powers would furnish forth bravely some score of ordinary critics. We do not know him personally, but we suspect him for a man who has one or two pet prejudices on which he prides himself. These sometimes allure him out of the strict path of criticism,[7] but, where they do not interfere, we would put almost entire confidence in his judgments. Had Mr. Poe had the control of a magazine of his own, in which to display his critical abilities, he would have been as autocratic, ere this, in America, as Professor Wilson[8] has been in England; and his criticisms, we are sure, would have been far more profound and philosophical than those of the Scotsman. As it is, he has squared out blocks enough to build an enduring pyramid, but has left them lying carelessly and unclaimed in many different quarries.

Remarkable experiences are usually confined to the inner life of imaginative men, but Mr. Poe's biography displays a vicissitude and peculiarity of interest such as is rarely met with. The offspring of a romantic marriage, and left an orphan at an early age, he was adopted by Mr. Allan, a wealthy Virginian, whose barren marriage-bed seemed the warranty of a large estate to the young poet. Having received a classical education in England, he returned home and entered the University of Virginia, where, after an extravagant course, followed by refor-

---

[6]Literally, a gall on oak trees caused by insects; the astringent gallotannic acid extracted from nutgalls was a core ingredient in ink until the twentieth century.

[7]We cannot but think that this was the case in his review of W. E. Channing's poems, in which we are sure that there is much which must otherwise have challenged Mr. Poe's hearty liking. [Lowell's note.]

[8]John Wilson (1785–1854), prominent critic for *Blackwood's Edinburgh Magazine*.

mation at the last extremity, he was graduated with the highest honors of his class.[9] Then came a boyish attempt to join the fortunes of the insurgent Greeks, which ended at St. Petersburg, where he got into difficulties through want of a passport, from which he was rescued by the American consul and sent home. He now entered the military academy at West Point, from which he obtained a dismissal on hearing of the birth of a son to his adopted father, by a second marriage, an event which cut off his expectations as an heir. The death of Mr. Allan, in whose will his name was not mentioned, soon after relieved him of all doubt in this regard, and he committed himself at once to authorship for a support. Previously to this, however, he had published (in 1827) a small volume of poems,[10] which soon ran through three editions, and excited high expectations of its author's future distinction in the minds of many competent judges.

* * *

Mr. Poe has that indescribable something which men have agreed to call *genius*. No man could ever tell us precisely what it is, and yet there is none who is not inevitably aware of its presence and its power. Let talent writhe and contort itself as it may, it has no such magnetism. Larger of bone and sinew it may be, but the wings are wanting. Talent sticks fast to earth, and its most perfect works have still one foot of clay. Genius claims kindred with the very workings of Nature herself, so that a sunset shall seem like a quotation from Dante or Milton, and if Shakespeare be read in the very presence of the sea itself, his verses shall but seem nobler for the sublime criticism of ocean. Talent may make friends for itself, but only genius can give to its creations the divine power of winning love and veneration. Enthusiasm cannot cling to what itself is unenthusiastic, nor will he ever have disciples who has not himself impulsive zeal enough to be a disciple. Great wits are allied to madness only inasmuch as they are possessed and carried away by their demon, while talent keeps him, as Paracelsus did, securely prisoned in the pommel of its sword. To the eye of genius, the veil of the spiritual world is ever rent asunder, that it may perceive the ministers of good and evil who throng continually around it. No man of mere talent ever flung his inkstand at the devil.

---

[9] In fact, Poe left Virginia after one semester.
[10] Poe's *Tamerlane, and Other Poems.*

When we say that Mr. Poe has genius, we do not mean to say that he has produced evidence of the highest. But to say that he possesses it at all is to say that he needs only zeal, industry, and a reverence for the trust reposed in him, to achieve the proudest triumphs and the greenest laurels. . . .

Mr. Poe has two of the prime qualities of genius, a faculty of vigorous yet minute analysis, and a wonderful fecundity of imagination. The first of these faculties is as needful to the artist in words, as a knowledge of anatomy is to the artist in colors or in stone. This enables him to conceive truly, to maintain a proper relation of parts, and to draw a correct outline, while the second groups, fills up, and colors. Both of these Mr. Poe has displayed with singular distinctness in his prose works, the last predominating in his earlier tales, and the first in his later ones. In judging of the merit of an author and assigning him his niche among our household gods, we have a right to regard him from our own point of view, and to measure him by our own standard. But, in estimating his works, we must be governed by his own design, and, placing them by the side of his own ideal, find how much is wanting. We differ with Mr. Poe in his opinions of the objects of art. He esteems that object to be the creation of Beauty,[11] and perhaps it is only in the definition of that word that we disagree with him. But in what we shall say of his writings we shall take his own standard as our guide. The temple of the god of song is equally accessible from every side, and there is room enough in it for all who bring offerings, or seek an oracle.

In his tales, Mr. Poe has chosen to exhibit his power chiefly in that dim region which stretches from the very utmost limits of the probable into the weird confines of superstition and unreality. He combines in a very remarkable manner two faculties which are seldom found united; a power of influencing the mind of the reader by the impalpable shadows of mystery, and a minuteness of detail which does not leave a pin or a button unnoticed. Both are, in truth, the natural results of the predominating quality of his mind, to which we have before alluded, analysis. It is this which distinguishes the artist. His mind at once reaches forward to the effect to be produced. Having resolved to bring about certain emotions in the reader, he makes all subordinate parts tend strictly to the common centre. Even his mystery is mathematical to his own mind. To him x is a known quantity all along. In any picture that he paints, he understands the chemical properties of all his colors.

---

[11] Mr. P.'s proposition is here perhaps somewhat too *generally* stated. — *Ed. Mag.* [Lowell's note.]

However vague some of his figures may seem, however formless the shadows, to him the outline is as clear and distinct as that of a geometrical diagram. For this reason Mr. Poe has no sympathy with *Mysticism*. The Mystic dwells *in* the mystery, is enveloped with it; it colors all his thoughts; it affects his optic nerve especially, and the commonest things get a rainbow edging from it. Mr. Poe, on the other hand, is a spectator *ab extrà.*[12] He analyzes, he dissects, he watches

> ———— "with an eye serene,
> The very pulse of the machine,"[13]

for such it practically is to him, with wheels and cogs and piston-rods all working to produce a certain end. It is this that makes him so good a critic. Nothing baulks him, or throws him off the scent, *except now and then a prejudice.*

This analyzing tendency of his mind balances the poetical, and, by giving him the patience to be minute, enables him to throw a wonderful reality into his most unreal fancies. A monomania he paints with great power. He loves to dissect these cancers of the mind, and to trace all the subtle ramifications of its roots. In raising images of horror, also, he has a strange success; conveying to us sometimes by a dusky hint some terrible *doubt* which is the secret of all horror. He leaves to imagination the task of finishing the picture, a task to which only she is competent.

> "For much imaginary work was there;
> Conceit deceitful, so compact, so kind,
> That for Achilles' image stood his spear
> Grasped in an armed hand; himself behind
> Was left unseen, save to the eye of mind."[14]

We have hitherto spoken chiefly of Mr. Poe's *collected* tales, as by them he is more widely known than by those published since in various magazines, and which we hope soon to see collected. In these he has more strikingly displayed his analytic propensity.

Beside the merit of conception, Mr. Poe's writings have also that of form. His style is highly finished, graceful and truly classical. It would be hard to find a living author who had displayed such varied powers. As an example of his style, we would refer to one of his tales, "The

---

[12]From the outside.

[13]Slightly misquoted from William Wordsworth, "She was a Phantom of Delight" (1807): "And now I see with eye serene / The very pulse of the machine. . . ."

[14]From William Shakespeare's *Rape of Lucrece* (1594), a narrative poem.

House of Usher," in the first volume of his "Tales of the Grotesque and Arabesque." It has a singular charm for us, and we think that no one could read it without being strongly moved by its serene and sombre beauty. Had its author written nothing else, it would alone have been enough to stamp him as a man of genius, and the master of a classic style.

*   *   *

Beside his "Tales of the Grotesque and Arabesque," and some works unacknowledged, Mr. Poe is the author of "Arthur Gordon Pym," a romance, in two volumes, which has run through many editions in London; of a system of Conchology, of a digest and translation of Lemmonnier's Natural History, and has contributed to several reviews in France, in England, and in this country. He edited the Southern Literary Messenger during its novitiate, and by his own contributions gained it most of its success and reputation. He was also, for some time, the editor of this magazine, and our readers will bear testimony to his ability in that capacity.

Mr. Poe is still in the prime of life, being about thirty-two years of age, and has probably as yet given but an earnest of his powers. As a critic, he has shown so superior an ability that we cannot but hope that he will collect his essays of this kind and give them a more durable form. They would be a very valuable contribution to our literature, and would fully justify all we have said in his praise. We could refer to many others of his poems than those we have quoted, to prove that he is the possessor of a pure and original vein. His tales and essays have equally shown him a master in prose. It is not for us to assign him his definite rank among contemporary authors, but we may be allowed to say that we know of none who has displayed more varied and striking abilities.

From A Fable for Critics

There comes Poe, with his raven, like Barnaby Rudge,[1]
Three fifths of him genius and two fifths sheer fudge,
Who talks like a book of iambs and pentameters,
In a way to make people of common sense damn metres,

---

[1] In Charles Dickens's *Barnaby Rudge* (1841), the titular character owned a raven, likely an inspiration for Poe's choice of the bird in his famous poem.

Who has written some things quite the best of their kind,
But the heart somehow seems all squeezed out by the mind,
Who-But hey-day! What's this? Messieurs Mathews[2] and Poe,
You mustn't fling mud-balls at Longfellow so,
Does it make a man worse that his character's such
As to make his friends love him (as you think) too much?
Why, there is not a bard at this moment alive
More willing than he that his fellows should thrive;
While you are abusing him thus, even now
He would help either one of you out of a slough;
You may say that he's smooth and all that till you're hoarse,
But remember that elegance also is force;
After polishing granite as much as you will,
The heart keeps its tough old persistency still;
Deduct all you can, *that* still keeps you at bay;
Why, he'll live till men weary of Collins and Gray.

RUFUS GRISWOLD

Death of Edgar A. Poe

After a failed career as a minister Rufus Wilmot Griswold (1815–1857) took up journalism and discovered success as a literary critic, one whose reviews often rivaled those of Poe for their intensity and ferocity. Griswold was most famous in his own day as an editor of anthologies, especially the influential and popular The Poets and Poetry of America *(1842) and* Prose Writers of America *(1847). Today, of course, Griswold is most remembered as Poe's literary executor and biographer, ironic since he explicitly sought to erase Poe's legacy while serving in those capacities. An anonymous reviewer in the (Philadelphia)* Saturday Museum *predicted that Griswold would ultimately be "forgotten, save only by those whom he has injured and insulted, he will sink into oblivion, without leaving a landmark to tell that he once existed; or if he is spoken of hereafter, he will be quoted as the unfaithful servant who abused his trust." That 1843 prophecy—likely written by Poe's friend Henry B. Hirst, but almost certainly attributed by Griswold to Poe—would prove remarkably accurate.*

[2]Cornelius Matthews (1817–1889), one of the founders of the Young America movement.

But at the time of Poe's death in 1849 Griswold's influence in the American literary scene was powerful indeed, making his assessment of Poe's career and personality especially devastating for the late author's friends and admirers. The first of the two assessments from Griswold was published anonymously in 1849, under the pseudonym "Ludwig" in the New-York Daily Tribune. *The second is from Griswold's hastily produced biography of Poe from 1850.*

Edgar Allan Poe is dead. He died in Baltimore the day before yesterday. This announcement will startle many, but few will be grieved by it. The poet was well known, personally or by reputation, in all this country; he had readers in England, and in several of the states of Continental Europe; but he had few or no friends; and the regrets for his death will be suggested principally by the consideration that in him literary art has lost one of its most brilliant but erratic stars.

The family of Mr. Poe—we learn from Griswold's "Poets and Poetry of America," from which a considerable portion of the facts in this notice are derived—was one of the oldest and most respectable in Baltimore. David Poe, his paternal grandfather, was a Quartermaster-General in the Maryland line during the Revolution, and the intimate friend of Lafayette, who, during his last visit to the United States, called personally upon the General's widow, and tendered her acknowledgments for the services rendered to him by her husband. His great-grandfather, John Poe, married in England, Jane, a daughter of Admiral James McBride, noted in British naval history, and claiming kindred with some of the most illustrious English families. His father and mother,—both of whom were in some way connected with the theater, and lived as precariously as their more gifted and more eminent son—died within a few weeks of each other, of consumption, leaving him an orphan, at two years of age. Mr. John Allan, a wealthy gentleman of Richmond, Virginia, took a fancy to him, and persuaded his grandfather to suffer him to adopt him. He was brought up in Mr. Allan's family; and as that gentleman had no other children, he was regarded as his son and heir. In 1816 he accompanied Mr. and Mrs. Allen [*sic*] to Great Britain, visited every portion of it, and afterward passed four or five years in a school kept at Stoke Newington, near London, by Rev. Dr. Bransby. He returned to America in 1822, and in 1825 went to the Jefferson University, at Charlottesville, in Virginia, where he led a very dissipated life, the manners of the college being at that time extremely dissolute. He took the first honors, however, and went home greatly in debt. Mr. Allan refused to pay some of his debts of *honor*, and he hastily quitted the country on a Quixotic expedition to join the Greeks, then struggling for liberty. He did not reach his original destination, however, but made his way to St. Petersburg, in Russia, when he became involved in difficulties, from which he was extricated by the late Mr. Henry Middleton, the American Minister at that Capital. He returned home in 1829, and immediately afterward entered the Military Academy at West-Point. In about eighteen months from that time, Mr. Allan, who had lost his first wife while Mr. Poe was in Russia, married again. He was sixty-five years of age, and the lady was young; Poe quarreled with her, and the veteran husband, taking the part of his wife, addressed him an angry letter, which was answered in the same spirit. He died soon after, leaving an infant son the heir to his property, and bequeathed Poe nothing.

The army, in the opinion of the young cadet, was not a place for a poor man; so he left West-Point abruptly, and determined to maintain himself by authorship. He printed, in 1827, a small volume of poems, most of which were written in early youth. Some of these poems are quoted in a review by Margaret Fuller, in *The Tribune* in 1846, and are justly regarded as among the most wonderful exhibitions of the precocious development of genius. They illustrated the character of his abilities, and justified his anticipations of success. For a considerable time, however, though he wrote readily and brilliantly, his contributions to the journals attracted little attention, and his hopes of gaining a livelihood by the profession of literature were nearly ended at length in sickness, poverty and despair. But in 1831, the proprietor of a weekly gazette, in Baltimore, offered two premiums, one for the best story in prose, and the other for the best poem. — In due time Poe sent in two articles, and he waited anxiously for the decision. One of the Committee was the accomplished author of "Horseshoe Robinson," John P. Kennedy, and his associates were scarcely less eminent than he for wit and critical sagacity. Such matters are usually disposed of in a very off-hand way: Committees to award literary prizes drink to the payer's health, in good wines, over the unexamined MSS, which they submit to the discretion of publishers, with permission to use their names in such a way as to promote the publisher's advantage. So it would have been in this case, but that one of the Committee, taking up a little book in such exquisite calligraphy as to seem like one of the finest issues of the press of Putnam, was tempted to read several pages, and being interested, he summoned the attention of the company to the half-dozen compositions in the volume. It was unanimously decided that the prizes should be paid to the first of geniuses who had written legibly. Not another MS. was unfolded. Immediately the "confidential envelop" was opened, and the successful competitor was found to bear the scarcely known name of Poe.

The next day the publisher called to see Mr. Kennedy, and gave him an account of the author that excited his curiosity and sympathy, and caused him to request that he should be brought to his office. Accordingly he was introduced: the prize money had not yet been paid, and he was in the costume in which he had answered the advertisement of his good fortune. Thin, and pale even to ghastliness, his whole appearance indicated sickness and the utmost destitution. A tattered frock-coat concealed the absence of a shirt, and the ruins of boots disclosed more than the want of stockings. But the eyes of the young man were luminous with intelligence and feeling, and his voice, and conversation, and manners, all won upon the lawyer's regard. Poe told his history, and his ambition, and it was determined that he should not want means for a suitable appearance in society, nor opportunity for a just display of his abilities in literature. Mr. Kennedy accompanied him to a clothing store, and purchased for him a respectable suit, with changes of linen, and sent him to a bath, from which he returned with the suddenly regained bearing of a gentleman.

The late Mr. Thomas W. White had then recently established *The Southern Literary Messenger*, at Richmond, and upon the warm recommendation of Mr. Kennedy, Poe was engaged, at a small salary—we believe of $500 a year—to be its editor. He entered upon his duties with letters full of expressions of the warmest gratitude to his friends in Baltimore, who in five or six weeks were astonished to learn that with characteristic recklessness of consequences, he was hurriedly married to a girl as poor as himself. Poe continued in this situation for about a year and a half, in which he wrote many brilliant articles, and raised the *Messenger* to the first rank of literary periodicals.

He next moved to Philadelphia, to assist William E. Burton in the editorship of the *Gentleman's Magazine*, a miscellany that in 1840 was merged in *Graham's Magazine*, of which Poe became one of the principal writers, particularly in criticism, in which his papers attracted much attention, by their careful and skillful analysis, and generally caustic severity. At this period, however, he appeared to have been more ambitious of securing distinction in romantic fiction, and a collection of his compositions in this department, published in 1841, under the title of "Tales of the Grotesque and Arabesque," established his reputation for ingenuity, imagination and extraordinary power in tragical narration.

Near the end of 1844 Poe removed to New-York, where he conducted for several months a literary miscellany called "The Broadway Journal." In 1845 he published a volume of "Tales" in Wiley and Putnam's Library of American Books, and in the same series a collection of his poems. Besides these volumes he was the author of "Arthur Gordon Pym," a romance: "A New Theory of Versification;" "Eureka," an essay on the spiritual and material universe: a work which he wished to have "judged as a poem;" and several extended series of papers in the periodicals, the most noticeable of which are "Marginalia," embracing opinions of books and authors; "Secret Writing," "Autography," and "Sketches of the Literati of New-York."

His wife died in 1847, at Fordham, near this City, and some of our readers will remember the paragraphs in the papers of the time, upon his destitute condition. His wants were supplied by the liberality of a few individuals. We remember that Col. Webb collected in a few moments fifty or sixty dollars for him at the Union Club; Mr. Lewis, of Brooklyn, sent a similar sum from one of the Courts, in which he was engaged when he saw the statement of the poet's poverty; and others illustrated in the same manner the effect of such an appeal to the popular heart.

Since that time Mr. Poe has lived quietly, and with an income from his literary labors sufficient for his support. A few weeks ago he proceeded to Richmond in Virginia, where he lectured upon the poetical character, &c.; and it was understood by some of his correspondents here that he was this week to be married, most advantageously, to a lady of that city: a widow, to whom he had been previously engaged while a student in the University.

The character of Mr. Poe we cannot attempt to describe in this very hastily written article. We can but allude to some of its more striking phases.

His conversation was at times almost supra-mortal in its eloquence. His voice was modulated with astonishing skill, and his large and variably expressive eyes looked repose [*sic*] or shot fiery tumult into theirs who listened, while his own face glowed, or was changeless in pallor, as his imagination quickened his blood or drew it back frozen to his heart. His imagery was from the worlds which no mortal can see but with the vision of genius. Suddenly starting from a proposition exactly and sharply defined in terms of utmost simplicity and clearness, he rejected the forms of customary logic, and by a crystalline process of accretion, built up his ocular demonstrations in forms of gloomiest and ghastliest grandeur, or in those of the most airy and delicious beauty—so minutely, and distinctly, yet so rapidly, that the attention which was yielded to him was chained till it stood among his wonderful creations—till he himself dissolved the spell, and brought his hearers back to common and base existence, by vulgar fancies or by exhibitions of the ignoblest passion.

He was at all times a dreamer—dwelling in ideal realms—in heaven or hell—peopled with creatures and the accidents of his brain. He walked the streets, in madness or melancholy, with lips moving in indistinct curses, or with eyes upturned in passionate prayers, (never for himself, for he felt, or professed to feel, that he was already damned), but for their happiness who at the moment were objects of his idolatry—or, with his glances introverted to a heart gnawed with anguish, and with a face shrouded in gloom, he would brave the wildest storms; and all night, with drenched garments and arms wildly beating the winds and rains, he would speak as if to spirits that at such times only could be evoked by him from the Aidenn[1] close by whose portals his disturbed soul sought to forget the ills to which his constitution subjugated him—close by that Aidenn where were those he loved—the Aidenn which he might never see, but in fitful glimpses, as its gates opened to receive the less fiery and more happy natures whose destiny to sin did not involve the doom of death.

He seemed, except when some fitful pursuit subjected his will and engrossed his faculties, always to bear the memory of some controlling sorrow. The remarkable poem of *The Raven* was probably much more nearly than has been supposed, even by those who were very intimate with him, a reflexion and an echo of his own history. He was that bird's

> ——Unhappy master,
> Whom unmerciful disaster
> Followed fast and followed faster,
> Till his songs the burden bore—
> Till the dirges of his hope, the
> Melancholy burden bore
> Of "Nevermore," of "Nevermore."

Every genuine author in a greater or less degree leaves in his works, whatever their design, traces of his personal character: elements of his immortal being, in which the individual survives the person. While we read the pages of the *Fall of the House of Usher*, or of *Mesmeric Revelations*, we see

---

[1] Eden.

in the solemn and stately gloom which invests one, and in the subtle metaphysical analysis of both, indications of the idiosyncrasies,—of what was most remarkable and peculiar—in the author's intellectual nature. But we see here only the better phases of this nature, only the symbols of his juster action, for his harsh experience had deprived him of all faith in man or woman. He had made up his mind upon the numberless complexities of the social world, and the whole system with him was an imposture. This conviction gave a direction to his shrewd and naturally unamiable character. Still, though he regarded society as composed altogether of villains, the sharpness of his intellect was not of that kind which enabled him to cope with villainy, while it continually caused him by overshots to fail of the success of honesty. He was in many respects like Francis Vivian in Bulwer's novel of "The Caxtons."[2] "Passion, in him, comprehended many of the worst emotions which militate against human happiness. You could not contradict him, but you raised quick choler; you could not speak of wealth, but his cheek paled with gnawing envy. The astonishing natural advantages of this poor boy—his beauty, his readiness, the daring spirit that breathed around him like a fiery atmosphere—had raised his constitutional self-confidence into an arrogance that turned his very claims to admiration into prejudice against him. Irascible, envious—bad enough, but not the worst, for these salient angles were all varnished over with a cold repellant cynicism, his passions vented themselves in sneers. There seemed to him no moral susceptibility; and, what was more remarkable in a proud nature, little or nothing of the true point of honor. He had, to a morbid excess, that desire to rise which is vulgarly called ambition, but no wish for the esteem or love of his species; only the hard wish to succeed—not shine, not serve—succeed, that he might have the right to despise a world which galled his self conceit."

We have suggested the influence of his aims and vicissitudes upon his literature. It was more conspicuous in his later than his earlier writing. Nearly all that he wrote in the last two or three years—including much of his best poetry—was in some sense biographical; in draperies of his imagination, those who had taken the trouble to trace his steps, could perceive, but slightly concealed, the figure of himself.

*   *   *

We must omit any particular criticism of Mr. Poe's works. As a writer of tales it will be admitted generally, that he was scarcely surpassed in

[2] *The Caxtons: A Family Picture* (1849) by Edward Bulwer-Lytton (1803–1873).

ingenuity of construction or effective painting. As a critic, he was more remarkable as a dissecter of sentences than as a commentater upon ideas: he was little better than a carping grammarian. As a poet, he will retain a most honorable rank. Of his "Raven," Mr. Willis[3] observes, that in his opinion "it is the most effective single example of fugitive poetry ever published in this country, and is unsurpassed in English poetry for subtle conception, masterly ingenuity of versification, and consistent sustaining of imaginative lift." In poetry, as in prose, he was most successful in the metaphysical treatment of the passions. His poems are constructed with wonderful ingenuity, and finished with consummate art. They illustrate a morbid sensitiveness of feeling, a shadowy and gloomy imagination, and a taste almost faultless in the apprehension of that sort of beauty most agreeable to his temper.

We have not learned of the circumstance of his death. It was sudden, and from the fact that it occurred in Baltimore, it is to be presumed that he was on his return to New-York.

"After life's fitful fever he sleeps well."[4]

LUDWIG.

Preface [to "Memoir of the Author"]

Hitherto I have not written or published a syllable upon the subject of Mr. Poe's life, character, or genius, since I was informed, some ten days after his death, of my appointment to be his literary executor. I did not suppose I was debarred from the expression of any feelings or opinions in the case by the acceptance of this office, the duties of which I regarded as simply the collection of his works, and their publication, for the benefit of the rightful inheritors of his property, in a form and manner that would probably have been most agreeable to his own wishes. I would gladly have declined a trust imposing so much labor, for I had been compelled by ill health to solicit the indulgence of my publishers, who had many thousand dollars invested in an unfinished work under my direction; but when I was told by several of Mr. Poe's most intimate friends—among others by the family of S. D. Lewis, Esq., to whom in his last years he was under greater obligations than to any or to all

---

[3] Nathaniel Parker Willis (1806–1867), a prominent American author and editor, and a friend to Poe.

[4] William Shakespeare, *Macbeth*, act 3, scene 2.

others—that he had long been in the habit of expressing a desire that in the event of his death I should be his editor, I yielded to the apparent necessity, and proceeded immediately with the preparation of the two volumes which have heretofore been published. But I had, at the request of the Editor of "The Tribune," written hastily a few paragraphs about Mr. Poe, which appeared in that paper with the telegraphic communication of his death; and two or three of these paragraphs having been quoted by Mr. N. P. Willis, in his Notice of Mr. Poe, were as a part of that Notice unavoidably reprinted in the volume of the deceased author's Tales. And my unconsidered and imperfect, but as every one who knew the subject readily perceived, very kind article, was now vehemently attacked. A writer under the signature of "George R. Graham," in a sophomorical and trashy but widely circulated Letter, denounced it as "the fancy sketch of a jaundiced vision," "an immortal infamy," and its composition as a "*breach of trust.*" And to excuse his five months' silence, and to induce a belief that he did not *know* that what I had written was already published *before I* COULD *have been advised that I was to be Mr.* Poe's *executor,* (a condition upon which all the possible force of his Letter depends,) this silly and ambitious person, while represented as entertaining a friendship really passionate in its tenderness for the poor author, (of whom in four years of his extremest poverty he had not purchased for his magazine a single line,) is made to say that in *half a year* he had not seen so noticeable an article,—though within a week after Mr. Poe's death it appeared in "The Tribune," in "The Home Journal," in three of the daily papers of his own city, and in "The Saturday Evening Post," of which he was or had been himself one of the chief proprietors and editors! And Mr. John Neal, too, who had never had even the slightest personal acquaintance with Poe in his life, rushes from a sleep which the public had trusted was eternal, to declare that my characterization of Poe (which he is pleased to describe as "poetry, exalted poetry, poetry of astonishing and original strength") is false and malicious, and that I am a "calumniator," a "Rhadamanthus," etc. Both these writers—John Neal following the author of the Letter signed "George R. Graham"—not only assume what I have shown to be false, (that the remarks on Poe's character were written by me *as his executor,*) but that there was a long, intense, and implacable enmity betwixt Poe and myself, which disqualified me for the office of his biographer. This scarcely needs an answer after the poet's dying request that I should be his editor; but the manner in which it has been urged, will, I trust, be a sufficient excuse for the following demonstration of its absurdity. [Griswold follows with a series of letters he claims he received from Poe, several of them clearly invented, designed to prove the value Poe placed on his friendship and to endorse the version of Poe he would put forth in the "Memoir" to follow.]

CHARLES BAUDELAIRE

New Notes on Edgar Poe

Charles Baudelaire (1821–1867), author of the poetic volume Les Fleurs du Mal *(1857), was one of France's most influential literary artists. A poet and a critic, Baudelaire's biography in many ways resembles Poe's insofar as he too had combative relations with his family, was frequently in financial straits, and was challenged for not living up to his artistic potential. He was a great admirer of Poe's work—an appreciation that culminated in his exacting and influential translations of Poe's work, including many of the tales,* The Narrative of Arthur Gordon Pym, *and* Eureka. *The essay below is extracted from the preface to his second volume of translations from 1857.*

I.

*　*　*

Let new literatures develop among the immense colonies of the present century and there will result most certainly spiritual accidents of a nature disturbing to the academic mind. Young and old at the same time, America babbles and rambles with an astonishing volubility. Who could count its poets? They are innumerable. Its blue stockings? They clutter the magazines. Its critics? You may be sure that they have pedants who are as good as ours at constantly recalling the artist to ancient beauty, at questioning a poet or a novelist on the morality of his purpose and the merit of his intentions. There can be found there as here, but even more than here, men of letters who do not know how to spell; a childish, useless activity; compilers in abundance, hack writers, plagiarists of plagiaries, and critics of critics. In this maelstrom of mediocrity, in this society enamored of material perfections—a new kind of scandal which makes intelligible the grandeur of inactive peoples—in this society eager for surprises, in love with life, but especially with a life full of excitements, a man has appeared who was great not only in his metaphysical subtlety, in the sinister or bewitching beauty of his conceptions, in the rigor of his analysis, but also great and not less great as a *carica-ture*. — I must explain myself with some care; for recently a rash critic, in order to disparage Edgar Poe and to invalidate the sincerity of my admiration, used the word *jongleur*[1] which I myself had applied to the noble poet as a sort of praise.

From the midst of a greedy world, hungry for material things, Poe took flight in dreams. Stifled as he was by the American atmosphere, he wrote at the beginning of *Eureka*: "I offer this book to those who have put faith in dreams as in the only realities!" He was in himself an admirable protest, and he made his protest in his own particular way. The author who, in "The Colloquy of Monos and Una," pours out his scorn and disgust for democracy, progress and civilization, this author is the same one who, in order to encourage credulity, to delight the stupidity of his contemporaries, has stressed human sovereignty most emphatically and has very ingeniously fabricated hoaxes flattering to the pride of modern man. Considered in this light, Poe seems like a helot who wishes to make his master blush. Finally, to state my thought even more clearly, Poe was always great not only in his noble conceptions but also as a prankster.

II.

For he was never a dupe! I do not think that the Virginian who calmly wrote in the midst of a rising tide of democracy: "People have nothing to do with laws except to obey them," has ever been a victim of modern wisdom; and: "The nose of a mob is its imagination. By this, at any time, it can be quietly led" — and a hundred other passages in which mockery falls thick and fast like a hail of bullets but still remains proud and indifferent. — The Swedenborgians congratulate him on his "Mesmeric Revelation," like those naïve Illuminati who formerly hailed in the author of the *Diable amoureux* a discoverer of their mysteries; they thank him for the great truths which he has just proclaimed — for they have discovered (O verifiers of the unverifiable!) that all that which he has set forth is absolutely true; — although, at first, these good people confess, they had suspected that it might well have been merely fictitious. Poe answers that, so far as he is concerned, he has never doubted

---

[1] Wandering minstrel.

it.—Must I cite in addition this short passage which catches my eye while scanning for the hundredth time his amusing "Marginalia," which are the secret chambers, as it were, of his mind: "The enormous multiplication of books in all branches of knowledge is one of the greatest scourges of this age, for it is one of the most serious obstacles to the acquisition of all positive knowledge." Aristocrat by nature even more than by birth, the Virginian, the Southerner, the Byron gone astray in a bad world, has always kept his philosophic impassibility and, whether he defines the nose of the mob, whether he mocks the fabricators of religions, whether he scoffs at libraries, he remains what the true poet was and always will be—a truth clothed in a strange manner, an apparent paradox, who does not wish to be elbowed by the crowd and who runs to the far east when the fireworks go off in the west.

But more important than anything else: we shall see that this author, product of a century infatuated with itself, child of a nation more infatuated with itself than any other, has clearly seen, has imperturbably affirmed the natural wickedness of man. There is in man, he says, a mysterious force which modern philosophy does not wish to take into consideration; nevertheless, without this nameless force, without this primordial bent, a host of human actions will remain unexplained, inexplicable. These actions are attractive only *because* they are bad or dangerous; they possess the fascination of the abyss. This primitive, irresistible force is natural Perversity, which makes man constantly and simultaneously a murderer and a suicide, an assassin and a hangman;—for he adds, with a remarkably satanic subtlety, the impossibility of finding an adequate rational motive for certain wicked and perilous actions could lead us to consider them as the result of the suggestions of the Devil, if experience and history did not teach us that God often draws from them the establishment of order and the punishment of scoundrels;—*after having used the same scoundrels as accomplices!* such is the thought which, I confess, slips into my mind, an implication as inevitable as it is perfidious. But for the present I wish to consider only the great forgotten truth—the primordial perversity of man—and it is not without a certain satisfaction that I see some vestiges of ancient wisdom return to us from a country from which we did not expect them. It is pleasant to know that some fragments of an old truth are exploded in the faces of all these obsequious flatterers of humanity, of all these humbugs and quacks who repeat in every possible tone of voice: "I am born good, and you too, and all of us are born good!" forgetting, no! pretending to forget, like misguided equalitarians, that we are all born marked for evil!

Of what lies could he be a dupe, he who sometimes—sad necessity of his environment—dealt with them so well? What scorn for pseudo-philosophy on his good days, on the days when he was, so to speak, inspired! This poet, several of whose compositions seem deliberately made to confirm the alleged omnipotence of man, has sometimes wished to purge himself. The day that he wrote: "All certainty is in dreams," he thrust back his own Americanism into the region of inferior things; at other times, becoming again the true poet, doubtless obeying the ineluctable truth which haunts us like a demon, he uttered the ardent sighs of the fallen angel who remembers heaven; he lamented the golden age and the lost Eden; he wept over all the magnificence of nature shrivelling up before the hot breath of fiery furnaces. . . .

III

Such a social environment necessarily engenders corresponding literary errors. Poe reacted against these errors as often as he could, and with all his might. We must not be surprised then that American writers, though recognizing his singular power as a poet and as a storyteller, have always tended to question his ability as a critic. In a country where the idea of utility, the most hostile in the world to the idea of beauty, dominates and takes precedence over everything, the perfect critic will be the most respectable, that is to say the one whose tendencies and desires will best approximate the tendencies and desires of his public—the one who, confusing the intellectual faculties of the writer and the categories of writing, will assign to all a single goal—the one who will seek in a book of poetry the means of perfecting conscience. Naturally he will become all the less concerned with the real, the positive beauties of poetry; he will be all the less shocked by imperfections and even by faults in execution. Edgar Poe, on the contrary, dividing the world of the mind into pure *Intellect*, *Taste*, and *Moral Sense*, applied criticism in accordance with the category to which the object of his analysis belonged. He was above all sensitive to perfection of plan and to correctness of execution; taking apart literary works like defective pieces of machinery (considering the goal that they wished to attain), noting carefully the flaws of workmanship; and when he passed to the details of the work, to its plastic expression, in a word, to style, examining meticulously and without omissions the faults of prosody, the grammatical errors and all the mass of dross which, among writers who are not artists, besmirch the best intentions and deform the most noble conceptions.

For him, Imagination is the queen of faculties; but by this word he understands something greater than that which is understood by the average reader. Imagination is not fantasy; nor is it sensibility, although it may be difficult to conceive of an imaginative man who would be lacking in sensibility. Imagination is an almost divine faculty which perceives immediately and without philosophical methods the inner and secret relations of things, the correspondences and the analogies. The honors and functions which he grants to this faculty give it such value (at least when the thought of the author has been well understood) that a scholar without imagination appears only as a pseudoscholar, or at least as an incomplete scholar.

Among the literary domains where imagination can obtain the most curious results, can harvest treasures, not the richest, the most precious (those belong to poetry), but the most numerous and the most varied, there is one of which Poe is especially fond; it is the *Short Story*. It has the immense advantage over the novel of vast proportions that its brevity adds to the intensity of effect. This type of reading, which can be accomplished in one sitting, leaves in the mind a more powerful impression than a broken reading, often interrupted by the worries of business and the cares of social life. The unity of impression, the totality of effect is an immense advantage which can give to this type of composition a very special superiority, to such an extent that an extremely short story (which is doubtless a fault) is even better than an extremely long story. The artist, if he is skillful, will not adapt his thoughts to the incidents but, having conceived deliberately and at leisure an effect to be produced, will invent the incidents, will combine the events most suitable to bring about the desired effect. If the first sentence is not written with the idea of preparing this final impression, the work has failed from the start. There must not creep into the entire composition a single word which is not intentional, which does not tend, directly or indirectly, to complete the premeditated design.

There is one point in which the short story is superior even to the poem. Rhythm is necessary to the development of the idea of beauty, which is the greatest and the most noble aim of poetry. Now, the artifices of rhythm are an insurmountable obstacle to the detailed development of thought and expression which has truth as its object. For truth can often be the goal of the short story, and reasoning the best tool for the construction of a perfect short story. That is why this type of composition, which is not as high on the scale as pure poetry, can provide more varied results, more easily appreciated by the average reader. Moreover, the author of a short story has at his disposal a multitude of tones, of nuances of language, the rational tone, the sarcastic, the humorous, which are repudiated by poetry and which are, as it were, dissonances, outrages to the idea of pure beauty. And that is also why the author who seeks in the short story the single goal of beauty works only at a great disadvantage, deprived as he is of the most useful instrument, rhythm. I know that in all literatures efforts have been made, often successful, to create purely poetic short stories; Edgar Poe himself has written some very beautiful ones. But they are struggles and efforts which serve only to prove the strength of the true means adapted to the corresponding goals, and I am inclined to believe that in the case of some authors, the greatest that can be chosen, these heroic attempts spring from despair.

IV

"*Genus irritabile vatum!*[2] That poets (using the word comprehensively, as including artists in general) are a *genus irritabile*, is well understood; but the why, seems not to be commonly seen. An artist *is* an artist only by dint of his exquisite sense of Beauty — a sense affording him rapturous enjoyment but at the same time implying, or involving, an equally exquisite sense of Deformity or disproportion. Thus a wrong — an injustice — done a poet who is really a poet, excites him to a degree which, to ordinary apprehension, appears disproportionate with the wrong. Poets *see* injustice — never where it does not exist — but very often where the unpoetical see no injustice whatever. Thus the poetical irritability has no reference to 'temper' in the vulgar sense but merely to a more than usual clear-sightedness in respect to Wrong: — this clear-sightedness being nothing more than a corollary from the vivid perception of Right — of justice — of Proportion — in a word, of the beautiful. But one thing is clear — that the man who is *not* 'irritable' (to the ordinary apprehension) is *no poet*."[3]

Thus the poet himself speaks, preparing an excellent and irrefutable apologia for all those of his race. Poe carried this sensibility into his literary affairs, and the extreme importance which he attached to things poetic often led him to use a tone in which, according to the judgment

---

[2] "Irritable tribe of poets"; from Horace's *Epistles* 2.2.102.
[3] This long quote is from Poe's "Fifty Suggestions," *Graham's Magazine* (1849).

of the weak, a feeling of superiority became too evident. I have already mentioned, I believe, that several prejudices which he had to combat, false ideas, commonplace opinions which circulated around him, have for a long time infected the French press. It will not be useless then to give a brief account of some of his most important opinions relative to poetic composition. The parallelism of error will make their application quite easy.

But above all, I must point out that in addition to the share which Poe granted to a natural, innate poetic gift, he gave an importance to knowledge, work, and analysis that will seem excessive to arrogant and unlettered persons. Not only has he expended considerable efforts to subject to his will the fleeting spirit of happy moments, in order to recall at will those exquisite sensations, those spiritual longings, those states of poetic health, so rare and so precious that they could truly be considered as graces exterior to man and as visitations; but also he has subjected inspiration to method, to the most severe analysis. The choice of means! he returns to that constantly, he insists with a learned eloquence upon the adjustment of means to effect, on the use of rhyme, on the perfecting of the refrain, on the adaptation of rhythm to feeling. He maintained that he who cannot seize the intangible is not a poet; that he alone is a poet who is master of his memory, the sovereign of words, the record book of his own feelings always open for examination. Everything for the conclusion! he often repeats. Even a sonnet needs a plan, and the construction, the armature, so to speak, is the most important guarantee of the mysterious life of works of the mind.

*   *   *

But there is another heresy which, thanks to the hypocrisy, to the dullness, and to the baseness of human minds, is even more formidable and has a greater chance of survival—an error which has a hardier life—I wish to speak of the heresy of teaching a lesson which includes as inevitable corollaries the heresy of passion, of truth, and of morality. A great many people imagine that the aim of poetry is a lesson of some sort, that it must now fortify the conscience, now perfect morals, now in short prove something or other which is useful. Edgar Poe claims that Americans especially have supported this heterodox idea; alas! There is no need to go as far as Boston to encounter the heresy in question. Even here it attacks and breaches true poetry every day. Poetry, if only one is willing to seek within himself, to question his heart, to recall his memories of enthusiasm, has no other goal than itself; it cannot have any other, and no poem will be so great, so noble, so truly worthy of the name of poetry as that which will have been written solely for the pleasure of writing a poem.

*   *   *

This extraordinary elevation, this exquisite delicacy, this accent of immortality which Edgar Poe demands of the Muse, far from making him less attentive to the technique of execution, have impelled him constantly to sharpen his genius as a technician. Many people, especially those who have read the strange poem called *The Raven*, would be shocked if I analyzed the article in which our poet, apparently innocently, but with a slight impertinence which I cannot condemn, has explained in detail the method of construction which he used, the adaptation of the rhythm, the choice of a refrain—the shortest possible and the most suitable to a variety of applications, and at the same time the most representative of melancholy and despair, embellished with the most sonorous rhyme of all (nevermore)—the choice of a bird capable of imitating the human voice, but a bird—the raven—branded with a baneful and fatal character in popular imagination—the choice of the most poetic of all tones, the melancholy tone—of the most poetic sentiment, love for one dead, etc.—"And I shall not place the hero of my poem in poor surroundings," he says, "because poverty is commonplace and contrary to the idea of Beauty. His melancholy will be sheltered by a magnificently and poetically furnished room."[4] The reader will detect in several of Poe's short stories curious symptoms of this inordinate taste for beautiful forms, especially for beautiful forms that are strange, for ornate surroundings and oriental sumptuousness.

I said that this article seemed marred by a slight impertinence. Confirmed advocates of inspiration would be sure to find in it blasphemy and profanation; but I believe that it is for them especially that the article has been written. Just as certain writers feign carelessness, aiming at a masterpiece with their eyes closed, full of confidence in disorder, expecting that words thrown at the ceiling will fall back on the floor in the form of a poem, so Edgar Poe—one of the most inspired men I know—has made a pretense of hiding spontaneity, of simulating coolness and deliberation. "It will not be regarded as a breach of decorum on my part"—he says with an amusing pride which I do not consider

---

[4]All quotes from "Philosophy of Composition" are very loose, and Baudelaire felt it appropriate to rework some of Poe's claims in his own words.

in bad taste—"to show that no one point in its composition is referable either to accident or intuition—that the work proceeded, step by step, to its completion with the precision and rigid consequence of a mathematical problem." Only lovers of chance, I say, only fatalists of inspiration and fanatics of *free verse* can find this *attention to detail* odd. There are no insignificant details in matters of art.

As for free verse, I shall add that Poe attached an extreme importance to rhyme, and that in the analysis which he has made of the mathematical and musical pleasure which the mind derives from rhyme, he has introduced as much care, as much subtlety as in all the other subjects pertaining to the art of poetry. Just as he has shown that the refrain is capable of infinitely varied applications, so also he has sought to renew, to redouble the pleasure derived from rhyme by adding to it an unexpected element, the strange, which is the indispensable condiment, as it were, of all beauty. He often makes a happy use of repetitions of the same line or of several lines, insistent reiterations of phrases which simulate the obsessions of melancholy or of a fixed idea—of a pure and simple refrain introduced in several different ways—of a variant refrain which feigns carelessness and inadvertence—of rhymes redoubled and tripled and also of a kind of rhyme which introduces into modern poetry, but with more precision and purpose, the surprises of Leonine verse.[5]

It is obvious that the value of all these means can be proved only through application; and a translation of poetry so studied, so concentrated, can be a fond dream, but only a dream. Poe wrote little poetry; he has sometimes expressed regret at not being able to devote himself, not more often, but exclusively, to this type of work which he considered the most noble. But his poetry always creates a powerful effect. It is not the ardent outpouring of Byron, it is not the soft, harmonious, distinguished melancholy of Tennyson for whom, it may be said in passing, he had an almost fraternal admiration. It is something profound and shimmering like a dream, mysterious and perfect like crystal. I do not need to add, I presume, that American critics have often disparaged his poetry; very recently I found in a dictionary of American biography an article in which it was adjudged esoteric, in which it was feared that this muse in learned garb might create a school in the proud country of utilitarian morality, and in which regret was expressed that Poe had not applied his talents to the expression of moral truths in place of spending

---

[5] Poetry based on internal rhyme.

them in quest of a bizarre ideal, of lavishing in his verses a mysterious, but sensual voluptuousness.

We are all familiar with that kind of sharp riposte. The reproaches that bad critics heap upon good poets are the same in all countries. In reading this article it seemed to me that I was reading the translation of one of those numerous indictments brought by Parisian critics against those of our poets who are most fond of perfection. Our favorites are easy to guess and every lover of pure poetry will understand me when I say that in the eyes of our antipoetic race Victor Hugo would be less admired if he were perfect, and he has succeeded in having all his lyric genius forgiven only by introducing forcibly and brutally into his poetry what Edgar Poe considered the major modern heresy—*the teaching of a lesson.*

SARAH HELEN WHITMAN

From Edgar Poe and His Critics

Although largely remembered today because of her friendship with and brief engagement to Poe toward the end of his life, Sarah Helen Whitman (1803–1878) was herself a well-respected American poet and essayist. A New Englander who lived her entire life in Rhode Island, she socialized with many prominent members of the American transcendentalist movement, including Margaret Fuller and Ralph Waldo Emerson. Her work was widely published and occupies a prominent position in Griswold's anthology The Female Poets of America *(1848). Her collection* Hours of Life, and Other Poems *(1853) included many of the verses she wrote about Poe in the aftermath of their broken engagement and following his death. Whitman was one of Poe's strongest defenders, publishing* Edgar Poe and His Critics *in 1860 as a direct repudiation to Griswold's earlier character assassinations. Whitman also provided her correspondence with Poe to his early biographer and fellow defender, John Henry Ingram.*

Dr. Griswold's Memoir of Edgar Poe has been extensively read and circulated; its perverted facts and baseless assumptions have been adopted into every subsequent memoir and notice of the poet, and have been translated into many languages. For ten years this great wrong to the dead has passed unchallenged and unrebuked.

It has been assumed by a recent English critic that "Edgar Poe had no friends." As an index to a more equitable and intelligible theory of the idiosyncrasies of his life, and as an earnest protest against the spirit of Dr. Griswold's unjust memoir, these pages are submitted to his more candid readers and critics by

ONE OF HIS FRIENDS.

*   *   *

The well written, but very brief memoir prefixed to the Illustrated Poems, and the various sketches that have, from time to time, appeared in the French and English periodicals, are all based on the narrative of Dr. Griswold, a narrative notoriously deficient in the great essentials of candor and authenticity. "It is a rare accomplishment," says one of our most original writers, "to hear a story as it is told; still rarer to remember it as heard, and rarest of all *to tell it as it is remembered.*" If Dr. Griswold's Memoir of Edgar Poe betrays the want of any, or *all*, of these accomplishments—if its remorseless violations of the trust confided to him are such as to make the unhallowed act of Trelawney[1] towards the enshrouded form of the dead Byron seem guiltless in comparison, we must nevertheless endeavour to remember that the memorialist, himself, now claims from us that tender grace of charity that he was unwilling, or unable, to accord to the man who trusted him as a friend.

It is not our purpose at present specially to review Dr. Griswold's numerous misrepresentations, and misstatements. Some of the more injurious of these anecdotes were disproved, during the life of Dr. Griswold, in the *New York Tribune* and other leading journals, without eliciting from him any public statement in explanation or apology. Quite recently we have had, through the columns of the *Home Journal*, the refutation of another calumnious story, which for ten years has been going the rounds of the English and American periodicals.

We have authority for stating that many of the disgraceful anecdotes, so industriously collected by Dr. Griswold, are utterly fabulous, while others are perversions of the truth, more injurious in their effects than unmitigated fiction. But, as we have said, it is not our purpose at present to revert to these. We propose simply to point out some unfounded critical estimates which have obtained currency among readers who have but a partial acquaintance with Mr. Poe's more

[1] Edward John Trelawny (1792–1881), English writer and biographer of the Romantic poet Lord Byron.

imaginative writings, and to record our own impressions of the character and genius of the poet, as derived from personal observation, and from the testimony of those who knew him. Although he had been connected with some of the leading magazines of the day, and had edited for a time with great ability several successful periodicals, Mr. Poe's literary reputation at the North had been comparatively limited until his removal to New York, in the autumn of 1847, when he became personally known to a large circle of authors and literary people, whose interest in his writings was manifestly enhanced by the perplexing anomalies of his character, and by the singular magnetism of his presence.

* * *

It is not to be questioned that Poe was a consummate master of language—that he had sounded all the secrets of rhythm—that he understood and availed himself of all its resources; the balance and poise of syllables—the alternations of emphasis and cadence—of vowel-sounds and consonants—and all the metrical sweetness of "phrase and metaphrase."[2] Yet this consummate art was in him united with a rare simplicity. He was the most genuine of enthusiasts, as we think we shall presently show. His genius would follow no leadings but those of his own imperial intellect. With all his vast mental resources he could never write an occasional poem, or adapt himself to the taste of a popular audience. His graver narratives and fantasies are often related with an earnest simplicity, solemnity, and apparent fidelity, attributable, not so much to a deliberate artistic purpose, as to that power of vivid and intense conception that made his dreams realities, and his life a dream. The strange fascination—the unmatched charm of his conversation—consisted in its *genuineness*. Even Dr. Griswold, who has studiously represented him as cold, passionless, and perfidious, admits that his conversation was at times almost "supra-mortal in its eloquence"; that "his large and variably expressive eyes looked repose or shot fiery tumult into theirs who listened, while his own face glowed, or was changeless in pallor, as his imagination quickened his blood or drew it back frozen to his heart."[3]

* * *

[2] From the eighth book of Elizabeth Barrett Browning's (1806–1861) long poem *Aurora Leigh* (1856).
[3] Griswold, p. 271.

We have said that the charm of his conversation consisted in its genuineness—its wonderful directness and sincerity. We believe, too, that in the artistic utterance of poetic emotion he was at all times passionately genuine. His proud reserve, his profound melancholy, his unworldliness—may we not say his *unearthliness* of nature—made his character one very difficult of comprehension to the casual observer. The complexity of his intellect, its incalculable resources, and his masterly control of those resources when brought into requisition for the illustration of some favorite theme, or cherished creation, led to the current belief that its action was purely arbitrary—that he could write without emotion or earnestness at the deliberate dictation of the will. A certain class of his writings undeniably exhibits the faculties of ingenuity and invention in a prominent and distinctive light. But it must not be forgotten that there was another phase of his mind—one not less distinctive and characteristic of his genius—which manifested itself in creations of a totally different order and expression. It can hardly have escaped the notice of the most careless reader that certain ideas exercised over him the power of fascination. They return, again and again, in his stories and poems and seem like the utterances of a mind possessed with thoughts, emotions, and images of which the will and the understanding take little cognizance. In the delineation of these, his language often acquires a power and pregnancy eluding all attempts at analysis. It is then that by a few miraculous words he evokes emotional states or commands pictorial effects which live forever in the memory and form a part of its eternal inheritance. No analysis can dissect—no criticism can disenchant them.

As specimens of the class we have indicated read "Ligeia," "Morella," "Eleanora." Observe in them the prevailing and dominant thoughts of his inner life—ideas of "fate and metaphysical aid"—of psychal and spiritual agencies, energies and potencies. See in them intimations of mysterious phenomena which, at the time when these fantasies were indited, were regarded as fables and dreams, but which have since (in their phenomenal aspect simply) been recognised as matters of popular experience and scientific research.

In "Ligeia," the sad and stately symmetry of the sentences, their rhythmical cadence, the Moresque sumptuousness of imagery with which the story is invested, and the weird metempsychosis which it records, produce an effect on the reader altogether peculiar in character and, as we think, quite inexplicable without a reference to the supernatural inspiration which seems to pervade them. In the moods of mind and phases of passion which this story represents we have no laboured artistic effects; we look into the haunted chambers of the poet's own mind and see, as through a veil, the strange experiences of his inner life; while, in the dusk magnificence of its imagery, we have the true heraldic blazonry of an imagination royally dowered and descended. In this, as in all that class of stories we have named, the author's mind seems struggling desperately and vainly with the awful mystery of Death.

*   *   *

The thought which informs so many of his tales and poems betrays its sad sincerity even in his critical writings, as, for instance, in a notice of Undine in the "Marginalia." Yet it has been said of him that "he had no touch of human feeling or of human pity," that "he loved no one but himself"—that "he was an abnormal and monstrous creation,"—"possessed by legions of devils." The most injurious epithets have been heaped upon his name and the most improbable and calumnious stories recorded as veritable histories. Ten years have passed since his death, and while the popular interest in his writings and the popular estimate of his genius increases from year to year, these acknowledged calumnies are still going the round of the foreign periodicals and are still being republished at home. We believe that with the exception of Mr. Willis's generous tributes to his memory, some candid and friendly articles by the Editor of the *Literary Messenger*, and an eloquent and vigorous article in *Russell's Magazine* by Mr. J. Wood Davidson, of Columbia, S.C. (who has appreciated his genius and his sorrow more justly perhaps than any of his American critics) this great and acknowledged wrong to the dead has been permitted to pass without public rebuke or protest.

*   *   *

The peculiarities of Edgar Poe's organization and temperament doubtless exposed him to peculiar infirmities. We need not discuss them here. They have been already too elaborately and painfully illustrated elsewhere to need further comment. How fearfully he expiated them only those who best knew and loved him can ever know. We are told that ideas of right and wrong are wholly ignored by him—that "no recognitions of conscience or remorse are to be found on his pages." If not *there* where, then, shall we look for them? In "William Wilson," in "The Man of the Crowd," and in "The Tell-Tale Heart," the retributions of conscience are portrayed with a terrible fidelity. In yet another of his stories, which we will not name, the fearful fatality of crime—the dreadful fascination consequent on the indulgence of a perverse will is portrayed with a relentless and awful reality. May none ever read it who do not need the fearful lesson which it brands on the memory in characters of fire! In the relation of this remarkable story we recognise the power of a genius like that which sustains us in traversing the lowest depths of Dante's "Inferno." The rapid descent in crime which it delineates, and which becomes at last involuntary, reminds us of the subterranean staircase by which Vathek and Nouronihar reached the Hall of Eblis,[4] where, as they descended, they felt their steps frightfully accelerated till they seemed falling from a precipice.

Poe's private letters to his friends offer abundant evidence that he was not insensible to the keenest pangs of remorse. Again and again did he say to the Demon that tracked his path, "Anathema Maranatha,"[5] but again and again did it return to torture and subdue. He saw the handwriting on the wall but had no power to avert the impending doom.

HENRY JAMES

Charles Baudelaire

Henry James (1843–1916), the American novelist and critic, is one of the most important theorists and practitioners of literary realism. James began his career writing for major American magazines, including the Atlantic Monthly, *which originally published the serialized version of his masterpiece* The Portrait of a Lady *in 1880–1881. Born in New York, James spent most of his life in Europe and many of his novels including* Daisy Miller *(1879),* The American *(1877),* Roderick Hudson *(1875), and* The Portrait of a Lady *describe the experiences of Americans abroad. His ideas about the aesthetics of fiction, articulated in "The Art of Fiction" (1884) and the Prefaces to the New York Edition of his novels, became dominant for much of the twentieth century and still exert a powerful influence on the theory and practice of fiction today. His 1876 essay on Baudelaire, from which the excerpt below is drawn, was originally published in* The Nation. *In his scathing denunciation of Baudelaire for his "lurid landscape and unclean furniture," James critiques Baudelaire for precisely the same kind of inattention to moralism for which Baudelaire praises Poe.*

[4]Allusion to William Beckford's 1787 novel, *Vathek, an Arabian Tale.*
[5]From 1 Cor. 16:22.

For American readers . . . , Baudelaire is compromised by his having made himself the apostle of our own Edgar Poe. He translated, very carefully and exactly, all of Poe's prose writings, and, we believe, some of his very valueless verses. With all due respect to the very original genius of the author of the "Tales of Mystery," it seems to us that to take him with more than a certain degree of seriousness is to lack seriousness one's self. An enthusiasm for Poe is the mark of a decidedly primitive stage of reflection. Baudelaire thought him a profound philosopher, the neglect of whose golden utterances stamped his native land with infamy. Nevertheless, Poe was vastly the greater charlatan of the two, as well as the greater genius.

GEORGE BERNARD SHAW

Edgar Allan Poe

Awarded the Nobel Prize for Literature in 1925, George Bernard Shaw (1856–1950) was the author of more than sixty plays, including Pygmalion *(1912), his most famous work and the basis for the even more famous play and film* My Fair Lady. *Shaw began his literary career as a critic, writing art, music, book, and theater reviews, and in 1895 he became the theater critic for London's* Saturday Review. *Shaw was also a member of the Fabian Society, a socialist organization that advocated for gradual social change as opposed to revolution. The society was instrumental to the foundation of the Labour Party and the London School of Economics, and its members included many other prominent artists and writers of the day, including H. G. Wells and Virginia Woolf. Shaw's essay on Poe was published in 1909 in the British magazine* The Nation, *a century after Poe's birth.*

There was a time when America, the Land of the Free, and the birthplace of Washington, seemed a natural fatherland for Edgar Allan Poe. Nowadays the thing has become inconceivable: no young man can read Poe's works without asking incredulously what the devil he is doing in that galley. America has been found out; and Poe has not; that is the situation. How did he live there, this finest of fine artists, this born aristocrat of letters? Alas! he did not live there: he died there, and was duly explained away as a drunkard and a failure, though it remains an open question whether he really drank as much in his whole lifetime as a modern successful American drinks, without comment, in six months.

If the Judgment Day were fixed for the centenary of Poe's birth, there are among the dead only two men born since the Declaration of Independence whose plea for mercy could avert a prompt sentence of damnation on the entire nation; and it is extremely doubtful whether those two could be persuaded to pervert eternal justice by uttering it. The two are, of course, Poe and Whitman; and there is between them the remarkable difference that Whitman is still credibly an American, whereas even the Americans themselves, though rather short of men of genius, omit Poe's name from their Pantheon, either from a sense that it is hopeless for them to claim so foreign a figure, or from simple Monroeism. One asks, has the America of Poe's day passed away, or did it ever exist?

*   *   *

Edgar Allan Poe was not in the least a Philistine. He wrote always as if his native Boston was Athens, his Charlottesville University Plato's Academy, and his cottage the crown of the heights of Fiesole. He was the greatest journalistic critic of his time, placing good European work at sight when the European critics were waiting for somebody to tell them what to say. His poetry is so exquisitely refined that posterity will refuse to believe that it belongs to the same civilization as the glory of Mrs. Julia Ward Howe's lilies or the honest doggerel of Whittier. Tennyson, who was nothing if not a virtuoso, never produced a success that will bear reading after Poe's failures. Poe constantly and inevitably produced magic where his greatest contemporaries produced only beauty. Tennyson's popular pieces, *The May Queen* and *The Charge of the Six Hundred*, cannot stand hackneying: they become positively nauseous after a time. *The Raven, The Bells,* and *Annabel Lee* are as fascinating at the thousandth repetition as at the first.

Poe's supremacy in this respect has cost him his reputation. This is a phenomenon which occurs when an artist achieves such perfection as to place himself *hors concours*.[1] The greatest painter England ever produced is Hogarth, a miraculous draughtsman and an exquisite and poetic colorist. But he is never mentioned by critics. They talk copiously about Romney, the Gibson of his day; freely about Reynolds; nervously about the great Gainsborough; and not at all about Rowlandson and Hogarth,

---

[1] Unrivaled; beyond competition.

missing the inextinguishable grace of Rowlandson because they assume that all caricatures of this period are ugly, and avoiding Hogarth instinctively as critically unmanageable. In the same way, we have given up mentioning Poe: that is why the Americans forgot him when they posted up the names of their great in their Pantheon. Yet his is the first—almost the only name that the real connoisseur looks for.

* * *

In his stories of mystery and imagination Poe created a world-record for the English language: perhaps for all the languages. The story of the Lady Ligeia is not merely one of the wonders of literature: it is unparalleled and unapproached. There is really nothing to be said about it: we others simply take off our hats and let Mr. Poe go first. . . .

Poe's limitation was his aloofness from the common people. Grotesques, negroes, madmen with delirium tremens, even gorillas, take the place of ordinary peasants and courtiers, citizens and soldiers, in his theatre. His houses are haunted houses, his woods enchanted woods; and he makes them so real that reality itself cannot sustain the comparison. His kingdom is not of this world.

Above all, Poe is great because he is independent of cheap attractions, independent of sex, of patriotism, of fighting, of sentimentality, snobbery, gluttony, and all the rest of the vulgar stock-in-trade of his profession. This is what gives him his superb distinction. One vulgarized thing, the pathos of dying children, he touched in *Annabel Lee*, and devulgarized it at once. He could not even amuse himself with detective stories without purifying the atmosphere of them until they became more edifying than most of Hymns, Ancient and Modern. His verse sometimes alarms and puzzles the reader by fainting with its own beauty; but the beauty is never the beauty of the flesh. You never say to him as you have to say uneasily to so many modern artists: "Yes, my friend, but these are things that men and women should live and not write about. Literature is not a keyhole for people with starved affections to peep through at the banquets of the body." It never became one in Poe's hands. Life cannot give you what he gives you except through fine art; and it was his instinctive observance of this distinction, and the fact that it did not beggar him, as it would beggar most writers, that makes him the most legitimate, the most classical, of modern writers.

It also explains why America does not care much for him, and why he has hardly been mentioned in England these many years. America and England are wallowing in the sensuality which their immense increase of riches has placed within their reach. I do not blame them: sensuality is a very necessary, and healthy and educative element in life. Unfortunately, it is ill distributed; and our reading masses are looking on at it and thinking about it and longing for it, and having precarious little holiday treats of it, instead of sharing it temperately and continuously, and ceasing to be preoccupied with it. When the distribution is better adjusted and the preoccupation ceases, there will be a noble reaction in favor of the great writers like Poe, who begin just where the world, the flesh, and the devil leave off.

YVOR WINTERS

Edgar Allan Poe: A Crisis in the History of American Obscurantism

An American poet, Yvor Winters (1900–1968) is remembered today more for his critical contributions than his verse. Receiving his Ph.D. from Stanford University in 1934, Winters then joined the Department of English there, where he taught for four decades. His students included many of the major poets of the twentieth century, such as Thomas Gunn, Philip Levine, Donald Justice, and Robert Pinsky. His critical work in many ways revolutionized academic practice, as Winters turned his critical eye toward his own contemporary literary artists—writing about Ezra Pound, T. S. Eliot, Marianne Moore, and Wallace Stevens—as opposed to focusing solely on the writers of the past. He was infamously blunt and dogmatic in his critical appraisals, characterizing Eliot's prosody, for example, as "limp versification" in his essay collection In Defense of Reason *(1947). The essay below was published in the academic journal* American Literature *in 1937.*

I am about to promulgate a heresy; namely, that E. A. Poe, although he achieved, as his admirers have claimed, a remarkable agreement between his theory and his practice, is exceptionally bad in both. I am somewhat startled, moreover, to awaken to the fact that this is a heresy, that those who object to Poe would do well to establish their position now if ever. Poe has long passed casually with me and with most of my friends as a bad writer accidentally and temporarily popular; the fact of the matter is, of course, that he has been pretty effectually established as a great writer while we have been sleeping. The menace lies not, primarily, in his impressionistic admirers among literary people, of whom he still has some, even in England and America, where a familiarity with his language ought to render his crudity obvious, for these individuals in the main do not make themselves permanently very effective; it lies rather in the impressive body of scholarship, beginning, perhaps, with Harrison, Woodberry, and Stedman, and continuing down to such writers as Campbell, Stovall, and Una Pope-Hennessy.[1] Much of this scholarship is primarily biographical, historical, and textual; but when a writer is supported by a sufficient body of such scholarship, a very little philosophical elucidation will suffice to establish him in the scholarly world as a writer whose greatness is self-evident.

*　*　*

The problem is a simple one. Most of Poe's essential theory is summarized in three essays: "The Poetic Principle," "The Philosophy of Composition," and "The Rationale of Verse." Important statements can be found elsewhere, and I shall draw upon other essays, but these essays contain most of the essential ideas. Furthermore, the essential statements recur repeatedly in other essays, frequently almost verbatim. By confining oneself largely to these essays, by selecting the crucial statements, by showing as briefly as possible their obvious relations one to another, one can reduce Poe's aesthetic to a very brief and a perfectly accurate statement. In doing this I shall endeavor in every case to interpret what he says directly, not with the aid of other writers whose theories may have influenced him and by aid of whose theories one may conceivably be able to gloss over some of his confusion; and I shall endeavor to show that this direct approach is fully justified by his own artistic practice.

The passages which I shall quote have all been quoted many times before; I shall have to beg indulgence on that score and ask the reader to examine once and for all their obvious significance.

---

[1]James A. Harrison (1848–1911) and George Edward Woodberry (1855–1930) are the authors of the standard Poe biographies available in the early years of the twentieth century. Edmund C. Stedman (1833–1908) was a poet and critic and coeditor with Woodberry of the ten-volume *Works of Edgar Allan Poe* in 1895. Killis Campbell (1872–1937) helped galvanize Poe's place in the literary canon through his graduate seminars on Poe at the University of Texas, publishing *The Mind of Poe and Other Studies* in 1933. Campbell's student Floyd Stovall (1860–1974) was one of the most prominent Poe scholars of the first half of the century, ultimately appointed Edgar Allan Poe Professor at the University of Virginia in 1955. Una Pope-Hennessy (1876–1949) was a British writer and historian, and the author of *Edgar Allan Poe, 1809–1849: A Critical Biography* (1934), which, along with Stovall's *Mind of Poe*, was very much on Winters's mind as he wrote this essay.

Any study of Poe should begin with a statement made in connection with Elizabeth Barrett's *A Drama of Exile*. He says: "This is emphatically the thinking age; indeed it may very well be questioned whether man ever substantially thought before."[2] This sentence displays an ignorance at once of thought and of the history of thought so comprehensive as to preclude the possibility of our surprise at any further disclosures. It helps to explain, furthermore, Poe's extraordinary inability to understand even the poetry of ages previous to his own, as well as his subservience in matters of taste to the vulgar sentimentalism which dominated the more popular poets of his period, such poets as Moore, Hood,[3] and Willis,[4] to mention no others. One seldom encounters a writer so thoroughly at the mercy of contemporaneity. . . .

II

*   *   *

Briefly, Poe implies something like this: the proper subject-matter of poetry is Beauty, but since true Beauty exists only in eternity, the poet cannot experience it and is deprived of his subject-matter; by manipulating the materials of our present life, we may *suggest the existence of Beauty*, and this is the best that we can do. As we may discover from other passages, especially in "The Philosophy of Composition," Poe had certain definite ideas in regard to which forms of human experience lent themselves best to this procedure, and also in regard to the rules of the procedure. Having decided, in an astonishing passage to which I shall presently return, that a melancholy tone most greatly facilitated his purpose, he wrote: "'Of all melancholy topics, what, according to the *universal* understanding of mankind, is the *most* melancholy?' Death—was the obvious reply. 'And when,' I said, 'is this most melancholy of topics most poetical?' From what I have already explained at some length, the answer, here also is obvious—'When it most closely allies itself to *Beauty*: the death, then, of a beautiful woman is, unquestionably, the most poetical topic in the world . . .'" (p. 229). In other words, we are not concerned

---

[2]From Poe's review of *A Drama of Exile* in *Broadway Journal* (January 4, 1845). Her poem "Lady Geraldine's Courtship," included in the collection mentioned, served as the model for the meter of Poe's "The Raven."

[3]Clement Moore (1779–1863), American author of "A Visit from St. Nicholas" ("'Twas the Night before Christmas"); Thomas Hood (1799–1845), British humorist and poet.

[4]Nathaniel Parker Willis (1806–1867), American author and editor.

with understanding human experience; we are seeking, rather, the isolated elements, or fragments, of experience which may best serve as the ingredients of a formula for the production of a kind of emotional delusion, and our final decision in the matter is determined again by our inability to distinguish between the subject and the style of poetry, by the conviction that beauty is the subject of poetry.

The reader should note carefully what this means; perhaps he will pardon me for restating it: the subject-matter of poetry, properly considered, is by definition incomprehensible and unattainable; the poet, in dealing with something else, toward which he has no intellectual or moral responsibilities whatever ("Unless incidentally," says Poe, poetry "has no concern whatever either with Duty or with Truth"), should merely endeavor to *suggest that a higher meaning exists*—in other words, should endeavor to suggest the presence of a meaning when he is aware of none. The poet has only to write a good description of something physically impressive, with an air of mystery, an air of meaning concealed.

An air of mystery, of strangeness, will then be of necessity, not an adjunct of poetic style, but the very essence of poetic style. In "Ligeia" there occurs the well-known passage which it is now necessary to quote: "'There is no exquisite beauty,' says Bacon, Lord Verulam, speaking truly of all the forms and *genera* of beauty, 'without some *strangeness* in the proportion'" (p. 49). But in Poe's terms, strangeness and beauty are, from the standpoint of the practical poet, identical. . . .

* * *

In "The Philosophy of Composition" Poe gives us a hint as to his conception of originality of style. After a brief discourse on originality of versification, and the unaccountable way in which it has been neglected, he states that he lays no claim to originality as regards the meter or the rhythm of "The Raven," but only as regards the stanza: "nothing even remotely approaching this combination has ever been attempted" (p. 231). Again we see Poe's tendency to rely upon the mechanically startling, in preference to the inimitable. This fact, coupled with his extraordinary theories of meter, which I shall examine separately, bears a close relationship to what appears to me to be the clumsiness and insensitivity of his verse. Read three times, his rhythms disgust, because they are untrained and insensitive and have no individual life within their surprising mechanical frames.

Before turning to the principal poems for a brief examination of them, we should observe at least one remark on the subject of melancholy. In "The Philosophy of Composition" after stating that, in planning "The Raven," he had decided upon Beauty as the province of the poem, Poe writes as follows:

> Regarding, then, Beauty as my province, my next question referred to the *tone* of its highest manifestation—and all experience has shown that this tone is one of *sadness*. Beauty of whatever kind, in its supreme development, invariably excites the sensitive soul to tears. Melancholy is thus the most legitimate of all the poetical tones. (p. 228)

Now if the reader will keep in mind the principles that we have already deduced; namely, that Beauty is unattainable, that the poet can merely suggest its existence, that this suggestion depends upon the ingenious manipulation of the least obstructive elements of normal experience—it will at once be obvious that Poe is here suggesting a reversal of motivation. That is, since Beauty excites to tears (let us assume with Poe, for the moment, that it does), if we begin with tears, we may believe ourselves moved for a moment by Beauty. This interpretation is supported solidly by the last two sentences quoted, particularly when we regard their order.

"The Philosophy of Composition" thus appears after all to be a singularly shocking document. Were it an examination of the means by which a poet might communicate a comprehensible judgment, were it a plea that such communication be carefully planned in advance, we could do no less than approve. But it is not that; it is rather an effort to establish the rules for a species of incantation, of witchcraft; rules whereby, through the manipulation of certain substances in certain arbitrary ways, it may be possible to invoke, more or less accidentally, something that appears more or less to be a divine emanation. It is not surprising that Poe expressed more than once a very qualified appreciation of Milton.

V

In his criticism of Hawthorne's *Tales*, Poe outlines his theory of the short story. He defends the tale, as preferable to the novel, on the same grounds as those on which he defends the short poem in preference to the long. He states the necessity of careful planning and of economy of means.

He says: ". . . having conceived, with deliberate care, a certain unique or single *effect* to be wrought out, he [the skillful literary artist] then invents such incidents—he then combines such events as may best aid him in establishing this preconceived effect." Now the word *effect*, here as elsewhere in Poe, means impression, or mood; it is a word that connotes emotion purely and simply. So that we see the story-teller, like the poet, interested primarily in the creation of an emotion for its own sake, not in the understanding of an experience. It is significant in this connection that most of his heroes are mad or on the verge of madness; a datum which settles his action firmly in the realm of inexplicable feeling from the outset.

"Morella" begins thus: "With a feeling of deep yet most singular affection I regarded my friend Morella. Thrown by accident into her society many years ago, my soul, from our first meeting, burned with fires it had never before known; but the fires were not of Eros, and bitter and tormenting to my spirit was the gradual conviction that I could in no manner define their unusual meaning or regulate their vague intensity." And "Ligeia": "I cannot, for my soul, remember how, when, or even precisely where, I first became acquainted with the lady Ligeia. Long years have since elapsed, and my memory is feeble through much suffering" (p. 48). "The Assignation": "Ill-fated and mysterious man!—bewildered in the brilliancy of thine own imagination, and fallen in the flames of thine own youth." "The Tell-Tale Heart": "True!—nervous—very, very dreadfully nervous I had been and am; but why *will* you say that I am mad?" (p. 173) "Berenice": ". . . it *is* wonderful what stagnation there fell upon the springs of my life— wonderful how total an inversion took place in the character of my commonest thought" (p. 41). "Eleonora": "I am come of a race noted for vigor of fancy and ardor of passion. Men have called me mad; but the question is not yet settled, whether madness is or is not the loftiest intelligence—whether much that is glorious—whether all that is profound—does not spring from disease of thought—from moods of mind exalted at the expense of the general intellect." Roderick Usher, in addition, is mad; "The Black Cat" is a study in madness; "The Masque of the Red Death" is a study in hallucinatory terror. They are all studies in hysteria; they are written for the sake of the hysteria.

VII

On what grounds, if any, can we then defend Poe? We can obviously defend his taste as long as we honestly like it. The present writer is willing to leave it, after these few remarks, to its admirers. As to his critical theory, however, and the structural defects of his work, it appears to me certain that the difficulty which I have raised is the central problem in Poe criticism; yet not only has it never been met, but, so far as one can judge, it has scarcely been recognized.

There are, I believe, two general lines of argument or procedure that may be used more or less in support of Poe's position; one is that of the Alterton-Craig Introduction, the other is that (if I may cite another eminent example) of Professor Floyd Stovall.

The argument of the [Alterton-Craig] Introduction appears to be roughly that Poe is an intellectual poet, because: first, he worked out in *Eureka* a theory of cosmic harmony and unity; second, related to this, he held a theory of the harmony and unity of the parts of the poem; and third, he devoted a certain amount of rational effort to working out the rules by which this unity could be attained.

But this intellectuality, if that is the name for it, is all anterior to the poem, not in the poem; it resides merely in the rules for the practice of the obscurantism which I have defined. The Introduction cites as evidence of Poe's recognition of the intellectual element in poetry, his essay on Drake and Halleck, yet the intellectuality in question here is plainly of the sort which I have just described. As a result, Professor Craig's comparison of Poe to Donne, Dryden, and Aquinas, is, to the present writer, at least, profoundly shocking.

The only alternative is that of Professor Stovall, as well as of a good many others: to accept Poe's theory of Beauty as if it were clearly understood and then to examine minor points of Poe criticism with lucidity and with learning. But Poe's theory of Beauty is not understood, and no casual allusion to Plato will ever clarify it.

T. S. ELIOT

From Poe to Valéry

A central figure of literary modernism, T. S. Eliot (1888–1965) was a poet, critic, editor, and playwright. Born in St. Louis, Eliot studied philosophy at Harvard University and at the Sorbonne in Paris, and like other prominent American artists of his generation, he was an expatriate, becoming a British citizen in 1927. Eliot published his first book of poetry Prufrock and Other Observations *in 1917 with the financial and critical support of Ezra Pound. Five years later, Eliot published* The Waste Land, *a poem whose fragmented, allusive, and improvisatory mode perfectly captured the emerging modernist poetic style. Capitalizing on the success from its publication, Eliot became the founding editor of the elite British literary journal the* Criterion. *Eliot's literary and critical voice dominated the first half of the twentieth century, and he offered the following essay as a lecture at the Library of Congress in 1948, the same year he was awarded the Nobel Prize in Literature.*

What I attempt here is not a judicial estimate of Edgar Allan Poe; I am not trying to decide his rank as a poet or to isolate his essential originality. Poe is indeed a stumbling block for the judicial critic. If we examine his work in detail, we seem to find in it nothing but slipshod writing, puerile thinking unsupported by wide reading or profound scholarship, haphazard experiments in various types of writing, chiefly under pressure of financial need, without perfection in any detail. This would not be just. But if, instead of regarding his work analytically, we take a distant view of it as a whole, we see a mass of unique shape and impressive size to which the eye constantly returns. Poe's influence is equally puzzling. In France the influence of his poetry and of his poetic theories has been immense. In England and America it seems almost negligible. Can we point to any poet whose style appears to have been formed by a study of Poe? The only one whose name immediately suggests itself is Edward Lear.[1] And yet one cannot be sure that one's own writing has *not* been influenced by Poe. I can name positively certain poets whose work has influenced me, I can name others whose work, I am sure, has not; there may be still others of whose influence I am unaware, but whose influence I might be brought to acknowledge; but about Poe I shall never be sure. He wrote very few poems, and of those few only half a dozen have had a great success: but those few are as well known to as large a number of people, are as well remembered by everybody, as any poems ever written. And some of his tales have had an important influence upon authors, and in types of writing where such influence would hardly be expected.

I shall here make no attempt to explain the enigma. At most, this is a contribution to the study of his influence; and an elucidation, partial as it may be, of one cause of Poe's importance in the light of that influence. I am trying to look at him, for a moment, as nearly as I can, through the eyes of three French poets, Baudelaire, Mallarme and

[1] Edward Lear (1812–1888), English writer and illustrator, famous for nonsense verse and limericks.

especially Paul Valéry.[2] The sequence is itself important. These three French poets represent the beginning, the middle, and the end of a particular tradition in poetry. Mallarme once told a friend of mine that he came to Paris because he wanted to know Baudelaire; that he had once seen him at a book-stall on a quai, but had not had the courage to accost him. As for Valéry, we know from the first letter to Mallarme, written when he was hardly more than a boy, of his discipleship of the elder poet; and we know of his devotion to Mallarme until Mallarme's death. Here are three literary generations, representing almost exactly a century of French poetry. Of course, these are poets very different from each other; of course, the literary progeny of Baudelaire was numerous and important, and there are other lines of descent from him. But I think we can trace the development and descent of one particular theory of the nature of poetry through these three poets and it is a theory which takes its origin in the theory, still more than in the practice, of Edgar Poe. And the impression we get of the influence of Poe is the more impressive, because of the fact that Mallarme, and Valéry in turn, did not merely derive from Poe through Baudelaire: each of them subjected himself to that influence directly, and has left convincing evidence of the value which he attached to the theory and practice of Poe himself. Now, we all of us like to believe that we understand our own poets better than any foreigner can do; but I think we should be prepared to entertain the possibility that these Frenchmen have seen something in Poe that English-speaking readers have missed.

My subject, then, is not simply Poe but Poe's effect upon three French poets, representing three successive generations; and my purpose is also to approach an understanding of a peculiar attitude towards poetry, by the poets themselves, which is perhaps the most interesting, possibly the most characteristic, and certainly the most original development of the esthetic of verse made in that period as a whole. It is all the more worthy of examination if, as I incline to believe, this attitude towards poetry represents a phase which has come to an end with the death of Valéry. For our study of it should help towards the understanding of whatever it may be that our generation and the next will find to take its place.

Before concerning myself with Poe as he appeared in the eyes of these French poets, I think it as well to present my own impression of his status among American and English readers and critics; for, if I am

---

[2]Charles Baudelaire (1821–1867); Stéphane Mallarmé (1842–1898); Paul Valéry (1871–1945). See p. 276 for Baudelaire's contribution to this debate.

wrong, you may have to criticise what I say of his influence in France with my errors in mind. It does not seem to me unfair to say that Poe has been regarded as a minor, or secondary, follower of the Romantic Movement: a successor to the so-called "Gothic" novelists in his fiction, and a follower of Byron and Shelley in his verse. This however is to place him in the English tradition; and there certainly he does not belong. English readers sometimes account for that in Poe which is outside of any English tradition, by saying that it is American; but this does not seem to me wholly true either, especially when we consider the other American writers of his own and an earlier generation. There is a certain flavour of provinciality about his work, in a sense in which Whitman is not in the least provincial: it is the provinciality of the person who is not at home where he belongs, but cannot get to anywhere else. Poe is a kind of displaced European; he is attracted to Paris, to Italy and to Spain, to places which he could endow with romantic gloom and grandeur. Although his ambit of movement hardly extended beyond the limits of Richmond and Boston longitudinally, and neither east nor west of these centres, he seems a wanderer with no fixed abode. There can be few authors of such eminence who have drawn so little from their own roots, who have been so isolated from any surroundings.

I believe the view of Poe taken by the ordinary cultivated English or American reader is something like this: Poe is the author of a few, a very few short poems which enchanted him for a time when he was a boy, and which do somehow stick in the memory. I do not think that he re-reads these poems, unless he turns to them in the pages of an anthology; his enjoyment of them is rather the memory of an enjoyment which he may for a moment recapture. They seem to him to belong to a particular period when his interest in poetry had just awakened. Certain images, and still more certain rhythms, abide with him. This reader also remembers certain of the tales—not very many—and holds the opinion that *The Gold Bug* was quite good for its time, but that detective fiction has made great strides since then. And he may sometimes contrast him with Whitman, having frequently re-read Whitman, but not Poe.

As for the prose, it is recognised that Poe's tales had great influence upon some types of popular fiction. So far as detective fiction is concerned, nearly everything can be traced to two authors: Poe and Wilkie Collins.[3] The two influences sometimes concur, but are also responsible for two different types of detective. The efficient professional policeman

[3]Wilkie Collins (1824–1889), British novelist and friend of Charles Dickens.

originates with Collins, the brilliant and eccentric amateur with Poe. Conan Doyle owes much to Poe, and not merely to Monsieur Dupin of *The Murders in the Rue Morgue*. Sherlock Holmes was deceiving Watson when he told him that he had bought his Stradivarius violin for a few shillings at a second-hand shop in the Tottenham Court Road. He found that violin in the ruins of the house of Usher. There is a close similarity between the musical exercises of Holmes and those of Roderick Usher: those wild and irregular improvisations which, although on one occasion they sent Watson off to sleep, must have been excruciating to any ear trained to music. It seems to me probable that the romances of improbable and incredible adventure of Rider Haggard[4] found their inspiration in Poe—and Haggard himself had imitators enough. I think it equally likely that H. G. Wells, in his early romances of scientific exploration and invention, owed much to the stimulus of some of Poe's narratives—*Gordon Pym*, or *A Descent into the Maelstrom* for example, or *The Facts in the Case of Monsieur Valdemar*. The compilation of evidence I leave to those who are interested to pursue the enquiry. But I fear that nowadays too few readers open *She* or *The War of the Worlds* or *The Time Machine*: fewer still are capable of being thrilled by their predecessors.

What strikes me first, as a general difference between the way in which the French poets whom I have cited took Poe, and the way of American and English critics of equivalent authority, is the attitude of the former towards Poe's oeuvre, towards his work as a whole. Anglo-Saxon critics are, I think, more inclined to make separate judgements of the different parts of an author's work. We regard Poe as a man who dabbled in verse and in several kinds of prose, without settling down to make a thoroughly good job of any one *genre*. These French readers were impressed by the variety of form of expression, because they found, or thought they found, an essential unity; while admitting, if necessary, that much of the work is fragmentary or occasional, owing to circumstances of poverty, frailty, and vicissitude, they nevertheless take him as an author of such seriousness that his work must be grasped as a whole. This represents partly a difference between two kinds of critical mind; but we must claim, for our own view, that it is supported by our awareness of the blemishes and imperfections of Poe's actual writing. It is worth while to illustrate these faults, as they strike an English-speaking reader.

---

[4]Henry Rider Haggard (1856–1925), British writer of adventure and "lost world" novels.

Poe had, to an exceptional degree, the feeling for the incantatory element in poetry, of that which may, in the most nearly literal sense, be called "the magic of verse." His versification is not, like that of the greatest masters of prosody, of the kind which yields a richer melody, through study and long habituation, to the maturing sensibility of the reader returning to it at times throughout his life. Its effect is immediate and undeveloping; it is probably much the same for the sensitive schoolboy and for the ripe mind and cultivated ear. In this unchanging immediacy, it partakes perhaps more of the character of very good verse than of poetry—but that is to start a hare which I have no intention of following here, for it is, I am sure, "poetry" and not "verse." It has the effect of an incantation which, because of its very crudity, stirs the feelings at a deep and almost primitive level. But, in his choice of the word which has the right *sound*, Poe is by no means careful that it should have also the right *sense*. I will give one comparison of uses of the same word by Poe and by Tennyson—who, of all English poets since Milton, had probably the most accurate and fastidious appreciation of the sound of syllables. In Poe's *Ulalume*—to my mind one of his most successful, as well as typical, poems—we find the lines

> It was night, in the lonesome October
> Of my most immemorial year.

Immemorial, according to the *Oxford Dictionary*, means: "that is beyond memory or out of mind; ancient beyond memory or record: extremely old." None of these meanings seems applicable to this use of the word by Poe. The year was not beyond memory—the speaker remembers one incident in it very well; at the conclusion he even remembers a funeral in the same place just a year earlier. The line of Tennyson, equally well known, and justly admired because the sound of the line responds so well to the sound which the poet wishes to evoke, may already have come to mind:

> The moan of doves in immemorial elms.

Here *immemorial*, besides having the most felicitous sound value, is exactly the word for trees so old that no one knows just how old they are.

Poetry, of different kinds, may be said to range from that in which the attention of the reader is directed primarily to the sound, to that in which it is directed primarily to the sense. With the former kind, the sense may be apprehended almost unconsciously; with the latter kind—at these two extremes—it is the sound, of the operation of which upon us we are unconscious. But, with either type, sound and sense must cooperate; in even the most purely incantatory poem, the dictionary meaning of words cannot be disregarded with impunity.

An irresponsibility towards the meaning of words is not infrequent with Poe. *The Raven* is, I think, far from being Poe's best poem; though, partly because of the analysis which the author gives in *The Philosophy of Composition*, it is the best known.

In there stepped a stately Raven of the saintly days of yore;
(p. 24)

Since there is nothing particularly saintly about the raven, if indeed the ominous bird is not wholly the reverse, there can be no point in referring his origin to a period of saintliness, even if such a period can be assumed to have existed. We have just heard the raven described as *stately*, but we are told presently that he is *ungainly*, an attribute hardly to be reconciled, without a good deal of explanation, with *stateliness*. Several words in the poem seem to be inserted either merely to fill out the line to the required measure, or for the sake of a rhyme. The bird is addressed as "no craven" quite needlessly, except for the pressing need of a rhyme to "raven" — a surrender to the exigencies of rhyme with which I am sure Malherbe[5] would have had no patience. And there is not always even such schoolboy justification as this: to say that the lamplight "gloated o'er" the sofa cushions is a freak of fancy which, even were it relevant to have a little gloating going on somewhere, would appear forced.

Imperfections in *The Raven* such as these — and one could give others — may serve to explain why *The Philosophy of Composition*, the essay in which Poe professes to reveal his method in composing *The Raven* — has not been taken so seriously in England or America as in France. It is difficult for us to read that essay without reflecting, that if Poe plotted out his poem with such calculation, he might have taken a little more pains over it: the result hardly does credit to the method. Therefore we are likely to draw the conclusion that Poe in analysing his poem was practicing either a hoax, or a piece of self-deception in setting down the way in which he wanted to think that he had written it. Hence the essay has not been taken so seriously as it deserves.

Poe's other essays in poetic esthetic deserve consideration also. No poet, when he writes his own *art poétique*, should hope to do much more than explain, rationalise, defend or prepare the way for his own

---

[5]François de Malherbe (1555–1628), a French poet whose work established classical rules of versification and vocabulary that held sway for centuries.

practice: that is, for writing his own kind of poetry. He may think that he is establishing laws for all poetry; but what he has to say that is worth saying has its immediate relation to the way in which he himself writes or wants to write: though it may well be equally valid to his immediate juniors, and extremely helpful to them. We are only safe in finding, in his writing about poetry, principles valid for any poetry, so long as we check what he says by the kind of poetry he writes. Poe has a remarkable passage about the impossibility of writing a long poem — for a long poem, he holds, is at best a series of short poems strung together. What we have to bear in mind is that he himself was incapable of writing a long poem. He could conceive only a poem which was a single simple effect: for him, the whole of a poem had to be in one mood. Yet it is only in a poem of some length that a variety of moods can be expressed; for a variety of moods requires a number of different themes or subjects, related either in themselves or in the mind of the poet. These parts can form a whole which is more than the sum of the parts; a whole such that the pleasure we derive from the reading of any part is enhanced by our grasp of the whole. It follows also that in a long poem some parts may be deliberately planned to be less "poetic" than others: these passages may show no lustre when extracted, but may be intended to elicit, by contrast, the significance of other parts, and to unite them into a whole more significant than any of the parts. A long poem may gain by the widest possible variations of intensity. But Poe wanted a poem to be of the first intensity throughout: it is questionable whether he could have appreciated the more philosophical passages in Dante's *Purgatorio*. What Poe had said has proved in the past of great comfort to other poets equally incapable of the long poem; and we must recognize that the question of the possibility of writing a long poem is not simply that of the strength and staying power of the individual poet, but may have to do with the conditions of the age in which he finds himself. And what Poe has to say on the subject is illuminating, in helping us to understand the point of view of poets for whom the long poem is impossible.

The fact that for Poe a poem had to be the expression of a single mood — it would here be too long an excursus to try to demonstrate that *The Bells*, as a deliberate exercise in several moods, is as much a poem of one mood as any of Poe's — this fact can better be understood as a manifestation of a more fundamental weakness. Here, what I have to say I put forward only tentatively: but it is a view which I should like to launch in order to see what becomes of it. My account may go to explain, also, why the work of Poe has for many readers appealed at a particular phase of their growth, at the period of life when they were just emerging from childhood. That Poe had a powerful intellect is undeniable: but it seems to me the intellect of a highly gifted young person before puberty. The forms which his lively curiosity takes are those in which a pre-adolescent mentality delights: wonders of nature and of mechanics and of the supernatural, cryptograms and cyphers, puzzles and labyrinths, mechanical chess-players and wild flights of speculation. The variety and ardour of his curiosity delight and dazzle; yet in the end the eccentricity and lack of coherence of his interests tire. There is just that lacking which gives dignity to the mature man: a consistent view of life. An attitude can be mature and consistent, and yet be highly sceptical: but Poe was no sceptic. He appears to yield himself completely to the idea of the moment: the effect is, that all of his ideas seem to be *entertained* rather than believed. What is lacking is not brain power, but that maturity of intellect which comes only with the maturing of the man as a whole, the development and coordination of his various emotions. I am not concerned with any possible psychological or pathological explanation: it is enough for my purpose to record that the work of Poe is such as I should expect of a man of very exceptional mind and sensibility, whose emotional development has been in some respect arrested at an early age. His most vivid imaginative realisations are the realisation of a dream: significantly, the ladies in his poems and tales are always ladies lost, or ladies vanishing before they can be embraced. Even in *The Haunted Palace*, where the subject appears to be his own weakness of alcoholism, the disaster has no moral significance; it is treated impersonally as an isolated phenomenon; it has not behind it the terrific force of such lines as those of François Villon when he speaks of his own fallen state.

* * *

Now, . . . I believe that the *art poétique* of which we find the germ in Poe, and which bore fruit in the work of Valéry, has gone as far as it can go. I do not believe that this esthetic can be of any help to later poets. What will take its place I do not know. An esthetic which merely contradicted it would not do. To insist on the all-importance of subject-matter, to insist that the poet should be spontaneous and irreflective, that he should depend upon inspiration and neglect technique, would be a lapse from what is in any case a highly civilised attitude to a barbarous one. We should have to have an esthetic which somehow comprehended and transcended that of Poe and Valéry. This question does not greatly exercise my mind, since I think that the poet's theories should arise out of his practice rather than his practice out of his theories. But I recognise first that within this tradition from Poe to Valéry are some of those modern poems which I most admire and enjoy; second, I think that the tradition itself represents the most interesting development of poetic consciousness anywhere in that same hundred years; and finally I value this exploration of certain poetic possibilities for its own sake, as we believe that all possibilities should be explored. And I find that by trying to look at Poe through the eyes of Baudelaire, Mallarme, and most of all Valéry, I become more thoroughly convinced of his importance, of the importance of his work as a whole. And, as for the future: it is a tenable hypothesis that this advance of self-consciousness, the extreme awareness of and concern for language which we find in Valéry, is something which must ultimately break down, owing to an increasing strain against which the human mind and nerves will rebel; just as, it may be maintained, the indefinite elaboration of scientific discovery and invention, and of political and social machinery, may reach a point at which there will be an irresistible revulsion of humanity and a readiness to accept the most primitive hardships rather than carry any longer the burden of modern civilisation. Upon that I hold no fixed opinion: I leave it to your consideration.

ALLEN TATE

The Poetry of Edgar Allan Poe

A poet, literary critic, and professor of English, Allen Tate (1899–1979) was an extraordinarily influential scholar in the establishment of American literature as an academic field. Like Poe, he was a Southerner, having been born in Kentucky and educated at Vanderbilt University, and like Poe, his Southern identity was crucial to his writing. Tate wrote biographies of both Stonewall Jackson and Jefferson Davis (1928 and 1929), and his most well-known poem is "Ode to the Confederate Dead" (1928). Along with his teacher John Crowe Ransom, Tate was a member of a group of conservative Southern writers called the Fugitives who idealized the antebellum agrarian South. Many within this group, including Tate and Ransom, were also central figures in the literary critical school known as New Criticism, which argued that the essence of literature was in its language and that the task of interpretation was to unpack the multiple meanings of a text's language. The essay below was one of a number that Tate wrote about Poe, an author for whom Tate had considerable appreciation. In an earlier essay, "Our Cousin, Mr. Poe" (1949), although he admits that Poe "never produce[d] a poem or a story without blemishes," he also identifies Poe as presaging the modern "nightmares" against which he and the Fugitives railed. The essay below was originally published in 1968 in the Southern literary magazine Sewanee Review, *and also served as the introductory essay to Tate's edited collection* Edgar Allan Poe: Complete Poetry and Selected Criticism.

In 1948 T. S. Eliot, in a lecture "From Poe to Valéry," said in substance that Poe's work, if it is to be judged fairly, must be seen as a whole, lest as the mere sum of its parts it seem inferior. There is much truth in this; but it puts an unusual strain upon the critic. I believe that I have read, over many years, everything that Poe wrote, but I have never been aware of it all at any one time; nor am I now, as I approach a discussion of the poems. Do the poems increase or diminish one's sense of Poe's greatness if considered apart from the prose, as if the prose did not exist? European critical practice would forbid such a separation, and would compel us to see the poems as one expression of a complex personality responding to the undeveloped society of the New World. This would have been Taine's "method" and, later in the nineteenth century, the method of Georg Brandes.[1] These critic-historians frequently produced elaborate commentaries and "explanations" of an author more interesting than the works of the author himself. That has not been an achievement of modern American criticism. We worry the single poem almost to death; we substitute what Poe himself called "analysis" for "passion"; yet the results have been on the whole rewarding, in that large numbers of persons who never read poetry before have learned how to read it and enjoy it. And we have developed more than any other age a criticism of criticism. But we have not done so well with the larger works like the novel, or even the nouvelle. We do not see the larger works, nor the collected works of an author as a whole.

I shall therefore try to "introduce" readers to the poetry of Edgar Allan Poe as I myself was introduced to it in boyhood, when I read almost anything out of curiosity; that is to say, Poe was in the house and I read him as I read the Rover Boys. But the difference, which appeared only much later, was that I retained Poe, whereas the Rover Boys, Tom Swift, and G. A. Henty soon became a blank; of this sort of author I

[1]Hippolyte Taine (1828–1893), a French critic, and Georg Brandes (1842–1927), a Danish critic.

remember only that Tom Swift had an electric rifle. There was, of course, Natty Bumppo;[2] but he was not, any more than Tom, a book, but a character of the mythical order of George Washington, different but not literature. One does not know, at the age of fourteen, that there is such a thing as literature; but at or at about that age I remember finding somewhere on a top shelf in the dingy parlor three small volumes by Edgar Allan Poe. They may have been part of the infamous Griswold edition; at any rate they were not the complete works. One volume contained some of the more famous tales, as well as the stories of ratiocination, like "The Murders in the Rue Morgue" and "The Mystery of Marie Roget." These stories gave the adolescent mind the illusion of analytical thought. Some of the others, such as "The Premature Burial" and "The Facts in the Case of M. Valdemar," raised questions that seemed at fourteen the deepest enquiries possible into the relation of body and soul: pseudo-philosophy for the unformed and ignorant mind. How a child's reading of Poe's prose tales affected his reading of the poems I shall try to explain, or at least to describe, in a moment.

One of the three volumes contained *Eureka*; the work in fact took up the entire book; and it was the first essay in cosmology that I read. It led just a little later to Ernst Haeckel's *The Riddle of the Universe*, the crassest materialistic cosmogony produced in the nineteenth century, and then to Herbert Spencer's *Synthetic Philosophy*. But *Eureka* is the only piece of adolescent reading in popular astronomy to which I have returned in age; and I still take it seriously. I have wondered why the modern proponents of the Big Bang hypothesis of the creation have not condescended to acknowledge Poe as a forerunner. Big Bang presupposes an agent to set off the explosion of the primordial atom; and that is what Poe presupposed in his fundamental thesis for *Eureka*: "In the original unity of the first thing lies the secondary cause of all things, with the germ of their inevitable annihilation." But the concluding phrase presupposes something else, which is characteristic of Poe in all phases of his work: "inevitable annihilation." The cosmos will shrink back into spatial nothingness, taking man along with it; and hence man, having returned to the original nothing, which is God, will be God. The last twenty or so pages of *Eureka* have a lurid, rhetorical magnificence unmatched by anything else that Poe wrote. For *Eureka* is Poe's elaborate, pseudo-systematic attempt to give his compulsive theme of annihilation scientific and philosophical sanctions.

---

[2]Protagonist in the *Leatherstocking* novels by James Fenimore Cooper (1789–1851).

The theme of annihilation is always attractive to young persons: from about twelve to sixteen, annihilation or simply romantic death at the end of sentimental love—an adolescent posture of disorder set against the imposed order of the family or of adult society into which the child resists entrance. This posture of disorder is never quite rejected in maturity, and it is the psychological and moral basis of what today is called Existentialism. One reason why Americans may be a little bored with French Existentialism is that we have always been Existentialists, or have been since the time of Poe, who discovered it in us. For Existentialism assumes—among other things—that man has no relation to a metaphysical reality, a kind of reality that he cannot know even if it existed; he is therefore trapped in a consciousness which cannot be conscious of anything outside itself. He must sink into the non-self. Poe sinks into the vortex, the maelstrom, suffocation of premature burial or of being walled up alive; or he sinks into the sea. We know Coleridge's influence on Poe. How apt for Poe's purposes was the "lifeless ocean" of Coleridge! And the death of a beautiful woman was, for Poe, the most "poetical" subject for poetry—or, as we should say today, the archetypal subject. One of his best lyrics begins, "Thou wast that all to me, Love, / For which my soul did pine. . . ." His love is dead, of course, and he is left alone, ready for loss of breath, loss of consciousness, loss of identity—never more anything outside himself. . . .

There are four poems by Poe that I believe everybody can join in admiring: "The City in the Sea," "The Sleeper," "To Helen" (the shorter and earlier poem of that title), and "The Raven"; one might include "Ulalume," but less as distinguished poetry than as Poe's last and most ambitious attempt to actualize in language his *aloneness.*

"To Helen" is somewhat more complex than the critics have found it to be, or found it necessary to point out. However, the similarity to Landor[3] has been frequently remarked, but nobody knows whether the influence was direct. (Whether the poem was addressed to an older lady who was kind to Poe when he was a boy is irrelevant.) The direct address is to "Helen," inevitably Helen of Troy whether or not Poe had her in mind; and the tact with which she is described is Homeric. She is not described at all; she is presented in a long simile of action, in which her beauty is conveyed to the reader through its effect on the speaker of the poem. There is nothing else in Poe's work quite so well done as this. In the second stanza one might detect a small blemish (the poem

[3]Walter Savage Landor (1775–1864), English poet.

is so nearly perfect that it invites close scrutiny): the phrase "thy Naiad airs" might be better if the noun were in the singular—"thy Naiad *air*," meaning that her demeanor or bearing is that of a Naiad; the plural has a slight connotation of the colloquial "putting on airs." Helen brings the wanderer home to his native shore, which is the ancient world: the Landoresque perfection of the two last lines of the second stanza has not been surpassed. But the complexity of feeling, unusual in Poe, comes in the last stanza with the image of Helen as a statue in a niche, perhaps at the end of a hall, or on a landing of a stairway. She has all along been both the disturbing Helen and, as a marble, a Vestal Virgin holding her lamp: she is inaccessible. The restrained exclamation "Ah, Psyche" is one of the most brilliant effects in romantic poetry. "Ah" has the force of "alas": alas, that Helen is now in a lost, if holy land, as inaccessible and pure as she herself is. But who is Psyche? She is usually identified with Helen, and she may be Helen, but at the same time she is the Psyche of Eros and Psyche; and Poe must have known the little myth in Apuleius: she could be an archetype of suprasensual love by means of which the classical, sensual Helen is sublimated. (In "Ulalume" Psyche appears again, as the sister of the poet.) Poe wrote the poem when he was not more than twenty-one; he pretended to Lowell that he had written it when he was fourteen; but whenever he wrote it he never before nor afterwards had such mastery of diction and rhythm. I need not point out that the theme of the poem is isolation of the poet after great loss.

Poe's aesthetic theory has not been overrated, but it has been complicated by certain scholars who have tried to show that the theory implies systematic thought; he was, on the contrary, not a systematic critical thinker but a practical critic who on the whole was limited by the demands of book-reviewing, by which he made a great part of his living. The essay most popular in his time was "The Poetic Principle," actually a lecture, what we know today as a "poetry reading with commentary." Poe was the first itinerant American poet who thus became known to hundreds of people who never read a line of his writing. The "Letter to Mr. B.," written when he was about twenty, is a simplified theft from Chapter XIV of *Biographia Literaria*. His review of Hawthorne states brilliantly the necessity for organic unity in fiction, a principle applicable also to poetry. His theory of prosody, which he developed in "The Rationale of Verse," founders on a misconception of the caesura. In the long run his theory of poetry is quite simple: "the rhythmical creation of Beauty" is the end of poetry, which is most completely realized in that most poetical of subjects, the death of a beautiful woman, or more often, in his own verse, the beautiful woman's corpse. He derived his psychology from his intellectual climate: Intellect-Feeling-Will. Since the aim of poetry is pleasure, not instruction, both intellect and will are eliminated, and emotion is the limited province of poetry. Poe was the first romantic expressionist in this country: the poet must not think in his poetry; he could be allowed to think only of the means by which the emotionally unthinking subject-matter reaches the reader as an effect. The intellect thus operates in technique but not in the poem itself.

It has not been pointed out by the biographers and critics that, although Poe attacked the genteel preaching of Longfellow and Lowell as the "heresy of the didactic," he was himself paradoxically a didactic poet, a grim and powerful one at that. He is constantly telling us that we are all alone, that beauty is evanescent, that the only immortality may be a vampirish return from the grave, into which we must sink again through eternity. In "The Haunted Palace" we are taught that the intellect cannot know either nature or other persons. In "The Conqueror Worm" we are taught that life is a "drama" in which we think we are the protagonists; but the actual hero is death in the guise of a gigantic Worm. This is the human "plot." If, as Poe says in *Eureka*, "the universe is a plot of God," and man participates in the plot as a conscious actor, then the purposeless activity of man has as its goal the horror of death and bodily corruption.

It is no wonder, then, that Poe wrote so few poems. There are not many ways to deliver his message of spiritual solipsism and physical decay if the poet limits himself to romantic expressionism. The "rhythmical creation of Beauty" means very little, if anything, as a general aesthetic principle; it means in Poe's poetry the expression of a Pure Emotion which creates in the reader a pure emotional effect, about which we must not think, and about which we must do nothing. Of the poems which I have mentioned as being among his best, there is no need to discuss at length "The Sleeper," which many critics consider a masterpiece. There is bad writing in it—"The lily lolls upon the wave"; "And this all solemn silentness"—yet it remains Poe's best treatment of the beautiful female corpse. The "lady" will be taken to a vault where her ancestors lie, against which she had "thrown, In childhood, many an idle stone." This is the only poem in which the dead lady has any life before her appearance on the bier or in the tomb. We can almost believe that she was at some remote time a human being; yet why at the end we are told that she was a "child of sin" I cannot discover.

If Poe wrote any "great" poems they are surely "The City in the Sea" and "The Raven." "The City in the Sea" was first published in 1831 as "The Doomed City"; revised and republished in 1836 as "The City of Sin"; "The City in the Sea" is the title in the 1845 edition of the poems. The recurrent symbolism of the vortex that one finds everywhere in the prose tales appears infrequently and incompletely in the poems; but here it receives its most powerful expression in verse. The nineteenth-century critics—Edmund Clarence Stedman, for example—thought the poem a masterpiece; Edwin Markham put it beside "Kubla Khan." But there is nowhere in the poem evidence of Coleridge's magisterial certainty and control. In the first five lines there is a doggerel movement—"Where the good and the bad and the worst and the best / Have gone to their eternal rest." I have written elsewhere that "everything in Poe is dead"; in this poem everything is dead; for the poem might be entitled "The City of Death." Here we go beyond the lovely dead woman to dead humanity; and all nature, as well, is dead. When this dead city slides into the sea we, presumably, go down with it into the vortex: into oblivion. This archetype of life after death is as old as recorded humanity. In Dante the sea to which we return is the will of God; in Poe it is a dire apocalyptic vision in which we suffer "inevitable annihilation."

*   *   *

In conclusion I can add very little to the criticism of "The Raven," a poem so badly, even vulgarly written in many passages that one wonders how it can be a great poem, which I believe it to be. We have here the two necessary elements—the beautiful, dead, "lost Lenore" and the *poète maudit* who with perfect literary tact is confronted with, I dare to say, the demon of the youthful poem "Alone." It is the same demon, this time come down from the clouds and taking the form of a bird that imitates human speech without knowing what the speech means:

And his eyes have all the seeming of a demon's that is dreaming . . .

This poem—a late poem, written in 1844—is the one poem by Poe which is not direct lyrical, or romantic, expressionism. It has dramatic form and progression: the poet conducts a dialogue with his demon; it is the only poem by Poe which leads the reader through an action. In classical terms, the plot is simple, not complex; it is a simple plot of

Recognition in which the poet, examining all the implications of the bird's "Nevermore," recognizes his doom.

Henry James said that admiration of Poe represented a "primitive stage of reflection" (p. 291). One agrees; but one must add that without primitive reflection, however one defines it, one cannot move on.

E. L. DOCTOROW

Our Edgar

Best known for his historical novels Ragtime *(1975) and* Billy Bathgate *(1989), both of which were made into Hollywood films, E. L. Doctorow (1931–2015) was the author of almost a dozen novels along with numerous stories and essays. Doctorow's parents named their son, Edgar Laurence, after Poe because of their own fondness for the writer. Doctorow recollects reading Poe at a young age, saying that Poe's work inspired him to become a writer. A professor of English at New York University, Doctorow unsuccessfully fought to preserve the house on 85 Amity Place, New York City, where Poe lived and which is now owned by NYU. But his admiration for Poe is coupled with no small degree of contempt, as Doctorow also describes Poe as the United States' "greatest bad writer." His description of Poe as "like some relatives who won't go away" captures the ambivalence that many readers feel toward Poe, too close to turn away but too uncouth to openly embrace. This essay was originally published in 2006 in the* Virginia Quarterly Review, *a literary quarterly founded in 1925 in connection with the University of Virginia.*

Edgar Allan Poe, that strange genius of a hack writer, lived in such a narcissistic cocoon of torment as to be all but blind to the booming American nation around him, and so, perversely, became a mythic presence in the American literary consciousness.

Poe's life was an unremitting disaster. Orphaned at the age of two, he was the dysfunctional foster child of an unforgiving surrogate father. A gambler and a drinker, he was booted out of the University of Virginia. He took it on himself to drop out of West Point. When he married it was to a cousin, a tubercular child of thirteen. Committing himself to the freelancer's life, he lived at the edge of poverty. A Southerner, he stood forever outside the ruling literary establishment of New England.

Poe's baleful yet wary expression in his most famous photo shows a man who believed he was born to suffer. If circumstances in his life were not propitious to suffering he made sure to change them until they were. Deep in his understanding, almost as to be unconscious, was a respect for the driving power of his misery—that it could take manifold forms in ways he didn't even have to be aware of, as if not he but it could create. That goes well beyond his conscious understanding of what he called the Imp of the Perverse—the force within us that causes us to do just what brings on our destruction.

His fiction can be so spectacularly horror-ridden as to suggest its origin in his dreams. Premature burials, revenge murders, and multiple-personality disorders abound. In proportion to his total output, Poe kills more women than Shakespeare. He kills them and they come back. They haunt, they avenge, they forgive. They are born one from another and merge again in death. Alive they are entombed. Dead, they are dentally abused. Loved or hated, alive or ghostly, they are objects of intense devotion. He would claim, on occasion, to have written some of these pieces with enough distance to make him laugh. Another of his delusions. In his "Philosophy of Composition" he says the supreme subject for a poem is the death of a beautiful woman. It can be but it doesn't have to be. Another poet could write supremely of the death of a hired man. Another of the death of a civilization.[1] In fact, as a poet, our Edgar is not the poet Melville is, to say nothing of Whitman or Dickinson. He is not a major. He did not produce enough to be a major poet and he may even be too much of a prim prosodist to be considered a minor poet. "The Raven" is to poetry as Ravel's Bolero is to music: rhythmic and hypnotic on first hearing, a mere novelty ever after. Or evermore. . . .

I do not forget Poe wrote for a living. His output was prodigious—fiction, criticism, verse—and he was never unaware of what the market would entertain. (It was his lifelong dream to be the owner/publisher of a magazine.) So he was, even in the steepest, most driven examples of his dark tales, fully cognizant of the Gothic convention he was working. But if he wrote only for the money he would be like so many other hacks. If Poe is a hack he is a genius hack, genius being a kind of helplessness to do anything but flow through the brain circuits

---

[1] "Death of a hired man" is a reference to a poem by that name by Robert Frost (1874–1963). "The death of civilization" is a reference to a recurring motif in the poetry of T. S. Eliot. [Doctorow's note.]

it has made for itself. Again and again he invents the imagery for impossible love, for unrelenting hate, for doom and despair. His contributions to the short story are the unmodulated voice — he starts high and ends high — and the embellished situation that serves for a plot. He pours the universal dread of existence into the forms of gothic fiction; that is what he does and it is the deepest source of his literary identity. It is why, when we think of Poe, we think of "Ligeia" or "Usher," or "William Wilson," "The Cask of Amontillado" rather than his metaphysical treatise *Eureka*, or the adventures of *Arthur Gordon Pym*. He is a test-tube sample of the nature of creativity, if any scientist wanted to boil it down to its salts: how we can be writing with both faculties of the brain, the surface, editorial intellect, and the impulsive, not clearly understood hallucinatory life produced in the brain's deepest recesses. So Poe knew what he was doing and didn't know, at the same time. He is an allegory for all literary life.

*   *   *

W. H. Auden,[2] in his essay on Poe in *The Dyer's Hand*, believes Poe is ill-served by the attention readers give to the Gothic warhorses. He decides the tales of destructive passion, such as "The Fall of the House of Usher," and the stories of ratiocination, such as "The Purloined Letter," are of a piece. "The heroes of both exist as unitary states — Roderick Usher reasons as little as Auguste Dupin feels." And neither has what Auden calls "an historical existence."

But there is an almost narcotized dream-state imaging in the gothic pieces that even the fustian rhetoric cannot dim. Auden himself would seem to agree when he asserts that the "operatic prose" of Poe's horror tales is essential for preserving their illusion. All the more reason that readers would imprint on the supernatural stories of hideous passion and do no more than enjoy or admire the feats of ratiocination. We would still have Poe if he never wrote a detective story. But we would not have him without his dead women and rotting manses and vengeful maniacs.

We mark the worst of his writerly sins in the stories that constitute his quintessential achievement. His overwrought style is so filled with an essayist's rhetorical vines and brambles that you have to slash and hack if you're to make your way through the story. The verbosity, the undisciplined rhetoric, the drift into haranguing essay, the purple passages — in

[2]Wystan Hugh Auden (1907–1973), Anglo-American poet and critic.

sum, the grandiosity of his tales—can sometimes seem intended only to assure Poe of his own existence. I write therefore I am. The tales may differ according to the identity of their narrators, or the time that passes within each; there is always a crucial decor, and there is the loneliness of voice of the short story, the automatic circumscription of the surrounding world that comes from the brevity of the piece; and there is the drift to stasis, in a story such as "Usher," that is basically an elaborated situation. But a Poe production is always unmistakably his. To find a rationale for all his operatics in the so-called Europeanized bias of his writing is to make a mistake: Of a generation slightly in advance of Poe's own, Heinrich von Kleist in Germany was writing tales that, even in the heavily consonantal and syntactically burdensome German language, raced along from one lean hunting-dog sentence to the next.

*   *   *

Edgar Allan Poe was of the new American consciousness to a far greater extent than Fenimore Cooper. He is as much an exemplar of the new consciousness, as much a formative master of the New World consciousness as Thoreau, Emerson, Whitman, Dickinson, or Twain. Emotionally solipsistic as Poe was, and with little sympathy for the idea of a democratic republic, he is one of those American writers of the nineteenth century who are de facto prophets created by their new country to speak in its voice. They were not that far removed in time from the impertinent Revolution and the still breathtaking social reality of a land severed from kingship and so from the lineage claimed by kings. They understood freedom as unencumbered though perhaps unblessed by an ecclesiastical culture. Their personalities differed, and in literary address and in what interested them they couldn't have been more diverse. But each of their minds saw through to the metaphysical disquiet that comes with a secular Democracy, a country written down on paper, a country in a covenant not with God but with itself. And whether in pain, or gloom, or elation or morbidity or bitter satire, they accepted it.

These authors could disdain the democratic mob around them, as did Poe, who given all that room, all that sky and air, sent his words out from the sealed crypt of his own brain; or they could open their arms as rhapsodists, theologically self infatuated from the use of words, which was the case with Emerson; or they could be self-consecrating, as Walt Whitman certainly was, all his life the singer of himself. Twain, unlike Hawthorne, did not find the tragedy in churchly rectitude; he was a merciless skeptic for whom the ordinary pieties were a form of fraud.

Dickinson uses her words as stitches, as if life is a garment that needs mending. And in Herman Melville—well, there the reportage most dramatically enlarges upon Poe and anticipates much of our own. The universe he reports is as amoral and monstrous as the featureless megalithic head of the white whale.

All of these voices together, were they one, would suggest a bipolar mental disorder. Nevertheless they constitute the demanding literary project of a secular nation. Poe's work no less than the others' teases out the risky ontological premises of the Enlightenment. Whatever his or any of his fellow authors' religious hopes or conflicts might have been, as writers they prophesy the modernist future implicit, if not entirely intentional, in the documentations of the Founding Fathers.

The philosopher Richard Rorty has suggested that the metaphysic of the American civil religion is pragmatism. To temporize human affairs, to look not up for some applied celestial accreditation but to look forward, ground level, in the endless journey, to resist any authoritarian restriction on thought—that is the essence of the civil religion, an expansive human inquiry that sees humankind putting all the work and responsibility for the value of life on its own shoulders. Well, what is that idea, what *metaphor* (for it is more apt), than a son without a father or a mother, the orphan being forever without consolation for his existence, and the only love requisite to his longing beyond his reach? On his own Poe essayed a poetics, a psychology, a cosmology that, altogether, might be viewed as a grandiose attempt to fill in post-Enlightenment meaninglessness. It was irrepressible, wild, excessive, and petrified. His poetics, which anticipated the New Criticism by a century, makes of poetry a humanly made artifice of sounds and rhythms and images. The derived and grandiose boyish cosmology of *Eureka* is his Bible. And living in the freedom of the happiest and most advanced social constructions, the Democracy that Lincoln would call the last best hope of mankind, Edgar Poe, with his dark tales, laid out its unavoidable nightmares.

These are the stories of Edgar Allan Poe.
Not exactly the boy next door.[3]

---

[3] From Lou Reed's "Edgar Allan Poe," located on the singer's album dedicated to Poe, *The Raven* (2003).

J. GERALD KENNEDY

From Poe in Our Time

One of the foremost scholars of Poe, J. Gerald Kennedy is the Boyd Professor of English at Louisiana State University. He is the author and editor of several important books about Poe, including The Narrative of Arthur Gordon Pym and the Abyss of Interpretation *(1995);* Poe, Death, and the Life of Writing *(1987); and, most recently,* Poe and the Remapping of Antebellum Print Culture *(2012). The essay that follows was originally published as the introduction to his invaluable edited collection of essays about Poe for Oxford University Press,* A Historical Guide to Edgar Allan Poe. *He has also written extensively about Ernest Hemingway and F. Scott Fitzgerald.*

Despite persisting disagreement about Edgar Allan Poe's literary achievement, no American writer of the antebellum period enjoys greater current popularity and recognizability. One hundred fifty years after the author's death, cartoon characters Garfield and Bart Simpson entertain young television viewers by reciting "The Raven," and the new National Football League team in Baltimore owes its team nickname and logo to that famous poem. The compact disc "Tales of Mystery and Imagination" by the Alan Parsons Project has dazzled rock fans with its pulsating interpretations of Poe texts; such Roger Corman films as *The Fall of the House of Usher* and *The Masque of the Red Death* (both featuring Vincent Price) have become cult classics; and Generation-X readers, especially those attracted to the "Goth" counterculture, revel in Poe's dark fantasies. Apart from Frederick Douglass, he is the only American writer of his era yet featured on the popular Arts and Entertainment "Biography" series. Why does his work from the 1830s and 1840s seem so fresh and compelling to readers in the new millennium? Why has his influence on popular culture remained pervasive and enduring? Why does Poe haunt us still?

Like the enigma of "The Purloined Letter," the answers to these questions are both obvious and subtle. In the most immediate sense, Poe appeals to the popular imagination because he scares us to death. The yen for sensation feeds our fascination with terror; just as moviegoers rush to the latest horror film to be frightened out of their minds, so too they read Poe's hair-raising tales of shipwreck or premature burial to experience the frisson of near-encounters with annihilation.

Long ago Aristotle speculated that tragedy produced catharsis through an audience's sympathetic identification with the doomed hero: the spectacle of agony and death on some level frightens us, yet we feel cleansed by the sacrificial scene we have witnessed. Symbolically someone else has suffered in our place. Perhaps for the same reason a sensational tale like "The Masque of the Red Death" produces exhilaration when we emerge from its absorbing horror unscathed by the deadly pestilence. "Sensations are the great things after all," Poe's Mr. Blackwood advises Psyche Zenobia, the aspiring magazinist in "How to Write a Blackwood Article" (p. 64). Psychiatrist Herbert Hendin called the 1970s the "age of sensation," and his analysis of American life still seems accurate enough at century's end. Hendin contends that in a materialistic, success-oriented culture, the desire to be impervious to unsettling feelings, to control one's personal life by avoiding emotional commitments, produces a craving for escapist sensation: "Through different ways and in many forms people seek out fragmented sensory experience as a way of . . . escaping completely the involvement with feeling."[1] If Hendin's theory does not pertain to all readers of Poe, it nevertheless characterizes our own epoch in a way that explains the contemporaneity of the author's sensationalism.

But the reasons for Poe's continuing appeal are in fact more deeply rooted in American history and culture. Writing in the wake of Charles Brockden Brown, Catherine Maria Sedgwick, and James Fenimore Cooper, all of whom depicted episodes of bloody cruelty, Poe was yet the first important American writer to foreground violence and to probe its psychological origins. Especially in stories like "The Tell-Tale Heart" and "The Black Cat," he portrayed brutality from the subject position of the perpetrator, fetishizing the desire for power or "ascendancy" over an adversary. If, as Richard Slotkin has argued, the violence of American culture was initially imported in the name of God, wealth, and Anglo-Saxon civilization, then exercised in wresting the land itself from Native peoples, and finally domesticated in cruelties enacted upon African slaves to make that land profitable, then Poe's emphasis on murder, revenge, mutilation, and torture patently mirrors a deep-seated national disposition. We need to remind ourselves that he produced his violent fiction in the 1830s and 1840s, when the U.S. government was either confining Indians to reservations, "removing" them west of the Mississippi, or (in the case of the Seminoles) remorselessly decimating

---

[1] Herbert Hendin, *The Age of Sensation* (New York: McGraw-Hill, 1977), 325. [All notes in this selection are Kennedy's.]

them; this was the same era when the perpetuation and extension of slavery were being defended by Southern apologists and challenged by abolitionists determined to expose the barbarities of the "peculiar institution." As we see unmistakably in *The Narrative of Arthur Gordon Pym* (1838) and the unfinished "Journal of Julius Rodman," Poe was keenly conscious of both controversies and the hostilities they aroused.

As a crucial component of American identity, the "internal flaw of violence" has been traced by historian Richard Maxwell Brown to the frontier ethos of standing one's ground and meting out personal justice. Connecting the "glorified gunfighters" of the Wild West with U.S. military interventions in Korea, Vietnam, Grenada, and the Persian Gulf, Brown shows how the American repudiation of English common law, and specifically its obligation "to retreat 'to the wall' at one's back" before killing in self-defense, became in the nineteenth century, at fabled places like the O.K. Corral, a fierce cultural imperative to confront the enemy and slay him—not only to defend one's life but also to protect private property and capitalist values.[2] If Poe prefers European settings and avoids explicitly nationalistic subjects, his tales nevertheless render in graphic detail the quick American impulse to violence. When the narrator of "The Black Cat" buries an ax in his wife's brain or when Hop-Frog (in the tale by that name) incinerates the king and his seven ministers dressed as apes, Poe anatomizes the psychology of revenge, flaunts atrocity, and depicts the recrudescence of our national "internal flaw."

In a culture of hate crimes, automatic weapons, high school slaughter, and gang wars, violence seems ubiquitous and contagious, the handiest form of instant self-empowerment. Violence has now perhaps become so commonplace in American life that many cannot perceive its strangeness or singularity as a cultural trait. (Such is the ongoing frustration of those who would ban handguns and restrict the availability of all firearms.) The glorification of Rambo, the Terminator, or John McClane (the *Die Hard* hero)—all cool exponents of redemptive violence—temporarily fosters the illusion of blood justice and assuages our anxiety about the gratuitous, random violence abroad in the real world around us. Meanwhile, movies like *Pulp Fiction* or *Natural Born Killers* glamorize cold-blooded murder as the ultimate entertainment, while *Fargo* turns the shredding of a body into a visual gag. We need only return to Poe tales like "The Man That Was Used Up," which playfully reveals a military hero to be no more than a mutilated lump, or "A Predicament,"

---

[2]Richard Maxwell Brown, *No Duty to Retreat: Violence and Values in American History and Society* (New York: Oxford University Press, 1991), 4, 39, 156.

which makes a joke out of the narrator's decapitation, to appreciate the author's stunningly modern treatment of violence.

The curious modernity (or postmodernity) of Poe's writing derives, however, from more than his reliance upon sensation and violence. For example, his fascination with madness and perverseness resonates with our heightened Western, post-Freudian awareness of the unconscious and the irrational. From the Holocaust to Jonestown and Kosovo, much of the century's history seems inspired by mass insanity. Foucault argues that after Sade and Goya, we can trace the emergence of a madness in modern art that constitutes a judgment on the unreason of modernity itself: "The world that thought to measure and justify madness through psychology must justify itself before madness, since in its struggles and agonies it measures itself by the excess of works like those of Nietzsche, of Van Gogh, or Artaud."[3] In *Madness and Modernism*, psychologist Louis A. Sass describes a provocative parallel between schizophrenia and modern culture, suggesting that the twentieth century, characterized by "the pursuit of extremes, by exaggerated objectivist or subjectivist tendencies, or by unrestrained cerebralism or irrationalism," has assumed on a vast social scale many of the features of schizophrenic experience.[4] As one of the first writers to treat madness as a recurrent subject, Poe explores the varieties of insanity and illustrates symptomatic phobias, obsessions, and hallucinations in such narratives as "Berenice," "Ligeia," and "William Wilson." His most famous tale, "The Fall of the House of Usher," presents a multilayered allegory of the disordered mind in which the house itself may be understood as the domain of unreason, its physical collapse analogizing the psychological disintegration of Roderick Usher, who in turn metaphorizes his loss of reason in the poem "The Haunted Palace." The analogy extends to the burial of Usher's sister Madeline and her return from the underground vault, for the utter madness that she represents cannot be indefinitely repressed in the unconscious. Poe thus portrays in "Usher" a distinctly modern world that seems (to borrow Sass's terms) altogether solipsistic, dehumanized, and "derealized"—a realm of the bizarre.

. . . Relentlessly problematizing the distinction between madness and sanity, Poe anticipates the unreality of the twentieth century, in which megalomaniacs such as Adolf Hitler, Joseph Stalin, Pol Pot,

---

[3]Michel Foucault, *Madness and Civilization: A History of Insanity in the Age of Reason* (New York: Vintage, 1973), 289.

[4]Louis A. Sass, *Madness and Modernism: Insanity in the Light of Modern Art, Literature, and Thought* (New York: Basic Books, 1992), 38.

Saddam Hussein, and Slobodan Milosevic have reconstructed entire societies as paranoid formations, and in which deranged killers like Charles Manson or Jeffrey Dahmer have briefly become media celebrities in part because they personify the psychopathology of our own century of atrocity. When the narrator of "The Black Cat" describes the "spirit of perverseness" ("this unfathomable longing of the soul to *vex itself*—to offer violence to its own nature—to do wrong for the wrong's sake only" [p. 180]), he may be said to describe a defining force in modern culture.

Poe's appeal to late-twentieth-century readers, however, derives not only from his projections of violence or insanity but also from his articulations of estrangement and doubt. It has been nearly fifty years since David Riesman's *Lonely Crowd* described the alienation of modern urban life, and more recent studies—like Robert N. Bellah's much-discussed *Habits of the Heart*—have documented the fragile, often superficial nature of postmodern community, as well as the recurrent American tendency toward solitude about which Crevecoeur worried two centuries ago. Estrangement figures importantly, of course, in Poe's narrative scheme, and his isolated, reclusive protagonists rarely participate in the activities of a larger society. While this tendency may be ascribed to his Gothic models, it also reflects contemporary cultural and socioeconomic changes. The foster son of a dry-goods merchant, Poe witnessed the "market revolution" (as Charles Sellers terms it) that saw a family-based subsistence economy give way to an aggressive capitalist system bringing entrepreneurial opportunity but also cutthroat competition and profit-driven exploitation. These same pressures gripped the literary world: without international copyright laws, publishers "pirated" works by celebrated British novelists and compelled American authors to write for the periodical market. As he continued the futile quest for support of his own monthly journal, Poe proclaimed: "The whole tendency of the age is Magazine-ward" (*ER* 1414). In satires like "The Business Man" and "Diddling," however, he exposed the crass, rapacious nature of nascent capitalism, and he recognized the intractably adversarial nature of economic rivalries—including conflicts between periodical owner-publishers and authors like himself, obliged to labor in what he bitterly called "the magazine prison house."

As a denizen of Philadelphia and New York, the author was also fascinated by the material aggregation of capital—the construction of the modern industrial city—and wrote about such phenomena as the omnibus, street paving, and cabs, although he surmised at once the social consequences of urban growth and the anomie that it would foster. His tale "The Man of the Crowd" conveys a prescient awareness of metropolitan alienation, in which a voyeuristic narrator regards passersby simply as social types, describes the city as a desolate, dehumanized place, and fixes his attention upon a singular character who seems paradoxically to personify both absolute loneliness and fear of solitude. This stranger who speaks to no one is said to be "the type and the genius of deep crime" because he "refuses to be alone" (p. 128). As we see in the Dupin detective stories, all set in Paris, Poe associated the modern city with the proliferation of crime and the detective forces required to contend with the volume, variety, and impersonality of urban felonies. The mutilation of Madame L'Espanaye and her daughter in "The Murders in the Rue Morgue" and the discovery of a young woman's waterlogged corpse in "The Mystery of Marie Roget" associate horrific violence with a specifically urban context. In this sense Poe anticipates the grim vision of contemporary television cop shows like *N.Y.P.D. Blue* or *Homicide*, in which the city figures as a lonely, dangerous place inhabited by ruthless, inhuman types ready to kill anyone who gets in their way.

Although C. Auguste Dupin advises the prefect of police and gathers information from the Parisian newspapers, there is little sense here or elsewhere in Poe of productive social relations. Indeed, the vast majority of his tales represent alienated figures ensconced in remote, indefinite settings, absorbed in private fantasies or obsessions—the nineteenth-century equivalent of cyberspace. Jean Baudrillard has declared that the dominance of electronic mass media and the profusion of mass culture in postmodernity mark the end of the social and the disruption of the political through the proliferation of "simulacra," digitized images that problematize the real as they construct a virtual reality. As Shawn Rosenheim and Terence Whalen have both suggested in recent books, Poe brilliantly foresaw the information age, the computer, and the use of code or encryption to achieve new forms of privileged communication. Rosenheim has emphasized the connections between Poe's obsession with cryptography and the development of modern surveillance and intelligence gathering. Whalen underscores the author's complicated desire to protect his privacy while appealing to a mass public, and his discussion of Poe and Charles Babbage (who devised an early calculating machine) suggests that the magazinist anticipated the rise of an economy based on the use-value of information. Now that the Internet has made this unimaginable flow of data a reality, more people communicate with each other than ever before, but they do so privately and electronically, gazing at a cathode-ray tube that simulates presence and social interaction while leaving the user in perfect solitude. . . .

SCOTT PEEPLES

Lionizing: Poe as Cultural Signifier

Scott Peeples is professor of English at the College of Charleston. He has written two important books about Poe, Edgar Allan Poe Revisited *(1998) and* The Afterlife of Edgar Allan Poe *(2004), from which the following essay is taken and to which we refer readers interested in delving further into the story of Poe's critical reputation. Peeples's dissertation at Louisiana State University was directed by J. Gerald Kennedy.* The Afterlife of Edgar Allan Poe *won the Patrick F. Quinn Award for a Distinguished Book of Poe Scholarship.*

Not long after my book *Edgar Allan Poe Revisited* was published, the manager of a Montblanc boutique contacted me about giving a talk to tie in with their new Meisterstück Edgar Allan Poe writing instrument. Eager to promote my book and secretly hoping for a deep discount, I gave her a copy to use as part of a window display and spent a half hour telling her about Poe's interest in autography, his own meticulous penmanship, his dreams of anastatic printing allowing writers to self-publish without typesetting, the implications of Poe's titling his prospective magazine first the *Penn*, then the *Stylus*, and so on. The relationship never got past that meeting: my hopes of owning a Montblanc pen were unrealized, the manager kept a copy of my book but never displayed it, and there was no public lecture on Poe and pens. More recently, a middle school teacher asked if I would come talk to two hundred seventh graders about Poe; after discussing a few possible dates, we settled on October 31. Then she asked if I generally dressed up as Poe for these occasions.

I mention these incidents not to emphasize the distance between the academic Poe and the pop-culture Poe, but to help make the case that the two are in close proximity. It is easy to imagine a bearded, bespectacled English professor—me, for instance—sarcastically dismissing, say, Michael Jackson's ambition of playing Poe. But that same professor might also find himself talking seriously about how Poe scholarship might help sell ridiculously expensive pens or wondering if Michael Jackson still needs a consultant. And while I did not portray Poe for the seventh grade, I did take along a bag of visual aids and hand props; after my presentation, I joined my host's home room to watch *The Simpsons'* rendition of "The Raven." It is true that the current popular image of Poe—drug abuser as well as alcoholic, lunatic, and Gothicist to the exclusion of all else—is at odds with most of the academic writing I have described in the last three chapters. At the same time, the Poe whose caricature decorates Barnes & Noble shopping bags has always drawn students to his work, helped keep him in print, made publishers a little more interested even in academic writing about him. But beyond that, scholars in recent years have been paying more attention to what might be called "the Poe effect," the creation and maintenance of Poe's image, the various ways this image interacts with popular culture and with Poe's writing. As Mark Neimeyer puts it, "the popular exploitation of Poe can be seen as adding another dimension to the element of the uncanny already present in the author's writings since these productions are all strangely Poe and not Poe at the same time."[1]

This recent interest in the Poe effect has occurred largely because of the trends discussed in the previous chapter. Research emphasizing the "cultural work" of fiction and poetry has helped blur the boundaries between high and middle and low brow, between literary text and subliterary context; for example, although many more academic essays continue to be written on Poe's "The Fall of the House of Usher," serious scholarly attention is also paid to Roger Corman's low-budget film adaptations of "Usher" and other Poe tales.[2] Don G. Smith's *The Poe Cinema* attests not only to the popularity of Poe's mystique as a source for films but also interest in the films themselves. And websites such as Peter Forrest's *House of Usher* and *The Poe Decoder* combine emphasis on academic scholarship and sightings of Poe in the broader cultural landscape.[3] At the 2002 International Poe Conference sponsored by the Poe Studies Association, panelists presented work on Poe's connections to the World Wrestling Federation, hard-boiled detective fiction, Dario Argento's slasher films, and Bob Dylan. At the same conference, guest speaker E. L. Doctorow angered much of the audience by referring to Poe as "our best bad writer." Many must have feared that the old battle over Poe's "place"

---

[1]Mark Neimeyer, "Poe and Popular Culture," in *The Cambridge Companion to Edgar Allan Poe*, ed. Kevin J. Hayes (Cambridge: Cambridge UP, 2002), 222. [Unless otherwise indicated, all notes are Peeples's.]

[2]See, for instance, Cyndy Hendershot, "Domesticity and Horror in House of Usher and Village of the Damned," *Quarterly Review of Film and Video* 17 (2000): 221–27, and Maren Longbella's M.A. thesis "Poe, Corman, Todorov: The Fantastic from Literature to Film" (U of North Dakota, 1990), as well as Don G. Smith's discussions of Corman's films in *The Poe Cinema: A Critical Filmography of Theatrical Releases Based on the Works of Edgar Allan Poe* (Jefferson, NC, and London: McFarland, 1999).

[3]As of this writing, the best clearinghouse for Poe websites is Heyward Ehrlich's "A Poe Webliography: Edgar Allan Poe on the Internet," http://andromeda.rutgers.edu /~ehrlich/poesites.html.

would have to be fought yet again—even our best bad writer would not rank in the top ten, or even top thirty. But this characterization, echoing as it does the earlier assessments by T. S. Eliot and Allen Tate, deserves serious consideration, however much one admires Poe's writing. I believe Doctorow was attempting to explain Poe in terms other than literary greatness as usually conceived. Perhaps his point was not to demote Poe to a lower tier of the pantheon but to try to get at why Poe's writing defies the usual assessments of literary merit, making him impossible to rank; to try to understand why, despite his frequent technical clumsiness, Poe sticks with so many readers, particularly readers who happen to be writers, graphic artists, musicians, filmmakers, and so on. The cultural-studies Poe scholars share that interest: why is Poe so adaptable, and in what surprising forms do his work and image appear? More specifically, how is Poe reinterpreted by Vincent Price or Lou Reed? Why does Poe appear in mainstream culture as a misunderstood Southern Romantic Poet in the 1900s and as the godfather of slasher films half a century later? If, as Allen Ginsberg claimed, "Everything leads to Poe," the paths connecting Poe to everything must be worth exploring.

* * *

By [1936], Poe's image was shifting decisively from the tortured romantic poet to the godfather of the macabre, thanks largely to a trio of Universal films starring Bela Lugosi and Boris Karloff: *The Murders in the Rue Morgue* (1932), *The Black Cat* (1934), and *The Raven* (1935). About two dozen Poe-related films had been made by the early 1930s, but these Hollywood blockbusters, produced during the first golden age of horror films, cemented Poe's place in modern pop culture. None of the three had much in common with the works from which they took their titles, but, particularly in the case of *The Raven*, they did much to reshape Poe's image.

Their most notable American predecessor is D. W. Griffith's *The Avenging Conscience* (1915), a film that weaves together several Poe stories, primarily "The Tell-Tale Heart," into a cautionary tale in which a young man apparently murders his uncle/guardian to clear the way for marriage and freedom.[4] But luckily for the young man, his crime, as

---

[4]Griffith directed the first Poe biopic, the one-reel *Edgar Allan Poe*, in 1909, in which Poe writes "The Raven" after a raven flies into his room, then hurries out to sell the poem to buy food and medicine for the dying Virginia (Smith, *The Poe Cinema* 8).

well as his eventual exposure, the suicide of his would-be bride Annabel, and the frightening visions of devils who torment him in retribution, all turn out to be a dream; he awakens grateful and hopeful of a bright future. *The Avenging Conscience* is ahead of its time in its emphasis on Poe's macabre fiction, but to the extent that it creates any image of Poe, it is that of a moralist: murder and hellish retribution are contained within the dream, employed strictly as a warning. At the end of the film, we are surprised not only to learn that most of the action has been a dream but that the dreamer is in fact Poe, and this Poe is after all a romantic poet: he is last seen lying by a river, reading lines from "Annabel Lee" to his future wife.

In contrast, Universal's *The Raven*, directed by Louis Friedlander, interprets both the title poem and Poe's fiction as if its creator were the Marquis de Sade.[5] Lugosi plays Dr. Richard Vollin, a mad genius whose twin obsessions are Poe and torture. He first appears in the film reciting "The Raven" as the camera moves back from the image of a gigantic shadow on the wall cast by the statuette of a raven on his desk. "The raven," he tells a visitor, "is my talisman." Later, he interprets the poem for a group of guests, some of whom he plans to torture and kill (with the help of Karloff's character, Edmund Bateman). He explains that the raven represents Poe's torment over being deprived of the love of his life, but he strays somewhat from the text: "When a man of genius is denied of his great love, he goes mad. His brain . . . is tortured. So he begins to think of torture—torture for those who have tortured him."

Of course, this is just what he has in mind for Judge Thatcher, who is trying to protect his daughter from Vollin, as well as the daughter's fiancé and the daughter herself. To help with the dirty work, he has entrapped Bateman, an escaped convict, who poses as his servant until the guests retire and the mayhem begins. Vollin explains Bateman's hideous appearance to his guests: during the war, "Arab bandits . . . mutilated him and tortured him. They have a genius for devising torture. It's almost the equal of Edgar Allan Poe." But in fact Vollin himself has mutilated Bateman, and he seeks to replicate Poe's tortures in his vengeful scheme. Since there is actually little torture in Poe's plots, Vollin draws inspiration from only one story, "The Pit and the Pendulum." The father gets the pendulum, while the lovers are to be crushed in a room with enclosing walls (there is no pit, however). At the height of his maniacal glee, Vollin declares, "Poe conceived it. I have done it, Bateman! Poe, you are

---

[5] Marquis de Sade (1740–1814), French politician and writer, most famous for his novels celebrating libertinism, including *Justine* (1791).

avenged!" Vollin thinks the spirit of Poe lives in him, and the film does nothing to contradict that belief. No one points out, for instance, that the other torture devices scattered around Vollin's basement have no relation to anything in Poe's fiction, much less Poe's personal desires. At this moment, though, Poe becomes a byword for gothic horror among moviegoers. As Neimeyer observes, *The Raven* is not only about a kind of Poe-esque madness but perhaps "just as much about a latter-day popular obsession with Poe, a sort of metafictional comment on Hollywood's and, more generally, popular culture's focus on and exploitation of frequently distorted views of the writer and his works."[6] Indeed, filmmakers, playwrights, graphic artists, and teachers have followed Dr. Vollin's lead in making "Poe" signify torture, murder, insanity, and perversity.

Especially filmmakers—and especially those at American International Pictures, which made thirteen Poe-inspired films between 1960 and 1971, most of them directed by Roger Corman and starring Vincent Price.[7] Universal had used Poe's name to market the Lugosi films in the 1930s, but by the 1960s, Poe's reputation was sufficiently gothicized that AIP made his association with horror the primary focus of their ad campaigns. The trailer for *The Masque of the Red Death* promises "A Masquerade of the Macabre / An Orgy of Savage Lusts / Conceived by the Master Designer of Evil Desires / Edgar Allan Poe." The *Premature Burial* trailer explains, "Only Edgar Allan Poe, who knew intimately the tortures of madness, could create such ever-increasing suspense." Some of the films deviate considerably from the plots of Poe's stories, while others ignore them altogether, as the series solidified the false impression of Poe as a writer of narrow range: the macabre, savage lusts, evil desires. AIP even published novelizations of the screenplays, so that Poe's new fans could buy and read *The Pit and the Pendulum* by Lee Sheridan and Richard Matheson.

While the AIP films were consistently unfaithful to their literary source material, they were faithful to their own advertising. In *Masque of the Red Death*, Price's Prospero casually orders the torture of prisoners, shoots an arrow into the neck of a nobleman who begs entrance into his castle, commands revelers to imitate the animals he thinks they resemble, and so on. (The savage lusts are more implied than depicted, thanks to the production code prohibiting onscreen sex or nudity.) The

---

[6] Mark Neimeyer, "Poe and Popular Culture," 217.

[7] Corman directed eight of the AIP Poe films; Price starred in eleven of them, including seven of the eight directed by Corman (Mark Neimeyer, "Poe and Popular Culture," in *The Cambridge Companion to Edgar Allan Poe*, ed. Kevin J. Hayes [Cambridge and New York: Cambridge UP, 2002], n. 224). [Editors' note.]

titillation of sex and torture also drive Corman's *The Pit and the Pendulum*, in which one of Price's characters (he plays both father and son) tortures and kills his wife and brother for committing adultery. In Corman's films, torture epitomizes the broader presence of "evil," a word Poe generally stayed away from. Prospero's Satan-worship, for instance, plays a large part in Corman's *Masque*, although Poe makes no reference to it. Roderick Usher, standing in a room hung with portraits of his ancestors, tells his visitor, "Evil is not just a word. It is a reality. . . . It can be created, it was created by these people." As is never the case in Poe's fiction, "evil" is its own explanation.

As much as these films distort the stories and play to the lowest common gothic denominators, they remain popular even among academics. As Neimeyer argues, Corman and Price's work "is one of the highpoints in the commodification of Poe, imposing a theatrically gothic aspect on the writings, much in the tradition of Victorian illustrations, and making him a favorite to a wide range of audiences."[8] Price's charismatic performances often transcend the clumsy scripts, and Corman certainly knew how to make a visual impact despite modest budgets. The films are always colorful but claustrophobic: they might not follow Poe's plots or his intellectual or psychological twists and turns, but the best ones do *look* like Poe stories. Indeed, the ambitious yet low-budget feel of the Poe series (and the rest of Corman's oeuvre) anticipated the aesthetic of much independent film of the late twentieth and early twenty-first centuries. Perhaps for that reason, Corman's work has inspired a number of scholarly books, articles, and dissertations, again demonstrating the dissolving of boundaries between academic and popular cultures. Despite their availability on VHS and DVD, these films that provided shared cultural (semi-)literacy for baby boomers are little-known to high school and college students of the twenty-first century; even so, they fueled Poe's continued popularity and shaped an enduring, if somewhat misleading, image of his works. In its second and third generations, this image has taken the form of Eric Draven (played by Brandon Lee) in the 1994 film *The Crow*, the WWF star known as Raven, and the Baltimore NFL team, all of which, like the 1934 film, transform a poem about "mournful and neverending remembrance" (as Poe described it) into a sinister, violent figure (albeit one you might want to root for).[9] It shows up in countless

[8] Mark Neimeyer, "Poe and Popular Culture," 218.
[9] At Maryland Public Television's impressive "Knowing Poe" website, one can watch a video of members of the Baltimore Ravens reciting "Quoth the raven, 'Nevermore.'" http://knowingpoe.thinkport.org/library/news/ravens.asp.

productions—stage, screen, website, and print—throughout the world. (To give one example, I saw a lavish Catalan musical entitled *Poe* in Barcelona in 2002, based loosely on "The Fall of the House of Usher" but, with its employment of demons, a dream sequence, torture chamber, and sexual content, clearly inspired by Poe-related films more than by Poe's writing.)

At about the same time Poe became a staple of B-movie horror, he found another pop-culture niche in comic books ranging from *Classics Illustrated* to *Tales from the Crypt*. Poe's tales were ideally suited to the former publication, which attempted to attract young readers to classic literature; *CI* adapted "The Pit and the Pendulum," "Hans Pfaall," and "Usher" in the August 1947 number and "The Gold-Bug," "The Tell-Tale Heart," and "The Cask of Amontillado" in June 1951.[10] Poe became a favorite of the less staid, more graphically compelling horror comics in the 1950s and 1960s: *The Haunt of Fear, Nightmare, Chilling Tales, Creepy, Eerie, Chamber of Darkness*, and so on.[11] Thomas Inge argues that "[w]ithout Poe, the entire horror genre of the comic book might not have developed as it did," but the corollary could also be argued—that without horror comics, Poe's late-twentieth-century image might not have developed as it did. While slightly more faithful to Poe's plots than films tended to be, the horror comics' artists played up the sex and violence more than even Corman did. Popular magazine fiction from this period reinforced Poe's gothic image: in Manly Wade Wellman's "When It Was Moonlight" (published in the fantasy magazine *Unknown* in 1940), Poe investigates a case of premature burial only to discover—and vanquish—a female vampire, while Michael Avallone's "The Man Who Thought He Was Poe" (*Tales of the Frightened*, 1957) features a Poe aficionado who plots his wife's murder, only to be tricked by her and entombed in a refrigerator.

Comic and graphic artists, as well as popular fiction writers, continue to gravitate toward Poe. "The Raven and Other Poems" relaunched *Classics Illustrated* in 1990, with "The Fall of the House of Usher" appearing later that year. Jason Asala began a Poe comics serial in 1996, using Poe as a fictional main character whose adventures allude to Poe stories, and in 1997 Maxon Crumb released a book of his interpretations of seven stories and poems. More recently, *Rosebud Graphic Classics*

---

[10] Earlier, in 1944, "Annabel Lee," "The Bells," and "The Murders in the Rue Morgue" had appeared in separate issues. See M. Thomas Inge, "Poe and the Comics Connection," *Edgar Allan Poe Review* 2.1 (2001): 5.

[11] Inge, "Poe and the Comics Connection," 8–13.

devoted its first issue (2001) to Poe, with illustrations by Crumb, Rick Geary, Gahan Wilson, and others. The illustrations range from deliberately silly to sinister, but, in a departure from earlier comic book practice, nearly all accompany original Poe text.[12]

* * *

Alfred Hitchcock, who, like Poe, was a serious, multi-dimensional artist with a one-dimensional popular reputation, expressed his admiration of Poe in a 1960 article: "[I]t's because I liked Edgar Allan Poe's stories so much that I began to make suspense films. Without wanting to seem immodest, I can't help but compare what I try to put into my films with what Poe put in his stories; a perfectly unbelievable story recounted to readers with such a hallucinatory logic that one has the impression that this same story can happen to you tomorrow."[13] In a recent article comparing Hitchcock and Nabokov, James A. Davidson discusses Poe as their most significant common literary influence. While Davidson does not explicitly link Poe to the other commonalities he sees in Hitchcock and Nabokov — game theory, cameo appearances and self-reference, use of the doppelgänger and unreliable narrator — they are all prominent in Poe's work as well. Davidson points out that in *Marnie*, Hitchcock alludes to Poe by giving the title character the last name of Edgar (a change from the book on which the film is based) and sets the action in three cities and one state in which Poe lived: Baltimore, New York, Philadelphia, and Virginia. Perhaps Hitchcock also had Poe biography in mind when he chose a story in which childhood trauma (an assault on the mother, as opposed to Poe's mother's death) creates psychological disorders in the adult Marnie Edgar. Otherwise, despite the Poe allusions, Marnie is less Poe-esque than, for instance, *Psycho*, which places Norman Bates in a role similar to the narrators of "The Tell-Tale

[12]The exceptions are Geary's "Tell-Tale Heart," which excerpts Poe's story, Spain Rodriguez's "The Inheritance of Rufus Griswold," and Clive Barker and Mark A. Nelson's "New Murders in the Rue Morgue," with text originally published by Barker in 1984. The most notable inheritor of the pulp-Poe tradition is Stephen King, who, for instance, reworked "The Cask of Amontillado" as "Dolan's Cadillac" (1989). On popular fiction that refers to or is obviously indebted to Poe, see Tony Magistrale and Sidney Poger, *Poe's Children* (New York: Peter Lang, 1999), as well as John E. Reilly's "Poe and Imaginative Literature" and his essays, "Poe in American Drama: Versions of the Man," in *Poe and Our Times*, ed. Benjamin F. Fisher (Baltimore: Edgar Allan Poe Society, 1986), 18–31, and "Poe in Literature and Popular Culture," in *A Companion to Poe Studies*, ed. Eric W. Carlson (Westport, CT: Greenwood, 1996), 471–93.

[13]Sidney Gottlieb, ed., *Hitchcock on Hitchcock* (Berkeley: University of California Press, 1997), 143.

Heart" and "The Black Cat," or *Vertigo*, with its emphasis on obsession, doubling, and the fantasy of a woman returning from the dead.

Another intriguing instance of an experimental filmmaker explicitly referencing Poe is Federico Fellini's short film "Toby Dammitt," the last of the trilogy making up *Histoires Extraordinaires* (1967; released in the U.S. as *Spirits of the Dead*). The first two films, Roger Vadim's "Metzengerstein" and Louis Malle's "William Wilson," are relatively faithful to Poe's stories, although both are more sexually provocative than anything in Poe. "Toby Dammitt," as indicated in the film's titles, is "liberally adapted from 'Don't Wager Your Head to the Devil,'" which is itself a translation of a translation of Poe's title "Never Bet the Devil Your Head." Like Poe's story, Fellini's film ends with a man named Toby Dammit being decapitated by a hidden cable as he attempts a daring stunt; and in both, the devil walks off with the head. Fellini's Toby (Terence Stamp), however, is a hedonistic, alcoholic young actor just arrived in Rome to work on a film, a "Catholic western" in which he will presumably play Christ. After being hounded by photographers at the airport, then interviewed on an inane television show and honored at a nightmarish parody of an awards ceremony (the Italian Oscars, or "Golden She-Wolves"), Dammit races out of town in a new Ferrari. He ends up at a bridge that has been partially washed away, creating a chasm, and on the other side he sees a young girl dressed in white and playing with a large white ball. He had seen this vision before, on his arrival at the airport, and had told the TV interviewer that "for me, the devil is friendly and joyful. He's a little girl." He tries to jump the chasm but of course doesn't see the cable stretched across it.

Although Fellini seems concerned primarily with satirizing the movie industry and celebrity culture, he also evokes sympathy for Dammit, a Shakespearean actor on the skids who is victimized by fawning but demanding show-business people as well as his own demons. During the awards ceremony, a beautiful, mysterious woman approaches him and immediately pledges herself to him: "I'll take care of you always. . . . You won't be alone anymore because I'll be with you always. Whenever you put out your hand, you will find my hand." Although he nods off as she finishes this speech (Was she a dream all along? A dream within a dream?), he clearly longs for the stability she spoke of: "A wonderful woman . . . she took my hand. She stroked my hand. She said, 'I'm here for you. I'm the woman of your dreams.' But I'm not waiting for you." Dammit fits the romantic artist role that Poe himself tried to appropriate from Byron and that Baudelaire successfully promoted after Poe's death. Already an old story by 1967, it has become even more familiar after the premature deaths of self-destructive visionary rock stars, Jim Morrison and Kurt Cobain in particular: a young, hedonistic, world-weary male artist, uncomfortable with celebrity, pursued by demons, in desperate need of a nurturing woman, kills himself rather than witness his own decline. Don G. Smith rightly observes that "the image of the pale, silver-haired, red-lipped child as Satan will haunt viewers for a very long time," but equally haunting is the long sequence leading up to that final frame, in which Dammit's face and maniacal laughter reveal his total desperation: having been a zombie throughout the film, he comes to life only as he races toward his death.

Although I have tried to distinguish what I see as more creative uses of Poe from the generally formulaic works of melodramatic stage biographies, horror movies, and mystery novels, I still contend that no rigid line can be drawn between the pop-culture Poe and the academic or avant-garde Poe. For instance, as popular as Fellini is, he is regarded as an art-film director today, especially in the U.S., yet when "Toby Dammit" was marketed as part of *Spirits of the Dead*, American International, its U.S. distributor, billed the trilogy as another in the series of titillating B-movies: "Edgar Allan Poe's Ultimate Orgy. An adventure in terror beyond your wildest nightmares."[14] Other examples are easy to find. Dario Argento's film *Opera* (1987), which not only alludes to Poe's fiction but, according to film critic Michael Sevastakis, "reaches a visual equivalent of Poe's elegantly wrought prose style," combines the aesthetics of low-budget slasher films with surrealism and Hitchcockian symbolism.[15] *The Simpsons'* interpretation of "The Raven" (1990) with James Earl Jones has probably been watched by more people than any other adaptation of a Poe work, and yet some of its biggest fans are professors who relish, for instance, the postmodern humor of Homer-as-narrator reading a book entitled "Forgotten Lore." One could argue that Matt Groening's parodic treatment of the poem is appropriate to its almost comically overwrought style (and yet it still scares Homer). Lou Reed and Robert Wilson's *POEtry* (2001), a rock opera based on Poe's life and

[14]Smith, *The Poe Cinema*, 186.

[15]Michael Sevastakis, "A Dangerous Mind: Dario Argento's Opera (1987)." *Kinoeye*, 24 June 2002. 28 paragraphs. Accessed 16 May 2003. http://www.kinoeye.org/02/12/sevastakis12.html. Sevastakis notes that Argento "has always felt 'a great affinity with Poe,' saying 'I understand his pain.' His notorious declaration, 'I like women, especially beautiful ones . . . being murdered . . . ,' has been coupled with Poe's infamous dictum, 'The death of a beautiful woman is, unquestionably, the most poetical topic in the world.'" I am also indebted to John Rocco's presentation, "The Origin of All Horror: Poe and Narrative Film from Griffith to Hitchcock to Argento," International Edgar Allan Poe Conference, Towson, MD, 4 October 2002.

works, has one foot in the avant-garde and one foot in mainstream rock and roll, like much of Reed's work. On *The Raven* (2003), the double-CD spinoff of *POEtry*, Reed adapts Poe to his personal mythology, emphasizing self-destructive impulses, the unleashing of repressed desires, and the guilt that follows. The rewrites of Poe poems and stories (including "The Raven") are for the most part bathetic, but some of Reed's original songs with thematic links to Poe work better. On "Guilty," Reed declaims over a tight rock groove and Ornette Coleman's beautifully off-kilter saxophone: "Guilty / I'm paralyzed with guilt / It runs through me like rain through silk / Guilty / My mind won't leave me alone / My teeth rot and my lips start to foam / 'Cause I'm so guilty . . . What did I say? What did I do? / Did I ever do it to you? / Don't turn your back / I can't look you in the eye / I—I—I—I guess I'm guilty as charged." Unfortunately, despite Reed's obviously sincere identification with Poe, most of *The Raven* is as pretentious and shallow as the previous grand attempt at a Poe-rock concept album, the Alan Parsons Project's *Tales of Mystery and Imagination* (1976).[16]

One final example, returning to the 2002 International Poe Conference: the night before E. L. Doctorow's talk, the conference participants attended a performance of "Three Tales by Poe" ("MS. Found in a Bottle," "The Man of the Crowd," and "The Tell-Tale Heart") presented by Puppetsweat Theater, a group that combines shadow puppetry with video, original soundtracks, and live narration. Their performance was rigidly faithful to the texts and easily accessible—they would have been a hit at the middle school where I struggled with my hand props. But at the same time, their interpretations of the stories were original and visually compelling in the manner of expressionist cinema. The cutouts used to cast shadows on a large screen were held by dancers who created various effects with the positioning of the props and with the motions of their bodies. The direction emphasized the long periods of inactivity and waiting in "The Man of the Crowd" and "The Tell-Tale Heart," creating palpable suspense. "The Man of the Crowd" featured the disconcerting image of a throng of men in bowler hats walking down a city street, each of them with Poe's face superimposed on their own. Meanwhile, in a long period without narration, the soundtrack consisted of almost whispered, rhythmic vocal sounds that

[16]A more successful Poe project by contemporary musicians and actors is *Closed on Account of Rabies* (Paris/Mouth Almighty/Mercury Records, 1997), produced by Hal Willner, who also produced Reed's *The Raven*. Most of the double-CD consists of unabridged readings of Poe's works with musical settings. Readers include Iggy Pop, Marianne Faithfull, Dr. John, and Christopher Walken.

turned out to be the recorded text of the story with the vowels removed from the speaker's voice. This combination of effects captured perfectly the disconcerting, claustrophobic feel of Poe's story.

. . . [T]here are as many pop-culture Poes as there are lit-crit Poes, as his image and his works have accommodated—or been forced to accommodate—changing times and a variety of approaches. Why has Poe proved so resilient, so present, over 150 years after his death? Gerald Kennedy suggests that Poe, writing "at the historical moment when public education and a secular, capitalistic mass culture had begun to supplant organized religion as the principal influences of thought and belief," simply anticipated a number of the predicaments and preoccupations of modern culture,[17] including dislocation from history, spiritual uncertainty and death anxiety, and a fascination with science, exploration, and information. Shawn Rosenheim's book *The Cryptographic Imagination: From Edgar Poe to the Internet* (1997) places Poe at the center of a history of encoding and decoding, with clear implications for his current academic importance and wider popularity: "Detective fiction and science fiction are among the most popular literary forms of the last three centuries; by tracing their origins back to the cryptographic values encoded in their formation, we discover specific links among cryptography, Poe's innovations in genre, and the effects of technology on literature" (3). In short, Poe continues to fascinate a wide range of readers and popular culture continues to reinvent him because Poe's work took off in so many directions, which is why "everything leads to Poe." Strictly as an icon, Poe is a marketer's dream, especially after Lugosi and Price: his name, even his face, simultaneously signifies the thrill of a campfire ghost story and the erudition of great literature.[18] If that pairing seems paradoxical, the paradox is fitting for a writer who, in his literary theory and ambitions as a magazinist sought to unite elite literary taste with bad taste, which he saw as crucial to mass circulation. In 1835, Poe defended the horrific conclusion of his story "Berenice" to his prudent future employer T. W. White, owner of the *Southern Literary Messenger*: "[T]o be appreciated you must be read, and these things are invariably sought after with avidity" (*L* 1:58). Over a century and a half later, they still are.

---

[17] J. Gerald Kennedy, ed., *A Historical Guide to Edgar Allan Poe* (New York: Oxford University Press, 2001), 14.

[18] Neimeyer, "Poe and Popular Culture," 206.

The Controversy over Race; or, What Did Poe Have to Say about African Americans and Slavery?

As we saw in the previous section, for many decades the debate surrounding Poe largely focused on issues of aesthetics and his place in the pantheon of great American writers. While this discussion continues to be a fruitful one for reasons addressed by both Kennedy and Peeples in their contributions to that section, Poe's place in the pantheon is now fully secure.

Well into the twentieth century, Poe was defined by both his fans and detractors as a writer largely disconnected or disinterested in the larger social and political concerns of his day. Canonized during a period in which the dominant critical methodology in American criticism largely eschewed historical contexts in favor of formal attention to the text itself, there was little interest in revising this understanding of Poe (for a fuller discussion of the New Criticism, see the introduction to the previous section). There were important exceptions to this, of course, most importantly Ernest Marchand's reassessment of "Poe as Social Critic" in 1934. But it would not be until the rise of new historicism in the 1980s—which privileged historical context and refused the distinction between literature and other cultural texts—that scholarship on Poe began to read Poe's work systematically in relation to the cultural logic of the time. Beginning most influentially with the scholarship of John Carlos Rowe and Joan Dayan, Poe's work began to be examined in terms of his engagement with what was undeniably the most pressing issue of his day: African American slavery.

With this shift in focus in Poe studies, we also see a shift in the Poe texts of interest to critics. Poe's one novel, *The Narrative of Arthur Gordon Pym*, which had already received a newfound critical attention in the 1960s and 70s after more than a century of relative critical neglect, became a central text in critical debate, as more than any other text by Poe, *Pym* seemed to offer access to his theories of race. A fascinating and confounding novel, those theories proved far from self-evident, and in 1988 a major conference was devoted entirely to *Pym* (resulting in an influential edited collection in 1992). At the core of the conference and the essays that emerged from it was a debate about what the novel had to say about race and slavery, from which Rowe's call to arms—"Poe was a proslavery Southerner and should be reassessed as such in whatever approach we take to his life and writings"—emerged as especially influential (117).

In 1989, Joan Dayan had made a similar call to what would prove an unsympathetic audience at the annual Poe Society meeting, expanding the new critical gaze to include not only *Pym* but also Poe's tales and even his love poems. Dayan gives her own account of this experience in her influential essay, "Amorous Bondage: Poe, Ladies, and Slaves" (1994), which leads off the readings in this section. The Poe Society, like other author societies, had been established to preserve the legacy of a beloved author, with meetings largely devoted to debating issues of authorship and interpretation. As scholarly concerns began shifting to Poe's responses to slavery and the highly charged debates of his day, the Poe Society increasingly found itself having to wrestle with issues that its founders in the 1920s and 30s had believed were largely irrelevant to the writer's work.

Indeed, this belief was part of what made Poe especially appealing for critics of Tate's generation: here was an antebellum Southern writer who seemed to have little or no interest in slavery, precisely what the southern literary movement of the 1920s and 30s most needed. And indeed, in contrast to many of his contemporaries, Poe had relatively few explicit comments on race and slavery in his literary works or correspondence. But by the late 1980s, Poe's inoculation seemed to be wearing off (and, as we will see in the next section, Poe's reputation had been coming under increasing assault by feminist scholars since the 1970s).

The question of what, exactly, Poe *had* said about race and slavery took on new importance for both sides of this emerging debate. Along with the revival of interest in *Pym* and previously neglected stories like "The Man Who Was Used Up" and "How to Write a Blackwood Article," Poe's editorial career at the *Southern Literary Messenger* came under new scrutiny. Poe had served as editor of the influential Southern journal for a little over a year, beginning in late 1835 (it was here that he first began serializing *Pym*), and he would maintain a productive relationship with the journal even after he relocated to New York. Since its founding by publisher Thomas White in 1934, the *Messenger* had attracted contributions from prominent proslavery advocates, eager for the platform a literary journal provided. Among the early contributors were fierce proslavery advocates such as Beverly Tucker and Thomas Dew, and the journal regularly reviewed proslavery work, including, during Poe's tenure, what has come to be known as the "Paulding-Drayton review."

This review of James Kirke Paulding's *Slavery in the United States* and *The South Vindicated* by William Drayton was published in the *Messenger* in April 1836. As was common practice at the time, the review was published anonymously. For years it elicited little attention from Poe scholars, even as Poe scholars differed as to whether it was written by Poe or by Tucker. The debate heated up in 1974 with the publication of Bernard Rosenthal's "Poe, Slavery, and the *Southern Literary Messenger*: A Reexamination," in which he offered the strongest argument to date for Poe's authorship.

As we will see in this section, Rosenthal's attribution of the review to Poe was far from the last word, and the debate would continue over the next three decades in large measure because the stakes were so high. If the review *was* by Poe, it would offer the clearest picture of Poe's attitudes about slavery, a topic on which he is often quite evasive or conspicuously silent. It is with the presumption of Poe's authorship that Dayan calls the review the "five of the most disturbing pages Poe ever wrote." If, on the other hand, the review was *not* by Poe, it is still the case that Poe did little if anything to distance himself from the sentiments expressed within and might, as Jared Gardner suggested in 1998, have "wanted readers to believe the anonymous essay was by him" (133). Nonetheless, there is a big difference between being the kind of proslavery ideologue who could write the Paulding-Drayton review and the kind of "average racist"—and first-time editor eager to please powerful authors and publishers—that Terence Whalen argues for in his important contribution to this debate. Indeed, based in large measure on the textual analysis offered by Whalen in his chapter "Average Racism," included in this section, critical consensus leans toward Tucker, and not Poe, as the author of the review.[1] But the debate is far from fully resolved and the review continues to loom large in almost all discussions of race and Poe, as we will see as the conversation that unfolds over the course of this section.

As with the other controversies that Poe more explicitly courted, the controversy surrounding his thinking on race and slavery remains frustratingly and fascinatingly unresolved into the twenty-first century—which explains the eagerness to pin down attribution for the Paulding-Drayton review. The debate also exposes some larger questions with which a critical enterprise newly interested in the political work of literature has had to wrestle—questions which remain largely unresolved today. Does definitive evidence of the biographical author's thoughts on a highly charged political and ethical issue provide a key for unlocking the meaning of literary texts that engage, often elliptically, with issues of race and slavery? In the absence of such proof, do the literary texts themselves provide us with sufficient evidence from which to reconstruct the author's opinions and beliefs on the most pressing issues of his day? Is it the responsibility of the literary critic to do so? If so, toward what end? Is it to purge the canon of authors whose political beliefs readers today find abhorrent? After all, slavery is an issue on which many Southern writers (and no small number of Northern writers, including Paulding) went on record defending, often in rapturous terms. What do we gain when we attribute similar convictions to literary authors who went out of their way, it would seem, to avoid such declarations of conviction? These and related questions will be raised repeatedly by the essays in this section.

We open with Dayan's 1994 "Amorous Bondage," which is an essay that speaks almost as much to the controversy in the third section as it does to our focus here, bringing together, as she does, Poe's attitudes about African American slaves with his fears and fantasies about white women. While Dayan is unflinching in her criticism of what she sees as a cover-up on the part of many in the Poe critical establishment of certain unpleasant aspects of his life and beliefs, her account of Poe's own attitudes is actually more nuanced than many of her critics credit. The previous year, in an essay for *Poe Studies*, Dayan had offered her answer to the question of Poe's gender politics by aligning Poe with a feminist practice insofar as his work critiques the subordination of woman even as he

---

[1] For reasons of space, Whalen's detailed argument for Tucker as the author is not included in the excerpts reprinted in this section, but interested readers are encouraged to seek out his argument in Sections II and III of the chapter excerpted below.

reproduces dominant society's images of women as passive victims. In "Amorous Bondage" shifting her critical methodology toward an increasingly historicist approach, Dayan is more critical of Poe's politics, especially with regard to race, but for her the evidence of Poe's convoluted thinking on race, whether provided from the Paulding-Drayton review or from his poetry and tales, says less about Poe himself than about the ways in which the institution of slavery perverted the thinking of all it touched, even the man who could have been its most creative critic.

Dayan's writings on Poe and slavery remain touchstones for most of the essays that follow. Yet outside of the contentious debates over the authorship of the Paulding-Drayton review, few will try explicitly either to rescue Poe from what they perceive to be Dayan's unfair attribution of proslavery ideology to the author or to advance the case for Poe as a committed racist. What emerges from the debate are something like shades of gray. For example, Lesley Ginsberg, focusing on "The Black Cat" at the center of historicist argument that draws on a range of other texts and contexts—including debates surrounding pets and the treatment of animals and abolitionist literature from the period—explores a Poe who is simultaneously committed to reproducing and critiquing the logic of American racism.

Terence Whalen's chapter from his influential *Edgar Allan Poe and the Masses* is a significant contribution to Poe studies for the case it makes regarding the authorship of the contentious review in the *Southern Literary Messenger*. Alongside this technical and meticulous textual analysis, however, is a potentially more explosive claim that lies at the heart of the selection published here. Whalen challenges his fellow Poe scholars to move beyond the question of whether Poe is or isn't racist, and instead think in more complex terms about the *kinds* of racism that circulated in the antebellum South (and in equally fierce if often more surreptitious currents in the antebellum North) and the relationship between institutions of racism and the literary marketplace with which Poe was in constant, fraught negotiation.

Paul Gilmore's essay on the story "Hop-Frog" continues Whalen's analysis of Poe's relationship to the literary marketplace, but sees him as more fundamentally engaging with issues of race and slavery. "Hop-Frog," one of Poe's last stories, had often been read as an allegory of Poe's own servitude and suffering at the hands of the literary marketplace and the Boston elites who controlled it and as a gruesome revenge fantasy directed against those same forces. Following the growing interest in Poe's attitudes about race and slavery, "Hop-Frog" also became increasingly of interest as an allegory for slavery: here the titular character has been stolen from a far-off land and enslaved to entertain the king. Dayan, for example, referred to the story as representing Poe's "envisioned revenge for the national sin of slavery" (p. 366), whereas Paul Christian Jones, in a 2001 essay, reads the story as a kind of hoax in which the reader is drawn into dangerous sympathy with Hop-Frog, using techniques familiar to abolitionist writing from the period, only to have his true, savage nature unleashed suddenly at the end. As Jones concludes, the story "ultimately reaffirms the status quo by arguing that slavery, despite some masters' abusive behavior, is preferable to giving slaves freedom and the means for violent retribution" (254).

Gilmore's essay offers a reading that reconciles the tradition of reading the story as being about the literary marketplace with the more recent understanding of the story as speaking about race and slavery. Ultimately, Gilmore discovers a Poe who is simultaneously fully implicated in the racist ideology of his peers and contemporaries and yet paradoxically finds himself identifying with, rather than against, the character who is coded as the racial other. Indeed, as Gilmore concludes, in a gesture that brings us back to some of the issues raised in our first section, Poe had found identifications of himself as a "savage Indian" effective in staking his place in the critical marketplace. For Gilmore, Poe found the commercial value of race to be simultaneously absurd *and* valuable.

The final contribution to this section similarly works to reconcile two competing traditions in Poe scholarship. Here Maurice Lee brings into productive dialogue the "metaphysical Poe"—the Poe who dominated the early generations of criticism—with the "historical Poe" obsessed with and plugged into the central debates of his time and place, chief among them race and slavery. Surprisingly, Lee turns to a story that few critics have ever addressed in terms of race, Poe's earliest tale, "Metzengerstein." Despite being set worlds away from the antebellum United States, Lee argues, this story offers arguably Poe's most thorough and (because early) unguarded statements about the slavery controversy and the mounting sectionalism that would ultimately drive his nation to war after his death. But Lee goes further, suggesting that Poe's thoughts about slavery and race are inextricable from his engagement with transcendentalist metaphysics.

Ultimately this ongoing critical controversy takes us far from the questions with which it began—was Poe a proslavery ideologue—toward messy, troubling, and contradictory insights into both the author and the culture of which he was very much a part. But this messiness, we suggest, provides us more meaningful insights into the ways in which the racism of an author's time co-opts and shapes him, and the ways in which authors themselves challenge or contribute to the stories a dominant culture tells about racial others and about the institutions by which it exploits or enslaves them. In Poe's case, many of our authors suggest, we must accept that he both challenges *and* contributes to the racism of his time, and neither his challenges nor his contributions are as legible as we might wish them to be.

WORKS CITED

Gardner, Jared. *Master Plots: Race and the Founding of an American Literature, 1787–1845.* Baltimore: Johns Hopkins UP, 1998. Print.

Jones, Paul Christian. "The Danger of Sympathy: Edgar Allan Poe's 'Hop-Frog' and the Abolitionist Rhetoric of Pathos." *Journal of American Studies* 35 (2001): 239–54. Print.

Marchand, Ernest. "Poe as Social Critic." *American Literature* 6 (1934): 28–43. Print.

Rosenthal, Bernard. "Poe, Slavery, and the *Southern Literary Messenger*: A Reexamination." *Poe Studies* 7 (December 1974): 29–38. Print.

Rowe, John Carlos. "Poe, Antebellum Slavery, and Modern Criticism." *Poe's Pym: Critical Explorations.* Ed. Richard Kopley. Durham: Duke UP, 1992. Print.

FURTHER READING
IN THE CONTROVERSY

Dayan, Joan. "Romance and Race." *The Columbia History of the American Novel.* Ed. Emory Elliott. New York: Columbia UP, 1991. 89–109. Print.

Goddu, Teresa A. "The Ghost of Race: Edgar Allan Poe and the Southern Gothic." *Gothic America: Narrative, History, and Nation.* New York: Columbia UP, 1997. Print.

———. "Rethinking Race and Slavery in Poe Studies." *Poe Studies/ Dark Romanticism* 33 (2000): 15–18. Print.

Kennedy, J. Gerald, and Liliane Weissberg, eds. *Romancing the Shadow: Poe and Race.* Oxford: Oxford UP, 2001. Print.

Leverenz, David. "Poe and Gentry Virginia." *The American Face of Edgar Allan Poe.* Ed. Shawn Rosenheim and Stephen Rachman. Baltimore: Johns Hopkins UP, 1995. 210–36. Print.

Morrison, Toni. *Playing in the Dark: Whiteness and the Literary Imagination*. Cambridge: Harvard UP, 1992. Print.

Nelson, Dana D. "The Haunting of White Manhood: Poe, Fraternal Ritual, and Polygenesis." *American Literature* (1997): 515–46. Print.

JOAN DAYAN

Amorous Bondage: Poe, Ladies, and Slaves

Colin (Joan) Dayan is the Robert Penn Warren Professor in the Humanities at Vanderbilt University where she teaches courses in the Department of English and the Law School. An elected fellow in the American Academy of Arts and Sciences, she is the author most recently of The Law Is a White Dog: How Legal Rituals Make and Unmake Persons *(2011). Her important book on Poe,* Fables of Mind, *was published in 1987. As the essays throughout this volume make evident, Dayan's work on Poe has been among the most influential of the past generation. The 1994 essay below was first published in the scholarly journal* American Literature.

> The *order of nature* has, in the end, vindicated itself, and the dependence between master and slave has scarcely for a moment ceased.
>
> –THOMAS R. DEW, *Review of the Debate in the Virginia Legislature* (1832)

In October 1989 I presented the Annual Poe Lecture at the Enoch Pratt Library in Baltimore. As part of the memorial to Poe's death, we walked to the grave and put flowers on the ground—wondering if Poe was really there, for some say the body has been removed. We then proceeded to the Library where I was to deliver the Sixty-Ninth lecture on Poe. I had titled the talk "Poe's Love Poems." In writing it, in thinking about those difficult last poems of Poe—unique in the history of American poetry—I turned to what I called "his greatest love poem," the much-contested review of Paulding's *Slavery in the United States* published in the *Southern Literary Messenger* in April 1836.[1] Tra-

---

[1] Edgar Allan Poe, review of *Slavery in the United States* by J. K. Paulding and *The South Vindicated from the Treason and Fanaticism of the Northern Abolitionists* by

ditionally these lectures are published as monographs by the Poe Society of Baltimore. A month after my talk, I received a letter from the Society saying that they wanted to publish the proceedings but advised that I limit the paper to the "fine analysis of the love poems" and cut out the dubious part on slavery.

I realized then that the process of how we come to read or understand our fondest fictions results from a sometimes vicious cutting or decorous forgetting. I have not been allowed to forget my attempt to talk about the "peculiar institution" behind Poe's most popular fantasies. I have received letters from male members of the Poe Society arguing that Poe did not write the proslavery review. Three years ago, after I spoke on Poe at the Boston Athenaeum, an unidentified man appeared before me, saying: "I enjoyed your talk, but Poe had nothing to do with such social issues as slavery." He then referred to an ongoing communication he had had with another Poe critic following my talk in Baltimore, adding that I had "overstepped the bounds of good taste and discretion by contaminating the purest love poems in the English language."[2]

William Drayton, *Southern Literary Messenger*, April 1836. Reprinted in *Complete Works of Edgar Allan Poe*, ed. James A. Harrison (New York: Thomas Y. Crowell & Co., 1902), 8:265–75. Although the review is often noted as the "Paulding Review," Bernard Rosenthal argues that it is more accurate to refer to it as the "Paulding-Drayton Review," since the other book under review (*The South Vindicated*) once thought to be anonymous is now known to be by William Drayton, to whom Poe dedicated his *Tales of the Grotesque and Arabesque*, 1839–40. See Rosenthal, "Poe, Slavery, and the *Southern Literary Messenger*: A Reexamination," *Poe Studies* 7, 2: 29–38. Here I refer only to Paulding's *Slavery in the United States* since I believe that Poe responds primarily to that text. For my full analysis of Poe's review, see "Romance and Race" in *The Columbia History of the American Novel*, ed. Emory Elliott (New York: Columbia Univ. Press, 1991), 94–102. [All notes in this selection are Dayan's.]

[2] Not until 1941, when William Doyle Hull claimed in his doctoral dissertation at the University of Virginia that Nathaniel Beverley Tucker wrote the Paulding review did scholars question Poe's authorship. See William Doyle Hull, "A Canon of the Critical Reviews of Edgar Allan Poe in the *Southern Literary Messenger* and *Burton's Gentleman's Magazine*, with an examination of his relationships with the proprietors" (Ph.D. diss., University of Virginia, 1941). Previous to Hull's work, the review was included in James A. Harrison's Virginia edition of Poe's work, and both Hervey Allen in *Israfel* (1929) and Arthur Hobson Quinn in his *Critical Biography* (1941) discuss the Paulding review as Poe's work. After Hull, the institutional erasure of Poe, slavery, and the South has continued in the Library of America edition of Poe's *Essays and Reviews* (1984), which omits the review. I cannot rehearse the arguments for and against Poe's authorship of the review here, but direct the reader to the excellent, still unsurpassed analysis by Bernard Rosenthal cited in note 1. A marvel of restorative historiography and detection, Rosenthal's essay remains the most convincing unraveling to date of the enigmatic review. Besides emphasizing Poe's friendship with proslavery apologists like Thomas Dew and

As these continuing confrontations demonstrate, the very questioning of authorship raises questions about Poe, property, status, superstition, and gentrification, questions that put Poe quite squarely in dialogue with the romance of the South and the realities of race. Just as the
ideology of Southern honor depended upon fantasies of black degradation, racist discourse needed the rhetoric of natural servility to confirm
absolute privilege. As I will argue, for Poe the cultivation of romance
and the facts of slavery are inextricably linked.

I don't want to sound like Poe in his protracted discussion of his
infamous performance at the Boston Lyceum in *The Broadway Journal*
for nearly two years, but I do want to draw our attention to the coercive
monumentalization of certain writers—specifically, how necessary Poe
(and "his ladies") remain as an icon to the most cherished and necessary
ideals of some men. Here is Floyd Stovall writing on "The Women of
Poe's Poems and Tales": "They are all noble and good, and naturally
very beautiful. . . . Most remarkable of all is their passionate and enduring
love for the hero."[3] It is perhaps not surprising that some Poe critics—the
founding fathers of the Poe Society, for example—sound rather like the
proslavery ideologues who promoted the ideal of the lady as elegant,
white, and delicate. Poe's ladies, those dream-dimmed, ethereal living
dead of his poems, have been taken as exemplars of what Poe called
"supernal Beauty"—an entitlement that he would degrade again and
again. Think about Lady Madeline Usher returning from the grave as a
brute and bloodied thing, reduced from a woman of beauty to the fren-
ziedly iterated "*it*" of her brother Roderick. Many of the dissolutions
and decays so marked in Poe's tales about women subvert the status of
women as a saving ideal, thus undermining his own "Philosophy of
Composition": the "death[, then,] of a beautiful woman is, unquestionably, the most poetical topic in the world" (p. 229). No longer pure
or passive, she returns as an earthy—and very unpoetical—subject.

Nathaniel Beverley Tucker and his attachment, even if vexed, to the idea of Virginia aristocracy, Rosenthal demonstrates that the letter of 2 May 1836, used by Hull and others
to prove Tucker's authorship of the review, must refer to a different essay. Among the
many other details he adduces to question Hull's contention, Rosenthal demonstrates
that there remains a "basic chronological inconsistency in relation to the letter and the
appearance of portions of the April *Messenger* in the *New Yorker*" (31–32). See also John
Carlos Rowe, "Poe, Antebellum Slavery, and Modern Criticism" in *Poe's "Pym": Critical
Explorations*, ed. Richard Kopley (Durham: Duke Univ. Press, 1992), 117–41, which
came to my attention after this essay was completed.
   [3]Floyd Stovall, "The Women of Poe's Poems and Tales," *Texas Studies in English* 5
(1925): 197.

IT DOTH HAUNT ME STILL

Let us take my experience as prelude to a rereading of Poe that depends absolutely on what has so often been cut out of his work: the institution of slavery, Poe's troubled sense of himself as a southern aristocrat, and, finally, the precise and methodical transactions in which he revealed the threshold separating humanity from animality. As I will demonstrate, his most unnatural fictions are bound to the works of natural history that are so much a part of their origination. Read in this way, Poe's sometimes inexplicable fantasies become intelligible. Poe's gothic is crucial to our understanding of the entangled metaphysics of romance and servitude. What might have remained local historiography becomes a harrowing myth of the Americas.

When we read about masters and slaves in the justifications of slavery which proliferated following the Nat Turner rebellion in Virginia on 21 and 22 August 1831, called by most Southerners the "insurrection" or "servile insurrection," women are very often absent from the discussion. Yet the Southern lady, pure, white, and on her pedestal, remained the basis out of which developed the proslavery philosophy. It was she, that amorphous yet powerfully contrived vessel of femininity, who represented the refined and artificial wants of civilized society. The patriarchal defense of the intimate relation between master and slave found itself coordinate with the insistence on the subordination of women. Here is George Fitzhugh, writing in 1850 what would become part of his acclaimed *Sociology for the South*: "A state of dependence is the only condition in which reciprocal affection can exist among human beings. . . . A man loves his children because they are weak, helpless and dependent. He loves his wife for similar reasons. When his children grow up and assert their independence, he is apt to transfer his affection to his grand-children. He ceases to love his wife when she becomes masculine or rebellious; but slaves are always dependent, never the rivals of their master."[4]

I now turn briefly to the disputed review of James Kirke Paulding's *Slavery in the United States* and William Drayton's *The South Vindicated from the Treason and Fanaticism of the Northern Abolitionists*. Here, Poe explicitly makes philosophy out of color: turning the negro inside out, he makes metaphysics out of a biological trait. The mark of blackness

---

[4]Originally published as "Slavery Justified by a Southerner," later included in *Sociology for the South, or The Failure of Free Society* (1854). Cited here from *Slavery Defended: The Views of the Old South*, ed. Eric L. McKitrick (Englewood Cliffs: Prentice Hall, 1962), 45.

compels him to elucidate the propriety of possession, a belief that underlies his most popular rituals of terror. Poe begins his review with the French Revolution, arguing that "property" is what everyone wants most, and that such desire is dubiously called the "spirit of liberty." He calls this Revolution—which made its first triumph "the emancipation of slaves"—"this eccentric comet," nearly the same words used by Thomas Jefferson in *Notes on the State of Virginia* to describe the negro's imagination.[5]

But the crucial section of the Paulding review remains Poe's analysis of the "patriarchal character." His strangely sober take on "moral influences flowing from the master and slave" depends on what he calls "the peculiar character (I may say the peculiar nature) of the negro."[6] We can go further. Poe suggests that the enslaved want to be mastered, for they love—and this is the crucial word for Poe—to serve, to be subservient. Dependence is necessary to reciprocal affection, yet note that Poe does not comment on Paulding's excursus on women as "guardian angels," whose "appropriate sphere is their home, and their appropriate duties at the cradle of the fireside." Indeed, Poe says nothing about what preoccupies the conclusion of Paulding's book: his disquisition on women abolitionists who have "prostituted" (his word) themselves by "assuming the character of a man."[7] What Poe does do, however, before getting back to Paulding, is to describe the "essential" negro. He notes an inscrutable power "which works essential changes in the different races of animals." Like Jefferson he faces the conundrum of color, pausing to consider "the causes which might and should have blackened the negro's skin and crisped his hair into wool."[8]

Poe then turns to that well-worn familial argument, which he describes as the "loyal devotion on the part of the slave" and "the master's reciprocal feeling of parental attachment to his humble dependent." These "sentiments in the breast of the negro and his master," Poe explains, are stronger than they would be under like circumstances between individuals of the white race: "That they [these sentiments] belong to the class of feelings 'by which the heart is made better,' we

[5]Thomas Jefferson, in *Notes on the State of Virginia,* talks about the "wild and extravagant" imagination of the negro which, "in the course of its vagaries, leaves a tract of thought as incoherent and eccentric, as is the course of a meteor in the sky" (ed. William Peden [New York: Norton, 1954], 189).

[6]Poe, review of Paulding, 270.

[7]James Kirke Paulding, *Slavery in the United States* (New York: Harper and Brothers, 1836), 309.

[8]Poe, review of Paulding, 270–71.

know. How come they? . . . They grow by the habitual use of the word 'my,' used in the language of affectionate appropriation, long before any idea of value mixes with it. It is a term of endearment. That is an easy transition by which he who is taught to call the little negro 'his,' in this sense and *because he loves him*, shall love him *because he is his*."[9] It seems at first that the language of affectionate appropriation says simply that you love most what you own. But Poe goes further: he suggests that you own what you love. For unlike George Fitzhugh, Thomas Dew, or Beverley Tucker, Poe is not simply speaking of desirable and ready submission, he is busy making convertible love and possession.

MUD AND SPIRIT

I might have titled this essay "Mud and Spirit," for Poe's textual cruxes have always to do with conversions between matter and spirit, between the utmost carnality and absolute ideality. The debate in *Eureka* about the suspension in cosmic rhythms between matter and not matter is grounded in enlightened disquisitions on the physiognomies of man and brute and, more precisely, in the character of a man and the nature of the negro. In most natural histories—for example Buffon's *Histoire Naturelle* or those other strangely unnatural "natural histories" of the Caribbean—as in the works of Southern theologians and proslavery advocates, the negro approximated the most destitute and most needy of all animals. For Edward Long in his extraordinary *History of Jamaica* (1774), negroes, excluded from the rest of mankind, were signal for a particular kind of exaltation. According to Long, from these degradations, from "mere inert matter," we can ascend "into the animal and vegetable kingdoms," until finally we proceed "from analogy" to "matter endued with thought and reason!"[10]

What is most striking and of course most infamous in Long's meditation is that the word *negro* calls up a disturbingly minute analysis of body parts and gradations of being, until finally he draws an analogy between the negro and the orangutan. "The oran-outang's brain," he claims, "is a senseless *icon* of the human; . . . it is meer matter, unanimated with a thinking principle."[11] Thomas Dew, Poe's friend and professor of political economy at William and Mary College, warned that

---

[9] Poe, review of Paulding, 271–72.
[10] Edward Long, *The History of Jamaica, or General Survey of the Antient and Modern State of that Island* (London, 1774; reprint, New York: Arno, 1972), 2:356, 372.
[11] Long, 2:30.

even with "the free black . . . the animal part of the man gains the victory over the moral, and he, consequently, prefers sinking down into
the listless, inglorious repose of the brute creation."[12]

When Long wrote about what he called the progression "from a
lump of dirt to a perfect human being," he meant the move from matter to man. But what is the relation between those "creatures" constituted as brute exemplars of matter and the rarified vessels of spirit,
those species of "true womanhood" who haunt the learned discourse
on race as the absolute perfection so antithetical to—and yet as subordinated as—that lump of dirt? What do we gain by forcing proximity
on those categories and claims the naturalists so rigorously separated?

Perhaps all of Poe's work is finally about radical dehumanization:
You can dematerialize—idealize—by turning humans into animals or
by turning them into angels. As Poe proves throughout *Eureka* and in
his angelic colloquies, matter and not matter are convertible. Further,
both processes, etherealization or brutalization (turning into angel or
brute), involve displacement of the human element. We are dealing with
a process of sublimation, either up or down. Animality, after all, emerges
for most nineteenth-century phrenologists, theologians, and anthropol-
ogists in those beings who are classified as both human and beast: luna-
tics, women, primates, black men, and children. What remains unmentioned, and uncoded, is the manhood at the center of these operations.
It is this powerfully absent construction that Poe intentionally probes.
He, the white epistemologist of the sublime, the enlightenment "universal man," haunts Poe's writings. It is his divisions, as well as his projections, that Poe confounds.

Thus the unbelievable overturning of the law of identity and contradiction that I have argued to be central to Poe's work can now be
considered as more than a fable of mind. Poe's reconstructions depend
upon experiences that trade on unspeakable slippages between men and
women, humans and animals, life and death. Poe deliberately undermines the taxonomic vocations of male supremacy and thus attributes
to it a troubling, ambiguous vitality.

---

[12]Thomas Dew, *Review of the Debate in the Virginia Legislature*, in *Slavery Defended*,
30. After the Nat Turner rebellion, Virginia's legislators debated openly during January
and February 1832, with antislavery spokesmen arguing for colonization of the blacks in
Liberia and stressing the destructive effects of slave labor. In the end, most delegates
accepted the proslavery argument that colonization was too costly to implement. It is
generally agreed that Dew's expert analysis of the debates with his conclusions and rec-
ommendations defeated once and for all western Virginia's gradual emancipationists and
ushered in a decade of repressive slave controls (the "black laws") and expanded patrol
and militia systems.

"MY TANTALIZED SPIRIT"

Poe's tales about women—"Morella," "Ligeia," "Berenice," "The Fall of the House of Usher," and "Eleonora"—are about the men who narrate the unspeakable remembrance: not the gun-toting, masterful cavaliers or gentlemen of southern fictions of the gentry, but the delicate acolytes of erudite ladies or the terrified victims of the lady revenants. In these tales, possession, multiple hauntings, and identity dissolutions suspend gender difference as a component of identity. The memorial act demands a willing surrender to an anomalous atmosphere where one thing remains certain: the dead do not die. They will not stay buried. In Poe's tales these awfully corporeal ghosts are always women. As we read the compelling narratives of the men who wait and watch for the inevitable return, we sense how much the terror depends on the men's will to remember, their sorcerer-like ability to name and to conjure the beloved, who is, of course, the exemplar for later "white zombies."

Poe's ideal of "indefinitiveness," his turn to the "ethereal," "ideal," "breath of faery," or "mystic," is most weirdly disrupted in his poetry. The three poems that trouble me most are the second "To Helen," "For Annie," and "To ——." Terms such as "saintliness," "sweet," "ideal," or "feminine perfection" (often used by critics to describe the women of Poe's poems) obscure how deliberately Poe fragments and dissolves conventional images of "womanliness." In these poems Poe reveals the progress of perfection: its absolute dependence on the imperfect. In "To Helen," we move from a lady's "upturn'd" face in a landscape of dying, smiling roses, with faces also "upturn'd," to the progressive elimination of the world of nature: "The pearly lustre of the moon went out: / The mossy banks and the meandering paths, / The happy flowers and the repining trees, / Were seen no more." Every part of the lady is obliterated, except for her eyes: "*Only thine eyes remained.* / They *would not* go—they never yet have gone / . . . . / They follow me—they lead me through the years. / They are my ministers—yet I their slave" (*PT* 96).

There is something less than ideal or sanctifying about these eyes. They recall the eyes of the Lady Ligeia or Berenice's teeth forever imprinted on the narrator's mind. In the process of abstraction, once every piece of nature named is blotted out, no woman remains but only what Poe calls "less than thou." Woman, "the fair sex," and the "romance" she bears can only be experienced as fragment. Freed from marriage, domesticity, and any possible relation to property, the beloved is reduced to a

haunting remnant. But what happens to the poet? Yielding himself passive to the lovelight, as does the death-obsessed imaginist of "For Annie,"
Poe renders himself up as "slave" to those omniscient eyes: "Their office
is to illumine and enkindle—/My duty, to be saved by their bright
light." The bereaved lover thus figures himself through a servitude articulated as salvation.

As a way to read the surrender of these love poems, I want briefly
to recall the rhetoric of redemption in Poe's Paulding-Drayton Review.
In the scenes of suffering that conclude the review, Poe appreciates the
all-consuming etiology of possession. As the master weakens, the servant remains fixed in a relentless, nearly superhuman deathwatch. How
different are such spectacles of feeling from Poe's representation of the
compulsive lover in these poems, or in the bedside vigils of "Ligeia"
and "Morella"? For Poe, adoration is always a deadly business. When he
wrote his review, Poe merely reiterated the sentimental decor necessary
for maintaining the illusion of mastery. But by the time he composed
these late poems, he had apprehended the ruse of sentiment and not
only exposed, but satirized the inalienable bond between the illusions
of reverent attachment and the matter of human bondage.

In "To ——" written to Marie Louise Shew in 1848, Poe fantasizes about being swallowed up by the object of his affections. A strange
turn takes place midway through the poem. He takes the name that
he will not name, "two foreign soft dissyllables"—Lady "Marie
Louise"—(she remains unnamed in the published version) as prod to
his undoing:

> . . . And I! my spells are broken.
> The pen falls powerless from my shivering hand.
> With thy dear name as text, though bidden by thee,
> I cannot write—I cannot speak or think,
> Alas, I cannot feel; for 'tis not feeling,
> This standing motionless upon the golden
> Threshold of the wide-open gate of dreams,
> Gazing, entranced, adown the gorgeous vista,
> And thrilling as I see upon the right,
> Upon the left, and all the way along
> Amid empurpled vapors, far away
> To where the prospect terminates—*thee only.* (p. 28)

Here we have another strange vanishing ritual, which like that of "To
Helen" seems to mock the progress of corporeality from matter to
man. The more closely Poe analyzes and purifies his notions, the more

he tries to establish a solid foundation, the more he loses himself in fantasy. Poe's unlinked Great Chain completely mixes men, nature, women, reason, and dreams. Not only does feeling summon dissolution, but Poe takes heartfelt affection and turns it into lust. What Southerners dignified by the name love, Poe rather unceremoniously presents as fierce, inhuman desire. In "To ——" he animates not feeling or thought, but instead wildly physicalized passion that has far from salutary effects on the soul.

The poet trades his subjectivity, his very power to speak or write, for the most fleshly part of his beloved, looking into her heart of hearts. Poe has coerced feeling into image; as in "To Helen," we are left with a strangely fetishized kernel of womanhood, those scintillant "star eyes." Here, "thee" is implicitly the "heart" that can be reached only through penetration "adown the gorgeous vista" into a tunnel-like space that thrills as it constrains, "upon the right / Upon the left, and all the way along / Amid empurpled vapors, far away / To where the prospect terminates—."

Why does Poe so often present himself in these later poems as a "slave" to the images he has created? What does he mean by this posture of enfeeblement, his claim of impotence? What I will suggest is that Poe articulates a specific relation of domination, where the speaker who has defined himself as possessor is in turn defined by his possession. I quote two passages of variously willed passivity: a stanza from "To Annie" and a passage from a letter to Sara Helen Whitman.

> Sadly, I know
>   I am shorn of my strength,
> And no muscle I move
>   As I lie at full length—
> But no matter!—I feel
>   I am better at length. (p. 30)

> Oh God! how I now curse the impotence of the pen—the inexorable *distance* between us! I am pining to speak to *you*, Helen,— to you in person—to be near you while I speak—gently to press your hand in mine—to look into your soul through your eyes—and thus *to be sure* that my voice passes into your heart.[13]

[13]Edgar Allan Poe, *The Letters of Edgar Allan Poe*, ed. John Ward Ostrom, vol. 2, rev. ed. (New York: Gordian, 1966), 396.

To gain a voice necessitates the writer's becoming the beloved. Getting into her mind will ensure that his voice gets into her heart. To want to be in the place of another is to be possessed. Or put another way, if you can't have her, then you can become her. Poe understands the law of the heart, the power in the word *my*. And in nearly all of Poe's dealings with ladies, whether in letters (recycled to various "real" beloveds), poems, or tales, he has possessed all the others so fully that they become the same, not only interchangeable with each other, but with Edgar Poe.

Yet if we put "To Helen" or "For Annie" in their Southern context, we can go further. Nathaniel Beverley Tucker, proslavery apologist and professor of law at William and Mary, who befriended Poe and was his greatest supporter when Poe edited the *Southern Literary Messenger* in 1835–36, wrote much about "obedience to the law of Love." In his "Moral and Political Effect of the Relation between the Caucasian Master and the African Slave," the terms of contrast are again limited to the benevolent master and grateful servant paradigm. But in *George Balcombe*, a romance of Missouri and Virginia, published in 1836, Tucker included women—and especially "genuine feminine devotion"—in his philosophy of feeling. He asked his male readers to seek those women who reject the "'ologies' of female radicals," and prefer "to learn the housewifely duties and plain old fashioned sense of a Virginia lady." Referring to unmarriageable "learned ladies," George Balcombe warns that there are "'secrets in heaven and earth not dreamed of in their philosophy.'" Instead, the uncorrupted—and "uncultivated"—woman will beware "*intellectual distinction, or distinction* of any kind," for such "a feeling unsexes her." This *real* woman "reads her Bible, works her sampler, darns her stockings, and boils her bacon and greens together."[14]

Before turning to Poe's review of Tucker's *George Balcombe*, I want to emphasize that Tucker's portrayal of the lady depends for its effect on another favorite subject of the gentleman George Balcombe: the zealous and appreciative negro. Balcombe's most lengthy disquisitions concern wives and slaves. What is the "noblest of God's works"? Balcombe has the answer: "a *right woman—a genuine unsophisticated woman.*"[15] The "established order of the universe," Balcombe's magisterial hierarchy, depends absolutely on distinguishing superior and inferior beings: "I see gradations in everything. I see subordination everywhere."

[14]Nathaniel Beverley Tucker, *George Balcombe, A Novel,* 2 vols. (New York: Harper & Brothers, 1836), 1:88, 277, 275, 278.
[15]Tucker, 1:273.

Within this created order, rising in a climax of subordination, white men are on top. Men of "delicacy" marry only women who know their place. Only these women can enjoy the bonds of matrimony, and only grateful negroes can be graced with "that strong tie . . . spun out of the interchange of service and protection." Those born slaves actually "feel themselves inferior," and that sentiment alone is "the *rationale* of the filial and parental bond."[16] Finally, Balcombe clinches his argument about negroes, tradition, and "inextinguishable affection" by joining women with blacks in happy servitude: "Is gratitude abject? Is self-abandoning, zealous devotion abject? If the duties of heaven require these sentiments, and its happiness consist in their exercise, which of us is it that is but a little lower than the angels—the negro or the white man? . . . Let women and negroes alone, and instead of quacking with them, physic your own diseases. Leave them in their humility, their grateful affection, their self-renouncing loyalty, their subordination of the heart, and let it be your study to become worthy to be the object of these sentiments."[17]

Poe reviewed *George Balcombe* in *The Southern Literary Messenger* in 1837. Most of the review is plot summary. Although Poe says nothing about Tucker's theory of servitude, he does pay attention to the women characters. The ever-blushing Mary Scott, who was "'beautiful and intelligent—gay, sprightly and impassioned,'" Poe praises as "imbued with the spirit of romance." Remarking on Elizabeth, whom he describes as "the shrinking and matronly wife of Balcombe," he concludes: "She is an exquisite specimen of her class, but her class is somewhat hacknied." Poe's favorite character is Ann, the proper Virginia lady, who in Balcombe's words is "'wise, generous, and delicate.'" Poe concludes his judgment of Tucker's ladies by asserting: "Upon the whole, no American novelist has succeeded, we think, in female character, even nearly so well as the writer of George Balcombe" (*ER* 956, 975–76).

Like women characters in the works of John Pendleton Kennedy and William Gilmore Simms, Tucker's proper ladies are passive and accommodating, utterly dependent on the men who regulate their destiny. In *George Balcombe*, Tucker's portrayal of the ideal wife reflects the character of her husband: "while her husband's light was above the horizon, [she] hid herself beneath it, or if she appeared at all, modestly

---

[16]Tucker, 2:164–65.
[17]Tucker, 2:166.

paled her lustre in his presence."[18] But when Poe yields himself up to the "bright light" of Helen, he shifts the entire patriarchal argument to the domain that seems relevant to him, namely, the reversibility of supremacy. In Poe's mechanics of love, heartfelt men become vague and impotent, while beloved women become shadowy or reduced to pieces of prized and sexualized symbolic matter. In a time when many argued for sharper categorizations and more hierarchy, when ladies, slaves, and men endured ever more difficult trials of definition, Poe managed to confound and de-naturalize the so-called "natural order" of things. In prostrating himself before the fetishized women of his poems or creating powerful intellects, mystics, and witches like Ligeia and Morella, Poe worked changes on the subservient women praised by his fellow Southerners.

As we have seen, Poe is preoccupied with repeated and varied postures of enfeeblement: a deliberate weakness that leaves only feeling, an obsession with the heart that links the white male writer, the white woman of his dreams, and the ungendered, unmentioned black. Without mentioning blacks, Poe applies the accepted argument on the "nature" of negroes and the "spirit" of women—both feeling, not thinking things—to the white men usually excluded from such categorization.[19]

When Poe dwells repeatedly on the extremes of savagery and cultivation, brute possession and tender affection, he refers to a long history of racialist writings, including those by natural historians such as George Buffon and Edward Long. Buffon described "Negroes" as "naturally compassionate and tender."[20] Edward Long discussed at length the "courteous, tender disposition" of the orangutan, debasing black women in the process. Long tells his readers that orangutans "sometimes endeavour to surprise and carry off negroe women into their woody retreats." He then turns to these negroes, to whom he grants not a trace of affectionate feeling, describing them as "libidinous and shameless as monkies, or baboons." Entertaining no question as to whether or not a black

---

[18]Tucker, 1:275.

[19]Some proslavery advocates, however, deprived the black even of feeling. William Beckford Jr. (not the Beckford of Fonthill, author of *Vathek*), in his *Remarks Upon the Situation of the Negroes in Jamaica* (London: T. and J. Egerton, Military Library, 1788), arguing against emancipation in the West Indies, wrote: "A slave has no feeling beyond the present hour, no anticipation of what may come, no dejection at what may ensue: these privileges of feeling are reserved for the enlightened" (84).

[20]George Louis Leclerc Buffon, *A Natural History of the Globe, of Man, of Beasts, Birds, Fishes, Reptiles, Insects, and Plants*, ed. John Wright, trans. W. Kendrick, 3 vols., new edition with improvements from Geoffrey, Griffith, Richardson, Lewis, Clark, Long, Wilson (Boston: Gray and Brown, 1831), 1:163.

female would accept an ape for a husband, Long assures his readers that "hot" negro women seek out these animals to "embrace."[21]

If white women were imaged by advocates of slavery as emptied of all qualities that could attach them to physical reality while black women became vessels for the carnality that was expelled from icons of pure womanhood, Poe takes the blushing belle and makes her both passionate and suspiciously white, with a deathly, unnatural pallor that makes whiteness as negative and opaque as what Jefferson had described in *Notes on the State of Virginia* as an "immoveable veil of black." Further, Poe's voice as poet reconstitutes itself, the male lover in nineteenth-century America, as a wholly negative consciousness, obeisant to the law of the heart.[22] The law, as Poe defines it, however, has more to do with lust than propriety, and he substitutes monomaniacal frenzy for the delicately modulated feelings of the "civilized" Southerner.

There is a two-pronged program here. First Poe plays with the possibility of one thing passing into another and vice versa—the *convertibility* so much a part of his project. The superior male mind erected over the bodies of women continuously purified or defiled, and blacks alternately sentimentalized or cursed, turns into the very objects once posited as external to it. Second, Poe repeats, exaggerates, and transforms the immutable, romanticized attributes white women are granted by men. He dramatizes the fact of appropriation, and thereby undefines the definitions that mattered to civilized society. It is not surprising, then, that one Poe reviewer writing in 1856 reflected: "In perusing his most powerful tales, the reader feels himself surrounded by hitherto unapprehended dangers; he grows suspicious of his best friends; all good angels appear turning to demons."[23]

DYING TO SERVE

To read much of nineteenth-century literature is to encounter conceits of servitude. From Caleb Williams's anguished and ambiguous declaration to Falkland's "Sir, I could die to serve you!" to Jane Eyre's

---

[21] Edward Long, 2:360, 364, 361, 383.

[22] Besides Hegel's elaboration on "The Law of the Heart, and the Frenzy of Self-Conceit," 391–400, his concept of the "Beautiful Soul" in his *Phenomenology of Mind*, trans. J. B. Baillie (New York: Harper and Row, 1967) is also useful here. For Hegel the "identity" of the "Beautiful soul" comes about "merely in a negative way, as a state of being devoid of spiritual character." The "'beautiful soul' . . . has no concrete reality" (676).

[23] *North American Review* 83 (October 1856): 432.

"I'd give my life to serve you," to a Bartleby who quite literally dies to serve while refusing to do so, readers who thought they would escape to fictions, or romances, found themselves treated to scenes of mastery and servitude. Even the supernatural in many gothic tales had its real basis in the language of slavery and colonization, put forth as the most natural thing in the world. One has only to read the 1685 *Code noir* of Louis XIV, that collection of edicts concerning "the Discipline and Commerce of Negro Slaves in the French Islands of America," to understand how what first seems phantasmagoric is locked into a nature mangled and relived as a spectacle of servitude. Its surreal precisions in human reduction (how best turn a man into a thing), like Long's anatomical permutations on monkey, man, horse, and negro, demonstrate how unnatural the claims to right and property actually were.

The *Code noir* or *Black Code* is a document of limits.[24] Unlike the racist disquisition on blacks as lacking the finer feelings of a tender heart, the Code is not concerned with the tangled semantics of charitable servitude or lurking debauchery. We read instead sixty articles that take us into a chilling series of qualifications: prohibitions that permit, limitations that invite excess, and a king's grandiloquence that ensures divestment. There is no time for discussions of innate inferiority, natural difference, or nightmares of contamination. For the blacks and slaves in French America are introduced not as persons, but as a special kind of property: a "thing," according to Roman law, juridically deprived of all rights. Once acquired by a planter, legally divested of their self and removed from their land, slaves became the planter's possession. Alternately defined as chattels and as real property, they were sometimes movable assets (part of the planter's personal estate) and sometimes unmovable, disposed of as if real estate, or in especially macabre cases, as if garbage.

If the *Black Code* turned a human into a thing, a piece of movable property, it could be argued that "the law of the heart" accomplishes the same end. For the law of the heart remains inseparable from the fact of property. Southern proslavery apologists appreciated the special privileges that accompanied possession, as did some abolitionists, who

---

[24]Note that in three hundred years the *Code Noir* has not been translated into English. Most significantly, this codification of methodical divestiture remains so difficult to find that it has vanished from historiography. I first read the *Code Noir* in a collection that included the additional royal edicts, 1699–1742: *Recueils de reglements, édits, declarations et arrêts ... concernant le commerce, l'administration de la justice, la police des colonies françaises de l'Amérique ... avec Le Code Noir et l'addition au dit Code* (Paris: Chez les libraires associés, 1745).

could never quite liberate their objects of pathos from domination. The acclaimed dispossession of Stowe's *Uncle Tom's Cabin* works only as long as the "negro" is kept forever separate in essence from the Anglo-Saxon, locked in the precincts of affectionate service, impressionable spirituality, and childlike simplicity. Stowe's fantasy, brimful of just pity, remains entirely affirming and satisfying to the "superior" white ego. How different, after all, is Stowe's representation of Tom stretched out supine on the veranda in order to be close to the dying Eva—what Miss Ophelia calls "sleeping anywhere and everywhere, like a dog"—from Poe's portrayal in the Paulding-Drayton Review of the bond between master and servant?

Poe's dramatizations of possession—a reciprocal devouring of self and other—reminds us of the force of language, especially literary language, to allow the covert continuation of domination. Fictions of sentiment and idealizations of love, the special realm of right-minded women and domesticated blacks, are linked in unsettling ways to the social realities of property and possession. Poe knew how the sanctifying of women depends upon a more sinister brutalization, or spectralization. His narrators in "Ligeia," "Berenice," and "Morella," for example, demonstrate how the language of love can animate and sustain utter servility.

Sentiment, as Poe confirmed in "The Black Cat," is not only coercive but also despotic. The rare and special love between slave and master, man and wife, based on the law of property, becomes the medium by which perfect submission becomes equivalent to a pure but perverse love. A slave, a piece of property, a black pet, once loved in the proper domestic setting, effects an excess of devotion, an inextricable bond that proslavery apologists—and even Captain Delano in Melville's *Benito Cereno*—argued can never be felt by two equals. Of course, Poe writes "The Black Cat" to demonstrate how destructive is the illusion of mastery: just as the pet of perfect docility turns into "a brute beast," "a man, fashioned in the image of the High God," is dependent on and utterly enslaved by the very thing he has so lovingly brutalized (p. 183).

NO PLACE OF GRACE

We need to reread Poe's romantic fictions as bound to the realities of race, keeping "every thing . . . within the limits of the accountable—of the real," as he urged in "The Philosophy of Composition" (p. 233). There is a logic to his excessive attention to blood, things dirtied, and bodies mutilated. Lurking in every effusion of ennobling love is the terror of literal dehumanization: not only the Burkean sublime or the Calvinist's rhetoric of sensation, but that most terrific conversion, the reduction of human into thing for the ends of capital.

*　*　*

The facts of race intrude almost imperceptibly, yet persistently into Poe's romance. "God's plan for securing the hearts of his creatures," to quote George Balcombe, Poe insists is analogous to the polemicist's plot to justify human bondage. But he reserves his greatest scorn for those who condemn slavery while continuing to restrict blacks to the status of objects: recipients of the charity of white men who continue to be masters. As "critical reader of the transcendentalist ideologies of his time," Poe's compulsive satire on the "pundits," on their mystifying language and cant, was fueled by the abolitionist leanings of those he called the "Frogpondians": Emerson, Thoreau, Lowell, and especially Longfellow.[25]

Emerson's 1844 address on the tenth anniversary of the emancipation of the negroes in the British West Indies preceded Poe's Lyceum debacle by about a year. For Emerson, the mettle of white men has been proved by their largesse on "behalf of the African": "Other revolutions have been the insurrection of the oppressed; this was the repentance of the tyrant. It was the masters revolting from their mastery."[26] Not only is Emerson idealizing, and decontextualizing, a far more disturbing history, but what he calls "elevation and pathos" keeps whites quite secure in their superiority while blacks, though no longer called slaves, remain inferior. Invited to the Boston Lyceum, Poe deliberately insults his audience by reading "Al Aaraaf" (which he introduced by saying he wrote it at nineteen years old), renamed "The Messenger Star of Tycho Brahe" for that "drunken" spectacle.[27] Poe's blustering and offensive performance no doubt had its sources not only in envy, insecurity, and aesthetic debate, but in his disapproval of Emerson's high-

---

[25] I am referring throughout to Poe's argument against the transcendentalists as elucidated in my *Fables of Mind* (New York: Oxford, 1987).

[26] Ralph Waldo Emerson, "Emancipation in the British West Indies," *The Complete Works of Ralph Waldo Emerson* (Cambridge: Riverside Press, 1904), 11:146.

[27] Poe then retold the story in two consecutive articles of *The Broadway Journal*. For an account of this episode, see Arthur Hobson Quinn, *Edgar Allan Poe: A Critical Biography* (New York: Cooper Square Publishers, Inc., 1969), 487ff.

minded celebration of West Indian emancipation as a "piece of moral history."

Poe's attack in *Eureka*, carrying further his condemnation of those he called the oracles of "higher morality," those "thinkers-that-they-think," who wander "in the shadowy region of imaginary truth," remained grounded in his disdain for those he condemned in his reviews as "the small coterie of abolitionists, transcendentalists and fanatics in general." After all, what he attacked as "the frantic spirit of generalization" was one of the major accusations of proslavery advocates in the South who called the Northern abolitionists fools of abstraction who knew nothing of the particulars of Southern slavery. In order to understand Poe's unceasing condemnation of the Bostonians as a "knot of rogues and madmen," we need to reread literary history as regional debate.

Poe's obsessive attacks on Longfellow—and especially his critique of the poem "The Slave in the Dismal Swamp" in his 1845 review of Longfellow's *Poems of Slavery* (1842)—come not only from envy or aesthetic discretion, as some have suggested, but the acute knowledge of the facts behind Longfellow's romantic sentimentalism. The Dismal Swamp, sometimes called "the Great Dismal," was for a long time the receptacle of runaway slaves in the South. Poe no doubt read Samuel Warner's "Authentic and Impartial Narrative," an account of Nat Turner's "Horrid Massacre," published in 1831. Warner's description of the "very large bog, extending from N. to S. near 30 miles, and from E. to W. at a medium about 10 miles," where cypress and cedar cast an "everlasting shade," could well be a source for Poe's ghastly landscape of "Silence—A Fable" (composed in 1832 and published in 1835). Even birds do not fly over this gloomy swamp, "for fear of the noisome exhalations that rise from this vast body of filth and nastiness. These noxious vapors infect the air round about." Warner then exclaims, "It is within the deep recesses of this gloomy Swamp, 'dismal' indeed, beyond the power of human conception, that the runaway Slaves of the South have been known to secret themselves for weeks, months, and years, subsisting on frogs, tarrapins, and even snakes!"[28]

Poe must have known about the scouring of the swamp in pursuit of slaves, of the hounds that scented unsuccessfully after Nat Turner.

---

[28] Samuel Warner, "Authentic and Impartial Narrative of the Tragical Scene Which Was Witnessed in Southampton Country (Virginia) on Monday the 22nd of August" in *The Southampton Slave Revolt of 1831: A Compilation of Source Material*, ed. Henry Irving Tragle (Amherst: Univ. of Massachusetts Press, 1971), 296–98.

Yet, as so often in his writings, Poe misrecognizes or disavows the facts
he knows, condemning Longfellow for writing "a shameless medley of
the grossest misrepresentation. When did Professor LONGFELLOW
ever *know* a slave to be hunted with bloodhounds in the *dismal swamp*?
Because he has heard that runaway slaves are so treated in CUBA, he
has certainly no right to change the locality" (*ER* 763). But some of
what Poe says matters, for Longfellow's poem purifies the place. He
cleans up the mire. The vessel for squalor, the bearer of putrefaction in
"The Slave in the Dismal Swamp" is his "poor old slave, infirm and
lame," who hides in an unreal landscape:

> Where will-o'-the wisps and glowworms shine,
>   In bulrush and in brake;
> Where waving mosses shroud the pine,
>
> . . . .
>
> All things above were bright and fair,
>   All things were glad and free;
> Lithe squirrels darted here and there,
> And wild birds filled the echoing air
>   With songs of Liberty![29]

Longfellow's picture of the "hunted Negro," like other portraits of the
pathetic hero so popular in the North, allows the reader pity but also
distance from the poeticized object of emotion.[30]

Poe did not accept Longfellow's translation of the Dismal Swamp
into an Edenic scene contaminated by one spot of deformity, the slave.
Indeed, Poe's dark, stagnant waters, the "morass" and "wilderness" in
"Silence — A Fable," at "the boundary of the dark, horrible, lofty forest," reiterates the locale of the hunted. . . .

When we note varying denigrations of blacks in Poe's early works,
it becomes even more unsettling that issues of race, like those of gender, have not figured significantly in Poe criticism.[31] But then, much

---

[29] Henry Wadsworth Longfellow, *Poems on Slavery* (Cambridge: John Owen, 1842),
1:285.

[30] No one has demonstrated more powerfully than Winthrop D. Jordan in *White
Over Black* how excessive sentimentality diminished the possibility of action or ethics in
the antislavery program: "A romantic sentimentalism was a symptom of, and perhaps a
subtle yet readily intelligible social signal for, a retreat from rational engagement with the
ethical problems posed by Negro slavery" (New York: Norton, 1977, 370–71).

[31] Dana D. Nelson's *The Word in Black and White: Reading "Race" in American
Literature 1638–1867* (New York: Oxford Univ. Press, 1992) came to my attention after
I completed this essay. Her rigorous redefinition of "race" in both fictional and nonfic-
tional works of Anglo-American writers is crucial to understanding the metaphysics of

that is necessary to the sanctification of something called "literariness"—those texts that are praised as art not politics—is risked if we put Poe in his place, if we avoid the romantic image of a genius in "Dream-Land," "Out of SPACE / out of TIME" (*PT* 79). For instance, in "The Journal of Julius Rodman," the "faithful negro" Toby is described "as ugly an old gentleman as ever spoke—having all the peculiar features of his race; the swollen lips, large white protruding eyes, flat nose, long ears, double head, pot-belly, and bow legs" (*PT* 1242). And of course, there is the orangutan in "Murders in the Rue Morgue," whose strange gibberish at first suggests "primitive" vocables: "it might have been the voice of an Asiatic—of an African" (p. 145).[32] In Poe's review of Robert Bird's *Sheppard Lee*, a story of metempsychosis, lost bodies, and wandering spirits—an obvious source for Poe's "The Gold Bug"—Poe discusses the "negro servant, Jim Jumble . . . a crabbed, self-willed old rascal, who will have every thing his own way." In Bird's story, as Poe represents it in his review, Jim Jumble "conceives that money has been buried by Captain Kid, in a certain ugly swamp, called the Owl-Roost. . . . The stories of the negro affect his master to such a degree that he dreams three nights in succession of finding a treasure at the foot of a beech-tree in the swamp" (*ER* 390–91). Sheppard Lee's failure to find the treasure, falling dead, and then turning into a ghost and looking for yet another body to inhabit (briefly possessing the corpse of a "miserable negro slave" called "Nigger Tom"), will be revised in Poe's tale of Legrand, who does the conceiving, and the manumitted black servant Jupiter, who knows (*nose*) nothing—unable to tell his left eye from his right—concluding with a final, successful treasure hunt.[33]

---

whiteness, the rewriting of race as aesthetics, and the connections in America between race, romance, and nation. See especially "Ethnocentrism Decentered: Colonial Motives in *The Narrative of Arthur Gordon Pym*," 90–109. In yet another turn on Poe and race, Toni Morrison in *Playing in the Dark: Whiteness and the Literary Imagination* (Cambridge: Harvard Univ. Press, 1992), claims Poe as crucial "to the concept of American Africanism" (32).

[32] As I have argued in "Romance and Race," Poe's Dupin knows how to detect unadulterated barbarism, and the descriptions of the affectionate, yet easily enraged orangutan who loves to mimic his master and violate women refer readers to the familiar fantasies of consanguinity between black men and apes. As Edward Long puts it in his *History of Jamaica*: "an oran-outang . . . is a human being . . . but of an inferior species . . . he has in form a much nearer resemblance to the Negroe race, than the latter bear to white men" (103).

[33] See Robert Montgomery Bird, *Sheppard Lee* (New York: Harper and Brothers, 1836), 1:36–38, and esp. 2:156–77, where Sheppard Lee enters the body of Tom, saying, "If thou art dead, my sable brother, yield my spirit a refuge in thy useless body!" Awakening as Tom in the chapter "In which Sheppard Lee finds every thing black about

Yet even though Poe used racist stereotypes in stories like "The Man That Was Used Up," "The Gold Bug," or "Murders in the Rue Morgue," I suggest that he exercised these images in order to tell another story. Let us take as example "The Man That Was Used Up: A Tale of the Late Bugaboo and Kickapoo Campaign" (1839). Not only does Poe describe the dismemberment and redemption of Brigadier General John A. B. C. Smith, but he writes the "other" into the white hero's tale, putting those called "savages" or "things" into the myth of Anglo-Saxon America. Reduced to "an odd-looking bundle of something" (p. 84) by the Bugaboo and Kickapoo Indians in a "tremendous swamp-fight away down South" (doubtless, an allusion to the Dismal Swamp; p. 80), the General is put together every morning by Pompey, his black valet. With each successive body part replaced, the General regains the voice of the consummate Southern gentleman while remaining utterly dependent on the "old negro" (p. 84) he debases. He calls Pompey "dog," then "nigger," then "scamp" (p. 85), and finally, once all his parts are reassembled, "black rascal" (p. 86).

When Poe was "dying" for "Annie," he was writing his most horrible tale of retribution, "Hop-Frog; or, The Eight Chained Ourang-Outangs" (1849). What Mabbott regards as "a terrible exposition of the darkness of a human soul" is Poe's envisioned revenge for the national sin of slavery.[34] As we have seen, orangutans were deemed the most appropriate analogues for blacks. Here Poe literalizes what natural historians perceived as bestial similitude and prophesies the apocalypse of "servile" war so feared by Southerners. In the fiery climax of "Hop-Frog," eight cruel masters get turned into orangutans by an enslaved dwarf "from some barbarous region . . . no person ever heard of" (p. 214). Just as the unidentifiable "gibberish" of the orangutan murderer in the Rue Morgue "might have been the voice of an Asiatic—of an African," this unheard of place refers implicitly to Africa. Tarred and flaxed, the masters are burned to "a fetid, blackened, hideous, and indistinguishable mass" (p. 221). The blind spot of most critics to slavery and its justifications as ground for the turn in "Hop-Frog" is exemplified when Mabbott reflects: "The manner of chaining apes described is not mentioned by any authorities consulted."[35]

him," Lee, expecting to be "the exemplar of wretchedness," finds instead the surprise of humane and gentle treatment by a "good-natured" and "'right-born master,'" thus replicating the hyperbolized scenes of plantation life so dear to the proslavery argument.

[34]See discussion of "Hop-Frog" in Dayan, "Romance and Race," 103–04.

[35]Thomas Ollive Mabbott, ed., *Collected Works of Edgar Allan Poe* (Cambridge: Harvard Univ. Press, 1978), 3:1344.

The dependence of much gothic fiction on Calvinist theology and apocalyptic text can be particularized as the relation between a "suffering"—alternately degraded and idealized—"servant" and an omniscient master. In Poe's narrations of domination, enslavement compels convertibility, where, as Hegel argued in his *Phenomenology*, the distinction between master and slave is transformed: "just as lordship showed its essential nature to be the reverse of what it wants to be, so, too, bondage will, when completed, pass into the opposite of what it immediately is."[36] Aware of the perils of mastery, Poe repeats the conversion narrative so much a part of material possession. As with Poe's tales about avenging women—those beloveds who haunt and possess the lover—"Hop-Frog" inverts and reconstitutes what Orlando Patterson has called "the idiom of power."[37]

"WHEN LADIES DID NOT WALK BUT FLOATED"

* * *

Like those Southern gentlemen who kept "black wenches" and "white ladies" neatly categorized, Poe does not explicitly connect the idea of race to that of gender, yet he suggests such a coupling in his fictions and poetry. Although he reviews both Margaret Fuller and Lydia Maria Child, he never mentions their essays against slavery or their comparison of violated slaves to women subordinated in marriage. Only once in a review does Poe link the institution of marriage and that of slavery. Reviewing Longfellow's *Poems on Slavery*, he describes "the Quadroon Girl" as "the old abolitionist story—worn threadbare—of a slaveholder selling his own child." He adds, "a thing which may be as common in the South, as in the East, is the infinitely worse crime of making matrimonial merchandise—or even less legitimate merchandise—of one's daughter" (*ER* 285).

What Poe seldom did in his criticism, he accomplished in his fictions. Let us recall that in "Ligeia" Poe's blond Lady Rowena of Tremaine is married off for money: "Where were the souls of the haughty family of the bride, when, through thirst of gold, they permitted to pass the threshold of an apartment so bedecked, a maiden and a daughter so

---

[36]Hegel, 237.
[37]See Orlando Patterson, *Slavery and Social Death: A Comparative Study* (Cambridge: Harvard Univ. Press, 1982), 17–34.

beloved?" (p. 55). A "lady" like Ligeia becomes the site for a crisis of racial identity. In life, Ligeia "came and departed as a *shadow*" (p. 48), and before her bodily "return," the narrator envisions "a *shadow* . . . such as might be fancied for the shadow of a shade" (p. 57). That Ligeia would not tell her lover about her family, or ever reveal her "paternal name" makes this lady sound as if she might well be Poe's rendition of the favorite fiction of white readers: the "tragic mulatta" or "octoroon mistress."[38]

In "Ligeia," Poe signals the same physiognomic traits as did taxonomists of color in the Caribbean and the South: hair, eyes, and skin. Ligeia has "the raven-black, the glossy, the luxuriant and *naturally-curling tresses*" (p. 49) also used by Stowe when describing Harry in *Uncle Tom's Cabin* and by Child in her portrayal of Rosabella in *A Romance of the Republic* and Rosalie in "The Quadroons," with her "glossy ringlets of . . . raven hair." In *A Romance of the Republic* miscegenation is safely reinscribed as nature's delightful caprice and the charming ability to speak many languages, to be mixed up or "polyglot." The female products of white and black coupling are represented as compounds of flowers blended, shaded, or striped in "mottled and clouded" hues and color naturalized as an "autumnal leaf" or the color of a pear made golden by the sun. Here, the origin myth for the mulatta is a "tropical"—never African "ancestry."[39]

[38]Note that the offspring of a "misalliance" between a white man and a black female slave followed the condition of the mother. In laws trying to curb interbreeding, light-colored women were prohibited from using the name of the father. Especially problematic is the use of the term *mulatto*. Virginia Domínguez writes in *White By Definition: Social Classification in Creole Louisiana* (New Brunswick, N.J.: Rutgers Univ. Press, 1986), that "Limited lexical options meant that the term *mulatto* was used to denote anyone who did not appear all white *or* all black" (49). In Europe and the United States, and in most of the Caribbean by the late 1700s, the general term *mulatto* was used to metonymize varying nuances of skin color and extent of blood mixture. Note, however, that colonial taxonomies were far from lexically limited but bear witness to a frenzied nomenclature of color. According to Moreau de Saint-Méry's theoretical taxonomies of color in *Description de la partie française de l'Isle Saint-Domingue*, mulatto was one of eleven categories of 110 combinations ranked from absolute white (128 parts white blood) to absolute black (128 parts black blood), pushing the invisibility of color differentiation to fantastic extremes. Such a system not only displaced the human element from the hybrid offspring of colonial coupling, but became a desperate attempt to redefine whiteness. This analysis of rituals of color and black codes is elaborated in my *Haiti, History, and the Gods* (forthcoming, Univ. of California Press, 1994).

[39]Surely one of the most problematic uses of women by well-intentioned abolitionists was their conversion of the racist portrayal of a demonic and lascivious ape-woman into a sentimental heroine, processed as the refined, potentially salvageable, but ever fallen "tragic mulatta."

Ligeia's eyes, like those of the sensuous Creole beauties described by numerous observers, are large and expressive. But Poe goes further: "far larger than the ordinary eyes of *our own race*. They were even fuller than the fullest of the *gazelle eyes* of the tribe of the valley of Nourja-had" (p. 49). Mabbott notes that Poe alludes "to *The History of Nou-riahad* by 'Sidney Biddulph' (Mrs. Frances Sheridan)" and then quotes from this text that describes Nourjahad's "seraglio" as "adorned with a number of the most beautiful female slaves, . . . whom he purchased at vast expense."[40] Ligeia's sirenlike voice, the reiterated "'strangeness'" in her beauty, and her passion all suggest a racial heritage that would indeed be suspect, but Poe's rhapsodic and tortured circlings around the *whatness* of eyes that are linked to those of a dark tribe suggest how masterful had become the euphemisms for marks of blackness in a land preoccupied with construing purity out of impurity. If we recall Poe's elaborate, phantasmagoric decor of the bridal chamber wrought for the new bride Rowena with its "few ottomans and golden candelabra, of Eastern figure" (p. 55), we are reminded that the scene for Ligeia's resurrection is indeed a harem devoted to the memory and perpetua-tion of a submission far more grounded in a particular and "peculiar" institution than has previously been noted.

Could a white lady of sufficient piety be described as having such "wild eyes," "wild desire," and "wild longing"?[41] Ligeia's "skin rival-ling the purest ivory" links her further to the dubious status of women of color. How can you detect color in a white "suspect"? As colors faded and hair and eyes became closer to those of "pure" whites, new distinctions had to be invented. The attempt to name, label, and classify the degrees of color in between the extremes of black and white resulted in fantastic taxonomies of a uniquely racialized enlightenment. The epistemology of whiteness, absolutely dependent for its effect on the detection of blackness, resulted in fantasies about secret histories and hidden taints that would then be backed up by explicit codes of law. And since it was not always possible to detect black blood in lightened skin, natural historians assured their readers that the tone of whiteness was different: unnatural, less animated, dull or faded, white but pale or closer to yellow, with a tint ranging from grayish yellow to yellowish white like ivory. This gothic obsession with identity and origins . . . gets

---

[40]Mabbott, 2:332.
[41]I am indebted here to my student Jennifer Ellis's analysis of Ligeia in her paper, "Rereading Poe's Textual Body in 'Ligeia,' and Ligeia's Body as Text: Doubling and the Racial Unconscious" (December, 1992).

its metaphors and the myth of its ambiguities from the mottled discourse of racial identity.

Further, if matrimony remains a woman's sole purpose, even a Southern writer like Tucker in *George Balcombe* suggests, though indirectly, the horrific slippages that Poe deliberately intensifies. According to Tucker's gentlemen, a proper woman is endowed with primitive qualities that civilized society hones into generous sentiments. Docile, she learns to cherish her husband's superiority and subordinate herself to the "master feeling of her heart." A turn to God, "the great King above all gods," clinches these bonds of affection. God loves and asks nothing in return from "us helpless worms" except "our hearts."[42] Poe takes this fiction and exposes it as coordinate with the most terrifying possession. In Poe's tales about women, marriage turns what was cherished into what is scorned. In this process of reciprocal repulsions, the "Conqueror Worm" gets into the heart, "seraphs sob at vermin fangs," and as beastliness reveals itself to be the true if concealed ground of immaculate femininity, the Great House collapses.

Poe demonstrates that if justifications of slavery depended on making the black nonhuman and unnatural, women were also subject to the mind of man. They would always remain on the side of the body, no matter how white, how rarified or ethereal, or how black, earthy, and substantial. They can be hags or beauties, furies or angels. They are nothing but phantasms caught in the craw of civilization, and Poe's gothic literalizes the way that racialist terminology — and the excesses of a system that depended on discourses of gender purity for its perpetuation — generated its own gods and monsters.

GETTING BACK TO RICHMOND

Though Poe left Richmond in 1827, he returned home in 1835 and became editorial assistant, principal book reviewer, and finally editor of *The Southern Literary Messenger*. In 1830 the total population of Virginia was 1,211,405, of whom 694,300 were white, 47,348 were "free persons of color," and 469,757 were black slaves. Further, the 1820 census figures for Richmond demonstrate the high percentage of African Americans in the city of Poe's youth: about two-thirds of the

---

[42]Tucker, *George Balcombe*, 2:51–52; 1:71–72.

households owned slaves.[43] So, Poe's Virginia could be argued to be a very African place.

Nat Turner's 1831 rebellion—in Southampton, some seventy miles below Richmond—along with accounts of butchery and, very often, stories of "unoffending women and children" victims were summoned whenever the question of emancipation was raised. And since emancipation in the British West Indies had been finalized in 1834, a year before Poe's return, we can imagine that many proslavery advocates found themselves faced with a double bind: rebellion or emancipation. It could be argued that folks in the Virginia Tidewater knew more about the revolution in Saint-Domingue than many in the Northern states, since proslavery newspapers and pamphlets compared "General Nat's" failed insurrection to the successful working of blood by Dessalines in Haiti in 1804, "when in one fatal night more than 1000 of the unfortunate white inhabitants of the island of St. Domingo (men, women and children) were butchered by the Negroes!"[44]

Some Virginians even feared that some of the refugees of Saint-Domingue who settled in Southampton had brought their negroes with them. "Over ten thousand emigres from that island fled to the southern States, bringing with them new elements of fear of slave uprisings."[45] The *Virginia Gazette and General Advertiser*, for example, published frequent accounts of women tortured by black insurgents, their eyes gouged out with corkscrews and bellies ripped open to reveal unborn children to their dying mothers.[46] Although Southern newspapers tended to underplay white-sponsored atrocities during the last years of the war for independence, they did report General Rochambeau's use of bloodhounds from Havana, Cuba, to disembowel black prisoners in his spectacular arena set up on the grounds of the old Jesuit monastery at Cap Français. Most of the French colonists—nearly 25,000—seeking refuge in the United States ended up in Philadelphia, Baltimore, Charleston, New Orleans, and Norfolk. As the exiled white Martiniquan lawyer and historian Médéric Louis Elie Moreau de

[43] Richard C. Wade, *Slavery in the Cities: 1820–1860* (New York: Oxford Univ. Press, 1964), 20.

[44] Warner, 293–94, 54

[45] Clement Eaton, *The Freedom of Thought Struggle in the Old South* (1940; reprint, New York: Harper and Row, 1964), 90.

[46] See Alfred N. Hunt, *Haiti's Influence on Antebellum America: Slumbering Volcano in the Caribbean* (Baton Rouge: Louisiana State Univ. Press, 1988), 38–40, and Winthrop Jordan, *White Over Black*, 375–80, for excellent summaries of white reactions in the United States to the black revolution in Saint-Domingue.

Saint-Méry noted, Norfolk was especially attractive, since "the inhabitants of this place have shown a constant affection for the French."[47]

Poe returned to Richmond as fear of black terror and retribution spread. Note that in the review of *Slavery in the United States*, though Poe refers to "recent events in the West Indies" and talks of "the parallel movement here," he nowhere refers to the Nat Turner insurrection. Perhaps Poe knew that his readers would too readily recall the Turner rebellion and white vengeance in southeastern Virginia, the inhuman carnage that finally cost many innocent blacks—some estimate about 200—their lives. As Poe worked on the *Southern Literary Messenger*, increasing circulation from five hundred to about thirty-five hundred, what became known as the Great Southern Reaction of the 1830s and 1840s created a closed, nearly martial society intent on preserving its slave-based civilization.

Slave trading in the city of Richmond was frequent and had reached its height in Virginia during the 1830s. Some have argued that Virginia slave traders enjoyed an affluence rivaled only by tobacco merchants of the previous century: "Prior to 1846, the Bell Tavern, on the north side of Main just below Fifteenth, was the scene of a great many of these deplorable spectacles."[48] Poe must have frequently walked past the Richmond slave market, which was only two blocks away from the offices of the *Southern Literary Messenger*. He doubtless witnessed slave auctions and experienced the terror of those led through the streets, chained in slave coffles, readied for their journey to the Deep South.

We have evidence of Poe's relationships with the leading proslavery advocates in Virginia, but what about his relationship to those variously represented in the Virginia Slavery Debate of 1831–1832 as "pets," "play-mates of the white children," "the merriest people in the world," "valuable property," or "monsters"? How can we begin to think about those who left no written records but were a constant presence, whose existence though distorted or erased informed Poe's unique brand of gothic narrative in ways that have been ignored?

Poe's guardians, the Allans, had at least three household servants (all slaves, but at least one of these was owned by someone else and bonded to Mr. Allan). On 1 January 1811, Mr. Allan hired a woman

[47]Moreau de Saint-Méry, *Voyage aux États-Unis de l'Amérique, 1793–1798*, ed. Stewart L. Mims (New Haven: Yale Univ. Press, 1913), 55–56.

[48]Virginius Dabney, *Richmond: The Story of a City* (New York: Doubleday & Company, 1976), 111.

named Judith from Master Cheatham for 25 pounds, "to be retained and clothed as usual under a bond of £50."[49] According to some accounts, Judith was Edgar's "Mammy," perhaps the "Juliet" or "Eudocia" mentioned by receipts and the bills of sale as being in John Allan's household. Whatever her name, she sometimes took him to the "Old Church on the Hill" grounds where he spent many late afternoons. After all, his foster mother Fanny Allan was often too ill to attend to Poe. Though we hear about Poe's dead mother Eliza and all those subsequent, surrogate pale mothers (especially Jane Stannard and Fanny Allan in Richmond), we are never reminded of the black woman in the house. When Poe was awaiting entry into West Point in 1829, living with Maria Clemm in Baltimore, he sold a slave. In April 1940, the *Baltimore Sun* published the record of the bill of sale of "a negro man named Edwin," calling it an "Item for Biographers." The article begins: "While examining some entries in an underground record room at the Courthouse a few days ago a Baltimore man who wishes his name withheld quite by chance came across an old document relating to Edgar Allan Poe, which seems thus far to have entirely escaped the poet's biographers."[50] Many Virginia accounts of the Nat Turner rebellion blamed its occurrence on superstition and religious fanaticism. But these written accounts of the "extraordinary" beliefs of negroes, shared by many whites, probably mattered less to Poe than his daily encounters with slaves in his own house or on the plantations he visited. Poe's gothic, his unique tools of terror, finally have less to do with "Germany" or the "soul," as he once proclaimed in the Preface to his "Tales of the Grotesque and Arabesque," than with African American stories of the angry dead, sightings of teeth, the bones and matter of charms, the power of conjuring. Let me add that such stories, merging with early Christian folk beliefs transplanted to the South, as well as the frenzy of revivals with whites and slaves caught up in the Holy Spirit, might also have encouraged the strangely sentient landscapes of Poe, his obsession with the reciprocities between living and dead, human and animal, the possessions and demonic visitations of his most well-known tales.[51]

[49] I am grateful to Jean M. Mudge for this information.
[50] I thank Jeffrey Savoy of the Poe Society of Baltimore for sending me this article.
[51] The biography that deals most with the contact between the young Poe and slaves is Hervey Allen's *Israfel: The Life and Times of Edgar Allan Poe*, 2 vols. (London: Brentano's Ltd., 1927). Note that the revised, one-volume edition of *Israfel* published in 1934 excludes these discussions of Poe and his African American surround.

DIALOGUE WITH THE DEAD

In writing *Fables of Mind: An Inquiry Into Poe's Fiction*, I struggled with the philosophical and religious cruxes in Poe's tales. Philosophy meant Locke. Religion meant Calvin and Edwards. The path to enlightenment was clear. I could explain the dark hauntings, the spectral return of a Ligeia who took possession of the physical Rowena by looking at Calvin's insistence on visibility in the flesh, by Locke's paradoxes on identity, and even Newtonian mechanics. Yet what if we turn to the equally critical ground in Poe's past, that of African American belief? In "Unspeakable Things Unspoken," Toni Morrison notes the presence, the shadow, the ghost from which most critics have fled.[52] In a world where identities wavered between colors, where signs of whitening and darkening were quickly apprehended by all inhabitants, enlightenment depended on shadows. The gods, monsters, and ghosts spawned by racist discourse redefined the supernatural. What the white masters called sorcery was rather an alternative philosophy, including spiritual experiences shared by both blacks and whites. The most horrific spirits of the Americas were produced by the logic of the master filtered through the thought and memory of slaves.

After "Ligeia" was published in 1839, Poe sent it to Philip Cooke and asked whether or not the ending was intelligible. What most dismays Cooke about the ending is the way "the Lady Ligeia takes possession of the deserted *quarters* . . . of the Lady Rowena." He explains, "There I was shocked by a violation of the ghostly proprieties . . . and wondered how the Lady Ligeia—a wandering essence—could, in quickening *the body* of the Lady Rowena . . . become suddenly the visible, bodily, Ligeia."[53] Consider the ending: Ligeia with her "huge masses of long and dishevelled hair" and "wild eyes" enters and takes the place of the "fair-haired, the blue-eyed Rowena." Seeing the quickening, risen flesh, the narrator thinks, "Can it be Rowena?" only to recognize Ligeia. Familiar with stories of the returning dead, Poe worked them into the tale he called his "best." The spirit so fills the living body that no trace remains of the once-alive vessel; taken by the spirit, the body reacts. Its gestures and lineaments conform to ghostly demands. We are no longer dealing with a narrator in trance, a madman who hallucinates, a drugged murderer, but the scene of possession. Not by a white

---

[52]Toni Morrison, "Unspeakable Things Unspoken: The Afro-American Presence in Literature," *Michigan Quarterly Review* 28 (Winter 1989): 12.

[53]Philip Cooke to Poe, 16 September 1839, in *Complete Works of Edgar Allan Poe*, 50.

master—the affectionate appropriator of Poe's disputed review—but by a spirit, conjured and rising up, like Ligeia, from quiescence to revenge.

I grew up in the South and recall the terrors that constitute knowledge, the awful concreteness of the spirit and theories that needed no John Locke to reveal wandering souls or shape-shifting identities. Who are the ghosts to drag you down? Blood on the carpet, a look at the moon that could kill you, circumscribed by fear of women who left their skin at the door—haints more present than the living. The question is how to bring what has been constituted as mere foolishness or worse into the study of a literary text without turning practice into cliché, without turning African American belief into a trope in yet another scholarly exercise. I conclude with two slave stories recorded by Moreau de Saint-Méry before he left Saint-Domingue for the United States. These stories of genesis suggest that cosmologies of color were not the property of whites alone:

> According to them, God made man and he made him white; the devil who spied on him made another being just the same; but when he finished the devil found him black, by a punishment of God who did not want his work to be confounded with that of the Evil Spirit. The latter was so irritated by this distinction, that he slapped the copy and made him fall on his face, which flattened his nose and swelled his lips. Other less modest negroes say that the first man came out black from the hands of the Creator and that the White is only a negro whose color has deteriorated.[54]

Poe's racialized gothic—the terrors of whiteness in Poe's Pym, the shadows and shades in fairyland, the blurring of privilege and perversion in tales about ladies who turn into revenants and lovers who turn into slaves—requires that we rethink the meaning of color and the making of monsters, as well as question the myths of the masters who still haunt the halls of the academy.

---

[54]Moreau de Saint-Méry, *Description topographique, physique, civile, politique et historique de la partie française de l'isle Saint-Domingue* (1797; reprint, Paris: Société de l'Histoire des Colonies Françaises et Librairie Larose, 1984), 1:58.

LESLEY GINSBERG

Slavery and the Gothic Horror of Poe's "The Black Cat"

Chair of the Department of English and associate professor at the University of Colorado, Colorado Springs, Lesley Ginsberg has published numerous essays on nineteenth-century American literature and culture and early American literature and culture, including two influential essays on Poe's story "The Black Cat." The essay below originally appeared in American Gothic: New Interventions in a National Narrative, *edited by Robert K. Martin and Eric Savoy (Iowa City: University of Iowa Press, 1998).*

As Leslie Fiedler put it more than thirty years ago, "the proper subject" of the "American gothic" is "slavery" (378). In this essay I shall argue that behind the gothic machinery of Poe's "The Black Cat"—with its graphic and "damnable atrocity," its "PERVERSENESS," its murdered corpse, "clotted with gore"—are resounding echoes of antebellum slavery discourses, allusions which allow the story to be read not only as an examination of the narrator's purported "peculiarity of character" but also as an investigation into the peculiar psychopolitics of the master/slave relationship, a bond whose sentimentalized image was at the heart of the South's proslavery rhetoric (p. 178).

Not only does "The Black Cat" reproduce the struggle between a helpless dependent and an abusive tyrant which figures so prominently in both gothic fictions and abolitionist discourses, but the crumbling edifice of denial exposed by the narrator's confession deconstructs the sentimental strategies of repression so common to antebellum rhetoric. Like many of Poe's gothic tales, "The Black Cat" (1843) cries out for contextualization: critics have shown that the story reflects contemporary sensationalist fictions, parodies the temperance confessional, and critiques the growing acceptance of the insanity defense in antebellum courtrooms (Reynolds, Matheson, Cleman). But the tale also invokes other discourses central to the 1830s and 1840s, including its rehearsal of the scene of pet abuse so often featured in antebellum child-rearing manuals and its repetition of the obsessive pitting of black against white, dependency against freedom, and animal against human which fueled contemporary debates over chattel slavery and social reform. As David Walker famously puts it to his "beloved brethren" (7) in a phrase which mirrors "The Black Cat's" compulsive iterations of the domestic battle between a black "*brute beast*" and its human owner ("a man, fashioned in the image of the High God" [p. 183]), the horror of slavery is its dehumanization: while "all the inhabitants of the earth are called *men*, we and our children are *brutes*!!" (Walker 7).

When the *Richmond Enquirer* repeatedly describes Nat Turner and his accomplices as a gang of "banditti" (qtd. in Tragle 43, 58, 145), the inaccuracy of this term and its muted reference to the standard public enemies of British gothic fiction belie the extent to which southern discourse was all too ready to conflate the real horrors of slavery and insurrection with the conventions of Radcliffean[1] cliché. As the *Enquirer* reports, using imagery which is as conspicuously literary as it is flagrantly removed from southeastern Virginia, these real-life rebels "remind one of a parcel of blood-thirsty wolves rushing down from the Alps" (qtd. in Tragle 43). In a rhetorical gesture which transforms rebel slaves into wild beasts and dissolves fact into fiction, the editors of the *Enquirer* participate in the production of a cultural convention: the creation of a national gothic narrative whose conspicuously fictive framework masks the real horror of race war at the core of the peculiar institution.

"Why?, Why?, Why?, the papers asked in long and repetitious articles which habitually described those who had revolted as 'banditti'" (Tragle 4). As historian Henry Irving Tragle notes, the overwhelming question which vexed southern newspapers, the riddle which ostensibly impelled Thomas Gray to extract Turner's confession, was the seemingly unsolvable enigma of motive. For, as the *Enquirer* muses, Turner acted "without any cause or provocation, that could be assigned"; the *Richmond Compiler* concurred when this newspaper submitted that "[t]heir ultimate object . . . [is] not yet explained." In his teasing introduction to the *Confessions*, Gray commiserates with the frustration of readers who have seen "the insurgent slaves . . . destroyed, or apprehended, tried, and executed . . . without revealing anything at all satisfactory, as to the motives which governed them." As Gray empathizes with his puzzled patrons, "[p]ublic curiosity has been on the stretch to understand . . . the motives" of the "great Bandit" and his gang: "[e]verything connected with this sad affair was wrapt in mystery, until [Gray adds in a transparent advertisement for his pamphlet] Nat Turner . . . was captured" (qtd. in Tragle 43–44, 48, 303).

By persistently describing the rebellious slaves as a gang of thieving banditti, southern reporters have already imputed a motive, but the repeated assertions that the insurrection was motiveless betray the poverty

---

[1] Anne Radcliffe (1764–1823), English writer and a pioneer of the Gothic novel.

of the plunder hypothesis, while the paltry consolations provided by southern pundits underscore their failure to mollify white anxiety. As Gray puts it ominously in his introduction to the *Confessions*, in a characterization of Turner which seems lifted out of the pages of Charles Brockden Brown's gothic novel *Wieland*, "whilst every thing upon the surface of society wore a calm and peaceful aspect, a gloomy fanatic was revolving in the recesses of his own dark, bewildered and overwrought mind, schemes of indiscriminate massacre to the whites" (qtd. in Tragle 304).

Yet when he imagines a "society" whose "surface," at least, was "calm and peaceful," Gray proffers his own version of the familiar fictions surrounding southern plantation life. As if tuned to the pulse of slaveholding apprehensions, Gray's insistence that Turner was but a uniquely deranged extremist became the most popular explanation for the rebellion: like a deadly but incommunicable disease, the revolt was no more than "a sudden . . . outbreak of fanaticism and subtle craft," soothes the *Constitutional Whig*. Beneath a headline proclaiming "THE BANDIT TAKEN!" the *Enquirer* effectively stifles any nascent debate over the causes of the insurrection by declaring that "[n]o man" can read Turner's account of the rebellion "without setting Nat Turner down as a wild fanatic." If Turner was just a crazed enthusiast, slave owners could continue to deny the far more frightening conclusion that the cause of the revolt was built into the very structure of the peculiar institution. Gray concludes the narrative with the ringing judgment of the court: "your only justification," proclaims the court chairman, as Turner's death sentence is pronounced, is that "you were led away by fanaticism" (qtd. in Tragle 90, 136, 319). But even as the court attempts to give its authoritative answer to the vexing question of Turner's motives, the circulation of his narrative offers at least the possibility that readers could recover another story buried within the *Confessions*, despite its controlling layers of introductions, official documents, and formal dictation supplied by Gray. To paraphrase Poe's later treatment of the paradoxical invisibility of the obvious in his most famous ratiocinative tale, "The Purloined Letter" (1844), in an echo of that document which haunted Turner's rebellion, the Declaration of Independence, perhaps the secret of Turner's motive remained opaque because the answer was just "'A little *too* self-evident'" (p. 187).[2]

Nat Turner's revolt prompted fearful southerners to launch a verbal and ideological counterattack which was manifested in an outpouring

---

[2]Turner had originally planned the revolt for "the 4th July" (see Tragle 310). [Ginsberg's note.]

of proslavery literature as well as a series of debates in the Virginia state legislature on the subject of emancipation, which the legislature predictably deemed impossible, though not without significant opposition. Many delegates, particularly those who represented the western parts of the state, favored either some form of gradual abolitionism or various schemes of deportation and colonization (Leverenz 213–14, Freehling 122–169). Horrified by the implications of these intellectually freewheeling debates, Thomas R. Dew (then a twenty-nine-year-old professor at the College of William and Mary) published a response in the *American Quarterly Review* that reads as a species of proslavery damage control. Soon reprinted with added commentary in pamphlet form, Dew's *Review of the Debate in the Virginia Legislature* (1832) became what Lewis P. Simpson calls "the prototypical document in a literature that was to flow unceasingly from Southern pens for the next thirty years" (169). Indeed, if Dew's treatise can be said to have provided a rhetorical template for the aspiring southern gentleman, his experience also demonstrated that identification with the discourse of white supremacy offered no hindrance to a markedly meteoric rise; four years later Dew ascended to the presidency of the college while concurrently forging a name for himself in the periodical press as a prominent contributor to the *Southern Literary Messenger*—a sideline which coincided with Poe's stint as editor of that magazine. And if Dew's chronicle of the debates can be read as an articulation of some of the South's most cherished fictions, it is worth noting that Dew quotes at least one participant who frames his opinion of emancipation in an argument which explicitly invokes gothic literature:

> To turn ["the negro"] loose in the manhood of his physical passions, but in the infancy of his uninstructed reason, would be to raise up a creature resembling the splendid fiction of a recent romance; the hero of which constructs a human form with all the physical capabilities of man, and with the thews and sinews of a giant, but . . . finds too late that he has only created a more than mortal power of doing mischief, and himself recoils from the monster which he has made. (Quoted in Dew 105)

In an allusion to a novel which sounds suspiciously like Mary Shelley's *Frankenstein* (1818), this Virginian participates in the creation of what could be called a national gothic narrative of slavery. And by invoking Shelley's novel, whose layers of frame narratives enclose the monster's own damning tale at its center, this extraordinary moment in the debates belies the fear on the part of these southern patriarchs that their control over the discourse of slavery was being challenged by the voices of those who were traditionally mute: women, children, slaves, and, by extension, animals.

At the core of proslavery ideology was the equating of slaves with animals. J. K. Paulding's *Slavery in the United States* (1836) asserts that the "woolly-headed race"—that familiar, hackneyed phrase which itself evokes an animal-like image—is burdened with an immutable "inferiority"; blacks are rightly "classed as the lowest in the scale of rational beings" (280). In *The South-West* (1835), Joseph Holt Ingraham approvingly notes that the field slave, whom he ranks as "but little higher than [a] brute . . . the last and lowest link in the chain of the human species," is commonly traded from "one [master] to another" like "a purchased horse." A provincial northerner, as Ingraham remarks, might look upon "a band of negroes, as upon so many men. But the planter, or southerner, views them in a very different light" (254, 194, 260). As William Drayton concurs in his vitriolic *The South Vindicated* (1836) in a stunning example of southern repression in the teeth of Turner's revolt, "[t]he slave, besotted, servile, accustomed to degradation, and habituated to regard his master with deference and awe, does not presume to dream of contending with him" (299).

Yet if proslavery advocates were wont to dehumanize blacks, abolitionists would consistently exploit the horror of slavery's challenge to the limit between human and animal. "The Black Cat" appeared two years before Frederick Douglass's *Narrative*, while Douglass toured the North delivering those speeches that culminated in the publication of his rhetorical transformation from the "beast-like stupor" of slavery to the full humanity of freedom, as Douglass famously reiterates the slave's lament, "O, why was I born a man, of whom to make a brute!" (1966–67). Theodore Dwight Weld's encyclopedic *American Slavery As It Is* (1839) documents the sufferings of slaves who are worked like "droves of 'human cattle,'" then "herded at night like swine" (76, 19). In his expert revision of abolitionist tropes, Douglass persistently equates slaves and animals: "horses and men, cattle and women, pigs and children" are all valued as if "holding the same rank in the scale of being" (1958). For Douglass, humanization was inextricably bound to literacy and the authorizing power of his *Narrative*. But like the condemning wail of the "brute beast" who convicts his owner with "a voice from within the tomb!" (p. 183, 185), Douglass narrates his first act of physical resistance in terms that are as gothic as they are Christian: "[i]t was a glorious resurrection, from the *tomb* of slavery" (1971, my emphasis). By imagining the assertion of his humanity as a return from the grave,

Douglass allows us to reread the irrepressible voice of the dead in "The Black Cat" as an explicit metaphor for the silences and repressions upon which the peculiar institution was built.

If southern ideology rested heavily on the supposed animal-like nature of black people, proslavery rhetoric was quick to sentimentalize the relationship of master and slave by repeated allusions to the cloying imagery of the bonds between humans and domesticated animals, especially pets. In Ingraham's romantic depiction of slavery, "slave children are pets in the house, and the playmates of the white children in the family" (126). J. K. Paulding (Poe's friend and literary champion during his tenure at the *Messenger*) thought highly enough of Ingraham's sentiments that he reprints this passage in full in his own treatise on slavery (223). Ingraham's much-loved passage is also echoed almost verbatim in "The Black Cat," when the narrator tells us that his cat was his "favorite pet and playmate" (p. 179).

Though southerners were apt to romanticize dependency, their most potent defense of slavery was the domestic fiction of the happy slaveholding family. As Dew sentimentally affirms, "[T]he slave . . . generally loves the master" (113). And in a stunning passage which conflates slavery and the dependency of childhood, Drayton declares, "We are all, in early life, slaves" (82). As George Fitzhugh puts it, all dependents are slaves: "[w]ives and apprentices are slaves; not only in theory, but often in fact," just as "[c]hildren are the slaves to their parents, guardians and teachers" (though in Fitzhugh's trivialization of slavery, "[t]hree-fourths of free society are slaves") (88–89, 91, 90). But it was not only southerners who represented family government on the antidemocratic model of master and slave. Samuel Goodrich, one of the period's premiere publishers of children's literature, articulates a similar vision in *Fireside Education*, a child-rearing guide popular enough to have gone through six editions by 1841. As Goodrich asserts, familial government is rightly "despotic, giving absolute authority to the monarch parents over their subject children" (26). And in his children's periodical *Merry's Museum*, Goodrich inundates the child reader with stories of loving dependency. The January 1843 edition includes a version of that tale so dear to southern apologists, entitled "Fidelity of a Negro Servant," the story of a vassal who is freed when his white "master" suffers financial disaster. But the grateful "negro" refuses to desert: " '[n]o, master, we will never part.' " The same issue includes a short essay on "EQUALITY" which flatly proclaims: "absolute equality" is "impossible." "Equality does not mean that a woman shall be equal to a man, or a child the same as a man." Though "[i]t is said in our Declaration of Independence, that 'all mankind [*sic*] are created equal,'" this part of the Declaration is not "literally true" (37–38).

While the narrator's alcoholism links "The Black Cat" to the temperance confessional, his struggle with "the Fiend Intemperance" (p. 179) also echoes those ubiquitous antebellum domestic guides whose relentless focus on emotional temperance implicitly highlights the dangers of familial tyranny. But as abolitionists argued, the intoxication of absolute power bred the intemperate abuses for which slavery was infamous—in a corollary to the atrocities in "The Black Cat," both Lydia Maria Child's *Anti-Slavery Catechism* (1835) and Weld's *Slavery As It Is* report incidents of eye gouging as well as outright murder (Child, *Catechism* 5; Weld 20, 77). As Weld puts it, "Arbitrary power is to the mind what alcohol is to the body; it intoxicates." For Weld, power is just as addictive as drink: "the more absolute the power, the stronger the desire for it." Power, Weld concludes, "is such a fiery stimulant, that its lodgement in human hands is always perilous" (115, 116).

At the same time as the abolitionist critique of power circulated on the fringes of respectable middle-class discourse, antebellum domestic guides struggled to justify traditional family government by lauding those parents who wielded their powers with discretion. To illustrate "the happy effects which may flow from firm, yet just and kind treatment of a disobedient child" by his omnipotent but temperate parents, Goodrich's *Fireside Education* includes a version of the scene of pet abuse so familiar to antebellum child-rearing guides, in this case an episode lifted from Catharine Maria Sedgwick's novelistic child-rearing manual, *Home*. In a fit of anger, young Wallace Barclay plunges his sister's kitten into a vat of boiling water; his elder brother first rescues the animal, but, "seeing its misery," he allows it to die in the hot water, a gesture of his "characteristic consideration." Wallace's father banishes him to his room with a curse that emphasizes the humanizing mission of parental absolutism: " '[y]ou have forfeited your right to a place among us. Creatures who are the slaves of their passions are like beasts of prey, fit only for solitude' " (26–27). Guilty of "murderous cruelty to an innocent animal" (Goodrich 26) dehumanized, like the narrator of "The Black Cat," by an act of wanton violence against an "unoffending brute" (p. 180), Wallace finally redeems himself by subduing his temper.[3]

---

[3] I am indebted to Marianne Noble for pointing out that the very scene which Goodrich reprints from Sedgwick's *Home* reappears in the opening pages of Maria Cummins's

*   *   *

For abolitionists, the keeping of forcibly domesticated animals had uncomfortable echoes of slavery. In *The Mother's Book* (1831), Lydia Maria Child concedes that caring for pets is a key step in the "cultivation of the affections," but Child also admits that she has moral qualms about the ethics of pet keeping: "I cannot think it right to keep creatures that must be confined in cages and boxes." And when Child reports a scene of pet abuse, she emphasizes the specter of parental tyranny: "I once saw a mother laugh very heartily at a kitten, which a child of two years old was pulling backward by the tail. At last, the kitten, in self-defense, turned and scratched the boy. He screamed, and his mother ran to him, and beat the poor kitten." As Child glosses, "the kitten was struck for defending herself; this was . . . a lesson of tyranny to the boy" (*Book* 6–7, 5–8, 7–8).

More tellingly, Child's abolitionist-leaning children's magazine includes stories which make the link between slavery and pet ownership explicit. In 1831, the *Juvenile Miscellany* offered the child-reader a story called "The Prisoners Set Free," authored by Hannah F. Gould, in which the Elsworth children decide to liberate their beloved caged pets (though as one child complains, in an echo of proslavery sentimentality, "I didn't keep my little Bonny because I was angry with him, but because I loved him"). Their mother affirms there is "no doubt" that her children's "little captives longed for freedom as much as the poor Africans do, who have to live and die in bondage to white men" (206–07). And if this story asserts that keeping formerly wild animals as pets reproduces the conditions of slavery, it is worth recalling that the pet-owning household in "The Black Cat" keeps not only domesticated creatures (like the cat and a "fine dog") but also "birds, gold-fish, rabbits," and, significantly, a "small monkey," whose position as a captive reads as a clear echo of slaveholding ideology, which, as David Walker complains, routinely classed blacks with "the tribes of *Monkeys*" and "*Ourang-Outangs*" (p. 179; Walker 10).

As Shawn Rosenheim points out, the etymological root of the word orangutan—so central to both "The Murders in the Rue Morgue" (1841) and Poe's grim "Hop-Frog" (1849), in which a formerly fawning servant ("forcibly carried off" in his youth from a home in "some barbarous region") summarily immolates his oppressors after symbolically

---

best seller *The Lamplighter* (Sedgwick 14–27; Cummins 10–12). See also Merish (28–29n9). [Ginsberg's note.]

reversing roles by costuming them as "ourang-outangs" in "chains" (pp. 217, 218)[4]—signifies not merely an animal but a "*wild man*" (Rosenheim 159), or, as the OED has it, an uncivilized "man of the woods." In Rosenheim's terms, what separates orangutans from humans "is less biology than culture, epitomized by the possession of language" (159); in other words, the dynamics of domestication is a model in miniature of the enslavement of the uncivilized Other (as well as the transformation of speechless, unsocialized infancy into adulthood). Further, representations of pet keeping trope those missionary impulses which were typically invoked to gloss involuntary servitude with a patina of sacredness; if (as Dew puts it in a telling syllogism) "the acquisition of dominion over the inferior animals" is "a step of capital importance in the progress of civilization," it "may with truth be affirmed, that the *taming* of man . . . is more important than the taming and using the inferior animals [sic], and nothing seems so well calculated to effect this as slavery." . . .

Like the southern version of Turner's revolt, "The Black Cat" seems to give us a terrifying example of a crime which challenges the logic of causality and a murderer whose criminality appears mysteriously motiveless. Like Turner, the narrator expresses no remorse, and by offering a confession which crazily collapses the murder of his wife with the slaying of his cat, the narrator begs to be dismissed as a lunatic. Yet this narrative quirk structurally reproduces the rhetoric of inversion and denial which allowed the *Enquirer* to describe rebel slaves as banditti and enabled southerners to indulge their wish that the insurrection was the motiveless work of "a complete fanatic" (Tragle 317). Further, when the narrator attempts to spook us with a black nemesis whose identity is tantalizingly obscure (is the second one-eyed cat a different pet, one of Poe's creepy undead, or the literal return of a shell-shocked creature who failed to die in the first place?), this narrative gesture mimics the dynamics of racial essentialism, which sometimes risks the destruction of individual particularity by predicating the self upon the oft-artificial category of race.[5] At the same time, the cat's mysterious subjectivity mocks the agitation of southerners who feared that every black could suddenly turn (to pun badly) into another Nat Turner; politicians admitted that Turner "had only furthered the 'suspicion attached to every slave,' the 'withering

---

[4]See also Dayan ("Amorous Bondage," p. 346) and Leverenz (232–33). [Ginsberg's note.]

[5]For a different yet illuminating treatment of the tension between the universal and the particular as they are played out within and through "The Black Cat," see Elmer (156–64). [Ginsberg's note.]

apprehension' that an 'insurgent' might lurk in any neighborhood, in any household" (Freehling 156). But if the South was haunted by Turner, the gothic exaggerations of the narrator's drama with a dark animal whom he owns allow his story to be read as the nightmarish return of the South's inescapable repressions: "I started, hourly, from dreams of unutterable fear, to find the hot breath of *the thing* upon my face, and its vast weight—an incarnate Night-Mare that I had no power to shake off—incumbent eternally upon my *heart!*" (p. 183). Figured as both a "creature" and a "*thing*," the cat, like a slave, is variously a beloved "pet," a "beast," a "child," and a "black object" (pp. 178, 179, 185, 181). While the narrator's bouts of "unutterable fear" invoke the aesthetics of the gothic sublime, his hyperbole recalls that other antebellum "Night-Mare," the one which was embodied "incarnate" in the brutalized body of the slave and inscribed in the condemning words of the slave narrative. Just as the "informing voice" of a formerly mute creature is that which consigns the narrator "to the hangman" (p. 186), the proliferation of slave narratives throughout the antebellum period threatened masters with the accusing voices of their previously muzzled "beasts of burden," in Garrison's metonym for the slave (Douglass 1933). Finally, the "pen-knife" (p. 179) which the narrator uses to cut out his pet's eye not only links "violence and the act of writing" (Benfey 36) but also suggests that the narrator imagines his black dependent as a discursive competitor.

Not only is Ingraham's oft-quoted proslavery formula repeated when the narrator tells us that "Pluto—this was the cat's name—was my favorite pet and playmate," but in a devastating mockery of southern sentimentality the narrator adds that "[t]here is something in the unselfish and self-sacrificing love of a brute, which goes directly to the heart of him who has had frequent occasion to test the gossamer fidelity of mere *Man*" (p. 178). Even the name Pluto recalls one of the few black people to appear in any of Poe's tales—"the old negro called Jupiter," who provides a bit of blackface humor in one of Poe's most popular antebellum stories, "The Gold-Bug," published less than two months before "The Black Cat." Like the hero of Goodrich's "Fidelity of a Negro Servant," Jupiter could not be "induced to abandon his young 'Massa,'" though he had previously been "manumitted." Further, the associative link between Jupiter and Pluto suggests that Poe may have been reviving the problem of dependency which lies dormant within "The Gold-Bug," but "The Black Cat" radically undermines the sentimental vision of paternal masters and grateful slaves which Poe invokes in this other, only minimally gothic tale. The pet owner in "The

Black Cat" degenerates from a child caretaker "noted" for his "docility and humanity" (p. 178) to a torturer and a murderer, while the happy dependent of the proslavery imagination not only bites the hand that feeds it, as Pluto first "inflicts a slight wound" upon the narrator's "hand with his teeth" (p. 179), but the brutalized animal, like Jupiter's dark double, finally condemns his owner by giving voice to the deeper horrors perpetrated by his master.

With its psychodramas of power and helplessness, "The Black Cat" reproduces the structural inequalities of the antebellum family, a doubling which is manifest when the protagonist is undone by the "scream" of a boughten creature, a dependent whose "cry" sounds suspiciously "like the sobbing of a child" (p. 185). As Poe's foray into that most stubborn of "sentiments"—the "spirit of perverseness"—implies (p. 180), the romance of dependency can so easily devolve into a horror story of abuse. In accordance with the abolitionist/feminist critique of absolute power, "The Black Cat" highlights the implicit dangers of familial tyranny: "I grew, day by day, more moody, more irritable, more regardless of the feelings of others. I suffered myself to use *intemperate language* to my wife. At length, I even offered her personal violence" (p. 179, my emphasis). Drunk with the thrills of petty domestic tyranny, the narrator immediately shifts his attention from wife to pet in a sequence whose crazy logic constitutes a confession that all dependents risk conflation within the brutal hierarchies of antebellum racial and sexual conventions: "[m]y pets, of course, were made to feel the change in my disposition. . . . I made no scruple of maltreating the rabbits, the monkey, or the dog. . . . even Pluto began to experience the effects of my ill-temper" (p. 179). And when read against abolitionist children's literature, the hyperbolic description of Pluto's murder in "The Black Cat" convicts the narrator of the same error made by young Caroline in the "The White Kitten with a Black Nose"—the confounding of persons and animals. To kill a cat with "tears streaming" and with "the bitterest remorse at . . . heart," to frame this act as "a sin—a deadly sin" which forever bars the perpetrator from the gates of heaven, is to reenact the deeper sin of slavery—the equating of humans with animals (p. 180).

Juxtaposed to the narrator's maudlin account of Pluto's death, his cold-blooded report of his wife's murder reads as an indictment of the dehumanizing effects of both domestic slavery and antebellum family government. In a final gesture of identification, his wife attempts to ward off the fatal ax originally "aimed at the animal," but "[g]oaded by the interference," the narrator "burie[s] the axe in her brain" (p. 184).

Never graced with a name, the murdered woman dissolves with terrifying speed from a "wife" to a "body" to an "it": the narrator toys with the possibilities of "packing it in a box, as if merchandize," an image which implicitly recalls slavery's commodification of human worth (p. 184). In a haunting perversion of the happy positivism of child-rearing manuals, the narrator's early training as a loving pet owner seems to have failed, though these guides insist that pet keeping teaches lifelong "kindness" (Sigourney 35). But as the abolitionist critique of this child-raising formula suggests, the act of keeping a pet may only transform pet owners into tyrannical domestic monsters. While the narrator's putative search for causality seems both gratuitous and perverse, "The Black Cat" needs no Dupin to unravel its secrets, for the cause of the narrator's brutality is walled up within the very structure of inequality upon which antebellum domesticity—and its dark double, domestic slavery—were built.

Like one of Poe's revenants, the specter of racism continues to haunt the Poe canon; even the most tentative perusal of Poe's oeuvre reveals a plethora of racist asides and bigoted formulas. From Robert Carter's angry letter to the *Liberator* denouncing Poe's unabashedly prosouthern puff of the *Southern Literary Messenger* (Thomas and Jackson 521, 520) to the nuanced assessments of contemporary critics, the debate over Poe's relation to proslavery ideology remains one of the most hotly contested issues in Poe scholarship. While the subject demands scrutiny (one more thorough than I can possibly present within the limits of this essay), I invoke this critical specter to suggest not only that "The Black Cat" invites us to deconstruct racist codes as they devolve into sheer horror but that the struggle between absolute dependency and absolute power so central to Poe's gothic fictions might also allow us to reconstruct Poe's vexed affiliation to the rhetoric of the antebellum southern elite. If, as David Leverenz remarks, Poe's work consistently attacks what he calls "gentry fictions of mastery" (212)—and here Leverenz skillfully conflates both the literature of the South as well as those gentry ideologies of aristocratic privilege predicated on the "starkly binary opposition" of " 'black' and 'white' " (223)—I would argue that to examine the psychosocial dynamics of race in Poe's fiction is not merely to display the "postabolitionist expectations" (218) of a hopelessly "Yankee" (214) naïveté. Rather, I suggest that the dilemma of race is at the core of Poe's gothic as well as his markedly conflicted attitude toward his own equivocal status as a literary professional.

Take, for example, Poe's distressing praise for Ingraham's *The South-West*, articulated in a review written for the *Southern Literary Messenger*.

When confronted by Ingraham's renditions of subhuman, animal-like slaves, Poe asserts that Ingraham "has spoken of slavery as he found it" and "discovered, in a word, that . . . the slave himself is utterly incapable of feeling the moral galling of his chain" (122).[6] Yet as unpardonable as this proslavery cliché may be, Poe's pronouncement must also be read in terms of the pressures under which it was produced. In a coincidence which invites us to rethink the strain of writing for the *Messenger* (Poe joined the magazine in August 1835), Thomas Dew's infamous *Review* was published by one T. W. White of Richmond—probably the same T[homas] W[illis] White who would soon launch the *Messenger*. The power struggles between Poe and White which led to Poe's abrupt dismissal from the magazine are notorious; further, the *Messenger* derived much of its support from some of slavery's most prominent apologists, including Dew, Paulding, and Nathaniel Beverley Tucker. When reviewing *The South-West* (a work which Paulding had already singled out for praise in his *Slavery in the United States*), Poe would have known that to be silent about Ingraham's portrait of the South's most crucial institution would be tantamount to professional suicide. As a conspicuously hired hand at the *Messenger*, our insecure young critic obligingly played out his role as mouthpiece for the slaveholding status quo.

At the same time, the act of entering into the editorial persona gave Poe the opportunity to identify with his putative father, John Allan, as well as Allan's circle of Richmond merchant-aristocrats, a class which enthralled Poe throughout his life even as it continued to reject him. And as the disinherited, never legally adopted son of this member of the Virginian elite, Poe was intimately acquainted with the limits of southern paternal benevolence, despite the wishful prose of slavery's apologists. Yet if Poe put up with the indignities of poverty and a marginal social reputation, the daily humiliations of writing for hire continued to chafe. In a letter to Judge Robert T. Conrad soliciting patronage for his ill-fated *Penn Magazine*, Poe takes care to mention that though he imagines his new magazine will be modeled "somewhat on the plan of the Richmond 'Southern Literary Messenger,'" the Poe of the *Messenger* was a counterfeit Poe: "I have been led to make the attempt of establishing it [the *Penn Magazine*] through an earnest yet natural desire of rendering myself independent. . . . So far I have . . . been forced to model my thoughts at the will of men whose imbecility was evident to all but themselves" (Poe, *The Letters* 153–154). Though Ste-

---

[6]Attributed to Poe in Thomas and Jackson (185). [Ginsberg's note.]

phen Rachman might argue that Poe's plaint is merely a confession of his artistic method (what Rachman convincingly shows is often the practice of plagiarism), I cite this letter for its more prosaic value as an example of the financial burdens under which Poe labored throughout his career (Ostrom, Whalen) and the concomitant ideological encumbrances which clogged the very politicized atmosphere of the antebellum periodical industry.

Further, in Poe's puff of the *Messenger* (*Broadway Journal*, 22 March I 854)—that notice which would so enrage the abolitionist Robert Carter—it is difficult not to hear the sneering tones of cynicism if not outright parody: Poe outrageously asserts that the *Messenger*'s "subscribers are almost without exception the elite . . . of the Southern aristocracy, and its corps of contributors are generally men who control the public opinion of the Southerners on *all* topics" (qtd. in Thomas and Jackson 520). While Carter alights on the political threat to "Northern democratic freemen" inherent within Poe's naked appeal to elitism (Poe is guilty of using "contemptible cunning" in the "alluring statement, that the supporters of the Messenger are 'the elite of the Southern aristocracy'"), Carter ignores the parodic implications of Poe's notably overdetermined language, including the obvious hyperbole contained in Poe's claim that the *Messenger* "controls" public opinion "on all topics." As Poe's one-time partner in the *Broadway Journal*, Charles Briggs, would joke about Carter's complaint: "[t]he Southern Lit[erary] Messenger . . . is as innocent of meaning of any kind as a blank sheet of paper" (both qtd. in Thomas and Jackson 521–522). Yet when Carter attacks the *Messenger* for its proslavery slant ("[i]ts principles are of the vilest sort, its aim being to uphold the 'peculiar institution,' to decry the colored race, [and] to libel abolitionists"), his critique also suggests that Poe may well have had to conform to the magazine's reigning ideology, an ideology which for Poe was already fraught with psychological temptation because the assumption of such views was a clear prerequisite to adoption by the southern elite. I do not mean to excuse Poe's racism or to force it, still breathing, back into its late unquiet grave; rather, I wish to suggest that the disjunction between Poe's proslavery pronouncements and the writer who produced fiction which plays out the proslavery agenda to its most horrifying conclusions might allow us to imagine a Poe whose relation to race was far more complex than it might at first appear.

Finally, when the narrator invites us into the gothic interior of his "most wild, yet most homely narrative" (p. 178), he does so in terms which presage the very linguistic contradictions that enabled Freud to develop a theory of the uncanny.[7] As Freud laboriously demonstrates, the word *unheimliche* means both homelike and unhomelike (221–227)—wild yet homely, to paraphrase Poe. "The Black Cat" has already undergone a Freudian analysis of sorts by critics, most notably Marie Bonaparte, and the narrator's misogyny seems tailored for Freudian treatment; the vacant eye sockets iterated throughout "The Black Cat" recall Freud's definition of castration anxiety ("the fear of damaging or losing one's eyes"), while Freud's assertion that "the *unheimlich* place" of female sexuality is really the familiar "entrance to the former *Heim* [home] of all human beings" throws the narrator's sexual fears into sharp relief (231, 245). But I make brief reference to Freud's treatment of the uncanny because I'd like to suggest that "The Black Cat" can also be read as the reflection of a collective form of psychosis, a manifestation of what could be called the political uncanny. In Freud's terms, the uncanny is inextricably linked to repression: he defines it as "that class of the frightening which leads back to what is known of old and long familiar" (220). The repeated southern renderings of Turner's revolt as the strange and inexplicable eruption of one person's craziness can thus be read as a form of the political uncanny, whereby southerners turned the event into a gothic horror story precisely because they were actively engaged in repressing the deeper horrors at the heart of the peculiar institution, a "familiar" fact of southern life walled up in the cellar of the collective antebellum psyche. To put it another way, when Poe dedicates his *Tales of the Grotesque and Arabesque* (1839) to Colonel William Drayton, author of *The South Vindicated from the Treason and Fanaticism of the Northern Abolitionists* (1836), Poe almost invites us to link the psychological machinery of the American gothic to the political machinations of American racism.[8] Further, if we accept that what often appears to be uncanny is really well known, the seemingly uncanny and compulsively repeated scenes of domestic violence throughout "The Black Cat" reveal nothing less than that familiar story of familial abuse, a tale which has its double in the model of domestic

[7] Compare Madden. [Ginsberg's note.]
[8] Poe's biographers appear quietly baffled by his decision to dedicate the volume to Drayton; Quinn notes the dedication and mentions that according to Drayton family tradition, Poe and the Colonel were friendly. Though Silverman's biography offers an otherwise complete discussion of the prefatory pages to the *Tales of the Grotesque and Arabesque* (the epigraph from Goethe on the title page, the preface by Poe), Silverman oddly omits any mention of the dedication, nor does Drayton appear in his index (see Quinn 129, 275; Silverman, *Edgar A. Poe* 153–154, 175, 545). [Ginsberg's note.]

slavery. But like the murdered body at the center of "The Black Cat" which refuses to stay buried, the narrative itself fails to hide the gruesome remains of antebellum repressions. Thus "The Black Cat" both reproduces and critiques the cultural work of the American gothic.

WORKS CITED

Benfey, Christopher. "Poe and the Unreadable." *New Essays on Poe's Major Tales.* Ed. Kenneth Silverman. Cambridge: Cambridge UP, 1993, 27–44.

Bonaparte, Marie. *The Life and Works of Edgar Allan Poe.* Trans. John Rodker. London: Imago, 1949.

Child, Lydia Maria. *Anti-Slavery Catechism.* 1835. 2nd ed. Newburyport: Charles Whipple, 1839.

———. *The Mother's Book.* 1831. Rpt. New York: Arno, 1972.

Cleman, John. "Irresistible Impulses: Edgar Allan Poe and the Insanity Defense." *American Literature* 64.4 (1991): 623–640.

Cummins, Maria Susanna. *The Lamplighter.* 1854. Rpt. ed. Nina Baym. New Brunswick: Rutgers UP, 1988.

Dayan, Joan. "Romance and Race." *The Columbia History of the American Novel.* Ed. Emory Elliott et al. New York: Columbia UP, 1991, 89–109.

Dew, Thomas R. *Review of the Debate in the Virginia Legislature of 1831 and 1832.* Richmond: T. W. White, 1832. Rpt. Westport: Greenwood, 1970.

Douglass, Frederick. *Narrative of the Life of Frederick Douglass, an American Slave, Written by Himself.* 1845. Rpt. in *The Norton Anthology of American Literature.* Ed. Nina Baym et al. 4th ed. Vol. I. New York: Norton, 1994, 1932–1995.

Drayton, William. *The South Vindicated from the Treason and Fanaticism of the Northern Abolitionists.* 1836. Rpt. New York: Greenwood, 1969.

Elmer, Jonathan. *Reading at the Social Limit: Affect, Mass Culture, and Edgar Allan Poe.* Stanford: Stanford UP, 1995.

"Equality." *Merry's Museum and Peter Parley's Magazine* (January 1843): 37–38.

"Fidelity of a Negro Servant." *Merry's Museum and Peter Parley's Magazine* (January 1843): 4.

Fiedler, Leslie A. *Love and Death in the American Novel.* New York: Criterion, 1960.

Fitzhugh, George. *Sociology for the South, or the Failure of Free Society.*
    1854. Rpt. in *Antebellum Writings of George Fitzhugh and Hinton
    Rowan Helper on Slavery.* Ed. Harvey Wish. New York: Putnam's,
    1960.

Freehling, Alison Goodyear. *Drift toward Dissolution: The Virginia
    Slavery Debate of 1831–1832.* Baton Rouge: Louisiana State UP,
    1982.

Freud, Sigmund. "Das Unheimliche" (The uncanny). 1919. *The
    Standard Edition of the Complete Psychological Works of Sigmund
    Freud.* Ed. and trans. James Strachey and Anna Freud et al. Vol. 17.
    London: Hogarth Press, 1962, 218–252.

Goodrich, Samuel G. *Fireside Education.* 6th ed. London: William
    Smith, 1841.

G[ould], H[annah] F[lagg]. "The Prisoners Set Free." *Juvenile
    Miscellany* (May–June 1831): 201–210.

———. "The White Kitten with a Black Nose." *Juvenile Miscellany*
    (January–February 1832): 288–304.

Ingraham, Joseph Holt. *The South-West. By a Yankee.* Vol. 2. New
    York: Harper, 1835. Rpt. Ann Arbor: University Microfilms,
    1966.

Leverenz, David. "Poe and Gentry Virginia." *The American Face of
    Edgar Allan Poe.* Ed. Shawn Rosenheim and Stephen Rachman.
    Baltimore: Johns Hopkins UP, 1995, 210–236.

Madden, Fred. "Poe's 'The Black Cat' and Freud's 'The Uncanny.'"
    Literature and Psychology 39 (1993): 52–62.

Matheson, T. J. "Poe's 'The Black Cat' as a Critique of Temperance
    Literature." *Mosaic* 19.3 (1986): 69–81.

Merish, Lori. "Sentimental Consumption: Harriet Beecher Stowe and
    the Aesthetics of Middle-Class Ownership." *American Literary
    History* 8.1 (1996): 1–33.

Nelson, Dana. *The Word in Black and White.* New York: Oxford UP,
    1992.

Ostrom, John Ward. "Edgar A. Poe: His Income as Literary Entrepre-
    neur." *Poe Studies* 15.1 (1982): 1–7.

Paulding, James Kirke. *Slavery in the United States.* New York:
    Harper, 1836.

Poe, Edgar Allan. *The Collected Works of Edgar Allan Poe.* Ed. Thomas
    Ollive Mabbott. 3 vols. Cambridge: Belknap-Harvard UP,
    1969–1978.

———. *The Letters of Edgar Allan Poe.* Ed. John Ward Ostrom. Vol. I.
    New York: Gordian, 1966.

Quinn, Arthur Hobson. *Edgar Allan Poe*. New York: Appleton, 1941.

Rachman, Stephen. "'Es lasst sich nicht schreiben': Plagiarism and 'The Man of the Crowd.'" *The American Face of Edgar Allan Poe*. Ed. Shawn Rosenheim and Stephen Rachman. Baltimore: Johns Hopkins UP, 1995, 49–87.

Reynolds, David S. "Poe's Art of Transformation: 'The Cask of Amontillado' in Its Cultural Context." *New Essays on Poe's Major Tales*. Ed. Kenneth Silverman. Cambridge: Cambridge UP, 1993, 93–112.

Rosenheim, Shawn. "Detective Fiction, Psychoanalysis, and the Analytic Sublime." *The American Face of Edgar Allan Poe*. Ed. Shawn Rosenheim and Stephen Rachman. Baltimore: Johns Hopkins UP, 1995, 153–176.

Rosenthal, Bernard. "Poe, Slavery, and the Southern Literary Messenger: A Reexamination." *Poe Studies* 7.2 (1974): 29–38.

Rowe, John Carlos. "Poe, Antebellum Slavery, and Modern Criticism." *Poe's Pym*: Critical Explorations. Ed. Richard Kopley. Durham: Duke UP, 1992, 117–138.

Sedgwick, Catharine Maria. *Home*. 15th ed. Boston: James Munroe, 1841.

Sigourney, Lydia Huntley. *Letters to Mothers*. 6th ed. New York, 1845.

Silverman, Kenneth. *Edgar A. Poe: Mournful and Never-ending Remembrance*. New York: Harper Perennial, 1992.

Simpson, Lewis P. "The Mind of the Antebellum South." *The History of Southern Literature*. Ed. Louis D. Rubin, Jr., et al. Baton Rouge: Louisiana State UP, 1985, 164–174.

"The South-West." *Southern Literary Messenger* 2 (January 1836): 122–123.

Thomas, Dwight, and David K. Jackson. *The Poe Log: A Documentary Life of Edgar Allan Poe, 1809–1849*. Boston: G. K. Hall, 1987.

Tragle, Henry Irving. *The Southampton Slave Revolt of 1831: A Compilation of Source Material*. Amherst: U of Massachusetts P, 1971.

Walker, David. *Appeal . . . to the Coloured Citizens of the World*. 1829. Rpt. in David Walker's *Appeal*. Ed. Charles M. Wiltse. New York: Hill and Wang, 1965.

Weld, Theodore Dwight. *American Slavery As It Is: Testimony of a Thousand Witnesses*. 1839. Rpt. New York: Arno, 1968.

Whalen, Terrence. "Edgar Allan Poe and the Horrid Laws of Political Economy." *American Quarterly* 44 (1992): 381–417.

TERENCE WHALEN

Average Racism: Poe, Slavery, and the Wages of Literary Nationalism

Terence Whalen (b. 1959) is associate professor of English at the University of Illinois, Chicago, and is the author of numerous essays on nineteenth-century American literature and culture and an important volume in Poe studies, Edgar Allan Poe and the Masses *(Princeton University Press, 1999), from which this selection is excerpted. This book has become a landmark in the critical conversation about Poe, race, and the literary marketplace.*

Public opinion consists of the average prejudices of a community.

(COLERIDGE)

We would therefore propose . . . that history is not a text, not a narrative, master or otherwise, but that, as an absent cause, it is inaccessible to us except in textual form, and that our approach to it and to the Real itself necessarily passes through its prior textualization.

(FREDRIC JAMESON)

In recent years the political and racial meaning of Poe's work has been the focus of intense critical debate, and undoubtedly the positions generated from this debate will have enduring consequences, not only for Poe scholars, but for all those investigating the importance of race in American culture. As I have suggested . . . , Poe's lifelong struggle with the publishing industry constitutes a kind of deep politics that should matter more than his awkward and infrequent forays into partisan rhetoric. Poe, that is to say, should be distinguished from the public-spirited intellectuals of his age, for whereas these intellectuals embraced a wide variety of civic and political causes, Poe's political agenda was conspicuously confined to problems of production, ranging from the poverty of authors to the corruption of publishers to the emergence of a vaguely ominous mass audience. To put such a theory to the test, it is necessary to consider what is conventionally seen as the single most important political struggle of antebellum America, namely the struggle over slavery that divided North from South and that culminated, a dozen years after Poe's death, in a catastrophic civil war. In this chapter I argue that any investigation into Poe's racial views should begin by acknowledging that in the 1830s, there were multiple racisms and multiple positions on slavery even in the South. In order to understand the complex relation between race and literature, moreover, it is also necessary to account for the pressures of literary nationalism and a national literary market, because these pressures put constraints on commercial writers in all regions and contributed to the always unfinished formation of what might be called average racism. For Poe and other antebellum writers, average racism was not a sociological measurement of actual beliefs but rather a strategic construction designed to overcome political dissension in the emerging mass audience. In other words, publishers and commercial writers were seeking a form of racism acceptable to white readers who were otherwise divided over the more precise issue of slavery.

Fredric Jameson's admonition about the textual nature of history, cited in the epigraph to this chapter, suggests the general difficulty of unraveling such political intricacies of the past. In the case of Poe and race, this task has been rendered doubly difficult by the texts themselves, because most are ambiguous, some are unsigned, and at least one does not even exist. Of all these real and imaginary texts, none is more controversial than the so-called Paulding-Drayton review, an anonymous proslavery essay published in the April 1836 *Southern Literary Messenger*. On one side of the controversy stand those who attribute the review to Poe and who use it to document his "Southern" attitudes or, more explicitly, his virulent and flagrant racism. Many of these critics share some broad assumptions, not only about regionalism and ideology in antebellum America, but also about the aberrance of discredited doctrines from the past. It's not that they find racism literally unthinkable. Instead, it might be said that for these and other critics, racism is only thinkable as the thought of a Southerner.[1] On the other side of the dispute stand those who attribute the review to Beverley Tucker, law professor at the College of William and Mary and author of the first secessionist novel. The group favoring Tucker's authorship comprises both literary critics who seek to defend Poe from charges of racism, and historians who, apparently oblivious to the whole controversy, seek only

---

[1] I am turning a phrase from Stephen Greenblatt, who writes, "I am not arguing that atheism was literally unthinkable in the late sixteenth century but rather that it was almost always thinkable only as the thought of another." *Shakespearean Negotiations: The Circulation of Social Energy in Renaissance England* (Berkeley: University of California Press, 1988), 22. [All notes in this selection are Whalen's.]

to clarify Tucker's famous—or infamous—position on slavery and secession. As shall become clear, this ostensibly simple case of attribution
raises fundamental questions about the meaning of authorship, questions that no interpretive approach can answer without recourse to history itself.

The nature of the controversy is best illustrated by the glaring contradiction between two literary histories recently issued by Columbia
University Press. In the *Columbia Literary History of the United States*,
G. R. Thompson disavows Poe's authorship and then argues that an
1849 review of James Russell Lowell is "the only instance of Poe's taking any kind of stance on the issue of slavery" (269). In the *Columbia
History of the American Novel*, Joan Dayan identifies Poe as the author
of the Paulding-Drayton review, calling it "five of the most disturbing
pages Poe ever wrote," and relying upon it to expose his "ugly" theory
that "the enslaved want to be mastered, for they love—and this is the
crucial term for Poe—to serve, to be subservient" (p. 350).

Even by the most traditional definition of authorship, Thompson
and Dayan are both wrong. As I shall demonstrate in this chapter,
Thompson is in error because Poe did make several statements about
slavery, and Dayan is wrong because her interpretation is based on a
review that Poe did not write.[2] In order to explore all of the relevant
evidence, I initially reserve judgment about the legitimacy of "author"
and "authorial intent," for by holding the fate of these concepts in
abeyance, I am free to pose some basic questions: What can one know
about Poe's racial views? In what sense are Poe's expressed views properly his own? What, if anything, can be deduced from Poe's silences?
And how should an author's "racism" influence the interpretation of a
literary text? Although these questions lead to further inquiries into
authorship and literary nationalism, my ultimate aim in this essay is to
lay the groundwork for a more historically informed criticism of race, a
criticism that surpasses the prevailing rhetoric of praise and denunciation. In doing so I often find myself contending against those who, like

---

[2]Neither Thompson nor Dayan, I hasten to add, is completely culpable for these
mistakes. Thompson was making a quick point with a bit of hyperbole, and Dayan was
basing her arguments on a persuasive but flawed article by Bernard Rosenthal. In addition, both writers were prevented from qualifying or justifying their arguments in footnotes. For complete texts, see G. R. Thompson, "Poe and the Writers of the Old South,"
Columbia Literary History of the United States, ed. Emory Elliott (New York: Columbia
University Press, 1988), 262–77; and Joan Dayan, "Romance and Race," *The Columbia
History of the American Novel* (New York: Columbia University Press, 1991), 89–109.

myself, stress the social ramifications of Poe's work; but if political criticism is to be more than politics as usual, it must fulfill a special burden of proof when it turns outward to the unconverted and the undecided.

* * *

[In the first two sections of this essay, Whalen offers a lengthy and detailed argument for identifying Beverley Tucker, and not Poe, as the author of the anonymous Paulding-Drayton review in the *Southern Literary Messenger*; see the introduction to this section for a discussion of the debate.]

III. POE AND SLAVERY RECONSIDERED

The resilience of the misattribution [of Poe as the author of the Paulding-Drayton review] raises a number of important issues, not only about Poe's racism, but also about the peculiar function that the concept of racism plays in critical discourse today. As noted above, some critics tend to identify racism as a collection of proslavery assumptions held primarily by antebellum Southerners. More recently, critics have emphasized the similarities between antebellum texts and current political struggles, but the discourse on race and literature continues to suffer from several limitations. Due in part to the continuing urgency of the issue, many neglect the historical context of race and instead resort to moralizing apologies, blanket denunciations, or full-blown jeremiads. These approaches, however, present fewer difficulties than the pervasive view of racism as a private sin or psychological malady rather than a longstanding, systemic condition perpetuated by powerful political and economic forces. In keeping with this personalizing tendency, most interpretations of Poe's racism share some common assumptions: that he chose his racial attitudes freely or at least knowingly; that his attitudes could be expressed without constraint; and, by extension, that his expressions constitute a "true" record of his thoughts or feelings. These assumptions are open to attack from many theoretical positions, but I would like to proceed with a more basic investigation of the scene of literary creation. Aside from specifying the social determinations of racism, this investigation should help to clarify one of the most neglected issues in all of Poe criticism, namely the political and economic constraints on his writing.

In order to understand these constraints, it is necessary to recall Poe's predicament as editor or editorial assistant for the *Southern Literary Messenger*. Since this was also Poe's first full-time editorial job, it cast a powerful shadow over his entire career in the industry of letters. Thomas Willis White, proprietor of the *Messenger*, conceived of his magazine as both a catalyst and beneficiary of a mass literary market in the South, but he also worked hard to cultivate a reputation as a national periodical. This reputation had little to do with actual demand, because . . . White relied almost entirely on the South for revenue. In 1838, the middle year of White's proprietorship, 90 percent of paid subscriptions were sent to slave states or areas, leaving only 10 percent for paid delivery in free states. *The Messenger* did not travel far even within the South, for of all paying subscribers, 48.9 percent lived in Virginia, with 18.2 percent residing in Richmond alone. Why, then, did White portray the *Messenger* as a national magazine? For one thing, he depended on the North for exchanges, contributions, and editorial favors, which helps to explains why the parsimonious proprietor mailed so many free copies to the offices of Northern newspapers and magazines.[3] Notices in the Northern press enhanced the *Messenger*'s prestige, and since many Southern readers subscribed to Northern journals, this was also an effective (albeit circuitous) way to reach the target audience. For these reasons, White seldom passed up an opportunity to drop intimations of the *Messenger*'s "national" following. During a steamer ride up the James River, for example, White managed to convince antislavery travel writer J. S. Buckingham that although the *Messenger* was published in Richmond, it was "read extensively in every State in the Union."[4]

---

[3]Statistics are derived from the Lists of Payments for 1838 (the middle year of White's proprietorship). These show the economic predominance of the South, but since White exchanged with other magazines, and since he canvassed the entire nation for new subscribers, many free copies of the *Messenger* were distributed in the North. See the announcement on the July 1838 cover: "A large distribution of the current volume of the *Messenger*, having been made in every part of the Union, as specimens of the work, the Editor is unable to furnish new subscribers with the entire volume" ("Wanted Immediately," *Southern Literary Messenger* 4.7 [July 1838]: ii). In addition, White counted on Northern writers for copy and for favorable reviews.

[4]J. S. Buckingham, *The Slave States of America* (London: Fisher, Son, & Co., 1842) vol. 2 (of 2 vols.), 545. Buckingham was predisposed to accept this claim; before recounting his steamer ride with "T. K. White" (sic), he had already described the literary scene in Richmond: "Its monthly periodical, *The Southern Literary Messenger*, contains as many well-written articles as any similar publication in England; and in my judgement, after a regular perusal of it for two years—as I subscribed to all the leading reviews and magazines during my stay in the country, or procured them, as published, through the

   This marketing strategy sometimes left White straddling both sides
of the Mason-Dixon Line. In the *Messenger* Prospectus, for example,
White first affirms and then denies any sectional bias. . . . White knew
that many of his Southern readers were troubled by the growing sectional conflict, and he undoubtedly hoped to mollify these readers with
a declaration of nationalist sentiments. The Prospectus accordingly
exploits fears of Northern dominance, but at the same time it allows
liberal or cosmopolitan readers to identify themselves with the image—
if not the reality—of a progressive Southern intelligentsia.

   To maintain and expand his share of the Southern market, White
therefore had to please an audience that was much less homogeneous
than generally assumed, at least in regard to political affairs. The *Messenger*'s status as a literary magazine obviously made this task easier, for
one of the preeminent ideological attributes of literature is its ability to
present itself as a discourse free of ideology. Not surprisingly, White
exploited the ostensible neutrality of literature in the Prospectus, claiming that "*Party Politics* and controversial *Theology*, as far as possible, are
jealously excluded. They are sometimes so blended with discussions in
literature or in moral science, otherwise unobjectionable, as to gain
admittance for the sake of the more valuable matter to which they
adhere; but whenever that happens, they are *incidental* only; not *primary*." White, however, had so little confidence in his literary judgments that he generally deferred to Poe, and when he could not count
on Poe, he begged advice from trusted supporters like Beverley Tucker
and Lucian Minor. Perhaps because of his uncertainty about literary
quality, White often assumed the role of censor, and he paid special
attention to inflammatory political issues which might give offense and
thereby drive off subscribers.[5]

   A dispute over an article by "Nugator" (St. Leger Landon Carter)
illustrates the *Messenger*'s aversion to partisan politics. During this
period, the Democratic Party in Virginia still relied on the caucus system

---

booksellers—it is at least equal to any periodical, Northern or Southern, published in the
United States" (522).

   [5]For White's desire to maintain full editorial control, see his 2 March 1835 letter
to Lucian Minor, in David K. Jackson, "Some Unpublished Letters of T. W. White to
Lucian Minor," *Tyler's Quarterly Historical and Genealogical Magazine* 17 (April 1936):
227. For White's wariness about political writing, see, in addition to the material below,
White's letter to Minor, 31 March 1840: "If I was to insert my personal, and at last my
political, friends' addresses, I should raise at once a hornet's nest about my head and
ears, that I should not soon get clear of." Reprinted in Jackson, continuation of "Some
Unpublished Letters of T. W. White to Lucian Minor," *Tyler's Quarterly Historical and
Genealogical Magazine* 18 (July 1936): 48.

to nominate presidential candidates. In the April 1835 *Messenger*, Nugator claimed that the term "caucus" was derived from Cacus, son of Vulcan and "Prince of Robbers." Viewing this as a slur against nominee Martin Van Buren, a writer in the Richmond *Enquirer* attacked Nugator as a "Whig Etymologist" and warned White to keep the *Messenger* "pure and unspotted from the pollution of party politics."[6] The *Messenger* responded immediately. Acting on instructions from White, editor Edward V. Sparhawk wrote to the *Enquirer* and disavowed any political designs. Pointing out that the issue contained an editorial disclaimer, and that Nugator was actually a Democrat, Sparhawk attempted to shield the *Messenger* behind a nonpartisan veil. Denying any intention "to make the Messenger a vehicle of political discussion," Sparhawk maintained that the magazine was "happy to escape the atmosphere of Party, and breathe a calmer, if not a purer, air."[7] Ultimately, however, this apolitical stance was motivated less by purity than by profit, for as Sparhawk admitted in the letter, he feared that any involvement in "the strife of party politics" might "jeopardize the fair prospects of the Messenger."

Such fair prospects were imperiled by the growing controversy over slavery. Insofar as it emphasized the fundamental differences between North and South, the struggle over slavery obviously hindered the emergence of a truly national literary market. But as implied above, the slavery question also exposed internal divisions within the *Messenger*'s Southern audience. In such a market, economic and ideological forces became fused, and White accordingly attempted to cultivate an average racism that would appeal to a majority of his subscribers. Average racism, however, was easier said than done. White could safely defend the South from the attacks of Northern "fanatics," but he was less certain about whether he should represent slavery as a positive good or a necessary evil, or whether he should take a position on African colonization, that is, on plans to deport American blacks to the African colony of Liberia.

It might have been prudent to avoid such issues altogether, but this was not always possible. In February 1836, for example, Lucian Minor contributed an article purporting to review recent issues of the *Liberia Herald*. In his review, Minor praises the "unparalleled" success of Liberia, where once "a tangled and pathless forest frowned in a silence unbroken save by the roar of wild beasts," but where today English lit-

---

[6]"Purgator," *Richmond Enquirer*, 19 May 1835.
[7][Sparhawk?], *Richmond Enquirer*, 22 May 1835.

erature thrives, and with it "those comforts, virtues and pleasures which the existence of Literature necessarily implies."[8] For Minor, literature indicates the overall level of social development, and the newspaper in particular serves as "the most expressive sign of all." Even more expressive than newspaper itself, however, are the people who produce it. "What heightens—indeed what *constitutes* the wonder," Minor continues, is that the editors, printers and writers "are all *colored people.*"

By using the *Liberia Herald* as a method of "instancing the literary condition of the settlement," Minor was obviously endorsing the work of the American Colonization Society. Founded in 1816, the Colonization Society enjoyed support in both the North and South for more than a decade. By the 1830s, however, the project of African colonization had come under attack by those maintaining more extreme positions in the debate over slavery. In 1832, for example, abolitionist William Lloyd Garrison and proslavery economist Thomas Dew both denounced colonization as a cruel, unworkable, and prohibitively expensive solution.[9] Minor himself realized that his review might arouse controversy. After praising Liberia effusively, he accordingly disavowed any radical intent: "What we especially had in view, however, when we began this article, was neither rhapsody nor dissertation upon the march of Liberia to prosperity and civilization—unparalleled as that march is, in the annals of civilization—but a notice (a *critical notice*, if the reader please) of the aforesaid newspaper" (158).

The disclaimer was hardly palliative, and this left White in something of a predicament. Since he relied heavily on Minor for articles and editorial advice, he could not simply reject it. But he was also loathe to embroil the *Messenger* in a dispute which might anger his subscribers. Characteristically, White decided to compromise. He ordered Poe to revise or delete the more controversial sections of the review. He also gave Poe the job of informing Minor about these revisions, and Poe

---

[8]Lucian Minor, "Liberian Literature," *Southern Literary Messenger* 2 (February 1836): 158. It is worth noting, in this context, that Lucian Minor had several (Southern) relatives who opposed slavery. Lucian Minor's grandfather, Major John Minor of Topping Castle, had introduced a bill for the emancipation of slaves in the Virginia Legislature shortly after the Revolution. And Lucian's cousin, Mary Berkeley Minor Blackford, denounced both slavery and secession. Between 1832 and 1866, she kept a journal called "Notes Illustrative of the Wrongs of Slavery." See L. Minor Blackford, *Mine Eyes Have Seen the Glory* (Cambridge: Harvard University Press, 1954), 5, 46, & 263 n. 2.

[9]See Larry Tise, *Proslavery: A History of the Defense of Slavery in America* (Athens: University of Georgia Press, 1987), 70–74. Colonization nevertheless enjoyed much support in Virginia. In the 1830s the *Richmond Enquirer* even printed notices of the local chapter's weekly meetings.

dutifully told Minor that "it was thought better upon consideration to omit all passages in 'Liberian Literature' at which offence could, by any possibility, be taken" (*L* 1:83). This incident, it should be noted, suggests another motive behind Poe's "immaterial alterations" of the Paulding-Drayton review. If Poe censored a colonization article to avoid controversy in February, he may have censored Tucker's proslavery article for the same reason in April. In any event, Poe's revision of Minor's article was not entirely successful. In a review of the February *Messenger*, the *Augusta Chronicle* denounced "Liberian Literature" as being "altogether unsuited to our Southern region, and as indicating a dangerous partiality for that most pestiferous and abominable parent of the Abolitionists, the *Colonization Society*."[10] The handling of Minor's article nevertheless reveals something of the ideological constraints that the *Messenger* imposed upon even its most valued contributors.

Significantly, the *Messenger* placed similar constraints on proslavery advocates like Beverley Tucker. "Notes to Blackstone's Commentaries," one of Tucker's first substantial articles on slavery, appeared in the January 1835 *Messenger*. In the "Editorial Remarks" for this issue, the writer—probably James Heath—takes exception to Tucker's general line of argument. Since these remarks represent the *Messenger*'s official position at its commencement, they are worth quoting at length:

> The able author of the *"Note to Blackstone's Commentaries,"* is entitled to be heard, even on a subject of such peculiar delicacy. . . . Whilst we entirely concur with him that slavery as a political or social institution is a matter exclusively of our own concern . . . we must be permitted to dissent from the opinion that it is either a moral or political benefit. We regard it on the contrary as a great evil, which society will sooner or later find it not only its interest to remove or mitigate, but will seek its gradual abolition or amelioration, under the influence of those high obligations imposed by an enlightened Christian morality.[11]

White felt obliged to print a more scathing response to Tucker's article in the next issue. Signed by "A Virginian," the four-page rebuttal begins with a merciless refutation of Tucker's position. . . . Such incidents demonstrate that White could not prevent the *Messenger* from occa-

---

[10] 6 March 1836. Cited in Dwight Thomas and David K. Jackson, *Poe Log*, 193. Poe called the *Chronicle* reviewer a "scoundrel," and in a personal correspondence he assured Minor that his article on Liberian writing had been "lauded by all men of sense" (*Letters*, 1:88).

[11] *Southern Literary Messenger* 1 (January 1835): 254.

sionally becoming "a vehicle of political discussion." Nor could he arrive at an average racism that would satisfy both colonizationists and "positive good" theorists. He could only attempt to minimize his risks by restricting the number of articles on slavery, by censoring these articles whenever possible, by printing editorial disclaimers, and by encouraging any offended readers to respond with letters rather than canceled subscriptions.

*   *   *

The strictures on "party politics" applied to Poe as well, especially since he was not a privileged contributor but merely a paid assistant to White. It was Poe's job, moreover, to implement and articulate the *Messenger*'s editorial policies, and on one occasion he found himself explaining that "the pages of our Magazine are open, and have ever been, to the discussion of all general questions in Political Law, or Economy—never to questions of mere party."[12] Obviously, then, there were implicit and explicit constraints on what Poe could say about slavery. Even if he had been a ranting abolitionist or a rabid secessionist, he would never have been able to express these views in the *Southern Literary Messenger*. White's fear of political controversy called for positions that were less progressive than Minor's and less reactionary than Tucker's, and in fact all of Poe's remarks on slavery for the *Messenger* fall between these two extremes.

In his review of Anne Grant's *Memoirs of an American Lady*, for example, Poe quotes a romantic description of slavery in colonial New York, claiming that these "remarks on slavery . . . will apply with singular accuracy to the present state of things in Virginia."[13] In the quoted passage, Grant maintains that in Albany, "even the dark aspect of slavery was softened with a smile." Rosenthal sees this as being consonant with "the standard pro-slavery argument" (30), but as quoted in the *Messenger*, Grant distances herself from the proslavery position: "Let me not be detested as an advocate of slavery, when I say that I think I have never seen people so happy in servitude as the domestics of the Albanians" (511). Less important than the remarks themselves, however, is the regional identification of the speaker. Northern apologies

[12]Poe, "Editorial: Right of Instruction," *Southern Literary Messenger* 2 (June 1836): 445.
[13]Poe, review of Memoirs of an American Lady by Mrs. Grant, *Southern Literary Messenger* 2 (July 1836): 511.

for slavery were highly coveted by Southerners, and for a fledgling magazine such as the *Messenger*, these apologies had the added attraction of mitigating—or appearing to mitigate—sectional differences in the national literary market. In Joseph Holt Ingraham's *The South-West. By a Yankee*, Poe found another Northerner who was willing to pardon the peculiar institution. In an account of his travels through Louisiana and Mississippi, Ingraham pauses on several occasions to excuse, if not to defend, Southern slavery. After passing a group of slaves purchased in Virginia and bound for a plantation outside New Orleans, Ingraham remarks that "they all appeared contented and happy, and highly elated at their sweet anticipations." "Say not," Ingraham continues, "that the slavery of the Louisiana negroes is a *bitter* draught."[14] Such pronouncements inspired the following comment, which remains Poe's most explicit statement on slavery:

> The "Yankee," in travelling Southward, has evidently laid aside the general prejudices of a Yankee—and, viewing the book of Professor Ingraham, as representing, in its very liberal opinions, those of a great majority of well educated Northern gentlemen, we are inclined to believe it will render essential services in the way of smoothing down a vast deal of jealousy and misconception. The traveller from the North has evinced no disposition to look with a jaundiced eye upon the South—to pervert its misfortunes into crimes—or distort its necessities into sins of volition. He has spoken of slavery as he found it—and it is almost needless to say that he found it a very different thing from the paintings he had seen of it in red ochre. He has discovered, in a word, that while the *physical* condition of the slave is *not* what it has been represented, the slave himself is utterly incapable to feel the *moral* galling of his chain.[15]

---

[14]Joseph Holt Ingraham, *The South-West. By a Yankee*, 2 vols. (1835; New York: Harper and Brothers; Ann Arbor: University Microfilms, 1966), 1:190–91. Like Grant, Ingraham apologizes for slavery without advocating it: "Do not mistake me: I am no advocate for slavery; but neither am I a believer in that wild Garrisonian theory, which, like a Magician's wand, is at once to dissolve every link that binds the slave to his master, and demolish at one blow a system that has existed, still gaining in extent and stability, for centuries" (2:33).

[15]Poe, review of Joseph H. Ingraham's *The South-West. By a Yankee. Southern Literary Messenger* 2 (January 1836): 122. The next sentence suggests that Poe had read (though he did not review) Paulding's *Slavery in the United States*: "Indeed, we strongly agree with a distinguished Northern contemporary and friend, that the Professor's strict honesty, impartiality, and unprejudiced common sense, on the trying subject which has so long agitated our community, is the distinguishing and the most praiseworthy feature of his book." Paulding—the Northern contemporary and friend—quotes extensively from Ingraham. The longest excerpt (*Slavery in the United States*, 221–26) is immediately followed by a

Poe here follows a double strategy. He obviously seeks to defend the South from Yankee "prejudices," but at the same time he attempts to "smooth down" the growing sectional divide by appealing to the liberal opinions of "the great majority of well educated Northern gentlemen." His position on slavery likewise seems directed toward a racist majority. Without advocating any specific policy, he first concedes the "misfortunes" of slavery and then assures his readers that these misfortunes cause little injury to the slaves themselves. In other words, Poe dodges the slavery question by shifting the argument to common ground — only in this case the common ground is racism.

In many ways, Poe's statement accords with the "moderate" *Messenger* position articulated in 1835 by James Heath. Unlike Heath, however, Poe failed to advocate even the gradual elimination of slavery. He also seemed hesitant about taking a position on colonization. As editor of the *Messenger*, Poe frequently discussed other monthly magazines, and in the October 1835 *North American Review*, he stumbled upon a long and favorable review of Ralph Gurley's *Life of Jehudi Ashmun, Late Colonial Agent in Liberia*. After quoting a laudatory account of Ashmun's character, Poe admits that he is "willing to believe" this description, and he also concedes that Ashmun "was a noble martyr in the cause of African colonization." But Poe wonders why the reviewer selected this particular book:

> We doubt, however, if there are not a crowd of books daily issuing unnoticed from the press, of far more general interest, and consequently more worthy the attention of our leading Review than even *The Life of Ashmun*. We shall soon, perhaps, have a Life of some Cuffy the Great, by Solomon Sapient; and then the North American will feel itself bound to devote one half of its pages to that important publication.[16]

"Cuffy," derived from an African word for Friday, was a common given name among American blacks; in this context it may also allude to Paul Cuffee (1759–1817), a black shipowner, Quaker, and political activist

---

passage discussing the "galling bonds" of slavery (227), which probably inspired Poe's phrase about "the *moral* galling of his chain." In another passage echoed by Poe, Paulding refers to "Professor Ingraham" as "the candid and intelligent author of 'The South West'" (293). Poe's reference to "galling chains," it should be noted, puts him more in line with those who depicted slavery as a necessary evil than those — Tucker included — who defended slavery as a positive good.

[16]Poe, review of the *North American Review*, *Southern Literary Messenger* 2 (December 1835): 59.

who helped establish a colony of African Americans in Sierra Leone.[17] Poe's remarks up to this point therefore suggest a willingness to belittle any text supportive of African colonization. But then, as if stepping back from the threshold of partisan politics, Poe immediately modifies his position: "In expressing ourselves thus, we mean not the slightest disrespect to either Ashmun or his Biographer. But the *critique* is badly written, and its enthusiasm outré and disproportionate."

The rest of Poe's reviews in the *Southern Literary Messenger* have little or nothing to add to these brief statements, indicating that he avoided taking a specific position on slavery and instead attempted to embrace an average racism that would appeal to a majority of subscribers. Despite this evidence, many critics nevertheless accuse Poe of sharing the views of the most extreme proslavery advocates. Kenneth Alan Hovey, for example, contends that Poe's social views "are essentially identical" to those expressed by Beverley Tucker in the Paulding-Drayton review ("Critical Provincialism," 347). Others identify Poe with the proslavery, anti-colonization position of Thomas Dew, political economist and President of the College of William and Mary. Joan Dayan notes that Poe corresponded with Dew and wrote the introduction to his "Address" for the *Southern Literary Messenger*.[18] John Carlos Rowe refers to Poe's "undisputed admiration" for Dew, and Dana Nelson observes that Poe revealed his true sentiments "particularly in his stance on works by the noted Southern defender of slavery, Thomas R. Dew." All of these critics echo Bernard Rosenthal's claim that "Perhaps the most telling fact about Poe's position on slavery is his record of

---

[17] "Cuffies" is the common transliteration of the African name; it was a common practice to name children after days of the week. See Peter Wood, *Black Majority: Negroes in Colonial South Carolina from 1670 through the Stono Rebellion* (New York: Norton, 1975); Gary B. Nash, *Forging Freedom: The Formation of Philadelphia's Black Community, 1720–1840* (Cambridge, MA: Harvard University Press, 1988), 301 n. 26; and David DeCamp, "African Day-Names in Jamaica," *Language* 43 (1967): 139–49. My thanks to Ted Pearson and Kathy Brown for this information.

[18] "Romance and Race," 96. Dayan insinuates that Poe is guilty by association. She does not, of course, insinuate that Poe was an abolitionist because he corresponded with Lowell and Longfellow, or because he favorably reviewed the work of Lydia Maria Child. In addition, Dayan identifies Dew as author of *Vindication of Perpetual Slavery*, a book that—if one by that title even exists—no one else attributes to Dew. Dew actually wrote an essay called "Abolition of Negro Slavery," *American Quarterly Review* 12 (1832): 189–265; this was later expanded and published by Thomas W. White as the *Review of the Debate in the Virginia Legislature of 1831–1832* (Richmond: T. W. White, 1832), and subsequently reprinted many times, most notably in a collection called *The Pro-slavery Argument* (Charleston: Walker, Richards, & Co., 1852).

public admiration for Thomas R. Dew, the man most fully identified with the extreme and articulate slavery apologetics of Poe's day."[19]

Aside from insinuating guilt by association, this position rests upon a fundamental misconception of Poe's work and work-related constraints at the *Messenger*. Thomas Dew was an important supporter of the magazine, for in addition to contributing articles directly, he was also in a position to influence many other subscribers and potential subscribers. And since he was president of the College of William and Mary, the *Messenger* could not offend Dew without imperiling the substantial patronage of college faculty, students, and alumni. Even if Poe had wanted to express disapproval of Dew, White would never have permitted it. Moreover, the particular text upon which this whole argument rests was originally composed not by Poe but by Dew himself, a fact overlooked by nearly everyone. The text in question is Poe's October 1836 review of Dew's welcoming address to the entering class. In order to write the review, Poe asked Dew for a copy of the address (published in the next issue of the *Messenger*) and for general information about the college. Dew responded with what we would today call a press release, and Poe merely revised it for his review. Dew's letter was reprinted in the standard edition of Poe's works, and it is a simple matter to identify the blatant similarities between Poe's review and Dew's press release. In a 1941 dissertation on the canon of Poe's critical works, which Rosenthal explicitly cites, William Hull in fact demonstrates that the six basic points in Poe's review are all derived, nearly verbatim, from the letter by Dew.

* * *

Further arguments about Poe's racism have been based on his alleged review of John L. Carey's *Domestic Slavery*. The problem here concerns not authorship but existence, for the review was never published, and no manuscript copy has ever been located. Rosenthal and Nelson nevertheless contend that the review demonstrates Poe's "proslavery sympathies."[20] This claim merits special consideration, because it is one of the most egregious examples of the guilt-by-association strategy practiced by Rosenthal and theoretically justified by Rowe.

---

[19] Rowe, "Poe, Antebellum Slavery, and Modern Criticism," 119–20; Nelson, *The Word in Black and White*, 91; Rosenthal, "Reexamination," 30.

[20] See Rosenthal, "Reexamination," 30; and Nelson, *The Word in Black and White*, 91.

Reports about the purported content of the review are based on Poe's
June 1840 letter to Joseph E. Snodgrass, editor of the *American Museum*
and later of the *Baltimore Saturday Visiter*. Snodgrass had sent Poe a
copy of Carey's book so that he might review it for Burton's *Gentleman's Magazine*. In a letter to Snodgrass, Poe explained why the review
did not appear:

> Mr. Carey's book on slavery was received by me not very long
> ago, and in last month's number I wrote, at some length, a crit-
> icism upon it, in which I endeavored to do justice to the author,
> whose talents I highly admire. But this critique, as well as some
> six or seven others, were refused admittance into the Magazine
> by Mr. Burton, upon his receiving my letter of resignation. . . .
> I fancy, moreover, that he has some private pique against
> Mr. Carey (as he has against every honest man) for not long
> ago he refused admission to a poetical address of his which I
> was anxious to publish. (*Letters*, 1:138)

There are several reasons to question the sincerity of this letter. First,
Poe was eager to tarnish the reputation of his former employer; as he
later told Snodgrass, "Burton . . . is going to the devil with the worst
grace in the world, but with a velocity truly astounding" (*Letters*, 1:152).
Second, Poe was caught up in a network of puffing and promotion that
included both Carey and Snodgrass. In December 1839, Poe (relying
on Snodgrass as a go-between) had sent a copy of *Tales of the Grotesque
and Arabesque* to Carey, who was then editor of the *Baltimore American*; shortly thereafter, Carey responded by publishing a favorable review
(*Poe Log*, 281). In addition, Poe was at this time cultivating Snodgrass
as a supporter of his magazine project. When Snodgrass sent Carey's
book to Poe, that is, when Snodgrass acted as a go-between in the other
direction, Poe may have felt obliged to return Carey's original favor.
Given these circumstances, Poe may have felt that a disparaging review
would appear ungrateful to both Carey and Snodgrass—editors whose
support Poe still wanted. He would therefore have been inclined to
express a favorable opinion of Carey's book, and since the review was
not published, this approval—whether feigned or genuine—cost him
nothing. This in turn raises the possibility that Poe never reviewed
Carey's book at all. If Poe had written a review, Snodgrass would certainly have been willing to publish it in the *Visiter*; as indicated below,
Snodgrass ultimately went on to publish several reviews of Carey's
works. In other words, it is entirely possible that conclusions about

Poe's racism are being drawn from a review that never existed, for Poe may have responded to Snodgrass's inquiry with a complete, yet plausible, fabrication.

Disregarding these considerations, Rosenthal nevertheless claims that "even a review mildly sympathetic to Carey's views would place one in a position of sympathy with the South's pro-slavery orthodoxy."[21] Aside from its scanty foundation in fact, this argument suffers from two additional weaknesses which are characteristic of regionalist reasoning. First, it collapses the differences between a union-loving colonizationist like Carey and a positive-good secessionist like Tucker. As already demonstrated, in the 1830s there were several orthodoxies vying for dominance. . . .

Second and most importantly, images of a monolithic South falsify the true political terrain of the region. We have already seen some of the ideological dissension and diversity that characterized the *Messenger* in the 1830s; such diversity was even more pronounced in border states such as Maryland. Joseph Evans Snodgrass, for example, was actually attempting to encourage an antislavery movement within the South. The *Baltimore Saturday Visiter* had been marketed as a family newspaper devoted to art and literature, but by 1843, Snodgrass was publishing articles that defended and attacked slavery. In 1845 he used another book by John Carey (*Slavery in Maryland, Briefly Considered*) to solicit controversial reviews, two of which he later published separately as pamphlets. In the first of these (*A Letter on Slavery, Addressed to John L. Carey*), Dr. R. S. Steuart describes slavery as a kind of "tutelage," which prepares savages for civilization and which—in due time—should be gradually eliminated. Later that year, however, Snodgrass published *Slavery in Maryland: An Anti-Slavery Review*, which attacks Steuart's gradualist approach on moral and religious grounds. The author of this second pamphlet disputes the benevolence of slavery and further contends that colonization, or any plan to remove blacks from Maryland, would prove both cruel and unworkable. . . .

Poe's "associations," then, exposed him to a diversity of positions on slavery, but even this does not mean that such positions could be freely chosen or freely advocated, especially in the Southern literary market. In the *Anti-Slavery Review*, for instance, the author counsels against establishing a newspaper devoted exclusively to emancipation,

[21] Rosenthal, "Reexamination," 30.

for he believes that a general publication with a few articles on slavery would reach more Southern readers:

> [The question] cannot be investigated effectually without some organ of public communication by which information may be diffused and the various plans brought forward, and fully discussed before the people. It, however, appears to me that a newspaper devoted to this especial object, would not effect so much as the introduction of suitable essays into the columns of papers already established. A paper devoted to emancipation would probably have but a limited circulation in the South, and that chiefly among persons already convinced . . .[22]

Snodgrass himself used similar arguments to elicit financial contributions from such notable abolitionists as Wendell Phillips, E. G. Loring, and Maria Weston Chapman. In an unpublished 1846 letter to Chapman, Snodgrass discusses the cost of sending his paper to "slave-holders and pro-slavery men in their feelings":

> I was enabled by your funds to continue the Visiter to such, all along—at least as long as they were willing to receive it— contrary to any "cash rule"—for it may not be known to you that, with a few accessible cases in the cities and else where, I stop all papers sent out of Baltimore. You will say this ought not to have been done—so say I; but, however desirable to keep the paper in the hands of such, especially slaveholding people, I could do no better, and had therefore to succumb to the pressure of my circumstances. Were the friends of Reform to do their duty, papers of the Visiter's class would be purposely left in the hands of the Slaveholders, just so long as there seemed the least chance of getting the pay.[23]

As indicated by the rest of the letter, Snodgrass was seeking Northern patronage so that he could carry on his antislavery campaign without succumbing to the "cash rule." "We are," he complained, "too few and feeble to stand alone as yet." Circumstances proved him right. By discussing plans for the abolition of slavery, Snodgrass damaged both his reputation and the circulation of his paper. According to Dwight Thomas, many residents of Baltimore regarded Snodgrass as "a danger-

---

[22][Heath?], *Slavery in Maryland: An Anti-Slavery Review*, 4.
[23]J. E. Snodgrass to Maria Weston Chapman, 25 November 1846. Boston Public Library, Ms.A.9.2.22, p. 134. See also Snodgrass to Chapman, 17 March 1846, Ms.A.9.2.22, p. 31. Some of the money donated by Chapman was used to pay for *Slavery in Maryland: An Anti-Slavery Review*.

ous radical," and journalist Jane Swisshelm, a dangerous radical herself, remembered Snodgrass as "a prominent Washington correspondent, whose anti-slavery paper had been suppressed in Baltimore by a mob."[24]

As Poe learned in New York, pressure could also be exerted in the other direction. In 1845, Poe had become one of the editors of the *Broadway Journal*. For the March 22 issue, he wrote an extremely favorable notice of the *Southern Literary Messenger*, claiming that under his editorship it had enjoyed "a success quite unparalleled in the history of our five dollar Magazines." The *Messenger*'s subscribers, Poe continued, "are almost without exception the *élite*, both as regards wealth and intellectual culture, of the Southern aristocracy, and its corps of contributors are generally men who control the public opinion of the Southerners on *all* topics."[25] Poe's 1845 notice raised doubts about the political neutrality of both the *Messenger* and the *Broadway Journal*. It also aroused the anger of antislavery activists, who were disturbed to see such a notice in a paper that was supposedly friendly to their cause. Writing for the *Liberator*, Robert Carter responded with a full-scale attack. According to Carter, many other reformers had hoped that the *Broadway Journal* would support "the cause of Human Rights" by "properly rebuking evil and evil-doers." Instead, Carter complained, the *Broadway Journal* had entered into an unholy alliance with a Southern magazine whose "principles are of the vilest sort" and whose aims are "to uphold the peculiar institution, to decry the colored race," and "to libel the abolitionists."[26]

Carter was under the mistaken impression that the notice of the *Messenger* had been written by coeditor Charles Briggs, so Poe escaped from the incident relatively unscathed. Briggs's reaction, however, reveals much about the predicament of a magazine attempting to circulate among subscribers with diverse and conflicting views toward slavery. Briggs claimed to be "unqualifiedly opposed to slavery in every

---

[24]Dwight R. Thomas, *Poe in Philadelphia, 1838–1844: A Documentary Record*, diss., University of Pennsylvania, 1978 (Ann Arbor: UMI, 1978; 7816395), 635, see also 896–899; Jane Swisshelm, *Half A Century*, 2nd ed. (Chicago: Jansen, McClurg & Co., 1880; rpt. New York: Source Book Press, 1970), 132. Significantly, Snodgrass persisted in his antislavery activism into the next decade. In 1852, for example, Snodgrass ran as an elector at large (Maryland) for the ill-fated Free Soil presidential ticket of John P. Hale and George W. Julian. See the "Free Democratic" handbill reprinted in Roger Burns and William Fraley, " 'Old Gunny': Abolitionist in a Slave City," *Maryland Historical Magazine* 68.4 (winter 1973): 370.

[25]*Broadway Journal* 1 (March 22, 1845): 183.

[26]R.C. (Robert Carter), "The Broadway Journal," *Boston Liberator*, 28 March 1845.

shape,"[27] but despite constant prodding from his friend James Russell Lowell, he was unwilling to turn the *Broadway Journal* into an abolitionist paper. If the paper were to espouse such a position openly, reasoned Briggs, it would lose the very readers most in need of reform:

> In the little time that our Journal has been going, we have received considerable countenance from the south and yesterday a postmaster in the interior of North Carolina wrote to solicit an agency. Now we should turn the whole people south of the Potomac from us if in our first number we were to make too strong a demonstration against them; and all my hopes of doing good by stealth would be frustrated.[28]

Briggs, however, had other motives. When Lowell pressed him to take a more daring stand, Briggs invoked financial necessity: "You know that publishers and printers judge of propriety by profit . . . and my publisher and printer took alarm at the outset at my manifest leaning toward certain horrifying because unprofitable doctrines." After Carter's attack appeared in the *Liberator*, Briggs stated the case more bluntly: "I cannot afford to publish a radical reform paper, for I could get no readers if I did."[29]

The lesson in political neutrality first given at the *Messenger* was therefore repeated at the *Broadway Journal*, and Poe seems to have learned his lesson well. With the exception of the laudatory notice of the *Messenger*, Poe was as willing as Briggs to measure "propriety by profit." He did mount a controversial attack against Longfellow's supposed plagiarisms,[30] but he tended to shun divisive political issues. He showed great reserve, for example, in his account of David Lee Child's allegory against annexation, *The Taking of Naboth's Vineyard*. "The name of the author of this pamphlet," says Poe, "will remove all doubt as the meaning of Naboth's Vineyard. Every body will understand that

---

[27]Briggs to Lowell, 22 January 1845; quoted in Bette S. Weidman, "*The Broadway Journal* (2): A Casualty of Abolition Politics," *Bulletin of the New York Public Library* 73 (February 1969): 106.

[28]Briggs to Lowell, 22 January 1845; quoted in Weidman ("*The Broadway Journal*," 107). The line about doing "good by stealth" comes from Alexander Pope, *Imitations of Horace*, "Epilogue to the Satires," Dialogue I, line 135.

[29]Briggs to Lowell, 19 March 1845 and 10 April 1845; quoted in Weidman, "*The Broadway Journal*," 108, 110.

[30]See *ER*, 671–777. This crusade was in keeping with Poe's earliest criticism, and it may also have been a deliberate strategy to arouse interest in the magazine and especially in his forthcoming book. Briggs's letters seem to indicate that Poe convinced him that it would sell magazines.

Naboth is Mexico, and the Vineyard Texas."[31] Poe demonstrated a similar circumspection in his notice of James H. Hammond's *Two Letters on Slavery in the United States*. Declining even to write a complete sentence, Poe tersely describes this key proslavery document as "A nervously written pamphlet, the design of which is to show that slavery is an inevitable condition of human society."[32]

After this period, Poe made only two conspicuous statements about slavery, and unfortunately the context of these statements has been universally neglected. The references to slavery appear in reviews of Longfellow and Lowell, but in each case Poe made the remarks anonymously, or under cover of what we would today call plausible deniability. The first statement occurs in an unsigned review of Longfellow published in the April 1845 *Aristidean*, just one month after the attack of the *Liberator*. The review begins by disparaging Longfellow's Boston supporters, a group identified as "the small coterie of abolitionists, transcendentalists, and fanatics in general," or more pointedly as "the knot of rogues and madmen" (*ER* 760). Then commences an attack on Longfellow's latest poetic works. Referring specifically to *Poems on Slavery*, the reviewer accuses Longfellow of pandering to "those negrophilic old ladies of the north" with "a shameless medley of the grossest misrepresentation." Noting how easily a Northern professor can "write verses instructing the southerners how to give up their all with a good grace," the reviewer charges that Longfellow has confused slavery in the South with the treatment of slaves in Cuba. Longfellow, the reviewer continues, has "no right to change the locality, and by insinuating a falsehood in lieu of a fact, charge his countrymen with barbarity" (*ER* 762, 763).

In an apparent attempt to do "evil by stealth," the anonymous writer turns Briggs's strategy on its head. This review, however, must be used with caution, for it is evidently a collaborative production by Poe and Thomas Dunn English, editor of the *Aristidean*. Most passages seem to come directly from Poe, but there are enough inconsistencies to indicate the work of a second author. In all likelihood, Poe provided

---

[31] *Broadway Journal* 1 (5 April 1845): 210; rpt. in Pollin, ed., *Collected Writings*, 3:71.
   [32] *Broadway Journal* 2 (26 July 1845): 41; Pollin, ed., *Collected Writings*, 3:183. In a section of the letter dealing with slavery and the Bible, Hammond remarks: "On the contrary, regarding slavery as an established, as well as inevitable condition of the human society, [Christ and the Apostles] never hinted at such a thing as its termination on earth." Reprinted in *The Ideology of Slavery: Proslavery Thought in the Antebellum South, 1830–1860*, ed. Drew Gilpin Faust (Baton Rouge, LA: Louisiana State University Press, 1981), 174.

a rough draft, which English altered to suit his own designs.[33] This
arrangement apparently satisfied both parties, for Poe wanted the piece
to look as if it had been written by another hand. The Longfellow
review contains many third-person references to "Mr. Poe," and in a
subsequent notice of the *Aristidean*, Poe with some impudence attempts
to maintain this illusion:

> Some of the papers are exceedingly good—precisely what Maga-
> zine papers should be—vigorous, terse, and independent. . . .
> There is a long review or rather running commentary on Longfel-
> low's poems. It is, perhaps, a little coarse, but we are not disposed
> to call it unjust; although there are in it some opinions which, by
> implication, are attributed to ourselves individually, and with
> which we cannot altogether coincide.[34]

It is therefore difficult to decide whether to blame Poe or English for
such phrases as "negrophilic old ladies of the north."[35] But two points
are clear. First, the defense of the South is presented as a reaction to
a Northern attack, specifically an attack by a Boston gentleman who
could—without financial risk—turn poetry into a vehicle for political
criticism. Second, whether or not Poe "coincided" with the *Aristidean*
review, he certainly recognized that it might arouse some outcry, and
he accordingly sought to distance himself from any "horrifying because
unprofitable doctrines."

Poe repeated this strategy in his 1849 attack on James Russell Lowell's *A Fable for Critics*. In a review written expressly for the *Southern
Literary Messenger*, Poe denounces Lowell as "one of the most rabid of
the Abolition fanatics." Posing as a guardian of Southern sensibility, he
attempts to shield prospective readers from Lowell's "prejudices on the
topic of slavery." "No Southerner," Poe warns, "who does not wish to
be insulted, and at the same time revolted by a bigotry the most obstinately blind and deaf, should ever touch a volume by this author"
(*ER*, 819).

As with the Longfellow review, Poe intended this to be anonymous.
On several occasions, the writer refers to "Mr. Poe" in the third person,
and in his private correspondence, Poe stresses that he had the review

---

[33] For a more conservative estimate of Poe's contribution to the review, see Dwight
Thomas and David K. Jackson, *Poe Log*, 529.

[34] "The Aristidean," *Broadway Journal* 1 (3 May 1845): 285.

[35] Kenneth Silverman speculates that English may be the author of the phrase because
he spoke derogatorily of blacks on other occasions. See Silverman, *Edgar A. Poe*, 254,
491. To my ear, however, the alliterative slur sounds like the work of Poe, and the rest of
the review seems perfectly consistent with Poe's other critical writings.

published "editorially" (*L* 2:449). For the first time in years, then, Poe was in a position to write anonymously for a Southern audience. But instead of unleashing a pent-up defense of slavery, Poe uses the opportunity to discuss the perils of fanaticism in general: "His fanaticism about slavery is a mere local outbreak of the same innate wrong-headedness which, if he owned slaves, would manifest itself in atrocious ill-treatment of them, with murder of any abolitionist who should endeavor to set them free. A fanatic of Mr. L's species, is simply a fanatic for the sake of fanaticism, and *must* be a fanatic in whatever circumstances you place him." In other words, fanaticism is a national problem which merely expresses itself differently in different regions. But as indicated in the succeeding paragraph, what most disturbs Poe is the power of fanaticism to aggravate the cultural division between North and South, for this effectively deprives Southern writers of access to the national literary market: "It is a fashion among Mr. Lowell's set to affect a belief that there is no such thing as Southern Literature. Northerners—people who have really nothing to speak of as men of letters,—are cited by the dozen . . . Other writers are barbarians and are satirized accordingly—if mentioned at all" (*ER* 819–20). Even when writing anonymously, Poe found it easier to denounce abolitionism than to justify slavery, and when he did defend the South, he showed greater concern for Southern writers than for Southern institutions.

There are other stray references to race, ranging from a comment on African-American speech in his review of Sedgwick's *The Linwoods* to a matter-of-fact description of a slave uprising in his review of Bird's *Sheppard Lee*.[36] But given the vast bulk of his writings, these references are conspicuously few. Unable and unwilling to bear the risks of political speech, Poe succumbed to the pressures of a national literary market either by falling silent on controversial issues, or by searching for an average racism that could take the place of unprofitable doctrines about slavery. There were of course writers who rejected this strategy and profited nevertheless, but as G. R. Thompson has pointed out, Poe generally shied away from the literary sectionalism of such writers as Simms, Longfellow, and Harriet Beecher Stowe.[37] Of Poe's sixty-five

[36]Poe's review of *The Linwoods* appeared in the *Southern Literary Messenger* 1 (December 1835): 57–59; rpt. in *Complete Works*, 8:94–101. His review of Robert Montgomery Bird's *Sheppard Lee* appeared in the *Southern Literary Messenger* 2 (September 1836): 662–67; rpt. in *ER*, 389–403. Both of these reviews are discussed more extensively in the next chapter.

[37]Thompson argues that Poe lacked the "regionalist sentiment" of other Southern writers ("Poe and the Writers of the Old South," 268–69). Stowe's *Uncle Tom's Cabin*

tales, only two—"The Gold-Bug" and "A Tale of the Ragged Mountains"—are set in the South, and many of the rest seem to be set nowhere at all. Thompson attributes this antiregional stance to Poe's professionalism, but it should be noted that professional calculations are not necessarily honorable or just. For Poe, admission to the national literary market meant turning his back on the momentous political and social struggles of the day, except when such struggles impinged directly upon the material interests of a commercial writer. So if there is little cause to denounce Poe for his statements on slavery, there is likewise no reason to praise him for his professional silence. Patriotism may be the *last* refuge of scoundrels, but professionalism is oftentimes the first.

IV. CONCLUSION: THE WAGES
OF NATIONALISM

All of this suggests that Poe, far from being "the most blatant racist among the American romantics," was arguably among the most discreet. Illuminating in this regard is the case of Ralph Waldo Emerson. Following what is now a familiar pattern, one critic has recently attempted to "unmask" Emerson's racism by assembling an extremely partial and incriminating selection of his journal entries.[38] In 1822, for example, Emerson reported that he saw "a hundred large lipped, low-browed black men who, except in the mere matter of languages, did not exceed the sagacity of the elephant." Emerson also described blacks as being "preAdamite" and marked for extinction: "It is plain that so inferior a race must perish shortly." In 1848 Emerson even wrote that "It is better to hold the negro race an inch under water than an inch over."[39] These journal entries are more blatantly racist than anything in

---

was of course a phenomenal success, but a Boston publisher, accepting the logic of political and regional neutrality, turned it down because "it would not sell in the South" (William Charvat, *The Profession of Authorship in America 1800–1870*, 301).

[38] Kun Jong Lee, "Ellison's *Invisible Man*: Emersonianism Revisited," *PMLA* 107 (March 1992): 331–44. Lee disputes Philip Nicoloff's characterization of Emerson as "a relatively mild racist" (Nicoloff, *Emerson on Race and History*, 124; quoted in Lee, 334).

[39] Lee, "Ellison's *Invisible Man*: Emersonianism Revisited," 334. In Emerson's defense, it should be noted that many of these statements appear to be fragmentary or even experimental. In addition, Lee sometimes quotes Emerson totally out of context, as with an entry concerning the fate of blacks to "serve & be sold & terminated" (Lee, 334). The rest of the passage—omitted by Lee—argues for the opposite position: "But if the black man carries in his bosom an indispensable element of a new & coming civilization, for the sake of that element no wrong nor strength nor circumstance can hurt him, he will survive & play his part. So now it seems to me that the arrival of such men as Toussaint if he is pure blood, or of Douglas (sic) if he is pure blood, outweighs all the

Poe's private correspondence or anonymous reviews. And yet, such a collection of quotations should not be taken as proof that Emerson was more "racist" than Poe. The kind of selective citation used to denounce Emerson and even Lydia Maria Child as racists, I would argue, crosses the boundary from political criticism into sheer character assassination. Critical approaches based on character assassination, or on any ahistorical diagnosis of racism, may possess some marginal pedagogical and heuristic value, but these approaches also project current stalemates into both the past and the future. In other words, the fervent hunt for some blatant racist utterance reveals less about antebellum literature than about the contemporary practice of endlessly unmasking racism as a scandal, as an unsurpassable and perversely cathartic spectacle.

* * *

Poe's wariness toward slavery is . . . demonstrated by "A Predicament" and "The Gold-Bug," the only tales containing extensive depictions of African Americans. In "A Predicament," the companion piece to "How to Write a Blackwood Article," Poe parodies the affection between black servant and white mistress in order to disparage both characters. In lines that would have made Beverley Tucker blanche, Psyche Zenobia moves from the sentimental to the ridiculous:

> And Pompey, my negro!—sweet Pompey! how shall I ever forget thee? I had taken Pompey's arm. He was three feet in height (I like to be particular) and about seventy, or perhaps eighty, years of age. He had bow-legs and was corpulent. His mouth should not be called small, nor his ears short. His teeth, however, were like pearl, and his large full eyes were deliciously white. Nature had endowed him with no neck, and had placed his ankles (as usual with that race) in the middle of the upper portion of the feet. (p. 71)

By combining stereotypical attributes with more absurd qualities, Zenobia impugns not only Pompey, but also her own literary talents

---

English & American humanity. . . . Here is the Anti-Slave. Here is Man; & if you have man, black or white is an insignificance. Why at night all men are black." See *The Journals and Miscellaneous Notebooks of Ralph Waldo Emerson*, ed. Ralph H. Orth and Alfred R. Ferguson (Cambridge, MA: Harvard University Press, 1971), 9:125. In my view Lee also unfairly belittles the antislavery efforts of Lydia Maria Child (343, n. 7). This condemnation of Child makes use of the evidence, though not the complete argument, of George M. Frederickson, *The Black Image in the White Mind: The Debate on Afro-American Character and Destiny*, 1817–1914 (New York: Harper & Row, 1971), 37.

and womanly sentiments. Curiously, Poe seems to imply that her deficiencies in both these areas arise because she is insufficiently racist.
Instead of arousing revulsion or distaste, the catalog of Pompey's attributes provokes an outpouring of passion: "I thought of myself, then of
Pompey, and then of the mysterious and inexplicable destiny which surrounded us. I thought of Pompey!—alas, I thought of love!" (p. 72).
Zenobia begins her description of Pompey by claiming that she "likes
to be particular," but by the end of the passage her claim seems scandal-
ously ironic: however particular in her descriptions, she is none too
particular in her passions. Zenobia's affection for Pompey, to be sure, is
not what Beverley Tucker had in mind when he alluded to those exalted
feelings by which "the heart is made better."[40] Indeed, when Zenobia
and Pompey later fall and tumble together on the floor, one can imagine Tucker's mortification—until he recalled that Psyche Zenobia was
not a Southern Lady but only a Philadelphia authoress, and that Pompey was not a Southern slave but only a Northern servant. Upon realizing this, he perhaps would have found some humor in "A Predicament" and laughed along with his Northern counterparts at the
absurdity of Zenobia's quest to write "a genuine Blackwood article of
the sensation stamp" (p. 64). Significantly, this laughter would have
been fueled not only by racism, but also by sexism, nationalism, and
cultural elitism (*Blackwood's* was a popular Scottish literary magazine
which sold well in England and the United States).

In "The Gold-Bug," Poe shifts the scene to South Carolina. Once
again there is something vaguely comical about the master-servant relationship, although in this case there is no question of improper affections, at least not on the part of Legrand. The black servant Jupiter,
however, seems to embody "the staunch loyalty and heart-felt devotion"
celebrated by Beverley Tucker.[41] Aside from his extreme devotion to
Legrand, Jupiter's speech is apparently intended to represent a black dialect influenced by Gullah, a creole spoken by blacks on the coastal islands
of South Carolina and Georgia.[42] Indeed, in his review of Sedgwick's
The Linwoods, Poe objects to "the discrepancy between the words and
the character of the speaker," particularly in cases where the character is
black. After quoting a rousing speech by an African-American character

[40]"Slavery," *Southern Literary Messenger*, 338.
[41]Nathaniel Beverley Tucker, *The Partisan Leader*, ed. Carl Bridenbaugh (1836;
New York: Alfred A. Knopf, 1933), 142.
[42]On Jupiter's use of Gullah, see Marc Shell, *Money, Language and Thought: Literary and Philosophical Economies from the Medieval to the Modern Era* (Berkeley: University
of California Press, 1982), 5–23.

named Rose, Poe asks, "Who would suppose this graceful eloquence to proceed from the mouth of a negro woman?" (*ER* 1203). Poe evidently sought to correct this alleged discrepancy in "The Gold-Bug," and in his unsigned review of himself, he in fact singles out the "accurate" depiction of Jupiter:

> The characters are well-drawn. The reflective qualities and steady purpose, founded on a laboriously obtained conviction of Legrand, is most faithfully depicted. The negro is a perfect picture. He is drawn accurately—no feature overshaded, or distorted. Most of such delineations are caricatures. (*ER* 869)

In what sense is Jupiter a "perfect picture"? Presumably, Poe is referring to his dialect, his superstition, and perhaps his inability to tell right from left. In addition, Jupiter is "obstinate" and physically strong—at one point he even considers beating Legrand with a stick to cure his gold fever. But as indicated already, Jupiter's most important trait is his loyalty to Legrand. Significantly, this loyalty determines the narrator's response to Legrand's apparent madness: "Could I have depended, indeed, upon Jupiter's aid, I would have had no hesitation in attempting to get the lunatic home by force; but I was too well assured of the old negro's disposition, to hope that he would assist me, under any circumstances, in a personal contest with his master" (*PT* 575).

Taken in isolation, such behavior seems derived from plantation narratives, and some critics have accordingly described Jupiter as a "black slave."[43] But as Poe carefully specifies at the beginning of the story, Jupiter is actually free:

> [Legrand] was usually accompanied by an old negro, called Jupiter, who had been manumitted before the reverses of the family, but who could be induced, by neither threats nor promises, to abandon what he considered his right of attendance upon the footsteps of his young "Massa Will." It is not improbable that the relatives of Legrand, conceiving him to be somewhat unsettled in intellect, had contrived to instil this obstinacy into Jupiter, with a view to the supervision and guardianship of the wanderer. (561)

Recognizing the political divisions in the national audience, Poe shrewdly tries to have it both ways. On the one hand, he exploits conventions about the intimate, loyal bonds between white masters and black servants. On the other hand, he attempts to evade any outcry over such a

---

[43] See, for example, Toni Morrison, *Playing in the Dark: Whiteness and the Literary Imagination* (New York: Vintage Books, 1993), 58.

portrayal by making Jupiter free, and although Legrand is referred to as "master" on several occasions, never once in the entire story does Poe use the word "slave." In other words, Poe capitalizes on the average racism of his audience while neutralizing the sectional conflict over slavery. Through a crucial yet subtle change in Jupiter's legal status, Poe attempted to create a sanitized South that could circulate freely in the national literary market.

Obviously, such a strategy could extend beyond U.S. boundaries to the world at large. In his remarks on literary nationalism, Poe accordingly disparages not only the political determinants of culture, but even the demand for uniquely *American* themes and settings:

> Much has been said, of late, about the necessity of maintaining a proper nationality in American Letters; but what this nationality is, or what is to be gained by it, has never been distinctly understood. That an American should confine himself to American themes, or even prefer them, is rather a political than a literary idea — and at best is a questionable point. We would do well to bear in mind that "distance lends enchantment to the view." Ceteris paribus, a foreign theme is, in a strictly literary sense, to be preferred. After all, the world at large is the only legitimate stage for the autorial *histrio*. (*ER* 1076)

Immediately after using this Shakespearean allusion to make exalted claims about authorship, Poe returns to the crucial practical function of literary nationalism: "But of the need of that nationality which defends our own literature, sustains our own men of letters, upholds our own dignity, and depends upon our own resources, there cannot be the shadow of a doubt" (*ER* 1076). The phrase about upholding American dignity seems to have been thrown in for good measure; Poe's real argument is that given the absence of international copyright protection, American authors have a material or economic dependence upon a nationalist ideology. This explains why, in the prospectus for *Penn Magazine*, Poe promises to "support the general interests of the republic of letters, without reference to particular regions" (*ER* 1025).

*   *   *

. . . It is misguided to conceive of [Poe's] racism as an attitude or sentiment somehow separable from the constraints and pressures of the prevailing modes of production, especially in a nation that suffered antagonistic modes to coexist until the advent of civil war. By extension, it is misguided to conceive of literary production as occurring in some fantastic realm of freedom apart from the ideological and material forces that characterize a social formation. If nothing else, the recognition of these forces makes it possible to move beyond interpretations that are informed by hindsight but not by history. For example, the paucity of comments about race in Poe's private correspondence, along with the offhanded disparagement of abolitionist poets in his anonymous critical reviews, should cast doubt on interpretations of the final chapters of *Pym* as divine retribution for "the known offense of slavery" (Dayan, "Romance and Race," 109). I must also question Dayan's claim that "Poe remained haunted, as did Jefferson, by the terrible disjunction between the ideology of slavery . . . and the concrete realities of mutilation, torture, and violation" (102). If anything, Poe seems to have conjured up the haunting portrait of blackness as a means of appealing to multiple segments of the white literary audience. And as soon as the audience is described in these terms, it becomes clear that his racist representations have less to do with black-white relations than with the way white people relate to each other.

The way white people relate to each other: this is what haunts Poe, this is what motivates his fantasies of a neutral culture, and this, to an extent seldom acknowledged, is what burdens the current critical discourse on race. What matters about Poe is not so much his reticence on slavery, nor even his use of racist stereotypes—which are as infrequent as they are offhanded. Instead, the case of Poe matters because his utterances and silences were both part of a coherent strategy to expel politics from the literary commodity. This is why attempts to read politics back into Poe's work have proven so vexing. To make this task easier, critics still turn to the Paulding-Drayton review as the smoking gun that will convict Poe once and for all. When this doesn't succeed, blame is sometimes placed upon conspiratorial Poe scholars, who are seen as withholding or covering up incriminating evidence.[44] This [essay] is not designed to comfort the vexed, but I do hope that I have demonstrated two things: First, although Poe left behind a clear trail of what might be called circumstantial racism, he avoided—by habit and design—the kind of political speech practiced by fire-breathing

---

[44] John Carlos Rowe, for example, accuses Poe critics of repressing "the subtle complicity of literary Modernism with racist ideology," and Dana Nelson complains of "the recent trend to sweep Poe's politics under the rug" (Rowe, 136; Nelson, *The Word in Black and White*, 91). Curiously, Rowe himself is one of the critics Nelson accuses of depoliticizing Poe, although she bases her argument on *Through the Custom House*, published ten years before "Poe, Antebellum Slavery, and Modern Criticism."

secessionists like Beverley Tucker and by antislavery moralists like James E. Heath (both of whom Poe knew during his connection with the *Southern Literary Messenger*). From this follows the second point, namely that the "depoliticized" Poe is only partly the work of his interpreters. Observing the dictates of the "cash rule," Poe sometimes played to the average racism of the national audience, but more frequently he avoided altogether those "horrifying because unprofitable doctrines" about slavery. In other words, Poe's work was not simply depoliticized by modern critics; it was in many ways depoliticized from the start. This, I would suggest, must be the basis for all future political criticism of Poe. Paradoxically, this insight also justifies the ideological interpretations of Poe that I have been attacking throughout this chapter. Though there may be flaws in the evidence and assumptions of critics such as Rosenthal, Nelson, and Rowe, the case of Poe nevertheless demonstrates the importance of race in determining what literature is—the form and meaning of its sentences, the form and meaning of its silences.

Taken in context, the example of Poe reveals the error of viewing racism as a private demon to be exorcised through simple denunciation, or as a Southern disease to be eradicated through a liberal dose of enlightenment. All too frequently, such views lead to the creation of an interpretive procedure that merely diagnoses texts as being racism-positive or racism-negative. When the texts themselves resist such a diagnosis, critics sometimes resort to *ad hominem* arguments, which resolve textual ambiguity by invoking the alleged beliefs of the alleged author.[45] . . . To resolve the current tangle of error and simplification, it is necessary to step back from the purity of ahistorical criticism and to delve into the complexities of a painful and uncompleted past. In the case of Poe and other antebellum writers, such an approach reveals a world of Orwellian complicity far beyond the explanatory reach of praise and denunciation. In that world—and perhaps in our own—all racisms are equal, but some racisms are more equal than others.

---

[45] In the case of "Southern" literature, this approach often combines contradictory assumptions about free will and determinism, or about the unfettered romantic artist and the poor-devil writer imprisoned by history. In other words, Poe is racist because all southerners are racist, but he is damnable because he freely chose to be a racist.

PAUL GILMORE

A "Rara Avis in Terris": Poe's "Hop-Frog" and Race in the Antebellum Freak Show

Paul Gilmore is a professor of English at California State University, Long Beach, and is the author of two books on nineteenth-century American literature: Aesthetic Materialism: Electricity and American Romanticism *(Stanford University Press, 2009) and* The Genuine Article: Race, Mass Culture, and American Literary Manhood *(Duke University Press, 2001), from which the selection below is drawn. His recent essay "John Neal, American Romance, and International Romanticism" appeared in the journal* American Literature *in 2012.*

In a letter to his close friend Frederick Thomas, dated 14 February 1849, less than eight months before his own death, Edgar Allan Poe wrote, "Literature is the most noble of professions. In fact, it is about the only one fit for a man." After being "quite out of the literary world for the last three years," Poe felt quite "savage." Having "some old scores to settle," he was ready to return to the critical battles that had made him infamous. As his just-completed review of James Russell Lowell's *A Fable for Critics* indicates, the target of his critical savagery, as it had been for much of his career, would be the Boston literary establishment.[1] A week before he wrote to Thomas, Poe completed "Hop-Frog," one of his last short stories, whose eponymous hero's parting shot—"This is my last jest"—has often been read as his own final jab at his critics and the literary marketplace. Publishing "Hop-Frog" in *Flag of Our Union*, a Boston weekly newspaper he described as "not a *very* respectable journal, perhaps, in a literary point of view, but one that pays as high prices as most of the magazines," Poe hoped the story would help him financially so he could start his own literary magazine, the *Stylus*. "Hop-Frog" was Poe's attempt to cash in on the public's demand for sensational tales in order that he might escape that very public. The target of Poe's critical savagery in his letter to Thomas, however, points to his story's being not simply an allegory of revenge against the literary marketplace, but also an attempt to establish a kind

---

[1] Letter to Frederick W. Thomas, 14 February 1849, *The Letters of Edgar Allan Poe*, vol. 2, ed. John Ward Ostrom (Cambridge: Harvard UP, 1948), 427–28. Further references to the letters will be to this edition and will be given with volume and page number. [All notes in this selection are Gilmore's.]

of savage literary manhood defined against both the literary mass market and the Boston literary elite.

[Here] I argue that Poe attempts to negotiate the literary marketplace by drawing on one of the most popular commercial entertainment forms of the period, the presentation of human oddities for mass audiences. While "Hop-Frog," with its dwarf-jester, his midget friend, a king, and his ministers, may seem far removed from the United States of the 1840s, such characters would have been familiar to the audiences of popular museum attractions such as Tom Thumb (Charles Stratton). Most famously with Stratton, but more tellingly, I will argue, with attractions such as "What is It?," P. T. Barnum and other proprietors brought a variety of human anomalies to the centerstage. Drawing on such contemporary figures in constructing his fantastical revenge, Poe places himself squarely amidst scientific debates over human types, over human bodies and their meaning, and specifically over race. Poe uses the freak show to construct his allegorical revenge because of its commercial success, a success dependent on its ability both to exemplify and to stand outside the laws of science and, in particular, scientific descriptions of race. While not every "freak" displayed in antebellum popular museums was coded in racial terms, commentary and advertisements readily drew on notions of race to figure bodily difference. Because the racially exotic body in the museum was valuable in various, at times contradictory, ways, it occasionally transgressed racial lines and overturned the racial hierarchy of white mass market audience members and displayed racial other. Poe attempts to use this subversive element within the antebellum freak show to place himself outside the realm of mere commerce in a more purely aesthetic sphere, in the process appropriating racial difference to figure his artistic practice. By reading Poe's story through the popular museum and the popular museum through Poe's story, I explore both how Poe unwraps the commercial racial logic of the freak show, its commodification of the exotic, the different, and the abnormal, and how that logic offers us a different understanding of Poe's racial politics *and* aesthetics.

. . . With "Hop-Frog," Poe identifies the male artist with a commercialized, racial other in articulating a particularly masculinized model of aesthetic production.[2] . . . Poe paradoxically invokes a commercialized

---

[2]David Leverenz has suggested that "Hop-Frog" satirizes both Southern gentry and Northern capitalist models of manhood and hints at the sort of racial identification I foreground when he talks of Poe as a Sambo-trickster figure in "Hop-Frog." My concern is more with how Poe savages a capitalist mode while relying upon mass cultural forms to do so. See David Leverenz, "Poe and Gentry Virginia: Provincial Gentleman, Textual

racial figure in order to imagine an antimarket literary manhood, a type of masculine literary production imagined to elude the demands of the marketplace. Because the racialized, freakish body became valuable not only by substantiating an audience's claim to (white) normality, but by upsetting racialized notions of what the body signified and, thus, turning the tables on its audience, Poe could use it to fantasize his revenge against those who would simply render him a commodity. In attempting to create a space for a literary production more independent of the market, Poe embraces his commodified status through the freak show, realizing he has "no other capital to begin with than whatever reputation I may have acquired as a literary man." In this way, Poe imagines Hop-Frog's escape as a model for escaping the mass market's demands and establishing himself as an aesthetic arbiter beyond both the market's fluctuations and an effete antislavery elite's power. In reacting to both the mass literary market and a white Northern antislavery literati, Poe, a self-identified Southerner, appropriates mass cultural racial difference in constructing a vision of literary manhood.

"MY LAST JEST"

"Hop-Frog: or, The Eight Chained Ourang-Outangs" is the story of "a dwarf and a cripple" captured "from some barbarous region" and enslaved by a king who makes him serve as his jester (p. 214). Upon the occasion of the story, the king is having a masquerade ball and calls upon Hop-Frog to contrive costumes for him and his ministers. One of the king's favorite "jokes" (the king is a great joker) is to require Hop-Frog to drink alcohol because of its potent effect upon him. The king forces Hop-Frog to drink a draught of wine and commands Hop-Frog to come up with "characters" for him and his ministers to assume.

Aristocrat, Man of the Crowd," in *Haunted Bodies: Gender and Southern Texts*, ed. Anne Goodwyn Jones and Susan V. Donaldson (Charlottesville: UP of Virginia, 1997), 100–101. As Joan Dayan has remarked, Poe "questions what it means to speak, or to love, as a man. . . . he ironizes the very possibility of speaking for or as a man" (Joan Dayan, "Poe's Women: A Feminist Poe?" *Poe Studies* 26.1–2 [June/December 1993]: 1). While it may be, as Dayan argues, that "the point of much of Poe's writing" was "to mutilate what his society constructed as manhood" (9), I am interested in how he implies another model of literary manhood in the place of a normative, white, Northern, middle-class manhood. See also Eliza Richards's discussion of how in his poetry and criticism Poe attempted "to carve out a specifically masculine, poetic space" by "outfeminizing the feminine in a masculine rendition that inverts female poetic practice" (Eliza Richards, " 'The Poetess' and Poe's Performance of the Feminine," *Arizona Quarterly* 55.2 [summer 1999]: 18, 8).

Shaken by the wine, Hop-Frog fails to respond. When the king tells him to drink more wine, Trippetta, a beautiful female dwarf who is the king's pet and Hop-Frog's sole friend (and fellow captive from the "barbarous region"), attempts to intercede on his behalf. The king tosses the wine in her face and pushes her to the ground. Following an inexplicable grating noise, Hop-Frog drinks more wine and elaborates his idea for the king and his courtiers to be costumed as "the Eight Chained Ourang-Outangs" (p. 217). Hop-Frog helps them prepare for the masquerade, making their costumes out of tar and flax and chaining them together as apes caught in the jungle. At the height of the ball, the costumed "Ourang-Outangs" enter with great commotion, frightening most of the guests. Hop-Frog corrals the faux orangutans in the center of the ballroom and attaches them by their chain to a chain extending from a skylight. With a whistle, he leaps above the courtiers and, hanging onto the chain, is raised up by an unseen accomplice. Hop-Frog, now seething in anger, breaks the silence by emitting a low grating noise and then pretends to scrutinize the identity of the orangutans by bringing his flambeau closer. Because their costumes consist of tar and flax, the courtiers erupt in flames and are quickly reduced to a charred mass. Hop-Frog describes the king's offenses to Trippetta, tells his stunned audience that "this is my last jest," and then climbs out the skylight, presumably to join Trippetta in an "escape to their own country" (p. 221).

For years, critics have read Poe's story of revenge as an allegory either of a transhistorical battle of the imagination with reality or, more specifically, of Poe's own battles with the publishing industry and his American audience.[3] Throughout his literary career, Poe was teetering on the edge of financial ruin, and by the time he was writing "Hop-Frog" in January and February of 1849, his financial condition was especially precarious. As he told one friend, his primary reason for publishing the story was to "get out of [his] pecuniary difficulties."[4] At the

[3] J. R. Hammond identifies the story as "a powerful allegory: the king representing Reality, the eternal antagonist of the creative mind, and the jester representing Imagination, the creative artist who is maimed and imprisoned by the unthinking majority" (J. R. Hammond, *An Edgar Allan Poe Companion: A Guide to the Short Stories, Romances, and Essays* [Totowa, N.J.: Barnes and Noble Books, 1981], 90–91). See also Hervey Allen's reading of "sovereign Reality who makes the cripple of Imagination, whom he keeps as a jester" who, in turn, takes "terrible revenge" and escapes with " 'Fancy' " (Hervey Allen, *Israfel: The Life and Times of Edgar Allan Poe* [New York: George H. Doran Co., 1926], 641); and, more recently, Kenneth Silverman's gloss (Kenneth Silverman, *Edgar A. Poe: Mournful and Never-Ending Remembrance* [New York: HarperCollins, 1991], 406–7).

[4] Letter to Annie L. Richmond, 8 February 1849, *Letters* 2:425.

same time, in addition to struggling to stay on his financial feet, Poe was also attempting to accumulate enough capital to start his own journal, the *Stylus*, a dream he had pursued since the early 1840s. As he described the journal in a letter to a potential subscriber in April 1849, only a month after the publication of "Hop-Frog," the Stylus would give the public "what they cannot elsewhere procure"; it would "aim high—address the intellect—the higher classes," thus allowing its editor to "exercise a literary and other influence never yet exercised in America."[5] In particular, Poe argued that such a magazine would fill a niche created by "the universal *disgust* excited by what is quaintly termed the *cheap* literature of the day," those magazines that consisted of "the ludicrous heightened into the grotesque; the fearful coloured into the horrible: the witty exaggerated into the burlesque: the singular wrought out into the strange and mystical" (*ER* 1033).[6] Thus, at the time Poe was writing and publishing "Hop-Frog," his hopes had become almost singularly pinned upon the idea of raising enough subscribers to start his independent, elite journal.

In this way, "Hop-Frog" amounts to more than an attempt at escaping "pecuniary difficulties"; it was specifically part of an attempt to elude the very market that called for "terrible" tales such as "Hop-Frog" and that made "not . . . *very* respectable journal[s]" like *Flag of Our Union* so successful.[7] Read in this light, the story becomes an allegory of Poe's attempt to escape his own dependence on an unappreciative and exploitative mass audience. Just as Poe hoped that by producing a tale of the horrible, grotesque, and burlesque, such as the literary market called for, he could escape its power, so "Hop-Frog" tells the story of its "professional jester" (p. 214) giving his audience exactly what they want in order to escape their power.[8] Like Poe's mass audience, the king and his ministers have no time for the "refinements . . . of wit" (p. 213). "Over-niceties wearied them," as they can only appreciate "*breadth*," "*length*," and the "practical" (p. 213). Their attention is focused on the "*effect* produced"—especially "fright" (pp. 218, 217)—and they specifically call for literary/creative novelties rather

---

[5] Letter to Edward H. N. Patterson, [30?] April 1849, *Letters* 2: 439–40.

[6] Letter to Thomas W. White, 30 April 1835, *Letters* 1: 57–58.

[7] Poe describes the "subject" of "Hop-Frog" as a "terrible one" in his letter to Annie L. Richmond, 8 February 1849, *Letters* 2: 425.

[8] Terence Whalen's observation that Poe "viewed his texts as split or divided objects—one part containing literary value for the critical taste, the other part containing such matter as would render them profitable in the mass market" seems appropriate here (Terence Whalen, *Edgar Allan Poe and the Masses: The Political Economy of Literature in Antebellum America* [Princeton, N.J.: Princeton UP, 1999], 91).

than art: "We want characters . . . something novel. . . . We are wearied
with this everlasting sameness" (p. 215). Poe not only characterizes this
audience as incapable of seeing beyond "fright" and "effect" but also
suggests their blindness derives from their focus on commercial matters. Throughout the story, the king's ministers respond in affirmation
as a chorus with the refrain "Capital!," while the prime minister's lone
enunciation consists of "And now to *business*" (p. 216, my emphasis) as
he demands characters of Hop-Frog. Finally, Poe emphasizes this audience's limited capacity to appreciate Hop-Frog's creations by describing it as one undistinguishable, massive body. From the outset, Poe
lavishes great attention upon the size of the king and his courtiers, their
"large, corpulent" bodies, sarcastically distinguished by their "heavy
wisdom" (p. 214). At the end, with his declaration that he knows "who
these people *are*, now!" (p. 221, Poe's emphasis), Hop-Frog reveals
them as "a fetid, blackened, hideous, and indistinguishable *mass*" (p. 221,
my emphasis). In this way, Poe's king and his court—who respond
with "Capital!" to the idea of "fright" (p. 217)—parallel the mass market that Poe, at times, felt himself financially required to appease. Writing "Hop-Frog" in the same month in which he wrote to Thomas that
literature was the only profession "fit for a man," Poe projects his anxieties of economic emasculation onto the body of Hop-Frog, then imagining himself, through Hop-Frog, gaining revenge against those who
abuse beauty and truth. With "Hop-Frog," then, Poe attempts to create a space for a kind of intellectual aristocrat, a model of literary manhood defined by its defense of beauty—embodied, perhaps, in Trippetta's feminine form—against an unappreciative mass audience only
interested in capital and fright.[9]

[9]Given Poe's infamous identification of poetic beauty with women ("the death . . .
of a beautiful woman is, unquestionably, the most poetical topic in the world" [p. 229];
"[The Poet] feels [poetry] in the beauty of women" [*ER* 93]), it has become a common-
place to read Poe as objectifying women as simply disembodied symbols of transcendent
beauty, a reading given substance, perhaps, in his description of Trippetta as nearly bodiless, both in her small size and her grace: she was "of exquisite proportions, and a marvel-
ous dancer" and "on account of her grace and exquisite beauty," was "universally admired
and petted" (*PT* 900). Yet as Joan Dayan and others have pointed out, the women in
Poe's tales tend to be frighteningly and hauntingly material as they refuse to be the purely
spiritual angels of domestic ideology even in death. Poe's women, as Dayan puts it, "are
not mere symbols for" Beauty because "Poe does not sustain the eternal polarities, but
instead analyzes the slippage in too convenient oppositions" including gendered ones
(Dayan, "Poe's Women" 1). Several critics have used this refusal of immateriality on the
part of Poe's female characters to argue for seeing the tales as "an enlightened deconstruction of nineteenth-century gender roles" (J. Gerald Kennedy, "Poe, 'Ligeia,' and the
Problem of Dying Women," in *New Essays on Poe's Major Tales*, ed. Kenneth Silverman
[Cambridge: Cambridge UP, 1993], 114). For readings of a feminist Poe, see Cynthia

"MALTREATMENT RECEIVED AT THE HANDS OF THE POPULACE"

Such an allegory—of the male artist (Hop-Frog) gaining revenge against an abusive audience (the king and his ministers)—nicely echoes the story of Poe as a writer who had to play to the sensational demands of the market in order to survive, but whose truly artistic tales transcend the market's power. Where apologists from Baudelaire to David Reynolds have read Poe in this way, critics such as Terence Whalen have more recently begun to argue that Poe's oeuvre, including his aesthetic critique of the marketplace, was, in fact, made possible by the commercialized nature of mass culture.[10] While Poe frequently denounced a purely economic basis for judging literature and lamented the way market considerations deformed literary works, he just as often accepted the economically driven nature of the antebellum publishing industry and often boasted of the growth in circulation that publications such as *Graham's Magazine* achieved under his editorship. In the early 1840s, he complained that "It seems that the horrid laws of political economy cannot be evaded even by the inspired" (*ER* 211) and argued that "if the popularity of a book be in fact the measure of its worth, we should . . .

Jordan, *Second Stories: The Politics of Language, Form, and Gender in Early American Fictions* (Chapel Hill: U of North Carolina P, 1989), and Leland S. Person Jr., *Aesthetic Headaches: Women and a Masculine Poetics in Poe, Melville, and Hawthorne* (Athens: U of Georgia P, 1988). My point is not to question Poe's destabilization of gender oppositions, but to argue that in challenging one dominant mode of literary manhood, he erects another model through the invocation of racial difference in the mass cultural sphere.

[10]See, for example, David Reynolds's contention that unlike the sensational literature he draws on, Poe's work "transcends its time-specific referents because it is crafted in such a way that it remains accessible to generations of readers" (David S. Reynolds, "Poe's Art of Transformation: 'The Cask of Amontillado' in Cultural Context," in *New Essays on Poe's Major Tales*, ed. Kenneth Silverman [Cambridge: Cambridge UP, 1993], 101). Also see David Reynolds, *Beneath the American Renaissance: The Subversive Imagination in the Age of Emerson and Melville* (Cambridge: Harvard UP, 1988). On the other hand, see especially Terence Whalen, "Edgar Allan Poe and the Horrid Laws of Political Economy," *American Quarterly* 44.3 (September 1992): 381–417. As Whalen has explored most fully, Poe's literary career at once grew out of the market conditions that structured literature in the antebellum era and protested against those conditions: "If Poe . . . tried to defend or create an autonomous realm for literature, it was an effort simultaneously doomed and motivated by the homogenizing pressures" of antebellum economic and literary production (391). I have found Whalen's discussion here immensely enlightening and helpful in thinking through Poe and the literary market. Jonathan Elmer has also recently considered Poe in relation to literary mass culture, but rather than being concerned with the political economy of mass culture, as Whalen is, he focuses on the democratic nature of mass culture, the tension between being part of a large, anonymous cultural whole and being an individual that was central to Jacksonian America. See Jonathan Elmer, *Reading at the Social Limit: Affect, Mass Culture, and Edgar Allan Poe* (Stanford, Calif.: Stanford UP, 1995).

admit the inferiority of 'Newton's Principia' to 'Hoyle's Games'" (*ER* 225–26). Yet only a few years earlier he seemed to embrace those "horrid laws" when he argued that the "effect" of a tale "will be estimated better by the circulation of the Magazine than by any comments upon its contents" and that "truth and honor form *no* exceptions to the rule of economy, that value depends upon demand and supply."[11]

The tension between these seemingly paradoxical views comes to a head in Poe's dream of establishing himself as editor of an independent journal. When Poe commented on the fact that "The history of all Magazines shows plainly that those which have attained celebrity were indebted for it to articles" of potentially "bad taste" consisting of "the ludicrous heightened into the grotesque; the fearful coloured into the horrible: the witty exaggerated into the burlesque: the singular wrought out into the strange and mystical," he was in fact defending his own tales, specifically "Berenice," in terms of their potential for helping a magazine's financial success.[12] Yet with the *Stylus* Poe apparently hoped that by gaining "a proprietary right" to his own magazine through the support of subscribers from "our vast Southern & Western Countries" he would escape his dependence upon the literate masses and a Northern literary elite, if not the literary marketplace.[13] Drawing on the commercial magazine form that had helped to place even "the inspired" at the mercy of "the horrid laws of political economy," Poe wanted to reinvent the form by appealing to an elite, regional audience and making it a vehicle for addressing ideas of truth and beauty. While critics have often read the *Stylus* as indicative of Poe's desire to inhabit an otherworldly aesthetic sphere outside the reach of the market, Whalen's work suggests that rather than trying to escape the market, Poe was simply trying to find the right market niche where the value of truth and beauty would fetch the best price.[14]

Thus, where David Leverenz has argued that "Hop-Frog" "satirizes emerging mass-market culture. . . . [and] capitalist constructions

[11] Letter to Thomas W. White, 30 April 1835, Letters 1:58; review of Beverly Tucker, *George Balcombe, Southern Literary Messenger*, January 1837, *Essays and Reviews* 978.

[12] Letter to Thomas W. White, 30 April 1835, *Letters* 1:57–58.

[13] Letter to Charles Anthon, ante 2 November 1844 (probably late October), *Letters* 1:266–72.

[14] As Whalen argues, "Poe's persistent struggle to influence the taste of the reading public was not so much a reactionary attempt to resurrect the old standards of literary value, but rather an effort to institute some new system of measurement that would enable the articulation and sorting of a new mass of literary commodities" (Whalen, "Horrid Laws" 398).

of manliness [and] individuality," we need to see this satire as being both critical of emerging mass culture and concomitant notions of manhood *and* deeply embedded within them.[15] "Hop-Frog" displays this dependence on mass market forms not simply in its sensationalism and its publication in a cheap weekly newspaper, but through its invocation of popular museum culture. Despite its seemingly fairy tale cast of a king, his ministers, and a jester, Poe's story of the display of half-man, half-beast orangutans, a deformed acrobatic dwarf, and a beautiful, talented midget to a mass audience would have resonated with American audiences familiar with the display and promotion of abnormal humans by popular museum proprietors like P. T. Barnum.[16] Dwarves and midgets not only had served as jesters in European royal courts throughout the sixteenth, seventeenth, and eighteenth centuries (and even, in a few cases, into the nineteenth century), but had appeared in popular, commercial forums such as Bartholomew Fair since the early seventeenth century.[17] Early American museums, such as Charles Willson Peale's museum in Philadelphia, while taking a more scientific, democratizing approach, continued to display scientific abnormalities, and with Barnum's American Museum in the 1840s the American freak show, "the formally organized exhibition of people with alleged and real physical, mental, or behavioral anomalies for amusement and profit," came into its own.[18]

[15] Leverenz, "Poe and Gentry Virginia" 101.

[16] Poe implies his own familiarity with Barnum and his display of apes in a letter published in a Philadelphia newspaper, in which he described the face of one of his literary rivals as resembling "that of the best-looking but most unprincipled of Mr. Barnum's baboons" (quoted in Joseph Wood Krutch, *Edgar Allan Poe: A Study in Genius* [1926; New York: Russell and Russell, 1965], 129).

[17] Don Francisco Hidalgo, a dwarf, like Hop-Frog, served King Ferdinand VII of Spain as a jester until the mid-1840s, when he attempted to capitalize on Tom Thumb's success by staging a tour of his own through England and the United States (Richard Altick, *The Shows of London* [Cambridge: Harvard UP, 1978], 256). As Poe says in his story, "at the date of my narrative, professing jesters had not altogether gone out of fashion at court" (*PT* 899). Further, he states that "the animals in question [orangutans] had, at the epoch of my story, very rarely been seen in any part of the civilized world" (*PT* 904); according to at least one source, Barnum displayed the first live orangutan in America in 1846. See John Rickards Betts, "P. T. Barnum and the Popularization of Natural History," *Journal of the History of Ideas* 20.3 (June–September 1959): 353.

[18] This is the definition of the freak show offered by Robert Bogdan in his seminal *Freak Show: Presenting Human Oddities for Amusement and Profit* (Chicago: U of Chicago P, 1988), 9. Besides Bogdan and Altick, for discussions of the freak show more generally and the antebellum freak show in particular, see Rosemarie Garland Thomson, "The Cultural Work of American Freak Shows, 1835–1940," *Extraordinary Bodies: Figuring Physical Disability in American Culture and Literature* (New York: Columbia UP,

The antebellum freak show attracted patrons both by objectifying the bizarre and by making the bizarre seem normal. The most successful of Barnum's attractions, the young Tom Thumb, exemplifies this play between the familiar and the different. Throughout his career, Thumb performed as the American Yankee in miniature, "a perfect MINIATURE MAN, only TWENTY-EIGHT INCHES HIGH, perfect and elegant in his proportions, and weighing only FIFTEEN POUNDS!"[19] As Neil Harris argues, Thumb's popularity depended on the fact that, unlike most human oddities, "Crowds identified with him, rather than against him."[20] But Thumb's success was not simply dependent on his audience identifying with him; rather, it was his rendering of the familiar in *miniature*, with a difference, the fact that he seemed so familiar, yet so strange, that made him such a popular draw.[21] Audiences were delighted by Thumb's performances and recognized in him the middle-class traits they wanted to have themselves—intelligence, elegance, kindness, morality.[22] Yet they were reassured of their own normality not simply by his mirroring those traits, but also by his small size, by laughing not simply with him, but at his attempts at personating "large" world historical figures like Napoleon, Samson, and Hercules. In other words, as much as he was a petted favorite, like Trippetta, Thumb

---

1997), 55–80; Thomson, ed., *Freakery: Cultural Spectacles of the Extraordinary Body* (New York: New York UP, 1996); Leslie Fiedler, *Freaks: Myths and Images of the Secret Self* (1978; New York: Anchor Books, 1993); and Leonard Cassuto, "The Racial Freak, the Happy Slave, and the Problems of Melville's Universal Men," *The Inhuman Race: The Racial Grotesque in American Literature and Culture* (New York: Columbia UP, 1997), 168–216.

   [19] *Sketch of the Life, Personal Appearance, Character and Manners of Charles S. Stratton, The Man in Miniature, Known as General Tom Thumb* (New York: Van Norden and Amerman, 1847), 5.

   [20] Neil Harris, *Humbug: The Art of P. T. Barnum* (Chicago: U of Chicago P, 1973), 49.

   [21] For more on the logic of the miniature, see Susan Stewart, *On Longing: Narratives of the Miniature, the Gigantic, the Souvenir, the Collection* (1984; Durham, N.C.: Duke UP, 1993).

   [22] Much work has been done of late on Barnum's museum and the role it played in bringing together a cross-class audience of rising artisans, merchants, and clerks and their families in an environment that brought together high and low, Broadway and the Bowery, while promoting itself as "respectable"—middle-class. See, in particular, Bluford Adams's discussion in *E Pluribus Barnum: The Great Showman and the Making of U.S. Popular Culture* (Minneapolis: U of Minnesota P, 1997), 75–163, and Peter Buckley's chapter on Barnum in "To the Opera House: Culture and Society in New York City, 1820–1860," Ph.D. diss., SUNY Stony Brook, 1984. See also my prologue and my chapter on Thoreau.

was still an object on display, to be laughed at and identified against, as with Hop-Frog.[23]

If Thumb's audiences tended to identify with him, even as his size marked him as abnormal and, consequently, them as normal, Barnum encouraged his audiences to view other strange humans he exhibited as different in terms of race. While in Europe developing the fame and reputation of his biggest star in the mid-1840s, Barnum also remained busy with other projects. In August 1846 he announced the London exhibition of what he called the "wild man of the prairies," or "What is It?" Claiming the creature had been captured in California or the mountains of Mexico, Barnum prompted his audience's reactions to the dark-skinned, hairy man with a series of questions: "Is it an animal? Is it human? Is it an Extraordinary Freak of Nature? Or is it a legitimate member of Nature's Works? Or is it the long sought for link between man and the Ourang-Outang?"[24] It was quickly revealed, however, that this nondescript was actually the well-known American actor Harvey Leach, dressed in a hair costume with his skin stained underneath.

Leach stood only three feet, five inches tall, and, when he walked, he "waddled along, his hands touch[ing] the ground, in the manner of the higher primates," because one of his legs was six inches longer than the other.[25] Despite his deformity, Leach's "extraordinary muscular powers, especially in his arms" allowed him to "achieve some very remarkable feats of strength and agility."[26] Using his acrobatic skills, he had gained minor fame as Signor Hervio Nano on the New York and London stages in the early 1840s in roles such as Jocko, the Brazilian ape;

---

[23]For more on Thumb as feminized commodity for an increasingly feminine audience, see Lori Merish, "Cuteness and Commodity Aesthetics: Tom Thumb and Shirley Temple," in *Freakery*, ed. Thomson 185–203. As she argues, "In the performances of these diminutive prodigies, the cute emerged as a site for feminine identification as well as a strategy for domesticating (the) Otherness (of 'freak,' of child), annexing the Other to the Self" (188). According to Merish, the cute, "emerg[ing] in conjunction with the 'feminization' of commercial amusements" (195), "transforms transgressive subjects into beloved objects" (194). Poe figures the transgressive and beloved nature of the freak by splitting it into two gendered bodies, the masculine, deformed Hop-Frog and the feminine, beautiful (or cute) Trippetta.

[24]Quoted in Altick, *Shows*, 265. The fullest account of Barnum's "What is It?" exhibits is James W. Cook Jr.'s "Of Men, Missing Links, and Nondescripts: The Strange Career of P. T. Barnum's 'What is It?' Exhibition," in *Freakery*, ed. Thomson, 139–57.

[25]Altick, *Shows*, 265.

[26]Joseph N. Ireland, *Records of the New York Stage from 1750 to 1860*, vol. 2 (1866; New York: Benjamin Blom, 1966), 318.

Bibbo, the Patagonian ape; and "the Frog."[27] His best-known performance was as the Gnome Fly, wherein "he successively embodied a
gnome, a baboon, and a fly," a performance that ended with his making
"a wonderful flight, in magnificent costume . . . from the ceiling, back
of the gallery, to the back of the stage."[28] Leach died only six months
after his involvement in Barnum's "What is It?" hoax was revealed, and
commentators of the day attributed his death to his embarrassment at
his complicity in such a disreputable performance: "It killed Harvey
Leach, for he took it to heart and died."[29] As one historian of the American stage put it in 1866, he died "from maltreatment received at the
hands of the populace."[30]

The resemblance between Leach and Hop-Frog is striking. Like
Leach, because of "the distortion of his legs," Hop-Frog "could only
get along by a sort of interjectional gait—something between a leap
and a wriggle." Similarly, despite his troubles walking, Hop-Frog is also
a spectacular acrobat: "the prodigious muscular power which nature
seemed to have bestowed upon his arms . . . enabled him to perform
feats of wonderful dexterity, where trees or ropes were in question."
And like Leach, who regularly performed as an ape, Hop-Frog, it seems,
"resembled . . . a small monkey" (p. 214). Hop-Frog's narrative even
seems to evoke Leach's most famous role, the "The Gnome Fly," in
which he transformed himself from a gnome into a baboon and then
into a fly; at the end of his story, Hop-Frog transforms his audience,
rather than himself, into orangutans, but like Leach he escapes by making a "wonderful flight" far above an astonished crowd. Finally, Hop-
Frog's story reverses the popular narrative of Leach's demise. While
Leach dressed up as an orangutan-type creature and was destroyed by
his mass audience, Hop-Frog bedecks his audience as orangutans in
order to destroy them. . . .

[27] For Jocko, see George C. D. Odell, *Annals of the New York Stage*, vol. 4 (1834–
1843) (New York: Columbia UP, 1928), 482; for Bibbo, see Odell, 5:135; for the Frog,
see Odell 4:371.
[28] Odell, 4:368.
[29] Henry Mayhew, *London Labour and the London Poor*, vol. 3 (1861; New York:
Dover, 1968), 103.
[30] Ireland, 2:319, paraphrasing Francis Wemyss, who stated that "poor Leach [was]
maltreated, and died shortly afterwards" (Francis C. Wemyss, *Wemyss' Chronology of the
American Stage, from 1752 to 1852* [1852; New York: Benjamin Blom, 1968], 92).

"THE CONNECTING LINK BETWEEN
HUMANITY AND BRUTE CREATION"

. . . [T]he antebellum freak show was much more than a commercial attraction; it was a central site for the popularization of scientific ideas, especially scientific ideas about race. While cultural critics often complained of the tawdry, sensationalistic, and commercial nature of "museums" such as Barnum's, scientists like Louis Agassiz lent credibility to these institutions by celebrating their promulgation of natural science.[31] In fact, when Barnum's museum burned down in 1865, Agassiz and other scientists wrote a public letter lamenting the loss to the scientific community.[32] In particular, Barnum's display of amazing humans, including "wild" Indians from the western frontier, promoted the popular discussion and dissemination of scientific ideas concerning humankind.[33] . . . The popular museum brought together a cross-class, mixed gender, white urban audience, in the process normalizing ideas of the white middle-class family and decorous behavior. . . .

Exhibits such as Barnum's "What is It?" more clearly reinforced the ideas of racial hierarchy put forth by texts such as J. C. Nott and George Gliddon's *Types of Mankind* (1854). With Leach, Barnum—as in his later and more famous "What is It?" exhibit featuring African American William Henry Johnson—refused to define precisely what his nondescript was: "The thing is not to be called *anything* by the exhibitor. We know not & therefore do not assert whether it is human or animal. We leave that all to the sagacious public to decide."[34] Yet as the exhibit of

---

[31] See such comments as " 'museum' in the American sense of the word means [simply] a place of amusement" (quoted in Louis Leonard Tucker, " 'Ohio Show-Shop': The Western Museum of Cincinnati, 1820–1867," in *A Cabinet of Curiosities: Five Episodes in the Evolution of American Museums* [Charlottesville: UP of Virginia, 1967], 73), and the idea that American museums were "full of worthless and trashy articles" (quoted in Whitfield L. Bell Jr., "The Cabinet of the American Philosophical Society," *A Cabinet of Curiosities*, 22). For Agassiz's position as the most prominent scientist of the age, see Edward Lurie, *Louis Agassiz, A Life in Science* (Chicago: Phoenix Books, 1966), especially chapter 5, "Naturalist to America." As Bogdan notes, human curiosities' strangeness at once drew scientific censure for sensationalism and at the same time "scientific interest because they represented specimens, data to be examined in quest of answers to the pressing scientific questions of the day" (*Freak Show*, 151).

[32] See Betts, "P. T. Barnum," 357. See Betts more fully for a discussion of Barnum's role in popularizing science.

[33] In this way, as Bogdan notes, freak shows were especially "relevant to debates concerning the classification of human races and the place of various humans in the great chain of being" (*Freak Show*, 27).

[34] Letter to Moses Kimball, 18 August 1846, *Selected Letters of P. T. Barnum*, ed. A. H. Saxton (New York: Columbia UP, 1983), 35. See Cook, "Of Men," for the fullest discussion of Johnson. Also see Bogdan, *Freak Show*, 134–44; Adams, *E Pluribus Barnum*,

Johnson more explicitly foregrounds and as Leach's stained skin implies, such missing link figures clearly evoked a rather imprecisely defined racial order that ranked white audience members above darker-skinned, nearly subhuman others in some hierarchy of both humankind and creation itself. Confirming the racial science of the era, Leach's "What is It?" with his racially indeterminate exotic pedigree indicated to his audience that their normative white bodies were not just the standard for mankind, but were the superior models.[35]

Poe mirrors the racial coding of exhibits such as "What is It?" in describing Hop-Frog. Like Barnum, Poe is "not able to say, with precision, from what country Hop-Frog originally came." It was, he assures, "some barbarous region, however, that no person ever heard of—a vast distance from the court of our king" (p. 214). The racially other character of Hop-Frog is further suggested by his resemblance to black and Indian characters from elsewhere in Poe's work, almost all of whom are not simply of a different race, but horribly misshapen. For example, in *The Narrative of Arthur Gordon Pym* (1838), Dirk Peters, "the son of an Indian squaw" and "a fur-trader," is

> one of the most purely ferocious-looking men. . . . He was short in stature—not more than four feet eight inches high—but his limbs were of the most Herculean mould. His hands, especially, were so enormously thick and broad as hardly to retain a human shape. His arms, as well as legs, were bowed in the most singular manner, and appeared to possess no flexibility whatever. His head was equally deformed, being of immense size, with an indentation on the crown (like that on the head of most negroes), and entirely bald. (*PT* 1043)

Poe describes black characters similarly in *The Journal of Julius Rodman* (1840) and "How to Write a Blackwood Article" (1838). In *Rodman*, Toby is "as ugly an old gentleman as ever spoke—having all the peculiar features of his race; the swollen lips, large white protruding eyes, flat

---

157–64, for a discussion of Johnson in terms of Barnum's shifting antebellum politics (and his production of Boucicault's *The Octoroon*); and Bill Brown, *The Material Unconscious: American Amusement, Stephen Crane, and the Economies of Play* (Cambridge: Harvard UP, 1996), 215–18, on Crane's *The Monster* and its interplay between blackface minstrelsy and the bestialized black of the freak show.

[35] See Cassuto, Thomson, Cook, and Reiss for the best overviews of the racial character of the freak show. See also Bernth Lindfors, "Circus Africans," *Journal of American Culture* 6.2 (1983): 9–14. Thomson goes a bit too far, perhaps, in arguing that in the freak show, "no firm distinction exists between primarily formal disabilities and racial physical features considered atypical by dominant, white standards" ("Cultural Work," 14).

nose, long ears, double head, pot-belly, and bow legs" (*PT* 1242), while Pompey, in "Blackwood," is "three feet in height. . . . [and] had bowlegs and was corpulent. His mouth should not be called small, nor his ears short. . . . Nature had endowed him with no neck, and had placed his ankles (as usual with that race) in the middle of the upper portion of the feet" (p. 71). Rather than simply drawing upon grotesque stereotypes of blacks and Indians, Poe emphasizes their supposed biological difference through bowed legs, deformed hands, and short stature. Describing the dwarf Hop-Frog in terms of his exotic pedigree, distorted legs, "prodigious muscular power" (p. 214), and "large eyes" (p. 216), Poe all but defines him as yet another one of his deformed black or Indian characters.[36]

Poe's use of orangutans in "Hop-Frog" and elsewhere is particularly telling in this regard. Barnum advertised his own orangutan in 1846 as "the Grand Connecting Link between the two great families, the Human and brute creation," using almost the exact language he used to describe both Leach and Johnson as "What is It?": "the connecting link between humanity and brute creation."[37] Barnum displayed the costumed Leach and Johnson as links between human and orangutan because the orangutan already stood as a link itself between humans and other brutes. This liminal status of the orangutan is a recurring trope in Poe's oeuvre. Most famously, in "The Murders in the Rue Morgue" (1841) the murderer is thought to be an inarticulate madman or perhaps "an [Asiatic]" or "an African" (p. 145) before Dupin posits that it is an orangutan.[38] The orangutan was not simply seen as linking

[36]Toni Morrison has pointed out that Poe's use of "othering" here and elsewhere reveals "unmanageable slips" indicative of the ambivalent structure of these images of blackness (Toni Morrison, *Playing in the Dark: Whiteness and the Literary Imagination* [New York: Vintage, 1993], 58–59). As I will argue more fully below, these grotesque visions point to Poe's interest in the use of race for frightening, sensationalistic purposes along with any racism they demonstrate. Poe describes the Sioux, in Rodman, in somewhat similar terms: "In person, the Sioux generally are an ugly ill-made race, their limbs being much too small for the trunk, according to our ideas of the human form—their cheek bones are high, and their eyes protruding and dull" (*PT* 1222). As these different racial others indicate, I think it is important to keep the exotic locale of Hop-Frog's birth indefinite as Poe does, even as we see the parallels with descriptions of blacks and Indians. From this position, Dayan, perhaps, pushes it too far, when she says "this unheard of place refers implicitly to Africa" ("Amorous Bondage: Poe, Ladies, and Slaves," p. 366).

[37]Quoted in Betts, "P. T. Barnum" 353–54; in reference to Johnson, quoted in Bogdan, *Freak Show* 136.

[38]For the racial nature of the orangutan in "The Murders in the Rue Morgue," see Nancy A. Horowitz, "Criminality and Poe's Orangutan: The Question of Race in Detection," in *Agonistics: Arenas of Creative Contest*, ed. Janet Lungstrum and Elizabeth Sauer (Albany: State U of New York P, 1997), 177–95; Whalen, "Horrid Laws" 401; and

humans and other animals, but as being more closely related to irrational, inarticulate, primitive humans, specifically supposedly intellectually
inferior Africans. Barnum drew upon this supposed relationship when
he stated that the later "What is It?" was "found in the interior of Africa
in a perfectly natural state, roving about like a monkey or Orang Outang," and was of "mixed ancestry" as indicated by the fact that "while
his face, hands and arms are distinctly human, his head, feet and legs are
more like the Orang Outang."[39] In both "Hop-Frog" and the "What is
It?" exhibits, orangutans help to place the abnormal body in a racialized
hierarchy, somewhere between fully human white audience members
and lower animals. As Hop-Frog's revelation of his orangutans as a
"blackened mass" iterates, the half-man, half-beast orangutan was, in
the end, implicitly black or, at least, not-white.[40]

"Hop-Frog," however, reverses this racial coding. Instead of simply
emphasizing the abnormality of its "dwarf" and "cripple" by demonstrating his close proximity to orangutans and blacks, the story reveals
its ostensibly normal, fully human king and his ministers as monsters by
displaying them first as orangutans and then as a blackened mass. "Hop-
Frog," in other words, does not abandon the metonymic link between
race and monstrosity, but rather reveals the supposed men as monsters
while demonstrating the more powerful manhood of the exotic, abnormal other through his subtle plan of revenge. As Joan Dayan puts it, the
story ends with "The epidermic curse—the fatality of being black, or
blackened—[being] visited on the master race."[41] Yet what is most
striking about this narrative is Poe's identification with, rather than

---

Dayan, "Romance and Race," in *The Columbia History of the American Novel*, gen. ed.
Emory Elliott (New York: Columbia UP, 1991), 103. Similarly, in "The System of
Dr. Tarr and Professor Fether" (1844), a story "Hop-Frog" possibly alludes to when one
of the ministers suggests adding "feathers" to their costumes of tar (*PT* 904), Poe links
the insane with orangutans through the appearance of the tarred and feathered keepers of
the asylum (*PT* 716).

[39] *An Illustrated Catalogue and Guide Book to Barnum's American Museum* (New
York: n.p. [1864]), 111. See also David R. Brigham, *Public Culture in the Early Republic:
Peale's Museum and Its Audience* (Washington, D.C.: Smithsonian Institution Press,
1995), 130, for a description of the way orangutans and blacks were linked together in
Peale's Museum in 1799.

[40] Perhaps most infamously, Thomas Jefferson suggested the possibility of sexual
relations between black women and orangutans in *Notes on the State of Virginia*: "[blacks']
own judgment in favour of the whites, declared by their preference of them, as uniformly
as is the preference of the Oran-ootan for the black women over those of his own species"
(Thomas Jefferson, *Notes on the State of Virginia*, ed. William Peden [1787; New York:
Norton, 1972], 138). See Cook, "Of Men," for more on the liminal, racialized status of
orangutans in reference to the "What is It?" exhibits.

[41] Dayan, "Romance and Race" 104. See also her "Amorous Bondage" p. 346.

against, the exotified other. Poe's racial attitudes have been debated much of late, with most of the focus centering on *Pym* and its description of the black Tsalalians and a review of two proslavery volumes that appeared in the *Southern Literary Messenger* under Poe's editorship in 1836 and that may or may not have been written by him.[42] What is clear by nearly all accounts is that whether Poe wrote the review, which states that "Domestic Slavery" is "the basis of all our institutions," or not, he embraced, at times, many of the "standard proslavery arguments of his day."[43] Most infamously, Poe's Pym describes the completely black Tsalalians as "among the most barbarous, subtle, and bloodthirsty wretches that ever contaminated the face of the globe"

[42] Such criticism first began appearing in the late 1950s and early 60s, but then was displaced by deconstructionist versions of Poe that tore him away from any social context. For example, Leslie Fiedler, in *Love and Death in the American Novel* (1960), argues that "*theoretically* the tale of *Gordon Pym* projects through its Negroes the fear of black rebellion and of the white man's perverse lust for the Negro, while symbolizing in the red man an innocent and admirable yearning for the manly violence of the frontier; but in the working out of the plot, the two are confused. . . . Insofar as *Gordon Pym* is finally a social document as well as a fantasy, its subject is slavery; and this scene, however disguised, is the section of America which was to destroy itself defending that institution" (Leslie A. Fiedler, *Love and Death in the American Novel* [1960; London: Paladin, 1970], 368). For more recent treatments of race and Pym, see John Carlos Rowe, "Poe, Antebellum Slavery, and Modern Criticism," in *Poe's Pym: Critical Explorations*, ed. Richard Kopley (Durham, N.C.: Duke UP, 1992), 117–38; Sam Worley, "The Narrative of Arthur Gordon Pym and the Ideology of Slavery," *ESQ* 40 (1994): 219–50; Teresa A. Goddu, "The Ghost of Race: Edgar Allan Poe and the Southern Gothic," *Gothic America: Narrative, History and Nation* (New York: Columbia UP, 1997), 73–93; Jared Gardner, "Poe's 'Incredible Adventures and Discoveries Still Farther South,'" *Master Plots: Race and the Founding of an American Literature, 1787–1845* (Baltimore, Md.: Johns Hopkins UP, 1998), 125–59; and Dana Nelson, "Ethnocentrism Decentered: Colonial Motives in *The Narrative of Arthur Gordon Pym*," *The Word in Black and White: Reading "Race" in American Literature, 1638–1867* (New York: Oxford UP, 1993), 90–108. For an alternative account, which discounts the argument for Poe's authorship of the Paulding-Drayton review as outlined by Bernard Rosenthal in "Poe, Slavery, and the *Southern Literary Messenger*: A Reexamination," *Poe Studies* 7.2 (December 1974): 29–38, see Terence Whalen, "Subtle Barbarians: Poe, Racism, and the Political Economy of Adventure," in *Styles of Cultural Activism: From Theory and Pedagogy to Women, Indians, and Communism*, ed. Philip Goldstein (Cranbury, N.J.: Associated University Presses, 1994), 169–83. As in his other scholarship, Whalen calls for reading Poe in terms of an information explosion, including an explosion of information produced by exploration about exotic locales and peoples. The criticism I have found most useful on Poe and race is Dayan, "Amorous Bondage" [p. 346] and "Romance and Race," and Dana Nelson, "The Haunting of White Manhood: Poe, Fraternal Ritual, and Polygenesis," *American Literature* 69.3 (September 1997): 515–46.

[43] *Review of Slavery in the United States* by J. K. Paulding and *The South Vindicated from the Treason and Fanaticism of the Northern Abolitionists* [William Drayton], *Southern Literary Messenger* 2.5 (April 1836): 337; Rosenthal, "Poe, Slavery," 30. As Nelson and Goddu have pointed out and as I will touch on below, Poe's racism was far less regional than it was national. Reading his racism simply from his self-identification as a Southerner helps to obscure the way in which that racism was common nationwide.

(*PT* 1150). Poe's exotic, deformed Hop-Frog, with his initial meekness and ready servitude that turn into sly revenge, closely resembles the subtle barbarians of *Pym* who initially appear meek and malleable, but then slaughter the crew of the *Jane*. Because of his customary slipperiness, Poe's precise attitude toward Pym and, by extension, the Tsalalians is as debatable as his racial attitudes, and his depiction of Hop-Frog has similarly evoked contradictory reactions. But what is more certain is that unlike the Tsalalians or Pompey, Toby, or even Dirk Peters (who only becomes "white" [*PT* 1156] in the context of the completely black Tsalalians), Poe describes Hop-Frog as a fully individuated and complex subject. In constructing a model of savage literary manhood in his fantasy of revenge against the literary marketplace, Poe identifies his aesthetic self with a character defined as racially other.

"A TRIPLICATE TREASURE"

How do we make sense of this identification? Dayan reads "Hop-Frog" as Poe's "envisioned revenge for the national sin of slavery," understanding the reversal of master and slave as deriving from Poe's "increasingly subversive concerns" with "the perils of mastery" and "the reversibility of supremacy."[44] While Poe may well have been obsessed with "the perils of mastery," his more explicit critical concerns during the period had to do with getting "the means of taking the first step" toward establishing the *Stylus* and settling "some old scores," specifically with the Bostonian literary elite.[45] More fully fleshing out Barnum's engagement with contemporary racial science grants one way of understanding how the figure of the freakish other offered Poe a vehicle both for commercial success and for allegorical revenge against the Bostonians. Spe-

---

[44]Joan Dayan, "Amorous Bondage" p. 366; "Romance and Race" 93; "Amorous Bondage" pp. 367, 358. Dayan's most recent comments in "Poe, Persons, and Property," *American Literary History* 11.3 (1999): 405–25, bring her insights about the philosophical underpinnings of Poe's work closer to my interest in the economics of the literary. In this article, she articulates the ways in which "Poe demands a way of reading that escapes the binary bind of the racist or nonracist Poe" (412), suggesting instead that "Poe's fantasies of degeneration or disability, then, are never only about the enslavement of the African American" (419), but rather derive from his "obsession with possession, personal identity, and the will" (411). My concern is with how Poe's obsession with his own literary property and reputation as possessions circulated through mass cultural images of race and slavery.

[45]As Whalen notes, "given the enormous quantity of [Poe's] writings, there are precious few references to slavery, and many of these are made in the heat of a broader assault on a literary enemy who is 'vulnerable' for having abolitionist tendencies" (Whalen, "Subtle Barbarians" 183, note 23).

cifically, the reversal at the end of the story, when the objectified Hop-Frog makes his mass audience the spectacle themselves and calls into question their own humanity, reveals and draws on a subversive element embedded within contemporary displays of the body in the museum and central to those displays' commercial success. In other words, Poe draws on the popular museum and its reversal of racial hierarchies because its exotification and disruption of racial differences had proven commercially successful and could be used to satirize what Poe saw as the hubris and hypocrisy of a Northern, antislavery, literary elite. The commercialization and subversion of racial difference and hierarchy in the popular museum becomes a mode through which Poe can create a popular story in attempting to escape the power of both the literary masses and a Boston literary elite.

Poe suggests the literary market value of race in a letter on the marketing of the *Stylus*, three months after the publication of "Hop-Frog." There, he explains his "awaiting the *best opportunity* for [the *Stylus*'s] issue," by quoting Monk Lewis. Lewis, according to Poe, "once was asked how he came, in one of his acted plays, to introduce black banditti, when, in the country where the scene was laid, black people were quite unknown." He writes that Lewis's "answer was:—'I introduced them because I truly anticipated that blacks would have more *effect* on my audience than whites—and if I had taken it into my head that, by making them sky-blue, the *effect* would have been greater, why sky-blue they should have been.' "[46] Poe's point, it seems, is that the success of the *Stylus* depends on timing, on it producing the proper *effect*, an effect directly analogous to the sensation that racial others might cause in an audience of whites. Race sells because it produces a certain effect, namely fright, that is analogous to the effect produced by the right timing and right promotion in producing an elite literary journal. But it is not simply race that sells; it is the exotic, abnormal nature of the racial other that sells, the fact that he or she too is human, but does not appear to be.[47] Linking his elite literary journal to the appeal of racial difference, Poe identifies his aesthetic program with the market in the sensational and the sensational's transgression of the normal.

Poe fleshes out the commercial value of fright and exotified racial difference in describing Hop-Frog's value to his audience. Taking great

[46]Letter to George W. Eveleth, 26 June 1849, *Letters*, 2: 449–50.

[47]As Whalen puts it, Poe's comments suggest "how ideological and economic forces combined to determine the salability of racism" (*Poe and the Masses*, 143); in Whalen's view, "Poe capitalizes on the average racism of his audience while neutralizing the sectional conflict over slavery" (142).

care to describe that value precisely, Poe expands the literary market value of race that his citation of Monk Lewis suggests and complicates notions of the role of race in popular museums. As a "professional jester," Hop-Frog, Poe states, was a "triplicate treasure in one person" (p. 214). First, Hop-Frog gives the king "a jester to laugh *with*, and a dwarf to laugh *at*" (p. 214); Hop-Frog's objectified body allows the king both to identify with him in his jokes and to reconfirm his superiority through a bodily-marked hierarchy. Like Tom Thumb, Hop-Frog entertains his audience members, mirroring their own sense of themselves, and at the same time reinforces, through his deformed body, their sense of superiority. Yet Hop-Frog's body also marks him as different in another way. His diminutive size sets Hop-Frog apart because in "ninety-nine cases out of a hundred" jesters "are fat, round and unwieldy" (like the "mass[ive]" king and his ministers). Thus, "a lean joker [like Hop-Frog] is a *rara avis in terris*" (p. 213). According to Poe, then, Hop-Frog is a triplicate treasure (1) because his audience can identify with him and be entertained by him, (2) because his body seems to confirm their superiority by affirming the body as a stable marker of identity and cultural/racial hierarchies (they are civilized, he is barbarous), and (3) paradoxically, because his body does *not* confirm, but rather troubles such notions of stable bodily meaning, because he disrupts the linkage between jesters and rotundity. Unlike ninety-nine jesters out of a hundred, he is not fat.

While Hop-Frog's being a lean joker does not seem particularly subversive of antebellum ideas about the body, Poe's delineation of Hop-Frog's value, his status as a *rara avis*, suggests that part of the freak show's commercial success arose from its disruption of audience expectations about bodies and their meanings. We can use Hop-Frog's triplicate value then to understand the market value of Leach in "What is It?" better. One aspect of the cultural work of antebellum freakery was, as we have seen, its shoring up of the white bourgeois family as a normative standard for judging the world and other peoples, its confirmation of hierarchical, racialized divisions through its display of bodily difference. But as "Hop-Frog" indicates, this does not tell the whole story. In its invocation of what Neil Harris has called "the operational aesthetic," Barnum's exhibit leaves it "to the sagacious public to decide" precisely what "It" is and what "It" means.[48] Barnum first suggests that "It" upholds a natural order of things that consists of a great chain of

---

[48]See Harris, *Humbug* 59–91 on the operational aesthetic, and 85–88 for a discussion of this aesthetic in reference to Poe's hoaxes and detective stories.

being leading from God to civilized whites to displayed racial others to orangutans and then brute creation; that is, that as a link in the chain of being, It is "a legitimate member of Nature's works." Yet Barnum goes on to hint that It may not conform to the laws of nature at all, that it may be "an Extraordinary Freak of Nature." "Hop-Frog" emphasizes that one part of the freak's triplicate value was its subversion of such an order. Just as Hop-Frog's value is trebled because his body does not conform to the general law that jesters are "fat, round and unwieldy," so "What is It?" gains its commercial value, its power to attract paying customers, not simply by confirming their sense of superiority, but by challenging the order of nature that supposedly guarantees their superiority.

Because of the ways in which Barnum both courted scientific acceptance by providing specimens that confirmed scientific laws and needed sensational attractions that defied the laws of science, his exhibition of humans did not simply replicate given scientific theorems about race, but questioned the empirical grounds of those theorems. In particular, Barnum's exhibits displayed blackness both as nearly nonhuman and as potentially white, through both blackface minstrel shows, where whites became black, and the exhibition of albino African Americans or African Americans whose skins were turning white.[49] Barnum more directly addressed racial science in promotional biographies of Tom Thumb where he hinted that the American science of craniometry had little or no basis. Craniometry, as promoted by Samuel George Morton, was based on the idea that the interior volume of one's skull corresponded to one's intelligence. Morton used the measurement of skulls from ancient and contemporary skeletons to "prove" the continuation of racial stocks and the superiority of Caucasians. In this way, he became one of the chief theorists for the emerging American school of ethnology, the chief proponents of polygenism and strict, biologically understood racial distinctions in the antebellum period.[50] Barnum reasoned

[49]For example, see Barnum's account of "*White Negroes*," from 1864: "The history of this family seems almost miraculous. The father and mother both black, and distinctly African, yet each alternate child (and they have had fifteen) has been white and black; the white children's features being so decidedly Ethiopian as to preclude the possibility of doubt as to their being purely African" (*Illustrated Catalogue and Guide Book*, 114). For more on Barnum and his depictions of blackness, see Reiss, "P. T. Barnum," and my chapter on Thoreau.

[50]See Stephen Jay Gould, *The Mismeasure of Man* (New York: Norton, 1981), and William Stanton, *The Leopard's Spots: Scientific Attitudes Toward Race in America, 1815–1859* (Chicago: University of Chicago Press, 1960), for the best overviews of craniometry and the American school of ethnology. As they both point out, scientific racialism

that while it may be "natural to suppose that the smallness of [Thumb's] brain should limit the development of his intellectual facilities," Thumb's intelligence implied that there was no correlation between brain size and intellect, thus disrupting the pseudoscientific assumptions underlying the racial hierarchy of the types of mankind.[51] While exhibits of people like Harvey Leach and Tom Thumb primarily served to substantiate their audience's claims to superiority and normativity, one part of their attraction was their calling into question the assumptions behind such norms, a questioning that simultaneously refocused attention on the "normal" bodies of the audience and empowered that audience, rather than a scientific elite, to be the arbiters of scientific truth.

"Hop-Frog" more fully plays out this reversal, but locates aesthetic and scientific power in the creative but disempowered individual rather than with the masses or the elite. Because Hop-Frog's body confounds the normative identity of jesters as fat, the focus shifts, as the story proceeds, from his body to the massive bodies of the king and his courtiers. The nature of this shift is possibly suggested by the fact that Hop-Frog's mental acuity, like Tom Thumb's, calls into question the assumptions of craniometry, assumptions implied by the story's description of the doltish king's "constitutional swelling of the head" (p. 214). Whether referring to craniometric standards or simply metaphorically referring to the king's ego, Poe's story emphasizes that the supposedly normative body does *not* correspond to intellectual superiority. Reversing the order of things in its conclusion, "Hop-Frog" inverts the chain of being that Hop-Frog's body supposedly substantiates—the chain from the skylight leads to Hop-Frog who hovers above the spectacularized and objectified blackened orangutan-courtiers below.

Poe's racist statements and his apparent belief in phrenology, a pseudoscience that provided the underpinnings for craniometry, would seem to trouble such a reading of "Hop-Frog."[52] Poe argued in an

---

and proslavery thought during this period did not necessarily go hand-in-hand. See also George M. Fredrickson, "Science, Polygenesis, and the Proslavery Argument," *The Black Image in the White Mind: The Debate on Afro-American Character and Destiny, 1817–1914* (New York: Harper, 1971), 71–96.

[51] *Sketch of Life* 8. See Bogdan, *Freak Show* 151, for a fuller discussion of this point.

[52] Jared Gardner uses Poe's acceptance of phrenological tenets to support seeing his desire to hierarchize American writers through their penmanship (in "Autography") as parallel to Morton's project of ordering races through cranial measurement. While this argument provides an interesting and suggestive parallel, which I found useful for thinking through Poe's desire to become a national critic, I will argue that the empiricism of craniometry and its implicit idea of progress repelled Poe in a way phrenology itself did not. See Edward Hungerford, "Poe and Phrenology," *American Literature* 2 (1930–31): 209–31, for the fullest discussion of Poe's interest in phrenology. As Hungerford argues,

1836 review that phrenology "ranks among the most important [sciences] which can engage the attention of thinking beings" (*ER* 329), and later in the same review, he quotes approvingly a passage that seems to contain the seeds of craniometry: "Idiocy is invariably the consequence of the brain being too small, while in such heads the animal propensities are generally very full" (*ER* 332). Yet as Dana Nelson has recently shown in a striking reading of Poe's "Some Words with a Mummy" (1845), Poe also satirizes racial science (and especially craniometry): Poe uses the mummy's account of the ancient Egyptians' scientific and technological superiority to undermine the scientific coterie's thesis that "we are to attribute the marked inferiority of the old Egyptians in all particulars of science, when compared with the moderns, and more especially with the Yankees, altogether to the superior solidity of the Egyptian skull" (*PT* 817).[53] Dismissing craniometry in order to poke fun at Yankee scientists and their ideas of progress, Poe suggests that he did not blindly accept racial science but rather saw it as evidence of hubris.

*   *   *

. . . "Hop-Frog" and its confutation of the relationship between bodies and their scientific meanings raises questions about the proper investigative techniques and attitudes that scientists should take in investigating man, about the relationship between science and aesthetics, and about the authority of scientific and other "votaries." Hop-Frog's success, like that of Tom Thumb, serves to undermine the idea of using purely mathematical, empirical devices for measuring human beings: the king and his courtiers' emphasis on "*breadth*" and "*length*" (p. 213) reveals that they, like racial scientists, incorrectly depend simply on measurements to decide what "make[s] a man" (p. 218). Just as

---

phrenology is found in much of Poe's literary criticism and plays a central role in characterizing both Ligeia and Roderick Usher. Yet, as he also notes, Poe was quick to criticize or satirize the claims of both phrenology and physiognomy in stories such as "Lionizing" (1835); "The Business Man" (1840); "The Murders in the Rue Morgue" (1841); "Diddling Considered as One of the Exact Sciences" (1843); "The Literary Life of Thingum Bob, Esq." (1844); "Some Words with a Mummy" (1845); and "The Imp of the Perverse" (1845).

[53] As Nelson puts it, Poe has his mummy "tear down the modern [scientists]' sense of cultural, political, scientific, and racial progress" ("Haunting of White Manhood" 515) by "refus[ing] to be baited by an essentialist argument correlating bodily differences with intellectual and cultural ones" (535).

Barnum's presentation of Leach in "What is It?" called on the imagination of the "sagacious public" rather than the measurements of a scientific elite to decide what "It" truly is, Poe's Hop-Frog uses his imagination to overturn the empirically minded king and his ministers and to show who is a man and who is not.

But "Hop-Frog" does not leave it up to the sagacious public to decide. Instead, it is not simply Hop-Frog's valuable exotic nature that makes him a *rara avis*, but his creative aesthetic imagination that sets him apart from an elite (the king and his ministers) and the masses (the guests at the masquerade who are duped by the orangutans). The term *rara avis* hints at this aesthetic nature, for Poe used the term in a version of his "Philosophy of Furniture" (1840) to describe those few with refined enough tastes to appreciate true art; and the phrase in both its sound, *rara avis*, and meaning, "strange bird," recalls Poe's most famous poem and nickname, "The Raven."[54] Hop-Frog's revenge, then, does not so much dismantle scientific racism as imply the importance of aesthetics rather than empirical data for judging what makes a (literary) man. In doing so, it links aesthetics with racial otherness against both the unthinking masses and an imitative and self-congratulating tyrant. As suggested by his satires of Yankee scientists and writers who use craniometry and phrenology to claim superiority, that tyrant, for Poe, was the Boston literati with whom he had so often waged war and who, he felt, used questions concerning race to substantiate their own aesthetic claims and authority.

"OUR LITERARY MOHAWK, POE!"

In closing, I will attempt to explore how identifying his own artistic and critical practice with racial otherness allowed Poe to imagine a revenge specifically against the Bostonians. Poe's identification with a racially indeterminate native of a barbarous region in "Hop-Frog" was not unprecedented. In fact, throughout his career, he embraced a characterization of himself as being a "savage Indian" in his critical practice. As early as 1836, the *Cincinnati Mirror* commented on Poe's "savage skill" in "us[ing] his tomahawk and scalping knife" as critic and editor for *Southern Literary Messenger*, a comment Poe subsequently reprinted

---

[54]See "Philosophy of Furniture," *Collected Works of Edgar Allan Poe, vol. 2, Tales and Sketches, 1831–1842*, ed. Thomas Ollive Mabbott (Cambridge: Belknap Press/Harvard UP, 1978), 500 note t.

in that magazine to puff its sales.[55] Later, in 1846, the image recurred when Poe was called "the tomahawk man" and "the Comanche of literature."[56] Then in January 1849, at the same time Poe was writing "Hop-Frog," A. J. H. Duganne lampooned Poe in "A Mirror for Authors" with the lines, "With tomahawk upraised for deadly blow, / Behold our literary Mohawk, POE!"[57] As noted earlier, in his letter to Thomas written soon after he finished "Hop-Frog" in early February, Poe invokes this characterization of his criticism. Being "quite out of the literary world for the last three years," during which time he has "*said* little or nothing," has made Poe "savage—wolfish" and ready to settle "*some* old scores."[58] Calling himself savage, Poe proclaims himself ready to rejoin the "the race of critics," whom he elsewhere defines as exclusively "masculine—men" (*ER* 116). Identifying himself with a character figured as racially other in "Hop-Frog," Poe hoped to establish himself outside the reach of the literary mass market, just as identifying himself with another racial figure, the savage Indian, he hoped to settle some old scores, in particular those with antislavery Boston. With both, he hoped to clear a space for the *Stylus* and the authority it would wield, thus guaranteeing himself a place in the only profession "fit for a man."

About the same time Poe finished "Hop-Frog" in early February 1849, he completed a review of James Russell Lowell's *A Fable for Critics*, a satire of American letters that had appeared the previous October. In *A Fable*, Lowell had gently upbraided Poe for his criticism of Longfellow, but in Poe's letter to Thomas, where he states that he feels "savage," Poe points to the broader basis of his critique of Lowell: "Lowell is a ranting abolitionist and deserves a good using up."[59] It is not just

---

[55]Cited in Dwight Thomas and David K. Jackson, *The Poe Log: A Documentary Life of Edgar Allan Poe*, 1809–1849 (Boston: G. K. Hall, 1987), 201.

[56]Quoted in Killis Campbell, *The Mind of Poe and Other Studies* (Cambridge: Harvard UP, 1933), 59.

[57]Motley Manners, esq. [Augustine J. H. Duganne], "A Mirror for Authors," *Holden's Dollar Magazine* (January 1849): 22. See John E. Reilly's discussion of the satire, "Poe in Pillory: An Early Version of a Satire by A. J. H. Duganne," *Poe Studies* 6 (June 1973): 4–12. Reilly contends that Poe probably never saw the Duganne satire, but whether he saw Duganne's identifying him as a Mohawk or not, he was clearly familiar with the popular idea of him as a savage, scalping Comanche-like critics.

[58]Letter to Frederick W. Thomas, 14 February 1849, *Letters* 2: 428, his italics.

[59]Ibid. 427–28; in *A Fable for Critics*, Lowell cautions Poe that "You mustn't fling mud-balls at Longfellow so," after commenting that Poe's "heart [somehow] seems all squeezed out by the mind" (p. 267). See Sidney P. Moss, *Poe's Literary Battles: The Critic in the Context of His Literary Milieu* (1963; Carbondale: Southern Illinois UP, 1969), for an overview of Poe's critical wars with the Bostonians, including the "Longfellow War" of 1845–1846.

Lowell who *deserves* a good using up; it is his entire Boston clique, "the Frogpondians":

> I wish you would come down on the Frogpondians. They are getting worse and worse, and pretend not to be aware that there *are* any literary people out of Boston. The worst and most disgusting part of the matter is, that the Bostonians are really, as a race, far inferior in point of *anything beyond mere talent*, to any other *set* upon the continent of N. A. . . . . I always get into a passion when I think about [it]. It would be the easiest thing in the world to use them up *en masse*. One really well-written satire would accomplish the business:—but it must not be such a dish of skimmed milk-and-water as Lowell's.[60]

Sharpening his critical tomahawk, Poe fixed his aim on his favorite target, those "servile imitators of the English," the Bostonians.[61] But as this letter suggests and as his review of Lowell's *Fable* and criticism of Longfellow reiterate, Poe's attacks were as grounded in sectional and political controversies over slavery and in his dismissal of their work as weak and effeminate ("skimmed milk-and-water") as in his sense that his foes' writings were imitative. In reviewing Lowell's *Fable* for *Southern Literary Messenger*'s Southern audience, Poe notes that "the grounds of the author's laudations" can only be understood by realizing that "Mr. Lowell is one of the most rabid of the Abolitionist fanatics," warning that "no Southerner who does not wish to be insulted, and at the same time revolted by a bigotry the most obstinately blind and deaf, should ever touch a volume by this author." Poe goes on to complain that Lowell's "prejudices on the topic of slavery break out every where in this present book" as he refuses to "speak well . . . of any man who is not a ranting abolitionist" (*ER* 819). According to Poe, Lowell's prejudice against Southerners is shared by most Bostonians: "It is a fashion about Mr. Lowell's set to affect a belief that there is *no such thing* as Southern Literature" (*ER* 819), and accordingly, "All whom he praises are Bostonians. Other writers are barbarians and satirized accordingly—if mentioned at all" (*ER* 820). Poe criticizes Lowell not just for his weak and imitative writing, but for what he sees as a regional bias revealed in his fanatical abolitionism.

Throughout his critical battles with the Bostonians, Poe used their abolitionist leanings as part of a broader attack on their aesthetics, a

---

[60] Letter to Thomas, 2:427, his italics.
[61] Ibid.

critique he enunciated in terms of region and gender. Earlier, during the "Longfellow War," Poe had defended his accusations against Longfellow of plagiarism by attacking Longfellow's defenders and their abolitionism: "In no literary circle out of Boston—or, indeed, out of the small coterie of abolitionists, transcendentalists and fanatics in general, which is the Longfellow junto—have we heard a seriously dissenting voice on this point" (*ER* 760). In reviewing Longfellow's *Poems on Slavery*, Poe more explicitly characterizes that group in effeminate terms, arguing that Longfellow's poems are "intended for the especial use of those negrophilic old ladies of the north, who form so large a part of Mr. Longfellow's friends." In the next sentence, Poe seems to allude to one of these "ladies" when he states "The first of this collection is addressed to William Ellery Channing" (*ER* 761–62). A few years earlier, in another review that attacked "Boston critics" (*ER* 461), Poe had argued that Channing was "like an honest woman" (*ER* 459). Poe attempted to clear a space for himself as literary arbiter for the nation and to suggest an alternative form of literary manhood by characterizing the Bostonians as a clique of womanish, imitative abolitionists who refused to see beyond their narrow bounds, who viewed all others, especially Southerners, as barbarians.

As I have argued, in "Hop-Frog" Poe identifies himself with a character from a "barbarous region" partly in order to gain the financial means to establish the *Stylus*, a journal he envisioned as breaking the stranglehold of the Boston literary clique. He specifically planned to raise subscribers in the South and the West, and repeatedly alluded to the *Stylus* and the Frogpondians in the same breath.[62] Even in his earliest plan for an independent literary journal in 1840, he stressed its independent nature by promising not to yield "to the arrogance of those organized cliques which, hanging like nightmares upon American literature, manufacture, at the nod of our principal booksellers, a pseudo-public-opinion by wholesale" (*ER* 1025). In attempting to establish the *Stylus*, Poe was not simply interested in controlling an independent journal that would place him beyond the mass market's demands and allow him to become arbiter of American literary taste; he was specifically attempting to gain independence from and revenge against the Boston clique of "abolitionists, transcendentalists and fanatics." As he put it, in reviewing his own work, he envisioned "the whole

---

[62] See letters to George W. Eveleth, 15 December 1846, and 4 January 1848, *Letters* 2:333, 354, for both "South & West" and Frogpondians.

literary South and West . . . doing anxious battle in his person against the old time-honored tyrant of the North" (*ER* 1100).[63]

The title of "Hop-Frog" clearly resonates with Poe's epithet for his birthplace, Frogpondium, and Poe's central critical concerns with the Bostonian literary establishment, and his recent break with Providence poet Sarah Helen Whitman, which he blamed on her transcendentalist friends, suggests reading Hop-Frog's vengeful fury as directed at Boston and its literary establishment.[64] Consciously or unconsciously, the story draws some of its energy from Poe's distaste for the Boston literary clique. Identifying himself with a barbarian, as he had been recently described as "the literary Mohawk" and as he argued the Bostonians saw all others, Poe figuratively gains revenge over those he saw oppressing him, a group of tyrants whose aping ability recalls his characterization of Longfellow as "the GREAT MOGUL of the Imitators" (*ER* 761). Just as Poe had suggested that Longfellow deserved to be hanged (*ER* 717) for committing the "most barbarous class of literary robbery" (*ER* 678), that Channing should be "hung *in terrorem*" (*ER* 459), and that the entire Boston clique "hang[s] like nightmares upon American literature" (*ER* 1025), he has Hop-Frog hang the king and his ministers for their crimes against beauty and their abuse of his creative talents. Read in this light, "Hop-Frog" becomes the very satire Poe called for in his letter to Thomas.[65] With the horrified but delighted guests now standing in as a mass audience obsessed with the sensa-

[63]See Kenneth Alan Hovey, "Critical Provincialism: Poe's Poetic Principle in Antebellum Context," *American Quarterly* 39 (1987): 341–54, for an account of Poe's criticism as being based in regional controversies over notions of history that included the issue of slavery.

[64]The title has other possible sources, of course. For example, Tom Thumb had played in *Hop-o'-my-Thumb* and Leach had performed as "the Frog." See Harris, *Humbug* 102, and *Sketch* 14, on *Hop-o'-my-Thumb*. As Silverman notes in *Edgar A. Poe*, Poe's "turbulent feelings about Boston involved more than literature" (264). He quotes Bernard C. Meyer's "suspicion that ultimately [Boston] represented the underside of the ambivalence he felt toward the mother who abandoned him by her untimely death" (492). Such a reading might help to complicate Marie Bonaparte's oedipal reading of "Hop-Frog" (Marie Bonaparte, *The Life and Works of Edgar Allan Poe: A Psycho-Analytic Interpretation*, trans. John Rodker [1949; New York: Humanities Press, 1971], 510–13) and suggests another way of identifying Boston as the target of Poe's overdetermined rage.

[65]This connection is further suggested by the fact that when Poe finished "Hop-Frog" he almost immediately wrote to his confidante, Annie Richmond. Richmond, a resident of Lowell, Massachusetts, was one of Poe's few close friends in the area and would have understood his ironic glee at the geographic implication of his title—especially since it would be published in a cheap Boston publication—"The five prose pages I finished yesterday are called—what do you think?—I am sure you will never guess—Hop-Frog!" (Letter to Annie L. Richmond, 8 February 1849, *Letters* 2:425).

tional, and the king and his ministers representing the tyrannical Boston literati, Poe's fantasy of revenge allows him to vent his rage against two groups he felt his art and his financial stability imperiled by: the literary masses and the elite Bostonian taste-makers.

In envisioning this revenge by making his Bostonian adversaries the victims of an imagined slave revolt, Poe also satirizes their racial politics and suggests their hypocrisy about racial matters. "Hop-Frog" echoes Poe's repetition of the standard Southern accusation against abolitionists of fomenting slave revolt. In response to Longfellow's poem "The Warning," Poe writes that it "contains at least one stanza of absolute truth" in its depiction of slave revolt: "One thing is certain:—if this prophecy be *not* fulfilled, it will be through no lack of incendiary doggrel on the part of Professor Longfellow and his friends" (*ER* 764). Poe reiterates this idea of abolitionist "incendiary doggrel" in his celebration of Robert M. Bird's proslavery novel *Sheppard Lee* (1836) for its "excellent chapters upon abolition and the exciting effects of incendiary pamphlets and pictures among our slaves in the South," an episode that ends "with a spirited picture of a negro insurrection, and with the hanging of Nigger Tom" (*ER* 399). The repetition of the word "incendiary" recalls the literally incendiary nature of Hop-Frog's final revenge, his destruction of the king and his ministers by hanging them by a chain and then burning them up, thus suggesting the link between the violence in "Hop-Frog" and abolitionist rhetoric.

This reversal of things—the identification of Yankee abolitionists with slaveholders as the victims of a slave revolt—underlines Poe's view of the Frogpondians as hypocrites. Throughout his criticism, Poe implies that Longfellow and other Bostonian abolitionist authors are as tyrannical in literary and other matters as the worst slaveholders and, perhaps, are as dependent upon the commercial value of race, in the literary market, as Southern slaveholders are in the slave market. In his review of Lowell's *Fable*, for example, Poe argues, "His fanaticism about slavery is a mere local outbreak of the same innate wrongheadedness which, if he owned slaves, would manifest itself in atrocious ill-treatment of them, with murder of any abolitionist who should endeavor to set them free" (*ER* 819). Similarly, in criticizing Longfellow's "The Quadroon Story," the story of "a slaveholder selling his own child," Poe comments that "a thing which may be as common in the South as in the East, is the infinitely worse crime of making matrimonial merchandise—or even less legitimate merchandise—of one's daughter" (*ER* 763). Longfellow, of course, is not literally making merchandise of his daughter; rather he is making literary merchandise out of the story of a daughter in slavery.[66] While Southerners hold slaves in bondage as a kind of property, Longfellow and his junto, according to Poe, abuse the slaves by turning them into a kind of inferior literary property. Poe emphasizes that the question is one of property rights, of economics, by commenting that "No doubt, it is a very commendable and very comfortable thing . . . [to] write verses instructing southerners how to give up their all with a good grace . . . but we have a singular curiosity to know how much of his own, under a change of circumstances, the Professor himself would be willing to surrender" (*ER* 762–63). The Boston abolitionists are willing to convert slave stories into merchandise, cashing in on the value of race in the literary marketplace, but would actually feel no sympathy for their own slaves and would be unwilling to give up their own (literary) property.[67] . . .

Finally, in making an argument against an effeminized model of white middle-class manhood that he identifies with Boston's "negrophilic old ladies" like Longfellow, Lowell, and Channing, Poe turns to an antibourgeois figure, the non-normative, racialized body, in attempting to create an alternative model of literary manhood. To figure himself as a *rara avis* in the terris of antebellum literary culture, a culture he saw dominated by the mass market and by imitative and womanish Bostonians, Poe took on a savage persona that at once drew on and criticized the commercial success of sensationalized racial difference. Because such exhibits as "What is It?" depended not simply on substantiating racialized difference, but on titillating audiences with the possibility that such differences might be humbuggery, they could, at times, reverse the subject/object dichotomy, making audience members the object of scrutiny. It is because of this possible reversal that Poe turns to such figures for reimagining his struggle with the marketplace, in this way linking the artist with both racial otherness and slavery. "Hop-Frog" suggests that in the topsy-turvy world of the antebellum commercial museum, performances of racialized bodily difference did not simply stabilize hard notions of racial difference and racial hierarchy. Instead, because of their commodification of difference, because such

[66] Along these lines, Duganne satirized the Bostonian abolitionist poet John Greenleaf Whittier in "A Mirror for Authors," just prior to addressing Poe, "Were 't not for darkies sure his fame would darkle:. . . . But, oh! how frail 'Othello's occupation!' / When slavery falls—falls Whittier's avocation" (22).

[67] See Dayan, "Poe, Persons, and Property" for an extended discussion of how "All of Poe's fiction is about property and possession" (410) and a short commentary on "Hop-Frog" as "a final joke on the gentry both North and South, who with torturous ingenuity defined property in women, workers, and slaves, fixing them and their progeny in their status and location, kept low down in the hierarchy of entitlements" (412).

attractions became triplicate treasures, they simultaneously underwrote and undermined both the bodily based racial hierarchies of contemporary science and the subject/object distinction they depended on. Because of the ways in which the exotified body in the museum transcended scientific laws—particularly those of race—in order to draw more attention and, thus, more money, the exotic, museal body becomes a perfect figure for Poe's attempt at transcending and exploiting the market and fantasizing an alternative model of white literary manhood. Identifying himself with a figure of racial otherness from one of the most popular and commercially successful attractions of the era in a sensational tale of slave revolt, Poe satirizes both the racial politics of the antislavery Bostonian literary circles and the mass market in sensational literature in an attempt to establish himself in a position of literary authority. Becoming the barbarian they imagine him to be, Poe appropriates racial otherness as a mode for reclaiming his position in the only profession "fit for a man."

MAURICE S. LEE

Absolute Poe: His System of Transcendental Racism

Maurice Lee is professor of English at Boston University and author of two important books on nineteenth-century American literature: Uncertain Chances: Science, Skepticism, and Belief in Nineteenth-Century American Literature *(Oxford University Press, 2012) and* Slavery, Philosophy, and American Literature, 1830–1860 *(Cambridge University Press, 2005). He is also the editor of* The Cambridge Companion to Frederick Douglass *(Cambridge University Press, 2009). Lee has been writing about Poe since early in his career and continues to do so today, including an essay in the recent volume* Remapping Antebellum Culture: Poe at 200 *(Louisiana State University Press, 2013). The selection reprinted here originally appeared in the journal* American Literature *in 2003.*

A haunting image appears on the cover of the 1995 essay collection *The American Face of Edgar Allan Poe*. From a perspective slightly above the subject, we see a grainy, black-and-white figure with vaguely familiar features: disheveled hair, broad forehead, thin mustache, deep-set eyes. The picture is not unlike a still frame taken from a surveillance video, as if Poe had come back from the grave and was captured leaving a convenience store. The hazy image simultaneously suggests Poe's modern presence and historical alterity, a fitting introduction to an essay collection that signaled a shift in Poe studies from abstract, ahistorical universals toward "Poe's syncopated relation to American culture." Subsequent scholarship in this vein has rendered rich interpretation.[1] The problem is that Poe is becoming something of a divided figure, embedded in his era's material discourse but divorced from the metaphysics of his day. It may be possible, however, to bring into focus a more stubbornly historical Poe who not only participates in his era's political, economic, and mass cultural life but also uses historically available ideas to theorize his American world.

This world, as critics have increasingly found, was torn by slavery and race. Through varying degrees of interpretive will, blackness and bondage become powerfully political in a wide array of Poe's poetry, fiction, essays, and reviews. What is striking in these analyses is how often Poe's social proclivities appear to be beyond his control as ideology and unconscious desire determine textual meanings.[2] But what if Poe is a more self-conscious observer of slavery and race whose political vision is mediated by his philosophical beliefs? This is not to suggest that Poe achieves a coherent or commendable understanding of slavery. Far from it. The terror, disruption, and chaos that mark Poe's treatment of the institution originate from the tensions between his metaphysics and racism. On one hand, Poe maintains distinctions between black and white, slave and master, brutish object and reasoning subject. On the other, he indulges what *Eureka* (1848) calls "the appetite for Unity," the transcendental urge to synthesize dualities in an "absolute oneness" (*PT* 1280).

This essay traces Poe's divergent urges for metaphysical unity and racial difference. It begins with "Metzengerstein" (1832), an exemplary story that offers an early and surprisingly cogent position on the American slavery debate. However, the racist anti-abolitionism evident

---

[1] Shawn Rosenheim and Stephen Rachman, introduction to *The American Face of Edgar Allan Poe*, ed. Shawn Rosenheim and Stephen Rachman (Baltimore: Johns Hopkins Univ. Press, 1995), xii. Subsequent scholarship includes Jonathan Elmer, *Reading at the Social Limit: Affect, Mass Culture, and Edgar Allan Poe* (Stanford, Calif.: Stanford Univ. Press, 1995); Terence Whalen, *Edgar Allan Poe and the Masses: The Political Economy of Literature in Antebellum America* (Princeton, N.J.: Princeton Univ. Press, 1999); and J. Gerald Kennedy, ed., *A Historical Guide to Edgar Allan Poe* (New York: Oxford Univ. Press, 2001). [All notes in this selection are Lee's.]

[2] For a sense of the diversity of Poe scholarship on race that nonetheless offers a kind of consensus regarding Poe's lack of intention, see J. Gerald Kennedy and Liliane Weissberg, eds., *Romancing the Shadow: Poe and Race* (New York: Oxford Univ. Press, 2001).

in "Metzengerstein" and beyond conflicts with transcendentalist concept Poe borrows from Schelling and Coleridge. Here Enlightenment
dualisms threaten to collapse into romantic absolutism as blackness and
bondage are figured as dangers immanent in the unwitting white mind.
For Poe, the slavery crisis is a crisis of the unconscious, which he dramatizes with a repetition more compelling than compulsive. Poe, that
is, seems less an author bedeviled by buried racial fears than one who
prejudicially enacts a strategic metaphysics of race.

*   *   *

The facts of Poe' politics are open to argument but can look something like this: Poe himself never owned a slave and was ambivalent
about Southern plantation culture. In New York City, he was loosely
affiliated with the literary wing of the Democratic Party, even as he
resisted conscription by the nationalists of Young America. But while
Poe learned to resent the aristocratic mores he enjoyed as a youth in
Virginia, he also expressed reactionary ire against progressive causes in
general and abolitionism in particular. Poe lambasted the antislavery
movement in critiques of Lowell and Longfellow; his correspondence
with proslavery thinkers can imply his concurring beliefs; and he may
have condoned as writer or editor the disputed Paulding-Drayton review,
a text that celebrates chattel bondage as a positive good. For the most
part, Poe's literary practice and criticism support the racist stereotypes of
plantation fiction. At the same time, Terence Whalen offers an important
caveat. Aspiring to a national reputation and attuned to market forces,
Whalen's Poe generally manages to avoid the slavery controversy, displaying instead an "average racism" that a range of readers could support. One might doubt, however, Poe's willingness and ability to pan-
der consistently to popular tastes, especially given his lifelong penchant
for self-destructive behavior. More crucially, a larger question looms:
even if Poe eschews explicit discussion of the slavery conflict, to what
extent might the crisis have influenced his literary work?[3]

---

[3]See Terence Whalen, "Average Racism: Poe, Slavery, and the Wages of Literary
Nationalism," pp. 394–422. On Poe's ambivalence about plantation culture, see David
Leverenz, "Poe and Gentry Virginia," in *The American Face*, ed. Rosenheim and Rach-
man, 210–36. On Poe's relationship with the Young America movement, see Meredith
McGill, "Poe, Literary Nationalism, and Authorial Identity," in *The American Face*, ed.
Rosenheim and Rachman, 271–304. For Poe and slavery, see Whalen, *Edgar Allan Poe
and the Masses*, 111–46. Here and elsewhere, I rely for biographical information on Ken-
neth Silverman, *Edgar A. Poe: Mournful and Never-Ending Remembrance* (New York:
HarperCollins, 1991).

There has been some study of racial ideology in Poe's poetry and poetic theory, although Poe's prose represents his most sustained engagement of slavery and race.[4] *The Narrative of Arthur Gordon Pym* (1838) and subsequent stories receive much notice, but the focus on Poe's middle and later writings obscures a formative tale. Poe's first published story, "Metzengerstein," describes the horrifying death of a Baron who becomes obsessed with a mystical horse that materializes out of a tapestry. The tale does not seem particularly political, nor are its interests overtly American. In his preface to *Tales of the Grotesque and Arabesque* (1840), Poe probably had "Metzengerstein" in mind when he wrote that only one story in the collection favors that "species of pseudo-horror which we are taught to call Germanic." Here Poe associates "Metzengerstein" with E. T. A. Hoffmann's *phantasystück* tradition, a comparison scholars tend to accept if only to watch Poe burlesque such supernaturalism.[5] Yet by this token, Poe's slippery preface itself may be ironic, for despite "Metzengerstein"'s Hungarian setting and tongue-tying Teutonic names, its fantastical terror is not solely Germanic but also intensely American. Published five months after Nat Turner's revolt, "Metzengerstein" stands as Poe's first serious treatment of slavery and race, offered in the form of a cautious—and cautionary—political commentary.[6]

In the story, the families of Berlifitzing and Metzengerstein represent two "contiguous" and "mutually embittered" estates that had "long exercised a rival influence in the affairs of a busy government" (p. 33). This tense situation is analogous to political conditions in the United States as conflict between the North and South spiked in 1831, when

[4]See John Carlos Rowe, *At Emerson's Tomb: The Politics of Classic American Literature* (New York: Columbia Univ. Press, 1997), 42–62; and Betsy Erkkila, "The Poetics of Whiteness: Poe and the Racial Imaginary," in *Romancing the Shadow*, ed. Kennedy and Weissberg, 41–74.

[5]See Edward H. Davidson, *Poe: A Critical Study* (Cambridge: Harvard Univ. Press, 1957), 138; and G. R. Thompson, *Poe's Fiction: Romantic Irony in the Gothic Tales* (Madison: Univ. of Wisconsin Press, 1973), 39–44.

[6]Because "Metzengerstein" came soon after Turner's revolt, specific dates matter. Turner's uprising began 23 August 1831, with coverage in the popular press appearing quickly thereafter. Poe had been writing short fiction in Baltimore from as early as April 1831. On May 28, the *Saturday Courier* of Philadelphia announced the short-story contest for which Poe would submit "Metzengerstein," though details for the contest were not provided until July 9. We do not know when Poe submitted "Metzengerstein," but the deadline for the contest was December 1 and Poe had a history of procrastination. It is thus possible, and in my mind quite likely, that Poe did not finish his "Metzengerstein" manuscript until after he heard of Turner's revolt through various available sources (see Dwight Thomas and David Jackson, eds., *The Poe Log: A Documentary Life of Edgar Allan Poe, 1809–1849* [Boston: G. K. Hall, 1987], 120–24).

South Carolina threatened to nullify Andrew Jackson's tariff on the dangerous grounds that states' rights superseded federal authority. Commentators of the time recognized that the nullification crisis bore heavily on the slavery conflict, which was entering a new and more militant phase.[7] In 1831, David Walker's "Appeal" (1829) and William Lloyd Garrison's *Liberator* outraged the South. That same year, John Calhoun renounced his ambitions for national office, pursuing instead a sectional course increasingly marked by secessionist rhetoric and aggressive defenses of slavery. Most dramatically, Nat Turner's revolt stoked the slavery controversy, unifying proslavery forces and engendering harsher slave codes even while convincing many observers that slavery needed to end. In 1831, chattel bondage was seen as a threat to the Union by Americans in both the North and South, including the twenty-two-year-old Poe, who that year crossed the Mason-Dixon line twice before settling near Frederick Douglass in Baltimore to begin a career in prose.[8]

Poe's first production was "Metzengerstein," a story that speaks to American sectionalism by exploiting regional stereotypes. In the antebellum era, hunting and horsemanship were standard features of the Southern cavalier, and by 1831, the South was depicted as a passionate, feudal, failing place.[9] The Berlifitzing house is headed by a count who possesses "so passionate a love of horses, and of hunting, that neither bodily infirmity, great age, nor mental incapacity, prevented his daily participation." In stories such as "The Man That Was Used Up" (1839), "The Fall of the House of Usher" (1839), and "The Gold-Bug" (1843), Poe shows both fealty and resentment toward a South (and an adopted father) that was for him an occasional home in which he never felt fully welcome.[10] "Metzengerstein" expresses these turbulent feelings in the "loftily descended" but "infirm" Count Berlifitzing, whose "honorable" but "weaker" estate falls to its neighboring rival.

This rival, the Metzengerstein house, is headed by the young Baron Frederick who, among other immoral acts, purportedly sets fire to the Berlifitzing stables. Poe could be indulging a fantasy of vengeance against his adopted father, John Allan, and authority in general, but it is

---

[7] See Richard E. Ellis, *The Union at Risk: Jacksonian Democracy, States' Rights, and the Nullification Crisis* (New York: Oxford Univ. Press, 1987), 187–94.

[8] For the geographical proximity of Douglass and Poe, see J. Gerald Kennedy, "'Trust No Man': Poe, Douglass, and the Culture of Slavery," in *Romancing the Shadow*, ed. Kennedy and Weissberg, 225–57.

[9] See William Taylor, *Cavalier and Yankee: The Old South and American National Character* (New York: George Braziller, 1961), 51–55.

[10] See Silverman, *Edgar A. Poe*, 26–68; and Leverenz, "Poe and Gentry Virginia," 210–36.

also at this point that race and slavery irrupt into the tale. As the Baron listens to the crackling stables, he fixates on an ancient tapestry featuring an "unnaturally colored horse" that once belonged to a "Saracen ances- tor" of the neighboring Count. Against the backdrop of a Metzenger- stein stabbing a fallen Berlifitzing, the horse's eyes glare with a "human expression" and its teeth show through "distended lips" (p. 36). Spir- itualist gambits and horrifying teeth are, of course, favorite Poe tropes, but the racial connotations of the "Horse-Shade" increase when it takes physical form, seemingly emerging from the tapestry under the Baron's monomaniacal gaze.[11] The origins of the beast are unclear, except that it is branded with Berlifitzing's initials, indicating to one servant that the animal belonged to the "old Count's stud of foreign horses" (p. 36). The antebellum era linked horses and slaves as branded, bred, and brut- ish chattel—a fact decried on the masthead of the *Liberator*, which conflated slave and horse auctions—though this linkage stretched back in Southern thought from Thomas Jefferson to William Byrd, who warned as early as 1736 that African slaves require "tort rein, or they will be apt to throw their rider."[12] If, as "Metzengerstein" suggests, the horse represents a slave, then the Baron plays an abolitionist role, for just as Turner's Southampton revolt was blamed on "incendiary" abo- litionists, the Baron is an "incendiary" villain implicated in the disas- trous end of his neighbor's chattel institution.[13]

Poe's basic position is anti-abolitionist. Count Berlifitzing, decrepit though he is, dies attempting to rescue his horses. Like the loving mas- ters of plantation fiction, he is too fond of his chattel. The tale also broaches what was for many the most troubling prospect of abolition: slavery may be undesirable, but what happens with masterless slaves? This question arises time and again in the American slavery debate, particularly after Turner's revolt when the fear of free blacks made colo- nization a popular (albeit unworkable) scheme and states passed laws more severely restricting the rights of free persons of color. In 1832, Thomas Dew, an architect of proslavery thought, saw "[e]mancipation without deportation" as the single greatest danger to the South. Dew

---

[11]"Horse-shade" was a variant title Poe considered for the tale.

[12]William Byrd II to John Perceval, 12 July 1736, *The Correspondence of the Three William Byrds of Westover, Virginia, 1684–1776*, ed. Marion Tinling, 2 vols. (Charlottes- ville: Univ. of Virginia Press, 1977), 2:488. I am grateful to Albert Devlin for pointing out Byrd's letter. See also Thomas Jefferson, *Notes on the State of Virginia* (1785; reprint, New York: Harper, 1964), 133.

[13]"Incendiary Publications," *National Intelligencer*, 15 September 1831; reprinted in Eric Foner, ed., *Nat Turner* (Englewood Cliffs, N.J.: Prentice–Hall, 1971), 87–89.

could only imagine black-white relations in which "[o]ne must rule the other"; and he predicted that any "commingling of races" would inevitably bring about "barbarism."

Like Dew, "Metzengerstein" worries over the control and ownership of chattel. When the Baron first meets the mysterious steed, he immediately asks, "Whose horse?" to which a servant replies, "He is your own property. . . . at least he is claimed by no other owner" (p. 36). Despite the "suspicious and untractable character" attributed to the brute, the Baron then muses: "[P]erhaps a rider like Frederick of Metzengerstein, may tame even the devil from the stables of Berlifitzing" (p. 36). This line echoes a frequent complaint about abolitionists: Northern reformers foolishly think that they can handle intractable slaves, an optimism born of perfectionist ignorance, which leads to Metzengerstein's death. Obsessed with the horse to the scandalous point that he "disdained the company of his equals," Metzengerstein allows his "perverse attachment" to grow into a "hideous and unnatural fervor" exacerbated by the horse's "peculiar intelligence" and "human-looking eye" (pp. 38, 39). In 1853 William Gilmore Simms wrote: "The moral of the steed is in the spur of his rider; of the slave, in the eye of his master."[14] Such is not, however, the case in "Metzengerstein" when the Baron is mastered by his semihuman chattel and borne into his own burning palace. As the "ungovernable fire" dies to a "white flame," Poe ends "Metzengerstein": "[A] cloud of smoke settled heavily over the battlements in the distinct colossal figure of—a horse" (p. 40).

Responsibility for this terrible end falls on Baron Metzengerstein as Poe takes up what was becoming a national anti-abolitionist stand.[15] The Baron relishes the destruction of his neighbor and then slyly possesses his chattel, implying—as did some proslavery radicals—that the North practiced its own form of bondage and coveted the labor of free blacks. Deadly to himself and his rivals alike, Metzengerstein prefers the company of a brute, a fact that Poe describes in sexualized language, thus voicing an anti-abolitionist jibe he repeats in subsequent works.[16]

[14]William Gilmore Simms, *Egeria: Or, Voices of Thought and Counsel for the Woods and Wayside* (Philadelphia: E. H. Butler, 1853), 15.

[15]See Larry Tise, *Pro-Slavery: A History of the Defense of Slavery in America, 1701–1840* (Athens: Univ. of Georgia Press, 1987).

[16]See, for instance, "How to Write a Blackwood Article" (pp. 61–70) and Poe's 1845 review of Longfellow in *Edgar Allan Poe: Essays and Reviews* (New York: Library of America, 1984), 762; further references to *Essays and Reviews* will be cited parenthetically as *ER*. It should also be noted that these insults accuse white female abolitionists of sexual desire for black male slaves. In "Metzengerstein," the horse is male, recalling Eric Lott's claim that antebellum racist anxiety is marked by the conflicted attraction and repulsion

Of most importance, the Baron tragically discounts the savagery of the chattel he frees. Just as accounts of the Southampton revolt dwelled on Turner's "spirit of prophecy," Poe's story begins with an "ancient prophecy" predicting the fall of both houses (p. 33).[17] Like an abolitionist fanatic, however, the Baron ignores all warnings. He fails to tame the devilish brute that survives the fire of Berlifitzing's stables, bringing to pass the darkest fears of anti-abolitionists—that the emancipation of African slaves would destroy both North and South, that blacks would come to rule over whites, and that the United States would go up in flames in the shadow of slaves without masters.

Such is one political subtext of "Metzengerstein" that may not come as a total surprise. The fear of incendiary slave revolt looms over much of antebellum literature, and slave rebellion potentially lurks in a number of Poe texts—from vague indications in "Silence—A Fable" (1835), "The Fall of the House of Usher," and "The Black Cat" (1843) to *Pym*, "The Murders in the Rue Morgue" (1841), "The System of Doctor Tarr and Professor Fether" (1844), and "Hop-Frog" (1849).[18] Like these later works, "Metzengerstein" takes a racist, anti-abolitionist stand at least insofar as Poe dwells on black savagery and the dangers of masterless chattel. Reflecting the anxieties of post-Turner America, "Metzengerstein" fits a familiar Poe profile, even as the story remains distinctive in at least two critical ways. First, "Metzengerstein" shows

---

of white men for black male bodies (*Love and Theft: Blackface Minstrelsy and the American Working Class* [New York: Oxford Univ. Press, 1993], 53–55, 120–22, 161–68).

[17] See *Constitutional Whig*, 29 August 1831; reprinted in Henry Irving Tragle, ed., *The Southampton Slave Revolt of 1831: A Compilation of Source Material* (Amherst: Univ. of Massachusetts Press, 1971), 53.

[18] On the fear of slave revolts in antebellum literature, see Eric Sundquist, *To Wake the Nations: Race in the Making of American Literature* (Cambridge: Belknap Press of Harvard Univ. Press, 1993), 27–221. On this fear in Poe's "Silence—A Fable," see Joan Dayan, "Amorous Bondage: Poe, Ladies, and Slaves" (pp. 346–75); in "The Fall of the House of Usher," see David Leverenz, "Spanking the Master: Mind–Body Crossings in Poe's Sensationalism," in *A Historical Guide to Edgar Allan Poe*, ed. Kennedy, 112–14; in "The Black Cat," see Lesley Ginsberg, "Slavery and the Gothic Horror of Poe's 'The Black Cat'" (pp. 376–93); in *Pym*, see Toni Morrison, *Playing in the Dark: Whiteness and the Literary Imagination* (New York: Vintage, 1992), 31–59; Rowe, *At Emerson's Tomb*, 42–62; and Dana Nelson, *The Word in Black and White: Reading "Race" in American Literature, 1638–1867* (New York: Oxford Univ. Press, 1993), 90–108; in "The Murders in the Rue Morgue," see Elise Lemire, "'The Murders in the Rue Morgue': Amalgamation Discourses and the Race Riots of 1838 in Poe's Philadelphia," in *Romancing the Shadow*, ed. Kennedy and Weissberg, 177–204; in "The System of Doctor Tarr and Professor Fether," see Louis Rubin, *The Edge of the Swamp: A Study of the Literature and Society of the Old South* (Baton Rouge: Louisiana State Univ. Press, 1989), 162–67; and in "Hop-Frog," see Leland S. Person, "Poe's Philosophy of Amalgamation: Reading Racism in the Tales," in *Romancing the Shadow*, ed. Kennedy and Weissberg, 218–20.

that Poe's fiction addresses slavery from the beginning. Poe did not discover the national sin as a literary topic during the writing of *Pym*, nor is his early political commentary limited to lesser satirical pieces such as "Four Beasts in One" (1833). Blackness and bondage are for Poe more than abstracted symbol of evil, as he treats the presence of Africans in America as a national problem.

"Metzengerstein" is also distinctive in that its political argument seems remarkably coherent and specific compared to Poe's later narratives. Racial horrors and slavery tropes run amok in many Poe texts, often collapsing allegorical structure into ideological chaos. "Metzengerstein" reaches its own frantic end, but its political logic is sustained, revealing subtle but recognizable patterns of anti-abolitionism and registering not only racial terror but also a position on civic events. This politicized reading need not entirely conflict with Whalen's account of Poe's career. Even if a savvier, market-driven Poe shied away from the slavery controversy, the partisan and provincial "Metzengerstein" comes at the outset of Poe's professional life — before he knew the publishing world and before he formulated ambitious plans for a national literary magazine.[19] There is no indication that "Metzengerstein" was criticized for its politics, yet Poe's subsequent fiction is more circumspect in that it lacks as discernible an opinion on the slavery conflict. For Whalen, such obscurity is governed by the strictures of political economy. But "Metzengerstein" suggests that Poe is not a passive conduit for racist ideology, nor is his racism, average or otherwise, so easily separated from the question of slavery. There remains another explanation for Poe's tortured treatment of blackness and bondage: Poe struggles to assimilate his politics and metaphysics, an antinomy evident in "Metzengerstein," if only in nascent form.

*   *   *

To read "Metzengerstein" in light of the slavery crisis is not to say that the story is philosophically flat. Joan Dayan has written on both Poe's metaphysics and his politics, and although these lines of inquiry do not often cross, Dayan links Poe's writing on color and servitude to "the mysteries of identity" and "the riddle of body and mind."[20] Can

---

[19] In *Poe and the Masses*, Whalen argues that Poe's writings were governed by political economy before Poe entered the publishing industry. This may be so, although such claims seem stronger to me when applied to Poe's later career.

[20] Joan Dayan, "Poe, Persons, and Property," in *Romancing the Shadow*, ed. Kennedy and Weissberg, 121.

one ever know one's self? Is the self a stable entity? To what extent does the subject's mind constitute objective reality? Such questions are manifest in Poe's discussions of American race and slavery, just as race and slavery help generate his explorations of subjectivity. This dialectical relationship, so fundamental to American romanticism before the Civil War, points Poe toward a synthesis in which subject and object, white and black, master and slave become one. "Metzengerstein"'s metaphysics of race broach this troubling prospect as the story exposes the political threat of a horrible absolutism. Here again the tale's ambiguous steed plays a central role, for among its many manifestations, the horse can be a creature of transcendental idealism representing a dangerous blackness hiding in the white mind.

Famously, Kant posits a subjectivity that constitutes objective reality in that the structures of the mind organize, reveal, and—in this sense—make up the phenomenological order. This seems the case when Baron Metzengerstein, "buried in meditation," fixates on the tapestry horse, seemingly bringing it into the natural world. . . . Simply considered, this summoning scene can enact a general transcendentalist claim: reality is not passively perceived by the subject but actively constructed by it. As we shall see, Poe's theory of race relies on this Kantian conviction, particularly as extended by Schelling and disseminated by Coleridge, who together propound two ideas that are of special importance to Poe: absolute identity, a reality concept that synthesizes subject and object, and unconscious production, the means by which subjects unknowingly create the phenomenological world.

*　*　*

It makes sense that Schelling, more than any other German philosopher, had an early influence on Poe.[21] "Loss of Breath" (1832) and "How to Write a Blackwood Article" (1838) refer to Schelling by name. Poe's resistance to dualistic order in "Metzengerstein" and beyond dramatizes what in "Morella" (1835) is called "*Identity* as urged by Schelling" (*PT* 235)—that is, identity not only as self but also as an absolute truth that Schelling's *System of Transcendental Idealism* (1800) formulates as "the coincidence of an objective with a subjective."[22]

---

[21] For Poe's references to Schelling and the availability of Schelling in English, see Hansen and Pollin, *The German Face of Edgar Allan Poe*, 80.

[22] F. W. J. Schelling, *System of Transcendental Idealism*, trans. Peter Heath (1800; reprint, Charlottesville: Univ. of Virginia Press, 1978), 5.

Poe probably learned such absolutism from Coleridge. As early as 1831, Poe knew *Biographia Literaria* (1817), a book that praises Schelling's massive influence and pays homage to the point of plagiarism. Citing Schelling, Coleridge discusses absolute identity: "All knowledge rests on the coincidence of an object with a subject. . . . During the act of knowledge itself, the objective and subjective are so instantly united, that we cannot determine to which of the two the priority belongs."[23] This is an abiding dilemma for Poe and precisely the challenge of Metzengerstein's steed. Because the horse is both a phenomenon produced by the mind of Frederick Metzengerstein and a brutish, material beast from the stables of Wilhelm Berlifitzing, subjectivity and objectivity are joined in an inseparable union that can represent the absolute identity of Friedrich Wilhelm Schelling.

But whereas Schelling and Coleridge see such synthesis as harmonious, beautiful, and true, for Poe the union of subject and object is a horse of a different color:

[T]he Baron's perverse attachment to his lately-acquired charger—an attachment which seemed to attain new strength from every fresh example of the animal's ferocious and demon-like propensities—at length became, in the eyes of all reasonable men, a hideous and unnatural fervor. In the glare of noon—at the dead hour of night—in sickness or in health—in calm or in tempest—the young Metzengerstein seemed riveted to the saddle of that colossal horse, whose intractable audacities so well accorded with his own spirit. (p. 38)

Poe cannot celebrate a transcendentalism that synthesizes black and white. Just as the narrator of "William Wilson" (1839) murders himself and the twin whose "absolute identity" nearly "enslaved" him (p. 120, 119), "Metzengerstein" recoils from a master-slave pairing by killing both subject and object. Eschewing the ecstatic, lyrical flights that characterize synthesis in Schelling and Coleridge, Poe renders the union of subject and object in an idiom of racial horror as absolute identity becomes an analog for amalgamation and slave revolt.

Even worse, Poe hints that this hideous synthesis originates in Metzengerstein's unwitting mind, a possibility also theorized by transcendentalist thought. The concept of unconscious production was first

---

[23]Samuel Taylor Coleridge, *Biographia Literaria; or, Biographical Sketches of My Literary Life and Opinions,* in *The Collected Works of Samuel Taylor Coleridge, Vol. 7,* ed. James Engell and W. Jackson Bate, 16 vols. (Princeton, N.J.: Princeton Univ. Press, 1983), (I):252, (I):255.

explored by Fichte, for whom the subjective production of phenomena precedes the subject's knowledge of it. This explains why radical subjectivity is so counterintuitive to the uninitiated. Because our minds do not know that they spontaneously make up reality, only guided philosophical reflection can discover the truth-making process. Absolute identity is thus revealed when unconscious production becomes conscious, when subjectivity finally recognizes that it is indistinguishable from objectivity, a realization that effectively abolishes subject-object dualism.[24]

For Schelling and Coleridge, art is the means for discovering this absolutism. . . . For Poe, however, the unconscious-made-conscious-through-art is finally horrific, not so much because the Kantian and Burkean sublimes can be implicated in race but because a deadly blackness emerges from the unsuspecting white mind.[25] When Metzengerstein first glances at the tapestry horse, he does so "without his consciousness," and he cannot quell the "overwhelming anxiety" that makes it "impossible" to avert his gaze as he "mechanically" stares at the object of art that becomes the "uncontrollable" horse-shade (pp. 35, 40). Here the monomaniacal subject unconsciously produces the object of its demise, creating a self-generated, self-annihilating nightmare that culminates in the Baron's last ride. Schelling calls the unconscious-made-conscious "the holy of holies" that "burns in eternal and original unity, as if in a single flame."[26] "Metzengerstein" ends with the unholy union of white master and black slave, a pairing that perishes in an inferno of unnameable absolutism. "Metzengerstein" can play upon the horror of slave revolt, but absolute identity and unconscious production turn the screw once more. Distinctions of color and servitude become metaphysically untenable when an irrepressible, bestial blackness lives in the white subject, ready to spring into hideous synthesis through an uncontrollable and distinctly transcendental coming-to-consciousness.

* * *

[24]My sense of unconscious production has been aided by Roger Hausheer, "Fichte and Schelling," in *German Philosophy since Kant*, ed. Anthony O'Hear (New York: Cambridge Univ. Press, 1999), 1–24; Andrew Bowie, *Schelling and Modern European Philosophy: An Introduction* (New York: Routledge, 1993), 45–54; and Paul Redding, *The Logic of Affect* (Ithaca, N.Y.: Cornell Univ. Press, 1999), 123–26.

[25]See Laura Doyle, "The Racial Sublime," in *Romanticism, Race, and Imperial Culture, 1780–1834*, ed. Alan Richardson and Sonia Hofkosh (Bloomington: Indiana Univ. Press, 1996), 15–39. See also Erkkila, "Poetics of Whiteness," 65–67.

[26]Schelling, *System of Transcendental Idealism*, 231.

A similar dynamic is at work in "Ligeia." Ligeia is a maven of "transcendentalism" and also a figure of amalgamation, whose physical features conjure images of Africa and Arabia (pp. 49–50). Like Metzengerstein's steed, Ligeia can symbolize the possibilities of absolute identity insofar as she is both a material other and a product of the narrator's mind. Synthesizing subjectivity and objectivity under the narrator's transcendentally influenced eye, Ligeia's struggle to return from the dead models a process of unconscious production when her resurrection as dark phenomenon is dialectically enacted in the natural world and in the narrator's irrepressibly associative mind. In the end, his white subjectivity is subsumed by the gaze of Ligeia, whose "black" eyes are "far larger than the ordinary eyes of [his] own race" (p. 49). Is Ligeia an embodied black figure or the figment of a racist unconscious? The transcendentalism of Schelling and Coleridge suggests that the answer is *yes*.[27]

Even an aggressively satirical piece like "How to Write a Blackwood Article" does not eschew race when trying to "[s]ay something about objectivity and subjectivity" (p. 65). The story's narrator, Psyche Zenobia, is told to adopt "the tone transcendental" and shun "the tone heterogeneous," and to praise the harmony of "Supernal Oneness" while avoiding "Infernal Twoness" (p. 66). Poe associates such absolutism with both "Coleridge" and a "pet baboon" (p. 64), and he further conflates transcendentalism and race mixing in Zenobia's tale, "A Predicament." Not only is the bluestocking Zenobia a reformer in the Frogpondian mode but Poe links her philosophy to amalgamation when her grotesque black servant crashes into her breasts. Poe responds to this bawdy union by decapitating Zenobia, which she describes in sensational detail as she wonders whether her head or body represents her "proper identity" (p. 77). Faced with an absolute identity entailing the threat of racial unity, Poe retreats to an epistemology in which the division of subject and object is explicitly, violently demarcated. "How to Write a Blackwood Article" is clearly a burlesque, yet Poe's caricature of transcendental writing aptly describes some of his best work. Under the influence of Schelling and Coleridge, Poe desires the supernal truth and beauty of absolute oneness. At the same time, he does not let go of

[27]Dayan discusses race and "Ligeia" in "Amorous Bondage," p. 346.

dualistic formulations of slavery and race, making transcendence a philosophically attractive but politically threatening prospect.[28]

Teresa Goddu has shown how Cold War critics took the blackness
of classic antebellum texts not as an indication of race but as a metaphysical cipher.[29] The pendulum has swung in the opposite direction as
race and slavery now seem everywhere in Poe, though the politics and
philosophy of blackness seem to me inextricably tied. In the case of Poe,
dark romanticism is appropriately named. Hawthorne, Melville, and
Dickinson know how to pit Calvin against Concord. For Poe, race and
slavery remain fearsome facts that resist any blithe absolutism. This is
not to say that transcendental idealism cannot accommodate racism.
Kant maintained a racist taxonomy, as did Coleridge and Emerson, and
romanticism—European and American—can be profoundly implicated in racialist thought.[30] This did not prevent almost all transcendentalists from supporting abolitionism, from thus becoming both part of
the racism problem and part of the emancipation solution. In Poe, however, the power of blackness is too threatening a concern. Poe retains a
racist anti-abolitionism that mars his potentially transcendental plots,
pushing his idealism toward a hideous synthesis in which absolute identity and unconscious production undermine the mastery of white subjectivity, an embattled political and philosophical formation after Nat
Turner.

*   *   *

Poe reportedly once leapt twenty feet in the running broad jump.
To move from "Metzengerstein" to the end of Poe's career may require
a similar stunt. The preceding discussion schematically offers some
sense of the long middle ground. Poe's formal technique matures; his
aspirations for a national magazine swell; in 1845 the Longfellow War
and Poe's disastrous reading at the Boston Lyceum bring a more per-

---

[28]For a compatible reading of "How to Write a Blackwood Article," see Leverenz,
"Spanking the Master," 116–17.

[29]See Teresa Goddu, *Gothic America: Narrative, History, and Nation* (New York:
Columbia Univ. Press, 1997), 7–8.

[30]For more on Kant's racist taxonomy, see Charles W. Mills, *The Racial Contract*
(Ithaca, N.Y.: Cornell Univ. Press, 1997), 69–72; on Coleridge and racism, see Thomas,
Romanticism and Slavery Narratives, 89–104; and on Emerson and racism, see Anita
Haya Patterson, *From Emerson to King: Democracy, Race, and the Politics of Protest* (New
York: Oxford Univ. Press, 1997), 129–38. Recent transatlantic studies of romanticism
and race include Thomas, *Romanticism and Slavery Narratives*; and Debbie Lee, *Slavery
and the Romantic Imagination* (Philadelphia: Univ. of Pennsylvania Press, 2002).

sonal, polemical hostility to his views of New England reform. The vagaries of Poe's career make for a tragic and fascinating story. Yet it is hard to index his fictions according to the shifting fortunes of his life, in part because he tends to revisit earlier topics and narrative strategies, prompting some scholars to organize his texts thematically, not chronologically. This makes sense in the matter of slavery and race, for Poe's literary treatment is in many ways consistent. Although the political subtext of "Metzengerstein" appears to me exceptionally cogent, absolute identity and unconscious production when combined with color and servitude continue to cause ungovernable horror, not only in "Ligeia," *Pym*, and "How to Write a Blackwood Article" but also in such texts as "The Fall of the House of Usher," "The Murders in the Rue Morgue," "The Black Cat," "The System of Doctor Tarr and Professor Fether," "The Raven" (1845), and "Hop-Frog." These works need not be explicitly about the American slavery crisis to show unconscious white subjectivities rising toward a terrible, self-generated blackness. Race and transcendental philosophy are frequently entangled in Poe's imagination, though a singular departure may be *Eureka*, his challenging, seldom-loved "Prose Poem" whose rhapsodic cosmology potentially invokes an absolutism free from the anxiety of race (*PT* 1257). . . .

What remains unclear is why Poe continues to tangle metaphysics and politics. Why do his writings so stubbornly dwell on so disruptive an antinomy?

In 1923, D. H. Lawrence hinted at a powerful explanation: "Moralists have always wondered helplessly why Poe's 'morbid' tales need have been written. They need to be written because old things need to die and disintegrate, because the old white psyche has to be gradually broken down before anything else can come to pass." Lawrence recognized that "Poor Poe" subverts white subjectivity, and although he sometimes described Poe as performing this work "consciously," he also attributed this impulse to a primitive, irresistible, and almost pathological "need."[31] Harry Levin and Leslie Fielder saw this need as an unconscious "racial phobia," a view that continues to predominate Poe scholarship in more sophisticated forms.[32] John Carlos Rowe, Dana Nelson, David Leverenz, and J. Gerald Kennedy are among those critics

---

[31]D. H. Lawrence, *Studies in Classic American Literature* (New York: Viking, 1923), 65, 71.

[32]Harry Levin, *The Power of Blackness: Hawthorne, Poe, Melville* (New York: Knopf, 1958), 121. See also Leslie Fiedler, *Love and Death in the American Novel* (1960; reprint, New York: Anchor, 1992), 391–400.

who see Poe as both in and out of control insofar as the vision of his "semiconscious" texts remains obscured by his racism. Even Whalen, who ascribes to Poe a larger amount of intention, does not consistently theorize Poe's conscious relation to political conditions. Whether the method is Marxist or psychoanalytic, whether the agency is ideology or id, for scholars who entertain questions of intention, Poe's literary treatment of slavery and race seems to operate beyond his authorial will.[33]

There is always space for the unconscious, politically or psychoanalytically understood. There is surely some truth to the picture of Poe as a man at the mercy of some hidden perversity. Henry James, no stranger to the dramatic potential of coming to consciousness, associated the vulgar pleasures of Poe with a "primitive stage of reflection."[34] Perhaps we like Poe best this way. Bodies under the floorboards, beasts in the jungle, madwomen in the attic—it is gripping to watch a subject in the throes of the unconscious, especially when the unconscious threatens to stun us by degrees. And Poe knows. For him, as for Schelling and Coleridge, the dialectical process of coming to consciousness is a necessary element of art premised on an aesthetic theory based in transcendental subjectivity.

In 1842, a British critic in the *American Eclectic* wrote of German romantics: "They consider, that as Art is a production, a creation of the mind of man, the real way to set about its examination must be the investigation of those laws of the mind from whence it proceeds. . . . Thus it becomes itself a branch of psychology. . . . *They* [the Germans] examine the producing mind; *we* the work produced."[35] Poe's aesthetics often focus on the form of the object of art, a tendency that can align him with high modernists and New Critics. However, as much as any antebellum thinker, Poe follows the Germans in taking an interest in the subjectivity of the artist. As Poe suggests when calling *Biographia Literaria* "an important service to the cause of psychological science,"

---

[33]See John Carlos Rowe, "Edgar Allan Poe's Imperial Fantasy and the American Frontier," in *Romancing the Shadow*, ed. Kennedy and Weissberg, 75–105; Nelson, *The Word in Black and White*, 90–108; Leverenz, "Spanking the Master"; and Kennedy, "'Trust No Man,'" 253. Meredith McGill points out inconsistencies in Whalen's treatment of Poe's "authorial agency" in "Reading Poe, Reading Capitalism," *American Quarterly* 53 (March 2001): 145.

[34]Henry James, *French Poets and Novelists* (1878; reprint, New York: Macmillan, 1893), 60.

[35]"Hegel's Aesthetics: The Philosophy of Art, Particularly in Its Application to Poetry," *American Eclectic: or, Selections from the Periodical Literature of All Foreign Countries* 4 (July 1842): 71.

his aesthetics are closely related to his sense of the operations of the mind (*ER* 188).

Part of Poe's fame as a cryptologist and critic came in 1842 when his review of Dickens's *Barnaby Rudge* correctly predicted some features of the ending before the novel was entirely serialized. In playing prognosticator, Poe also pronounced on the unconscious production of literature: "This is clearly the design of Mr. Dickens—although he himself may not at present perceive it. In fact, beautiful as it is, and strikingly original with him, it cannot be questioned that he has been led to it less by artistical knowledge and reflection, than by that intuitive feeling for the forcible and the true" (*ER* 222–23). Here Poe's theory of artistic production relies not on conscious "knowledge" or "reflection" but on an "intuitive" mental faculty of which the author remains unaware. Such claims undermine the omnipotent intention Poe ascribes to the poet in "The Philosophy of Composition" (1846), a work that seems especially specious in light of other Poe texts. In "MS. Found in a Bottle" (1833), the narrator "unwittingly" paints "DISCOVERY" on a sail, suggesting in both production and product that writing uncovers the unconscious (*PT* 195). And in an 1836 review, as well as in later critical pieces, Poe further celebrates artistic effects that "arise independently of the author's will" (*ER* 263).[36]

Thus, unconscious production is a consciously theorized aspect of Poe's thought—both in his metaphysics of race and in his thinking on art. This does not, of course, exclude psychoanalytic or ideological readings of Poe, but it does suggest that Poe can be a remarkably canny subject whose texts are acutely self-aware of the play between the known and unknown mind. Considering the political position presented in "Metzengerstein," and considering Poe's continued attention to the unconscious production of beauty and blackness, texts that may seem haunted by Poe's lurking racial phobias can be taken as complex dramatizations of a psychology of mastery and racism, dramatizations driven by Poe's abiding refusal to integrate the differences of racial others into an absolute oneness. In this way, Poe rises from the couch and moves toward the analyst's chair. The story of many of his stories—and a narrative in the history of Poe criticism—is the gradual coming to consciousness of chattel bondage and race.

The problem is that such self-consciousness fails to raise Poe's moral conscience. How can an author so committed to the issue of race and

---

[36]See also Poe's 1836 review of Daniel Defoe (*ER* 202); and his 5 April 1845 installment in the Longfellow War (*ER*, 759).

subjectivity deny the subjectivity of racial others who become, for Poe, literal images of blackness in the white mind? Clearly, theoretical sophistication need not lead to convincing truth-claims or humanist convictions. Clearly, Poe can be placed within a tradition of transcendental racism, even if there is no necessary equivalence between romanticism and egregious racial views. One might also read Poe's philosophy of race as a kind of sublimation or ideological formation, thus reinscribing Poe's psychological system within an unconscious plot. Such claims might invoke some version of the intentional fallacy, although there are more specific, more historical grounds for retaining what Nelson calls "psychopolitical imperatives" as an explanatory factor in the structure and practice of antebellum racism.[37]

Addressing the fear of slave revolt in the post-Turner South, Alexis de Tocqueville wrote that the white man "hides it from himself."[38] Douglass, Melville, and Jacobs all notice this white repression of blackness, but the fact that these writers ascribe a "deep" psychology to the slavery crisis suggests that Poe himself had access to similar conclusions. There is always space for consciousness when the evidence interpreted by the analyst is available to the subject of analysis, even if the subject's sense of psychology is not phrased in the same modern idiom. One way to determine authorial intention is to look for patterns of reflection and recognition that indicate an extended look into the recesses of the mind. If my reading of Poe is right, Poe knows that race operates unconsciously. The difference between Poe and his savvy contemporaries is that he does not follow this insight toward a more progressive politics. A reason for this is that Poe's thinking is so aggressively phenomenological that for him to conclude that the horror of blackness is "only" a mental construction may not serve to subvert that construction as such but, rather, to establish it as the most convincing account of a reality maintained only through fierce denials of intersubjectivity that mark the limits of Poe's truth-claims, psychology, ethics, and art. In the end, the unconscious in Poe combines two implications of the word: the modern sense of the unrecognized mind and the etymological meaning that signals the negation ("un") of shared ("con") knowledge ("science").[39]

[37] Nelson, *National Manhood*, 206.

[38] Alexis de Tocqueville, *Democracy in America*, ed. J. P. Mayer and Max Lerner (1835; reprint, New York: Harper and Row, 1966), 329.

[39] For the connotations of *conscience*, see Jean Hagstrum, *Eros and Vision: The Restoration to Romanticism* (Evanston, Ill.: Northwestern Univ. Press, 1989), 3–28.

* * *

In 1800, Coleridge first used "unconscious" to indicate what the self does not know of itself. In 1822, he coined "subjectivity" to signify the consciousness of one's mind engaged in the act of perception. Coleridge did not invent these concepts, but he brought them to the United States with the help of other romantics who impressed, among others, Poe. In 1831, Carlyle proclaimed: "Unconsciousness is the sign of creation." In 1832, De Quincey coined the related term "subconscious."[40] In that same year, Poe published "Metzengerstein," commencing a prose career that would use romantic theories of the mind to explore the metaphysics of race and art. Poe's thinking is not exactly systematic, coherent, or analytically rigorous. Yet as Stanley Cavell has argued, Poe is perversely attuned to the skeptical potential of romantic philosophy, showing us "the recoil of a demonic reason, irrationally thinking to dominate earth. . . . not to reject the world but rather to establish it."[41] More specifically, Poe's creativity lies in the application of romantic idealism to antebellum culture, particularly the issue of slavery and race that was tearing the United States apart.

The slavery crisis thus helps to explain Poe's anomalous standing in antebellum literature. On the margins of Southern gentility, his racial views are too radically vexed for pastoral plantation fiction. Fearing transcendence, he could not join in the perfectionist projects of Concord. Such skepticism can leave Poe in the familiar company of Hawthorne and Melville, though an important difference is that Poe is a more insistent idealist, returning repeatedly to the troubling prospects of transcendental unity, particularly in *Eureka*'s vigorous, if ultimately tenuous, synthesis. When Hawthorne and Melville harass transcendentalism, they are overly conscious of Concord, and as a result, they tend toward satiric, reactive, and derivative critique. Emerson and his circle would pay some heed to the unconscious production of oneness.[42] Poe, however, pursued

---

[40]All references to first usages are based on the *OED*. See Thomas Carlyle, "Characteristics," in *John Stuart Mill and Thomas Carlyle*, ed. Charles W. Eliot (New York: P. F. Collier, 1909), 347. For helpful accounts of *subjectivity* and *unconscious*, see Raymond Williams, *Keywords: A Vocabulary of Culture and Society* (New York: Oxford Univ. Press, 1976), 259–64, 270–73.

[41]Stanley Cavell, *In Quest of the Ordinary: Lines of Skepticism and Romanticism* (Chicago: Univ. of Chicago Press, 1988), 138.

[42]See, for instance, Frederick Henry Hedge's selection and translation of a telling passage from Schelling: "It was long ago perceived that, in Art, not everything is performed with consciousness; that, with the conscious activity, an unconscious action must

romantic absolutism before the founding of the Transcendental Club. He would eventually meet the Frogpondians in polemical, defensive, and not always earnest ways, but this was long after he established an original relation to transatlantic transcendentalism. Poe's sense of absolute truth is not premised on a transparent eye, for his dramatic depictions of absolute identity are occluded by slavery and race, and his thinking is intensely attentive to the productive opacity of the unconscious mind. Poe's terror is of Germany. It is carried through England. And unrelieved from political anxiety, it is shaped by the American slavery crisis as Poe pursues a metaphysic, an aesthetic, and a psychology that for all his sophistication form a conscious and unconscionable system of transcendental racism.

It may be tempting to think of racism as irrational, unconscious, unenlightened, and therefore open to reform through reflection and education. However, to take this too much for granted is to make the mistake of Poe: to maintain a separate, masterful subjectivity by radically distancing others. It is probably easier to think of Poe as culturally, morally, and philosophically distant. It is easy to be swayed by his popular image—wine bottle in one hand, opium pipe in the other, lusting after relatives and shamelessly plagiarizing while muttering racial slurs and dying in the gutter. Poe may be a pathological figure, but the point that his writings make so well is that perversity is never far from reason. Enlightenment thinking, including its resistant relative transcendentalism, certainly can lead to liberating views and progressive political ends. Poe reminds the rational reader that this conclusion is by no means foregone, especially in the antebellum United States where plenty of racists thought hard about race and where the project of emancipation remained as yet unfinished.

---

combine; and that it is of the perfect unity and mutual interpenetration of the two that the highest in Art is born" (*Prose Writers of Germany* [1840; reprint, Philadelphia: Porter and Coates, 1847], 512). The passage is from Schelling's "On the Relation of the Plastic Arts to Nature" (1807).

The Controversy over Gender
and Sexuality; or, Why Is Poe So
Obsessed with Dead Women?

While interest in Poe's attitudes about race and slavery emerged late in the history of Poe studies, engagement with Poe and gender was a feature of the criticism from very early on. Poe invites such interest when he declares, as he famously does in "Philosophy of Composition" that "the death . . . of a beautiful woman is unquestionably the most poetical topic in the world" (p. 229). And the corpses of beautiful women do indeed pile up, in both his stories and his poems.

For generations, Poe's women were dismissed or admired as a manifestation of his Southern chivalry, as if this was a code requiring women to die in order that men might suffer over their corpses. The first period of more focused engagement with Poe's women emerged during the early years of psychoanalytic criticism. The early feminist psychoanalytic critic Lorinne Pruette in 1920 suggested that Poe in fact had no meaningful interest in his female characters at all: "These women are never human . . . they are simply beautiful lay figures around which to hang wreaths of poetical sentiments. His emotional interest lay in himself, rather than in outer objects" (380). And in what remains to this day the most ambitious (and, at times, outlandish) psychoanalytic treatment of Poe, Marie Bonaparte's *Life and Works of Edgar Allan Poe* (1933) systematically read Poe's women through a Freudian lens as a working through of guilt, fear, and repressed desire for the lost mother.

It would not, however, be until the full flowering of the contemporary feminist movement that Poe's attitude toward women would come under closer scrutiny for its political and social effects in place of or in addition to reading it as a psychological symptom to be diagnosed by the critic. Beginning in the early 1980s, feminist scholars like Beth Ann Bassein, who leads off our section, began increasingly to question the excuses and explanations that had been offered for the representation of women in Poe's work. Bassein makes the case especially forcefully, asking her reader to consider the ways in which Poe's stories (and Poe's place in the canon) serves to perpetuate associations of women with passivity and death and to consider the effects of these associations on young readers—especially young women.

Perhaps surprisingly, Bassein in many ways represents a minority position within feminist scholarship, as many scholars have identified a Poe whose attitudes about women and gender are at the very least ambivalent if not explicitly subversive. In fact, Joan Dayan, one of the more strident of the early critics in the race debate featured in the previous section in terms of charging Poe with proslavery sympathies, emerged early in the 1990s as the critic who perhaps goes furthest in arguing for a "feminist Poe." For Dayan, Poe's deconstruction of the female body is part of a larger project of deconstructing social power and identity constructions in nineteenth-century America.

Cynthia Jordan's Poe is considerably less developed a feminist than that which Dayan would recover, but she does see clearly in Poe the emergence of a writer increasingly conscious of the systematic ways in which women are silenced and interested in imagining the voicing of this "second story." For Jordan, Poe's narrators in the dying women tales are clearly villains and we are supposed to measure considerable distance between their attitudes and actions and those of the author who penned the stories. Especially intriguing, Jordan extends this line of argument to Poe's detective stories, and to Dupin in particular, reading him as an emerging androgynous male protagonist who is determined to seek out the second story a patriarchal society systematically and often brutally silences.

Compared to the debate over race, which focuses predominantly on Poe's fictions, the discussion of Poe and gender often works on the poetry. Leland Person's attention to the poetry moves the conversation beyond the misogynist versus feminist debate, toward a more nuanced assessment of the contradictions Poe brought to this topic just as fully as he did to race and slavery. At the heart of the poetry about women, Person finds an engagement with *masculinity* and the desires of and for the male body. These poems, Person suggests, are a series of extended exercises in transgender performance, ultimately allowing Poe to imaginatively inhabit the "masculine" and "feminine" position—at once, objectifier and object, lover and beloved—in a perfect narcissistic circle.

Eliza Richards turns our attention from women in the poetry to the numerous women poets with whom Poe interacted throughout his career. She focuses on the odd dissimilarity between the victimized women found in Poe's work and perpetuated by Poe criticism and the vocal, talented, and active women Poe actually knew, corresponded with, and wrote about as a literary critic. Briefly summarizing here the research that is more fully explored in her important 2004 book, *Gender and the Poetics of Reception in Poe's Circle*, Richards challenges Poe scholars to move beyond the biographical readings that focus only on the many important women in the author's life who died and instead focus on the women surrounding him who wrote, spoke, and in many cases lived to defend his legacy after his death. "How could this extensive engagement not have a significant impact on his work and its reception," she asks, "and why is that impact so rarely noted and almost never studied?" (p. 519). Most urgently, her essays ask, how might we see Poe and his fictional and poetical women differently if the historical women who surrounded him are able to speak fully in the criticism.

The 1990s were largely dominated by a scholarship that pushed back against the kind of feminist critique articulated by Bassein, but the new century has seen a return to some of the arguments raised by earlier feminist scholarship. In his 2006 essay, for example, Joseph Church expresses his frustration with what had become an overwhelming chorus on behalf of Poe as "actually enlightened about the plight of woman in the nineteenth century" (p. 525). Picking up Bassein's concerns from almost a quarter century earlier, Church insists that critics fool themselves by imagining a feminist Poe out to critique a patriarchal society when in fact he is exactly what his protagonists often present themselves as: men determined to silence and punish women, particularly women who pose a threat to masculine privilege. Working very much against Jordan, who saw Dupin as Poe's most *enlightened* male protagonist, Church reads Dupin as a man capable not only of punishing women but also of expunging any trace of the feminine within himself. Church's essay serves to remind us that the debate over Poe's gender politics is far from over. Few today would argue for a Poe who is explicitly antiracist, but many critics, especially feminist scholars, find in Poe an ally. Is this, as Church suggests, an example of critical wishful thinking? Or is Church, like Bassein before him, reading and hearing only part of what Poe has to say on the topic?

Even as these questions continue to inform the controversy surrounding Poe and gender, our final essay, Valerie Rohy's "Ahistorical," seeks to suggest how questions of gender and sexuality in Poe's tales might be torqued in entirely new directions by moving beyond the historicist paradigm that has dominated literary scholarship in the United States for much of the last generation. Rohy's essay emphasizes the idea of historical alterity and its significance to queer theory. The concept, in brief, has been taken to mean that our knowledge of the past can be distorted if we assume that institutions or concepts have the same meaning across history. This concern for ahistoricism is of particular concern for queer theorists because although the modern designations of "homosexual" or "gay" can be anachronistic, there is nevertheless the critical imperative to recover sexual identities and expressions that have been silenced by history. Rohy expresses concern that the respect for historical alterity has gone too far and has, in fact, curtailed the kinds of connections contemporary queer readers want to make with authors, characters, and stories from the past. Rohy turns to Poe's "Ligeia"—the most contentious story within this controversy—in order to validate an ahistorical approach and the queer anachronisms that become visible when we do so. Rohy argues further that this ahistorical approach is validated by the tale itself—in which a dead woman returns to possess the body of a living woman and past and present literally collapse into something approaching illegibility by story's end.

Rohy's essay seems to us an ideal note to end on, as it reminds us that the story of these controversies is far from over, and new answers and entirely new methodologies are always being discovered. It is now up to you to begin the work of writing the next chapters in these conversations, as Poe continues to fascinate, frustrate, and elude us deep into our new century.

WORKS CITED

Bonaparte, Marie. *Life and Works of Edgar Allan Poe, a Psycho-Analytic Interpretation*. 1933; London: Imago, 1949. Print.

Dayan, Joan. "Poe's Women: A Feminist Poe?" *Poe Studies/Dark Romanticism* 24 (1991): 1–12. Print.

Pruette, Lorine. "A Psycho-Analytical Study of Edgar Allan Poe." *American Journal of Psychology* 31 (1920): 370–402. Print.

Richards, Eliza. *Gender and the Poetics of Reception in Poe's Circle.* Cambridge UP, 2004. Print.

FURTHER READING
IN THE CONTROVERSY

Carter, Catherine. "Not a Woman: The Murdered Muse in 'Ligeia.'" *Poe Studies/Dark Romanticism* 36 (2003): 45–57. Print.

Doyle, Jacqueline. "(Dis)Figuring Woman: Edgar Allan Poe's 'Berenice.'" *Poe Studies/Dark Romanticism* 24 (1991): 13–21. Print.

Kot, Paula. "Feminist 'Re-Visioning' of the Tales of Women." *A Companion to Poe Studies.* Ed. Eric W. Carlson. Westport: Greenwood, 1996. 388–402. Print.

Renzi, Kristen. "Hysteric Vocalizations of the Female Body in Edgar Allan Poe's 'Berenice.'" *ESQ: A Journal of the American Renaissance* 58.4 (2013): 601–40. Print.

Stovall, Floyd. "The Women of Poe's Poems and Tales." *Studies in English* (1925): 197–209. Print.

Weekes, Karen. "Poe's Feminine Ideal." *The Cambridge Companion to Edgar Allan Poe.* Ed. Kevin J. Hayes. Cambridge: Cambridge UP, 2002. 148–62. Print.

BETH ANN BASSEIN

Poe's Most Poetic Subject

Beth Ann Bassein (b. 1925) is professor emerita at Southern Colorado State College, where she taught English and women's studies courses for twenty-five years. The following essay is taken from her 1982 book, Women and Death: Linkages in Western Thought and Literature. *She also published* The Matriarch's Power: A Cross-Cultural Literary Study *in 1993.*

Charles Baudelaire pronounced Edgar Allan Poe's attitude toward women chivalric, and scholars have repeatedly done likewise, even within the past three decades, without finding chivalry incompatible with his proclamation that the death of a beautiful woman is the most poetic subject to be found. Even when seeing his life and works as inextricably bound together, writers generally look upon what they consider his chivalrous approach as the accepted mode for a Southern gentleman and seem to have no special misgivings about his statement on what is suitable subject matter for poetry.[1] With a similar blind spot, educators who may condemn extremes in twentieth-century literature and life do not flinch at making Poe's poetry and fiction required reading in our schools. Others who regard death as the ultimate terror find his stories highly entertaining. When looking at Poe's own immediate predecessors and contemporaries, it is obvious that he was not unique in his interest in dead females. Other writers with similar interests can be found, and crime statistics, among numerous other sources, bear out this fact. What has escaped many is that his skills as a poet and fiction writer, his theories regarding art, beauty, and pain, and the enthusiasm of his audience have all helped perpetuate a view of woman that identifies her with the most passive state occurring, that of the dead, and thus creates negative conditioning for generation after generation of vulnerable readers. That Poe's works emerged from and fed into the much-read Gothic tale, which often makes woman a victim, goes without saying.

Anyone separating out the definitions of chivalry as Poe's critics use it, as history hands it down to us, and as Poe practiced and/or wrote about it would have to take into account varying circumstances and diverse customs. A rigid definition of the term would be difficult to formulate, but some valuable generalizations can be made about it. The element that Poe adds to the custom of chivalry may be viewed as contradictory to it, or as the other side of a coin that poses as one thing while participating in another. The reading of his tales given here will produce evidence in support of the latter view.

The linkage of women and death is not an absolute in the traditional chivalric pose. Chivalry often praised woman for her beauty and intelligence and sometimes for her faithfulness and chastity. Its purpose was ostensibly to protect the woman from ravishment or other types of harm. When the relationship between the knight and lady was adulterous, the woman adored was most often well stationed, independent, and capable of performing courtly rituals. Sometimes the two lovers vowed faithfulness until death, and their dual death functioned

---

[1] Lois Hyslop and Francis E. Hyslop, trans. and ed., *Baudelaire on Poe* (State College, Pa.: Bald Eagle, 1952), 110; Edward Wagenknecht, *Edgar Allan Poe* (New York: Oxford, 1963), 25; Edd Winfield Parks, *Edgar Allan Poe As Literary Critic* (Athens: University of Georgia Press, 1964), 62; and Arthur Hobson Quinn, *Edgar Allan Poe, A Critical Biography* (New York: Cooper Square Publishers, 1969), especially his discussion of Poe's "The Philosophy of Composition." While these writers equate chivalry with protection, courtesy, and adoration or the show of same, others such as Kate Millett see it as sugar-coated lip service to placate the oppressed. Susan Griffin calls it an old protection racket that could not exist without rape. [All notes in this selection are Bassein's.]

symbolically as the consummation of love.[2] For the most part, however, the relationship purported to spur the knight into performing deeds of valor and motivated women to perform an active role in court life. Problematical as we may now think the lady's role to be, she was a life-oriented person, and her lover was not totally obsessed with viewing her in the throes of death.

Death either as cancellation or as a spectre in woman's path would seem to add to her sense of hopelessness and make her doubt her own worth or that of any kind of productive action. As we see love and death becoming more closely allied in Romantic writers, the result makes for a negative outlook, but this coupling of love and death contains less of the one-sided obsession Poe depicts in his works. To label Poe chivalric in his attitude toward women is obviously to gloss over a special set of negatives which his depictions contain. As this discussion will illustrate, numerous works by Poe are not the product of a chivalric attitude that places women on pedestals and leaves them there. Instead, they picture her as annihilated, as a plague upon man, and simply as a catalyst for a deep-seated obsession wherein there are no reciprocated benefits for her.

Many efforts have been made to explain why Poe linked women and death. But of far greater significance are those aspects of his works that would shape the impressionable reader's concepts of women, aspects that relegate her to a kind of vehicle for imaginatively carrying both Poe and his readers into the throes of death, thereby limiting the woman to a death-oriented function. Some would even have us believe that Poe worshipped woman even as he imagined her undergoing death. Rather, one suspects that whatever courtesy and adoration Poe exercised before woman fell away as he worked himself into an empathetic death orgy over her expiration. To clothe him in chivalry is to shroud the negative with a positive that can only deceive the unwary.

It is possible to see Poe's works merely as his life rewritten; it is also possible to label and dismiss him as a case study in necrophilia or misogyny and to put him on the shelf with the peculiar. Much in his approach, however, suggests a sweeping attitude stretching much before and beyond his time, an attitude that takes lightly literature made up of nine parts satisfaction at the death of the female and one part (at most) courtesy and adoration. Poe is but one of many who accept an extremely exaggerated and totally unreasonable coupling of women and death, to say nothing of taking satisfaction from finding her so overcome.

[2]Wayland Young, *Eros Denied: Sex in Western Society* (New York: Grove, 1964), 211–14.

Medicine is only one example of a nonliterary field in which beauty and death have a special titillation. Several articles in *Blackwood's* magazine, which Poe read, coupled woman's beauty with disease. Margaret Alterton thinks Poe may have caught the suggestion for choosing his "most poetic topic" from medical articles found there. In "The Diary of the Late Physician," which incidentally "touched a chord of interest" in London, he could have found the suggestion that a greater thrill will result from diseased conditions if beauty is added. According to this article, more morbid pleasure can be produced if disease works on a beautiful woman.[3] With fascination the doctor describes developing cancer, calling attention to an eminent medical writer who thought the most beautiful women were usually the ones afflicted with this disease. Later, he is also fascinated with catalepsy in women:

> "Beautiful, unfortunate creature!" thought I, as I stood gazing mournfully on her, with my candle in my hand, leaning against the bed-post.[4]

Poets and thinkers on an artistic level and nearly contemporaneous with Poe mingled pleasure and pain. Keats finds beauty in melancholy; Coleridge's "Rime of the Ancient Mariner" features life-in-death as female; and the conservative Edmund Burke in his "On the Sublime and Beautiful" says beauty in distress is the most affecting kind.[5]

Poe spawned much interest, but one suspects the attraction to him sprang from like preoccupations, already rooted. In England, the Pre-Raphaelites were impressed not just by his style but by the pictures of his heroines. Dante Gabriel Rossetti stated that when he set out to write "The Blessed Damozel," he had to go beyond Poe's treatment of grief on earth, that he had "to reverse the conditions, and give utterance to the yearning of the loved one in heaven."[6] Swinburne and Morris showed Poe's influence, and later, Wilde and Beardsley exploited the chaste and ethereal coupled with cruelty.

*   *   *

[3]Margaret Alterton, *Origins of Poe's Critical Theory* (New York: Russell and Russell, 1965), 24.

[4]Ibid., 25.

[5]Edmund Burke, "On the Sublime and Beautiful," *The Harvard Classics* 24 (New York: Collier, 1909), Section IX, 94.

[6]Jerome Hamilton Buckley and George Benjamin Woods, eds., *Poetry of the Victorian Period*, 3d ed. (Chicago: Scott, Foresman, 1965), Notes, 505.

Some scholars explain Poe's interest in dead women by cataloging the deaths that occurred during his lifetime and by attempting to show how these affected him. The list is so extensive that we are left wondering how he could have escaped becoming blasé about death. His mother, Elizabeth Arnold Poe, died when he was three, having been deserted in July 1810 by Poe's father, who apparently disappeared at this point never to be seen again. Her husband's departure, her incipient tuberculosis, her being pregnant with Poe's sister, and her attempt to retain her glory on the stage brought her to death in December 1811. Acting as long as her strength lasted, she finally was bedridden:

> All the while her little son and her baby daughter were with her, hearing her cough and moan, witnessing her tears at the knowledge that she must soon leave them . . . on the aware, sensitive mind of her intelligent three-year-old son, the sights and sounds of the sickroom . . . the mother's despair and anguish, the gradual change in the familiar face, must have left their unforgettable mark.[7]

According to Frances Winwar, Poe's association with Jane Stanard, the mother of one of his friends, when he was fifteen did much to solidify his conception of the ideal of romantic womanhood. Jane is thought to have resembled Poe's mother and to have embodied for him a kind of purity and spirituality that evoked adoration. Poe seems to have thought Jane would guide him toward greater and greater heights as a poet and would stop any excesses that might pull him down. When she suddenly died in April 1824, he was distraught and for many weeks visited her grave every night.[8]

Frances Allan, his foster mother, died in 1829; his brother Henry in 1831 of tuberculosis; his grandmother Poe in 1835; and, probably most distressing of all for its lingering duration, his child-wife Virginia Clemm in 1847. Many believe that all these experiences with death colored his relationships with other women—Sarah Royster, Mary Devereaux, Frances Osgood, Helen Whitman, and Annie Richmond—by causing him to develop a strong dependence upon them, epitomized by his association with his Aunt Maria Clemm who often nursed him back to health or sobriety. He developed an acute fear of losing the person upon whom he depended, causing him to reenact her death repeatedly. It is believed that sexual passion was not part of these relationships to

---

[7]"Francis Winwar, *The Haunted Palace: A Life of Edgar Allan Poe* (New York: Harper, 1959)," 24.
[8]Ibid., 54–57.

any extent, if at all. Intelligence in these women interested him sporadically and often only slightly. Death came to define nearly the whole of his concept of female reality. Other men have limited woman to sex, breeding, or dissembling, but most women would prefer these functions to being thought of as a vehicle for experiencing death. Poe makes *memento mori* of women. He forces, up out of his being, fictional character after fictional character in the throes of death. He handled death like a jeweler absorbed in his merchandise. His reading of the graveyard poets, Keats and Coleridge, his interest in mesmerism which he sees as a death-like state, his preoccupation with calling the dead back to life, his belief that contemplating beauty is a high challenge which must be done in the presence of death, his tendencies to elevate his dead mother into something which she was not—an English lady—along with strong melancholy tendencies, all helped establish around him an aura of death that seemed to obsess and nourish him. The character, of course, that most obsessed him and most often moved from life to cadaver was woman. A look at a number of these women is a meaningful trip into a source of woman's crippled self-image.

The death woman appears in Poe's best known poems, and in "Romance" he claims to have met her in his youth when "I could not love except where Death / Was mingling his with Beauty's breath" (*PT* 55). He would have Lenore, the "queenliest dead that ever died" (p. 20), be alive, but the intensity of his sorrow and his requests that the Raven tell him if he will be united with her overwhelm the reader to such an extent that little life shines through. He returns to the tomb of his lost Ulalume and wonders if a demon has tempted him there, seemingly to suggest that it is a fiend in the tomb which holds him in its grip, not woman. A thousand roses in "To Helen" give out, "in return for the love-light, / Their odorous souls in an ecstatic death—" (95). Annabel Lee's highborn kinsmen bear her away from him, and he goes to lie in her tomb (p. 28). In these poems sound gives a compelling gloss to the corpse of woman. Almost all of us can remember reciting these poems at an early age.

In Poe's tales, however, the death woman gets much fuller treatment. We can assume that his statement about the most poetic topic also held for fiction. In "Berenice," Poe reduces his heroine to teeth just as street language has long turned woman into just a part of herself by designating her *cunt, skirt,* or any of dozens of other epithets most often suggestive of sexuality. Berenice's agility and beauty make little impression on the protagonist until she becomes emaciated by disease. Then her teeth hop out at him from a face that has lustreless, pupil-less eyes, a placid pale high forehead, and shrunken lips. Just as street language gives exaggerated efficacy to woman's sexual side, the protagonist speaks of the "sensitive and sentient power" of the teeth that can carry moral persuasion and restore peace to him (p. 46). So determined is he to have these teeth that he opens her tomb, only to find her alive (p. 47).[9] His guilt, of course, shows on his spade and his clothes. We assume he got the teeth at the expense of her life.

Marie Bonaparte and other Freudians played into Poe's sadism when, in connection with this tale, they discussed the sadistic, castrating vagina, once thought to be equipped with teeth.[10] One does not have to follow their thinking to see the protagonist's lukewarm, if not rejecting, attitude toward woman who is energetic and attractive, and his preference for woman in a diseased and finally dead state. If Poe had a chivalric attitude toward women and if by that is meant respect for them, it does not spill over into his depiction of the protagonist in this ugly little tale, either as a pose or with some degree of sincerity.

In "Morella," the heroine tastes of intelligence and fathoms the unearthly so subtly that she terrorizes the protagonist. Her erudition includes determining that one's identity persists beyond the tomb. She dies but not before leaving him a daughter to take her place; even if both have separate and different identities, neither is palatable because of an exaggerated intelligence, which is as much a part of these women as teeth were for Berenice. All erudition and no passion, the first Morella can only give birth to "the most hideous." As his wife's end approaches, the protagonist longs for her death. Fiendishly he prompts the death of the child by calling her by her mother's name, the sound of which is death-producing. His "long and bitter laugh" at the end is a "mad" and sinister I-got-ya-this-time response, perhaps because there will be no future child to trouble him as there had been when the mother died (*PT* 239). In this tale we find little chivalry.

"The Assignation" and "The Oblong Box," like the poems "Annabel Lee" and "For Annie," are about meeting the beloved in death. In "The Assignation," there is a kind of telepathic union when two lovers take poison. Evidently unable to see the Marchesa Aphrodite except under the stress of rescuing her child, the male lover retrieves the infant which she has let slip into the water. Although this woman seems to fit

---

[9]Poe indicates in "The Premature Burial" that being buried alive is believed to be the most horrible death possible.

[10]Marie Bonaparte, *The Life and Works of Edgar Allan Poe* (London: Imago, 1949), 218.

better than Berenice or Morella the goddess-to-be-worshipped stereo-
type (and her lover a brave knight doing a good deed), we scarcely see
her enough to realize her nature since she is at a distance from her lover
whom we constantly see in the company of the male character who tells
the story. She, "the adoration of all Venice" (*PT* 201), is adulterous, as
many women in the early chivalric tradition were, but she seems to have
more in common with adulterous female sinners, much written about
before and after Poe in nineteenth-century fiction, who have no choice
but death. The tale is told from a male perspective, and it is mostly
about males; the woman's role has its focus in death.

"Ligeia" presents an extravagant picture of woman's beauty, intelligence, and devotion, but even as Poe begins his laudatory description
of this heroine, he seems to undercut the idealization when he mentions the "ill-omened" marriage she has with the protagonist. Ligeia
has some "strangeness" about her (p. 49). Like most of Poe's women,
she gives but receives little from others; what she gives is a sense of the
importance of will which, if exercised with strength, she thinks can save
one from death. If this were Poe's only tale and if we read only the passages leading up to her illness, we might think Poe worshipped woman
and took great pleasure in her vitality of spirit and mind. However, not
only Ligeia but also Rowena, the new wife, dies in order that Ligeia
may live again and in order, it would seem, that the protagonist may
relish not one, but two, journeys into necrophilia. In opium fantasy and
influenced by the phantasmagoric effect of a new abbey, he is able to
will Rowena's return from death prior to willing her change into Ligeia.
The night he spends with Rowena, who lapses into death and returns
to life alternately and finally into Ligeia, is a rich orchestration of the
death process that Poe employs often but nowhere with such prolonged
intensity as in this case. Poe's most deeply felt and intense writing is not
on woman alive but on woman experiencing death.

"The Fall of the House of Usher," like other tales, does not point
to a conventional chivalric attitude toward women, nor does it make
the death of a beautiful woman anything more than what it often is—
a terror-producing experience. Poe's first-person narrator has another
necrophilic adventure; the whole story appears to be a trip into a grave.
The narrator visits a house of "excessive antiquity" reminiscent of
"some neglected vault" (p. 89). His cadaverous host Roderick Usher,
whose lips have a "surpassingly beautiful curve" (p. 90), makes him
aware of his "tenderly beloved sister" (p. 92) who, as was also the case
with the Marchesa Aphrodite, is never seen for more than a few seconds
and who is never revealed as more than a tortured victim who is buried

alive. We learn that she had been wasting away for some time with a lingering disease that had baffled the skill of doctors. Called a life-in-death symbol by various critics, she, like Poe's mother and wife Virginia, dies a slow death. Bonaparte, for example, who sees a very close link between sex and cruelty, says she was "a mother symbol to Poe Usher."[11] Provisions are made to have Madeline's corpse put in a vault within one of the main walls of the building, and the two men see to its being put there:

> The vault in which we placed it (and which had been so long unopened that our torches, half smothered in its oppressive atmosphere, gave us little opportunity for investigation) was small, damp, and entirely without means of admission of light; lying, at great depth, immediately beneath that portion of the building in which was my own sleeping apartment. (p. 97)

The night they discover they have buried Madeline alive is one of "singular" terror and beauty (p. 99). Missing in this tale is an element that is not altogether absent in Poe, excessive mooning over the loveliness of woman. A sickly smile quivers on the host's lips as he discovers that he has buried his sister; guilt and "madness" seize him, and when Madeline does come forth alive only to fall heavily upon the person of her brother, she becomes the instrument of his death. Madeline is given no feelings, or for that matter much substance as a human being; she is victim-destroyer. Poe spends greatly less time on Madeline than he does on his two male characters. That he does not allow either the sister or the brother to live suggests that they were perhaps involved with the mysteriously "terrible": incest likely in the manner of that in Byron's *Manfred*. This tale clearly shows why the Freudians found so much in Poe, as well as why Leslie Fiedler insisted that American literature was basically a homosexual one written by authors incapable of depicting a realistic woman.[12]

*   *   *

"The Oval Portrait" is of special significance because here Poe might be indicating that he realizes artists exploit women in the throes of death to produce art and that sadism and art are closely allied. In this

---

[11] Bonaparte, *Life and Works*, 249.
[12] Leslie A. Fiedler, *Love and Death in the American Novel* (New York: Criterion, 1960), 325–45.

work, the artist's canvas grows to perfection; his wife, the model, shrinks to death. She waxes pale and weak as her strength and beauty are transferred to the portrait. The painter grows "wild with the ardor of the work" and rarely removes his eyes from the canvas, "even to regard the countenance of his wife" (p. 160). Standing proudly over his accomplishment, he proclaims it Life, but when he turns to his wife, she is no more. When we watch the mounting obsession and pleasure in the artist, we become more and more aware that a woman is being used to produce that pleasure and ultimately profit. How much Poe felt this exploitation also explained his art is not clear; had it made much of a dent in his makeup, he might have written more on the subject than is found in "The Oval Portrait," a slight four-page account.

Anyone searching for relief from the death woman in Poe's tales should not turn to "The Murders in the Rue Morgue" where Madame L'Espanaye is mutilated and decapitated and her daughter is killed and stuffed head downward in the chimney; or to "The Mystery of Marie Rogêt" where a girl's corpse is found in the Seine after a rape-murder; or to "The Black Cat" where the wife is axed to death by her drunken husband as she stays his hand when he is about to kill the cat with which he is obsessed; or to "Scheherazade" where the main character stalls death by talking, but in the end is done in as we might expect. . . .

If Poe had the conventional chivalric attitude toward women with the attendant sincerity that many of his critics thought he had, this attitude is not much in evidence in his poems and fiction. That he did exploit the death of females is quite apparent in his works. The life-orientation of chivalry does not seem to be compatible with his noticeable emphasis on death. If all women had to read was a steady diet of Poe, they would likely develop so keen a sense of their demise that they would have only a negative approach to life. If women believed that Poe's attitude toward women was chivalric, then they would come to think of chivalry as something having to do with graves, gasping their last breath, and coming alive again. They would soon unmask chivalry, as the term has recently been used, as a ritual that elevates women in order to topple them with a more pronounced thud. It goes without saying that many people still do not view chivalry in this light, although the number that do has increased sharply.

The thoughtful reader would want to have little to do with Poe's works or any literature exploiting similar stereotypes. However, given the abundance of Gothic romances written by women, apart from all those written by men, and given the number of female readers of those Gothic tales, it can be said that repulsion from the stereotypes that the

Gothic tale perpetuates is not as strong as one would wish it to be. Interestingly, during periods of low emphasis on women's freedom, such as the fifties and early sixties, the publication of Gothic romances tends to increase. Perhaps the Gothic tale is thought to be necessary to uphold, through the support of identification, female capacity to go on in a victimized and subservient position.[13]

Poe does not, of course, hold up the entire weight of the Gothic tradition, for it existed long before him and branched into areas that he never treated. He did have considerable influence on this tradition, however, and it is time we addressed the question of what the legacy of that tradition has done to the image of women. It is important to analyze Poe's antagonisms,[14] his sexuality or lack of it, the influence the deaths in his family, the American literary preoccupation with death, or whatever caused him to write as he did. Since we can neither alter Poe nor his works, we should concentrate on what his pictures of women have done and will do to the self-image and aspirations of generations of readers. If attitudes are to be changed, we need to school ourselves in how they are shaped. It would be good to label him more according to what he was and to read him with full awareness of literature's power to mold thought and action. All that Poe has done to relegate women to the world of the dead must be exorcised.

CYNTHIA S. JORDAN

Poe's Re-Vision: The Recovery of the Second Story

Cynthia Jordan (1949–1993) was an associate professor of English, American studies, and women's studies at Indiana University. She was the author of Second Stories: The Politics of Language, Form, and Gender in Early American Fictions *(1989), which included work on numerous canonical American authors, including Benjamin Franklin, James Fenimore Cooper, and Edgar Allan Poe. The following essay was first published in the scholarly journal* American Literature *in 1987.*

---

[13]Janice Radway, "Dialogue: Is Popular Culture Social History?" in *Humanities* 1, no. 1 (January–February 1980): 14.

[14]Fiedler, *Love and Death in the American Novel*, 413. Fiedler thinks that Poe was in flight from a woman when he died.

While the longstanding debates over Hawthorne's treatment of women characters have been reinvigorated and refined by feminist critics in the last fifteen years or so, feminist criticism has as yet had little to say about Poe's women-centered fictions.[1] This lack of attention might have surprised—or more probably, annoyed—the egotistical Poe, since he himself suggested the terms by which his treatment of women characters might be compared with Hawthorne's. In an 1842 review of *Twice-Told Tales*, Poe praised "The Minister's Black Veil" as "a masterly composition" whose underlying meaning would probably be lost on most readers, for the "*moral* put into the mouth of the dying minister will be supposed to convey the *true* import of the narrative; and that a crime of dark dye, (having reference to the 'young lady') has been committed, is a point which only minds congenial with that of the author will perceive" (*ER* 575).

Poe's use of the term "crime" was perceptive in this instance and virtually prophetic of the direction Hawthorne's tales would take in the next few years. Nina Baym has observed, for example, that in "most of the stories written before . . . 1842, the destruction or damaging of the woman seems to result accidentally as a by-product." The question of the male character's having a "covert intention" to cause such harm, however, "cannot be entirely absent," especially since in the years which followed, Hawthorne's stories "escalate" the male character's ambiguous intentions to "an attitude more clearly hostile."[2] In stories such as "The Birthmark" (1843), "Rappaccini's Daughter" (1844), "Drowne's Wooden Image" (1844), "The Artist of the Beautiful" (1844), and "Ethan Brand" (1849), "crimes" against women are indeed laid bare.

A chronology of Poe's women-centered tales written during these same years suggests a reason for his apparently inside knowledge of Hawthorne's "true import" in 1842. Having already published "Berenice" (1835), "Morella" (1835), "Ligeia" (1838) and "The Fall of the House of Usher" (1839), Poe had clearly established his own "congenial" interest in the fictional possibilities to be found in covert crimes against ladies. With the publication of "The Murders in the Rue Morgue" in 1841, he had begun to highlight such crimes and would continue to

---

[1]Nina Baym has made the strongest and most persuasive case for regarding Hawthorne's treatment of women characters as feminist, in a series of articles, two of which will be cited below, and a full-length critical biography, *The Shape of Hawthorne's Career* (Ithaca: Cornell Univ. Press, 1976). . . . [All notes in this selection are Jordan's.]

[2]"Thwarted Nature: Nathaniel Hawthorne as Feminist," in *American Novelists Revisited: Essays in Feminist Criticism*, ed. Fritz Fleischmann (Boston: G. K. Hall, 1982), 64–65.

do so in the two subsequent detective stories in the Dupin series, "The Mystery of Marie Rogêt" (1842) and "The Purloined Letter" (1845). Thus the evolution of Hawthorne's women-centered tales followed the same pattern as Poe's: both authors gradually changed their fictional focus from covert to overt victimizations of women.

A brief look at individual works reveals more similarity between the authors, because the recurring crime in all of the above-mentioned tales is that one or more women have been criminally silenced; the speech that would allow them self-expression has been denied or usurped by male agents. Poe was especially prolific in creating images of violently silenced women, their vocal apparatus the apparent target of their attackers, who, in the earlier stories, are the storytellers themselves. One remembers the forcible removal of Berenice's teeth by her professed "lover"; the premature shroud that "lay heavily about the mouth" of Ligeia (p. 60)—and of Madeline Usher, no doubt; and later, the throat-cutting and strangulations in "The Murders in the Rue Morgue" and "The Mystery of Marie Rogêt." The psychological violence in such tales is no less pre-emptive. Morella's narrator-husband comes to a point where he can "no longer bear . . . the low tone of her musical language," and after she dies she is denied a place in his own speech: "Morella's name died with her at her death. Of the mother I had never spoken to the daughter . . ." (*PT* 238). Even in "The Purloined Letter," the least violent of Poe's tales about women, the Queen who sees her "letter" stolen before her very eyes cannot speak to save herself for fear of jeopardizing her position with the King, who fails to understand the crime taking place.

*   *   *

What I propose to do in this essay is to bring Poe into the critical arena on Hawthorne's coat-tails, as it were. Given the similar progression of his fictional focus from covert to overt crimes against women, and given his similar understanding of what in fact constitutes such "crimes," Poe's women-centered tales raise the same issues as Hawthorne's: "the imaginative limits" of male-authored fictions and "the responsibility of change." What makes Poe an equally apt candidate for a feminist inquiry is that, like Hawthorne, he incorporates those issues into his own discourse, and his fictional response to both problems is also to cross gender boundaries in order to tell "the woman's story."

Poe's villainous narrators in tales like "Berenice," "Morella," and "Ligeia" do indeed tell one-sided stories, and the warped nature of their sexual crimes has been well documented.[3] Poe's search for a solution to such crimes is my main subject here, and "The Fall of the House of Usher" marks the beginning of that search. Starting with Roderick Usher, Poe began his experiments with the androgynous male character whose developing empathy with a woman enables him to reject one-sided male-authored fictions and finally to engender a new fictional form—a second story that provides a text for female experience. In the Dupin tales that follow, in which the task of solving crimes against women calls for a detective with an awareness that other men lack, the androgynous Dupin becomes virtually a feminist critic. In Dupin, Poe created a new caretaker of social and political order, and Dupin fulfills these responsibilities by going beyond the imaginative limits of the male storytellers around him and recovering the second story—"the woman's story"—which has previously gone untold. Whether that act of recovery establishes Poe as a writer of feminist sensibility is an issue I will take up in my conclusion.

II.

The crime against the Lady Madeline Usher is that she is prematurely entombed, and while Roderick has traditionally been considered solely responsible, he is but a character in the story himself, and his actions are at least in part the product of his narrator's construction. That is, while critics have credited him with a variety of personal motives for trying to kill his "tenderly beloved sister" (p. 92), including self-defense, euthanasia, and a vampiristic "creative impulse,"[4] the fact remains that he could not have incarcerated Madeline without the narrator's help, as Roderick himself comes to realize: "*We have put her living in the tomb!*" (p. 102). Thus it is the male narrator's actions in this story, his influence over Roderick and his misogynist strategies of textual control, that first warrant a reader's attention—and suspicion.

---

[3] Michael Davitt Bell has shown the narrators of "Berenice," "Morella," and "Ligeia" to be "lover-murderers," repulsed by sexuality, in *The Development of American Romance: The Sacrifice of Relation* (Chicago: Univ. of Chicago Press, 1980), 101, 112–17. See also Terence J. Matheson, "The Multiple Murder in 'Ligeia': A New Look at Poe's Narrator," *Canadian Review of American Studies* 13 (1982), 279–89.

[4] J. O. Bailey, "What Happens in 'The Fall of the House of Usher'?," *American Literature* 35 (1964): 445–66; Maurice Beebe, "The Universe of Roderick Usher," in *Poe: A Collection of Critical Essays*, ed. Robert Regan (Englewood Cliffs, N.J.: Prentice-Hall, 1967), 129–30; and Daniel Hoffman, *Poe Poe Poe Poe Poe Poe Poe* (New York: Doubleday, 1972), 310–11.

A boyhood friend of Roderick, the narrator arrives on the scene at the outset to bolster his friend's waning manhood, and from hints variously placed in his narration, it soon becomes clear that he views Roderick's acute nervous condition as arising from his sister's presence, perhaps from her overcloseness or her unmanly influence. The long-standing critical consensus regarding the narrator is that he is a well-intentioned man of reason, valiantly, albeit naively, trying to make sense of a world skewed by irrational forces.[5] His animosity towards Madeline, however, which is foreshadowed in his first description of the mansion upon his arrival, seems if anything unreasonable, irrational. The "vacant and eye-like windows" (p. 87), the "fine tangled web-work" of fungi "hanging . . . from the eaves" (p. 89), and the crack which runs from roof to foundation prefigure Roderick's "luminous" eyes, his "hair of a more than web-like softness and tenuity" (p. 90), and his oddly split personality, all of which seem ominous enough to the narrator. But he experiences "a shudder even more thrilling than before" when he looks at the reflection of the House in the tarn, the "remodelled and inverted images" (p. 87) which represent Madeline, Roderick's physical and psychological counterpart. In particular, the "silent tarn" (p. 89) foreshadows Madeline's ill-fated exclusion from the narrator's story, for she will be buried at a "great depth" (p. 97) in the House, in a chamber that lies beneath the surface of the tarn and of the narrative.

The narrator's first encounter with Madeline confirms the conflict between the male storyteller and the lady of the House, for he frames the encounter as one between mutually exclusive presences. "I regarded her with an utter astonishment not unmingled with dread. . . . A sensation of stupor oppressed me," he tells us, and the effect of his presence on her is equally oppressive: "on the closing in of the evening of my arrival at the house, she succumbed . . . to the prostrating power of the destroyer." What is of interest here is the periphrastic description of her lapse into a cataleptic-speechless-stupor and the narrator's passive construction in the phrasing that follows: "the lady, at least while living, would be seen by me no more." Without implicating himself as an agent in her immediate demise, the narrator uses language covertly to

---

[5]See, for example, Charles Feidelson, Jr., *Symbolism and American Literature* (Chicago: Univ. of Chicago Press, 1953), 35; Joel Porte, *The Romance in America: Studies in Cooper, Poe, Hawthorne, Melville, and James* (Middletown, Conn.: Wesleyan Univ. Press, 1969), 62; and Stefano Tani, *The Doomed Detective: The Contribution of the Detective Novel to Postmodern American and Italian Fiction* (Carbondale: Southern Illinois Univ. Press, 1984), 12.

relegate Madeline to a passive position in relation to himself, and in the next sentence he tries to exclude her from the text altogether: "For several days ensuing, her name was unmentioned by either Usher or myself" (p. 92). Although he ostensibly remarks on this to demonstrate his concern and sensitivity for his friend's grief over his sister's deteriorating condition, the effect is to show the narrator making sure that Madeline has no place in their masculine language or in this male-authored fiction.

Similarly, on the verge of her return from the tomb, the narrator will try not to hear what he dismisses as her "indefinite sounds" (p. 98) as she breaks through steel and a copper-lined vault, sounds which emanate from the tomb "beneath . . . [his] own sleeping apartment" (p. 97) on a night when he tries unsuccessfully to sleep. The suggestion here of a guilty conscience, or more specifically, of a consciousness plagued by its repressed underpinnings, is heightened by the fact that the narrator is awakened to such ominous sounds by the nightmare vision of "an incubus," which he wants to believe is "of utterly causeless alarm" (p. 98). His word is ill-chosen, however, or at least revealing of the psychological processes he has previously tried to conceal, for "incubus" is the archaic name for a male spirit that visited women in their sleep and aroused female sexuality. If his word choice is a conscious misnomer, that is, if he has substituted "incubus" for "succubus," the female counterpart supposed to visit sleeping men, then the choice is but another narrative strategy intended to exclude any female agency from his text. If, as seems more likely, we are to take "incubus" as an authentic report of a mind that is losing conscious control (for on this night of nights the return of the repressed is imminent), then Poe would seem to be suggesting that the narrator's homoerotic attraction to Roderick has caused him to see himself in some way feminized. If this is the case, then the nightmare status of this identification with female sexuality is no less proof of the narrator's misogyny—of his fear and hatred of the female sexuality incarnate in Madeline Usher.

It is Roderick who finally admits to hearing Madeline, and it is Roderick's growing consciousness of the crime perpetrated against his sister that finally allows her back into the text. Before he can make such an admission, however, he has first to undergo a mighty transformation for a fictional character and free himself of his narrator's control. Essentially, the conflict between the male storyteller and the female character is internalized in the androgynous Roderick, whose dual gender is depicted in behavior that is "alternately vivacious and sullen" and in a voice that varies "rapidly from a tremulous indecision" to a "species of energetic concision" also described as a "guttural utterance" (p. 91). That he is Madeline's twin more obviously implies a merging of gender identities in this story, and there are other suggestions of his partly feminine nature. Given the year of publication for "The Fall of the House of Usher," for example, when the "feminization of American culture" was well under way, the fact that Roderick is an artist is itself enough to insure his effeminate status.[6] In addition, his composition of a musical ballad is reminiscent of Morella and Ligeia, who had been characterized by their musical language, which their male narrators had also found unsettling. Poe's physical description of Roderick is in fact, as D. H. Lawrence recognized, very similar to that of the beautiful Ligeia.[7] He has the same large, pale brow; eyes "large, liquid, and luminous beyond comparison"; lips of "a surpassingly beautiful curve"; and "a nose of a delicate Hebrew model" (p. 90). Thus it is not surprising that the narrator speaks distastefully of his friend's "peculiar physical conformation and temperament" (p. 90) or that he will try to cure him of the effeminacy he denigrates as a "mental disorder" (p. 97).

We may speculate that it was the masculine side of Roderick's character, or rather, his desire for an exclusively masculine identity, that originally motivated him to summon the narrator to him, "with a view of attempting . . . some alleviation of his malady" (p. 88). Once the narrator is in authorial possession of the House, however, and Madeline's effeminizing influence has been dispatched, Roderick begins to have second thoughts about what he will finally come to see as the crime of masculine exclusivity, and his change of mind is imaged in his search for a narrative form that will allow him to express what the narrator has so artfully excluded.

Roderick's first attempt to communicate his inner turmoil after Madeline has been confined to her sick chamber, for example, is through a "perversion and amplification" of a waltz by Von Weber. That Roderick gives an unusual interpretation of this musical score suggests his desire to deviate from male-authored compositions. But the single-minded narrator characteristically refuses to confer such meaning on his friend's deviation from a masculine script and thus labels it merely a "perversion" (p. 93). The next of Roderick's creations we see, a small painting of an interior vault that suggests both Madeline's femaleness

---

[6] I have borrowed the phrase from Ann Douglas' *The Feminization of American Culture* (New York: Knopf, 1977), in which she discusses the feminized status of nineteenth-century American artists at length.

[7] *Studies in Classic American Literature* (Garden City, N.Y.: Doubleday, 1923).

and her fate, is illuminated, the misogynous narrator would have us believe, with "inappropriate splendor," and again he resists assigning meaning to his friend's subversive attempt to communicate otherness, claiming that Roderick's subject may be "shadowed forth, [only] feebly, in words" (p. 93). Roderick's third formal experiment, the musical ballad of "The Haunted Palace," has its own verbal component, which implies Roderick's growing abilities as a storyteller in his own right. But here, perhaps sensing a rival narrative voice for the first time, our narrator escalates his textual control. Acknowledging that there is an "under or mystic current of . . . meaning," he nevertheless exerts editorial authority over Roderick's text in phrasing that hints at partial censorship: "The verses . . . ran very nearly, if not accurately, thus:" (p. 94).

"The Haunted Palace," like "The Fall of the House of Usher," tells the story of a mind ("Thought's dominion") assailed and enervated by nameless "evil things," and as in the prose narrative, where Madeline's enshrouded body is graced by "the mockery of a faint blush upon the bosom and the face" (p. 97), "the glory / That blushed and bloomed / Is but a dim-remembered story / Of the old time entombed" (p. 95). The narrator of "The Fall of the House of Usher" has used his narrative strategies to suppress the "story" of Madeline's victimization, and Roderick's ballad, while it is an improvement over the nonverbal suggestiveness of his music and his painting, is no more explicit about the crime perpetrated against his sister: it tells its tale in symbolism, metonymy, allegory—all misnomers sanctioned historically by a male-dominant literary tradition. It is Roderick's task finally to retrieve that "dim-remembered story" from the obfuscating language of male-authored fictions, and to do so he must become fully conscious of his own complicity in the crime of excluding-by-misnaming. It was Roderick after all who had first invited the narrator's misogynistic intrusion into the House of Usher by labelling his "sympathies" with his lady sister a "malady" (pp. 97, 91).

Roderick's reviving sympathies with and for his sister precipitate her return from the tomb to the text, and in the climactic closing scenes of this tale, where Roderick at last acknowledges and renounces his crime, the narrator struggles to maintain his textual control. As Madeline makes headway up from the lower regions of the House, the narrator, finally showing his true colors, tries desperately to shut out her noisy return with the language of another male-authored fiction, "the only book immediately at hand." Trying to hold Roderick's divided attention with "a gentle violence" (p. 99), he reads him the story of

Ethelred, a manly hero and "conqueror," who is challenged by a dragon with "a shriek so horrid and harsh, and withal so piercing, that Ethelred had fain to close his ears with his hands against the dreadful noise of it" (p. 100). But Roderick here becomes virtually "a resisting reader." He rejects both the model of manliness the narrator has tried to impose upon him and the misnaming of the sound he hears, and he replaces the narrator's death-dealing text with a new, second story in a dramatic act of "re-vision"[8]:

> Not hear it?—yes, I hear it, and *have* heard it. Long—long— long—many minutes, many hours, many days, have I heard it— yet I dared not—oh, pity me, miserable wretch that I am! I dared not—I *dared* not speak! *We have put her living in the tomb!* . . . And now—to-night—Ethelred—ha! ha!—the breaking of the hermit's door, and the death-cry of the dragon, and the clangor of the shield!—say, rather, the rending of her coffin, and the grating of the iron hinges of her prison, and her struggles within the coppered archway of the vault! . . . *Madman! I tell you that she now stands without the door!* (p. 102)

By momentarily freeing himself of the narrator's control and authoring a second story that explicitly reveals the crime perpetrated against femaleness, Roderick has succeeded in bringing Madeline to the threshold of the narrator's tale. And indeed, the unmasked "Madman" in Poe's story is here forced to acknowledge in unambiguous words the irrefutable truth of Roderick's narrative: "without those doors there *did* stand the lofty and enshrouded figure of the lady Madeline of Usher. There was blood upon her white robes, and the evidence of some bitter struggle upon every portion of her emaciated frame" (p. 102, Poe's emphasis). The narrator is still not willing to admit his role in her long "struggle" for acknowledgment, however, any more than he is willing to wait around for her to speak her own mind. Claiming that Madeline and Roderick reunite only to die in each other's arms, this eminently unreliable narrator flees the chamber, the House, and his own misogynistic narrative endeavor.[9] "The Fall of the House of Usher" ends with

---

[8]Adrienne Rich, "When We Dead Awaken: Writing as Re-Vision," in *On Lies, Secrets, and Silence: Selected Prose 1966–1978* (New York: Norton, 1979), 35. I will give Rich's full definition of "re-vision" later in the text.

[9]G. R. Thompson has also argued the unreliability of the narrator, but for different reasons. He claims that the narrator gradually comes to accept Roderick's mad interpretations and that the scene of Madeline's return is thus a dual hallucination. See *Poe's Fiction: Romantic Irony in the Gothic Tales* (Madison: Univ. of Wisconsin Press, 1973),

the narrator's fragmented sentences, the last fragments of his control. But control, nevertheless, for his final act of "sentencing" is to dispatch Madeline and her too-familiar twin into the "silent tarn," out of mind and out of language one last time: "the deep and dank tarn at my feet closed sullenly and silently over the fragments of the 'House of Usher' " (p. 103).

In this tale, Roderick's growing abilities as a storyteller are paralleled by his growing terror at the implications of what he must finally do: act as a free agent and virtually rupture the narrative proper with a second story that lays bare the crime of male-authored fictions. The rupture is momentary, lasting just long enough to allow the woman character to get a foot in the door, but it is a significant moment in the evolution of Poe's artistry. Roderick Usher was a new character in Poe's repertoire, an androgynous spokesperson capable of giving voice to female experience and critiquing male-authored fictions which mute that experience, and despite what his madman-narrator must have hoped, his unusual talents were not so easily laid to rest. They would surface again two years later in the service of C. Auguste Dupin, Poe's great detective. The new genre that serves as a vehicle for this androgynous mastermind may be said to be Poe's own "second story," for it too is a new narrative form that critiques male-authored interpretive paradigms which fail to do justice to women. In the three detective stories published between 1841 and 1845, Poe moved from the timeless, dreamlike worlds of remote gothic mansions, turrets, and dungeons to the social realm of neighborhoods, shops, newspapers, and political intrigue, where the investigation of seemingly isolated crimes against women uncovers a network of covert gender-related "crimes" that pervades the entire social order. And Dupin, like Roderick Usher before him, is the detective-critic who brings such "crimes" to light.[10]

The epigraph to the first tale, "The Murders in the Rue Morgue," introduces the idea of crossing gender boundaries to recover the now "dim-remembered story" of female experience: "What song the Syrens sang, or what name Achilles assumed when he hid himself among

---

68–104, and "Poe and the Paradox of Terror: Structures of Heightened Consciousness in 'The Fall of the House of Usher,'" in *Ruined Eden of the Present: Hawthorne, Melville, and Poe*, ed. G. R. Thompson and Virgil L. Lokke (West Lafayette, Ind.: Purdue Univ. Press, 1981), 313–40.

[10]Tani, 4, likens Dupin to Roderick Usher on the grounds that each is a poet-figure suffering from a "diseased" imagination. For other readings of Dupin as a poet-figure, see Leslie A. Fiedler, *Love and Death in the American Novel*, 2nd ed. (New York: Stein and Day, 1966), 497; and Hoffman, 114–22.

women, although puzzling questions, are not beyond *all* conjecture" (p. 128). Like Roderick, Dupin exhibits a "Bi-Part Soul," which leads his narrator to imagine "a double Dupin," and he speaks in dual modes, his normal speaking voice "a rich tenor" which rises "into a treble" when he delivers his analysis of a crime, i.e., when he recounts the experience of a female victim (p. 132). That he represents a second draft of Roderick's character, however, is evident in his greater ability to speak, literally, for the silenced woman, to imagine her story in her own words. In "The Mystery of Marie Roget," for example, Dupin goes so far as to recreate the thought-pattern of the murdered Marie in the first-person: "We may imagine her thinking thus—'I am to meet a certain person . . .'" (*PT* 538).

The most significant difference between Dupin's ability to recover the story untold by male-authored fictions and Roderick's, however, is that the detective's skill is presented as the desired model. Unlike Roderick's closed-minded narrator, for example, Dupin's narrator greatly admires his friend's mental powers (as do the police), and Dupin in fact tries to teach his lesser-skilled narrator how to read in a new way. In this, the evolution of his character may be traced back to Ligeia, whose deeper knowledge of texts had threatened her narrator-husband by revealing his lesser abilities. In "Ligeia," the narrator had described his attempt to attain to Ligeia's knowledge as being like "our endeavors to recall to memory something long forgotten": "we often find ourselves *upon the very verge* of remembrance, without being able, in the end, to remember" (p. 50). In "The Murders in the Rue Morgue," Dupin tells his narrator his own partial interpretation of a newspaper text reporting the grisly murders of two women and asks for the man's conclusion: "At these words a vague and half-formed conception of the meaning of Dupin flitted over my mind. I seemed to be upon the verge of comprehension, without power to comprehend—as men, at times, find themselves upon the brink of remembrance, without being able, in the end, to remember" (p. 149). One critic has claimed that readers rightly identify with this "ostensible dummy," rather than with the detective, whom he sees as "grotesquely naive" in this story. He argues in particular that the story is a lesson in the dangers inherent in sexual repression: while the overly intellectual Dupin fails to see the obvious sexual nature of the crime and thus tries to rationalize the evidence in a way that the narrator finds incomprehensible, the narrator, who represents "every reader," more naturally sees evidence of rape. "Every reader," this critic explains, knows that "he" is potentially "capable of such actions" and all-too-humanly "finds himself excited by—and identifying with—" the putative rapist-murderer.[11] The similar phrasings above, however, suggest that Poe conceived of Dupin as being like Ligeia, or at least as thinking like her, and it seems unrealistic to fault a character who apparently thinks like a woman for failing to identify with or be excited by the idea of a rapist. Indeed, this seems to be the point of the similar phrasings, that men and women think and see things differently; specifically, that Dupin, like Ligeia, has mental abilities of which most "men" are unconscious, their conceptions merely "half-formed." He is thus able to read beyond the surface narrative of male-authored texts, to perceive the gap between text and reality. . . .

What I have called the gap between text and reality is, of course, a gender gap. In the Dupin tales, male-authored texts exclude femaleness because their authors are incapable of imagining women's experience; which is to say, they fail to recognize the various ways in which women are victimized. Such failures of imagination, recognition, and empathy are thus "crimes" in their own right, for although these male authors are less obviously misogynistic than Poe's earlier narrators, the texts they create continue to leave the woman's story untold, the overt crime unsolved. In "The Murders in the Rue Morgue," for example, Dupin is able to track down the murderer of the old woman and her daughter because he can recognize what has gone unnamed by the newspaper account of the crime: the strange "voice" of the attacker, which none of the "witnesses" could identify, is that of an orangutan. Once this fact is established, the detective is then able to recover the entire scenario— the second story, which reveals at last what the women actually suffered. Not surprisingly, that story presents a grim parody of what in Poe's tales constitutes normative masculine behavior. The trained animal had been acting out a masculine script, first flourishing a razor around the face of one of his victims, "in imitation of the motions of a barber"; then silencing both women when they put up a struggle; and finally trying to conceal all evidence of the crime (p. 157).

* * *

In the third and final tale in which Dupin appears, the "limited region" whose boundaries are set by masculine minds is shown to be the province of the Parisian police. Their failure to recover "the purloined letter" results, as Dupin explains, from the narrow "limits of the

---

[11] J. A. Leo Lemay, "The Psychology of 'The Murders in the Rue Morgue,'" *American Literature* 54 (1982): 177, 178, 187.

Prefect's examination—in other words, had the principle of [the let-ter's] concealment been comprehended within the principles of the Prefect—its discovery would have been a matter altogether beyond question" (p. 196). In this tale the plot-lines we have seen previously are reduced to their essence and the issue of gender conflict is in fact given a political dimension, for the crime is the theft of a text that right-fully belongs to the Queen; the thief is the Minister D——," who dares all things, those unbecoming as well as those becoming a man" (p. 188); and "the power thus attained," as even the Prefect of police recognizes, "has . . . been wielded, for political purposes, to a very dan-gerous extent" (p. 189). Once again Dupin, acting according to his "political prepossessions" as "partisan of the lady" (p. 201), is able to recover the lost text (and replace it with a clever substitute) because he alone can decode the artifice by which the woman has been disem-powered: the male criminal had merely disguised her "letter" to look as if it was his own. And once again this second story acts as a gloss upon the first. The Minister's conscious concealment of the Queen's letter is but the external manifestation of the police's interpretive paradigm, by which they unconsciously define all human action only according to "their *own*"—masculine—"ideas" of it. In Dupin's words, "They have no variation of principle in their investigations." Their unchanging principle is "based upon . . . one set of notions regarding human inge-nuity" (p. 195), and one set of notions, as the "double Dupin" demon-strates, is not enough to accommodate both halves of humanity.

This tale has a new ending, suggesting perhaps that Poe felt he had taken his critique of male-authored fictions to its logical conclusion: the victimized woman lives to benefit from Dupin's recovery of the second story, and the male criminal faces imminent retribution. As Dupin reveals at the end, for "eighteen months the Minister has had her in his power. She has now him in hers—since, being unaware that the letter is not in his possession, he will proceed with his exactions as if it was. Thus will he inevitably commit himself, at once, to his political destruction" (p. 201). Dupin's criticism of the police's interpretive paradigm, how-ever, is obviously not new; it merely rounds out the metaphorical argu-ments begun in "The Fall of the House of Usher." The police's "one set of notions," like the earlier depictions of "half-formed conception" and male-authored texts which failed to convey "but one meaning," repre-sents a blind spot in masculine interpretations of reality that keeps men from seeing how women are victimized. What the men in these tales cannot see, they cannot include in their own "story" of events, but the crime metaphor that provides the basis for Poe's detective tales insists on

500 THE CONTROVERSY OVER GENDER AND SEXUALITY

the criminal nature of such oversights. The death-dealing misogyny of Roderick Usher's narrator differs from the half-formed conceptions of Dupin's newspaper writers and police only in degree, not in effect. The second story, or perhaps finally, the second half of the human story, must be recovered by a mind capable of "looking back, of seeing with fresh eyes, of entering an old text from a new critical direction,"[12] and Poe's solution to the problem of such much-needed "re-vision" is the androgynous mind that had first so terrified Roderick Usher and had finally so distinguished C. Auguste Dupin.

III

I have twice referred to Adrienne Rich's definition of "re-vision" to help explain Roderick's and Dupin's recovery of the second story, so it seems only proper to repeat it here as she originally articulated it: "Re-vision—the act of looking back, of seeing with fresh eyes, of entering an old text from a new critical direction—is for women more than a chapter in cultural history: it is an act of survival. Until we can understand the assumptions in which we are drenched we cannot know ourselves. . . . We need to know the writing of the past, and know it differently than we have ever known it; not to pass on a tradition but to break its hold over us." Read in sequence, "The Fall of the House of Usher" and the three Dupin tales suggest that Poe was considering what [Judith] Fetterley has called "the responsibility of change" and experimenting with the idea of the androgynous mind which would be capable of imaginative re-vision. The androgynous Dupin accomplishes what Roderick Usher so tentatively began, a fully-specified critique of "the imaginative limits" of one-sided male-authored fictions. The end-product of such a critique is the recovery of "the woman's story," which, in the last tale in the sequence, breaks the hold of male domination and finally insures the woman's survival by restoring her honor and her socio-political power.

There is no question that Poe's depictions of acts of physical violence committed against women are particularly gruesome, and some feminist readers might feel that having to encounter such grisly surface details is too big a price to pay to get to the final acts of recovery and restoration Poe seems to have had in mind. A greater stumbling block to any acceptance of Poe as an author capable of feminist sensibility

---

[12] Rich, 35.

must surely be his now infamous statement that "the death . . . of a beautiful woman is, unquestionably, the most poetical topic in the world" (p. 229). Certainly at first glance it would seem to contradict any argument that his tales show an evolving feminist ethos, a growing awareness and renunciation of death-dealing male-authored fictions, and indeed, it appeared a year after "The Purloined Letter," in "The Philosophy of Composition," published in 1846. When feminist critics cite the statement, however, they tend to leave off the second half of the sentence: "—and equally is it beyond doubt that the lips best suited for such topic are those of a bereaved lover."[13] While I do not intend to justify the images of death which Poe habitually chose as a vehicle for his vision, I do believe that the halves of this statement constitute a conceptual whole which is not inconsistent with his use of the androgyny metaphor, and to argue this final point, I will extrapolate from Baym's reading of Hawthorne one last time: "The domain of his work is the male psyche, and throughout his writings 'woman' stands for a set of qualities which the male denies within himself and rejects in others. . . . The ability to accept woman—either as the 'other' or as part of the self—becomes in his writing a test of man's wholeness."[14]

The domain of Poe's work is also the male psyche, and the loss of "woman" throughout his writings represents a halving of "man's" soul, his human potential, and—for the male artist—his imagination. Telling the story of that loss seems to have been for Poe a compelling need, for he told it obsessively again and again and clearly derived a kind of perverse pleasure from doing so. Nevertheless, that such works are cautionary tales is confirmed by the heroic stature of his androgynous heroes. Roderick Usher does come to accept woman both as the "other" and as part of the self, but it is Dupin who stands finally as Poe's greatest achievement. "The double Dupin" represents his creator's fullest expression of the need for wholeness and the need to tell not only the story of loss, but the second story as well: the story of recovery and restoration, "the woman's story." I have to conclude that Poe's ability to tell both stories, or both halves of the human story, is—like Hawthorne's—the sign of what we would today call feminist re-vision.

[13]See, for example, Sandra M. Gilbert and Susan Gubar, *The Madwoman in the Attic: The Woman Writer and the Nineteenth-Century Literary Imagination* (New Haven: Yale Univ. Press, 1979), 25.
[14]"Hawthorne's Women: The Tyranny of Social Myths," *Centennial Review* 15 (1971): 250–51.

LELAND S. PERSON

Poe's Poetics of Desire: "Th' Expanding Eye to the Loved Object"

The author of Aesthetic Headaches: Women and a Masculine Poetics in Poe, Melville, and Hawthorne *(1988) and* Henry James and the Suspense of Masculinity *(2003), Leland S. Person is a professor of English and comparative literature at the University of Cincinnati. In addition to his monographs, Person has edited several important volumes and editions, including (with J. Gerald Kennedy)* American Novels to 1870, *the fifth volume of* The Oxford History of the Novel in English *(2014); The* Cambridge Introduction to Nathaniel Hawthorne *(2007); and the Norton Critical Edition of* The Scarlet Letter *(2005). He is also the coeditor of* Poe Studies: History, Theory, Interpretation, *a journal devoted to Poe scholarship. The 1999 essay that follows was first published in that journal under its earlier title,* Poe Studies/Dark Romanticism.

I take my subtitle for this essay, "Th' Expanding Eye to the Loved Object," from a line in Poe's early poem "Stanzas" (1827), for it concisely characterizes my concern with object relations in his poetry—specifically, with the reflexive power of a "loved object" to create a subject, to "expand" a male "eye," through the medium of the gaze. The self-creative lines of desire in Poe's poetry do not travel straight or unambiguously, however, and I would like to begin with another of Poe's early poems, the 1829 "Alone," because it foregrounds a central problem in his poetics of desire—the problem of unreciprocated desire. "From childhood's hour I have not been / As others were," Poe's speaker claims;

> I have not seen
> As others saw—I could not bring
> My passions from a common spring—
> From the same source I have not taken
> My sorrow—I could not awaken
> My heart to joy at the same tone—
> And all I lov'd—*I* lov'd alone—
> (*PT* 60)

Daniel Hoffman says that in this "confessional meditation" Poe comes close to defining "the essential *Moi* who speaks in his best poems."[1] If

[1] Daniel Hoffman, *Poe, Poe, Poe, Poe, Poe, Poe, Poe* (Garden City: Doubleday, 1972), 31. Robert D. Jacobs, on the other hand, claims that, "[i]f self-expression is the end" in

so, that "essential" self seems constructed out of difference—a sense of different desire, of not being able to "bring" his passions from a "common spring." It is that sense of difference, represented in the desiring subject's vexed relation to its love objects, that I want to explore in some of Poe's poems about women.

In assessing Poe's representations of women and then speculating on the male subjectivity to be inferred from those represented objects, critics commonly begin with his infamous claim in "The Philosophy of Composition" (1846) that "the death . . . of a beautiful woman is, unquestionably, the most poetical topic in the world" (p. 229). They have disagreed, however, over where to place Poe on a misogynist-protofeminist spectrum—that debate often hinging on the issue of how much poetical and other pleasure Poe derived from the deaths of the beautiful women he himself had created. Cynthia Jordan and I have emphasized Poe's representation of male failures to subordinate and silence women, his depiction of female characters who resist objectification and death, because such representations suggest Poe's desire to grant female subjectivity a place in his writing. Joan Dayan has gone the furthest in analyzing the complexities of Poe's representation of women, arguing that he not only "destabilizes any sure identification of women" but also "questions what it means to speak, or to love, as a *man*."[2]

Many recent critics, however, stress the violence that Poe directs toward his female characters—especially the way death serves as a prerequisite for masculine creativity. Scrutinizing the conjunction of women, beauty, and death in Poe's writing, for example, Elisabeth Bronfen argues that his poetics "seem to endorse a spectatorship that ignores the referent, the non-semiotic body[,] and focuses its reading exclusively on the image as a self-reflexive, materialised sign." Paula Kot observes that Poe's aesthetic practice relies upon "silencing" the "feminine Other," even as it demonstrates the "inherently unstable distinction

---

Poe's early poems, Poe himself "is not sure of the self he has to express" ("The Self and the World: Poe's Early Poems," *Georgia Review* 31 [1977]: 639). [All notes in this selection are Person's unless otherwise indicated.]

[2] See Cynthia S. Jordan, *Second Stories: The Politics of Language, Form, and Gender in Early American Fictions* (Chapel Hill: Univ. of North Carolina Press, 1989), 133–51; Leland S. Person, *Aesthetic Headaches: Women and a Masculine Poetics in Poe, Melville, and Hawthorne* (Athens: Univ. of Georgia Press, 1988), 19–47; and Joan Dayan, "Poe's Women: A Feminist Poe?" *Poe Studies* 26 (1993): 1. Dayan observes that, "if women exist at all in [Poe's] letters, tale[s], or poems, they appear to be excuses for [his] continued fascination with himself" (2). However, she goes on to argue, "[u]sing his love letters and poems to repeat romantic cliché, Poe shows how the language of ideal love petrifies the lover as well as his object" (3).

between subject and object, viewer and viewed, male and female, reality and art."[3] Eliza Richards concludes that Poe predicates his poetic power upon women's deaths: "not only do poetic texts thematize the deaths of beautiful women, but beautiful women generate poetic texts." Characterizing Poe's "inherent misogyny," J. Gerald Kennedy considers his "sharply vacillating treatment of dying women"—swinging between idolatry, especially in the poetry, and violent aggression, in the tales—as part of a "neurotic paradigm" in which male "happiness and self-worth [have become] contingent on sustained female affection." In the absence of such affection, Kennedy discovers a conflicted male identity, a "grieving male" who "undergo[es] perpetual self-punishment for the unworthiness implied by the abandonment of the nurturing female" or who exacts revenge for his abject dependency.[4]

I would like to extend these insights into Poe's literary relationship with women by treating the death of a beautiful woman more as the beginning than as the end of his poetics of desire. Poe himself would declare in "The Poetic Principle" (1850) that "Love—the true, the divine Eros—the Uranian, as distinguished from the Dionaean Venus— is unquestionably the purest and truest of all poetical themes" (*ER* 93). Poe's poetry, especially the love poems, reflects the tension that his two claims about the "most poetical" suggest—the death of a beautiful woman, the birth of a vexed and vexing desire. Death and Love—each is the most "poetical," and each depends, in its poetic manifestation, upon desire between subject and object.[5] I want to investigate this tension by bringing together two lines of inquiry: the deconstructive insights into Poe's writing that have accumulated in recent years and

---

[3]Elisabeth Bronfen, *Over Her Dead Body: Death, Femininity and the Aesthetic* (New York: Routledge, 1992), 71; Paula Kot, "Painful Erasures: Excising the Wild Eye from 'The Oval Portrait,'" *Poe Studies* 28 (1995): 1, 4. Where Kot interests herself in the woman, or female object, in "The Oval Portrait," I wish to look at the reciprocal effects that women as objects have on the male subjects in Poe's poetry.

[4]Eliza Richards, "'The Poetess' and Poe's Performance of the Feminine," *Arizona Quarterly* 55 (summer 1999): 7; J. Gerald Kennedy, "Poe, 'Ligeia,' and the Problem of Dying Women," in *New Essays on Poe's Major Tales*, ed. Kenneth Silverman (New York: Cambridge Univ. Press, 1993), 113–29, esp. 113, 126, 117.

[5]In her analysis of Poe's statement that "'the death . . . of a beautiful woman is, unquestionably, the most poetical topic in the world,'" Bronfen reaches a similar conclusion. "The duplicity of the play of imagination that allows for the substitution of death through love," she argues, "such that it encompasses an idea, which allows one to guess at the figure of death beneath that of love, and a desire, which allows one to misrecognise death because what is visibly figured is not death itself but its double, love" (*Over Her Dead Body*, 63).

the gender studies, such as those I have mentioned, that have focused on his representation of women.

Poe's "'truth,'" comments Mutlu Konuk Blasing, is "only a self-authorized or textual truth—that is, a mere duplication and multiplication of the word's original 'untruth,' the spatial-temporal gap between the signifier and the signified."[6] Understanding the textuality, or "writer-liness," of Poe's poetry offers another way of recognizing Poe's narcissism and thereby the essential absence of the women who seem to be the subjects and the objects of his poetic writings. In "The Poetic Principle," for example, Poe rhapsodizes about the occasions when the poet recognizes the "true poetical effect," and follows with a lengthy catalog of objects that "induce" the proper feeling. That catalog concludes with a tribute to women that works itself to a climactic pitch of reverence:

> He feels it in the beauty of woman—in the grace of her step—in the lustre of her eye—in the melody of her voice—in her soft laughter—in her sigh—in the harmony of the rustling of her robes. He deeply feels it in her winning endearments—in her burning enthusiasms—in her gentle charities—in her meek and devotional endurances—but above all—ah, far above all—he kneels to it—he worships it in the faith, in the purity, in the strength, in the altogether divine majesty—of her *love*. (*ER* 94)

Poe had included a very similar passage in "Ligeia" (1838), a "circle of analogies" through which his narrator tries to explain the expression of Ligeia's eyes and the "sentiment" they cause in his imagination.[7] Poe borrows from himself, then, in "The Poetic Principle," and in both cases, it seems to me, there is at least as much emphasis on the male viewer's subjective feelings as on the female object's embodied subjectivity. Put another way, a woman's beauty serves as a narcissistic mirror for reflecting and heightening— "inducing," in Poe's own term—male desire. Since Poe plagiarizes himself in the later passage, however, he

---

[6] Mutlu Konuk Blasing, *American Poetry—The Rhetoric of Its Forms* (New Haven: Yale Univ. Press, 1987), 18.

[7] "I recognized it, let me repeat, sometimes in the survey of a rapidly-growing vine—in the contemplation of a moth, a butterfly, a chrysalis, a stream of running water. I have felt it in the ocean; in the falling of a meteor. I have felt it in the glances of unusually aged people. And there are one or two stars in heaven—(one especially, a star of the sixth magnitude, double and changeable, to be found near the large star in Lyra) in a telescopic scrutiny of which I have been made aware of the feeling. I have been filled with it by certain sounds from stringed instruments, and not unfrequently by passages from books" ("Ligeia," p. 51).

creates a closed circuit of narcissistic desire in which his own prose serves as the "loved object."

In a telling observation of 1843 Poe acknowledged that, while he defined poetry as the "rhythmical *creation* of beauty," it might "more properly" be called a "personification, for the poet only personifies the image previously created by his mind."[8] This is the case in "The Raven," as the bereaved lover torments himself through the ventriloquistic agency of the bird in the absence rather than the presence of the dead Lenore, who exists hardly even as a memory in the involuted game the speaker plays with the raven. Paradoxically, then, Poe writes narcissistically in those places where other-directed desire would seem most warranted. As Bronfen puts it, the "'death of a beautiful woman' marks the *mise en abyme* of a text, the moment of self-reflexivity, where the text seems to comment on itself and its own process of composition, and so decomposes itself."[9] I want to go one step further by focusing not so much on the text as on the male subject who finds his own desiring self decomposing in the absence of a "loved object."

Poe had commented in his preface to *"Tamerlane" and Other Poems* (1827) that the "smaller pieces" in the volume "perhaps savour too much of Egotism" and were written "by one too young to have any knowledge of the world but from his own breast."[10] Intensely self-reflexive in the way this youthful self-criticism suggests, Poe's love poems seem situated on the frontier of desire, at the border between self and other where desire may leave the gravity of the self, as it were, and enter the orbit of the other. This projection, however, poses a reflexive danger for the self: the dissociation of desire threatens a dissociation of identity. If a gendered identity derives from desire—is reflexive or mirrored—then how can a gendered self be constructed if the "other" is absent? Without a love object on which to focus the gaze of its "eye," how does the poetic *I* "expand"? Poe's Tamerlane admits that he "knew not woman's heart" even though he felt "lov'd, and loving," and when he leaves Ada, a "silent gaze" serves as his "farewell" (36)—a gaze, in other words, unable to speak its desire, unable to desire and mirror a male self. As Richards has shown, Poe's "evacuative aesthetic" depends upon "[d]raining" women and women poets of "substance" and transforming them into "marmoreal emblems, momentarily quieted so that

---

[8] Edgar Allan Poe, review of *The Poets and Poetry of America*, by Rufus Griswold, in *The Complete Works of Edgar Allan Poe*, edited by James A. Harrison (New York: Thomas A. Crowell, 1902), 11:225–26.

[9] Bronfen, *Over Her Dead Body*, 71.

[10] Edgar Allan Poe, *The Poets and Poetry of America*, 11: 225–26.

his own work might take center stage." Analyzing "The Raven," Richards notes the speaker's "narcissistic aestheticization of grief," but in figuring Poe's poetics as paradoxically dependent upon an absent woman, I think she does not explore the full extent of his aesthetic narcissism.[11]

As early as "Tamerlane" Poe teases out the vexed connection between desire and absence. Describing the awakening of his "passions" and the tyrannical effect they had on his developing nature, Tamerlane admits that he has "no words, alas! To tell / The loveliness of loving well!" He continues:

> Nor would I dare attempt to trace
> The breathing beauty of a face,
> Which ev'n to *my* impassioned mind,
> Leaves not its memory behind.[12]

In this poem, being or presence—a woman's "breathing beauty"—seems to melt away before the intensity of remembered desire, as if the goal of memory were to create a closed circuit of desire by disassociating the self from any desired "other," leaving desire to focus on itself. The poetic "I," coincident with its desiring "eye," desires itself, so to speak, in absentia. David Halliburton considers "Tamerlane" the "history of a being that negates itself," because "when Tamerlane deprives the other of fulfillment in love, he deprives himself equally." Robert Jacobs, on the other hand, considers Tamerlane "an egotist, like Melville's Ahab, who imposes himself upon what he sees"; his love for Ada "becomes an agency to reinforce his impulse to personal aggrandizement."[13] I certainly agree that "Tamerlane" is a self-absorbed poem, but I think it reveals a deeply conflicted subject, torn between self-centered and object-oriented identity, struggling to find itself desirable.

As much as "Tamerlane" mourns the loss of a woman's love, it investigates the problems of reconstituting and even remembering a self. Tamerlane can recall how his passions "[u]surp'd a tyranny," but he finds it difficult to recall the self that loved. "I have held to mem'ry's

---

[11] Richards, "Poe's Performance of the Feminine," 15.

[12] Person here is drawing on the early version of "Tamerlane" originally published in *Tamerlane and Other Poems* (1827) and there are several variations (including entirely different lines and stanzas) in this much-revised poem between this version and the canonical one, reprinted in this volume—including this stanza. The 1827 version of "Tamerlane" (to which Person refers throughout his discussion of the poem) can be found online at the Poe Society's website: http://www.eapoe.org/works/poems/tamerlna.htm. [Editors' note.]

[13] David Halliburton, *Edgar Allan Poe: A Phenomenological View* (Princeton: Princeton Univ. Press, 1973), 51, 63; Jacobs, "The Self and the World," 648.

eye / One object," he confesses, "until / Its very form hath pass'd me by." Since he has "reach'd to power," Tamerlane notes, other men have inferred his "innate nature" from those passions—his sublimation of desire in power and ambition. But Tamerlane claims that one person lived in his boyhood who perceived a different "innate nature," "[E'en then knew] this iron heart / In woman's weakness had a part" (p. 12). In citing his passage from boyhood to manhood as a disassociation from "woman's weakness," Poe confuses Tamerlane's male self with what it desires, suggesting what psychologists Liam Hudson and Bernadine Jacot call a failure of "dis-identification"—that is, a failure on a male child's part to "separate himself imaginatively from his mother" in order to experience "counter-identification" with his father.[14] Tamerlane seems poised precisely at such a critical moment, enabling Poe to elaborate the problems of short-circuited desire for gender identity formation. It is not only the "breathing beauty of a face" that Tamerlane cannot recall, or "trace." It is passion or desire itself, which he reconstitutes intellectually, transfiguring it as idealizing adoration—a feeling "such as angel minds above / Might envy" (p. 12). In thus externalizing desire and attributing it to angels, Poe separates desire from subjectivity and, the poem reveals, uncouples subjectivity in the process. "I had no being but in thee!" Tamerlane exclaims to Ada:

> All that I felt, or saw, or thought,
> Crowding, confused became
> (With thine unearthly beauty fraught)
> Thou—and the nothing of a name. ("Tamerlane," 1827,
>   section VIII)

Despite Tamerlane's protestations, however, his career when reconstructed in retrospect depends more upon Ada's absence than upon her presence—indeed, upon the narcissistic direction of desire toward the self:

> The passionate spirit which hath known,
> And deeply felt the silent tone
> Of its own self supremacy[.] ("Tamerlane," 1827, section IX)

In Ada's absence, this supreme, phallocentrically configured self becomes the object of its own desire. Driven by ambition, power, and

---

[14] Liam Hudson and Bernadine Jacot, *The Way Men Think: Intellect, Intimacy and the Erotic Imagination* (New Haven: Yale Univ. Press, 1991), 40.

pride, Tamerlane becomes a conqueror and empire builder. In his own words, however, that conquering self—a conquering "worm," it is tempting to call him—is regressive, narcissistic, locked into a developmental stage prior to any "dis-identification." Explicitly, he identifies himself with

> The soul which feels its innate right—
> The mystic empire and high power
> Giv'n by the energetic might
> Of Genius, at its natal hour[.] ("Tamerlane," 1827, section IX)

Internalizing Ada, moreover, Tamerlane uses her as a mirror to reflect and valorize this phallocentric self. He pictures to his "fancy's eye / Her silent, deep astonishment" when she hears that "Fame / Ha[s] gilded with a conquerer's name" the man she still loves. The constancy of reciprocated desire, at least in Tamerlane's imagining, seems to promise continuity of self. But Tamerlane, according to the note Poe furnishes, acquires his renown "under a feigned name"—Alexis (section XII). Even as conqueror, he is already not himself. The remainder of the poem, in fact, tells a tragic story of self-alienation. Even as Tamerlane's "proud hopes" have "reach'd a throne" and he has "clamber'd" to a "tottering height," he recognizes that his "wilder'd heart" is "far away," still identified with Ada (section XVI). Distancing desire from the self, identifying it with its object, Tamerlane loses the power to desire himself in Ada's absence. "Tamerlane" ends on a note of despair, with its hero on his death bed, alienated from a home that is a "home no more," his "broken-heart" drained of desire (section XVII).

"Tamerlane" presents a character, concludes Jacobs, "whose traits, revealed in his examination of his own consciousness, lead logically to ontological disaster—a failure in relation to others, and a consequent failure of the self."[15] Tamerlane's dying predicament seems prophetic, forecasting those of Poe's speakers in so many of his later poems about women. Although his male persona may proclaim in the 1831 "Paean," "I am drunk with love / Of the dead, who is my bride," Poe more often represents the absence—indeed, the disembodiment—of desire. In the second "To Helen" (1848), for example, so spiritualized is his vision of Helen Whitman that the power of the female gaze is defused. The speaker recalls "only the divine light" in her "uplifted eyes" (*PT* 95). In the earlier "Fanny" (1833), the female gaze had the power to kill the

---

[15] Jacobs, "The Self and the World," 652.

male observer, rendering him a "victim on love's altar slain, / By witching eyes which looked disdain." In "To Helen," the woman's gaze, disembodied and emptied of desire, promotes an undesirable and undesiring male self. Haunted though he is by the eyes that "*remained*," that "*would not* go," as he recounts, Poe eagerly becomes "their slave." His "duty," he claims, is "*to be saved* by their bright light" (*PT* 97). Like Tamerlane, this purified male self seems attenuated, as if reflexively mirroring the disembodiment of its love object through what Dayan, writing about "Fairy Land," calls the "desublimation of desire."[16] In "A Paean" Poe's speaker may advertise his love for the woman who lies "All motionless, / With the death upon her eyes," but the loss of a woman's embodied and reciprocally desiring gaze more often vexes male desire and male subjectivity.

Jacobs contends that by 1831 Poe had developed his "mature idiom, which uses rhetorical strategies to create a distance between the self that suffers and the self that tells," but many of Poe's later poems reflect the same problem with dissociated states of being and desire that we have seen in "Tamerlane" and other early poems.[17] In "The Sleeper" (1831), for example, Irene's inert and lifeless body is neither desirable nor desiring, and it leaves the speaker voyeuristically cruising the circumference of her embodied form. Unlike Whitman's twenty-ninth bather, who leaves the safety of her station behind the curtain to frolic fantastically and sexually with the male bathers, Poe's voyeur remains at a distance. Instead of emanating from within as an integral function of the self, desire in "The Sleeper"—while phallocentrically imaged—is disembodied. The poem, in other words, represents a drama of desire and the self, desire and the gaze, rather than a drama of the desiring self and its object. Irene's window may be "open to the night," but it is the "wanton airs"—indeed, the "bodiless airs"—that "Flit through [the] chamber in and out," enacting a gothic play of desexualized intercourse for the voyeuristic speaker. His distance from the sleeping Irene seems a function of fear—of the female body, the physicality of sex and death, a fear of being implicated in his own desires. He prays that Irene's sleep, "Which is enduring, so be deep," and above all that she will remain

---

[16]Joan Dayan, "From Romance to Modernity: Poe and the Work of Poetry," *Studies in Romanticism* 29 (1990): 416. In "Fairy Land," Dayan points out, the lady Isabel "disappears as a possible presence" when the speaker invites her to sit down. "What follows," according to Dayan, "is a move from an overworked, affective nature to an aggressive locus of desire, marked by a chatty meditation on a rose that will be torn asunder" (417), figuring the woman's sex "dismembered" (418).

[17]See Jacobs, "The Self and the World," 658.

asleep and rigidly objectified (p. 17). He fancies a realm of existence in which she will be safe from the physical realities of death and desire:

> I pray to God that she may lie
> Forever with unopened eye,
> While the pale sheeted ghosts go by!
>
> My love, she sleeps! Oh, may her sleep,
> As it is lasting, so be deep!
> Soft may the worms about her creep! (p. 17)

For all his frenzied pursuit of various women (Nancy Richmond, Helen Whitman, Elmira Royster Shelton, Sarah Lewis) toward the end of his life, Poe's late poetry registers a sense of loss—loss of "loved objects" and of the self that loves.[18] At the beginning of "Ulalume" (1847), for example, the speaker emphasizes the self-enclosed nature of his desiring state of mind: "I roamed with my Soul—/ Of cypress, with Psyche, my Soul" (*PT* 89). In this monologic dialogue with his own "soul," Psyche, the speaker, performs a verbal duet much like the student's with the raven. Desire for a "loved object"—the dead Ulalume—returns to the self and finds its object within the speaker's subjectivity in the form of a feminine soul. In "To Marie Louise," published in a less personal version as "To - - -" in the March 1848 *Columbian Lady's and Gentleman's Magazine*, Poe emphasizes the dissociative effects of love.

> Ah, Marie Louise!
> In deep humility I own that now
> All pride—all thought of power—all hope of fame—
> All wish for Heaven—is merged forevermore
> Beneath the palpitating tide of passion
> Heaped o'er my soul by thee. Its spells are broken—
> The pen falls powerless from my shivering hand—
> With that dear name as text I *cannot* write—
> I cannot speak—I cannot even think—
> Alas! I cannot feel.[19]

---

[18] Dayan observes that in the late love poems Poe "analyzes the inevitable reciprocities between the writer and his object of desire. Further, in turning Locke's investigation of personal identity into a question of sexual identity, Poe hopes to analyze what it means to feel love. The feeling is so corrosive that to experience it is to be before and outside any subject, or any object" ("Poe's Women," 4).

[19] As with "Tamerlane," there are multiple versions of this poem. For our edition, we used the published version from the *Columbian Lady's and Gentleman's Magazine* for March 1848. The lines Person quotes here are from an earlier manuscript version. [Editors' note.]

Even though Poe inscribes this love poem to an actual woman, he emphasizes the self-negating rather than self-creating effects of love. As Dayan notes, "Poe's utterance breaks down before the terrible risks of reciprocal desire"; instead of sponsoring creativity, the "palpitating tide of passion" disempowers the self, reducing the male subject to a death-in-life state in which he cannot write, speak, think, or even feel. "To Marie Louise" demonstrates the failure of desire to "expand" the "I" that "eyes" a woman—as if Poe were looking into the magic mirror of self-creative "loved objects" and seeing nothing. Poe's "final ecstasy," in Dayan's words, "encourages the reversal of gender positionings, as the speaker is somehow not yet classifiable fully as either subject or object, masculine or feminine, mind or heart."[20]

Having begun with the 1829 poem "Alone," it seems appropriate to close with two poems from the other end of Poe's career, "Annabel Lee" and "For Annie" (both from 1849). Both commemorate relationships to women. "Annabel Lee" apparently celebrates Poe's marriage to Virginia, although upon its completion he sent the poem to Nancy Richmond, for whom he had written "For Annie." At first glance "Annabel Lee" seems an exception to the argument I have been making. Despite the loss of his "loved object," Annabel Lee, the speaker reaffirms the self-creative ties that remain after death. "[O]ur love it was stronger by far than the love / Of those who were older than we," he asserts, and he continues to feel the "bright eyes" of the "beautiful Annabel Lee." The female gaze, which fails to sustain the male subject in many of Poe's poems, here sponsors continued creative energy. At the same time, internalizing the gaze of this "loved object" causes the speaker to join his "darling" in death, to "lie down," he says,

> by the side
> Of my darling, my darling, my life and my bride,
> In her sepulchre there by the sea[.] (p. 29)

As in "To Marie Louise," the male speaker's love for a woman climaxes in his own living death—his reduction to subject-as-object.

"For Annie" is unique in Poe's canon because, instead of the death of a beautiful woman, it features the death of a beautiful man—Poe himself, or at least his poetic persona—who celebrates his own demise as preferable to "the fever called 'Living,'" which "Is conquered at last" (p. 29). More important, objectifying the speaking subject as a dead

[20]See Dayan, "Poe's Women," 7, 8.

body pacifies and even kills desire—what he calls "that horrible, / Horrible throbbing" that he feels "At heart." The "worst" torture of "all tortures," he exclaims, is

> the terrible
> Torture of thirst
> For the napthaline river
> Of Passion accurst[.] (p. 30–31)

Killing desire by killing its subject enables Poe's speaker to discover an uncommon spring, as it were, from which to bring his passion. Becoming the object rather than the subject of desire, he finds a unique way to desire himself. He quiets the "accurst" torture of embodied passion and so discovers a safer form of desire-spiritualized and attributed to another. His spirit "lies happily," the speaker observes,

> Bathing in many
> A dream of the truth
> And the beauty of Annie—
> Drowned in a bath
> Of the tresses of Annie.
>
> She tenderly kissed me,
> She fondly caressed,
> And then I fell gently
> To sleep on her breast—
> Deeply to sleep
> From the heaven of her breast. (p. 31–32)

Like the raven-haired Ligeia revivified in Rowena, Poe feels reborn, as if he has actually incorporated Annie and her maternal desire—identifying, rather than "dis-identifying," with this maternal figure. After years of "mournful and never-ending remembrance" for absent or deceased women, Poe turns the tables, transgendering himself and playing both gender roles. He can desire and be desired at the same time. His heart, he claims,

> is brighter
> Than all of the many
> Stars in the sky,
> For it sparkles with Annie[.] (p. 32)

Where his heart once throbbed with a "[h]orrible throbbing" (p. 30), it now

> glows with the light
> Of the love of my Annie—
> With the thought of the light
> Of the eyes of my Annie. (p. 32)

Even though in so many other poems the female gaze frightens the speaker, here the power of the gaze has been disarmed—through the counteractive power of the speaker's imagination. In effect, he has incorporated the desire of an "other" subject, entwining it around his own objectified body. He still "loves alone," but he has divided desire so that it can come back to him narcissistically disguised in the desiring look of another. "For Annie," in other words, solves the problem posed in "Tamerlane" and in other poems by creating a circle of desire that operates by some principle of imaginative fusion. Poe becomes the subject of desire by playing possum—impersonating an object. In effect he becomes one of his own female characters, returned from the dead by the desiring gaze of another—an other that is actually himself.

ELIZA RICHARDS

Women's Place in Poe Studies

Associate professor of English at the University of North Carolina, Chapel Hill, Eliza Richards is the author of Gender and the Poetics of Reception in Poe's Circle *(2004) and the editor of* Emily Dickinson in Context *(Cambridge University Press, 2013). Richards publishes frequently on American poetry. The following essay was published in 2000 in the scholarly journal* Poe Studies/Dark Romanticism.

Women are everywhere and nowhere in Poe studies. A sign of this paradox, the figure of the dead woman has occupied Poe scholars of many generations and critical orientations. For some, she serves as a visible reminder of evacuated presence, a vital object of fascination so forceful that she must be neutralized. For others, she memorializes an unacceptable absence that Poe tries to remedy in vain. Either way, she is never fully forgotten, and she threatens or promises to rise again. The focal point of an incomplete process of nullification or resurrection, the dead woman is a symbol that foregrounds its literal referent. In various critical arguments she represents Poe's melancholic attachment to lost mothers; a linguistic "necrophilia," manifested in a compulsive repetition of maternal sounds like "Lenore"; writing as "a form of nympholepsy" that rehearses inscription's deadness and the writer's insatiable longing to enliven the memory of the beloved; thought's slippery and chronic conversions between body and spirit; the male imagination's desire to contain and control "a woman in her most challenging aspect" through aesthetic objectification, and the threatening return of repressed female vitality; the "moment of self-reflexivity" in the text when the figure overrides its reference to a palpable world and thus draws attention to the materiality of signs; a "dependency-desolation-retribution" complex in which Poe's male characters enact violent revenge on women because of their enthralling power; the force of idealized womanhood and its inextricable relation to total subjugation; sentimental discourse's claims to an unmediated transmission of affect, and Poe's sensational exposure of affect's dependence on the letter.[1] In each interpretation, literal and symbolic impulses remain bound in eternal conflict.

Poe biography echoes and underpins this central figure and its interpretations.[2] In narratives of his life, women fuel the writer's imaginative processes: they are his love objects and, therefore, his poetic inspiration. Recall the famous sequence of beloved women that he lost too soon to illness: his mother Eliza; his foster mother Fanny Allan; his childhood friend's mother Jane Stanard (the fabled inspiration for his first poem "To Helen"); his child bride Virginia (the possible inspiration for

---

[1] Citations for these oversimplified summaries of complex arguments are, in (chronological) sequence: Marie Bonaparte, *The Life and Works of Edgar Allan Poe: A Psycho-Analytic Interpretation*, trans. John Rodker (London: Imago, 1949); Mutlu Blasing, "Edgar Allan Poe, the Poet to a 'T,'" in *American Poetry: The Rhetoric of Its Forms* (New Haven: Yale Univ. Press, 1987), 17–35; J. Gerald Kennedy, *Poe, Death, and the Life of Writing* (New Haven: Yale Univ. Press, 1987), 76; Joan Dayan, *Fables of Mind: An Inquiry into Poe's Fiction* (New York: Oxford Univ. Press, 1987); Leland S. Person Jr., *Aesthetic Headaches: Women and a Masculine Poetics in Poe, Melville, and Hawthorne* (Athens: Univ. of Georgia Press, 1988), 23; Elisabeth Bronfen, *Over Her Dead Body: Death, Femininity and the Aesthetic* (New York: Routledge, 1992), 71; J. Gerald Kennedy, "Poe, 'Ligeia,' and the Problem of Dying Women," in *New Essays on Poe's Major Tales*, ed. Kenneth Silverman (New York: Cambridge Univ. Press, 1993), 127; Joan Dayan, "Amorous Bondage: Poe, Ladies, and Slaves" (pp. 346–75); Jonathan Elmer, *Reading at the Social Limit: Affect, Mass Culture, and Edgar Allan Poe* (Stanford: Stanford Univ. Press, 1995), 105–6. [All notes in this selection are Richards's.]

[2] Among the most important and comprehensive biographies of Poe are Hervey Allen, *Israfel: The Life and Times of Edgar Allan Poe* (New York: Farrar and Rinehart, 1934); Arthur Hobson Quinn, *Edgar Allan Poe: A Critical Biography* (1941; reprint, with an introduction by Shawn Rosenheim, Baltimore: Johns Hopkins Univ. Press, 1998); and Kenneth Silverman, *Edgar A. Poe: Mournful and Never-Ending Remembrance* (New York: HarperCollins, 1991). In *Collected Writings of Edgar Allan Poe*, vol. 1, Poems, T. O. Mabbott meticulously reconstructs the biographical circumstances surrounding Poe's poems, suggesting how crucial the knowledge of those circumstances has been for poetic interpretation.

"Annabel Lee"). Recall still other, frequently rehearsed, romantic interests: the enchanting, tubercular, childlike poetess Frances Sargent Osgood, whose name threads through a valentine poem by Poe; Marie Louise Shew, "The Beloved Physician," who nursed Poe's dying wife and then Poe in his grief, and whose initials entitle "To M. L. S."; Poe's Providence fiancée Sarah Helen Whitman, the subject of the second "To Helen"; Nancy Richmond, the young woman to whom Poe wrote begging for solace near the end of his life, and the anesthetizing healer in "For Annie." In each case, the life story and the poem reciprocally inform each other so that they are difficult, if not impossible, to separate.

By naming the poems after women he knew and the women he knew after his poems, Poe encourages the synthesis, and critics and biographers follow in his stead. Consolidating the link between Poe's life and letters, for example, T. O. Mabbott, in his definitive edition of the poems, fills in the blanks in Poe's titles with the names and initials of historical women. Though critical interpretations may diverge, they frequently identify Poe's ruptured psyche as the origin of his literary portrayals of men and women who are locked in a dynamic where one may live only at the expense of the other; the figure of the dead woman alludes, however obliquely, to the biographical mythology. Though biographical fascination with Poe may seem to be a naive or outdated indulgence, the 1999 International Poe Conference in Richmond, Virginia, included a trip to visit Jane Stanard's grave (among others).[3] The tombstone to which Poe returned remains a landmark to his female idolatry to which we turn. The thirty-something mother, probably unsuspecting of young Poe's devotion and his future fame, could not have dreamed that perennial busloads of strangers would visit her grave for a reason outside the purview of her own imagination. Something about Poe, and Poe studies, depends upon women, even as this dependence transmutes women into a figure of Woman that resides firmly within a space designated as Poe's mind. In order to inspire their own exegesis, by Poe or his critics, women need to remain silent.

This silence is particularly striking because a large number of highly verbal women, both literate and loquacious, surrounded Poe during his lifetime; indeed, some of the women who appear in his poems as mute objects of adoration were themselves prolific poets. Though they appear in Poe biographies, these women and their writings rarely enter Poe criticism without evoking a summary dismissal. This dismissal is espe-

---

[3] International Poe Conference, Richmond, Virginia; 7–10 October 1999.

cially notable since Poe himself responded at length to their work: much of his practical criticism, especially in his later years, was devoted to women writers from both sides of the Atlantic. A brief perusal of the Harrison edition produces reviews of works by Elizabeth Barrett Browning, Lucretia Davidson, Margaret Davidson, Amanda Edmond, Elizabeth Ellett, Hannah Gould, Sarah Josepha Hale, Felicia Hemans, Mary Hewitt, L. E. L., Stella Lewis, Mrs. R. S. Nichols, the Honorable Mrs. Norton, Frances Sargent Osgood, Catherine Sedgwick, Lydia Sigourney, Elizabeth Oakes Smith, and Amelia Welby (*Complete Works*, vols. 8–13). The Library of America edition of Poe's essays and reviews includes his comments on the work of other prominent women writers of the time, including (but not limited to) Elizabeth Bogart, Maria Brooks, Lydia Maria Child, Emma Embury, Margaret Fuller, Caroline Kirkland, Anne Lynch, and Ann Stephens.[4] Poe's interactions with this set of peers extend far beyond his criticism. While he was editor of the *Broadway Journal,* he frequently devoted the lead position to a woman's poem, often one that alluded to his relationships with women.[5] Poe wrote about women writers; he wrote to women writers; women writers contributed heavily to both the journals that he edited and those to which he contributed; he attended the literary salons of women writers; he became romantically involved with women writers. Individual cases of influence, such as the indebtedness of "The Raven" to Elizabeth Barrett's "Lady Geraldine's Courtship" have been noted, but Poe's engagement with women's writings was far more extensive and has gone largely unexplored.[6]

[4]Edgar Allan Poe, *Essays and Reviews,* ed. G. R. Thompson (New York: Library of America, 1984).

[5]Poe was assistant editor of the *Broadway Journal* by the end of February 1845 and sole editor by 25 October 1845 (Silverman, *Mournful and Never-Ending Remembrance,* 244, 274). A woman's poem occupies the lead position on 30 August, 6 September, 4 October, 1 November, 8 November, 15 November, and 29 November 1845.

[6]In an eloquent 1993 footnote, Joan Dayan describes a gap in Poe studies that persists: "Poe's women suffered oblivion and, known only through his work, were not, until recently, studied through their own literary productions. It's time that we substituted for Wagenknecht's *Man Behind the Legend* projects revealing 'the Women Behind the Legend.' Think about what it would mean to reread Poe from the ground of those women he read, wrote about, and wrote to. For example, read Poe's 'Eleonora' in the context of Frances Sargent Osgood's 'Ermengarde's Awakening,' or reconstitute Poe's 'love poems' through a careful reading of Sarah Helen Whitman" ("Poe's Women: A Feminist Poe?" *Poe Studies* 26 [1993]: 12 n. 24). I am currently completing a book that explores Poe's lyric exchanges with his female contemporaries. . . . For articles on that subject, see Eliza Richards, "'The Poetess' and Poe's Performance of the Feminine," *Arizona Quarterly* 55 (1999): 1–29; that article includes an examination of the relation

Nor did Poe's intimate connection to women writers end with his death, for the women who figured so prominently in his biography were important sources for it. The women writers whom Poe promoted promoted him in turn, especially after his death. Judging from *Poe's Helen Remembers* and *Building Poe Biography*, John Carl Miller's informative collections of source materials for John Ingram's landmark writings on Poe, women were among the most voluble and valuable contributors to the posthumous recuperation of Poe's literary reputation.[7] Sarah Helen Whitman's contribution was by far the most significant, rivaling Ingram's own. Ingram's "Providence" (as he addresses her in their extensive correspondence), Whitman provided him with original manuscripts by Poe; she recounted her conversations and interactions with Poe; she offered interpretations of the poet's works and of significant events in his personal and professional life; she also evaluated information from other sources. Her pivotal defense of Poe, *Edgar Poe and*

---

between Barrett's "Lady Geraldine's Courtship" and Poe's "Raven." See also Eliza Richards, "Lyric Telegraphy: Women Poets, Spiritualist Poetics, and the 'Phantom Voice' of Poe," *Yale Journal of Criticism* 12 (1999): 269–94.

On Poe's interactions with Frances Sargent Osgood, see Mary De Jong, "'Read Here Thy Name Concealed': Frances Osgood's Poems on Parting with Edgar Allan Poe," *Poe Studies* 32 (1999): 27–40; and De Jong, "Lines from a Partly Published Drama: The Romance of Frances Sargent Osgood and Edgar Allan Poe," in *Patrons and Protégées: Gender, Friendship, and Writing in Nineteenth-Century America*, ed. Shirley Marchalonis (New Brunswick: Rutgers Univ. Press, 1988), 31–58. On Osgood's "Life Voyage" as possible source for Poe's "Annabel Lee," see Buford Jones and Kent Ljungquist, "Poe, Mrs. Osgood, and 'Annabel Lee,'" *Studies in the American Renaissance*, ed. Joel Myerson (Charlottesville: Univ. Press of Virginia, 1983), 275–80. See also John Reilly's rebuttal in "Mrs. Osgood's 'The Life-Voyage' and 'Annabel Lee,'" *Poe Studies* 17 (June 1984): 23. In *Aesthetic Headaches*, Person argues that Poe's portrayal of female characters in his fiction manifests a "powerful if anxious attraction to the creative possibilities of relationship"; in support of his assertion Person cites Poe's epistolary exchange with Sarah Helen Whitman, in which Poe "grants her the power as the reader of his words to confirm his identity as a writer" (22). Her power as writer awaits fuller analysis; I begin such an exploration in "Lyric Telegraphy." Noelle Baker argues for a reevaluation of Whitman's achievements that goes beyond her association with Poe in "'This Slender Foundation . . . Made Me Immortal': Sarah Helen Whitman vs. Poe's Helen," *Poe Studies* 32 (1999): 8–26. In an essay stressing the "'worldliness'" of Poe's "biographical and fictional" existence, Person offers a historical perspective on Poe's gender representations (both masculine and feminine). Though he concentrates on measuring "Poe's female characters against the standard of True Womanhood" and the alternative "New Woman," Person notes Poe's personal and professional relationships with women, including his criticism of women writers. See "Poe and Nineteenth-Century Gender Constructions," in *A Historical Guide to Edgar Allan Poe*, ed. J. Gerald Kennedy (Oxford: Oxford Univ. Press, 2001), 129–65, esp. 131, 133–34.

[7] *Poe's Helen Remembers*, ed. John Carl Miller (Charlottesville: Univ. Press of Virginia, 1979); *Building Poe Biography*, ed. John Carl Miller (Baton Rouge: Louisiana State Univ. Press, 1977).

His Critics, written in response to Griswold's slander, inspired Ingram's later project.[8] Early Poe biography and criticism, whose mythologizing tendencies have profoundly influenced the tradition of Poe studies, is, to an unexamined degree, a product of women's memories, fantasies, and desires. We would learn much from exploring how they shape Poe's future reception, and, indeed, how Poe shapes his own reception by finding ways to appeal to a sympathetic female readership.[9]

These multiform interactions between Poe and women writers raise an overarching, twofold question: how could this extensive engagement not have a significant impact on his work and its reception, and why is that impact so rarely noted and almost never studied? While it may be overly simplistic to suggest that critics have actively exchanged the articulate woman for her marmoreal form in order to silence her, it is nevertheless true that critics have persistently literalized Poe's attraction to women writers, foregrounding their physical appeal at the expense of their words. An extreme but illustrative example is John Walsh's case for Fanny Osgood's illegitimate Poe-child, which is primarily based on textual evidence—the exchange of poems in the *Broadway Journal* orchestrated by Poe, known for his hoaxes; other published flirtatious writings by Osgood, known for her verbal coquetry; the mysterious bundle of letters that disappeared before we could read them; the gossip of Elizabeth Ellett and others.[10] Why, we might ask, is the possibility of a bodily child more intriguing than the possibility that a verbal exchange could provoke a scandal and invoke a paternal Poe? The conversion of scandal to an illegitimate child annuls investigation into the erotic powers of Poe's and Osgood's writing and the ways verbal eroticism fuels magazine circulation. It also forecloses the investigation of

---

[8]Sarah Helen Whitman, *Edgar Poe and His Critics* (1860; reprint, New York: Gordian Press, 1981), (see. pp. 285–90). In the reprint's introduction, Oral Sumner Coad tells us that "Mrs. Whitman wrote the first sound and informed appraisal of this complex personality, and one that still commands respect for its independence, its insight, and its balance, and not less for the generosity of spirit that called it into being" (19). Quinn calls it, "the first book in [Poe's] defence—which still remains not only a convincing personal tribute but also one of the most sympathetic and brilliant interpretations of his poetry and fiction" (*Edgar Allan Poe*, 572).

[9]Kent Ljungquist and Cameron Nickels gather and analyze Elizabeth Oakes Smith's comments on Poe in "Elizabeth Oakes Smith on Poe: A Chapter in the Recovery of His Nineteenth-Century Reputation," in *Poe and His Times: The Artist in His Milieu*, ed. Benjamin Franklin Fisher IV (Baltimore: Edgar Allan Poe Society, 1990), 235–46.

[10]John Evangelist Walsh, *Plumes in the Dust: The Love Affair of Edgar Allan Poe and Fanny Osgood* (Chicago: Nelson-Hall, 1980); De Jong explores some of the professional implications of the exchange in her "Lines."

the ways that gossip and scandal emerge from and motivate this burgeoning print medium.

One might even argue that the force of erotic attraction toward women's bodies stands in for and suppresses an even stronger attraction to and repulsion from their words. Poe's criticism of women writers offers another productive area of inquiry that is persistently deferred. When this body of work is not ignored entirely, which is frequently the case, it is dismissed with an intriguingly self-contradictory line of commentary: Poe is one of our most adept and astute early critics, but his judgment is fatally compromised when it comes to women writers. Critics assume that Poe was either paid to puff them, blinded by physical attraction, or simply out of his mind when it came to his assessment of female accomplishment. In Daniel Hoffman's words, Poe's

> own standards were not only high but a little odd: he couldn't keep himself from overpraising poetesses who wrote elegies to dead lovers, finding in the effusions of such nobodies as Mrs. Amelia Welby and Elizabeth Oakes Smith the nearly articulated intimations of the theme which became the sole burden of his own verse, and its undoing.

On the other hand, Hoffman claims that "Poe on poetic principles makes a lot of good sense."[11]

While Hoffman peremptorily dismisses the poetesses as unimpressive "nobodies," one need not look beyond his own characterization to postulate that serious consideration of their work might deepen our understanding of Poe. Hoffman suggests that Poe identifies so strongly with his female peers that he experiences the affinity as uncanny. In Hoffman's formulation, women operate as Poe's subconscious, on which he relies to intimate the ideas he eventually articulates. Such a formulation should open rather than foreclose inquiry about how ideas originate, and whether they emerge from within or outside of an individual subjectivity. Rather than accept Hoffman's absorption of the poetesses into Poe's own mental processes, we might return to the women's work to see what inspires Poe's interest. Hoffman's enforced disjunction

---

[11] Daniel Hoffman, *Poe Poe Poe Poe Poe Poe Poe* (Garden City: Doubleday, 1972), 96–97. I discuss this dismissive tendency and assess Poe's criticism of women writers in "Poe's Performance of the Feminine." With the goal of determining whether Poe was a "systematic critic," Ashby Bland Crowder examines his criticism of women writers and concludes that "there seems to be no significant difference between Poe's application of his critical standards to male and female authors" ("Poe's Criticism of Women Writers," *University of Mississippi Studies in English* 3 [1982]: 116).

between Poe's practical criticism and his critical principles begs the question of their precise relation. This particular uncoupling stands out because of the usual emphasis on a reciprocally informing relationship of literal and abstract thinking in Poe studies, as we have seen in the figure of the dead woman. Instead, in this specific case, the dismissal of Poe's admiring comments on women's writing stands in contrast, perhaps in direct inverse proportion, to the stress on the significance of his distilled poetic principles. This specific exception suggests that Poe's canonical status depends in some way on women writers' exclusion.[12] What might we say about canon formation if we examined the dynamic relation between the two bodies of work?

The tendency to ignore Poe's relations with women writers has become increasingly inexplicable with the renewed interest in his relation to the literary marketplace, which from Poe's own time has been personified in the figure of the female scribbler. The scribbler's prolixity and indiscriminacy provides a verbal register of the promiscuities of the free market, simultaneously mirroring it, expressing it, and profiting from it. Recent work continues to align women writers with the forces of commercialism against which genius must struggle: Ann Douglas's *Feminization of American Culture*, Michael Gilmore's *American Romanticism and the Marketplace*, and David S. Reynolds's *Beneath the American Renaissance* are landmark versions of this configuration.[13] At the same time, critics have sought to complicate this oppositional model, exploring the way that material and cultural conditions informed the literary output of antebellum writers. Given these tendencies, one would think that Poe's engagements with women writers might be analyzed for evidence of his immersion in market culture; for his attempts to harness their profit-making capabilities; for his desire to engage a popular audience. Does Poe apprentice himself to women writers? How does he modify their practices? Do the exchanges between Poe and women writers suggest a symbiotic, an adversarial, or some other kind of relationship? Surprisingly, these questions have not been asked or answered in studies of Poe's relation to the marketplace. Terence

---

[12]Meredith McGill suggests as much in a recent conference paper: "In Poe's account, women's poetry is essential to the coherence of the high male canon without necessarily being proper to it" ("'The Ruins of Shelley': Poe, Elizabeth Barrett Browning, and Poetic Inheritance," paper presented at the annual meeting of the American Literature Association, Baltimore, May 1999).

[13]Ann Douglas, *The Feminization of American Culture* (New York: Knopf, 1977); Michael Gilmore, *American Romanticism and the Marketplace* (Chicago: Univ. of Chicago Press, 1985); David S. Reynolds, *Beneath the American Renaissance: The Subversive Imagination in the Age of Emerson and Melville* (New York: Knopf, 1988).

Whalen's recent book-length study, *Edgar Allan Poe and the Masses*, for example, discusses Poe's ambivalent relation to market culture and scrutinizes a range of his interactions with male contemporaries without noting a single interaction with a woman writer. Jonathan Elmer's *Reading at the Social Limit* begins to explore the subject in his provocative analysis of the dialectical relation between Poe's sensational and Sigourney's sentimental literary forms, without exhausting the topic.[14] Cultural studies of Poe explore his engagement with the ideas of his times, but the ideas of his female contemporaries are consistently excluded from consideration. On what basis are some cultural relations dismissed, and others valorized? Shouldn't that basis bear re-examination?

How would the critical landscape shift if we considered the possibility that Poe was as earnest in his criticism of women writers as he was in his assessment of his male peers, for when was he fully in earnest? What would happen if we were to factor into an understanding of his critical perspectives his assertion that Elizabeth Oakes Smith's "Sinless Child" "*narrowly missed*" being the greatest American poem? That if the "greatest poems have not been written by women, it is because, as yet, the greatest poems have not been written at all"?[15] Even if one accepts the common critical assumption—itself meriting critical examination—that Poe applied a different set of criteria in judging works by women than he used in his assessment of his male peers, then that double standard should signal a starting point for investigation rather than grounds for dismissal of a significant portion of his work. These questions may arise in part because many of the women writers who interested him were poets, and recent cultural studies of Poe have not discussed Poe's devotion to poetry, which rivaled or even overshadowed his interest in prose. Surely the stir surrounding "The Raven" was one of the key moments in Poe's rise to celebrity and critical acclaim during his time. Why, then, are studies that focus on Poe's professional engagements with the literary marketplace restricted to his prose?

Poe's literary figuration of women has set the tone for the critical gestures that pursue it. Time and time again, his poems and stories draw

---

[14]Terence Whalen, *Edgar Allan. Poe and the Masses: The Political Economy of Literature in Antebellum America* (Princeton: Princeton Univ. Press, 1999); Elmer, "Poe, Sensationalism, and the Sentimental Tradition," chap. 2 of *Reading at the Social Limit*, 93–125.

[15]Poe, "Elizabeth Oakes Smith" and "Editorial Miscellanies," in *Essays and Reviews*, 911, 1114.

our attention to women's significant silence, and we, in turn, pay tribute to that silence by explicating it in the text, or visiting it on the tour. But Poe's sustained and significant engagement with women writers and their works might lead us to wonder, particularly in the light of recent attention to Poe's place in the literary culture of his time, how an examination of his multifaceted dialogue with his female contemporaries could contribute to current discussion of his work. Exploring such a topic would tell us much about the creation of the mythic Poe (that inconsolable mourner of lost women), that myth's significance for Poe criticism, and more generally, the cultural transmission of ideas and the formation of American literary history.

JOSEPH CHURCH

"To Make Venus Vanish": Misogyny as Motive in Poe's "Murders in the Rue Morgue"

A scholar of nineteenth-century American literature, Joseph Church is an associate professor in the English Department at the State University of New York, Binghamton. He is the author of Transcendent Daughters in Jewett's Country of the Pointed Firs *(1994) and of several essays on nineteenth-century American literature and culture. The 2006 essay that follows was originally published in the* American Transcendental Quarterly.

Despite his otherwise unconventional ways, in his personal life Edgar Allan Poe held the most conventional early nineteenth-century views about the subordinate place of woman in man's world. As Ernest Marchand concludes, "in all matters touching women, sex, marriage, 'morals,' no more conventional-minded man than Poe ever lived" (35). Poe makes explicit his assumptions about women's subservience in his remarks about their proper education:

The business of female education with us, is not to qualify a woman to be head of a literary coterie, nor to figure in the journal of a traveling coxcomb. We prepare her, as a wife, to make the home of a good, and wise, and great man, the happiest place to him on earth. We prepare her, as a mother, to form her son to walk in his father's steps, and in turn, to take his place among the good and wise and great. . . . Her praise is found in the happiness of her husband, and in the virtues and honors of her son. Her name is too sacred to be profaned by public breath. She is only seen by that dim doubtful light, which, like "the majesty of darkness," so much enhances true dignity. (*Complete Works* 8:14–15)

In his writings as critic and journalist, Poe assails powerfully intellectual women who esteem the "head" and ignore his orthodox strictures: according to Burton R. Pollin, Poe routinely mocks the "successful, professional woman," and thus derides Margaret Fuller, for example, as "absurd," a victim of a "fine phrenzy" (49–50). Ashby Bland Crowder observes in "Poe's Criticism of Women Writers" that Poe considered female writers in America "at best a mediocre lot" (111) and quotes his complaint that "'literary women . . . are a heartless, unnatural, venomous, dishonorable set, with no guiding principle but inordinate self-esteem'" (118 n26). In his own poetry and fiction, as readers have long noted, Poe often depicts the suppression or annihilation of women who because of overpowering beauty, intellect, or wealth depart from the conventional and threaten man's superior position. As Eliza Richards succinctly puts it, "Poe's male characters enact violent revenge on women because of their enthralling power" (10). Reviling signs of her autonomy, Poe understands woman as essentially subordinate to man, in Margaret Fuller's proto-Sartrean terms, "*for man*" (19). He reviles the autonomous woman in this world. Of course at times Poe idealizes some women, but he always requires that they lose their lives to serve an interest of man. In "Poe on Women: Recent Perspectives," Michael J. S. Williams helpfully details these interests and calls attention to Joseph Moldenhauer's representative argument that Poe's protagonists typically "'murder their beloved and lovely women . . . in order to further their perfection *as objets de virtu*'" (34). Addressing Poe's own psychological maneuvering, many critics, such as Marie Bonaparte, Elisabeth Bronfen, J. Gerald Kennedy, and Diane Long Hoeveler, convincingly argue that his hostile dramatizations in fact allegorize his efforts to subordinate elements of his psyche associated with woman— all that to him stands over against intellect and reason, above all, emotion, sensuality, the body—and that his psychological and social attitudes, bordering on misogyny, thus reinforce one another.[1]

---

[1] See Elisabeth Bronfen's *Over Her Dead Body: Death, Femininity and the Aesthetic*, J. Gerald Kennedy's "Poe, 'Ligeia' and the Problem of Dying Women," and Diane Long Hoeveler's "The Hidden God and the Abjected Woman in "The Fall of the House of Usher.'" [All notes in this selection are Church's.]

Recently, however, some have attempted to show Poe as actually enlightened about the plight of woman in the nineteenth century. In *Aesthetic Headaches: Women and a Masculine Poetics in Poe, Melville, and Hawthorne*, Leland S. Person, Jr., asserts that Poe challenges the premises of "conventional masculinity by demonstrating its weakness or impotence in the presence of strong women" (175). In "Poe's Women: A Feminist Poe?" Joan Dayan, after describing his several idealizations of dead women, asks, "But what are we to do with Poe's bleeding, raped, decapitated, dead, and resurrected women, brutalized, buried, cemented in cellars, and stuffed up chimneys?" She answers, "Poe is after nothing less than an exhumation of the lived, but disavowed or suppressed experiences of women in his society. . . . he lays bare the mechanics of cultural control in the Anglo-American experience" (10). And in *Second Stories: The Politics of Language, Form, and Gender in Early American Fictions*, Cynthia S. Jordan sees in Poe's work an "evolving feminist ethos, a growing awareness and renunciation of death-dealing, male-authored fictions" (150–51). Jordan, concentrating on his narratives of detection in her essay "Poe's Re-Vision: The Recovery of the Second Story," writes, "In the Dupin tales . . . in which the task of solving crimes against women calls for a detective with an awareness that other men lack, the androgynous Dupin becomes virtually a feminist critic. In Dupin, Poe created a new caretaker of social and political order, and Dupin fulfills these responsibilities by going beyond the imaginative limits of the male storytellers around him and recovering the second story — 'the woman's story' — which has previously gone untold" (p. 490).

I believe these conclusions mistaken. Far from working as a "feminist critic" to disclose the gendered "mechanics of cultural control" and to tell woman's untold story, Poe and his avatars such as Dupin work to punish and silence womankind in the world and its correlatives in the mind that threaten a masculinist ontology. We discern this unambiguous enterprise of suppression in a closer examination of Dupin's part in "The Murders in the Rue Morgue." Although less-sanguine commentators than Person, Dayan, and Jordan have called attention to the psychological hostility toward women in the tale, none has adequately set forth the extent of its misogyny. Bonaparte ultimately reduces the story's murder of two women to a fantasy of a Freudian "primal scene" (445). Terry J. Martin view the deaths through the lens of Dupin's "lack of mental proportion," his intellectual one-sidedness, that sets him in severe opposition to women generally; hence, Martin holds that the tale's murdered mother, whose "head is severed from her body, . . . vividly portrays Dupin's failure to integrate thought and feeling" (41–42). And in "The Psychology of 'The Murders in the Rue Morgue,'" J. A. Leo Lemay envisions the attacks on the women as primarily symbolizing the deleterious consequence of modern humankind's sexual repression. Lemay clarifies some of the psychological machinations, especially the unconscious doubling, in the story, but he deplorably errs when he claims that the women bring their murders upon themselves: "by their deliberate suppression of sexuality, by their denial of the body, [they] have created the monster who kills them" (186).

Most know the events in "Murders in the Rue Morgue": the brutal and evidently motiveless deaths of a Parisian mother and daughter have baffled the police until the brilliant Auguste Dupin solves the crimes by deducing and demonstrating that a sailor's escaped orangutan has carried out the carnage. Often overlooked, however, is the tale's leaving the women's deaths strangely unpunished. The man mistakenly arrested for the murders, the bank clerk Le Bon, of course gains instant release. The orangutan, a blameless creature, obtains a new home along the Seine in the Jardin des Plantes. And the sailor, although indirectly involved, proves guiltless, as Dupin insists from the first: "'Cognizant . . . of the murder'" although "'he was innocent of all participation in the bloody transactions'" (p. 152). The sailor even gets a "very large sum" (p. 157) from the Jardin for the animal. Women murdered, men rewarded and going free (the orangutan is a male; the name itself Malaysian for "man of the woods")—one suspects the likelihood of misogyny. Indeed, a closer reading of "The Murders in the Rue Morgue" reveals not only an intense ambivalence toward women in the tale but also Dupin's and the narrator's (and by extension Poe's) own misogynistic satisfaction in the deaths of the mother and daughter. In fact Poe's self-disclosing narrative depicts both Dupin's and the narrator's identifying with the sailor and his orangutan and their bloody deeds. Representing the author's interests, the men's aims differ only superficially in their object: Dupin would attack woman primarily in the world, the narrator in the psyche.

Although Lemay reaches a different conclusion, he makes a convincing argument that "the sailor and the orangutan are a double for Dupin. That also means, of course, that they are doubles for one another; and since Dupin is a double for the narrator, all four characters are symbolic doubles" (170). A risk of seeing too much doubling, however, is the loss of responsibility for action (no one is responsible for an act). Lemay goes on to argue that the two women also function as doubles of the four males: "all three sets of characters are symbolic doubles" (171). He claims that, combined, the six equal one genuine being in Poe's mind: the "implied final unity of the three couples—Dupin and the narrator, Madame and Mademoiselle L'Espanaye, and the sailor and the orangutan—suggests the proper ingredients of what, in Poe's vision, constitutes an achieved unified life" (173). But this conflation re-eliminates the women as such and makes investigation and ascription of responsibility for their murder futile.

Poe's great "analyst" (p. 128), Dupin, prefers an all-male world of the intellect—he lives hermetically with the narrator ("We existed within ourselves alone" [p. 132])—and in this realm where "mind struggles with mind" (p. 130), he exults in and excels at competitively establishing his mental superiority over other men. Poe's protagonist rises superior because together with his great reasoning powers he possesses a "*truly* imaginative" (p. 131) sensibility, an "ingenuity" that derives from his whole being, as it were, head and body both. He deems this imaginative acumen a male power, for when he bests the superficially rational Prefect of Police, he mocks the unimaginative man as castrated: "'I am satisfied at having defeated him in his own castle. . . . the Prefect is somewhat too cunning to be profound. In his wisdom is no stamen. It is all head and no body, like the pictures of the Goddess Laverna'" (p. 158). Dupin's attraction to events in the Rue Morgue involves more, however, than his competition with the Prefect: given his biases, and those of his creator, he must see in the circumstances of these two women, and modern women generally, their possession of new powers—intellectual, material, and sexual—and therein must experience an excruciating affront to man's, but above all, his own superiority.

In his satirical criticism Poe often attacks intellectual women, the so-called bluestockings, as, for example, in "Fifty Suggestions," where he writes, "When we think very *ill* of a woman, and wish to *blacken* her character, we merely call her 'a *blue*-stocking'" (*Complete Works*, 14:170). One notes the menace in his emphasized "black" and "blue." In "Murders in the Rue Morgue" he symbolizes the women's doomed association with intellect by having them, like Dupin and the narrator, reside on the top floor of their building, and, then, as Lemay suggests, allegorizing man's reasoning powers vanquishing woman's "mind" (171). Instructively, Poe locates meaningful, rational discourse in the two men and limits the two women to "'shrieks'" and "'screams'" (pp. 135, 137). In the tale the often insolvent Poe also takes aim at woman's material wealth. His Dupin could take no joy in learning that the mother and her daughter "have money" (p. 137) and own the large house in which they have lived. Dupin himself leads a materially impoverished life. Of an "illustrious family" (p. 131) now reduced to penury, he exists frugally on a "small remnant of his patrimony" (p. 131), a son forced in modern times to subsist on the resources of a fallen father. Again, given his masculinist philosophy, he must hold that these women, a mother and daughter and thus matrilineal, wrongly possess wealth and power and a future properly belonging to men, to fathers and sons patrilineally. Poe's tale in fact mocks the legitimacy of Madame L'Espanaye's wealth by several times repeating the rumor that she "'told fortunes for a living'" (p. 137), thus contrasting her fraudulent use of the mind to gain "fortunes" with Dupin's virtuous reasoning. And it is to the point that the women not only receive a large sum of money from the bank (delivered by Le Bon) just before their murder but also receive that sum in testicle-like sacks: the daughter "'took from [Le Bon's] hands one of the bags, while the old lady relieved him of the other'" (p. 138), as if the arrogant women have appropriated phallic power. From the standpoint of Dupin their illegitimate affluence and its attendant powers warrant a punishing attack.

Dupin also loathes these women because he could scarcely countenance their evident indifference if not antipathy toward men. One such as he must expect that women subordinate themselves to man, but in this case he finds the mother and daughter self-reliant. In this tale Madame L'Espanaye has no husband, her daughter no father, and, we learn, some years earlier the mother had summarily expelled their one male tenant for an "'"abuse of the premises"'" (p. 137). In short, the women apparently consider themselves superior to and satisfied without men: as their laundress recalls, the "'old lady and her daughter seemed on good terms—very affectionate towards each other'" (p. 137). This affection between the two obliquely hints at homoerotic values, women who have one another and need no man, and accordingly, in Poe's prejudicial handling, their family name—L'Espanaye—resonantly betokens "Lesbian." Lemay, too, notes this similarity (174), but he then works his way into a disturbing contradiction when he argues that although the women likely exist as lesbians they enact a "deliberate suppression of sexuality, by their denial of the body" (186). How is it that lesbianism and sexuality exclude one another? Yet he uses this argument to claim that the murderous orangutan symbolizes a kind of "return of the repressed," retribution for the women's fear of eros, their "continual suppression of the body and sex" (186). Lemay concludes, "The psychological level of the story suggests that a man's penis is the bludgeoning instrument of death. Not, to be sure, a real penis—but such a one as might exist in the imagination of a severely repressed female neurotic" (186). In a woman's mind? or in a man's? Poe's?

On the face of it Dupin himself shows no interest in eros, but he must assume that desirous man—made desirous by woman—succeeds with and subordinates her when and where he pleases. The story anatomically symbolizes this mastery when it has the gendarme remembering his "'endeavoring to gain admittance'" to the "'gateway'" of the "'screaming'" (p. 137) women: "'Forced it open, at length with a bayonet. . . . Had but little difficulty in getting it open, on account of its being a double or folding gate. . . . The shrieks were continued until the gate was forced—then suddenly ceased'" (p. 137). However, if women provoke but will not satisfy desire—as the L'Espanayes evidently will not (this mother, prima facie sexual, needs no man)—they stand superior to men. A portion of the tale's epigraph, taken from Browne's *Urn-Burial,* reads, "What song the Syrens sang . . . although puzzling questions, are not beyond all conjecture," indicating Poe's interest in probing and mastering the debilitating temptation of women. When Dupin observes, "'it is possible to make even Venus herself vanish from the firmament by a scrutiny too sustained, too concentrated, or too direct'" (p. 142), he ostensibly praises indirect means of analysis, but he leaves in place the idea that "direct" action, of the sort the orangutan takes, will make Venus vanish. Indeed, the animal does seek to make the mother and daughter disappear, throwing one out the window, shoving the other up the chimney. Insofar as Dupin identifies with the sailor and his "beast" (p. 155), he himself has resorted, however symbolically, to direct action, signifying in this case his frustration with more cerebral stratagems.

"The Murders in the Rue Morgue" carefully associates Dupin's avatars—the sailor and his male animal—with man's physical, sexual conquest of women. An hour before the murders, the mariner has been on a "sailors' frolic" (p. 155) in Paris; in the meantime, the orangutan has broken free and, with the returning sailor in pursuit, found the mother and daughter "in their night clothes" (p. 156). In Borneo the sailor had "passed into the interior on an excursion of pleasure" where he captures and takes "exclusive possession" of the orangutan, a creature of "intractable ferocity" (p. 155). The imagery implies that his taking sexual pleasure has brought to life an interior beast, one now requiring reconfinement because too-insistently demanding expression. On the night of the frolic in Paris, the sailor secludes the animal but returns to find "the beast occupying his own bed-room, into which it had broken from a closet adjoining, where it had been, as was thought, securely confined. Razor in hand, and fully lathered, it was sitting before a looking-glass, attempting the operation of shaving, in which it had no doubt previously watched its master" (p. 156). In this strange scene it appears as if the orangutan, shaving in the bedroom, grooms himself for his own frolic. Tellingly, he then makes his way to the dwelling of two women who scorn men: in an explosion of sexual symbolism he kills them, again, as if in punishment for their power, here not in material wealth (he leaves the gold lying on the floor), but in sexual autonomy.

While its master looks through the window to get at the "interior" (p. 156) not of Borneo but woman's dwelling, he witnesses in voyeuristic "anxiety" (p. 156) the beast let loose. The animal mounts a sexual psychodrama, attacking the women, rifling their drawers (implying underclothes), and hurling their bedding to the floor. With his phallus/razor he sets out to shave Madame L'Espanaye, "flourishing the razor about her face, in imitation of the motions of a barber" (p. 157). In his "The Psychology of 'The Murders in the Rue Morgue,'" Lemay views this scene as a symbolic rendering of a woman's own self-destruction. He notes that the figure of an imitative monkey's wielding a razor and cutting its own throat has a long tradition in humorous broadside ballads, insists on the woman's being a "severely repressed neurotic" (186), and preposterously concludes that "Madame L'Espanaye psychologically and symbolically decapitated herself . . . the orangutan's shaving is thus a splendid analogue for the murders" (184). But the episode in fact signifies Poe's misogyny, for in the brutal shaving he depicts the animal's now treating the resisting woman as if she were a counterfeit man. The tale thus mocks and punishes the women for aspiring to be men when they should be sexually subservient, just as it punishes them for appropriating man's treasured sack when they should be materially subordinate. When the animal sees blood (and all that would imply for eros), he uses the razor to decapitate the mother, signifying that, unlike man, she cannot possess both body and head. In further symbolical castrations he shatters "all the bones of the right leg and arm" (p. 140), and, turning to the daughter, chokes her in such a way that her "tongue [is] partially bitten through" (p. 140)—an image of self-castration forced upon her—enragedly punches her abdomen/womb (a "large bruise was discovered upon the pit of the stomach" [p. 140]), and finally thrusts her feet-first up the chimney. In her reading of this scene, Bonaparte emphasizes the maternal character of the room and argues that the chimney represents the mother's "vagina" (454), her "inner genital region" (455), but given Poe's misogyny we have to see the chimney as phallic and the daughter's inverted position an image of her being mockingly reborn via man.

As we should expect, Dupin tries to exculpate this ravage, blaming the women's screams for having "had the effect of changing the probably pacific purposes of the Ourang-Outang into those of wrath. . . . The sight of blood inflamed its anger into phrenzy" (p. 157). Such palliation, here only halfheartedly advanced (how can "probably pacific purposes" exist in a beast of "intractable ferocity"?), recurs more emphatically throughout "Murders in the Rue Morgue." For example, Poe's protagonist tentatively hypothesizes that the mother "could have first destroyed the daughter, and afterward have committed suicide" (p. 144). He rejects this solution for obvious reasons, noting that he speaks "'of this point chiefly for the sake of method'" (p. 144), but importantly he leaves the possibility openly declared: that the women killed themselves (no men responsible), a conclusion Lemay lamentably subtilizes when he argues that "Psychologically, the L'Espanayes cut off their own heads" (186). To the extent that an ultimately blameless animal carries out Dupin's interests, it is not surprising to hear the tale speculate that in hurling the mother from the room and hiding the daughter in the chimney even the beast may have been "conscious of having deserved punishment" and thus "desirous of concealing its bloody deeds" (p. 157). But the insistence on qualified innocence receives its greatest emphasis in Dupin's repeatedly asserting the sailor's innocent part in the women's death. He has good reason to do so if he sees in the man and animal his own culpable hostility toward women. We hear Dupin's self-referential and self-exculpating identification with the animal's owner when he declares to him, "'I perfectly well know that you are innocent of the atrocities in the Rue Morgue. It will not do, however, to deny that you are in some measure implicated in them. From what I have already said, you must know that I have had means of information about this matter—means of which you could never have dreamed. . . . You have done nothing which you could have avoided—nothing, certainly, which renders you culpable'" (p. 155). These "means of information," beyond the obvious reference to Dupin's acumen, I take to signify an identification, one heard when the Parisian Dupin confides, "'A Frenchman was cognizant of the murder'" (p. 152), one speaking French "'of a Parisian origin'" (p. 154).

Further evincing this identification is the uncanny way in which Dupin, reflecting upon the evidence, rapidly reconstructs the murders, even specifying the type of animal and the nationality of its master. Of course Poe's hero takes pride in drawing inferences and seeing into the thinking of others—says the narrator, "He boasted to me . . . that most men . . . wore windows in their bosoms" (p. 132)—but in this case he demonstrates an almost preternatural identification with the sailor. When he places a public notice directed to the attention of that man, Dupin not only readily envisions but bizarrely ventriloquizes his response: "He will reason thus:—'I am innocent; I am poor; my Ourang-Outang is of great value. . . . Should [the police] even trace the animal, it would be impossible to prove me cognizant of the murder, or to implicate me in guilt on account of that cognizance. Above all, *I am known'*" (p. 153). The emphasized words hint at self-disclosure, perspicacious Dupin's awareness that in the sailor's and orangutan's actions he sees his own interests. It is suggestive that he confides to the creature's master, "'I almost envy you the possession of him; a remarkably fine, and no doubt a very valuable animal. . . . I shall be sorry to part with him'" (p. 154). Dupin's name itself hints at doubling and division (duplicate, duplicity, duping), and early on the narrator wonders if his companion in fact possesses a "Bi-Part Soul": "I amused myself with the fancy of a double Dupin," perhaps the product of a "diseased intelligence" (p. 132). In this characterization of Dupin Poe self-reflexively hints at his own anxieties concerning a "diseased" mind, and represents that worry in the story's central clue, the nail that only appears to secure the women's window: this nail seems like any other, just as a human might seem like his or her fellows, but in fact, Usher-like, it possesses an invisible "'fissure'" in its "'head portion'" (p. 147).

Working to eliminate such anxieties at their source, Poe's tale emphasizes the initially baffling lack of motive for the murders—"'The police are confounded by the seeming absence of motive . . . that startling absence of motive in a murder so singularly atrocious as this'" (pp. 143, 150)—and then has Dupin's revelations dispose of the question entirely (apart from involving the blamelessly instinctual behavior of an animal). As Martin observes, "Dupin goes so far as to deny the idea of motive altogether. . . . The overall effect of his analysis is thus to negate all moral responsibility for the murders and utterly diminish their significance" (40). Yet Dupin's own misogynistic interests go far toward explaining if not the immediate reasons for, then at the least the man's satisfactions in, the deaths of women who have intellectual, material, and sexual power. Significant is the fact that Dupin shows neither sympathy for the victims nor interest in involving himself in this apparently "insoluble mystery" until he learns that "Le Bon had been arrested and imprisoned" for the murders. The narrator observes, "It was only after the announcement" of Le Bon's incarceration that the analyst "seemed [singularly] interested in the progress of this affair" (p. 141). Dupin has a personal connection to the bank clerk ("'Le Bon once rendered me a service for which I am not ungrateful'" [p. 142]), and now motivated to acquit this wrongly accused good man (Le Bon) and all men, including himself, Poe's analyst quickly resolves the crimes, makes pointless the question of motives, and thus releases all the men from responsibility. In effect the murders no longer count as criminal acts; the women's deaths go unpunished.

But what specific satisfaction has the narrator gained from the deaths of these women? Events in the tale suggest that the narrator has come to doubt his own masculinity, fears that he increasingly occupies woman's assumed position of subordination viz. his companion, and consequently identifies himself with the "powerful man" (p. 140), i.e., the orangutan, who destroys and rids the dwelling (psyche) of woman. The tale's epigraph includes an unusual reference to Achilles: "What song the Syrens sang, or what name Achilles assumed when he hid himself among women, although puzzling questions, are not beyond *all* conjecture" (p. 128). Poe's narrator, troubled at what he takes to be womanly attitudes arising within, fantasizes himself an Achilles among women, in other words, a powerful man merely and necessarily in the temporary guise of a woman. The man has come to Paris in the spring upon a brief visit when he meets and finds himself instantly captivated by Dupin. The narrator confesses, "I felt my soul enkindled within me by the wild fervor, and the vivid freshness of his imagination. . . . I felt the society of such a man would be to me a treasure beyond price; and this feeling I frankly confided to him" (p. 131). Indeed, he yields himself to Dupin's every "freak of fancy": "into this [*bizarreries*] . . . I quietly fell; giving myself up to his wild whims with a perfect *abandon*" (p. 132, Poe's italics). Clearly he has subordinated himself to the more masterful Frenchman, and in the symbolism of this tale has accepted the woman's position.[2] In a way the hyper-competitive Dupin, cheerful castrator of the Prefect, permits no other relation.

On an evening just before the murders the two men have been walking when Dupin suddenly enacts upon the narrator one of his pre-ternatural feats of mind-reading. "He boasted to me . . . that most men . . . wore windows in their bosoms," the narrator has said, but now it is his turn to be penetrated by an analyst who demonstrates "intimate knowledge" (p. 132) of the man's inner world. Part of what Dupin dis-

---

[2]See J. A. Leo Lemay's detailed argument for the "homosexual romance" (172) between Dupin and the narrator. It is also telling that Poe's narrator appears drawn to the "not [altogether] unprepossessing" (p. 154) sailor. He confides, "I pitied him from the bottom of my heart" (p. 155), but expresses no such compassion for the brutalized women.

closes involves the narrator's thinking about "Epicurus" (p. 134) and by association sensual pleasure, but the content is less important than the fact that Dupin can enter the interior of the narrator but the latter cannot do the same with his companion. The narrator finds himself in the passive/receptive position. And on that same evening the narrator gets knocked to the ground by a passerby but remains unable to assert an objection: he tells how a "fruiterer, carrying upon his head a large basket of apples, had nearly thrown me down" (p. 133); Dupin firmly corrects him, saying the fruiterer in fact "'thrust you upon a pile of paving-stones . . . [You] slipped, slightly strained your ankle, appeared vexed or sulky, muttered a few words . . . then proceeded in silence'" (p. 134). Immediately following the narrator's being knocked down and penetrated, the two companions become engrossed in—"arrested" (p. 135) by—the newspaper's account of the murdered women. Given Dupin's investment in these events, we can now surmise that in them the narrator gains from Dupin's penetrating attention being diverted, identifies with a lethally "powerful man," and symbolizes the annihilation of woman within his psyche. He would make Venus vanish within himself.

Poe suggests that Dupin himself risks and resists association with internal femininity. Poe's analyst triumphs in his interpretations because of reason and imagination, but in his metaphysics he must link the latter, with its endless variability, to woman as such. Thus he has the problem of how to be powerfully imaginative without being a woman. "Murders in the Rue Morgue" evasively addresses this dilemma and consequent anxiety by identifying Dupin with the orangutan and then tentatively associating the animal with androgyny. People at the scene of the murders recall having heard strange articulations: "'Could not be sure whether it was the voice of a man or of a woman'"; "'Could not be sure if it was a man's voice. It might have been a woman's'"; "'Was sure that the shrill voice was that of a man'" (p. 138); "'Might have been a woman's voice'" (p. 138). Poe's protagonist, too, when aroused, expresses himself in a shrill voice ("his voice . . . rose into a treble" [p. 132]). As Jordan approvingly deduces, Dupin himself herein evinces an androgyny ("crossing gender boundaries"), especially "when he recounts the experience of a female victim" (15). But for men in Poe's work this uncertainty about gender in fact signals both in the mind and in the world a danger not a desideratum. When in the tale it is demonstrated with certainty that the perpetrator is in fact a blame-less wild beast with the strength of a "very powerful man" (p. 140)—indeed, explicitly a "He"—all the men obtain deliverance, the women unrequited annihilation. And insofar as Poe represents his interests in those of these men, he convicts himself of a blameworthy misogyny.

WORKS CITED

Bonaparte, Marie. *The Life and Works of Edgar Allan Poe: A Psycho-Analytic Interpretation.* New York: Humanities, 1971.

Crowder, Ashby Bland. "Poe's Criticism of Women Writers." *University of Mississippi Studies in English* 3 (1982): 102–19.

Dayan, Joan. "Poe's Women: A Feminist Poe?" *Poe Studies* 26:1–2 (1993): 1–12.

Fuller, Margaret. *Woman in the Nineteenth-Century and Other Writings.* Oxford: Oxford UP, 1994.

Jordan, Cynthia S. *Second Stories: The Politics of Language, Form, and Gender in Early American Fictions.* Chapel Hill: U of North Carolina P, 1989.

Lemay, J. A. Leo. "The Psychology of 'The Murders in the Rue Morgue.'" *American Literature* 54:2 (1982): 165–88.

Marchand, Ernest. "Poe as Social Critic." *American Literature* 6 (1934): 28–43.

Martin, Terry J. "Detection, Imagination, and the Introduction to 'The Murders in the Rue Morgue.'" *Modern Language Studies* 19:4 (1989): 31–45.

Moldenhauer, Joseph. "Murder as a Fine Art: Basic Connections between Poe's Aesthetics, Psychology, and Moral Vision." *PMLA* 83 (1968): 284–97.

Person, Leland S., Jr. *Aesthetic Headaches: Women and a Masculine Poetics in Poe, Melville, and Hawthorne.* Athens: U of Georgia P, 1988.

Poe, Edgar Allan. *The Complete Works of Edgar Allan Poe.* 17 vols. Ed. James A. Harrison. New York: AMS, 1965.

———. "The Murders in the Rue Morgue." *Tales of Horror and Suspense.* Mineola, NY: Dover, 2003.

Pollin, Burton R. "Poe on Margaret Fuller in 1845: An Unknown Caricature and Lampoon." *Women & Literature* 5:1 (1977): 47–50.

Richards, Eliza. "Women's Place in Poe Studies." *Poe Studies* 33:1–2 (2000): 10–14.

Williams, Michael J. S. "Poe on Women: Recent Perspectives." *Poe Studies* 26:1–2 (1993): 34–40.

VALERIE ROHY

Ahistorical

Author of Lost Causes: Narrative, Etiology, and Queer Theory *(2014),* Anachronism and Its Others: Sexuality, Race, Temporality *(2009), and* Impossible Women: Lesbian Figures and American Literature *(2000), Valerie Rohy is professor and chair of the Department of English at the University of Vermont. She has published extensively on gay/lesbian studies, queer theory, and nineteenth- and twentieth-century American literature, and coedited* American Local Color Writing, 1880–1920 *(1998). The following essay was first published in 2006 in* GLQ: A Journal of Lesbian and Gay Studies.

> They are always there, specters, even if they do not exist, even if they are no longer, even if they are not yet.
>
> —JACQUES DERRIDA, *Specters of Marx*

Along the way to its gothic conclusion, "Ligeia" (1838) produces one of the strangest bedroom scenes in American literature. In the tale that Poe declared "undoubtedly the best story I have written," a nameless narrator endures the loss of his first wife, Ligeia, and the death of her hapless replacement, Rowena, before witnessing an impossible revival.[1] As he watches at her deathbed, Rowena's shrouded form stirs, rouses, and relapses into a lifeless state as "time after time, until near the period of the gray dawn, this hideous drama of revivification was repeated" (p. 60). Recounting the various acts of this drama, the impatient narrator would "hurry to a conclusion" (p. 60), but Poe takes his time. The cycle of "alarming recurrence" that began with Rowena's illness ends only when, the narrator reports, "the thing that was enshrouded advanced boldly and palpably into the middle of the apartment" (pp. 57, 60), in so doing revealing that the body has become Ligeia's.

This last indelible image of Ligeia rising from Rowena's deathbed cannot, however, match the spectacle that we do not see directly. Proving that there were *two* women in that bed, Poe's conclusion retroactively reveals a queer intimacy. Now we see why, as Rowena strained for

---

[1] Poe's remark on "Ligeia" appears in Arthur Hobson Quinn, *Edgar Allan Poe: A Critical Biography* (New York: Appleton-Century, 1941), 496. [All notes in this selection are Rohy's.]

life, "each agony wore the aspect of a struggle with some invisible foe" (p. 60), if not why that foe got rather more than friendly. Ligeia bends Rowena's body to her will in a corporeal exchange whose rhythms of excitation and exhaustion can hardly be understood outside the realm of the sexual.[2] Attentive to the symptoms of Rowena's arousal, the narrator reports: "There was now a partial glow upon the forehead and upon the cheek and throat; a perceptible warmth pervaded the whole frame" (p. 59). The "warmth," the "glow," the flush, the sighs, the "tremor," and the "pulsation" announce an event, he says, of "unspeakable horrors"—a moment of intercourse between two women who share one body (pp. 59, 60). Prefiguring later tropes of lesbian sexuality, their relation appears as a predatory form of occult possession, companion of arcane horrors and half-seen monsters.[3]

There needs no ghost come from the grave, though the odds of that are good, to tell us that a Poe story is perverse. But the apparition of queer sexuality in "Ligeia" raises the epistemological stakes in a text already consumed by not knowing. From its first line, "I cannot, for my soul, remember" (p. 48), to its ending, regarded as a "mystery" (p. 50) by Poe's narrator and generations of skeptical readers, "Ligeia" is about uncertainty. As if forgetting were the precondition of remembering, the labor of narration begins under the sign of lack, founded on that "I cannot." In life, Ligeia is as obscure as the apparition she will become; after years spent studying her "expression," the narrator finds himself unable to "define that sentiment, or analyze, or even steadily view it" (p. 50). In death, she returns in "wild visions," as "shadowlike" as the scene of resurrection that the narrator will insist he "distinctly saw" but also "might have dreamed" (pp. 58, 59, 60). Like the spectacle of that return, the text's queer effects resist empirical proof. As Ligeia's spirit enters her body, Rowena sighs and stirs, but what does that mean? The scene seems sexual, but *it cannot be*. It shows a weird intimacy between women, but *surely we are imagining it*. It is impossible—and yet, as the narrator wonders at Rowena's revival, "Why, *why* should I doubt it?" (p. 60). Is lesbian sexuality more implausible

[2] Other readings that discuss lesbianism in "Ligeia" are Ralph J. Poole, "Body/Rituals: The (Homo)erotics of Death in Elizabeth Stuart Phelps, Rose Terry Cooke, and Edgar Allan Poe," in *Soft Canons: American Women Writers and Masculine Tradition*, ed. Karen L. Kilcup (Iowa City: University of Iowa Press, 1999), 239–61; and Camille Paglia, *Sexual Personae: Art and Decadence from Nefertiti to Emily Dickinson* (New Haven: Yale University Press, 1990), 338–39.

[3] See Andrea Weiss, *Vampires and Violets: Lesbians in Film* (New York: Penguin, 1993), 85; and Patricia White, *Uninvited: Classical Hollywood Cinema and Lesbian Representability* (Bloomington: Indiana University Press, 1999), 63.

than Poe's gothic plot, more preposterous than metempsychosis and the resurrection of the dead?

In historical terms, perhaps it is. Despite the appearance of sapphic love in nineteenth-century French novels—Balzac's *Girl with the Golden Eyes* and Théophile Gautier's *Mademoiselle de Maupin* were both published three years before "Ligeia"—in 1838 the lesbian had been neither named as such nor conceptualized as "a personage, a past, a case history."[4] Poe's tale comes nearly half a century before the first mentions of female homosexuality in American medical journals and much longer before scholarly notions of queer theory and queer desire.[5] How then can we know that the eerie frisson of "Ligeia" is not a backward projection of contemporary concerns? What can protect the reader from the careless assumption of "an ahistorical, or transhistorical, homosexuality"?[6] What indeed, since the uncanny return, the temporal reversal, and all that is dismissed as ahistorical in much recent criticism are precisely what makes Poe's text so queer. I mean to take such historical questions seriously, not to avoid charges of anachronism but to meet them, by examining the anachronism that operates in "Ligeia" and in queer literary history. Poe's lesbian effect is an optical illusion, visible only from one historical vantage point, but just the same it hangs before our eyes. Turning to "Ligeia," I want to hold that angle of vision, neither denying nor confirming what it seems to show, because my subject is not, finally, the truth value of the lesbian effect in Poe's tale but the angle of vision itself. Such a reading cannot speak to history, but it can speak to historicism. A historically "illegitimate" approach may suggest how "Ligeia" anticipates and proleptically answers questions about historical illegitimacy—may suggest, that is, how its anachronistic narrative structure and its invitation to a certain backward glance address queer theory's temporal concerns.

How can the text's perversity be so elusive and so obvious? Nothing could be less mysterious than the "mysteries of the will" described in Poe's epigraph. Woman, as they say, will have her will, and Ligeia is all will, all appetite. That this desire, purportedly a lust for life, must signify as sexual needs no witness but Will Shakespeare, whose sonnets turn

---

[4]Michel Foucault, *The History of Sexuality*, trans. Robert Hurley, vol. 1 (New York: Vintage, 1990), 43. On Balzac and Gautier see Lillian Faderman, *Surpassing the Love of Men: Romantic Friendship and Love between Women from the Renaissance to the Present* (New York: Morrow, 1981), 264–68.

[5]Carroll Smith-Rosenberg, *Disorderly Conduct: Visions of Gender in Victorian America* (New York: Knopf, 1985), 272.

[6]Estelle B. Freedman, "The Historical Construction of Homosexuality in the United States," *Socialist Review* 25 (1995): 31.

on the bawdy pun: "will" as wish or purpose, as male or female genitals, as carnal desire. In the words of sonnet 135, Ligeia has "*Will* to boot, and *Will* in overplus"; she is nothing if not too much.[7] The double double entendre of the epigraph, "the will therein lieth, which dieth not" (p. 47), sets Ligeia's body and desire against the narrative closure conventionally found in death and consummation. Although her return cannot last—the narrator tells us early on that she "is no more" (p. 48)—she is always excessive, always so much more. Her "gigantic volition" renders Ligeia "more than womanly" (pp. 51, 53), and in the old phallic sense of *will* it can hardly do anything else. But she need not be so well endowed to overstep the narrow bounds of nineteenth-century feminine propriety, for she is a woman of "immense," "astounding" learning—with an intellect, the narrator says, "such as I have never known in woman" (p. 51)—and exempt from the law of the father, unmarked by a "paternal name" (p. 48).

Both more and less than womanly, Ligeia makes a mockery of motherhood. While Rowena's rhythm of climax and collapse evokes sexual intercourse, this sequence of spasmodic "struggle" followed by "terrific relapse" also conjures labor and childbirth (p. 60). In an 1839 letter to Poe, Philip P. Cooke took the hint, remarking on the image of Ligeia's spirit "quickening *the body of the Lady Rowena*."[8] That "quickening" registers a grotesque pregnancy, in which Ligeia is both the child born out of Rowena's body and the paternal agent of insemination. Changing the deathbed to a ghastly parody of the childbed, Ligeia mimes birth in the service of death and of an impossible, still more deathly life: this woman giving birth to herself delivers not the future but the past. Small wonder that Ligeia has a vexed relation to heterosexual love, even by the generous standards of Poe's oeuvre. The narrator, for his part, explains that his wife's will to live reflects only her "idolatry" for him: "In Ligeia's more than womanly abandonment to a love, alas! all unmerited, all unworthily bestowed, I at length, recognized the principle of her longing, with so wildly earnest a desire, for the life which was now fleeing so rapidly away" (p. 53). This tangled passage credits Ligeia's vitality to her heterosexual devotion; it claims that her eventual return from the dead bespeaks a normal love, however

---

[7] *The Riverside Shakespeare*, ed. G. Blakemore Evans (Boston: Houghton Mifflin, 1974), 1774. On Shakespeare's notion of *will* see Joel Fineman, *Shakespeare's Perjured Eye: The Invention of Poetic Subjectivity in the Sonnets* (Berkeley: University of California Press, 1986), 26–28, 292–93.

[8] Quoted in I. M. Walker, ed., *Edgar Allan Poe: The Critical Heritage* (New York: Routledge and Kegan Paul, 1986), 112.

abnormal its proportions. Her conjugal bond, the narrator argues, forms the governing premise of her lust for life, the premise that her will to live merely imitates or allegorizes. Yet predicting the final moment when a revived Ligeia will cast off her veil, "shrinking from [his] touch" (p. 61), he admits that her love for him is at best a dim echo of her "eager vehemence of desire for life — *but* for life" (p. 52).

If the perversity of Poe's bedroom scene seems gratuitous, an accidental side effect of the "real" narrative, that apparent insignificance recalls the narrative function of lesbian sexuality. In the heterosexual plot whose favorite end is reproduction, female homosexuality is at best irrelevant (a meaningless by-product of the plot) and at worst obstructive (a detour that delays or obviates its conclusion). Regarded as endlessly unproductive, it cannot be an end in itself. Ligeia may have her reasons to claim Rowena's body, but the effect of lesbian eros born of their encounter becomes the obscene waste material of a story that in the end has no use for it. In fact, the shadow of queer enjoyment in "Ligeia" misdirects the plot at the moment of its most crucial turn. Peter Brooks has argued that delay, deviance and bad object choice belong to the middle of narrative structures, where they work to delay closure.[9] Such heteronormative conventions, Judith Roof writes, reduce sexual deviance to useless foreplay, a time of lingering "in the field of pleasure that constitutes part of the narrative's 'détour.'"[10] In Brooks's view, this detour serves narrative closure by deferring it and thus rendering the postponed conclusion more satisfying. But this is so only when the narrative obstacle, like a youthful delinquency or infatuation, cedes its place in due time to proper ends. The hetero narrative, Paul Morrison suggests, resists "any teleology that is simply for pleasure, any sexual economy in which pleasure does not work toward its own effacement."[11] Like the "gigantic" will that drives it, the lesbian effect of Poe's text exists "simply for pleasure," detached from narrative aims. To go on in defiance of sexual norms is to go back; desires that cannot die signal a malignant cycle of return. If in the wake of the AIDS crisis straight culture has figured gay male sexuality as a lively death wish, Poe represents Ligeia's desire as a morbid life wish.

---

[9] Peter Brooks, *Reading for the Plot: Design and Intention in Narrative* (New York: Knopf, 1984), 98–100.

[10] Judith Roof, *Come as You Are: Sexuality and Narrative* (New York: Columbia University Press, 1996), 36

[11] Paul Morrison, *The Explanation for Everything: Essays on Sexual Subjectivity* (New York: New York University Press, 2001), 62.

As plainly as "Ligeia" bears the hallmarks of deviance, the collocation of these terms with each other and with lesbian desire, not to say
lesbian identity, belongs to the twentieth century. Such rare qualities
would not have signified in 1838 what they might have meant a half
century later, when sexology found female masculinity symptomatic of
sexual inversion, or still later, when the refusal of motherhood joined
the diagnostic rubric. Early-nineteenth-century American culture would
have judged as deviant any woman whose appetites so far exceeded
heterosexual ends, but not until the twentieth century were reproductive status and gender identity taken as expressions or determinants of
object choice and sexual identity.[12] A lesbian reading of "Ligeia" cannot
then make Ligeia a lesbian, nor can a queer reading make her queer,
since history precludes any trace of desire that in 1838 would answer to
those more modern names. Instead, a backward, "ahistorical" approach
offers an occasion to revisit the time lines of queer literary history: the
straight-arrow rhetoric against anachronism, the turn back toward retrospection and queer temporality, the Victorian association of sexual
deviance with temporal deviance, and contemporary queer accounts of
identification, anachronism, and alterity. Directing our eyes to anamorphic images—forms intelligible only when viewed aslant—"Ligeia"
offers an allegory of its own reading, including the queer reading structured by temporal obliquity. Seen from the wrong time, Poe's story
confronts the modern reader with an instance of *historical* anamorphosis, and with it a refracted view of the strategic anachronism through
which queer theory has lately adjusted the angle of its gaze on the past.

ALWAYS HISTORICIZE?

The queer past was overdetermined from the first, not least by the
reparative impulse of "making up lost time," from whose pathos the
most rigorous historicism is not exempt.[13] Inspired by visions of those

---

[12] Judith Halberstam contests the conflation of gender identity and expression with
sexual object choice in *Female Masculinity* (Durham: Duke University Press, 1998),
45–73.

[13] Laura Doan and Sarah Waters, "Making Up Lost Time: Contemporary Lesbian
Writing and the Invention of History," in *Territories of Desire in Queer Culture: Refiguring Contemporary Boundaries*, ed. David Alderson and Linda Anderson (Manchester:
Manchester University Press, 2000), 13. On issues in queer history and historiography
see also Susan McCabe, "To Be and To Have: The Rise of Queer Historicism," *GLQ* 11
(2005): 119–34; Annamarie Jagose, *Inconsequence: Lesbian Representation and the Logic
of Sexual Sequences* (Ithaca: Cornell University Press, 2002), 8–24; Lisa Duggan, "The
Discipline Problem: Queer Theory Meets Lesbian and Gay History," *GLQ* 2 (1995):

silenced in former ages, queer scholars sought to discover loves, in the words of one landmark book, "hidden from history."[14] As Michel Foucault has argued, however, the past's continuity with the present cannot be assumed. Attentive to historical alterity, the dangers of metanarrative, and the disjunction between an earlier register of homosexual acts and a modern rubric of gay identity, queer criticism has largely translated Foucault in a cautionary tone.[15] It warns against the hasty assumption of commonalities between present and past same-sex desires and refuses as "ahistorical" or "anachronistic" readings that would project modern concepts back in time. In this logic, historicism, now broadly cognate with social constructionism, becomes the hallmark of progressive politics. Hailed as the universal defense against universalism, historicism promises respect for difference, particularity, and pluralism where the ahistorical would impose tyrannical conformity.

To grasp the influence of this argument, one need only track the recurrence of the words *ahistorical* and *anachronistic* in the queer criticism of the past fifteen years. The rise of historicist methodologies in queer literary studies in the 1990s brought a set of apotropaic gestures—the perfunctory nod to historical cautions, the pointed aside on a rival's anachronism, the dutiful apology for an unavoidable retroversion—that by now have been honed and condensed to a stylized, almost *purely* gestural form. Where the ahistorical is concerned, distinguished scholars from widely different critical positions seem to share a common language. When Eve Kosofsky Sedgwick notes that the "modern view of lesbians and gay men as a distinctive minority population is of course importantly anachronistic in relation to earlier writing," we are asked to remember something that *of course* everyone already knows (and to remember that we already know it), because, however wellknown, this important point must endlessly be acknowledged.[16] . . .

179–91; and Jennifer Terry, "Theorizing Deviant Historiography," *differences* 3, no. 2 (1991): 55–74.

[14] See Martin Bauml Duberman, Martha Vicinus, and George Chauncey Jr., eds., *Hidden from History: Reclaiming the Gay and Lesbian Past* (New York: New American Library, 1989); and Foucault, *History of Sexuality*, 42–44.

[15] I have no quarrel with the notion of historical alterity; indeed, I will suggest that anachronism is most valuable precisely when it stages an uncomfortable confrontation with alterity. However, the common conflation of historicism, social constructionism, and the notion of alterity, like the conflation of the ahistorical and the anachronistic, produces a Manichaean scheme in which any unorthodox reading of temporality can be accused of stupidly positing a past identical to the present.

[16] Eve Kosofsky Sedgwick, *Epistemology of the Closet* (Berkeley: University of California Press, 1990), 51. As Sedgwick notes in a later essay, historicism often seems to appreciate the contingency of everything except itself. I borrow a phrase from her

From this point of view, the dangers of anachronistic projection might be personified in Poe's narrator, who in his yearning for the past abandons fact for "the suggestion of a vivid imagination" and allows his "labors" to take "a coloring from [his] dreams" (p. 58, 55). But what else might "Ligeia" tell us about history and retrospection? What makes anachronism so "appalling" and "relentless" a threat? And how might queer theory interpret the desire and disgust underlying notions of the ahistorical? Such questions do not deny the value of queer literary history, nor do they presume that all accounts of the past can be equally credible. Rather, they speak to the critical discourse in which something called historicism is defended as the sole ethical possibility and something called the ahistorical is denounced by a shaming rhetoric whose vehemence seems at times to outstrip its object. Queer reading requires attention to historical specificity, but it does not demand a defense of an authentic past against the violation of backwardness.

It is worth noting the tendency, in that defensive effort, to treat *ahistorical* and *anachronistic* as synonymous and thus to obscure the difference between a neglect of history and a violation of chronology. When *ahistoricism* becomes another word for *anachronism*, the lack of engagement with the past becomes indistinguishable from the guilty overcathexis that clings too closely to it; an overinvestment in history mirrors an indifference to it; and, by implication, the improper treatment of history is tantamount to the outright rejection of it.[17] Rightly or wrongly, the anachronistic use of contemporary terms is now first among the intellectual offenses designated as ahistorical. Naming the scholarly fault of retrospective projection, it marks the guilty party as old-fashioned, decked out in the trappings of the scholarly past. Anachronism is anachronistic, out of step with the times, a throwback to the essentialism that, like those other styles of the 1970s and 1980s, we can't quite admit we ever liked. In the twenty-first century, we are told, the history that will be — the history of "an emerging futurity" — is not

---

epigrammatic reading of Fredric Jameson's injunction: "*Always* historicize? What could have less to do with historicizing than the commanding, atemporal adverb 'always'?" ("Paranoid Reading and Reparative Reading; or, You're So Paranoid, You Probably Think This Introduction Is about You," in *Novel Gazing: Queer Readings in Fiction*, ed. Eve Kosofsky Sedgwick [Durham: Duke University Press, 1997], 5).

[17] The conflation can have troubling effects, as Lisa L. Moore suggests: "This caution against anachronism has most often taken the form of an ahistorical prohibition against reading sex between women in history" (*Dangerous Intimacies: Toward a Sapphic History of the British Novel* [Durham: Duke University Press, 1997], 11).

anachronistic but properly sequential.[18] The discontinuous, genealogical history held up as a shield against progressivism has become a mark
of progress, relegating "transhistorical" thinking, like a primitive belief—
or like literary close reading—to the pages of the history whose lessons
it has failed to learn.[19]

Here the rhetoric against anachronism begins to sound like the
theories that have historically labeled homosexuality regressive and premature, belated and derivative—in short, out of order. Annamarie Jagose outlines the ways in which "regulatory technologies of sequence,"
enforcing the rule of linear progression, accommodate the "drive to
secure heterosexuality as chronology's triumph."[20] This temporal discipline governs the phobic myths that variously deem homosexuality a
form of regression, a violation of narrative form, a case of arrested development, a threat to futurity, and a "bad copy" of heterosexual love. While
straight culture at its own convenience finds homosexuality primitive or
derivative, too early or too late, it is the old idea of queer retrogression
that most clearly echoes in the complaint against scholarly anachronism. In the nineteenth century, sexologists such as Richard von Krafft-
Ebing drew on post-Darwinian theories of primitivism and arrested development extant in scientific racism to represent homosexuality as an
atavistic sign of evolutionary and individual regression.[21] In *Three Essays
on the Theory of Sexuality* Freud too mapped a developmental trajec-
tory in which inversion appears as a kind of atavism, ineluctably bound
to the past. Taking homosexuality as evidence of "a predominance
of archaic constitutions and primitive psychical mechanisms," he attributes inversion to childhood, the historical past, and early evolutionary

[18]Valerie Traub, "The Rewards of Lesbian History," *Feminist Studies* 25 (1999):
392. This view is not universal; those lesbian scholars, like Zimmerman, who attribute
ahistoricism to queer theory tend to regard both as new and unwelcome developments
that threaten established lesbian history.
[19]Louise Fradenburg and Carla Freccero, "Introduction: Caxton, Foucault, and the
Pleasures of History," in *Premodern Sexualities*, ed. Louise Fradenburg and Carla Freccero (New York: Routledge, 1996), xv.
[20]Jagose, *Inconsequence*, 102, 112. Jagose's acceptance of the argument against the
ahistorical—she questions any reading that "finds the modern category of 'lesbian'
anachronistically written across preceding sexual systems of female eroticism" (10)—is
the one troubling thread in a masterful discussion of sequence and temporality in heteronormative discourses. While she frames the critique of historical anachronism as a counter
to homophobic discourses of lesbian atemporality, I see that critique of anachronism as
an extension and a reflection of the temporal model on which homophobic rhetoric is
founded.
[21]Jennifer Terry, *An American Obsession: Science, Medicine, and Homosexuality in
Modern Society* (Chicago: University of Chicago Press, 1999), 30–39.

stages.[22] That notion extends far beyond psychoanalysis: as Guy Hocquenghem explains, heteronormative society, its sexual time lines measured by the sovereign goal of reproduction, deems homosexuality "a regressive neurosis, totally drawn towards the past."[23] From Victorian sexology to right-wing radio, homosexuality has been made to figure the corruption of history, the retroactions of anachronism and arrested development, and all that violates the developmental chronology we might call *straight time.*

Despite its complicity in the diagnosis of homosexual backwardness, psychoanalysis—no stranger to charges of ahistoricism—also sought to acknowledge the central place of retrospective processes in both private and public anamnesis. Where psychic formations are concerned, Freud insists that time runs no straight course and that cause may lie far from effect. In processes of *Nachträglichkeit,* uncanny returns of the repressed, screen memories, and the persistence of memory that Freud compares to impressions on a "mystic writing-pad," the past recurs in the present, and the present invents the past.[24] The Oedipus complex, for example, must be approached through belated reconstructions of early childhood: "Whenever someone gives an account of a past event, even if he is a historian, we must take into account what he unintentionally puts back into the past from the present or from some intermediate time, thus falsifying his picture of it."[25] Going back in memory, we build a history that anticipates what is to come, a history that will in time forget its own retrospective construction and assume the naturalized status of linear temporality. Although retrospection here implies a "falsifying" projection "back into the past," for Freud memory is nothing but falsification—that is, nothing but representation. Because anachronism structures all psychic life, the ahistorical—like the propensity for homosexual attraction—is typical, not exceptional. Freud's understanding that the normal is pathological and the pathological is normal may be his greatest and most humane insight: everyone fails at development, everyone is subject to sexual perversity, everyone falls back in time. Under these circumstances, straight hegemony must

[22] Sigmund Freud, *Three Essays on the Theory of Sexuality* (1905), in *The Standard Edition of the Complete Psychological Works,* ed. and trans. James Strachey, 24 vols. (London: Hogarth, 1953–74), 7:146.

[23] Guy Hocquenghem, *Homosexual Desire,* trans. Daniella Dangoor (Durham: Duke University Press, 1993), 108.

[24] Sigmund Freud, "A Note upon the Mystic Writing-Pad," in *Standard Edition,* 19:227–32.

[25] Sigmund Freud, *Introductory Lectures on Psycho-analysis* (1916), in *Standard Edition,* 16:336.

represent anachronism as deviance in order to displace the burden of the ahistorical onto others—queers and people of color, each differently stigmatized as "primitive"—and to claim for itself the role of truth, not falsification, the path of progress, not regression.

Although no one now denies that historiography's backward glance colors the past with traces of the present, that reminder changes the case against scholarly anachronism. When compelled by an ethical imperative to read the past *on its own terms*, the practice of historical criticism is impossible *on its own terms*. Historical alterity is, after all, a recent invention; the conviction that past ages are noncontinuous with modernity is a hallmark of modernity.[26] To apply such theories retroactively to texts whose own view of time more nearly matches what is now called continuism can only in the most paradoxical sense constitute a "respectful" acknowledgment of the texts' historicity. In "Song of Myself" Walt Whitman declares that "these are really the thoughts of all men in all ages and lands" and imagines the poet's subjectivity extending across time and space: "Here or henceforward it is all the same to me, I accept Time absolutely."[27] Whitman's dream of universal connection among "all men in all ages" may indeed be a product of his age, but the theory that would protect Whitman's age from contamination by the present imposes, in that prophylactic effort, a contemporary notion of the past's fragile specificity.

The Whitman example suggests not that we should be more truly historical but that there is no truly historical historicism. As its canniest practitioners acknowledge, historicism is always to some degree ahistorical—or rather, anachronistic. A screen memory of the public sphere, historiography cannot cease to transfer ideas of the present to the past. And if historiography without anachronism is impossible, then resistance to anachronism is resistance not to the other of historicism but to an abject aspect of its own methodology, a projected image of its own atavism. The impossibility of a "true" historicism, however, does not undermine charges of anachronism but ensures their effective

---

[26]In Terry Eagleton's formulation, "The belief that our beliefs are bound up with a historical form of life is itself a belief bound up with a historical form of life" ("The Estate Agent," *London Review of Books*, March 2, 2000, 10; see also Fradenburg and Freccero, "Introduction," xv).

[27]Walt Whitman, *Leaves of Grass*, ed. Harold W. Blodgett and Sculley Bradley (New York: New York University Press, 1965), 45, 51. Freedman contrasts a "respectful" deference to the past with the error of "ahistorical" approaches ("Historical Construction of Homosexuality," 31).

performance. This rhetoric has no outside; it interpellates everyone as a guilty subject of temporal self-governance and measures all against a standard that none can meet. Perhaps that is why Haggerty styles himself at once the cop and the criminal of historicism, why Sedgwick must "of course" insist on something that, even in 1990, everyone already knew. The charge of anachronism recurs endlessly because no one is ever innocent of it. In this respect the historical argument mirrors the fundamental logic of sexual discipline, in which no one's hetero credentials are ultimately above suspicion and in which, under the threat of an ineradicable perversity, to be heterosexual is always to be policed by one's vulnerability to being seen otherwise.[28] Faced with its own uncertainty, straight culture seeks a categorical distinction from the deviance whose backwardness might oppose reproductive futurity. Although in the queer historicist version of this logic it is not the future that must be rescued but the past, the same pathos of untenable boundaries informs each—whether the counterfactual, hegemonic fantasy of straight families' vulnerability to the predations of homosexuality or queer theorists' defense of a hard-won history.

It may seem that a properly historical queer theory is the one anodyne for doctrines of primitivism and regression that devalue gay and lesbian desires, or that undoing hurtful theories of queer anachronism means rejecting anachronism as such. Indeed, with greater awareness of its own not-knowing, the critique of anachronism might serve as a reminder that, to revise Sedgwick's axiom, we can't know in advance what the past will turn out to have been.[29] But when the insistence on historicism is, first and foremost, an effort to put the past first and foremost, it mimes the heteronormative demand for proper sexual sequencing. Construing retroaction as abomination, it upholds the illusion of a true, unidirectional history, whose effect of veracity and realism is in fact sustained by the very retroaction it condemns. Resistance to phobic definitions of homosexuality as anachronistic does not require the same temporal logic that has sustained such diagnoses; instead, resistance might mean a turn away from the discipline of straight time, away from the notions of historical propriety that, like notions of sexual propriety, function as regulatory fictions.

---

[28] See Eve Kosofsky Sedgwick, *Between Men: English Literature and Male Homosocial Desire* (New York: Columbia University Press, 1985), 88–89; and Morrison, *Explanation for Everything*, 5.
[29] Sedgwick, *Epistemology of the Closet*, 27.

THE LAST SHALL BE FIRST

While objections to the ahistorical continue in queer criticism, they are increasingly joined by discussions of "queer time." Revisiting anachronism, scholars seek to open a space for temporal variation in queer methodologies by recognizing the fictional status of linear time and the fact of our retrospective investment in the past.[30] With a few exceptions—Terry Castle's claim that the lesbian "is not a recent invention" explicitly opposes the queer theory epitomized, in her view, by Foucault and Judith Butler—the majority take their cue from poststructuralist theory.[31] In "The History That Will Be," Jonathan Goldberg borrows from Derrida to trace the proleptic and analeptic effects inherent in historiography. Even empire-building metanarratives include temporal distortion: origins are retroactively constructed, and events unfold in the future perfect, anticipating their own significance (as Whitman says to a historian, "I project the history of the future"). Queer reading, accordingly, might "open the historical text to its multiples" by noting the double temporality that determines "the relation between the writing of history as prediction and as retrospection."[32]

With the goal of rereading queer history, other scholars have stressed the power of identification, desire, and affective attachment to forge connections across time. In their introduction to *Premodern Sexualities* Louise Fradenburg and Carla Freccero question the past's categorical alterity and the assumption that only an armature of alienation can prevent its contamination by present scholars. They do not defend

---

[30]Judith Halberstam traces a "queer sense of temporality" through an archive of lived experiences, subcultural communities, and representational practices in her book *In a Queer Time and Place: Transgender Bodies, Subcultural Lives* (New York: New York University Press, 2005), 187. On this experiential sense of queer time see also Stephen M. Barber and David L. Clark, "Queer Moments: The Performative Temporalities of Eve Sedgwick," in *Regarding Sedgwick: Essays on Queer Culture and Critical Theory*, ed. Stephen M. Barber and David L. Clark (New York: Routledge, 2002), 1–53. Other significant work seeks to revalue formerly disavowed identifications with the past: see Elizabeth Freeman, "Packing History, Count(er)ing Generations," *New Literary History* 31 (2000): 727–44; and Heather K. Love, "'Spoiled Identity': Stephen Gordon's Loneliness and the Difficulties of Queer History," *GLQ* 7 (2001): 487–519. Projects that address queer history in terms less directly concerned with anachronism include Scott Bravmann, *Queer Fictions of the Past: History, Culture, and Difference* (New York: Cambridge University Press, 1997); and Christopher Nealon, *Foundlings: Lesbian and Gay Historical Emotion before Stonewall* (Durham: Duke University Press, 2001).

[31]Terry Castle, *The Apparitional Lesbian: Female Homosexuality and Modern Culture* (New York: Columbia University Press, 1993), 8.

[32]Whitman, *Leaves of Grass*, 4; Jonathan Goldberg, "The History That Will Be," *GLQ* 1 (1995): 385–403; see also Goldberg, introduction to *Queering the Renaissance* (Durham: Duke University Press, 1994), 1–14.

anachronism—indeed, they caution against "transhistoricist nostalgia"—
but by inviting queer critics to acknowledge identificatory and pleasurable links with the past, their essay functions as an apologia for any work
whose historical cathexes caused it to be dismissed as "transhistorical."[33]
No less than critical intimacy with the past, the violation of the chronological rule of law has changed from a scholarly blunder to a strategic possibility. In *Getting Medieval* Carolyn Dinshaw imagines tactile,
erotic, affective connections across time as the bases of a new historiography, reclaiming transhistorical reading as a "queer historical impulse"
distinct from simple identification with the past.[34] As Dinshaw explains
in a later essay, "Since I am trying to explore unconventional temporal
possibilities in history writing, I do not tremble at the very concept of
anachronism but rather want to investigate its potential productivity."
Toward that end, her study seeks "to demonstrate the simultaneous
copresence of different chronologies in any moment."[35]

*   *   *

Queer theories of retrospection speak to "Ligeia" because the text
so pointedly anticipates them. Structured by hysteron proteron, the rhetorical effect of temporal inversion, the narrative advances backward. In
"The Philosophy of Composition," an essay that opens by pointing
out Dickens's "backwards" writing, Poe says that his own poem "The
Raven" "may be said to have its beginning—at the end" (p. 230). The
same might be said of "Ligeia." Counting back from its sensational
denouement, the narrative trades on inversions of chronology, retracing Ligeia's monstrous journey from death to life. Poe may allude to
conventional emplotment in the narrator's fantasy of his wife's learning as a "delicious vista . . . down whose long, gorgeous, and all untrodden path, I might at length pass onward to the goal" (p. 52), but the
story's own course is nothing of the kind. Ligeia's death obstructs that
straight and narrow road to knowledge, leading both narrator and text
to the less productive pleasures of regression and return. In place of
progress "onward," the narrator gets "a circle of analogies" that circle
back in time: "My memory flew back" (pp. 50, 56). Against the
teleological path of human life from birth to death, the text moves

---

[33]Fradenburg and Freccero, "Introduction," xvii–xix.
[34]Carolyn Dinshaw, *Getting Medieval: Sexualities and Communities, Pre- and Postmodern* (Durham: Duke University Press, 1999), 1, 34.
[35]Carolyn Dinshaw, "Got Medieval?" *Journal of the History of Sexuality* 10 (2001):
209.

from death to birth. Ligeia "is no more" at the tale's beginning, but she lives at the end: her will bequeaths to the future the unending persistence of the past.

Fulfilling all too literally the biblical promise, "Ligeia" ensures that the last shall be first for its reader. We must enter into the text's anachronism, placing the end of the story in relation to the later moment of its beginning and understanding its beginning as an effect of its earlier end. The meaning of Ligeia's will stays veiled until it is materialized in her macabre return, and, like the meaning of that insatiable will, the lesbian effect appears *après coup*. Only later do we learn what must have happened in the "bed of death" and solve the puzzle of the moment when "she who had been dead, once again stirred" (pp. 58, 60). Only in retrospect, when we learn that a second woman has been with Rowena all along, does that deathbed present a different sort of bedroom scene. Regarded in hindsight, the encounter between Ligeia and Rowena leaves a ghostly afterimage. This backward logic enacts in narrative terms Freud's notion of deferred action or *Nachträglichkeit*, the process through which a past moment belatedly assumes significance. In this fractured temporality, an event may "occur" long after its actual date, and the work of memory may re-create the past it pretends merely to recall. Patricia White suggests that the deferred action of *Nachträglichkeit* offers one model for the contemporary viewing of lesbian figures in the cinema of the past. What White neatly terms "retrospectatorship" mimics the psychic process whereby "an unconscious 'scene' becomes meaningful in retrospect, [when] it is opened onto and transformed by experience in the present."[36] Where lesbian representation is concerned, she argues, this act of historical retrospection is not an error but a strategic practice, resisting the allegation of presentism that would construe all "reading back" as illegitimate "reading into."[37]

Retrospectatorship could then describe our reading of "Ligeia," a text that yields its most arresting visions after the fact. But the story itself offers another model for this backward glance. Its temporal illusions can be read as a form of anamorphosis, the optical effect in which a meaningless blot assumes its true form when observed from a certain oblique angle. As Stephen Greenblatt notes in his reading of Hans Hol-

---

[36]Patricia White, "Hollywood Lesbians," interview by Annamarie Jagose, *Genders* 32 (2000), www.genders.org/g32/g32_jagose.html. White develops her theory of retrospectatorship in *Uninvited*, 196–205. *Nachträglichkeit* also figures in Brett Farmer's theory of gay spectatorship and fantasy (*Spectacular Passions: Cinema, Fantasy, Gay Male Spectatorships* [Durham: Duke University Press, 2000], 55–56, 71–73).

[37]White, *Uninvited*, 15.

bein's *Ambassadors*, the painting's anamorphic image appears in proper perspective as an "unreadable blur," but becomes meaningful through the "radical abandonment of what we take to be 'normal' vision."[38] Poe's own example of anamorphosis concerns the outré furnishings of the home to which the narrator brings Rowena. Here the tapestries, "changeable in aspect," produce a "phantasmagoric effect," appearing "Arabesque only when regarded from a single point of view": "To one entering the room, they bore the appearance of simple monstrosities; but upon a farther advance, this appearance gradually departed; and, step by step, as the visitor moved his station in the chamber, he saw himself surrounded by an endless succession of the ghastly forms which belong to the superstition of the Norman" (p. 56). In a curious cultural shift, the patterns look Eastern or European according to the visitor's position. The tapestries' "appearance," "aspect," and "forms" respond to the observer's line of sight, just as their meaning depends on their relation to a spectator—or a reader. After all, what better purpose for this long, seemingly gratuitous excursus on interior decorating than a lesson in how to read "Ligeia"? (Scholars who identify "Ligeia" as orientalist are thus following Poe's directions: the text, like the draperies it depicts, reveals its "arabesque" patterns to a single vantage point.)[39] And like the "ghastly forms" of the bridal chamber, the text's lesbian effect appears from the right angle—that is, from the wrong angle. Its phantasmagoric forms invisible to the straight gaze, "Ligeia" reserves its clearest visions for those who look aslant.

While Poe's account of anamorphosis presumes a viewer who enters and advances, Jacques Lacan tells a story of withdrawal and retrogression. His own discussion of *The Ambassadors* includes instructions to the viewer who would discover the painting's secret: "Begin by walking out of the room in which no doubt it has long held your attention. It is then that, turning around as you leave—as the author of the *Anamorphoses* describes it—you apprehend in this form . . . What? A skull."[40] The anamorphic form appears through a lapse of attention; it is unintelligible when sought directly. Only in hindsight can one recognize the death's-head, emblem of the gaping hole in symbolic reality and the

---

[38] Stephen Greenblatt, *Renaissance Self-Fashioning: From More to Shakespeare* (Chicago: University of Chicago Press, 1980), 18–19.

[39] See, e.g., Malini Johar Schueller, "Harems, Orientalist Subversions, and the Crisis of Nationalism: The Case of Edgar Allan Poe and 'Ligeia,'" *Criticism* 37 (1995): 601–23.

[40] Jacques Lacan, *The Four Fundamental Concepts of Psycho-analysis*, ed. Jacques-Alain Miller, trans. Alan Sheridan (New York: Norton, 1981), 88.

intolerable lack around which our own subjectivity is structured. This revelation turns on a turn: it is when "turning around as you leave" that you see the skull for what it is. Lacan explains that "the secret of the picture is given at the moment when, moving slightly away, little by little, to the left, then turning around, we see what the magical floating object signifies" (92). The physical turn that exposes the secret of *The Ambassadors* becomes in "Ligeia" another sort of return, which turns back the clock to confront a *historical* anamorphosis. Only when we regard the scene of Rowena's revival from the moment of Ligeia's reappearance can Ligeia's will appear morbid and the "unspeakable horrors of that night" (p. 60) seem distinctly queer. Like the past events whose temporal displacement Freud's theory of *Nachträglichkeit* seeks to explain, the perverse effects of the text appear when observed from the wrong time, through the specific obliquity of belatedness.

Viewing the 1838 text from the twenty-first century, we find our own retrospectatorship already inscribed in Poe's tale. Traub's "strategic anachronism" and White's "retrospectatorship" can apply to "Ligeia," but "Ligeia," with its own instructions for reading aslant, applies no less to them. The text calls for a historical version of the "anamorphic reading" that, as Slavoj Žižek writes, reveals through a shift in perspective the trauma or scandal that symbolization otherwise occludes.[41] . . .

MEMENTO MORI

As an impossible, anticipatory response to the queer theory of our time, Poe's invitation to look awry is also an encounter with alterity. Both sides of the critical debate have largely presumed that anachronism contravenes historical alterity, that ahistorical methods shore up contemporary identities by affording readers opportunities for sentimental investment and narcissistic reflection. Traub notes that scholarly anachronism is often impelled by the search for a "useable past" in which the present finds the reassurance of "personal affirmation, homo life support," and Halperin guardedly acknowledges the "queer project of identifying with and reclaiming non-heteronormative figures from the past."[42] All fantasy and identification across time may be anachronistic, but not all anachronism must serve these ends. Despite the iden-

[41]Slavoj Žižek, *The Plague of Fantasies* (New York: Verso, 1997), 75.
[42]Traub, *Renaissance of Lesbianism*, 27; Halperin, *How to Do the History of Homosexuality*, 16.

tificatory lure of Ligeia's "immense" learning for the queer scholar, she cannot be a lesbian, and for more than historical reasons. We cannot say that she loves Rowena, only that she uses her. She does not want to *have* Rowena (even when, as they say, she wants her body); she wants to *be* Rowena (to be in her place, replacing her replacement). Rowena is not an end in herself but a means to an end—that is, in Poe's own endgame, a means for Ligeia to avoid ending. What she wills is her own will's power, and what she desires is desire itself.

However queer Ligeia's turn from heterosexuality, then, queerer still is her refusal of object choice as such; however appalling her return from death, more appalling is the will that drives it, traversing "the field of a pure and empty want."[43] Ligeia's meeting with Rowena produces the somatic signs of arousal without the armature of object choice usually mistaken for sexuality tout court; it shows something like lesbian sexuality stripped of anything like same-sex attraction. What is sex between women who don't really want each other? One answer: a straight fantasy. Indeed, Poe's bedroom scene, structured by the voyeuristic presence of its male observer, resembles mass-marketed lesbian tableaux. As a corporeal event without affect or interiority, it evokes the pornographic dream of a lesbianism manifested in acts, not identities, and conveniently dissociable from the "real," ultimately heterosexual status of the actors. In this sense, the scene would merely describe Poe's desire, saying nothing about the true love of the fictional Ligeia or the factual experience of American women in 1838. But there is another answer to the question—what is sex between women who don't really want each other?—and it is lesbianism. The idea, of course, is absurd, if not dangerously dehumanizing, countering as it does the liberal rhetoric of subjectivity, interiority, and personal fulfillment that anchors gay rights arguments in the public sphere. That is exactly why it should be pursued.

In fact, the spectral lesbian effect of "Ligeia" makes visible what such well-intentioned arguments tend to repress or romanticize. Poe's fantasy reflects reality despite itself. The perversity of Ligeia's will, which spurns the promise of satisfaction in favor of "the reproduction of desire as such," is the perversity of all desire.[44] That Ligeia does not really want Rowena but something else in no way negates the sexual

[43]Jacques Lacan, *Feminine Sexuality: Jacques Lacan and the École Freudienne*, ed. Juliet Mitchell and Jacqueline Rose, trans. Jacqueline Rose (New York: Norton, 1982), 131.
[44]Žižek, *Looking Awry*, 7.

valence of the scene, for as Lacan reminds us, sexual desire is always the desire for something else.[45] The object of desire, whatever it may be, is never more than contingent. When an oblique gaze reveals in "Ligeia" a ghostly figure, the counterpart of Holbein's memento mori, what returns there is the blind, meaningless insistence of desire beyond any object. Oriented only toward its own continuance, Ligeia's will enacts the sheer force of desire's quest to sustain itself, a quest in which the object, hetero or homo, must be secondary and substitutive. The object is an effect and not a cause of desire, never adequate to satisfy the will that persists. . . .

. . . Poe's camp-gothic aesthetic effectively disguises the true horror of the story—what could be less frightening than how obviously it intends to frighten, how thickly its lurid colors are applied? Yet "Ligeia" is a horror story, not because it shows love between women but because it doesn't. The text's real monstrosity is not its reanimation of the dead, or even its hint of necrolesbianism, but the objectless, grimly instinctual dimension of desire to whose existence both testify.

When Poe's narrator struggles to understand "the principle of her longing," the essence of Ligeia's desire "but for life," by deciphering the greater principle of which that desire is an emblem or an effect, he fails because the answer is *nothing*. Ligeia's will refers to nothing, signifies nothing, seeks nothing except its own persistence. Accepting no conclusion and knowing no satisfaction, it describes the aspect of desire that is most drivelike and inhuman. Lee Edelman contends that heteronormative society compels queers to embody the future-negating energies of the death drive: "As the name for a force of mechanistic compulsion whose formal excess supersedes any end toward which it might seem to be aimed, the death drive refuses identity or the absolute privilege of any goal. Such a goal, such an end, could never be 'it'; achieved, it could never satisfy."[46] Ligeia's will "for life" cannot constitute a death drive in any literal sense—but then, the death drive is never literal. This relentless, mechanical lust, this desire as unconcerned with the narrator as Rowena, this will whose repetitive rhythms exceed anything we might imagine as its object—*this* is the death's-head in "Ligeia." This is the skull that grins obscenely from the anamorphic spot, as a reminder of what we cannot see because we daily take pains not to see it: the endless, ultimately objectless energy of desire. There is nothing distinctly queer about this, but everything queer about its legibility in a society that must deny the impossibility of desire's satisfaction in order to defend the aims of heteronormative reproduction. Only in the form of the monster, the grotesque, and the pervert can straight society recognize the perfectly ordinary but intolerable logic of sexuality as such.

Queer communities, however, are no less reluctant to confront this image. Long after essentialist notions of sexual identity have been dismantled, the authenticity of object choice and the possibility of sexual satisfaction remain central to queer culture. Fantasies of a simple, sentimentalized homosexuality—whether in the coming-out story's happy ending or in the politically expedient discourse of gay familialism—must refuse to recognize the anamorphic blot whose message is not death itself but the deathly insatiability of desire. This, then, is the alterity of the present, the difference that haunts the now of queer theory. In *Specters of Marx* Derrida notes that while ghostly figures indicate an uncanny return, this temporal violation does not befall a historically innocent moment. The ghost is no anomaly, but a strange reminder of what Derrida calls the "non-contemporaneity of present time with itself (this radical untimeliness or this anachrony on the basis of which we are trying here to *think the ghost*)."[47] If, as some historians would have it, the past is always other to the present, the present is no less other to itself.

Rather than impose a narrative of continuous time or render the past identical to the present, then, an anamorphic reading of "Ligeia" can bring into focus the anachrony of the present. The case against scholarly anachronism assumes that historical criticism maintains a rigorous awareness of alterity, while ahistorical reading offers identification's guilty pleasures and a comforting, if phantasmatic, sense of the familiar. In "Ligeia" the opposite is true. Reading anachronistically, going temporally awry, we find a certain lesbian effect, but that effect unsettles what today's queer discourse takes for granted about sexuality. In place of any reassuring reflection of modern sexual identity or

---

[47] Jacques Derrida, *Specters of Marx: The State of the Debt, the Work of Mourning, and the New International*, trans. Peggy Kamuf (New York: Routledge, 1994), 25. For Castle, ghosts figure the homophobic repression of real, embodied lesbian life (*Apparitional Lesbian*, 2–8). But as Mandy Merck suggests in an astute response to Castle, the defense of embodiment against such specters may mean "the veritable petrification of the subject and its desires" ("The Queer Spirit of the Age," in *Literature and the Contemporary: Fictions and Theories of the Present*, ed. Roger Luckhurst and Peter Marks [Harlow: Longman, 1999], 209).

sustaining identification, Poe's story shows a ghostly figure, its own memento mori, in which returns the alienating force of sexuality as such. The anachronism named as ahistorical is not bound, in other words, to an essentially conservative work of identification and self-affirmation; it need not project cherished values backward or repeat what we already know. Instead, the critical engagement with historical anamorphosis can open our own queer moment to alterity, serving the "denaturalization of the present" promised by Halberstam's theory of perverse presentism.[48]

When, like Lacan standing before *The Ambassadors*, we turn back to look once more at "Ligeia," whose every contour we think we know, the text produces, in place of Holbein's death's-head, an anamorphic lesbian image. Both in that specter of queer sexuality and in the ways that it eludes our grasp, the text confronts us with alterity—the alterity not only of history but also of our own desire. Reading "Ligeia" from the wrong angle, we may catch a backward glimpse of the discourses that, in Poe's time and our own, braid together narrative, developmental, and historical time lines: the retrospectatorship of recent queer theory, the normative construction of homosexuality as regressive in nineteenth-century rhetoric, and the scholarly effort to defend literary history against perverse anachronism. At the same time, the phantasmagoric effects of "Ligeia" hold out the possibility of readings that, informed by psychoanalysis and by "queer historical impulses," might recognize, aslant and at a distance, the queer figures that still burn in our field of vision.

[48] Halberstam, *Female Masculinity*, 53.

How to Write about Critical Controversy over the Work of Edgar Allan Poe

In our introductory essay, we discussed *why* studying critical controversies can increase your engagement with literary texts and the wider world of literary and cultural criticism in which your teachers and many other readers live. In this essay, we offer some suggestions about *how* to contribute to the controversies yourselves. We will focus our advice primarily on how to write about controversies because, if you are like most people, you will find writing more challenging than speaking, but we believe that our advice can also be useful for participating in class discussions and in conversations outside the classroom. Our advice will cover some general principles and some specific techniques not just for managing an argument but for doing so in response to the arguments of others.

GETTING DIALOGIC, OR, ARGUMENT AS TRIANGULATION

Let us suppose that your teacher, after discussing with you and your classmates the essays in this book on the controversy over Poe's attitudes toward race, gives you an assignment to write a five-page paper making your own contribution to that debate. How should you proceed? Consider the following responses to the assignment by three different students. (1) Student A decides that the most important thing to do is to say something original about Poe's work; therefore, she states her thesis early in the paper and then spends the rest of it presenting the textual evidence that supports it. Along the way she drops in footnotes that indicate which critics in this text agree with her opinion and which ones do not. (2) Student B decides that the most important thing to do is to show the complexity of the debate and so he spends most of the paper summarizing what others have said, making some reference to Poe's texts, but saving his own opinion for the last few paragraphs. Indeed, to impress the teacher Student B goes to the library to find more essays on Poe's texts so that he can include their views in his summary. (3) Student C decides that the most important thing to do is to assess the merits of all the previous critics and she spends most of the paper analyzing the logic of their arguments, giving high marks to those she agrees with and low marks to those she disagrees with. Only at the end does she say anything about her own ideas about Poe's texts and her comments are brief.

Although each approach has some merit, each, in our view, has a major flaw. Student A's, which we will call the *solo flyer model*, mentions and occasionally quotes or summarizes several critics and their debate but does not really grapple with their ideas. Her references to that debate are not integral to her argument, but added on, because she has learned that English teachers like footnotes. Since the solo flyer paper does not respond to the debate, the chances of its being recognized as a substantial contribution are very low, even if it does have original things to say. Student B, whose approach we will call the *shrinking violet model*, does not give enough emphasis to his own contribution to the debate and allows his paper to be dominated by the opinions of others. Consequently, although student B's approach is likely to require more hours of work than student A's, his paper, too, is unlikely to substantially contribute to the debate. Student C's approach, which we will call the *metacritic model*, builds on the positive features of the shrinking violet model and adds virtues that the solo flyer model lacks, but it moves her own ideas about Poe's texts and their features to the background of the discussion. Consequently, although Student C's paper can shed light on the strengths and weaknesses of others' positions, it, too, is unlikely to say anything substantially new and insightful about Poe's work itself.

Although the solo flyer and the shrinking violet models are, in one sense, very different, they both have the same flaw: they are insufficiently *dialogic*, by which we mean that they both do a poor job of relating the writer's ideas to those of others. The metacritic model is dialogic in the sense that it actively engages with others' arguments but insufficiently dialogic in another sense: it does not add Student C's own ideas about Poe's work to the conversation. Critical debates are like conversations; to be a good conversationalist you need to do three interrelated things: (1) make what you say responsive to what others in the conversation have been saying; (2) make what you say relevant to the main issues under discussion; and (3) make your own argument recognizable as a response to one or more others.

In fact, listening closely to others (or closely reading their texts), thinking about your own take on the main issues, and then attempting to do justice to that take in a way that is also responsive to others' ideas is the best way to find something worthwhile to say. We're sure that you've had the experience of joining a conversation on a topic that you did not think you had much investment in, only to discover, after listening to others, that you actually had a strong opinion and wanted to express it. In that experience, the listening helped you discover your own take, but the success of your contribution will depend on your being able to combine that take with your response to others' ideas. Of course not all conversations, critical or otherwise, work in exactly that way, but the example does underline the point that an excellent strategy for finding something worthwhile to say is to work dialogically among the text, the ideas of others, and your own ideas.

Another way to express these points is through an analogy between constructing an argument and drawing a triangle. A successful critical argument, like a triangle, has three legs, and a good writer, like a good geometrician, pays attentions to all three: the text and its features, others' ideas about those things, and the writer's own ideas about both the text and others' ideas (see Figure 1). If you work with only two legs of the argument—your ideas and the text; others' ideas and the text; your

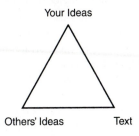

Figure 1. Argument as Triangulation.

ideas and others' ideas—your contribution will be as incomplete as a triangle with only two legs, which of course would not actually be a triangle. If you attend to all three legs, however, you are likely to command the attention of the other debaters.

CHOOSING A POSITION: AGREEING, DISAGREEING, DOING BOTH

In one sense, the process of making a critical argument is very simple. If you think about situating your ideas about a text in relation to others' along a spectrum from complete agreement to complete disagreement, you can see that there are a limited number of general positions to take: strongly agree, strongly disagree, and partially agree and partially disagree. We advise you to decide which of these three options you want to take and stick to that plan as you write. If you find yourself shifting to one of the other options, no problem; just revise your essay so it sticks to that one.

At the same time, each of these three simple positions—agree, disagree, do both—is open to a countless number of variations and complications, because there are multiple ways of handling each leg of the argumentative triangle. To illustrate, here are the main responses and just a few of their variations. The variations are rarely mutually exclusive; almost all of them can be combined within a single response.

1. You can strongly disagree with another critic's argument, saying in effect, "No, that's just wrong." In developing this position, you contrast the other critic's ideas about the text with your own and offer reasons why your ideas are more persuasive. You can establish those reasons in various ways: (a) by showing that your interpretation of the critic's main textual evidence offers a more precise or more coherent account of it; (b) by bringing into the discussion significant relevant textual evidence that the critic's argument neglects and that leads to a different conclusion; and (c) by arguing that the context within which the critic reads the evidence is not appropriate. You can of course also make the case by combining two or more of these strategies.

Yvor Winters, in "Edgar Allan Poe: A Crisis in the History of American Obscurantism," provides an excellent example of strong disagreement in his case against what he saw as the dominant view of Poe as a great writer. After establishing the details of that view—one built on the accumulation of an "impressive body of scholarship" that is primarily "biographical, historical, and textual" (p. 295)—Winters turns to key passages in Poe's theoretical texts and argues that they show him to be a deficient thinker (he obscures rather than clarifies ideas) and that his artistic practice is in line with this deficient thought. In effect, Winters uses strategy (b) above. Having made his case against Poe, Winters then turns to consider possible defenses against his criticisms, taking up the work of two critics who view Poe as a great writer. The first defense is that Poe is a special kind of intellectual poet and the second that he has an appealing idea of Beauty. Winters counters the first defense with a version of strategy (c), contending that Poe's intellectuality is of a trivial sort and to be found only in his theory not in his poetry. And he counters the second defense with a version of strategy (a), contending that his readings of Poe's discussions of Beauty illustrate not his strengths but his deficiencies.

2. You can say, "No, but . . ." or "Yes, but . . ."; that is, you can partially agree and partially disagree (and lead with no or yes, depending on the degree of your disagreement). In using this tactic, you acknowledge what you find valuable in another critic's argument, and then bring in your own ideas about the text to complicate or modify that argument. More specifically, you can develop the agreement by (a) pointing to positive features of the critic's argument such as her use of textual evidence, or (b) extending the critic's argument to some issue or part of the text that she has not addressed. You can develop your disagreement by using one or more of the strategies for strongly disagreeing described above. Paul Gilmore, in "A 'Rara Avis in Terris': Poe's 'Hop-Frog' and Race in the Antebellum Freak Show," offers an exemplary model of the "Yes, but" response. He accepts the arguments of Joan Dayan and others that Poe often endorsed proslavery attitudes and that this stance is reflected in his attitudes toward race in his fiction. Gilmore then adds his very important *but*, as he argues that in "Hop-Frog," a story in which Poe uses the title character to explore his concerns about the literary marketplace, "Poe identifies his aesthetic self with a character identified as racially other" (p. 440).

3. You can say, "Yes, and . . ."; that is, you can agree and develop the agreement along the lines in number 2(b). In this response, you want to show both that you're building on the previous critic's case and making your own contribution to the debate through the analysis of textual material that has been neglected or not sufficiently explored by the previous critic—or not sufficiently considered from an important critical perspective. Leland S. Person, in "Poe's Poetics of Desire: 'Th' Expanding Eye to the Loved Object,'" provides a valuable example of the "Yes, and" response. After succinctly reviewing previous work on

"Poe's literary relationship with women," Person describes his own project: "I would like to extend these insights . . . by treating the death of a beautiful woman more as the beginning than as the end of [Poe's] poetics of desire" (p. 504). Person's extension, with its attention to the way the love poems constitute a transgendered and ultimately narcissistic performance, significantly advances the conversation about Poe and gender.

DEALING WITH MULTIPLE OTHERS

As these examples indicate, a range of options are available to you whether you are engaging with just one other critic or with more than one, but there are also some common strategies for dealing with more than one. Here are two such ways:

1. After summarizing the other critics' positions, you can identify and focus on something significant that they have in common: a view of a certain part of the text, an assumption about what is important in the text or the criticism of it, or some other such issue. You can be explicit and straightforward about the underlying issue and your relation to it: "Despite their different concerns, X and Y identify Z as a crucial element of the text, and their views of it are largely the same. However, by considering evidence of the text that both essays neglect, I will argue for a different view of Z." Alternatively, you can treat two or more critical positions that are not in agreement and argue that both are flawed because they fail to account for some important textual evidence that you will consider. Terence Whalen, in "Average Racism: Poe, Slavery, and, the Wages of Literary Nationalism," demonstrates one way to make this move. After noting the two main critical views of Poe's attitudes toward race, Whalen contends that they are "both wrong" and goes on to make the case for a "more historically informed" approach to reading an author's attitudes toward race, one that goes beyond "the prevailing rhetoric of praise and denunciation" (p. 396).

2. After identifying a generally shared critical practice or interpretation, you can suggest that a new approach represents a critical advance. Joan Dayan, in "Amorous Bondage: Poe, Ladies, and Slaves," offers a good model of this strategy. She provides telling evidence of how most previous critics had separated questions of Poe's aesthetics from questions about his racial and gender politics, and then demonstrates how important those questions about politics are to any assessment of Poe's work.

As with any art, the best way to develop skill in critical argument is through practice. As you get accustomed to handling the triangulations among texts, your ideas about them, and others' ideas about them, you are likely to find yourself becoming better at both reading and writing critical arguments. Your reading skills will develop because you will be more attuned to the moves other critics make as they express their takes on texts, and this greater awareness will enhance your own ability to make similar moves in your writing. Furthermore, the more you practice, the more you will realize that, whether you want to praise or denigrate a particular text, whether you agree or disagree with others' takes on it, your engagement with both the text and others' ideas about it is crucial to the development of your own thinking.

Gerald Graff
James Phelan

About the Editors

Jared Gardner is professor of English at the Ohio State University and the author of *Master Plots: Race and the Founding of an American Literature, 1787–1845* (1994), *Projections: Comics and the History of Twenty-First-Century Storytelling* (2012), and *The Rise and Fall of Early American Magazine Culture* (2012). At Ohio State he directs the Popular Culture Studies program and works closely with the Billy Ireland Cartoon Library & Museum.

Elizabeth Hewitt is associate professor at the Ohio State University and the author of *Correspondence and American Literature, 1770–1865* (2004) and the coeditor of *The Collected Writings of Charles Brockden Brown Vol. I: Letters and Early Epistolary Writings* (2013). She is currently completing a book on the literature of early American finance and, with Jared Gardner, Volume VI of *The Collected Writings of Charles Brockden Brown: The American Register and Other Writings, 1807–1810*.

ABOUT THE SERIES EDITORS

Gerald Graff is professor of English and Education at the University of Illinois at Chicago. He developed his pedagogy of "teaching the conflicts" at Northwestern University, where he was a professor of

English, and the University of Chicago, where he was George M. Pullman Professor of English and Education. He is one of the most eminent figures in literary studies and education today, as his election as president of the Modern Language Association attests. His influential books include *Literature Against Itself* (1981), *Professing Literature* (1987), *Beyond the Culture Wars* (1992), and *Clueless in Academe* (2003). With Cathy Birkenstein, he authored the best-selling textbook *They Say/I Say: The Moves That Matter in Academic Writing* (first published in 2006 and now in its third edition).

James Phelan is Distinguished University Professor of English at the Ohio State University. Editor of the award-winning journal *Narrative* and coeditor of the Ohio State University Press series on the Theory and Interpretation of Narrative, he has also written extensively about narrative and its elements as well as its affective and ethical effects. His books include *Worlds from Words* (1981), *Reading People, Reading Plots* (1989), *Narrative as Rhetoric* (1996), *Living to Tell about It* (2005), *Experiencing Fiction* (2007), *Narrative Theory: Core Concepts and Critical Debates* (2012, coauthored with David Herman, Peter J. Rabinowitz, Brian Richardson, and Robyn Warhol), and *Reading the American Novel, 1920–2010* (2013).

Professors Graff and Phelan are coeditors of *Adventures of Huckleberry Finn: A Case Study in Critical Controversy* (Second Edition, 2004) and *The Tempest: A Case Study in Critical Controversy* (Second Edition, 2009).

Acknowledgments (*continued from p. iv*)

Beth Ann Bassein. "Poe's Most Poetic Subject" (1982) from *Women and Death: Linkages in Western Thought and Literature* by Beth Ann Bassein. Copyright © by Beth Ann Bassein. Reproduced with permission of Greenwood Press, in the format Republish in a book via Copyright Clearance Center.

Joseph Church. " 'To Make Venus Vanish': Misogyny as Motive in Poe's 'Murders in the Rue Morgue' " from *American Transcendental Quarterly*, Volume 20, No. 2, June 2006. Copyright © by Joseph Church 2006. Reprinted by permission of the author.

Joan Dayan. Excerpts from "Amorous Bondage: Poe, Ladies, and Slaves" by Joan Dayan from *American Literature*, Volume 66, No. 2, pp. 239–73. Copyright © 1994 by Duke University Press. All rights reserved. Republished by permission of the copyright holder, Duke University Press. www.dukeupress.edu

E. L. Doctorow. "E. A. Poe" by E. L. Doctorow from *Creationists: Selected Essays, 1993–2006* by E. L. Doctorow. Copyright © 2015 by ICM. Used by permission. All rights reserved.

T. S. Eliot. Excerpts from "From Poe to Valéry" by T. S. Eliot from *The Hudson Review*, Volume 2, No. 3, Autumn 1949. Copyright © Estate of T. S. Eliot. Permission granted by Faber & Faber Ltd.

Paul Gilmore. Excerpts from "A 'Rara Avis in Terris': Poe's 'Hop-Frog' and Race in the Antebellum Freak Show" from *The Genuine Article: Race, Mass Culture, and American Literary Manhood* by Paul Gilmore, pp. 98–124. Copyright © 2001 by Duke University Press. All rights reserved. Republished by permission of the copyright holder, Duke University Press. www.dukeupress.edu

Lesley Ginsberg. Excerpts from "Slavery and the Gothic Horror of Poe's 'The Black Cat' " by Lesley Ginsberg from *American Gothic: New Interventions in a National Narrative*. Copyright © 1998 by the University of Iowa Press. Used with permission.

Cynthia S. Jordan. Excerpts from "Poe's Re-Vision: The Recovery of the Second Story" from *American Literature*, Volume 59, No. 1, pp. 1–19. Copyright © 1987 by Duke University Press. All rights reserved. Republished by permission of the copyright holder, Duke University Press. www.dukeupress.edu

J. Gerald Kennedy. "Introduction: Poe in Our Time" by J. Gerald Kennedy from *A Historical Guide to Edgar Allan Poe*, edited by J. Gerald Kennedy (2001). Copyright © 2000 by J. Gerald Kennedy. By permission of Oxford University Press, USA.

Maurice S. Lee. Excerpts from "Absolute Poe: His System of Transcendental Racism," from *American Literature*, Volume 75, No. 4, pp. 751–81. Copyright © 2003 by Duke University Press. All rights reserved. Republished by permission of the copyright holder, Duke University Press. www.dukeupress.edu

Scott Peeples. Excerpts from "Lionizing: Poe as Cultural Signifier" from *The Afterlife of Edgar Allan Poe* by Scott Peeples (Rochester, NY: Camden House, 2004). Copyright © 2004 by Scott Peeples. Reprinted by permission of Boydell & Brewer, Inc.

Leland S. Person. "Poe's Poetics of Desire: 'Th' Expanding Eye to the Loved Object' " from *Poe Studies*, 34:1–2 (2001), 1–7. Copyright © 2001 Washington State University. Reprinted with permission of Johns Hopkins University Press.

Eliza Richards. "Women's Place in Poe Studies" from *Poe Studies*, 33:1–2 (2000), 10–14. Copyright © 2000 by Washington State University. Reprinted with permission of Johns Hopkins University Press.

Valerie Rohy. Excerpts from "Ahistorical" from *GLQ: A Journal of Lesbian and Gay Studies*, Volume 12, No. 1, pp. 61–83. Copyright © 2006 by Duke University Press. All rights reserved. Republished by permission of the copyright holder, Duke University Press. www.dukeupress.edu

Allen Tate. Excerpts from "The Poetry of Edgar Allan Poe" by Allen Tate. First published in *The Sewanee Review*, Volume 76, No. 2, Spring 1968. Copyright © 1968 by Allen Tate. Reprinted with the permission of the editor and the author.

Terence Whalen. "Average Racism: Poe, Slavery, and the Wages of Literary Nationalism" from *Edgar Allan Poe and the Masses: The Political Economy of Literature in Antebellum America* by Terence Whalen. Reproduced with permission of Princeton University Press in the format Book via Copyright Clearance Center.

Yvor Winters. "Edgar Allan Poe: A Crisis in the History of American Obscurantism" from *American Literature*, Volume 8, No. 4, pp. 379–401. Copyright © 1937 by Duke University Press. All rights Reserved. Republished by permission of the copyright holder, Duke University Press. www.dukeupress .edu